Introductory Economics

Sixth Edition

Introductory Economics

Sanford D. Gordon

Professor of Economics, Russell Sage College
Executive Director, New York State Council on Economic Foundation

George G. Dawson

Emeritus Professor of Economics,
Empire State College, State University of New York

D. C. Heath and Company

Lexington, Massachusetts   Toronto

To Alice and Shirley

Preface

The Sixth Edition of *Introductory Economics*, like earlier editions, is designed for students taking their first course in economics. The text continues to use an analytical and problem-solving approach, with the mathematics largely confined to simple geometric models, bar graphs, and schedule analyses. Careful distinctions are made between the body of the theory developed and the application of that theory to solving problems.

As in the Fifth Edition, the text remains relatively short. However, no basic theory has been omitted. Indeed, the text contains everything needed for a well-balanced and interesting course. Every possible effort has been made to provide the very latest data in all tables, graphs, and examples.

Changes from the Fifth Edition

Those changes made in the Fifth Edition in order to facilitate learning have been carried over into the Sixth Edition. For example, the Appendix to Chapter 1 provides a step-by-step orientation to the role and meaning of graphs in economics, and the Appendix at the end of the book explores "Economics in Careers." As in the Fifth Edition, the inside cover serves as a motivational device by raising relevant questions to stir the curiosity of the student. Answers to these questions can easily be found by checking the page referred to in the text.

The Sixth Edition incorporates the most significant changes made in the text to date. New learning aids include marginal notes that reinforce important concepts found in the text, graphs that are easier to read, and boxed items that identify and explain common mistakes. A significant innovation not found in other texts is the infusion of *global economics throughout the text* rather than in only one or two chapters. This new approach reflects the growing importance of a world economy.

To make this new edition more meaningful and exciting to the student, a new feature called "Controversy in Our Times" has been introduced. Such issues as mergers and acquisitions, nuclear energy, and the public debt are discussed in these sections. Other relevant topics on which new material has been added include federal tax reform, the value-added tax, employee buyouts, comparable worth, the deficit, the public debt, indicative planning in France and Japan, and changes in the Chinese economy. New examples and illustrations have been added throughout the text. Sections on deregulation and the theory of rational expectations have been expanded. A simple graphic summary of the causes of the agricultural depression of the mid-1980s serves as an excellent review of demand and supply. More emphasis is given to the special economic problems of women, minorities, and the "new poor." Much of Chapter 15 on formulating modern economic policy has been rewritten. Indeed, not a single chapter in the Sixth Edition has escaped change.

Learning Aids

The book continues to be student-oriented. Those features that proved helpful to readers of earlier editions have been retained:

- a list of learning objectives that serves as an outline of the chapter ("Chapter Objectives")
- an introduction to each chapter. Many of these introductions contain provocative questions that connect economic theory to real-world concerns.
- a list of the main points covered in each chapter ("Chapter Highlights")
- a list of the important concepts and people discussed in each chapter ("Key Terms and Names")
- a set of review questions that test the student's understanding of the principles covered in each chapter ("Questions")
- a set of projects that test the student's ability to apply those principles ("Problems")
- an end-of-book list of terms that precisely defines the concepts presented in the book, including over 400 new items ("Glossary of Economic Terms").

Also of importance are four review models: demand and supply, long-run equilibrium, pricing the factors of production, and national income determination. Each review model takes the student step by step through the development of the model and ends with a problem or policy analysis. Taken together, these models represent the core of introductory economic theory.

Supplements

The *Instructor's Guide with Test Items* suggests ways in which the textbook can be used. It provides chapter summaries, methods of approaching the content, questions for discussion, and a sequential list of concepts. This supplement also includes a complete test item file with more than 1,100 test questions (multiple choice and true/false), 300 more items than were in the Fifth Edition. For the first time the difficulty of each of the test questions is indicated by the designation easy (E), moderately difficult (M), or hard (H). As in the past, a page reference to the text is included.

The *Study Guide for Introductory Economics* by Philip R. Robbins and John A. Tribble, has also been revised. The Study Guide contains lists of objectives identical to those in the book, summaries of the chapters, self-tests, applications and problems, and "Food for Thought" sections. Crossword puzzles have been added to help vocabulary building.

Acknowledgments

Although this book is fully the responsibility of the authors, it is nevertheless the product of many minds and influences. Our primary acknowledgment rightfully belongs to the thousands of students whose insight and experience have guided us. We also want to thank the many instructors of economics who have used our book and who took the time to send us thoughtful and useful comments. Many of their suggestions have been incorporated into this edition. Special thanks are due Daniel Rosen and Richard Trainer, Federal Reserve Bank of New York, who provided information for Chapters 13 and 14, and to the following teachers for extensive critiquing of the manuscript of this edition: Paige W. Christiansen, New Mexico Institute of Mining and Technology; David A. Dieterle, University of Nebraska, Lincoln; Robert Drago, University of Wisconsin, Milwaukee; Herb Frizol, Rantoul Township High School, Rantoul, Illinois; Dennis Muraoka, California State University, Long Beach; and Timothy Payne, Western Washington University. The text is very much improved as a result of their efforts.

Finally, we wish to express our thanks to the staff of D. C. Heath and Company for their fine editorial assistance in the development and production of this book and its ancillaries—not an insignificant task.

Contents

Figures

Tables

Introductory Economics

PART

The Framework
of Economics

Economics: What It Is and What It Tries To Do

At the beginning of each chapter, a short introduction by the authors covers in general terms what the chapter is about, how the concepts introduced relate to broad theory, the relevance of the content to you as a member of society, and specific learning goals you should set for yourself within the chapter. Exploring new ideas is easier if you have some idea of what to expect.

As you become deeply involved in economics, you will observe that it provides a way of looking at problems—a pattern of thought—not exactly like that of any other social science. As you complete each chapter, try to explain the economist's approach. See whether these first discoveries stand the test of time when you reexamine them later in the course. You will also be able to identify very quickly the controversy associated with economic problems. Ask yourself why economists with similar training disagree. Does this disagreement mean that there are no correct answers? What do we mean by "correct answers"? Many of you may emerge from this course with more questions than you had when you began. This curiosity is the sign of a good introduction to economics.

Chapter 1 introduces you to economics. It explains what economics is and whether it is an art or a science, and it explores the central questions economics tries to answer. The factors of production, which make up our resources, are identified, the production possibilities curve is explained, and the important economic concept of opportunity cost is explored. The chapter then examines an economic system in general and the U.S. economic system in particular. You will learn what an economic model is and how such a model can answer the questions *What? How?* and *For whom?* Finally, you will be introduced to the approach and pattern of organization that will be followed in this study.

In the appendix to this chapter, you will be introduced to graphs and how to read and work with them. Give this section careful study. It should help you understand the more complex graphs that follow.

Chapter Objectives

When you have completed this chapter, you should be able to:

- Provide a working definition of economics that includes the central economic problem.
- Describe when economics is a science and when it becomes an art.
- Give a working definition of an economic system.
- Define an economic model.
- List the four factors of production and define each.
- Explain what a production possibilities curve shows about outputs.
- Show how opportunity costs help in economic decision making.
- Discuss the main features of Adam Smith's economic model of classic capitalism.
- Explain at least one big difference between Smith's model of classic capitalism and the present U.S. economic system.

A   The Professional Economist: Deity or Dunce?

"An economist is someone who doesn't know what he's talking about, but makes you think it's *your* fault." "An economist is a person who has no idea what's happening in the present but predicts what will happen in the future." "If you made all economists lie down end to end, they'd never reach a conclusion." These are some of the many humorous comments that suggest that professional economists are far from omniscient.

Yet, when economic activity declines, the public turns to economists for explanations as to why. More important, it wants a quick and easy solution that will hurt no one. Frequently there is much consensus among economists on the why but less on the remedy. Perhaps the most serious criticism of all came from an honored member of the profession, Gunnar Myrdal, winner of the Nobel Memorial Prize in Economic Science. Myrdal stated: "I am rather distressed by the confusion among my colleagues. . . . They try to tell what the world will be like at the end of this century, which, of course, nobody can scientifically investigate."[1]

Without doubt, some economists have foolishly made predictions without "hedging their bets," and indeed too few are capable of communicating clearly with the general public. Martin Feldstein, former chairman of the President's Council of Economic Advisers, recently said: "One of the great mistakes of the past 30 years . . . has been an excessive belief in the ability to forecast."[2] During a recent 14-year period, the average error in forecasts of our economic growth was only 1.7 percent, however.

Many factors can cause an original forecast to miss the mark—a long strike, a major crop failure, an unexpected change in government economic policy, an increase in oil prices, an international crisis, and so on. If time permits, the forecasters can take these changes into account, revise the values in their equations, and induce their computers to spew out a new prediction to replace the old. In any event, if the forecasts are not perfect, they are certainly better than nothing. Furthermore, the forecasts made by trained statistical economists are usually better than those made by noneconomists. Therefore, even if they do not tell exactly what will happen, they usually give pretty good "ball park" figures. The mistake on the part of government officials, business leaders, and others who rely upon the forecasts is expecting them to be exact. Instead, they should

[1]*New York News,* October 13, 1974, p. 92.

[2]*Time,* August 27, 1984, p. 42.

be viewed as approximations, and users of the forecasts should be aware of the assumptions upon which they are based.

 Although economists' predictions are not exact, they are more often right than wrong.

No one could have predicted the Arab oil embargo of 1973–74,[3] which profoundly affected prices and the balance of payments. Economists could not have foreseen weather conditions (even the weather forecasters have trouble at times) and other factors that sent food prices soaring. What they can and *should* do is recognize that any predictions are tentative and subject to unforeseen elements. In short, there should be plenty of *ifs, ands,* and *buts* in any economic forecast.

Now that we have conceded some fault on the part of economists, let us note emphatically that the consumers of the economists' services (government officials, business people, newspaper reporters, and the public in general) must also bear some of the blame. First, they expect too much. Second, they often misinterpret objective economic reports. Third, they sometimes fail to follow sound advice when it is forthcoming, and then blame economists because the problem persists.

Everyone should realize from the start that economists are not all-knowing deities who can always give accurate predictions. For instance, those of us in the profession are constantly plagued at social gatherings by people who want infallible advice on what stocks to buy in order to get rich quickly and without any risk whatever. Although studies have shown economists do better than the average investor, very few have enough confidence in their skills at predicting market trends to substitute investing for making a living as an economist.

Regarding the second point, many people have not been trained to read carefully, weigh evidence dispassionately, and look at all sides objectively. Thus economists constantly find themselves mis-

quoted and misinterpreted. Although most news people try to be honest, accurate, and complete, in their haste to meet deadlines and to provide exciting headlines they often take material out of context or err in reporting. Economists then spend a great deal of their time moaning: "But I didn't say that!"

 Economics is complex, yet people want simple answers.

Now for the third point—the failure to follow good advice. In the mid-1960s President Johnson announced his determination to "escalate" the war in Vietnam and at the same time carry on with his Great Society program—both of which would involve heavy federal spending at a time of high employment. Economists by the hundreds warned that inflation (a general price rise) would result unless taxes were raised both to help pay for the added expenditures and to curb spending by the people. The president ignored this advice. By the time the administration was convinced that a tax increase was necessary, inflation was almost out of hand. It was like trying to slow a car by applying the brakes when the vehicle is three-fourths of the way down a steep hill and has been gaining momentum, instead of doing so at the top of the hill when it is still moving slowly. Thus a tax increase that might have been effective when it was suggested was less potent when it was finally applied; yet many blamed the economists for this. After all, if your physician prescribes a certain medicine and you refuse to take it, can you blame the doctor if your ailment persists?

 Good economics and good politics frequently differ.

Well, then, if economists are not deities who can make perfect predictions or always come up with infallible solutions, what good *are* they? First, let us identify three types of economics—"pure" economics, economic ethics, and applied economics. The first is strictly the realm of the professional economist. Pure economics deals with the question What exists? Economic ethics asks, What *ought* to be? Applied economics deals with the question How can we, by applying the principles and tools of pure economics, achieve the

[3]Nevertheless, economist Lawrence Klein correctly predicted that the embargo would result in a recession and a higher rate of inflation.

goals economic ethics have established? In a democratic society, everyone (potentially at least) has a voice in setting economic goals. Theoretically, one person's opinion is as good as another's, and all votes count equally. For example, society might decide through some sort of democratic procedure that every individual and household is entitled to a certain minimum level of living. (Economists might be somewhat more realistic in establishing goals, for they usually are better aware of the costs involved and the limitations a scarcity of productive resources imposes.)

Whether or not economists agree with the goals society establishes, they can do much toward their achievement. To stay with our example of the goal of a guaranteed minimum level of living, pure economics could be used to do such things as find out the existing levels of living, try to ascertain causes for poverty, identify the existing resources for dealing with the problem, try to find laws or relationships (such as the relationship between high incomes and education), and suggest possible alternative courses. Economists could point out the trade-offs involved. For example, they might suggest that one way of ending poverty would be to have the government take much higher taxes from the wealthy and the upper-middle classes and simply transfer money in direct welfare payments to the poor. This might be a quick solution, but it might also produce less investment, so in the future the economy as a whole would fail to grow rapidly, resulting in less wealth for everyone to share. An alternative might be to educate and train the poor to raise their productivity. This would take more time, but in the long run the entire economy would be more prosperous and there would be a bigger total pie for everyone to share. There are many other possibilities; the decision as to which to accept is made through the political process.

 Economists do not set society's goals, but they can suggest how to achieve them.

Most of the criticism leveled against economists is focused on their failures in forecasting the direction of the economy as a whole. However, more economists work for businesses and government and devote most of their time to pro-jecting the costs and benefits of alternative approaches to very specific problems. Questions such as whether to buy new machines or to add additional labor in the production process are being studied constantly by business economists. Determining the economic impact of putting a bridge across a river or of building a civic center in town requires economists as well as environmentalists and urban planners. The successes of economists in these ventures are constant and valuable, but they fail to get the same attention that national forecasting does.

 Economists are as involved with individual parts of the economy as with national economic performance.

When society, through its political machinery, decides what course to follow, applied economics takes over. For instance, professional economists might analyze existing tax structures (if the former course is chosen) and advise the government on how best to change them to achieve the desired goal of transferring money wealth from the rich to the poor.

Those who lack an understanding of basic economics, or are unable to obtain the services of a professional economist, often make serious mistakes. Every year, small businesses collapse by the hundreds. This is usually because of inept management and a failure to recognize such factors as implicit costs as well as explicit costs in running a firm, elasticities of demand, or realities of the competitive market. "Common sense" is not always a good substitute for sound economic analysis. "Common sense" tells the noneconomist that if the government lowers taxes it will reduce its revenue, but the economist Walter Heller was able to convince President Kennedy that a tax cut could actually bring an increase in the tax revenue. Heller correctly predicted that a tax cut would give people more money to spend, that this "marginal" income would indeed be spent and put into circulation, and that as it circulated it would create more income for more people and thus *raise* the amount the government would receive, thanks to this multiplier effect! More important, the tax cut stimulated the economy and thus provided jobs for the unemployed.

In summary, economists are neither deities nor dunces, but highly trained professionals whose work is essential to our economy. As one executive stated: "Economists are as essential to conducting your business as meteorologists are for anticipating weather patterns. The alternative would be flying blind."[4]

[4]*Time,* August 27, 1984, p. 44.

B Economics as a Discipline

Why Should You Study Economics?

As you skim the pages of this book, you will see graphs and charts, facts and figures. As you examine some sections closely, you will probably ask, Why should I study economics? Will this study help me in any way? Psychologists have found that students are better able to learn when they see a purpose in learning. Therefore, examining possible answers to these questions is a good way to start.

Citizens Influence Economic Policies of Government

In a democracy, we as citizens are expected to participate, at least indirectly, in decision making. In voting for representatives or in supporting a political party, we are endorsing certain principles and supporting particular solutions to problems. Should school taxes be increased? What kind of tax reform is best for the poor? The middle class? The rich? Will raising gasoline taxes reduce consumption? What should we do to avoid a recession?

These questions, although usually asked within a political framework, have an economic nature. They are as important as the money in our pockets, and just as personal. Their answers will affect the amount of money we make and the amount of money we must spend. We rely on newspapers to keep us informed so that we can make rational decisions about public questions. But there is little in the newspapers and there is little government activity that does not have an economic origin. No one can avoid the influence of economics on public issues and policy.

THAT WAS BOB JOHNSON... THE FAMOUS ECONOMIST, WHO WILL BE WITH US NEXT WEEK AND THE WEEK AFTER AND THE WEEK AFTER THAT, OR HOWEVER LONG IT TAKES UNTIL HE MAKES A CORRECT PREDICTION!

news magazine

T.V.

RAESIDE FOR ROTHCO

Consumers and Producers Influence Economic Policies of Business

Even though the influence of government policy on your life may seem remote at present, you are deeply involved in economics. When you shop, you are interested in the goods you get and the prices you pay for them. When you work, you are concerned about the amount of your paycheck. What you buy as a consumer and earn as a worker helps to shape economic decisions and policies of U.S. businesses. Although studying economics may not provide you with a method of earning a living, it can help you better understand your roles as a consumer and a producer so that you can be more effective in both roles.

Economics: Science or Art?

Science is frequently described as (1) an organized body of knowledge from which (2) generalizations may be developed and used for (3) predicting and (4) controlling behavior. Economists score high marks in 1 and 2—they collect a massive number of facts and organize them in an orderly manner. This can be verified by glancing through government, business, labor, and banking publications. In reviewing these data, economists will try to find some generalization, principle, law, or theory (they are all the same). A study of what happens to price if either the supply or the demand of a product changes leads to the laws of supply and demand. At the end of this course you will probably agree that economists have been productive in developing a large body of theory. Having accumulated the facts and formulated the theory, how successful has the profession been in predicting and controlling?

As you have already read, the forecasting record of economics is spotty, because economics, even at its best, is not an exact science. Like the meteorologist, the economist is more often right than wrong. However, because the economy depends on so many factors outside its control—foreign policy, major catastrophies, the weather—controlled experiments are not possible and therefore the outcome cannot be certain.

 Like medicine, economics is part science and part art.

To cope with the many variables, economists make assumptions, one of which is that all things hold constant except the variable being studied. Economists start their analysis of a problem with a statement of their assumptions and end with "all other things being equal."

Models and the Real World

To analyze problems such as cause and effect, economists use models or theories. Sometimes these models are expressed in words, such as "With an increase in demand, supply remaining the same (an assumption), price will rise." This same idea can be expressed as a table or schedule (Table 2–3) or a graph (Figure 2–7). Sometimes mathematical equations are used, such as the one found in Chapter 12, to help determine the level of national income.

A model is developed to help economists analyze and better understand the economy. Like a set of plans, it is a simplified version of the real thing. Remember that a model is not reality. It may look good on paper, but if it differs from the real world it is unlikely that it will work. We will be using economic models frequently.

 Models are simplified representations of the real world.

Policy Economics

Controlling behavior is *policy economics*. Correct policy depends on the accuracy of predictions, the application of the right economic principle or theory, and a lot of luck in that environmental factors, which are not exclusively economic, must not change. Economists must weigh all these variables and sense how they will interact.

An additional complication for economists is the conflicting values found in society. If inflation and unemployment are both problems, which of the two is the more serious? Answering this question will be important in deciding the right policy.

Although economics may be the only social science included among Nobel prizes, its ability to predict and control is limited; therefore, selecting the right policy to cope with economic problems is probably more of an art than a science.

What Economics Is

Economics is classified as a social science. Like political science, sociology, and geography, it concerns people's attempts to organize the environment to satisfy their needs. Economics concentrates on satisfying material needs such as the need for food and shelter. Specifically, it concerns *production, distribution, and consumption of goods and services.*

Scarcity and Choice

Unfortunately for the world, there are limited resources, too few to satisfy wants. Therefore choices have to be made as to how to allocate our scarce resources to maximize the satisfaction of our wants. When choices are made, alternatives are given up (see the discussion of opportunity costs at the end of this section). Economics as a discipline provides a way of determining how to allocate our scarce resources *effectively* and *efficiently.* If effective, we will be producing products that will best satisfy our wants. If efficient, we will be getting the most value (output) from our resources (inputs).

Economics is the study of choosing among alternative ways in which scarce resources may be allocated to maximize the satisfaction of wants.

The Central Problem of Economics

Although definitions are useful in delineating the scope of an academic discipline like economics, they are sometimes weak in pointing out the purpose and direction of the discipline. In living, people are faced with certain basic problems. In trying to find answers, they gather facts, organize them, discover related questions, and develop methods for solving problems. Collectively, these procedures, the body of knowledge, and the attitudes developed add up to a discipline—for example, *economics.* However, the discipline develops because people are searching for answers.

Let us now review the questions that economists try to answer.

For Individuals

All of us at some time allow ourselves the luxury of daydreaming. A common tendency in these dreams is to picture ourselves as able to afford all the things we associate with wealth. A look through a mail-order catalogue or a visit to a large department store whets our appetite for a never-ending list of products. However, nothing can bring us back to reality sooner than reaching into our pockets and finding how little we have to work with. *The problem we are faced with is that our resources, here identified as money, are limited.* The only way we can resolve our problem is to make choices. After looking at our resources, we must examine our list of wants and identify the things we need immediately, those we can postpone, and those we cannot afford. As individuals, we face the central problem involved in economics—*deciding just how to allocate our limited resources to provide ourselves with the greatest satisfaction of our wants.*

For Nations

Nations face the same problem. As a country's population grows, the need for more goods and services grows correspondingly. Resources necessary to production may increase, but there never are enough resources to satisfy the total desires of a nation. Whether the budget meeting is taking place in the family living room, in the city hall, in the conference room of the corporation board of directors, or in the chamber of the House of Representatives in Washington, the basic problem still exists. We need to find methods of allocating limited resources in order to satisfy unlimited wants.

A short time ago economists divided goods into two categories, free and economic. The former, like air and water, were in such abundance that economists had no concern for them. After all, economics is the science of scarcity and what to do about it. Today many of these "free goods" are in reality very expensive to use. Pollution has made clean air and water expensive for producers who have to filter their waste products, for consumers who ultimately pay for the producers' extra costs, and for taxpayers who pay for the government's involvement in cleaning the environment or keeping it clean.

In the 1980s, almost all goods are scarce. Only by effort and money can they be obtained in the form people wish.

Meeting the needs of people and nations from resources available leads to the basic activity of *production*. In trying to meet unlimited wants from limited economic goods, production leads to new problems in economics.

 Scarcity and choice are what economics is all about.

The Big Questions: What? How? For Whom?

Three questions are closely associated with the central problem of unlimited wants and limited resources. We shall call them the problems of *What, How,* and *For whom*. Whether we study the simple subsistence economy of a South Pacific island or the complex system of an industrialized nation, we must see how the problem of *What* to produce is solved. If economics deals with studying the satisfaction of material wants, then, the student may well ask, what material wants shall be met? Should the people submit an annual list? Should a central planning committee decide? How much freedom should the people have in deciding? The question of what to produce is basic and exists

What Economists Do

Economists study the way a society uses scarce resources such as land, labor, raw materials, and machinery to provide goods and services. They analyze the results of their research to determine the costs and benefits of making, distributing, and using resources in a particular way. Their research might focus on topics such as energy costs, inflation, business cycles, unemployment, tax policy, or farm prices.

Some economists who are primarily theoreticians may use mathematical models to develop theories to explain the causes of inflation. Most economists, however, are concerned with practical applications of economic policy in a particular area, such as finance, labor, agriculture, transportation,

energy, or health. They use their understanding of economic relationships to advise business firms, insurance companies, banks, securities firms, industry associations, labor unions, government, and others.

Being able to present economic and statistical concepts in a meaningful way is particularly important for economists whose research is policy directed. Economists who work for business firms may be asked to provide management with information needed to make decisions on marketing and pricing of company products; to look at the advisability of adding new lines of merchandise, opening new branches, or diversifying the company's operations; to analyze the effect of changes in the tax

laws; or to prepare economic and business forecasts.

Economists who work for government agencies assess economic conditions in the United States and abroad and estimate the economic impact of specific changes in legislation or public policy.

Besides the jobs described above, an estimated 15,000 persons hold economics faculty positions in colleges and universities, according to data from the National Science Foundation.

Employment of economists is expected to grow about as fast as the average for all occupations through the mid-1990s. Most job openings will result from the need to replace experienced economists who transfer to other occupations, retire, or leave the labor force for other reasons.

Source: U.S. Department of Labor, Bureau of Labor Statistics, *Occupational Outlook Handbook,* 1984–85 edition, p. 8.

because we have limited resources and unlimited wants.

 Every economy seeks answers to the questions *What to produce? How to produce? For whom to produce?*

If we answer the question *What,* we must then consider the question *How:* How do we produce the goods and services we have decided on? Production, even in a simple society, can be difficult to achieve. It involves getting the right kind and amount of ingredients together at the right time and place to produce the things we want. We have to be careful not to waste these ingredients because they are scarce. Inefficient production will mean that there will not be enough resources left over to satisfy other wants. More will be said about these ingredients shortly.

After deciding what to produce and how to produce it, we still have an important question to answer: *For whom* is this production meant? The *For whom* is a question of *distribution.* Will everyone get an equal portion? Should production be distributed according to need? If so, how do we determine need? Who gets steak and who gets hamburger is as basic as *What* and *How.*

Factors of Production

Although nations may choose different economic systems, all must be concerned with producing. Any discussion of economic systems requires an understanding of what have been described as the ingredients of production. All production involves four separate *factors:* natural resources, labor, capital, and entrepreneurship.

Natural Resources

Natural resources—the materials nature provides—are necessary for the production of the things we want. Some economists prefer to call this factor *land.* The minerals in the ground, forests, waterfalls, and fertile soil are all examples of a nation's resources; they are important in determining its production, particularly because they are becoming more scarce.

Labor

To adapt natural resources for human use, we must apply work. This is done by *labor,* the second factor of production. The skill and the amount of labor will also be important in determining production. India has more than twice the labor force of the United States, but the greater skill of the U.S. worker leads to far more productivity. Superior education has allowed the United States to capitalize on the use of machines.

Capital

The third factor of production is *capital.* Most people think of capital as money. To the economist, *capital is any man-made instrument of production*—that is, a good used to further production. Frequently it will mean a tool or a machine. It can also mean the rolled steel that is used in automobile production. If great amounts of capital are placed in skilled hands, productivity can be increased tremendously.

Entrepreneurship

The fourth factor of production is entrepreneurship. People engaged in this function are referred to as *entrepreneurs* (enterprisers). It is their responsibility to initiate production, to organize the other factors of production, and to operate the productive establishment. An entrepreneur who produces goods and services efficiently will not only make a profit, the reward for the risk taken, but also serve society by helping to satisfy wants.

When we have these four factors, we have the ingredients of production.

 All production involves factors: natural resources, labor, capital, and entrepreneurship.

The Production Process

Putting the factors of production together to satisfy consumer wants at the right time, in the right place, and at the right price is what production is about. Much of this course will be devoted to finding out how this is done. For now let us review a production process to make sure we understand

Production involves four factors, all of which contribute value to the final product and must be paid for.

what the factors of production are and how they will be used in the process.

Suppose we have as our final product educated people to provide the human resources to carry out the functions of our society. A great deal of this "production" in the western society is done through training in schools and colleges. In this case the natural resources—the ingredients that are "worked on"—would be you, the students. Your teachers or professors would be labor, seeking to develop your knowledge, skills, and reasoning powers. The classrooms, chairs, books, pens, and blackboards are examples of capital, the manufactured tools that labor uses to help in the production process. But who will initiate the idea? Determine the need for this service? Get the ingredients together (the students, the instructors, the schedule that brings the right number of students together in a classroom equipped for learning, the assurance that credit will be given for work done, etc.)? This is the role of the entrepreneur.

There are times when an item's function will determine what role the item will play. A car is a consumer product when used for personal transportation. If the car is used as a taxi, it is capital, a man-made instrument to further production (in this case, transportation). A baseball bat used in sand lot ball is a consumer item, but in professional baseball it is capital. What is oil when it is in the ground? When it is used to drive machines? When it is used to heat your house?

How do we allocate these factors of production, limited resources, to satisfy our wants?

The Need for an Economic System

To answer the central problem of limited resources and unlimited wants and the related questions of *What, How,* and *For whom,* we need rules, or guiding principles. Such principles usually reflect the values that people hold. We find that the American people hold a broad range of values. Most students of U.S. history agree that individual freedom and the sanctity of private property rank highest among values. Some people today place equality and promoting the general welfare high on the list. In the Soviet Union, the best interests of the state and collective ownership of property are emphasized. Values such as these, and more specifically the principles that stem from them, provide the direction for answering the big questions in economics. The way a nation answers these questions determines its *economic system.*

 Economic systems provide answers to the big questions.

What Kind of Economic System?

An economic system must determine who is to produce the goods and services. If business people produce all, we have an exclusively private enterprise system, which we classify as *capitalism,* or a market system. The emphasis of this system is on private ownership and operation of factors of production and the allocation of resources by decisions made in the market. If, on the other hand, government owns the means of production and distribution, the system is labeled *socialism,* or a command system.

Because no country has all its production coming exclusively from either the private or the public (government) sector, it may be said that all countries have more or less *mixed economies.* However, this does not mean they are the same. Far from it. In the United States, the largest portion of our goods and services comes from businesses—private enterprises—and a much smaller, though important, portion (primarily services) comes from government. Some of the government enterprises with which we come in close contact are educational and library facilities and the postal system. Although our economy is mixed, we usually label it *capitalism, mixed capitalism, private enterprise,* or *free enterprise.* These terms are characteristic of economies in which production stems primarily from business, and in which government has a smaller role.

In the Soviet Union, most means of production are owned and operated by the government, and very little originates with private enterprise. Because of this emphasis on government production, the USSR calls its system socialism. Most economically developed countries of the world have economic systems that are somewhere between that of the U.S. and that of the USSR.

The Production Possibilities Curve—A Tool for Economic Analysis

As was pointed out earlier in this section, every society has to make choices. It can't produce everything its people want, so it must choose among various possible goods and services. The *production possibilities curve* is an economic model that helps us to see what we have to sacrifice in order to produce more goods of a certain type. We make the assumption that the resources in our society are fixed, as is our level of technology.

At any particular time, there is a limit to the amount of goods and services that a nation can produce with its existing resources. This may be referred to as its *production possibilities frontier.* If a nation is fully and efficiently using its existing

resources, it is producing on the production possibilities frontier. A decision must be made, however, about the *types* of things produced. If we are fully and efficiently using our resources and we decide that we need more military hardware, we can increase our stock of military goods only by decreasing our production of something else. Capital, labor, and materials will be shifted away from the production of some other item (such as passenger cars) to the production of tanks, planes, guns, and so on. To get more military goods, we must sacrifice nonmilitary goods. The *real cost* of the new military hardware will be the nonmilitary goods we sacrifice. If we decide to promote economic growth by increasing our stock of capital goods, we must sacrifice consumer goods to do so. The production possibilities curve is a convenient device for illustrating this point.

Figure 1–1 illustrates an imaginary production possibilities frontier. Capital goods are shown on the vertical axis, consumer goods on the hor-

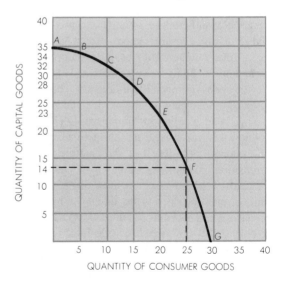

Figure 1–1   Production possibilities curve
We have divided the nation's output into two types of goods—capital goods and consumer goods. In this imaginary situation, the curve shows how many units of each type can be produced if the nation is fully and efficiently using its resources. At point A, we can produce 35 units of capital goods but no consumer goods. At point G, we can produce 30 units of consumer goods but no capital goods. At point F, we can have 14 units of capital goods and 25 units of consumer goods.

izontal. If the nation were producing at point *A* on the production possibilities curve, it would turn out 35 units of capital goods, but no consumer goods at all. This would hardly be desirable, for the people would have machines, tools, factories, and so on, but no shoes, food, and other items that provide immediate consumer satisfaction. If the nation produced at point *G*, it would turn out 30 units of consumer goods, but no capital goods at all.[5] Society would enjoy a great deal of food, clothing, cosmetics, and other consumer goods, but it would come to regret this in the future. Existing capital goods would wear out, and eventually there would be a decline in the output of consumer goods because the capital items needed to produce them would be disappearing. Since both extremes are undesirable, where should a nation produce on its production possibilities curve? There is no simple answer. Each society must make a choice, and ideally it should try to strike the right balance between capital and consumer goods. If, in this case, the nation chose point *F* on the curve, it would produce 14 units of capital goods and 25 units of consumer goods. About 36 percent of its total output would be devoted to capital formation.

In choosing to sacrifice consumer goods to produce more capital items (or vice versa), society must consider the *law of increasing costs*. To see how this works, we can construct a table based on the curve in Figure 1–1 showing the various production possibilities. Table 1–1 shows the alternatives open to society by indicating how many units of consumer goods the nation can have if it produces a certain number of units of capital goods. It also shows how much of one item we must

sacrifice to get more of the other. At each step, check the table against the curve in Figure 1–1.

When we moved from point *A* to point *B*, we sacrificed 1 unit of capital goods to gain 5 units of consumer goods. When we moved from *B* to *C*, we sacrificed 2 units of capital goods to gain 5 units of consumer goods. Moving from *C* to *D*, we gave up 4 units of capital goods to get 5 more units of consumer goods. At each succeeding step, the sacrifice of capital goods becomes greater. Finally, we have to sacrifice 14 units of capital goods to get 5 more units of consumer goods. Why does this occur? It occurs because productive resources are not always perfectly adaptable to alternative uses. At first, as we shifted some of our resources from the production of capital goods to the production of consumer goods, we experienced a large gain in the latter. We took resources that were not well suited to producing capital goods and began using them more efficiently to turn out consumer goods. After a time, however, we started to shift away from the production of capital goods resources that were really not well suited for the production of consumer goods. Thus, the real cost of producing more consumer items rose, for we had to sacrifice larger and larger numbers of capital goods. (The curve is sometimes called a *transformation curve* because, in effect, we are transforming capital goods into consumer goods when we take resources away from the production of the former to increase the output of the latter.)

 A nation producing along its production possibilities curve is achieving at highest efficiency.

Up to this point, we have assumed that the nation is using its productive resources fully and efficiently. Of course this is not always true in real life. If there is unemployment or if technical inefficiency exists, the nation will not be producing at some point on the curve. It will be producing somewhere *inside* the curve.

The solid black curve in Figure 1–2 shows us what the nation *could* be producing if it were using all resources efficiently. The point marked *U* shows where it is actually producing. In this case, it is producing 10 units of capital goods and 10 of consumer goods. If the nation could achieve

Table 1–1   Production possibilities schedule

Possibilities	Capital goods	Consumer goods	Sacrifice of capital goods	Gain of consumer goods
A	35	0	0	
B	34	5	1	5
C	32	10	2	5
D	28	15	4	5
E	23	20	5	5
F	14	25	9	5
G	0	30	14	5

full employment, or use its resources with maximum efficiency, or do both simultaneously, it could produce much more of both items. Note the arrow marked *X*. This arrow indicates that the nation could increase its output of consumer goods from 10 to about 21 and still produce 10 units of capital goods. Note arrow *Z*. This arrow shows that the nation could raise the output of capital goods to about 26 and still produce 10 units of consumer goods. There are many other possible combinations. Arrow *Y* suggests that the nation could have 19 units of capital goods and about 16 units of consumer goods. In any event, unemployment, underemployment, and inefficiency result in a denial to the public of goods and services that could otherwise be enjoyed. (If we were to draw a production possibilities curve for the United States showing a serious recession, would production be at a point *on* or *inside* the curve?)

It is difficult to say exactly which point on the curve is best for a nation, because conditions are always changing. However, every nation should attempt to achieve a good balance between capital and consumer goods. Suppose a nation chooses to devote its productive capacity very largely to consumer goods, at the expense of capital formation. Its consumers might be affluent for a while, but economic growth can be retarded. As a nation grows economically, its production possibilities curve shifts outward. New workers entering the labor force, new sources of raw materials, and new capital equipment increase the nation's productive capacity. The solid colored curve in Figure 1–2 illustrates the outward shift. Again, note that the nation can produce more capital goods

without sacrificing any consumer goods, or more consumer goods without sacrificing any capital goods, or it can produce more of both items. The nation might also fail to produce at some point on the new curve, meaning that unemployment, underemployment, or inefficiency exists.

One final note about the production possibilities curve. We have used it to illustrate the trade-

Figure 1–2   Unemployment and changing production possibilities

The point marked *U* inside the solid curve illustrates unemployment, when the nation is producing fewer goods and services than it can. If the nation moves towards full employment, it can have more capital goods, more consumer goods, or more of both. The colored curve shows that the nation has increased its productive capacity—its production possibilities frontier has moved outward.

off between capital goods and consumer goods and to stress the importance of capital formation for economic growth. The curve has several other uses. Whenever we can divide a nation's output into two categories, the curve becomes a useful tool for analysis. For example, we could put "military goods" on the vertical axis and "nonmilitary goods" on the horizontal. We could put "public goods" (government) on one axis and "private goods" on another, thus showing that in a full-employment economy the government could increase its share of the GNP only by reducing the share of the private sector. The curve could be used to show agricultural compared with non-agricultural production. Can you think of any other possible uses for this analytical device?

 Producing inside the production possibilities curve is underutilizing resources. Outward expansion of the curve reflects increased productivity or greater input of resources.

Opportunity Cost

In looking at the production possibilities schedule in Table 1–1, we learned that we could produce more capital goods if we sacrificed consumer goods and vice versa. This choice of alternatives is called a *trade-off*, i.e., trading one use of a resource for another. In each case costs are involved, a central theme in economics.

The value of what is given up or lost by a resource (or individual) when it is *used in the next best alternative way* is known as *opportunity cost*. If you give up an opportunity to work as a salesperson in order to work in a library, your opportunity cost is what you would have earned as a salesperson. The opportunity cost for a college education is not merely what you spend in out-of-pocket costs but also the earnings you forgo if you worked full time instead of going to college.

 Moving from one position to another on the production possibilities curve illustrates the concept of opportunity cost—giving up some of one thing to get more of another.

Opportunity cost involves more than money value. Time is a resource. Right now you are reading about economics. The time you spend on this chapter could be spent reading about history or watching television. Time is scarce and you must choose between alternatives. The opportunity cost for reading this chapter depends on the value of what you consider to be the next best alternative, history or television. Because economics is the study of how to maximize the use of scarce resources, opportunity cost is an important concept used in analyzing problems.

C The U.S. Economic System

Production—What?

With most of our production coming from business enterprises numbering about 16 million privately owned firms, how do we decide what to produce? In a country with 240 million people, each of whom has a variety of wants larger than the inventory list of a supermarket, the question *What* seems overwhelming. Even the thousands of items listed in mail-order catalogues do not begin to cover the numerous wants of people. Deciding what to produce under these circumstances appears impossible. Yet such decisions are being made all the time, along with decisions about

how much of each product to make. Not only have we been finding answers to these questions, but the indication is that our system is working comparatively well. The United States produces and consumes more goods and services than any other country in the world.

Every day business managers throughout the country decide what and how much to produce. They are very careful in their estimates because they realize that if their decisions are wrong they will lose money. They also realize that those who make the most accurate decisions will make the most money. What guidelines do they have to follow?

Individual Choices Determine Production

Business firms watch carefully what customers buy. Every time you buy something in a store, you are casting your dollar vote for that particular good. Actually, you vote many hundreds of times a year for the various products you buy. If very few people buy a product, that product will be defeated at the polls; that is, it will not be produced or it will be produced in a smaller quantity. Storekeepers do not order it again, and producers know they will have to cut down their production, change their product, or stop producing it. However, if a great many people buy a product, the cost of these many votes will result in storekeepers increasing their orders and producers increasing the amount manufactured. The buyers tell the sellers what they want, and the sellers in turn tell the producers.

You cast votes indicating your choice whenever you obtain something that is produced. Consider how many times you have purchased a phonograph record at your favorite music store. If you and your friends are particularly interested in a special record, the owner of the music store will have to increase his or her order for records to satisfy this single want of many people. You also find this same principle—of supply meeting demand—in a library. A librarian who has numerous requests for one book may have to order additional copies. The second order to the book publisher tells of an additional demand. These examples illustrate that both the kind and the amount of our production are determined by the choices people make in buying goods and services.

Production—How?

We have mentioned that all production involves four factors: natural resources, labor, capital, and entrepreneurship. If producers and sellers are to increase their business, they need to employ more of the factors of production—more iron ore, more machinists, more machines, and more supervisors. How can these factors be obtained? They can be secured from producers facing reduced demand or with money not currently in use. Producers who are increasing their business need more of the factors. They usually take them from those whose business is declining; they do so by offering more money.

 # Jeremy Bentham: Hedonism and Utilitarianism

Much of the philosophical basis for capitalism is found in hedonism and utilitarianism, concepts developed by an English philosopher and economist, Jeremy Bentham. He said that people are influenced by two forces, pain and pleasure. The basic principle of hedonism is that people seek their own greatest happiness. A person will continue to work until work will no longer buy enough pleasure to offset the pain it causes. To his analysis, Bentham added utilitarianism, the doctrine that all should strive for happiness for the greatest number of people. This principle minimizes self-interest and requires government to have a limited part in subordinating individualism to the common interest.

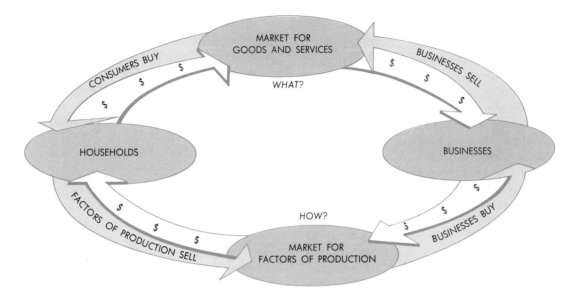

Figure 1–3   Circular flow of the economy
This simplified circular flow model of pure capitalism shows how a free-
enterprise economic system answers the questions of *What* and *How* to produce.
People from households go to the market as consumers to buy, and they go to
the market as suppliers of the factors of production to sell. Businesses go to the
market to sell their production, but they must first go to the market as buyers
to get the factors of production necessary to produce. The inner arrows show
the flow of money payments. The outer arrows show the flow of economic
resources—that is, production and factors of production. The flow of money
thus determines allocation of resources.

The Directing Computer: A Guide to Production

An example may help you to understand the circular flow of the economy, as it is diagrammed in
Figure 1–3. Try to imagine that floating above
our country is a directing computer carrying a
sensitive antenna. This instrument records every
single purchase that is made by every single buyer
in the entire country. It is registering the votes of
people for the goods and services they want. This
scientific instrument then determines whether the
factors of production are going in the right amount
to the places that are producing the goods and
services.

Let us suppose that consumers indicate an
increasing interest in new appliances and a
decreasing interest in new automobiles. This change
would be shown by the purchase of more appliances and fewer automobiles. Our computer, hav-

ing registered this change, would indicate that some
of the steel and the workers and the supervisors
now producing automobiles should be shifted to
producing appliances.

 The U.S. market system is consumer-
oriented.

We will be returning to the circular flow model
in Figure 1–3 frequently to show what part of the
economic system we are studying. In most cases
we will add to it so as to improve our understanding of how the economy is expected to operate.

Incentives Influence Production

A logical question you might ask at this point is,
How in a democracy can you shift people from
one industry to another? You cannot force people
to move, nor can you arbitrarily order that materials be redirected from one producer to another.

This is where our wonderful instrument comes to the rescue. Signals to offer more dollars are transmitted from our computer to the factors of production. The greater the need for factors of production to move from one industry to another— as from automobiles to appliances—the more the dollars offered to speed the change.

As a worker, you know that the more you earn, the more satisfactions you can derive from your income. Therefore, you will try to work at the job that will pay you the most. Because fewer automobiles are being bought, fewer auto workers are needed. Some of these workers will find themselves looking for another means of earning a living. Because demand for appliances has increased, thereby requiring more labor for their production, we shall find our workers following the signals— moving where more dollars are offered. The same would be true of steel and machines.

The computer, after recording the kind and quantity of our purchases, also determines the kind and amount of production needed to meet our demands. It determines whether factors of production are going in the correct combination to the right place to produce goods and services we want. It then suggests the necessary adjustments in the flow of our resources to the right place, in the right amounts, and at the right time. This is accomplished by directing additional resources where they are needed and redirecting resources when they are not needed, by adjusting the amount of dollars offered. Thus this payment provides an incentive for change.

Distribution—For Whom?

Why is our computer so successful? We are able to understand its success when we answer the question *For whom*. The production is there. For whom is it meant? The tall? The strong? The fair? No! With some exceptions, to be mentioned later, it will go to those who have the money—the dol-

---

Adam Smith and the Theory of Laissez-Faire

Adam Smith (1723–90) lived at a time when England's economy was undergoing a significant transition. During the seventeenth century, the Netherlands led England in commerce and France led England in manufacturing; in the next century England surpassed both.

During this time the economic philosophy dominant among the nations of Western Europe was mercantilism. This system, designed to increase a nation's supply of precious metals, required extensive government controls. Monopoly privileges, subsidies, and tariff protection were granted to a select few to encourage investment in new business ventures bringing monetary return.

By the middle of the eighteenth century, the conditions on which the mercantile system was based had begun to change in England. As businesses grew in power with the increase of trade and manufacturing, government protection was no longer so essential to them. At the same time, the Industrial Revolution was shaping a new era of production. It was on these new conditions that Adam Smith based his theories of laissez-faire.

Smith believed that individual initiative, motivated by the desire for profits, could result in a healthier national economy. If the economy were freed from the restraints of government interference, the factors of production could seek their maximum return. With supply and demand operating in a free competitive market, the problems of production and distribution could be solved most effectively. And because England was stronger than her neighbors and more efficient in production, she could afford to encourage free competition at home and overseas.

Smith is usually referred to as the father of modern economics. In giving meaning and order to the environment he lived in, he reflected the changes taking place in his day, and his ideas influenced the direction of future change and development.

lars—to buy it. Business people want to make big profits, workers want high wages, landlords want to collect as much rent as possible, just as you want your income raised in order to buy more of the things you want.

It would be nice if every person could have all individual wants satisfied. However, you will recall we said our needs seem unlimited—never ending—and our resources to produce are definitely limited. If we agree that we cannot all have everything we want, or even most of the things we want, and we know that we have to figure out some system of distributing the production, a question remains: Why should production be distributed on the basis of who has the most money? Some people have a great need for goods and services but do not have the money to obtain them.

Our System Provides Answers

The economic practices of the United States do give some answers to the question of how to meet needs, although not everyone considers these the best ways of distributing goods and services. Money payments are used as incentives to reward people for contributing to the well-being of our country. Workers toil to earn money to satisfy their needs; although they are working with their own self-interest in mind, they are also adding production that people want. The more they produce, the better they serve society. The more their services are in demand, the higher their wages will be. Business people try to produce the best possible products most efficiently. Therefore, they try to increase their profits by producing at as low a cost as they can and selling as much of their product as possible at the highest acceptable price.

Because other business people are also trying to produce efficiently the things that individuals want, there is competition for the buyer's dollars. Those who make the best products—the products that people want most—at the lowest price will get most of the dollars. The people of the country are being served by this competition, because through it they are getting what they want. Although the successful business person may be working for personal gain—earning more money—all society benefits from the efforts. Thus the worker and the business person, motivated largely by self-

interest and the desire for profit, both contribute to the material growth of the country.

Adam Smith and the Theory of Classical Capitalism

Most of the theory behind classical capitalism comes from a book entitled *The Wealth of Nations,* published the year our country declared its political independence—1776. Adam Smith, a professor at the University of Glasgow, Scotland, described and advocated the system of classical capitalism. The system Smith described, which became the basis of our economic system, depends on the *market* to answer the basic economic questions. The market is the place where buyers and sellers meet and where prices placed on the goods we want to sell and buy determine how we allocate our resources. The things we buy determine the *What*—buying the best products at the lowest prices. Those who have taken the factors of production and put them together in the most economical way to produce the goods the public wants determine the *How.* The money that goes to those who do the jobs we indicate we want done and who do those jobs better than others indirectly answers the question *For whom.*

 Pure capitalism works best if each person pursues his or her own self-interest.

The Limited Role of Government

What part does the government play in Smith's plan? Almost none. We frequently refer to this system as *laissez-faire,* a French expression meaning "hands off." It is expected that government will protect us from invasion by foreign countries and will protect our freedoms and our property. However, the original plan contemplated no interference with the free flow of production factors and production itself. The directing computer—or the "invisible hand," as Smith called it—was responsible for guiding everything to the places that wanted it most. Remember that need was determined by the most money offered. Only if the government stayed out of the marketplace could the questions *What, How,* and *For whom* be answered in a way that would ensure the most good for the most people.

The Classical Model: Theory and Practice

Is the economic system we now have in this country the system Adam Smith described as existing in eighteenth-century England? Do workers and business persons determine their wages and prices in the marketplace on the basis of the dollar amounts suggested by the directing computer? Does the government really stay out of the marketplace?

The answer to all these questions is *no*. Business firms do not always compete with one another. Neither do workers or landlords. We must also note that the government does not always stay out of the marketplace.

This system that Adam Smith and others described—laissez-faire, or classical capitalism—is what economists sometimes call a *theory* or a *model*. Earlier we pointed out that a model is developed to help us analyze or understand the economy better. It is, like models you are familiar with, a set of plans designed to work in a particular way. You have probably seen people look at a set of plans and remark, "It looks good on paper, but . . ." This remark means that things in real life do not seem to work out quite the way they are planned. Similarly, economists' models do not seem to work out exactly as planned. Not every situation can be anticipated, or all details included. When theories or plans involving people are made, many things can go wrong. This does not mean that we should throw away our plans. Because we know of little involving human beings that is perfect, we should make plans with the hope that they will be as close to perfect as possible. However, we should recognize our limitations and make changes accordingly.

The classical model described by Adam Smith has largely served as the basis for our nation's economic system. However, the model originally set forth by Adam Smith was further defined and amplified as a result of continued study of its operation. Other economists, such as Jean Baptiste Say, a French economist writing at the beginning of the nineteenth century, and Alfred Marshall, a British professor of political economy writing at the end of the same century, took Smith's model and added to it or changed it.

 Pure capitalism, *laissez-faire*, the market system, free or private enterprise, and the classical model are used interchangeably to describe our economic system.

The Classical Model: Practice and Change

The classical model—sometimes called capitalism, sometimes laissez-faire—developed as the private enterprise system that ultimately became characteristic of our economy. We shall have to examine this model more closely, because it has guided us in the past and will probably continue to guide us in the future. In addition, we must try to answer the questions how and why have we changed the model? We have not become slaves to blueprints, but rather have changed the blueprints somewhat to meet our needs.

There were many things that Adam Smith, writing over 200 years ago, could not have foreseen in our modern atomic age. There are times when economists expect people to behave in certain ways, but they do not. When these things happen, we must alter our plans to allow for the unexpected or for new developments. If our model is really good and seems to do most of the things it is designed to do, we do not dispose of it when we have trouble. Rather, we modify it in an effort to make it a better model, one that meets our current demands.

At times, big business and big labor unions have interfered with the operation of the free market—of the directing computer—and we have had to make adjustments. Sometimes we have needed things in this country, but businesses either have not had enough money to provide them or have not wanted to do so because of fear that they might lose money trying! At times, through no fault of their own, some people have been unable to create enough value in the marketplace to support themselves and their families. These are just a few examples of situations that have influenced us to alter our model and to consider further changes.

In Part Three you will be introduced to another model, which uses a different approach to answer the big questions of our economy. Those who favor the new approach criticize the classical model as being too far removed from the reality of the world. However, the defenders of the classical model claim that it has not been given a fair chance, and some say we should return to it rather than continue altering it.

 The theory and reality of economic systems differ.

Reasons for Economic Controversy

From this discussion it is obvious that economics, like other disciplines, has unresolved problems. Just as you find disagreement about values and interpretations among physicians, biologists, historians, and art critics, so there are differences among economists. If economists disagree, how can a student who is just being introduced to the subject draw conclusions about economic problems? Although this question can be answered by pointing out that disagreement exists in all subjects, there are at least two better answers. First, the tools, the method of approach, the facts, and the problems that all economists deal with are the same. *Differences in economics most frequently arise because of disagreements over values and judgments.* These differences will be pointed out at the end of some chapters after the problems have been identified, the facts presented, and the tools given for analyzing the problem. Second, the areas of agreement are far greater than the areas of disagreement. For these reasons, economists are able to function within the discipline and provide students with the tools to make intelligent decisions as a consumer, a producer, and a citizen.

Changing Values

In 1973, a small but important book appeared that caused people, particularly traditional economists, to question many of their basic values. Most of us have always assumed that bigger, or more, is better. We set as our goals to make more money and to own larger and more expensive cars and homes, more appliances, and more expensive

clothes. Nationally, economic success is measured predominantly by the size and growth of the value of all goods and services produced (GNP). E. F. Schumacher, in *Small Is Beautiful: Economics As If People Mattered,*[6] raised a fundamental question that some college students and environmentalists had found an answer to over a decade earlier. Does happiness or a better way of life for those living in a mature industrial country depend on growing material wealth?

The answer is not a simple one because economic growth involves change—from agriculture to industry, from small business with its personal relationships to giant enterprise with its impersonality of mass production, from simple and more identifiable goals to complex and interdependent objectives. Economic growth is the way to more material abundance, but frequently it must be paid for at a cost to our individuality and our environment. Put another way, there is a trade-off between the cost and the benefits, both in dollars and in happiness, that growth can offer. Economists frequently do cost-benefit analysis to determine whether a new investment should be made. As you approach the economic problems in your reading, you should think of the trade-offs that may have to be made when you evaluate solutions.

Looking Ahead

We shall now take a close look at parts of the U.S. economy, examining the classical model, some of its modifications, and some unanswered questions. In Part Three we shall look at another model—the Keynesian—and discuss its application to the U.S. economy as a whole. Our analysis will include a look at the critics of Keynes, the monetarists, supply-siders, and those who believe in rational expectations. Then we shall take a brief look at some of the economic problems we are facing in this decade. We shall conclude by considering the part the economy of our country has played and will continue to play in the world.

In each instance, we shall try to use the following approach:

[6]New York: Harper & Row, 1973.

1. In what way does the model answer the big questions *What, How, For whom?*
2. If the model applies, what does it prescribe? Has it undergone any particular changes? Does it differ appreciably from conditions in the real world?
3. Are there problems that have to be solved? What are they, what are possible solutions, and what are the trade-offs?
4. What has been the impact of the growth of a global economy on our country and on the rest of the world?

Appendix: Reading and Working with Tables and Graphs

You have probably heard the expression "A picture is worth a thousand words." The expression may not always be true, but we can at least agree that both words and pictures are used to communicate ideas. Poets and novelists are best at using words, and painters and photographers use visual expressions. Although economists use both words and pictures, economists are best known for communicating with other tools: tables, graphs, and equations. All three have a place in communicating ideas. Frequently they are used together and are accompanied by word descriptions.

Surveys of students who have been discouraged in their study of economics reveal that the major cause of their difficulty was their inability to understand graphs. It is our hope that this appendix will provide you with the skills that will enable you to *read* tables and graphs, since these tools often communicate ideas better than words. We will focus on tables and graphs, since few equations are used in an introductory course.

Variables and Relationships

Tables and graphs show relationships between variables. Here we will concentrate on two variables, an *independent* variable and a *dependent* variable. The value of an independent variable—for example, the number of calories a person consumes in a day—may change freely. The value of a dependent variable fluctuates with the value of the independent variable, in this case the weight of the individual consuming the calories. In economics the most frequently used independent variable is price. If price is changed, the quantity sold (the dependent variable) will also change.

 An independent variable may change freely; a dependent variable changes with changes in the independent variable.

Variables can be related in different ways. In the case of consuming calories and gaining weight, there is a *direct relationship*. The greater the number of calories consumed, the more likely it is that the individual will gain weight. Table A–1 shows both variables increasing or decreasing in the same direction. Price and quantity, however, show an *inverse relationship*. When price is increased, the

Table A–1*   Relationship of Calories to Weight

Calories consumed daily		Weight change weekly	
4,500	↑	+3	↑
4,000	↑	+2	↑
3,500	↑	+1	↑
3,000	↑	0	↑
2,500	↑	−1	↑
2,000	↑	−2	↑

*For average male, 18–35 years, 175 pounds, 70 inches tall.

Table A–2   Relationship of Price to Quantity

Price of TV set		Quantity of TV sets sold	
$800	↑	10	↓
700	↑	20	↓
600	↑	35	↓
500	↑	55	↓
400	↑	80	↓

quantity sold decreases. When price is decreased, the quantity sold increases. Table A–2 shows this inverse relationship.

All Other Things Being Equal

In both cases cited above we made assumptions about other variables. In our illustration using the relationship of calorie consumption and weight change, we used an "average male," 18–35 years, 175 pounds, 70 inches tall. If such a man led a very sedentary life, he might gain weight on a daily consumption of 3,000 calories. A football player in training might lose weight consuming 4,000 calories a day. In our example we have assumed that the characteristics of the person, including his activities and state of health, remained constant. Only the amount of calories he ate changed. The assumption we have made is that all other things have remained the same.

 Graphs show two variables. Other variables are held constant.

In our second case, the sale of TV sets, we assumed a particular time of year. Sales of TV sets are lower in the summer. The data in Table A–2 hold true only if all other things are equal.

From Tables to Graphs

Tables A–1 and A–2 show the relationship between two variables. Our next step is to "see" that relationship through the use of a graph. Most of the graphs in this text represent two quantities, which are shown by vertical and horizontal lines called *axes*. The axes meet at a point of origin, 0. Each axis is divided into regular intervals, or spaces, and the intervals are numbered.

 Graphs convert the numbers in tables into pictures showing relationships.

Figure A–1 shows the appropriate axes for Table A–1, and Figure A–2 shows the axes for Table A–2. The vertical axis is called the *y* axis. It represents the independent variable (in Table A–1, calories). The horizontal axis is called the *x* axis. It shows the dependent variable (in Table

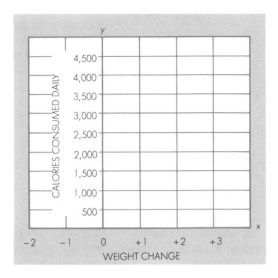

Figure A–1

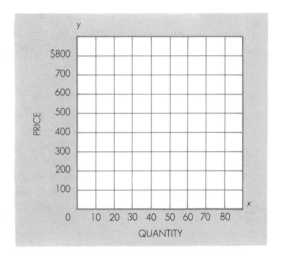

Figure A–2

A–1, weight). In order to get a visual picture of our table, we will have to use both vertical and horizontal axes and the appropriate numbers found in the table. Figure A–3 shows the information from Table A–1. We take the number 4,500 in the calorie column (the independent variable) and match it with the corresponding number +3 in the weight change column (the dependent variable). Follow the vertical, or *y*, axis in Figure A–3

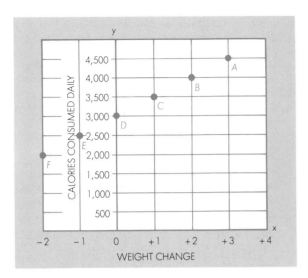

Figure A–3

The Slope of the Curve

One of the most important properties of a curve represented on a graph is its slope. Slope may be measured by identifying the change in the *y*, or independent, variable divided by the change in the *x*, or dependent, variable. Table A–3 and Figure A–5 show the demand for 42-inch TV sets in a large department store in one week.

As you will see in Chapter 2, demand curves are usually downward sloping and show an inverse relationship between price and quantity. However, the slope is often not uniform. In Figure A–5 the

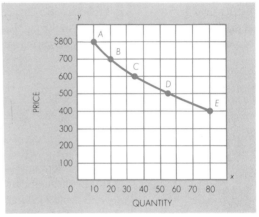

Figure A–4

until you reach 4,500. Now move horizontally to the right until you reach +3. You see a point, which we have labeled *A*, representing the two numbers 4,500 and +3. The *y* axis is labeled calories, and the *x* axis is labeled weight change.

Once the first point has been located, the rest is easy. Find 4,000 on the *y* axis and move horizontally to the right to +2. Note that these numbers correspond to the numbers in Table A–1. See the point *B?* Points *C*, *D*, *E*, and *F* are likewise derived from the numbers in Table A–1. (Points *E* and *F* to the left of the vertical axis are negative because the weight change is in pounds lost. However, we will not concern ourselves with negative values.)

In Figure A–4 we have plotted each of the two coordinate numbers, price and quantity. The numbers are taken from Table A–2, and each is labeled. Here we have gone a step further than we did in Figure A–3; we have connected all the points. In economics we call the line connecting points *A* and *E* a *curve*, even if it is straight as in Figure A–3. Note in Figure A–3 that the curve slopes upward as you move from left to right; an upward slope shows a direct relationship. In Figure A–4 the curve slopes downward; as price declines the quantity rises, an inverse relationship.

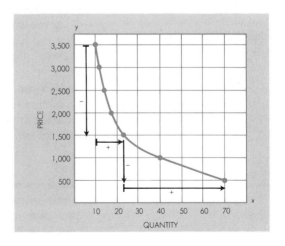

Figure A–5

TABLE A–3

Price	Quantity
$3,500	10
3,000	12
2,500	14
2,000	17
1,500	22
1,000	40
500	70

slope is very steep from $3,500 down to $1,500. A vertical arrow shows the drop in price from $3,500 to $1,500. The horizontal arrow is much shorter than the vertical arrow, because this change in price brings only a minor change in the number of sets sold, from 10 to 22. Clearly, lowering the price in this price range does little to stimulate sales, since few people can afford such a TV set.

 The slope of a curve shows the relationship between the two variables.

Now look at what happens to the slope of the curve when you move from $1,500 to $500. The second vertical arrow, showing the drop in price, is clearly shorter in length than the horizontal arrow showing the change in quantity sold. Clearly, a drop in price from $1,500 to $500 brings a major increase in the quantity sold. In this lower price range those in the middle class may choose to spend a little more money to get a much larger TV set, partially at the expense of not purchasing other goods. The slope of curves will be discussed in more detail in Chapter 2.

Chapter Highlights

1. Economists are highly trained professionals who aid decision makers through their ability to collect and analyze relevant data, to forecast, and to suggest solutions. Their success record, however, is mixed.
2. The study of economics helps you to understand your role as a consumer and producer and provides you with tools to make wise decisions as a citizen.
3. Economics is both an art and a social science. It is an organized body of knowledge from which generalizations based on data may be developed and used for predicting and controlling behavior. Like other sciences, it makes assumptions and uses models reflecting the real world. Its record on predicting and controlling behavior is spotty, and in this sense it is more like an art than a science.
4. Economics is concerned with the production, distribution, and consumption of goods and services.
5. Scarcity forces people to make choices. They must select alternative uses of resources in an effort to maximize the satisfaction of their wants.
6. Effective use of resources is producing products that best satisfy wants. Efficiency is getting the most output from the resources used.
7. The central problem in economics stems from the opposing conditions of limited resources and people's unlimited wants. To solve this problem individuals must make choices.

8. There are three related problems that every society must find answers to: *What* shall we produce? *How* shall we produce it? *For whom* shall we produce it?

9. All production involves four basic factors: natural resources, labor, capital, and entrepreneurship. Natural resources are the materials nature provides, labor is work applied to production, and capital is the man-made instruments used in production. Finally, entrepreneurs initiate and organize the other factors.

10. The production process involves putting the factors of production together at the right time, place, and price to satisfy consumer wants.

11. The production possibilities curve is an economic tool that shows the greatest amount of goods and services that a nation can produce at a particular time. If a nation produces less, it is not fully utilizing its resources. The curve also shows the trade-off in production between two types of goods.

12. Opportunity cost is the value of what is given up or lost by a resource (or individual) when that resource is used in the next best alternative way.

13. An economic system provides rules and guiding principles to help us answer the central and related questions. An economic system that depends primarily on private enterprise to supply production is called capitalism. When production comes mainly from government enterprise, the economic system is known as socialism. Most countries have mixed economies, although they may emphasize business or government.

14. The U.S. economy emphasizes production by private enterprise. Under this system, the *What* is determined by business people, who are influenced in their decisions by what consumers purchase in the market for goods and services. To produce these goods, businesses go to the market to buy the factors of production. Money payments are used as incentives to reward people for supplying the services that society wants.

15. Adam Smith, in *The Wealth of Nations*, set forth what has come to be known as the classical model. This model depends on a market free from government interference to answer the main questions. Government's role is to protect freedom and property and to defend against foreign invasion.

16. Many forces have worked to interfere with the freedom of the market and to cause alteration of the model. Although economists disagree somewhat about whether to go back to the original model, alter it further, or substitute a new model, they generally agree on facts, methods, and approaches to problems.

17. Some people now question whether economic growth is worth the possible sacrifices in other human values. Economists approach problems by considering the costs versus the benefits of solutions to problems.

Study Aids

Key Terms

scarcity
choice
effective
efficient
assumption
economics
model
central problem
what?
how?

for whom?
distribution
laissez-faire
Wealth of Nations
economic system
factors of production
production process
production possibilities curve
capitalism
incentives

private enterprise
circular flow
classical model
cost-benefit analysis
trade-off
opportunity cost

Questions

1. Of what value are economists to society? Why might they disagree on solutions to problems?
2. How may consumers use opportunity cost to deal with their problem of scarcity?
3. Define *economics* and then explain how the central problem in economics is the basic focus of this discipline.
4. Why is it difficult to classify any country as having a fixed economic system?
5. How does the production process work? Show the role each factor of production plays in the process.
6. Explain how the circular-flow model answers the basic questions *What, How,* and *For whom.*
7. What was Adam Smith's contribution to economics?

Problems

1. Ask five people what economics is and then evaluate their answers.
2. Explain how a business you are familiar with fits into the economic system.
3. Determine what the opportunity cost is for going to college.
4. Locate a graph relating to economics in a newspaper or magazine. What is the independent variable? The dependent variable? Is there a direct or inverse relationship between them?

Demand and Supply: An Answer to Resource Allocation

In the first chapter, after identifying what economics is and what problems it seeks to solve, we sketched the model that has extensively guided development of the U.S. economy. Now, a closer look at this classical model will show how it provides answers to the central problem of allocating our resources. Because our resources are limited and our wants are not, we must decide how we will use what we have. In our economic system, these choices should be determined by what people want and by the efficiency of the producing unit.

The *market* is the place or condition in which buyers and sellers meet to exchange commodities for the prices they agree on. The buyers' willingness and ability to purchase at certain prices is called *demand*. The sellers' offer to part with goods or services at certain prices is the *supply*. The numbers and independence of buyers and sellers determine the kind of competition. Our market structure, with its price system, is used to allocate our resources. How far are our resources actually allocated under our present system?

A few hints may help you in studying this chapter. Take a few products and services at random to see whether you understand the concept of elasticity. There is an easy-to-overlook distinction between a change in price and a change in demand. As you read, keep in mind that the law of diminishing marginal utility helps explain the downward-sloping demand curve, whereas the law of diminishing returns applies to the supply curve. Finally, use the step-by-step review with graphs at the end of the chapter to review visually the material covered.

Consider your own behavior as a consumer. When you buy hamburger, do you go where you can get it at the lowest price? How might your behavior distort or support the market mechanism? As a producer, how would you resolve the "trade-off" between the price and the quality?

Chapter Objectives

When you have completed this chapter, you should be able to:

- Describe the function of price in resource allocation.
- Define the term *market* and list and define the four types of markets.
- Define *demand* and discuss the relation of demand to the law of diminishing marginal utility.
- Define *supply* and discuss the relation of supply to the law of diminishing returns.
- Describe the effects on equilibrium price of elasticity and of changes in demand and supply.
- Evaluate whether the laws of supply and demand have been modified.

A The Market

Price: An Important Economic Influence

Price is a primary influence in determining allocation of resources in our free enterprise system. It determines what goods and services will be produced and how much of them. It influences the use of the four factors of production. In addition, price is most important in determining who gets what. A different way of stating this idea is to say that the price system answers the questions *What, How,* and *For whom.*

When we think of price, we often also think of value; and when we think of value, we may think of usefulness, or utility. The student of economics must distinguish among price, value, and utility. Although none of the three is exactly the same as the others, it is easy to see that they are closely related. *Utility* relates to the satisfaction that a good or service can provide. Both time and place affect utility. In December a bathing suit is likely to have less utility in Buffalo, New York, than in Miami. Yet in July it might be of greater value in Buffalo than in Miami.

If in addition to having usefulness, a good or service is relatively scarce, it has economic value. When we measure value in terms of other goods and services, we call it *exchange value*. When we measure that value in money, we call it *price.*

Conditions of Pure Competition

A market is a place or situation where buyers and sellers meet. It can be a market for goods and services, where consumers meet suppliers, or a market to which suppliers come to bid for the factors of production. For the classical model to work as planned, certain market conditions must be met:

1. There must be enough buyers and enough sellers acting independently so that the entry or exit of any one buyer or seller will not affect price.
2. The products offered for sale must be sufficiently alike for buyers to feel free to choose the product offered by any seller.
3. New sellers must be able to enter the market freely and existing sellers must be able to leave.
4. Buyers and sellers must be informed about prices, quantities, and quality.

These four conditions signify what economists call a *purely competitive market,* or *pure competition.*

Consumers Benefit from Competitive Prices

Pure competition serves the consumer well, because if sellers are to be successful, they must offer their products at the lowest prices. Charging one penny more than any other seller will mean no sales, because it is assumed there is no difference in quality between one product and another.

Society Progresses through Improved Efficiency

To obtain higher profits, sellers are encouraged to improve their products and produce them with more efficiency. The better the product and the lower the cost, the more money to be made. Such a goal, which at first appears selfish, is also in the best interests of the consumer. Those who favor this classical model call the desire to make more money by increasing efficiency and improving products *incentive*. They consider this a step toward a better society because it induces performance at the most efficient level. Others think such motivation runs counter to the spirit of brotherhood, pits people against their fellows, and is not a fair method of distributing production. The clash among several sets of values has resulted in modification of the classical model. We shall examine this synthesis after we have examined the classical model more closely and have taken a look at the market situations that actually exist.

Market Conditions Other Than Pure Competition

All competition that is not pure is called *imperfect competition*. Few markets in the United States meet the four conditions of pure competition. Agriculture, textiles, and certain retail fields come closest. Yet even in these areas there is some interference with the market freedom of the classical model.

Pure Monopoly

The opposite of pure competition is *pure monopoly*, which exists when the following conditions prevail:

1. Only one seller offers the product for sale, allowing considerable control over price by the seller.

2. There is no close substitute to which the buyer can turn.
3. Other competing businesses cannot enter the field.

Pure monopoly places the consumer at the mercy of the monopolist. With no place to turn, the consumer must be deprived of the product or pay the price the monopolist charges. Because prices are unchecked by competition, more of the consumer's limited resources are used. The consumer's position is further weakened in that the monopolist lacks incentive to improve the product, since the consumer has no alternative source of purchase. In this particular case, monopoly interferes with progress.

Fortunately for the consumer in the United States, there are today no large privately owned monopolies that are not regulated by government. Thus, in *public utilities* and transportation, the protective measures of the government are designed to safeguard the consumer. Public monopolies, such as the post office, mint, and fire department, are owned by the people. However, neither government regulation nor ownership provides the incentive for improving efficiency and lowering prices.

Before World War II, the Aluminum Company of America had a virtual monopoly on primary aluminum through its control of bauxite, the primary ingredient for making aluminum. However, unregulated national monopolies are now no longer a problem. In some cases, government action has helped to establish competition by creating an environment that has brought additional producers into the market. We can still find businesses having a virtual monopoly in their geographic areas—television stations, newspapers, and cement plants, for instance. The effect of these local monopolies on prices is debatable.

Monopolistic Competition

Most markets are found to be somewhere between pure competition and pure monopoly. Many sellers acting independently, with each trying to promote a product allegedly different from products of other sellers, create a market condition known as *monopolistic competition*. The manufacturers of name-brand aspirin plead with buyers not to ask simply for aspirin or for a combination-of-ingredients tablet, but to ask for their aspirin by name. The implication is that their aspirin is a special product. Consumers can substitute a different brand of tablet, but will they be getting the same product? Because substitution is not as easy under monopolistic competition as under pure competition, the seller has some control over price.

Oligopoly

The remaining market situations are classified as *oligopoly*. The prefix *oligo-*, "a few," suggests the meaning. An oligopoly exists when a few sellers have sufficient control over the market for a product so that changes in price by one will affect all other sellers. Examples of oligopolies are the "Big Three" in automobiles and the "Big Four" in rubber tires, linoleum, tin cans, and cigarettes. Although it is difficult for buyers to differentiate among products like tin cans, copper, and steel, there is an attempt to do so wherever possible. Serious barriers to entering the market exist, and little attempt is made to bring about changes in price, particularly reductions in price. Absence of pure competition does not eliminate changes in

price resulting from changes in the supply of goods offered, but it does lessen any such effect. Under conditions of oligopoly, the producer must be very careful that an action by any firm will not bring retaliatory action by others in the field.

Competition Among Buyers

Just as there are situations involving sellers that deviate from the classical model, so pure competition is not always found on the buyers' side. Frequently, suppliers of goods not used directly by consumers—tobacco farmers and ranchers, for instance—find themselves in market situations with few buyers, or even in a condition of *monopsony*, where there is only one buyer. In some industries, a few buyers meet a few sellers. The rubber tire industry, which is an oligopoly, must sell a major share of its product to automobile manufacturers, whose industry is also oligopolistic. When large retail chain stores contract with producers to manufacture an item under the store name, they exercise considerable control over price. Though competition among buyers has not been reduced as much as it has among sellers, we cannot ignore its reduction as a factor in influencing price.

B   How Demand Functions in the Classical Model

In our discussion of different market conditions, we showed that prices were influenced by the number of buyers and sellers. The interaction of demand and supply for all market conditions determines price. The purely competitive market is a good starting point for studying markets because:

1. Competition is a condition most Americans consider desirable, and we have pursued a policy of making our market more competitive.
2. Imperfect competition is affected by the same forces that affect perfect competition, but in a modified way.
3. We are all consumers and are affected by price.

 Competition is important if the market is to function efficiently.

The Nature of Demand

The computer registering the wants of consumers does not register the daydreams that people have about what they would buy if they had more money. Only when consumers have the purchasing power and are willing to part with their limited resources to obtain a good or a service at a given price does the computer react. This willingness of consumers to purchase certain amounts of a product at given prices at a particular time and place is called *demand*.

Consumers will purchase products based on

(1) the urgency of their need for the product, (2) the price of the product, (3) expectations of future prices, (4) the price of the substitutes, and (5) their income. The general rule of the *law of demand* is that *the lower the price of a given product, the more of this product the consumers will buy.* In the opposite situation, the higher the price, the less the consumers will buy.

Demand Is Subject to the Law of Diminishing Marginal Utility

Why do consumers buy products? They usually buy to satisfy a want. The utility of a product depends on its ability to satisfy wants. The greater the want satisfaction, the greater the utility. However, utility for a number of units of a given product, let us say bags of pretzels, is not the same. If you have eight bags of pretzels, each bagful you eat may increase your total satisfaction. However, the satisfaction you derive from the first bag of pretzels is likely to be greater than satisfaction from the second bag. The third will probably give you less satisfaction than the second, and the fourth less than the third, and so on. Even if you are particularly fond of pretzels, it is unlikely you would wish to consume the total number of bags of pretzels you have available. Once your hunger for pretzels is satisfied, each unit you consume will give you an ever-diminishing satisfaction, and therefore will have an ever-decreasing utility.

The word *marginal* is frequently used in economics. It refers to one more unit or one less unit. The marginal utility of bags of pretzels would be the degree of satisfying power—utility—of eating the last bag of pretzels you have had or the next bag you will have. The *law of diminishing marginal utility* states that as the number of units of a product a consumer has increases, the satisfying power for each extra unit decreases. You may be willing to pay 80 cents for the first small bag of pretzels that usually sells for 50 cents, but you will buy additional bags only at lower prices as your desire for them declines.

Other Factors Also Influence Demand

Although the law of diminishing marginal utility explains consumer purchases on the basis of

urgency of need and price of product, substitutes and the level of income of buyers also affect demand. If you are in a theater and want something to eat while watching the movie, you will probably go to the refreshment stand (a monopoly) and see what is for sale. Pretzels might be your first choice, but the 80-cent price seems too high. A small candy bar costs only 50 cents. Although the candy bar is not quite as satisfying as the pretzels to you, it is cheaper. The price of the substitute may cause you and other pretzel lovers to buy candy in spite of your preference for pretzels.

Suppose you are in the situation described above, but this time your funds are greater. You will probably splurge on the pretzels. Your added resources allow you to satisfy more of your wants. In the mid-1980s, fast-food chains grew so rapidly that supermarkets felt the impact; increased income allowed consumers to shift to more costly eating habits.

Demand Schedule

Some students may have received the impression that demand refers only to how much of a product consumers would buy at a particular price. This is not a correct interpretation. Our definition of *demand* was a "willingness" on the part of consumers to buy certain amounts of products at given prices. The fact that at 80 cents only a few pretzel lovers will buy bags of pretzels that they usually pay only 50 cents for does not mean that many have no desire for the pretzels. They just do not want to part with that much of their limited resources. However, if the price is dropped to 60 cents, many who were not willing to buy before may now want to purchase pretzels. If the price is reduced to 40 cents, a greater quantity of pretzels will be sold. At a still lower price, a still larger number will be sold, perhaps also to candy lovers buying pretzels as a substitute.

When we speak of the quantity of a product that consumers will buy at varied price levels, we are making use of the economist's concept of demand. When we list in a table the amounts consumers will buy of a product at various prices, in a particular market, and at a given point in time,

Table 2–1   Demand schedule for bags of
pretzels for one week

Price	Quantity
$.80	50
.70	150
.60	250
.50	350
.40	450

Increasing the price causes consumers to switch their
purchases to other goods.

we have a *demand schedule*. Table 2–1 is an
example of a demand schedule.

Demand Curve

Let us see what the demand schedule for pretzels
looks like when we place it on a graph. Figure
2–1 illustrates graphically the demand schedule
in Table 2–1. The vertical axis shows the five
different price levels; the horizontal axis shows
quantities at intervals of 100. We draw our demand
curve (or line) by locating a point on our graph
for each of the different price levels. We go up
the vertical axis, measuring price, until we come
to 80 cents. We then follow the horizontal line to
the right until we come to the right quantity for
80 cents—50. Because we have quantities identified only in intervals of 100 units, we locate our
point halfway between 0 and 100. Point A on Figure 2–1 shows the demand for bags of pretzels at
the price of 80 cents. We now locate points for
70 cents (B), 60 cents (C), 50 cents (D), and 40
cents (E). Next we connect points A, B, C, D,
and E, and we can see what the demand schedule
in Table 2–1 looks like on a graph. Can we tell
how many bags of pretzels will be sold at 53 cents?
Our demand schedule does not give us this information; but, if we measure on the vertical axis
three-tenths of the way between 50 cents and 60
cents and draw a horizontal line to the right, we
can get an estimate. The point at which our 53-
cent price line crosses our demand curve gives us
an approximation of the quantity that could be
sold. Is it closest to 260, 280, or 310?

Notice how the demand curve slopes downward as we move along to the right. This helps

explain the economics of the buying habits of consumers. Can you explain the economics of a sale
held by a retail merchant? As you move from left
to right on our demand curve, you should be able
to explain how the downward slope reflects the
law of diminishing marginal utility. Consider
yourself buying and eating successive bags of
pretzels. The diminishing utility of each (and
therefore your unwillingness to pay the same price
for another bag) should make diminishing marginal utility and the downward demand curve clear.

Changes in Demand

A change in demand means an increase or a
decrease in the number of units of a product that
can be sold throughout the range of prices at which
they are offered. It does *not* mean a change in the
number of units sold brought about by a change
in the price. An example will clarify the difference. When reports first came out linking cigarette smoking with lung cancer, there was a decline
in the demand for cigarettes. This is shown on a
graph as a shifting of the demand curve to the

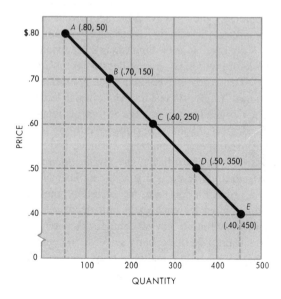

**Figure 2–1   Demand curve for bags of
pretzels for one week**

The downward-sloping curve shows consumers buying
more bags of pretzels as the price is reduced.

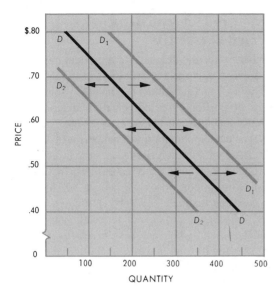

Figure 2–2 Changes in the demand curve

Changes in demand are shown by shifting the curve to the right, D_1, or to the left, D_2, from the original demand D. Explain how you can determine which of the two curves (D_1 or D_2) represents an increase in demand.

left. In Figure 2–2 the demand curve moves from D to D_2. Each new report brought about a further change in demand. The decrease in sales did not come about through a change in price, but rather through the change linking cigarette smoking with health; the decrease occurred at all prices. In contrast, a change in price, rather than a change in demand, would bring about a change in the quantity bought. This change is reflected by movement upward and to the left on the demand curve D in Figure 2–2; the curve itself does not move.

Causes for a Change in Demand

Changes in demand may be caused by (1) a change in people's taste; (2) a change in consumer income; and (3) a change in the market price for a substitute or complementary good. An important change has taken place in the demand for butter, particularly in the last 15 years. Advertising, inventions, and changes in style affect demand by changing people's tastes. How can producers protect themselves from a change in demand?

Changes in Price; Changes in Demand

A deep freeze hit Brazil in 1976, killing many coffee trees. This dropped the supply of coffee, thereby pushing the price to $4 a pound, more than double the usual price, within a few months. Sales dropped 17 percent, while price rose 100 percent. Coffee has a relatively inelastic demand.

The change in the price of coffee did not reduce the demand for it. It did lower the quantity sold because of the additional cost for satisfying that desire. *A change in price does not cause a change in demand.*

Tea is a substitute for coffee. The increased price for coffee caused some coffee drinkers to switch to tea. *A change in the price of a substitute,* coffee, *will cause a change in demand* for tea.

When the price of gasoline quadrupled in the 1970s, the demand for large, gas-guzzling cars dropped. When gasoline prices dropped in 1983, there was a modest increase in the demand for larger cars. *A change in price of a complementary good,* gasoline, *causes a change in demand* for large cars.

A change in demand will result in a new set of figures on the demand schedule. When we plot a new demand curve, we find the curve has shifted either to the right or to the left of the original demand curve. In Figure 2–2, which curve illustrates an increase in demand? Which curve illustrates a decrease? If you follow one price level, such as 50 cents, through all three demand curves, you can easily find the answer.

Price Elasticity of Demand

Not all demand curves look like the one shown in Figure 2–1. Let us look at the demand for salt instead of the demand for pretzels. The price of salt may vary from 20 cents a pound to 35 cents a pound. If your family uses between one and two pounds of salt a month, its expenditure for salt could fluctuate from 20 to 70 cents a month, depending on the quantities used and the prices paid. Another way of looking at the situation is to say that the cost of satisfying your family's need for salt can fluctuate from ⅔ cent to 2⅓ cents per day. There would probably be a very small decline in the sale of salt if the price increased 50 percent, or even 100 percent. The cost is so low, even at the highest price, that few people would deprive themselves. When the percentage change in price is greater than the percentage change in the quantity bought, we say that the demand for the product is inelastic.

 Elasticity is the responsiveness of quantity to changes in price.

An Example of Price Elastic Demand

The demand for expensive meats is usually quite different from that for salt. When the price of sirloin steak drops from $4 a pound to $3, a 25 percent reduction, sales are likely to increase by 100 percent (from, say, 500 pounds to 1,000 pounds). Shoppers will switch from hamburger to steak. When the quantity of products sold is very responsive to price changes, their demand is said to be *elastic*.

Factors Determining Price Elasticity

What makes the demand for a product inelastic? Usually the demand is inelastic when (1) it is difficult to find a substitute; (2) the outlay represents a small portion of an individual's budget; and (3) the product is considered a necessity. Any one reason or a combination will tend to make demand inelastic. Try these criteria on salt. In contrast, products that have many substitutes, that represent a large portion of the budget, and that are considered luxuries tend to be elastic in demand.

Most products do not fit neatly into either category, and what may have an elastic demand in one family may have an inelastic demand in another. Evaluate elasticity of demand for milk, a television set, your favorite magazine, a second car in a suburban family, and a first car for a low-income family in a metropolitan center. The influence of elasticity of demand may be seen in Cases I and II of the classical model in the Review Model at the end of the chapter.

A word of caution before you try to analyze the elasticity of a product: For most products, elasticity changes over a very broad price range. Demand for steak may be quite elastic when its price fluctuates between $4 and $3 a pound. As the price goes above $4, it becomes inelastic. There will be a relatively small change in the quantity of steak sold when the price goes above $5. The relatively few who can afford to pay such a high price, or the few who feel they must have steak because they just love it, will probably pay the additional money regardless of price.

Measuring for Price Elasticity

How can we be sure when a product is price elastic or inelastic? We can measure price elasticity by using the formula

$$\text{Price elasticity} = \frac{\% \text{ change in quantity}}{\% \text{ change in price}}$$

or

$$E_d = \frac{\% \Delta Q}{\% \Delta P}$$

where E_d = Price elasticity, Δ is the Greek letter delta standing for change, Q = quantity, and P = price.

The percentage change in quantity is derived by dividing the change in quantity by the original quantity:

$$\frac{\Delta Q}{Q} = \frac{500}{500} = 1$$

The percentage change in price is derived by dividing the change in price by the original price:

$$\frac{\Delta P}{P} = \frac{1}{4} = 0.25$$

Thus the price elasticity for sirloin steak as shown in our sale is

$$E_d = \frac{1}{0.25} = 4$$

If the price elasticity of demand is greater than 1, the product has an *elastic demand*. If the price elasticity is less than 1, the product has an *inelastic demand*. If the price elasticity is 1, the product has *unitary elasticity.*

The Revenue Test

The price elasticity of demand for a product can be determined by noting how a change in price affects revenue. The price times the quantity sold equals total revenue. If total revenue increases when price decreases, demand for a product is said to be *elastic*. When the price of steak is $4 a pound, the butcher sells 500 pounds, for a day's receipts of $2000 ($P \times Q = R$) from the sale of steak. When the price is dropped to $3 a pound, sales rise to 1,000 pounds a day. The butcher's revenue from steak for the day is now $3,000. The change in price of 25 percent brought about a larger change in quantity sold, + 100 percent, resulting in an increase in revenue. The demand for steak is elastic.

If total revenue decreases when price decreases, the demand for the product is said to be *inelastic*. At 60 cents, a grocer sells 100 cakes

of soap a day, yielding $60 revenue. He drops the price to 50 cents and increases sales to 110 units for a day. His total revenue decreases to $55 from the sale of soap. Additional deductions in price bring about greater decreases in total revenue. The demand for soap is inelastic.

If total revenue neither increases nor decreases with change in price, the product is said to have *unitary elasticity* of demand.

 Price elasticity of demand can be determined by changes in revenue resulting from changes in price.

Price Elasticity Shown on a Graph

We can plot the price elasticity of the demand for a product on a graph and show the impact of a price change on revenue. Figure 2–3 shows the demand for three different products, D, D_1, and D_2. When the price is set at $3, consumers buy 100 units of each product per day. Revenue is $300 for each ($P \times Q = R$).

When the price drops to $2, the sales for each unit increase. For D_1 the units sold increase to 130, but revenue declines to $260 ($2 \times 130 = $260). D_1 has an inelastic demand. Sales for D rise to 200 units, increasing revenue from $300 to $400. The demand curve for D is less steep, and the demand for the product is slightly elastic. The curve of D_2 is more horizontal than the others, indicating greater responsiveness to the change in price. Sales jump to 400 units, increasing revenue to $800 and indicating a very elastic demand.

A product could have a perfectly elastic or perfectly inelastic demand. The former would appear on a graph as a horizontal line showing that the product would sell an infinite amount without a change in price. A farmer might be able to sell all of his wheat at the market price but none at a higher price.

A rare drug that could cure cancer would be an example of a product whose demand is perfectly inelastic. Those needing it would pay any price to get it, but the quantity offered would be fixed.

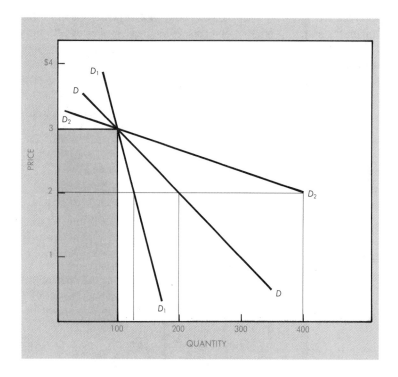

Figure 2–3   Impact of a price change on revenues for products with different demand elasticities

Reducing the price from $3 to $2 decreases revenue for a product with an inelastic demand, as in D_1, and increases revenue greatly for a product with a highly elastic demand, as in D_2. Compare the size of the shaded rectangle, where the price is $3, with the sizes of the rectangles for D_1 and D_2, where the price has dropped to $2. The size of the rectangle represents the size of the revenue. If you were manager of a store, which of the three products would you put on sale?

C How Supply Functions in the Classical Model

What Is Supply?

Just as demand deals with the consumer's willingness to buy, supply concerns itself with producers or sellers and their willingness to offer products for sale. Like demand, supply refers to a particular product offered in a given market at a given time and at different prices. We may define supply as the various amounts of products that a seller will offer for sale at specific prices at a

specified time and place. When we have this information, we can prepare a supply schedule, just as we prepared a demand schedule.

Factors Influencing Supply

Supply, like demand, is subject to change under a variety of conditions. Changes occur not in relation to price but in response to other events of the market.

Supply and the Time Factor

In considering supply, we must recognize that the time factor has an important effect on availability. For an accurate analysis of supply, we must know which of the following conditions applies to what is being offered for sale:

1. The product immediately available.
2. The short run, where producers or sellers can use their present facilities to increase or decrease the amount of the product.
3. The long run, where producers and sellers can increase their facilities to produce or sell more or less of the product, and where either additional producers or sellers or fewer producers or sellers may leave or enter the market.

When designer jeans were first introduced into the market, a few firms devoted a small part of their production facilities to them. No one could possibly have known how well this new style would catch on. A supply curve for the early designer blue jeans could be drawn. When it became apparent that they were going to be very popular, the producers already involved in making them used their existing facilities to turn out more. The supply curve for this situation is for the short run. When enthusiasm continued to mount, other producers decided that they should undertake production of the new fashions, and so additional facilities were used. This last situation would call for a supply curve for the long run.

Let us turn back to our computer. The intensity of the demand for new-fashioned pants is picked up on the antenna and registered on the computer. This information is relayed to business persons, who then realize they can earn additional dollars if they turn their efforts to producing these pants. However, such action takes time and reflects our three possible supply situations—present, short run, and long run.

The Law of Supply

There is a direct relation between price and quantity supplied. When suppliers can get a higher price than the current one for their product, they have incentive to go to the market to bid for additional factors of production. They will even bid higher than other bidders so they can offer more of their product for sale. The general rule for supply states that *producers will offer more of their product for sale as price rises and will offer less as price falls*.

Cost as a Factor in Supply

In a purely competitive market, the supplier of goods and services has no control over the market price, because he produces too little to influence market conditions. With no difference between his product and the products of his competitors, he will sell nothing if he charges above the market price and he will sell all if he charges at or below the market price. However, in considering the price, he must take cost of production into account. There are times when he may be willing to sell below his cost. This might happen when prices tumble for what he believes will be a short time. However, no business person can afford to lose money for a prolonged period. He must be constantly aware of his costs in relation to the market price if he is to compete successfully and earn a profit.

Many people have the impression that as production increases, costs per unit decrease. Though mass production has made this true in certain industries and at certain levels of production, both logic and practical experience have shown that costs per unit begin to rise beyond a certain level of production. Some economists refer to this principle as the *law of increasing costs*.

The reason costs rise as production goes up is complex, and we will explain it in Chapter 5. However, it is easy to recognize that as production goes up, the need for additional factors of production will also grow, resulting in competitive bidding in the marketplace for the factors of production. If a producer needs more skilled labor to produce more, and none of this labor is unemployed, the producer will have to get it from other sources. This can be done by offering higher wages. Higher bidding would also apply to the other factors of production. We must also recognize that not all labor is equally productive, just as not all land is equally fertile and not all ore is equally rich in the mineral wanted.

As production increases, costs to the supplier increase. Only the expectation of higher prices will cause him or her to increase production.

When output is low, producers will use the most efficient factors of production. As these factors of production grow scarcer, producers will have to use the less productive factors. Only when prices rise does it pay to use these less productive factors. Otherwise, the additional costs will be greater than the additional revenue.

Supply Schedule and Supply Curve

A *supply schedule* is a table listing the amount of a product that sellers will offer for sale at various prices in a particular market and at a given time. From the data in a supply schedule, we can draw a supply curve. Table 2−2 shows a supply schedule for bags of pretzels for a week. Figure 2−4 shows the supply curve drawn from this supply

Table 2−2   Supply schedule for bags of pretzels for one week

Price	Quantity
$.80	450
.70	350
.60	250
.50	150
.40	50

When the market price increases, suppliers can afford to increase the quantity they offer for sale.

schedule. This schedule may be compared with the demand schedule, and the supply curve compared with the demand curve in Figure 2−1.

Changes in Supply

A change in supply, like a change in demand, is a change in the quantity of the product at the different price levels. It is *not* a change in the quan-

Alfred Marshall and His Contribution to Price Theory

Alfred Marshall (1842–1924), for many years professor of economics at Cambridge University in England, is most noted for his contributions to the theory of price. Believing strongly that the best of all economic worlds is one in which the forces of supply and demand are able to operate in a free competitive market with a minimum of government interference, Marshall focused attention on the individual firm and the ways in which prices for its goods are determined. Borrowing from the classical economists Smith and

Ricardo the concept of the importance of cost on the supply side, and from the marginalists, of whom he was the greatest (see Section 8A), the concept of demand determined by marginal utility, he created a new synthesis for interpreting price formation. As an expert mathematician, he developed diagrams to aid in economic analyses.

Perhaps Marshall's greatest contribution was the recognition that the time element is extremely important in determining supply. For the immediate period, demand

is the main factor that determines price, because supply is fixed. As the time interval is lengthened, supply can be adapted to changes in demand, with cost of production kept in mind. For the short run, a business can alter its quantity by using existing facilities of production. In the long run, a business is able to change its production facilities, for example, by adding a new plant and equipment. Therefore, the supply side becomes more important as the interval of time is increased.

Marshall was not only an original thinker and a great synthesizer but also a great teacher. His most famous pupil was John Maynard Keynes, the most influential economist of the twentieth century (see the profile in Chapter 12).

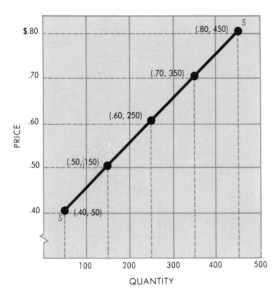

Figure 2–4   Supply curve for bags of pretzels for one week
The upward-sloping curve shows that the seller will offer more bags of pretzels as the price is increased.

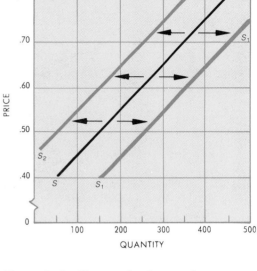

Figure 2–5   Changes in the supply curve
Changes in supply are shown graphically by shifting the original curve S to the right, S_1, or to the left, S_2.

tity offered brought about by a change in price. As we have previously seen, cost is a primary factor in determining supply. Changes in the cost of production, such as those brought about by wage increases or technological advances in machinery, will usually result in a change in supply.

Another factor is expectations about future prices. Business people do not know what prices will be; they only know what prices are. They plan their production on what they expect prices to be. If they expect prices to be above their costs, they produce with confidence. Falling prices will tend to discourage production. When beef prices declined in 1977, cattle ranchers reduced the size of their herds. The real impact on prices was not felt for two years.

 Changes in nonprice factors lead to a change in supply. A price change leads to a change in quantity.

A change in the demand for other goods can result in a change in supply. When men's vests became fashionable, manufacturers shifted more of their facilities to the production of this popular product.

Figure 2–5 shows changes in supply. Examine the curves and note which one shows the increase. Follow one price through all curves and see what quantities are offered.

Elasticity of Supply

Supply, like demand, may be *elastic* or *inelastic*. When the quantity of a product offered for sale varies little although big changes in price are made, the supply is inelastic. An inelastic supply curve appears as a steeply sloping or vertical curve, because the quantity offered changes relatively little with price changes.

If the quantity of a product offered for sale varies greatly when small changes in price are made, the supply is elastic. An elastic curve appears as a gently sloping or horizontal curve.

The formula for determining the price elasticity of supply is the same as that used for demand:

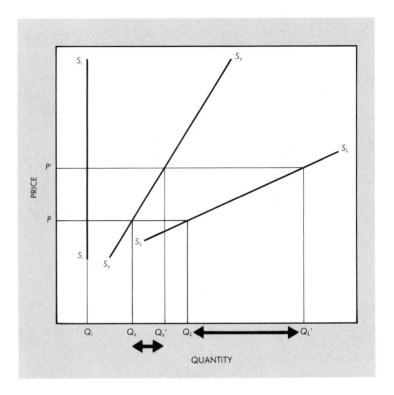

Figure 2–6   Supply elasticity and time
A price increase from P to P' for the immediate market period, S_i, has no effect
on quantity, Q_i. For the short run the higher price, P', motivates producers to
extend the use of their existing capacities and increase quantity from Q_s to Q'_s.
In the long run producers can increase their capacities so that the price increase
will motivate additional production from Q_L to Q_L'.

$$E_s = \frac{\% \Delta Q}{\% \Delta P}$$

where E_s is price elasticity of supply. If E_s is larger
than 1, the supply is price elastic; if it is less than
1, the price is inelastic; and if it is 1, the product
is unit elastic.

Although there are many causes for different
elasticities of supply, time is the most important.
For the immediate market period the producer has
a fixed quantity to offer, so the supply curve is
perfectly inelastic or vertical. In the short run

producers can work overtime using their existing
facilities. This increases their costs, but the costs
are covered by the higher prices they receive. The
supply curve rises sharply, showing some response
to price increases or some elasticity. In the long
run the producer can increase the number of
machines used or the size of the factory. Here the
supply curve slopes up gently and is most elastic.
Figure 2–6 shows the elasticity for each market
period.

 Time is the major factor in determining
the elasticity of supply.

D How Price Is Determined

Interaction of Supply and Demand

Supply and demand become especially significant when they are put together. Sellers offer products for sale when they anticipate demand. Buyers can convert their wants into demand only if there is supply. The two interact to create the market price and provide an answer to our basic problem of allocating our resources.

Let us put our supply schedule and demand schedule side by side and see how the laws of supply and demand determine price (see Table 2–3). The illustration given assumes a purely competitive market over a given period of time. As we look at Table 2–3, we see that at prices above 60 cents dealers will offer more bags of pretzels than consumers will buy, resulting in a surplus of bags of pretzels. Having a surplus means wasting limited resources. Sellers have a choice of cutting back their production, stopping production for a while, or cutting the price.

Below the price of 60 cents, consumers want more bags of pretzels than are offered for sale. Some who want pretzels will not be able to buy them, even if they are willing to pay more. Only at 60 cents does the number of bags of pretzels offered for sale equal the number of bags of pretzels buyers wish to purchase. When supply and demand equal each other, the market is at *equilibrium,* and the price at this point is the *equilibrium price.*

 The equilibrium price is where the quantity demanded by buyers is equal to the quantity offered by sellers.

We can graphically show the supply and demand schedules in Table 2–3 by drawing the supply and demand curves (see Figure 2–7). The equilibrium point is the point at which the supply and demand curves intersect. Any point above would leave a surplus; any point below would result in a shortage. When the forces of supply and demand are allowed to operate freely without any interference from government or groups formed to control prices, the *market will be cleared;* that is, there will be no shortage of buyers willing to pay the freely-arrived-at market price and no surplus of producers willing to sell at the freely-arrived-at market price.

Changes in Supply and Demand

Changes in the equilibrium price and quantity will occur when changes in supply or demand, or both, take place. This can be seen most easily in Figures 2–8, 2–9, and 2–10.

Figure 2–8 illustrates the effect of a given supply and changes in demand. An increase in demand shifts the curve to the right, as shown by the movement of the original demand D to the increased demand D_1. The intersection, which tells us the equilibrium price and quantity, shifts along the supply curve to a higher price and a greater

Table 2–3 Supply and demand schedules for bags of pretzels for one week

Quantity buyers would purchase	Price	Quantity sellers would offer	Surplus (+) or shortage (−)	Pressure on price
50	$.80	450	+400	↓
150	.70	350	+200	↓
250	.60	250	0	
350	.50	150	−200	↑
450	.40	50	−400	↑

What is the equilibrium price?

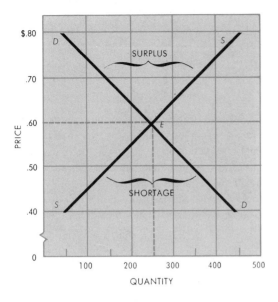

Figure 2–7 The equilibrium price and the quantity exchanged for bags of pretzels for one week

The price of bags of pretzels for one week in a purely competitive market will be at the interesection of the supply curve and the demand curve, or point E. At this equilibrium point, the market will be cleared. Any price above E will leave sellers with a surplus. Any price below E will produce a shortage for buyers.

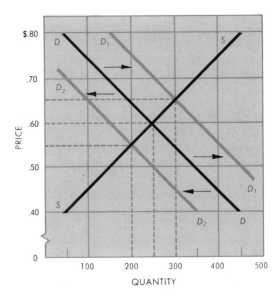

Figure 2–8 Change in demand and its effect on price and quantity

An increase in demand, D_1, supply remaining the same, results in an increase in price and an increase in quantity. A decrease in demand, D_2, supply remaining the same, results in a decrease in price and a decrease in quantity. These examples show the direct relationship between changes in demand and changes in the equilibrium price and quantity exchanged.

quantity of the product bought. The broken line connecting the new intersection with the vertical axis measuring price and the horizontal axis measuring quantity shows the new market condition, 65 cents and 300 units sold. Both price and quantity have increased with an increase in demand. A decrease in demand is shown by D_2. What are the new equilibrium price and quantity with D_2 as demand?

Compare the market situations of dealers in popular and classical records. Which of the record dealers has to be more alert to changes in demand?

Figure 2–9 illustrates the effect of a given demand and changes in supply. An increase in supply shifts the supply curve to the right, creating a new equilibrium price and quantity at the intersection of S_1 (the increased supply curve) and D (the unchanged demand curve). The change lowers the market price to 55 cents and increases the quantity sold to 300 units. Whether we increase

supply or demand, there will be an increase in quantity. It is easier to learn how to draw and interpret supply and demand curves than to memorize the relations involved. The classical model in the Review Model at the end of the chapter will explain further the effect of changes in supply and demand.

A decrease in supply is shown in Figure 2–9 by S_2. What influence can a new, more efficient machine have on the market? Successful research, it can be seen, helps both the producer and the consumer.

Figure 2–10 illustrates the effect of equal increases in supply and demand. The equal shifting of both curves to the right results in an increase in the number of units sold at the marketplace, but there is no change in price. If demand increases more than supply, both quantity and price will increase. Is the illustration in Figure 2–10 more likely to be characteristic of a short period or a long period? Why?

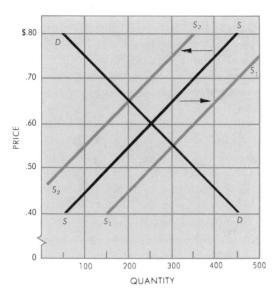

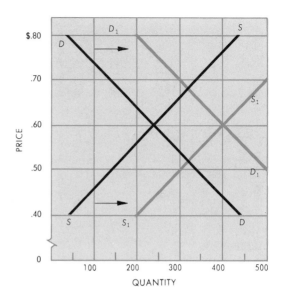

Figure 2–9   Change in supply and its effect on price and quantity

An increase in supply, S_1, demand remaining the same, results in a decrease in price and an increase in quantity. A decrease in supply, S_2, demand remaining the same, results in an increase in price and a decrease in quantity. These examples show the inverse relationship between changes in supply and changes in the equilibrium price, and the direct relationship between changes in supply and changes in quantity exchanged.

Figure 2–10   Change in supply and demand and the effects on price and quantity

An increase in supply and demand will result in an increase in the quantity exchanged. The equilibrium price will change when the changes in supply and demand are not equal.

Resource Allocation and the Classical Model

We are now in a better position to see how the classical model provides an answer to the allocation of our limited resources to meet our unlimited wants. In Figure 1–3, we showed a simplified model of how our economic system is supposed to operate. In Figure 2–11, we have added to the original model the forces of supply and demand in both our market for goods and services and our market for the factors of production. How are resources allocated by this system? How are prices determined?

If we turn once again to our computer, we now can see that the measurements made by the computer are measurements of demand—by consumers in the marketplace for goods and services and by businesses in the marketplace for the factors of production. After figuring out demand, the computer relays the amount of dollars that would be enough to induce businesses to offer sufficient supply in the marketplace to satisfy the wants of consumers. It also tries to bring enough factors of production into the marketplace to supply the ingredients necessary for production.

Have the Laws of Demand and Supply Been Repealed?

The law of demand states that as prices rise, fewer items will be sold—all other things being equal. But all other things are not always equal. A clever supermarket manager found that when he replaced a "20 cents" sign with "2 for 45 cents," sales immediately increased. At a garage sale one of the authors observed someone buying a used electric drill for $5 more than it would have cost to buy a new drill of the same make and model at a department store less than one mile away. The psychological factor of a "bargain" leads consumers to engage in irrational behavior.

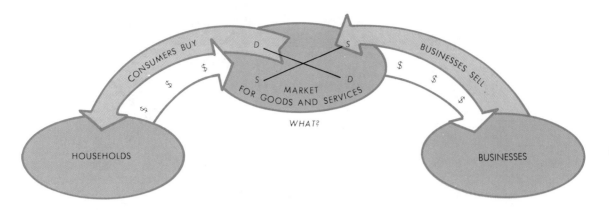

Figure 2–11   The circular flow of the economy with supply and demand

The classical model's answer to resource allocation is the market mechanism. Through the interaction of supply and demand, price determines the answers to our basic questions *What, How,* and *For whom.*

A few years ago when the Chrysler Motor Corporation was having a poor sales year, its president raised prices. ALCOA, the largest aluminum company, did the same thing about the same time. Both companies claimed that their costs were up because their production was down. However, the law of supply implies that costs rise with higher production.

If these examples can be multiplied many times, does it mean that the laws of demand and supply are no longer valid? Decidedly, no! In both demand and supply the qualification is *other things being equal.* We cannot assume that consumers are always rational, that business always tries to maximize profits, and that information about the market is well known. Consumers can be misled, or they may not know what prices are in other places. Sometimes the time and the place are more important than the price; a consumer may be willing to pay more to buy a product on Sunday or to avoid traveling a mile.

Business executives make decisions on the basis of their expectations of whether prices will rise or fall. Sometimes they sacrifice short-run profits for longer-run gains. Errors in judgment are not infrequent, as in the case of the Chrysler Corporation mentioned previously, where price rebates rather than increases were finally made.

Another factor is that a regional or national market may be influenced by world conditions that may not be known immediately, as was the case when the Soviet Union purchased wheat at a very low price just before a world shortage appeared. Finally, a superficial examination of the market may conceal conspiracies by producers to alter price.

Many of the factors that alter "other things being equal" will be examined in some detail in succeeding chapters. However, it is fair to conclude that if the following assumptions are met, the laws of demand and supply hold true.

Conditions Necessary for Making the Classical Model Work

If the classical model is to work as its creators intended, certain conditions must be met and certain assumptions must be made. If they are not, modifications in the model may be needed. What conditions and assumptions are necessary?

1. People are primarily economic beings with incentives to make money in order to satisfy their wants. They will take the highest-paying job available, go into the most profitable business, sell what the public wants most,

and, at least in the long run, sell at the highest price that will give them the greatest profit. They will buy products at the lowest price without showing favoritism to any seller.

2. The factors of production, including labor, are mobile and can be readily moved to the place that will offer the highest return. As consumers' wants change, the allocation of resources will shift to meet these new needs.

3. Both the market for goods and services and the market for the factors of production are free from control by government, by buyers, or by sellers. Nothing will interfere with the freedom of consumers and the factors of production. Business, too, will be free to enter or leave the market and to act independently in the market.

4. Knowledge is available to consumers so that they can determine what products best serve their needs and can thus make wise decisions.

5. Society will achieve its maximum happiness by allowing individuals to make most of the decisions on what to produce and how to produce it. This system contrasts with one in which society, acting collectively through government, makes the decisions about production.

Although the five conditions just stated do not exist in our environment in pure form, they are present to a far greater degree than in most other nations. Many people in our society think, talk, believe, and behave as if the classical model did exist in pure, or nearly pure, form. As a result, the classical model influences much of our behavior as consumers, as owners of the factors of production, and as citizens trying to influence economic policy. We often refer to incentives for producing, such as commissions to salespeople, bonuses for managers, and higher pay for extra hours of work.

We have antitrust laws to keep the market competitive. Both state and national governments make information easily available to consumers so that they can be more effective buyers. Not only do most Americans resent the government's going into business, but loud complaints are heard when the government's budget is increased, because such action often results in individuals' having fewer free choices.

The classical model, with its emphasis on a free market, cannot be dismissed merely because some controls have been instituted. Some of these controls, such as antitrust action, have helped to keep the market free. The classical model is a significant factor in determining our country's answers to the big economic questions, although modifications of it and substitutions from other models have added flexibility to our system.

Expansion to a World Market

With world trade having tripled during the last 25 years, it has become necessary to include a world market if our economic analysis is to be valid. As recently as 1970 the automobile market in the United States had five producers and was dominated by only three. By the mid-1980s, imports from Japan and Europe had increased competition significantly. In steel and textiles, imports were even more significant. In each of these cases, because costs were lower, the supply curve shifted to the right and resulted in a lower equilibrium price than there would have been with just domestic suppliers. One important factor in the slowing of the inflation rate during the first half of the 1980s was the expansion of trade to a world market.

Throughout this textbook we will make reference to the impact of moving into a global economy.

Demand and Supply

This is an exercise in the functioning of the price system: the classical model's answer to how to allocate our limited resources. Its purpose is to review how, in a free market, the forces of supply and demand determine price and distribution of resources. We review these concepts graphically.

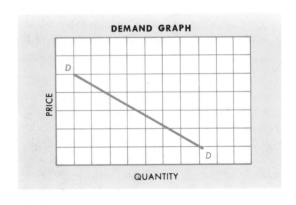

■ Consumers make their wants known by showing a willingness and an ability to purchase certain quantities of a product at different prices. This is known as *demand*, and it can be shown graphically. The curve is downward sloping because of the law of diminishing marginal utility.

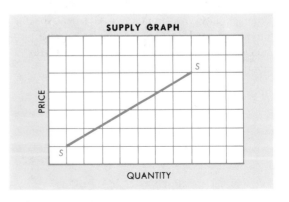

■ Business offers for sale certain quantities of a product at different prices. This is known as *supply*, and it can also be shown graphically. The curve is upward sloping because of the law of increasing costs.

Consumers and businesses meet at the market, where the demand for goods interacts with the supply of goods. The intersection of demand and supply is the *equilibrium* price. This price will clear the market. Any price above this point will leave a surplus of goods. Any price below this point will leave consumers wanting more. Note that the intersection of demand and supply shows (1) price and (2) quantity exchanged. If we change the price, we vary the quantity exchanged, altering our resource allocation.

A change in demand is an increase or a decrease in the number of units that will be sold throughout the range of prices offered. It can be caused by (1) a change in consumers' income, (2) a change in taste, and (3) a change in the market for substitutes or complements.

■ An increase in demand shifts the demand curve to the right.

■ A decrease in demand shifts the demand curve to the left.

A change in supply is an increase or a decrease in the number of units offered throughout the range of prices. Changes in supply are caused by (1) changes in cost, (2) expectations of profit, and (3) changes in demand for other goods.

■ An increase in supply shifts the supply curve to the right.

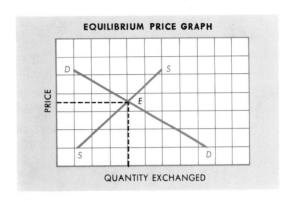

EQUILIBRIUM PRICE GRAPH

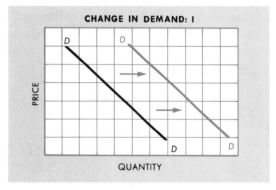

CHANGE IN DEMAND: I

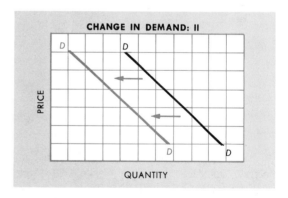
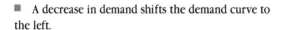

CHANGE IN DEMAND: II

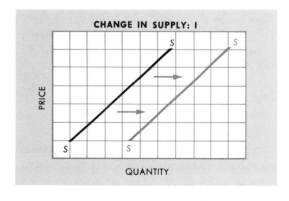

CHANGE IN SUPPLY: I

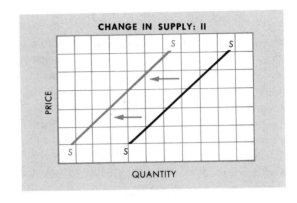

■ A decrease in supply shifts the supply curve to the left.

Some products are very responsive to price changes. A small change in price will bring about a major change in the quantity that is bought or offered for sale. Such products are said to have an *elastic demand* or an *elastic supply.* When this condition is shown graphically, the curves are more horizontal than vertical.

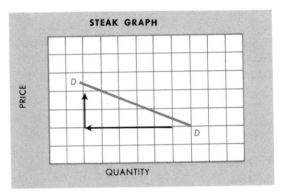

■ The demand for sirloin steak is highly elastic because substitutes can easily be found, it is not a necessity, and it may represent a large share of the food budget.

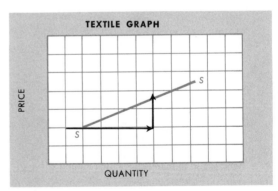

■ The supply of textiles is highly elastic because an increase in production is easily accomplished in a short time.

Products that respond very little to price changes are said to have an *inelastic demand* or an *inelastic supply.* This condition is shown graphically by curves that are more vertical than horizontal.

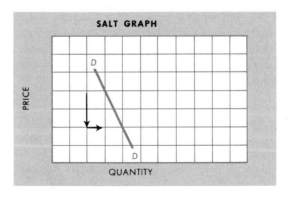

■ The demand for salt is highly inelastic because it represents a small share of the food budget and substitution is difficult.

Before we proceed with our case studies, a word of caution is necessary. The models that have been shown are not accurate pictures of the real world. They are simplified to help you understand better how elasticity and changes in demand and supply affect distribution and price.

Few products have supply and demand schedules that fit neatly into linear patterns. Most products have schedules that are expressed graphically by curves with slopes that change, particularly at the upper and lower price ranges. This simplification does not distort the basic ideas of the functioning of the price system.

- The supply of orchids is highly inelastic because of the time and difficulty involved in cultivating new plants.

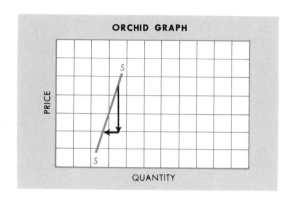

Case Studies

Herewith are two case studies from "the world that is," showing graphically the importance of changes in supply and demand and of the elasticity of demand. Complete Case I before starting Case II.

Case I: Agriculture

The demand *D* for most agricultural products tends to be highly inelastic. Thus a change in price will make little difference in the quantity consumers

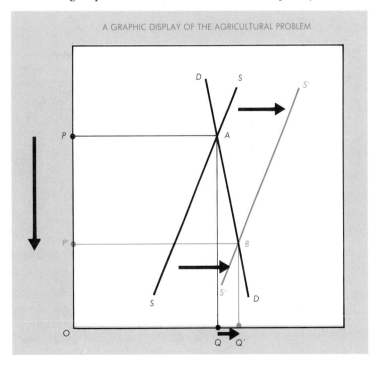

buy. The point where supply S and demand D intersect is the equilibrium price P, at which the market will be cleared of quantity Q.

Technological advances have increased the farmers' productivity. This is shown by a shift to the right in the supply curve from S to S'. The revenue of farmers when S is the supply curve is $OP \times OQ$, or the rectangle $OPAQ$. With the new supply curve S', revenue is $OP' \times OQ'$, or the rectangle $OP'BQ'$. Comparing the sizes of the two rectangles shows that collectively farmers make more by producing less.

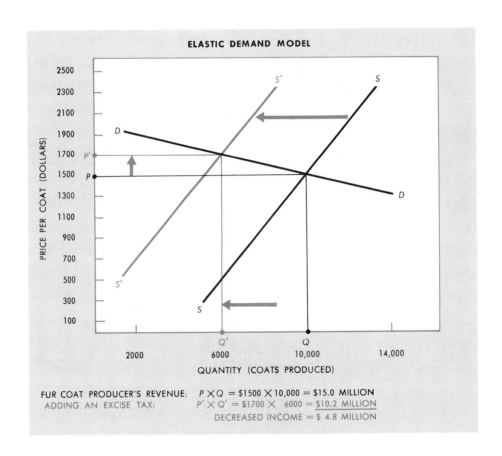

ELASTIC DEMAND MODEL

FUR COAT PRODUCER'S REVENUE: $P \times Q = \$1500 \times 10,000 = \$15.0$ MILLION
ADDING AN EXCISE TAX: $P' \times Q' = \$1700 \times 6000 = \underline{\$10.2 \text{ MILLION}}$
                                DECREASED INCOME $= \$ 4.8$ MILLION

Case II: Excise tax on fur coats

The demand for many kinds of fur coats is highly elastic. A small change in price will bring about a major change in the quantity bought. The equilibrium price is P, and the quantity exchanged is Q.

If the government decides to place an excise tax on fur coats, a supplier must add this cost to the price of each coat. This results in a new supply curve S'. The equilibrium price moves to P', a smaller *increase* than the *decrease* in the quantity Q' of coats sold. Because the demand for fur coats is elastic, the decrease in the supply curve causes the fur dealer to lose revenue.

$$(P \times Q) - (P' \times Q') = \text{change in income}$$

In addition, the government gets less revenue from the excise tax than it expected, because the elastic demand reduces considerably the quantity exchanged.

What products might the government put an excise tax on without significantly changing the quantity sold?

Chapter Highlights

1. Price measures values in money. Goods and services have economic value when they satisfy wants (utility) and are relatively scarce. Price plays a very important part in determining allocation of our resources.

2. A market is a place where buyers and sellers meet. There are markets for goods and services and markets for factors of production. Markets can be classified as pure competition, pure monopoly, monopolistic competition, and oligopoly. The number of buyers and sellers and their ability to influence price distinguish the type of market. Most markets fall somewhere between pure competition and pure monopoly. The classical model assumes pure competition. All competition that is not pure is called imperfect competition.

3. Demand is the willingness on the part of consumers to buy certain amounts of a product at certain prices in a given market. The general rule for demand is that the lower the price of a given product, the greater the quantity bought by consumers. This rule is explained by the law of diminishing marginal utility. Substitutes and the level of buyers' income also influence demand. A demand schedule lists the quantities of a product consumers will buy at various prices and can be plotted on a graph as a demand curve. Elasticity of demand is determined by the way price changes affect quantity. Changes in demand can be brought about in many ways.

4. Supply is the willingness on the part of sellers to offer certain amounts of products at certain prices in a given market. Supply schedules differ for products available immediately, for the short run, and for the long run. The general rule for supply states that producers will offer more of their product for sale as price rises. This is because costs, which greatly influence supply, will begin to rise after a certain level of production has been reached. Supply schedules can be plotted on graphs to give supply curves. They may be elastic or inelastic and may change because of costs.

5. When we put supply and demand together, we get the equilibrium price, which will clear the market of products. Changes in supply and demand bring about changes in price and quantity bought.
6. The classical model explains that it is the interaction of the laws of supply and demand at the market that determines allocation of our resources.
7. Certain conditions must be met if the classical model is to work. They include the economic motivation of human beings, mobility of factors of production, pure competition, and freedom for consumers and producers.
8. Expansion of global trade has increased competition and helped slow inflation.

Study Aids

Key Terms

demand	elasticity	imperfect competition
market	clearing the market	equilibrium
supply	increasing costs	change in demand
utility	economic value	classical model
price	exchange value	law of diminishing marginal
monopoly	incentive	utility
oligopoly	pure competition	
monopsony	monopolistic competition	

Questions

1. Classical capitalism depends on the market for answers to the basic economic questions.
   (a) What is the main function of the market in the U.S. economy?
   (b) What are the important considerations that determine the kind of competition that develops?
   (c) List and explain the various kinds of markets we have.
   (d) Why is competition essential to this system?
2. Competition is a keystone of the capitalist system.
   (a) What is the meaning of *competition?*
   (b) What are the various kinds of competition that may develop?
3. In our economy, supply and demand are important factors in determining price.
   (a) Draw a graph that shows the relation between a price increase and the quantity of an item that will be sold.
   (b) What factors besides price will determine the shape of the demand curve?
   (c) What influences in our economy determine the supply of any commodity or service?
4. Products have value for a variety of reasons. Sometimes the value of a product will change with circumstances. We identify value with prices. Account for the prices of the following:
   (a) roses in February
   (b) ice skates in May

(c) diamonds
(d) bread
(e) a day-old newspaper
5. In what kind of market would you place each of the following?
   (a) a gas and electric company
   (b) an orange grower
   (c) a local automobile dealer
   (d) an appliance manufacturer
   (e) the Boston Symphony Orchestra
6. Make a list of five products with elastic demand and five with inelastic demand. What accounts for the elasticity?
7. Over the years the demand for products changes. Can you identify some changes in consumer preferences? Explain why you think these changes have taken place.
8. The demand for a product may be elastic over one range of prices, but inelastic over another range. Why?
9. Explain the relation between cost and supply. Why does the time period influence supply? What factors are most likely to bring about a change in supply?
10. Explain how the equilibrium price is established for a product in a perfectly competitive market.

Problems

1. On graph paper, plot the following supply and demand schedules. Let each interval (box) represent one cent for price (start with 68) and let each interval represent 300 cans for quantity.

Demand and supply schedules for cans of frozen orange juice

Price per can	Demand	Supply
$.80	1,000	5,500
.79	1,100	4,800
.78	1,200	4,300
.77	1,400	3,800
.76	1,600	3,200
.75	1,900	2,700
.74	2,300	2,300
.73	2,600	1,900
.72	3,000	1,700
.71	3,500	1,500
.70	4,100	1,300
.69	4,700	1,100
.68	5,500	1,000

What is the market price for 6-ounce cans of frozen orange juice? If oranges are hurt by a frost and the supply drops 400 cans at each price level, what will be the new price?

2. What will be the effect on both price and quantity in the following situations? Are there situations below for which you do not have enough information to answer this question with respect to price and/or quantity?
   (a) increase in demand
   (b) decrease in supply
   (c) increase in demand and decrease in supply
   (d) decrease in demand and increase in supply
3. Sterling Electronics has dropped the price of its 25-inch TV sets from $500 to $450. Sales during the week increased from 150 to 300 sets. What is the elasticity of demand for these TV sets?

Economic Systems Other Than Capitalism

When economists classify economic systems, they are primarily concerned with how resources are allocated. At one extreme is a system operating on the market mechanism alone; at the other is one with a central planning agency. The former is called a market system, the latter a command economy. However, when we look at the real world we find no pure example of either. Most economies are mixed. Economists are also concerned with who owns the means of production. Is it owned individually, by corporations, by workers collectively, or by the government? Again there are no pure examples. Another way of viewing the problem is How does the system answer the three basic questions of *What, How,* and *For whom*?

What makes this analysis more difficult is that we must recognize the political context of an economic system. When we do so, we introduce the world of "isms." We have already referred to the classical model of capitalism. Capitalism and its variations fall into the category of market systems. But in addition to capitalism, there are three main economic systems: socialism, communism, and market socialism. Each of these systems has its own model that explains why it offers people the greatest hope for the future; each has had sufficient appeal to win millions of followers. In these systems, as in capitalism, there is a difference between the theory (the "ought-to-be") and the practice (the "is"). Each model has critics who oppose certain of its aspects but choose to keep its framework, preferring to modify the system rather than to change to another. Each system has elements of the command economy; each has its own model explaining why.

Before we can analyze these systems, we need to separate them from their accompanying political structures and the emotional overtones often generated by "isms." Once this is done, the basic differences among the systems will become apparent. These differences form a spectrum, with individualism and the free market at one extreme and collectivism and centralized control at the other.

How do you feel about government's siphoning off more and more of the middle- and upper-class incomes? Do you think U.S. citizens are less free today than they were 50 years ago when government services were fewer? Would you rather work for government or for private enterprise? Would you rather be a consumer of government or private enterprise production?

Chapter Objectives

When you have completed this chapter, you should be able to:

- Explain and describe the socialist, communist, and market socialist economic models.
- Evaluate capitalism from the standpoint of a socialist, a communist, and a market socialist.
- Present the capitalist critique of socialism, communism, and market socialism.
- Discuss the political and the economic spectra and categorize at least three countries with which you are familiar in terms of these two spectra.
- Compare the progress of the Soviet economy over the past 50 years with the progress of the U.S. economy.

A What Economic System? The Theory

In our present-day world, three principal economic systems compete with capitalism. They are *socialism, communism,* and *market socialism.* Each of these has developed a model explaining the logic of its own system. Each must, like capitalism, concern itself with scarcity and allocation of resources. Answers must be furnished for the *What, How,* and *For whom.* Production and distribution are as important to the socialist, communist, and market socialist economies as they are to the capitalist economy. We shall consider each of these systems from the point of view of its differences from capitalism or other systems, the model it follows, variations suggested for the model, and weaknesses inherent in the form.

Socialism

Socialism is found today in Norway, Sweden, Denmark, and Israel; it has existed in some degree at various times in Great Britain, Australia, New Zealand, The Netherlands, and Belgium. Most Western European nations have strong socialist parties that have held political power often enough to influence the economic system strongly. To many Europeans, socialism has a more favorable connotation than capitalism does, and several political parties oriented toward capitalism use the word *social* or *socialist* to make their cause more appealing.

Many underdeveloped nations, including India, have chosen socialism as their preferred system. The Socialist party in the United States has never been very successful at the polls, but many of the particular programs it has advocated have eventually become law.

Dissatisfaction with Capitalism

Modern socialist thinking developed largely as a protest against the misery that accompanied the Industrial Revolution. Instead of looking on the factory system as a way to improve the lot of the poor, early socialists considered it responsible for crowded slums and low wages. Most objectionable of all to them was the idea that laissez-faire policies would best serve the public interest. Specifically, the socialists objected to these aspects of capitalism:

1. Private ownership of the tools of production—that is, of capital—leads to increasing inequality of wealth. Having a great advantage over the worker in bargaining, the capitalist receives a larger portion of the "pie" than he or she deserves.
2. Profit rather than need is the motivation for production. Because of this, scarce resources may be wasted on goods and services that serve no useful purpose, while other goods and services that do have real utility, especially to poorer people, are in short supply.

3. Competition is often wasteful. Duplication of effort, built-in obsolescence, advertising, and shortsighted exploitation of natural resources to make a quick profit characterize capitalism's wasteful methods.
4. Planning by businesses on an individual basis leads to overproduction, causing business cycles. Cycles, in turn, lead to frequent depressions, which add to the waste of resources and a feeling of insecurity among workers.
5. The concentration of capitalistic wealth brings with it a concentration of political power. Greater concern is shown for property rights than for human rights.
6. Capitalism tends to lead to imperialism, as business people seek raw materials, markets, and places to invest their surplus capital. When their investments abroad are threatened, they call on their government to provide protection. Such involvements may lead to war.

The Socialist Model

In a socialist economy, the basic problems of scarcity and allocation of limited resources are solved by producing for use or need rather than producing for profit. With most of the means of production owned and controlled collectively, usually by government, production can be planned and distribution organized to assure fairness for all. Socialist theory states that instead of allowing the market to determine what shall be produced, how it shall be produced, and for whom the production is meant, the government should provide the answers. Plans are carefully drawn to avoid waste, and production is aimed at improving living standards. Inequalities of income are reduced because distribution does not allow the strong to take advantage of the weak. Overproduction, duplication of effort, and depressions are avoided, as competition is replaced by cooperation and planning.

 Pure socialism may be classified as a command economy because central planning allocates production.

Socialists believe in moving toward their goal of government ownership and control by gradual means and through democratic processes. The freedom of choice of the consumer and the producer may be curbed as the society moves from capitalism to socialism, but the decisions that citizens make when they go to the polls affect the economy even more than such decisions do under capitalism. When property is *nationalized*—taken over by the government—the owners are compensated. Socialists claim that only by doing away with private ownership of capital and the power derived from that ownership can the state become economically and politically democratic.

Variations of the Model

Primary differences of opinion exist among socialists about how extensive government ownership and control should be. These differences are reflected in the many forms of socialism, all varying in organization, methods, or emphasis.

The oldest and most idealistic form of socialism is known as *utopian socialism*. It is based on the belief that people can live together best in an environment that stresses cooperation over competition. Utopian socialists sought to set up communities in which people would work together in harmony with little or no direction by government. Robert Owen (1771–1858), of Wales, and the followers of Charles Fourier (1772–1837), of France, set up experimental communities in the United States, hoping to show by example the superiority of their system, so that other people might wish to live in the same way. The failure of these experiments and the lack of any strong formal organization, at a time when industrial organization was bringing about great changes, ruined any chances they may have had for success. Communal living has been revived as a lifestyle by some young people throughout the world.

 Utopian socialism has religious or humanistic appeal.

After the defeat of radical movements in Germany and England in the middle of the nineteenth century, a new attempt at social reform was made. Based on certain teachings of the Bible and directed primarily at workers, this movement was known as *Christian socialism*. According to its teachings, society should be organized on the principles of concern for humanity and belief in the brotherhood of people. Repudiating violence and class struggle, Christian socialists advocated use of the private property of the rich for the benefit of all. They supported a broad program of reform designed to lessen the sufferings of the poor.

Some of you may already be acquainted with another form of socialism—that of Karl Marx. Marx referred to his socialism as "scientific," claiming that his analysis was based on scientific reasoning. In his two famous works, *The Communist Manifesto*, written in collaboration with Friedrich Engels, and *Das Kapital*, Marx explained his criticism of capitalism and predicted its eventual destruction and its replacement by socialism. Much of the thinking of present-day communism is based on these writings.

Marx saw history not as a meaningless succession of events but as social change resulting from the struggle of classes. With the transition from agricultural to industrial production, a change in the dominant economic class was taking place. Marx felt that under capitalism economic power would become so concentrated that society would be divided between the few capitalists owning all the means of production and the masses of workers owning nothing.

Marx explained the concentration of wealth in industry by the doctrine of *surplus value*. All wealth, he argued, is produced by labor, with the other factors of production being passive or also the result of labor. Because workers are not paid the full value of what they produce, capitalists are able to accumulate this reservoir of surplus value—the difference between what the workers produce and what they earn. As this process continues, the middle class disappears and society becomes

 # Karl Marx, the Revolutionary

Karl Heinrich Marx (1818–83) was born in Trier, in the German Rhineland, the son of a middle-class family. At the age of seventeen, he began his college education at the University of Bonn, where, following his father's wish, he began the study of law. However, he soon changed to history and philosophy at the universities of Berlin and Jena, receiving his doctor's degree.

Marx had hoped to pursue an academic career; when this became impossible because of his radical ideas, he turned to journalism instead. His political views soon led to suppression of his newspaper by the government, whereupon Marx moved to Paris.

There he studied political economy, particularly the writings of French utopian socialists. Although their theories interested him, his own views were more extreme. While in Paris he met Friedrich Engels, who shared his opinions and who later collaborated with him to produce the famous *Communist Manifesto*. Exiled from France at the request of the Prussian government, Marx moved to Brussels. He returned to Germany during the Revolution of 1848. Expelled again, he settled in London. There he became active in workers' organizations and continued to develop his own theories.

In his later years, Marx spent most of his time in the British Museum, where he read and wrote, earning a meager living by preparing articles for the New York *Tribune*. He and his family suffered from poverty and poor health, but these circumstances did not deter him from writing his famous book, *Das Kapital*, and organizing and leading the International Working-men's Association, later known as the First International. The second and third volumes of *Das Kapital* were edited by Engels and published after Marx's death.

The influence of Karl Marx on the noncommunist world has been more in business cycles, stages of economic development, and interpretation of history than in advancing economic theory. However, the vast importance of his thinking to the development of the communist world gives his work a significance beyond its contributions to economics alone.

divided between capitalists (the exploiters) and workers (the exploited).

 Marx explained history as a series of class struggles between haves and have nots.

Because workers lack the means to buy back the goods they produce, overproduction soon leads to depressions. As this condition develops, the position of the workers becomes even more intolerable. Eventually the workers will unite and throw off capitalist domination by a revolution. With the capitalists gone, the means of production will be owned and operated by the workers. Because all people will be workers, there will be only one class. The struggle between classes will cease because the separation between owners of the means of production and workers will no longer exist. In effect, the new society will be "classless."

Toward the end of the nineteenth century a new movement in socialist thought appeared. Led by Eduard Bernstein in Germany and by Sidney and Beatrice Webb, George Bernard Shaw, H. G. Wells, and the Fabian Society in England, the new movement rejected Marx's class struggle and sudden revolution. In its place the *revisionists,* as they came to be called, favored a gradual evolution to socialism. Progress for society through education and political control gained at the polls was preferred to class struggle. The revisionists believed that in extending ownership of productive facilities the government must proceed slowly; in some cases, such as public utilities, municipal ownership was favored over national ownership. The policies of the present British Labour party have been greatly influenced by the thinking of the Fabian Society, which incorporated many revisionist ideas. However, much of Britain's production remains in private control and her government is democratic.

Socialist ideas were sometimes incorporated into political and economic movements, such as *anarchism, syndicalism,* and *guild socialism,* whose main emphases were on ideas other than socialism. Each sought to eliminate private property, and each had strong objections to the existing organization of government. The anarchists looked at the state as the source of all evil and wished to substitute for it self-governing groups living in voluntary association. The syndicalists wanted to organize workers into one big union that would carry out a general strike and overthrow capitalism. Each industry would then be run by workers in autonomous units; these would be federated for overall direction. Guild socialists recognized the need for government, but wanted to organize the society into producers and consumers, each with a national association. Industry was to be run by employees organized into guilds. Though significant in their time, these groups have little influence and importance today.

Weaknesses in the Socialist Position

Just as the socialist can find fault with capitalism, so the capitalist can point to weaknesses in socialist thought. In particular, the supporters of capitalism criticize these aspects of socialist theory:

1. Socialism lacks incentives for increasing effort, whereas under capitalism, private ownership of wealth, including capital, is a motivating force. Under collective ownership, unproductive members of society are subsidized by their more productive fellows, reducing incentive for both. In the system of private enterprise, the individual business person can see in a very direct way the rewards for energy and ability.

2. Substituting production for need in place of production for profit may sound altruistic, but who determines what need is? Even if that question could be resolved to everyone's satisfaction, the fact remains that profits are as great in industries producing necessities as in industries producing luxuries. In either case, profits will be made when individual consumers indicate their needs by buying what they wish. And isn't the will of the people expressed more clearly and directly by the individual vote in the marketplace than by the collective vote, even of a democratically elected government?

3. Although competition does produce some duplication and waste, it more than compensates by eliminating the inefficient producer and motivating those who stay in business to

improve their products and reduce their costs. The cost of advertising is more than compensated for by the increased market for goods resulting from economies of large-scale production, which result from the larger market.

Competition also yields an indirect benefit by offsetting political decisions. People frequently exercise more care in spending their own money than in evaluating the consequences of their choices in voting.

4. Overproduction and economic fluctuations can and do occur in socialist countries as well as in capitalistic countries. Modern capitalistic economic policy has reduced the average length and severity of recessions. Moreover, a capitalist system with its millions of producers has more flexibility to adapt to changing demand.

5. The concentration of wealth the socialists predicted has not taken place in capitalist economies. Instead, ownership of our giant corporations is becoming increasingly widespread. Today millions of workers in the United States are themselves capitalists.

6. At present capitalism shows no greater tendency toward imperialism than socialism does, as shown by the Cuban and Soviet intrusions into trouble spots. Many socialist countries have sought out private capital as an aid to development. Competition for raw materials and markets is more closely related to capital accumulation and trade than to the economic structure involved.

7. Although socialists strongly support freedom and democracy and reject communism because it ignores civil rights, the amount of regulation and central planning necessary in socialism reduces consumer sovereignty and limits the decisions of workers.

Freedom is more closely tied to the political traditions of a country than to the economic system it chooses. In such socialist countries as New Zealand, Denmark, and Israel, there is great respect for civil liberties. Likewise, the socialist charge that in capitalism there can be no real freedom because economic concentration leads to political concentration seems absurd when one looks at the number of elected officials, including U.S. presidents, who were opposed by "big business" interests.

 Socialism may exist in a political democracy.

Recent disclosures of economic influences on government policies, revealed in the investigations of the EPA and the fixing of milk prices, have badly shaken the confidence of people in the credibility of our economic and political institutions. In addition, the length and severity of our recession in the early 1980s make some of the criticisms of socialism seem less potent. Yet the ability of our system to adjust gradually as we discover our weaknesses may be viewed as its most fundamental strength.

Communism

On the surface, the theories of present-day socialism and communism seem marked more by similarities than by differences. Both systems make the same criticisms of capitalism. Both received impetus from the writings of Karl Marx. Perhaps the problem of distinguishing between the two systems is one of semantics, concerning the meaning and use of the term *socialism*. Both the Soviet Union and some Western European nations refer to their systems as socialist states, but the informed observer knows that the socialism of Western Europe and the socialism of the communist world are two different and incompatible systems.

Stages Leading to Communism

Unlike most socialists, who believed in progress by peaceful evolution, Marx believed the transition from capitalism to communism would follow a particular pattern and would be accompanied by a violent revolution. Communist theoreticians have classified this process in four stages.

The first stage is marked by the workers' overthrow of capitalism and is followed by their seizure of the government.

The second stage is characterized by the establishment of a *dictatorship of the proletariat*. A centralized authority is necessary because the majority of workers are not capable of ruling; direction by a small group of intelligent leaders—the Communist party—is required. Under the dictatorship, destruction of the capitalist class is completed and society is reorganized along socialist lines, with private ownership and profit abolished. The state now owns and operates the means of production.

In the third stage, the dictatorship of the proletariat is replaced through the establishment of a "socialist" society. The political state still exists, and, because there may still be opposition, it has considerable power; economic production, however, is controlled by the workers. Because production is still limited, output and payment are "from each according to his ability, to each according to his work."

The fourth and highest stage is that of the true "communistic" society. Production is in such abundance that work and payment are made "from each according to his ability, to each according to his need." The political state is no longer necessary because there is no longer any antagonism between classes. Administrators are needed, however, to supervise industrial complexes.

The communists of the USSR claim that they have now reached the third stage—socialism—and that they hope to have enough production to attain actual communism very shortly.

Differences between Socialism and Communism

The communists seek to end capitalism by revolution, whereas the socialists wish to do it through the ballot box, adhering to constitutional procedures. In socialism, education and persuasion are substituted for the militant class struggle the communists advocate. For the most part, socialists believe in an orderly transfer of the means of production from private to public ownership. This changeover can be accomplished by gradually increasing the size of the public sector, thereby allowing capitalism and socialism to live side by side during the transition.

One of the important differences between socialism and communism may be seen in the treatment of nationalized property. Under social-

ism, fair payment is made to the owners. Because communists look with disdain on capitalists, considering the property they own to be stolen from the people, they expropriate private property without any compensation. Furthermore, they do not accept a mixed economy (although they did in practice in Russia between the years 1921 and 1927) and they believe in total nationalization.

Finally, socialism has a high regard for the political freedom of the individual. It does not seek to control the total way of life of the people; instead, it is responsive to the popular will expressed through elections. Communism, on the other hand, is totalitarian, seeking to subject not merely economic affairs but all individual thought and activity to the good of the state.

 Communism is a command economy, but politically it is authoritarian.

Weaknesses of Communism

In our analysis of socialism we have already identified many of the weaknesses of communism. To these, other criticisms must be added:

1. Marx, with his materialistic interpretation of history, focused attention on how economic forces determined history. Those people who owned wealth or the means of acquiring wealth—land in an agricultural society, ships in a maritime state, machinery in an industrial nation—also controlled the forces of government and determined their policies and direction.

   There is little doubt that Marx made a substantial contribution to understanding history, because too little attention had been given to economic forces before his time. At the same time, he committed the error common to all those who seek a single answer—oversimplification. No single factor can possibly explain all historical development. Events result from multiple causes; no one factor has been predominant throughout history.

2. Marx predicted that the proletarian revolution to overthrow capitalism could come only in advanced capitalistic nations. If this were true, the United States, Britain, and Western Europe should have been the first to experi-

ence such revolutions. Instead, communism has developed most frequently in nations that are just beginning to move from feudalism into the capitalist stage.

3. Marx predicted that polarization of classes would grow to the point where almost all people would be industrial workers and the rest would be capitalists. Writing a hundred years ago, he did not foresee the growth of the *salariat,* or white-collar workers, who identify with the middle and upper classes. Today, the salariat constitutes the largest group of workers. To them, the class struggle as Marx envisioned it is almost meaningless.

4. Marx foresaw the decline of interest rates as accumulation of more and more capital would lead eventually to a shortage of new areas for investment. In contrast to Marx's expectations, good opportunities for investment continue to exist today, and interest rates tend to fluctuate in the same way and for the same reasons that they always have.

5. Marx predicted that only through revolution could there be any reforms for the workers. He failed to foresee the economic gains and humanitarian reforms that the democratic capitalistic nations have carried out without resort to force.

6. Marx and other communist theoreticians looked on capitalist theory as a rigid doctrine incapable of solving the basic problems of a dynamic society. The capitalism of today, in theory and also in practice, is not the same as the capitalism Marx observed or prophesied in the nineteenth century. Current communist theoreticians commit the same error as their predecessors, although it is likely that they do so for propaganda rather than out of sincere conviction.

Market Socialism

In the late 1930s some economists who looked favorably on public ownership of the means of production and centralized planning became disillusioned with the inefficiency in the Soviet economy. They could not accept capitalism because they believed private property led to a concentra-

tion of both economic and political power. On the other hand, they recognized that the communist central planning of the Soviet Union became grossly inefficient at a certain stage of development. Their solution called for public ownership of the means of production, with greater reliance on the market rather than on central planning for the allocation of resources.

 Market socialism combines elements of a market and a command system using collective ownership of the means of production.

A famous Polish economist, Oskar Lange, developed a model known as *market,* or *decentralized, socialism.* The major features of this type of economic organization are the following:

1. Primary but not exclusive reliance on government ownership of the means of production.
2. Decentralized decision making to provide for consumer sovereignty in buying, workers' choice in selection of occupation, and major control by plant and industry managers of the resources bought and the products produced and sold.
3. A central planning board to determine broad national economic policies such as the amount that should be spent on capital goods and consumer goods and what interest rates should be.
4. A major emphasis on the market's determining price, but with some government control over resources used in the manufacturing of products.
5. Differences in the wage structure, adjusted for greater equality in income through the tax system.

Can Market Socialism Work?

After a brief experiment with Soviet communism after World War II, Yugoslavia gave up its Five-Year Plan and gradually moved toward market socialism. The Yugoslavs felt that what Russia had done was substitute bureaucratic state capitalism for the capitalist class, with the working class equally exploited in both systems. Therefore, they decided they would place the means of production directly into the hands of the worker. Control of state enterprises was passed on to the workers, who elected "workers councils." These representative bodies are responsible for policy issues such as hiring management, pricing, and distributing income earned by the enterprise. This self-management arrangement gives each worker a self-interest in the success of the firm, because each worker shares in what is left after expenses, new investment, and taxes are paid out. If the residual (what our businesses call profits) is large, bonuses are given. If what remains is small, minimum wages are still drawn from reserves or funds provided by a local government.

This system is not totally decentralized. The central planning board provides coordination and some regulation of the economy by making decisions about the economic growth rate, the distribution of resources by industry and geography, the amount and type of foreign trade, taxes, government investment, and anti-monopoly laws. The national bank sets interest rates and provides money for investment. Most farms are owned by individual peasants, although cooperatives are encouraged. Small retail stores, such as repair shops and service-oriented firms such as restaurants, are often privately owned.

How Successful Has the Yugoslav Experiment Been?

It is too early to make any definite decision on how successful Yugoslavia has been in its market socialism plus worker management system because there have been no parallels to compare it with. We do know that its economic growth record has been quite good largely because of greater efficiency and large capital investments. Nevertheless, there have been major problems stemming from wide fluctuations in growth from year to year, shortages in skilled labor and a high unemployment rate for unskilled labor, firms operating with monopolylike power, and a high inflation rate. Many underdeveloped countries are watching this experimental economic system with interest.

B   What Economic System? The Reality

Having examined the models of the three principal competitors of capitalism, we are now ready to analyze the basic principles of these systems. An adherent of any one of these systems would tend to exaggerate the differences among them. If, however, we can remove ourselves from the emotional involvement often associated with a discussion of "isms," we can more clearly identify the real issues.

The Political and Economic Spectra

Every scientific discipline seeks to organize knowledge in such a way that it can be handled easily. Criteria are drawn up so that groups of ideas, bodies of knowledge, and systems can be categorized. When political scientists classify a country's political system as a democracy or an oligarchy, they take numerous characteristics into consideration and then adjudge which of these categories comes closest to describing the political state they are examining. Economists do the same thing in trying to classify a nation's economic system. No nation's system, political or economic, conforms exactly to the model.

The basic issue, both politically and economically, is the degree of freedom allowed the individual. In Figure 3–1 we can see the complete political spectrum as it moves from left to right. At the extreme left, we see the complete freedom of the individual and the absence of any governmental coercion. The condition in which government is absent is called *anarchism*. At the extreme right is *totalitarianism*—citizens have surrendered all freedom to a government that has total control over every aspect of their lives. *Absolute monarchy* is listed on the extreme right because it refers to rule by one person. *Constitutional monarchy,* as in Britain, can be just as liberal as other

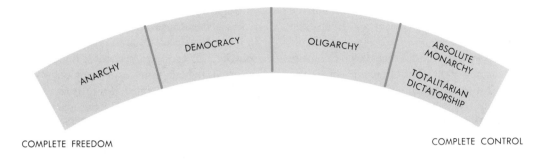

COMPLETE FREEDOM   COMPLETE CONTROL

Figure 3–1   The political spectrum

Anarchy offers the individual citizen complete freedom with no government
coercion. Totalitarianism subordinates the individual completely to the good of
the state.

democracies, because the constitution guarantees
the rights of the people. In an *oligarchy* the few
rule, whereas in a *democracy* the many rule. The
political spectrum defines the extent of personal
freedom the citizen has in relation to government
authority.

In Figure 3–2 we see the economic spectrum. Here the difference lies in who decides the
answers to the basic economic questions *What,
How,* and *For whom.* On the right side of the spectrum, consumers are king. Their decisions,
expressed by their purchases, and the response of

private enterprise, expressed by supply, determine the use of resources. It is the market
mechanism at work. Laissez-faire, or classical
capitalism, generally keeps the government out of
decision making as much as possible.

Mixed capitalism, sometimes called *welfare
capitalism,* favors decisions by consumers but
allows for some central planning. As we move
toward the left from mixed socialism to socialism
to communism, central planning increases and
reliance on the market mechanism declines. At
the extreme left, we see command central plan-

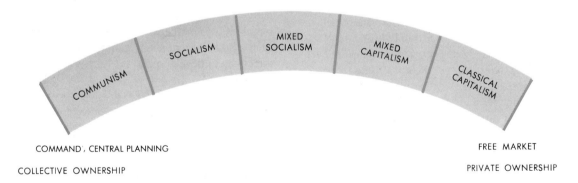

COMMAND, CENTRAL PLANNING   FREE MARKET

COLLECTIVE OWNERSHIP   PRIVATE OWNERSHIP

**Figure 3–2   The economic spectrum of decision making and
of the ownership of wealth**

Classical capitalism makes the consumer king and the regulator of the entire
market. Communism (before the state withers away) calls for the greatest
amount of central planning with very little consumer sovereignty. Classical
capitalism calls for a maximum of private ownership, whereas communism calls
for a maximum of collective ownership.

ning, where government makes almost all the decisions and consumer choices are given little attention.

Our economic spectrum is not complete unless we include the ownership of wealth. In Figure 3–2 we also see complete private ownership on one side and complete collective ownership on the other. Although no countries have either of these extremes, classical capitalism calls for a maximum of private ownership and communism calls for a maximum of collective ownership, particularly of capital goods. Again we see the different degrees of emphasis on ownership of wealth given by mixed capitalism, mixed socialism, and socialism.

Tying the Political and Economic Spectra Together

When we try to determine where to place a particular nation on the two spectra with freedom as one of the criteria, we must consider both its political and its economic system. Although the British Labour party strongly emphasizes central planning and believes in nationalizing some of its nation's basic industries, it can do these things only with approval of the British electorate and with just compensation to owners whose private property is lost to collective ownership. No such limits are placed on the Soviet government.

Either democracy or totalitarianism can exist as a political system with either private or collective ownership. The Fascists in Italy and the Nazis in Germany allowed private ownership of even the basic industries, but there was little freedom, even for the owners of businesses. Democracy can be practiced in nations that rely primarily on the market mechanism for the allocation of resources, such as our own, or in nations that have a great deal of central planning, such as Sweden.

Economic Systems Evolve

Advocates of a particular economic system may preach and work to have their system supplant what exists, but the chances of installing a completely new economic system are remote. Economic systems grow slowly, and only occa-

sionally can changes be speeded up. In the United States under Roosevelt's New Deal policies and in Great Britain under the Labour party policies between 1945 and 1951, several significant changes occurred. In both instances, the amount of central planning was accelerated. More recently, under the administrations of Ronald Reagan in the United States and Margaret Thatcher in Britain, the trend has been reversed. Government involvement in the economy has been reduced, and the free market has been substituted for governmental planning and regulation.

When the Communists took control in Russia in November of 1917, they tried to replace the existing system with pure communism. Their attempt was not successful. In 1921, Lenin, realizing the need for compromise, launched the New Economic Policy (NEP), which combined elements of both communism and capitalism. For the next seven years, limited private ownership and the profit motive were allowed to exist side by side with collective ownership. Gradually, central planning and collective ownership were increased, and by 1928 Stalin had restored solely communist principles.

Recent Changes

Each of the political-economic systems we have considered has changed from the model as originally conceived. The reality of the present may represent a prime departure from past theory. In each system, recent changes have indicated new directions of development.

Trend of the American Economy

Our nation's economy today is a far cry from what the classical economists envisioned. In Chapter 9 we will survey and discuss the changes in size and influence of our various levels of government. Today a third of the market value of all the production in the United States, called the *gross national product* (GNP), is spent by our local, state, and national governments. Services, particularly in health, welfare, education, and the broad field of research, are frequently controlled, subsidized, or owned by government. Government influence over economic groups—including labor, business, and professional groups—is considerable. Economic decisions are being made by individual consumers less often than previously, and planning takes place at all levels of government.

Are we losing our freedom and becoming totalitarian? Most social scientists would answer with a resounding *no*! They believe that what we have done is to transfer some of our decision making as consumers to decision making as citizens. Increased specialization and interdependence have forced us, sometimes reluctantly, to give up our individual sovereignty for the common good. So long as we have a free marketplace in which to learn the facts and evaluate ideas, and so long as we have the power through elections to reverse the trend, we need not fear the future.

 The U.S. economy is a mixed market system.

In spite of the trend toward central planning, the private sector of our economy is still twice as large as the public sector. Most of our economic decisions are still made by individual consumers and producers, and we continue to rely on the market mechanism to allocate most of our scarce resources. We may properly call our nation's economic system mixed capitalism.

Trend of the Soviet Economy

Since Stalin's death in 1953, trends in the Soviet Union have indicated a decrease in centralized planning. Still, each year the State Planning Commission, known as the "Gosplan," makes the basic economic decisions. It does so for both the short and the long term in close cooperation with party leaders. Thus economic planning reflects political decisions. Great attention is paid today to setting quotas and to considering the suggestions of regional councils and even of plant managers. Although consumers appear to have relative freedom in determining their own purchases, most consumer prices are determined not by supply and demand (at least not directly), but by the state. If more overcoats than jackets are made and consumers want more jackets, a tax is placed on jackets to discourage their purchase. The state permits the sale of certain food products—those grown by farmers on their own time and on specially designated land—in a free market, very similar

to our own. These private plots account for less than 3 percent of the land under cultivation but approximately 30 percent of the value of agricultural output.

Most Soviet workers are free to work where they wish, although some of them are required to work on special projects. Wide differences are found in the pay scales of Soviet workers. Scientists, plant managers, and skilled technicians have the highest incomes. The Soviet Union has adopted capitalistic incentive plans by paying *piece rates* (wages determined by output) and by offering various kinds of bonuses to managers who meet or exceed their production quotas.

A close check is maintained over the economy by the state control commission and the Gosbank, which handles all banking in the Soviet Union. The Gosbank works closely with the central planners, providing funds according to plan requirements. As you know, in our country the market mechanism determines the allocation of capital.

In the 1960s, first under Khrushchev and later under Brezhnev, the obsession with meeting production quotas and concentrating on heavy industry without regard to consumer demand changed in degree, if not in kind. Partly through opening up channels for criticism (which indicated gross inefficiencies in the system) and partly through the analysis and efforts of Evsei Liberman, a Soviet professor of economics, market research, using supply and demand for price adjustments, and decentralization of managerial decisions spread to many segments of the economy. Studies revealed that, because a complex bureaucracy fixed prices and wages, resources were not being allocated where they were most productive and most needed. Managers frequently operated well below their plants' capacity in order to escape the pressures of having their quotas raised regularly. Expenditures for capital investment were made without considering what the money would yield if it were used in some other way. Overproduction of some parts for a truck and underproduction of others resulted in fewer trucks. The production of too many large suits and too few small suits may have filled production quotas but satisfied too few consumers. Poor quality control left unsold merchandise on counters. Rising incomes made Soviet consumers more selective and they delayed their purchases.

Libermanism

A modified profit system, not nearly as extensive as the Yugoslavian one, was introduced—at the suggestion of Professor of Economics Evsei Liberman—in the Soviet Union in the 1960s. Under this system the producing unit as well as the Gosbank was charged for the materials and labor used. Cooperation between the producer and retailer to determine consumer wants was encouraged, and sales could be used to bring supply and demand into balance. The entire production process was recorded through an accounting system and profits could be determined.

Although some significant success has been recorded in increasing efficiency and improving the quality of goods through decentralizing decision making, big problems continue because the Soviet bureaucracy interferes with producing units.

Over 20,000 commodities are still planned centrally. This arrangement seriously interferes with allocating raw materials and capital in all the remaining industries. Incentives are geared to short-run gains and prices are too inflexible. The struggle between the central planners and the advocates of decentralizing decision making will continue. Political considerations more than total economic performance will probably determine the balance that will prevail. However, central planning and government ownership remain the key to that economic system.

Trends in Other Communist Countries

In the 1960s decentralization and a greater reliance on market forces worked their way into the Eastern European nations' economies, particularly Hungary. However, with a decline in the economic growth rates, there was a retrenchment of reforms, and new controls found their way back into the economy in the 1970s and 1980s.

 # Capitalism in the Soviet Economy

A number of myths exist about the Soviet economy. The distribution of income is considerably less equal than in most of the mixed economies in Western Europe but somewhat more equal than in the United States. Wage and salary differentials are considerable between the upper-income groups (such as top-level managers; scientists and stars of the theater, ballet, and concert stage), middle-income groups (such as physicians, teachers, and skilled workers); and lower-income groups (the semiskilled and unskilled workers). People are free to choose their own occupations and geographic locations. Wage differences motivate people to work at or move to less desirable places. Consumers may choose what they wish to buy, and there is private ownership of goods such as appliances and automobiles. However, consumers have little direct say in what is produced.

Professionals and artisans may work for themselves, but they may not hire anyone to work for them. Incentives in the form of bonuses for managers and payments to workers for their unit output (piece work) are accepted as part of the transition to full communism.

Changes in the Chinese economy have been very significant since the death of Mao Tse-tung in 1976. Admitting the failure of the "Great Leap Forward and Cultural Revolution," the new leaders moved to establish closer ties with the West, particularly the United States. Trade agreements, investment of capital, educational exchange programs, and decentralization of economic decision making have produced dramatic increases in productivity. Incentives are being tried, along with some autonomy for enterprise management. In agriculture, team efforts are being used in both growing and delivery of produce. A shift in priorities from military and heavy industries to agriculture and light industries, has increased the supply of consumer goods. The People's Republic of China may be the first large nation to find a midway position, shifting from communism toward a more market-oriented economy.

Trend of Socialism

Because early socialists were discontented with great inequality of wealth, one of their main objectives was achieving greater equality in the distribution of returns from production. They hoped to accomplish this by nationalizing the means of production so that profits, the alleged cause of inequality, could be shared by everyone. They also sought to provide for all a minimum standard of living as a means to economic and social security.

As we have seen, these objectives are no longer the goals of socialists exclusively. Such goals have in fact become a reality, or close to a reality, in many of the affluent nations, including those with mixed capitalism. Social legislation providing for the poorest members of society has been passed by a Conservative government in Britain and by both Republican and Democratic administrations in the United States. Socialist nations have, like our own, used the progressive income tax (levies set on the ability to pay) and the inheritance tax to achieve greater economic equality. Greater emphasis on increasing productivity and raising the GNP so that even the smallest individual share will provide a decent living standard has replaced the desire to make the distribution of wealth more nearly equal.

 Reliance on the market to improve efficiency has increased in many mixed economies.

Indicative Planning

Two countries, both with mixed capitalistic economies, have used elaborate planning to promote their national economic goals in general and their economic growth specifically. For many years France has been using a national economic plan developed by representatives of labor, industry, and government, with the help of technical experts. The purpose of this indicative planning is to coordinate economic activity voluntarily. Strongest control is exercised through investment of half the national effort plus consumer credit. French firms work closely with government, and they may get together with their competitors without worrying about the strict antitrust laws that we have.

Although the Japanese economy differs from the French in that many of its corporations assume a strong sense of paternalism with respect to workers, it too uses indicative planning. The Min-

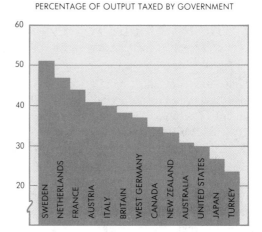

Figure 3–3   Taxes as a percent of production

One clue in determining what type of economic system a nation has is to look at the percentage of total output that is taxed by government. The decisions as to how that revenue is allocated are made by government. The use of the remaining production revenue is determined by consumers and businesses.

ister of Finance and the Ministry of International Trade and Industry (MITI) set priorities by selecting the "winning" and the "losing" industries in terms of growth potential. They then try to direct investment capital where they believe expansion is likely to take place in the future. Business and labor cooperate in the national interest.

In our country a number of leaders in government, business, and labor have called for such planning under the heading of "Industrial Policy." They say that if we are to compete successfully in the global economy, it will take the cooperative efforts of all forces in the economy, with government leadership and a relaxation of our antitrust laws.

Conclusion

What conclusion does our study of economic systems lead us to? Economic models are important because they supply the guidelines for answering the big economic questions. They designate the direction in which a society and its people think they should be moving. However, as we have seen, there is a difference between the theory and the reality of economic systems. The basic difference between systems is largely a matter of whether they use the market mechanism, with its emphasis on freedom and the individual, or the central planning, with its emphasis on collective decisions and collective ownership. Totalitarianism and democracy can exist with either private ownership or collective ownership.

Economic systems evolve over time. Capitalistic systems are using more central planning, and communist countries are experimenting with the market mechanism. British socialism has varied according to political climate, elections, and changing economic circumstances.

What we as citizens of a democracy must remember is that we have the power and responsibility to guide our economic system in the direction we believe will best accomplish our individual and national goals. It would be unfortunate if we failed, either through ignorance or through irresponsibility, to put forth the necessary effort, and thus to realize the benefits of our democratic heritage.

C The Problem: Progress or Weakness in the Soviet Economy?

There can be little doubt that the Soviet Union is in competition with the United States. Premier Khrushchev made an open challenge in 1957, calling it economic war. He claimed that the Soviet Union would soon surpass the United States in production and boasted that the Russians would "bury" us. Although Khrushchev's challenge is not much closer to reality today than it was in 1957, the underdeveloped countries of the world are aware of this challenge. Because many of them are not yet committed to either system, they are watching the progress of the two competing systems.

In trying to evaluate Soviet economic progress, we must be aware of certain problems. We must not assume that the goals of our mixed capitalistic system are the same as the goals of the Soviet system. We must recognize that resources, both human and natural, are not the same. Lastly, we are not certain about the accuracy of Soviet figures. In some instances, errors in comparison are made because methods and techniques in compiling statistics differ; in other instances, no data are available.

The Progress of the Soviet Economy

In the last sixty years, the Soviet Union has been transformed from a largely preindustrial, feudally organized nation to the second-largest industrial power in the world. It has introduced central economic planning on a scale never before attempted; its growth in production is unquestioned. Its average annual growth rate from 1961 to 1970 was 5.1, slightly higher than that of the European Community countries and about 25 percent higher than that of the United States. From 1971 to 1980

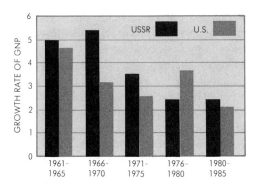

Figure 3–4 A comparison of the performance of the U.S. and Soviet economies

Because total output of the Soviet economy was only about 50 percent of that of the United States', the USSR must have nearly double our growth rate to catch up. In only one of the five-year periods shown above did our rate of growth exceed that of the Soviets, yet their output has fluctuated between 54 percent and 57 percent of ours. In per capita GNP, it is less than half that percentage. (Source: OECD and IMF.)

growth declined in most industrial countries. The average rate for the USSR was 3.1, for the United States about the same, and for Japan, a capitalistic country, 4.9 percent. From 1981 to 1984 our country had a slightly higher growth rate than the USSR—2.8 to 2.7—while Japan had a 4 percent growth rate.

Despite many claims that Soviet production is inefficient, much of that country's industrial expansion must be attributed to increases in output per worker, because the labor force has increased less rapidly than production. The same positive record is shown in productivity for each capital unit of input invested.

Besides increasing the output per unit of input (that is, creating more value per labor hour), the Soviet Union has increased the use of factors or potential factors of production. The growth of the percentage of adults participating in the labor force increased from slightly more than 50 percent in 1928 to 75 percent in 1980. During this same period, the percentage of the Soviet labor force devoted to agriculture decreased from 80 to 25 percent. This permitted a shift in the work force

to the industrial sector, accounting for significant gains in the Soviet gross national product.

Although most experts put the Soviet GNP at about 55 percent of ours, this comparison is not a true measure of the relative economic strength of the two nations. For the Soviet Union to achieve this rate of growth, the Soviet citizen has had to forgo many consumer goods. The standard of living of the Russian people is improving, but it has gained at a slower rate than parts of the economy designated by Soviet leaders as essential, such as Soviet military power.

Any underdeveloped country wishing to become highly industrialized must sacrifice current consumption for capital investment. This is exactly what the Soviet leaders have done. Consumption as a percentage of GNP is lower in the Soviet Union than in the United States, but capital investment is far greater. It is from this additional capital investment that increased productive capacity is obtained.

Differences between the two systems in the productive capacity of heavy industry are far less than the differences in GNP would seem to indicate. In the production of steel and new machine tools, the USSR is ahead of the United States. In coal and electricity, the gap has already been closed. The increase in the productive capacities of these basic industries may soon be reflected in higher living standards for the Russian people.

 Soviet progress has been greatest in heavy industry and defense at the expense of consumer goods.

There is no doubt that borrowing from the advanced technology of Western nations has helped the Soviet Union to progress. However, she has developed a large number—and in some fields such as engineering, a greater number than we have—of highly trained specialists in the sciences, engineering, and managerial operations, who provide new knowledge and techniques to sustain continuing development. In addition, the Soviet economy has been almost "depression-proof." By having full employment at all times, the Soviets appear to be avoiding the waste in human resources so common in western capitalistic countries. However, they sometimes achieve this through made or inefficient work such as sweeping streets with hand brooms.

Weaknesses in the Soviet Economy

The reforms associated with Evsei Liberman in the 1960s and early 1970s, which permitted some price fluctuations based on market conditions, disappeared as the bureaucracy of Brezhnev took hold. Central planning became stronger than ever. Prices on wholesale goods remained the same from 1967 to 1982, and retail food prices dated back even further. This rigidity, basically an attempt to repeal the laws of demand and supply, has led to long lines for scarce goods and the development of a hidden, or black-market, economy,[1] not very different from the situation that existed when our own country used controlled prices.

When one of the authors visited the Soviet Union, he left with the memory of consumers waiting in line for goods that were in short supply at prices that reflected state subsidies. Bread prices have not changed for 30 years, although the prices paid to farmers for grain have increased. This has led Soviet peasants to buy about 5 percent of the bread back to feed their animals rather than take the more expensive grain from their own fields.[2]

Soviet managers are known to bribe suppliers of their raw materials so that they can meet their factory quotas. Clerks in appliance stores are "tipped" to shorten the wait consumers have, and doctors, carpenters, and electricians take their state materials and put them to use for their private gain. Factories that lag behind their quotas speed up the quantity output by ignoring quality. Those that could exceed their quotas substantially are afraid to do so for fear their quotas will constantly be raised.

Military expenditures consume over 14 percent of the Soviet Union's gross national product,

in contrast to 6.3 percent for U.S. military expenditures. Not only does this drain natural resources and labor away from other parts of the economy, it siphons off the best scientists, engineers, and skilled labor needed for developing high-tech industries. The latter is a major weakness in the Soviet economy, requiring the USSR to import western technology.

Earlier we referred to the remarkable economic growth rate during the 1950s and 1960s. Part of the reason was the flow of surplus labor from agriculture to industry. Not only has this source of labor dried up, but the number of new workers joining the Soviet labor force has slowed from approximately 19 million in the 1970s to a projected 9 million in the 1980s. This compares to new entries into the work force in the United States of 24 million in the 1970s and a projected 11 million in the 1980s. To increase their gross national product, the Soviets will have to raise the output per worker.

As do all nations going through stages of development, the Soviet Union tapped its richest and least costly natural resources first. It must now explore less developed areas such as Siberia, which involves expensive transportation costs, and more costly sources from places already exploited. This general phenomenon, known to us as increasing costs (or, as we will see in Chapter 5, diminishing marginal productivity), will make future growth more difficult.

Perhaps the greatest weakness of the Soviet economy has already been referred to. It is the giant, inflexible bureaucracy that is trying to allocate production by central planning. This may have been suitable for the 1950s, when objectives were limited, but it is doubtful it can do the job in a complex economy. The need to provide incentives to increase productivity and apply the price system for efficient allocation of goods may put the Soviet system at a disadvantage in its attempt to increase its economic growth and overtake the United States.

Finally, the noneconomic consequences of forced industrialization and collectivization required coercion and subjection of millions of people. Although Soviet leaders have justified such ruthlessness as a means to an end—that the Soviet

---

[1]Gregory Grossman, "The 'Second Economy' of the USSR," in Morris Bornstein (ed.), *The Soviet Economy: Continuity and Change* (Boulder, Colo.: Westview Press, 1981), p. 88.

[2]Marshall I. Goldman, "The Failure of Soviet Leadership," *Challenge*, May/June 1984, p. 8.

Union has become the second industrial power in the world—it seems unlikely that such values would ever be acceptable to most people living in political democracies.

Considering an Answer

Comparing a variety of economic systems helps to clarify the strengths and weaknesses of each one. Points of likeness and difference among systems provide a basis for evaluation and give us more objectivity in analyzing the working of our own system. Distinguishing between economic and political aspects of these systems gives an added dimension to our analysis. Finally, by making such comparisons, we as individuals and citizens become more aware of what our values are.

The following questions will guide you in evaluating Soviet economic progress:

1. What criteria are most important to you as consumer, producer, and citizen in evaluating an economy? How does Soviet progress measure up according to these criteria?
2. Are the factors responsible for economic growth the same at all stages of development? What changes in these factors have taken place in the course of development in the USSR?
3. Are the recent changes in performance trends of the Soviet and U.S. economies likely to be temporary or permanent? Why?
4. How do your personal preferences and your own sense of values influence your evaluation of Soviet progress?

Chapter Highlights

1. The three principal economic systems competing with capitalism are socialism, communism, and market socialism. Each system has reasons for rejecting the other models and choosing its own way of answering the basic economic questions.

2. Socialism rejects production for profit and private ownership of the means of production. In their place, it puts collective ownership and production for need. Socialists prefer central planning to the free market in economic decision making. Unlike communism, it can live side by side with capitalism, nationalizing industry gradually through education and the ballot box. There are many forms of socialism.

3. Marx, the father of communism, believed that all history can be explained as a series of class struggles between those who own the means of production and those who seek power. Communists believe that capitalism can be overcome only by revolution. They envision society as moving into higher stages, eventually attaining communism. When that occurs, production will be so great that payment will be according to need. Much of what Marx predicted has failed to materialize.

4. Market socialism combines communism's public ownership of the means of production with capitalism's market system for the allocation of resources. In Yugoslavia the economy is decentralized, with workers' councils controlling the enterprise and group rewards given for efficiency. Some central control is provided by the central planning board. It is too early to evaluate the Yugoslav experiment, but

the economy suffers from monopolylike firms and high unemployment and inflation.

5. No nation falls completely into any one of these three systems. The political spectrum extends from complete freedom for the individual citizen in relation to the state to complete control by government. The economic spectra extend from a free market to command central planning and from complete private ownership to total collective ownership.

6. Systems in most countries are mixed, with differences existing within countries as well as between them. Changes in these systems tend to evolve gradually.

7. The dominant trend in the United States has been toward increased central planning but interrupted frequently by the desire and need to return to the market system. In the Soviet Union there was limited experimentation with the market, but that trend seems to have been reversed.

8. Many other communist countries, particularly Hungary and China, have moved toward decentralizing control, providing some incentives, and using some market forces to allocate resources.

9. The trend in socialism is to place less emphasis on nationalizing industry and more on equality of income and opportunity.

10. Indicative planning is found in some mixed capitalistic countries, most notably France and Japan. Economic groups are brought together by government to establish national economic priorities. Guidance rather than coercion is used.

11. There is disagreement on the progress of the Soviet economy, with evidence pointing to a slowdown from its remarkable early growth.

Study Aids

Key Terms and Names

socialism	proletariat	indicative planning
nationalization	revisionism	totalitarianism
scientific socialism	utopian socialism	collective ownership
syndicalism	Christian socialism	communism
welfare capitalism	anarchism	surplus value
social legislation	fascism	salariat
		market socialism

Robert Owen	Charles Fourier	*Das Kapital*
Karl Marx	Evsei Liberman	*Communist Manifesto*
Friedrich Engels	Fabian Society	Gosbank
	Oskar Lange	

Questions

1. In considering "isms," we have found close parallels between economic and political philosophies.
   (a) Explain the idea "Although there are close ties between economic and political systems, the characteristics of the two kinds of systems are not necessarily the same."
   (b) What questions does each kind of system attempt to answer?
2. Explain socialism's appeal in other parts of the world. Why have some Americans supported socialism at various times in our history?
3. There are several variations of socialist economic philosophy. Identify four different versions and describe the ways in which they differ from one another.
4. Identify the main economic ideas that Karl Marx set forth.
   (a) What are the four stages in the development of communism from capitalism?
   (b) What proof exists that some of these stages have not fully materialized?
5. What are the essential differences in the methodology used by socialists and communists in achieving their goals? Illustrate these differences by referring to specific countries or historical events.
6. What aspects of the Yugoslavian economy are like communism? Like capitalism? Would you like to be a worker in this system? What part does central planning play?
7. How does communism in the Soviet Union substitute central planning for the price system in allocating resources? What are the weaknesses of central planning?
8. What evidence is there of indicative planning in the United States? Given Japan's remarkable economic progress, should we be moving in that direction?

9. Explain the meaning of each of these statements:
   (a) "Communist countries are using capitalist ideas, capitalist countries are using central planning, and socialists are marking time."
   (b) "The particular conditions within each nation determine the degree of political and economic control exercised there."

Problems

1. Compare one of the communities established by the utopian socialists with a modern youth commune. What are the economic realities of each?
2. Compare the economies of Sweden ("the middle way"), Japan, and the Soviet Union. How are they similar? How and why do they differ? Consider the success of each in terms of basic economic goals.
3. The Roosevelt New Deal has been called the "road to socialism" and the "savior of American capitalism." List and explain the arguments supporting each point of view. Explain how time can change our values.
4. Select a national economy that closely approximates each economic theory. To what extent does actual practice in each country conform to theory? Why are many countries unable to adhere strictly to the theories they espouse?
5. Compare the ideas on the role of government expressed by F. A. Hayek in his *Road to Serfdom* with J. K. Galbraith's theories in *The New Industrial State*.
6. In what way did the Reagan Administration reverse the trend of centralization begun by Franklin D. Roosevelt?

PART

II

The Factors Responsible for Production

Business Enterprise

The focus of Part Two is on *microeconomics,* the study of individual units of the economy. Part Three, in turn, will deal with *macroeconomics,* the study of the nation's economy as a whole. Actually, our study of microeconomics began in Chapter 2 with an analysis of how demand and supply determine price. It continues in this unit with a consideration of how businesses maximize their profits and of the factors in the economy that are responsible for production.

In a *private-enterprise* economy the decisions as to what and how to produce are made mainly by entrepreneurs. They ascertain the probable trend of consumer wants and then proceed to organize the factors of production to satisfy these wants. Their motivation is profit; and if their decisions on the *What* and the *How* are correct, they will probably do well.

Businesses in the United States vary in size, organization, and product according to the many diverse needs of the consumer. Businesses are organized as single proprietorships, partnerships, or corporations, each having certain advantages and limitations. The Industrial Revolution, with its change in the methods of production, gave impetus to the modern corporation. It also led to business combinations that changed the pattern of competition from that assumed in the classical model. Government has responded to this change by trying to keep competition as close to the original model as possible. Where competition has been impractical, the government has tried to protect the consumer through regulation.

In view of the economic climate, would you prefer to go into business for yourself or work for someone else? Would you rather work for a big corporation or a family business? Should the size of businesses be limited?

Chapter Objectives

When you have completed this chapter, you should be able to:

- Explain the organizational differences among a single proprietorship, a partnership, and a corporation.
- Discuss the advantages and disadvantages of these three forms of business organization.
- Discuss the impact of changing technology on business structure.
- Define fixed costs and variable costs.
- Discuss the impact of high fixed costs on competition in the U.S. economy.
- Present and evaluate the cases for and against mergers and acquisitions.
- Discuss the means whereby government can seek to counterbalance big business, including the multinational firm, and foster more competition.
- Understand the role that small business plays in the U.S. economy.

A Characteristics of Business Enterprise

Production in the United States

A primary concern that we, as individuals, have with economics lies in deciding how well we can afford to live. If we are to achieve a high *standard of living,* it is necessary that the production of goods and services be maintained at a high level. In 1985, the GNP was nearly $4 trillion, one-quarter the value of all the world's production. This achievement is even more remarkable when you consider that it was carried out by only one-twentieth of the world's population. Most of this production came from U.S. business.

The Role of Business

The classical model calls for business owners to go to the market for goods and services to find out what consumers want and then, spurred on by the profit motive, to go to the market for the factors of production to produce the goods. About two-thirds of the value of the total GNP results from the decisions made by private enterprise. Although the decisions on the remainder of our production are determined by governments at the local, state, and national levels, most of this production comes from business enterprise. Our schools, our weapons of defense, and most of the purchased items in government budgets are produced by business. Throughout our history we have remained fairly consistent in favoring private enterprise over government enterprise with respect to the *What* and the *How* of production.

Variety of Business Enterprises

The sixteen million separate businesses in our country vary greatly in size and organization. The person who sells popcorn, ice cream, and hot dogs from a cart is in business, although total sales may amount to only a few thousand dollars a year. In contrast, the United States has giant corporations that do more business than is done in many countries. In 1985 Exxon sold more goods and services—about $100 billion worth—than were produced in Greece, Ireland, Chile, and Portugal combined.

Both the street vendor and Exxon are producing what they think their customers want. They are both in business to make as large a profit as they can; they both must take risks, invest money, and organize the factors of production. Although they have much in common, they are organized quite differently. To get a better understanding of business and the part that organization of a business plays, we shall take a hypothetical venture into business ourselves.

Starting a Business

Our chief purpose in going into business is to make a profit. This is done by supplying consumers with something they want but do not have, or something better than what they have. If there are mice but no mousetraps, build a trap. If there is a mousetrap, build a better or a cheaper one.

What to Produce

First we shall call a meeting to discuss the *What*. After listening to many suggestions, all of which prove unsatisfactory for one reason or another, we finally hit upon the idea for an adult game based on urban planning. According to the latest toy-trade journals, the demand has been growing for decision-making games for mature people. The game "Monopoly" caught on years ago. A more sophisticated game should catch the educated public's interest now. Let's give it a try! After organizing ourselves into a business firm, which is sometimes called an enterprise, we adopt the name "Build-a-City." As the organizers of the business we are known as *entrepreneurs* or, more simply, managers.

How to Produce

We are now ready to consider the means of producing—the *How* of a business enterprise. Our responsibility is to collect the factors of production and assemble them in the right amount, at the right time, and in the right place.

Adults are more likely to pay a higher price for a game for themselves than for one for their children, because they reason it will be used more often over a longer period of time. We shall use wooden models and package the game in a wooden box. This being the case, the principal natural resource we need is lumber. There is a mill nearby, but it is currently selling all the lumber it produces. If we are to divert the wood from its present use to our business, we must offer a slightly higher price than the present market price. We have increased the demand, but the supply of materials on hand remains the same.

In the labor market, we can attract workers by offering them jobs that will pay at least as much as they are currently earning, if not more. However, if there is unemployment in the area—if the supply of workers is greater than the demand—labor costs may be low, and we can hire workers at the going market rate.

We also need machinery and a factory. Usually, the more and better the machinery available to workers, the greater the production. Because machinery is not used to satisfy the consumer's needs but rather to make the goods that the consumer wants, it is called a *capital good* or a *producer good*. Goods used directly by consumers to satisfy their needs are called *consumer goods*.

To buy machinery and a building we obviously need money. When money is used by business to buy the things needed in production, it is called *capital*. When people ask us, "How much capital do you have?" they are not referring to the actual number of machines. They want to know how much money we have for man-made instruments of production—that is, machines, buildings, and goods made by others that are necessary for production.

 Money is the representation of capital when it is used for investment.

Raising Capital

At a meeting to discuss the cost of equipment, we soon discover that we do not have enough capital. The decision is made to go to a commercial bank to see whether the officials will lend us the amount of money we need. A primary function of commercial banks is to provide short-term capital to businesses. If we obtain a loan, we shall have to pay a price for its use, *interest*. Rate of interest is expressed as a percentage. If we borrow $100,000 at 12 percent interest for one year, we pay $12,000 for the money we borrow. Although interest is for the money borrowed, in the long run it is for the equipment and other things needed for our business.

Money is used in many other ways in the marketplace. The money we pay for the wood from the forest (natural resources) is called *rent*, and the money we pay our workers is called *wages*. We, the entrepreneurs, receive the money that is left, the *profits*. Payments to each of the factors of production are subject, at least partly, to supply and demand.

B Forms of Business Organization

Although we have proceeded with the initial steps in starting a business, we have neglected to answer one of the first and most important questions facing any business person. What kind of business organization shall we choose? There are three forms of organization from which to select: a *single proprietorship,* a *partnership,* and a *corporation.* Because each form has particular advantages and disadvantages, our choice can best be made after examining each form.

Single Proprietorship

To illustrate the various forms of organization possible, let us suppose that you alone are the one who thought of the idea of producing "Build-a-City" sets and want to start a company by yourself. Such a business is classified as a single proprietorship, the most common type of business organization and the easiest to set up. Figure 4–1 shows that nearly three-fourths of all firms use this form of organization. The approximately 11 million single proprietorships in the United States produce only 8 percent of all business receipts because most of these businesses are very small. You, as owner, are the boss and need not consult others in making business decisions. You cannot be fired. If you fail, it will be your own fault. On the other hand, if there is a profit, you will receive it all—a great incentive. Another advantage is that you do not have to pay a corporation income tax.

At first you may be happy to be the sole owner of a business. However, you soon recognize that there are serious drawbacks to such an organization. If your business is like many single proprietorships, you are likely to be bothered by a shortage of cash. This shortage may not be caused by incompetence or carelessness. Deficits are likely to occur when you attempt to meet the constant expenditures of the business. If business is bad, this is easy to understand. Your business, however, has been almost too good. You have had so many requests for "Build-a-City" sets that to meet this demand you have had to employ more of the

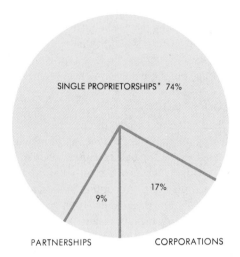

*Includes farmers and professional people in business for themselves.

Figure 4–1   Legal organization of business population in percentages
Source: U.S. Department of Commerce.

factors of production. In addition, your financial situation has been hurt because the merchants buying your sets have been slow in paying their bills. You might solve your production problem by enlarging your factory, buying a few more machines, and hiring additional workers. This would allow you to increase the size of your business sufficiently to meet the demand. If only you had more capital!

 Each of the business forms has advantages and disadvantages in comparison to the others.

As you consider enlarging your business, you may become aware of another disadvantage of the single proprietorship. It is nice to be your own boss, but it also means that all the responsibility is on your shoulders. You never seem to have any free time and are required to be a specialist in such diverse activities as buying, producing, and merchandising. You hire a managerial assistant to help share your responsibilities, but her interest in the business is not as personal as if she were an owner. Two additional disadvantages, unlimited liability and limited life, apply to both single proprietorships and partnerships. (These disadvantages will be considered in connection with partnerships.) It occurs to you that, although a partnership also has disadvantages, perhaps it would be a better form of organization for your purposes.

Partnership

What your business needs, if it is to expand more quickly, is additional capital and perhaps additional talent. As the present owner, you might interest several people in investing their money in your business and becoming partners. A partnership might also relieve you of some of the responsibilities, and the skills of several others might be pooled to help the business develop. Like a single proprietorship, a partnership does not have to pay a corporate income tax. This is a tax that is paid to the national government on the profits of the corporation. It is in addition to the tax you pay on the income you draw from the company.

Along with the advantages, partnerships have problems. Although partners share the profits according to a prearranged plan, you are not sure that each partner will devote a fair share of time and effort to the business. Partners do not always

Table 4-1 Comparison of forms of business organization

	Single proprietorship	Partnership	Corporation
Ease of organization	Easiest	Moderately difficult	Most difficult
Availability of capital	Least	Intermediate	Most (best able to raise capital)
Responsibility	Centered in one person	Spread among partners	Policy set by directors; president supervises day-to-day operation
Incentive to succeed	Centered in one person	Spread among partners	Spread among many
Flexibility	Greatest	Intermediate	Least
Ability to perform varied functions	Dependent on one individual's versatility	Dependent on capabilities of two or more	Best able to employ versatile individuals
Possibility of conflict in management	None	Most prone to conflict	Chain of command reduces internal conflict; wide ownership minimizes disagreement
Taxation	No corporate income tax	No corporate income tax	Corporate income tax
Distribution of profits or losses	All to proprietor	Distributed to partners in accordance with partnership agreement	Profits retained or distributed to stockholders as dividends; losses reduce price of stock
Liability for debts in event of failure	Unlimited	Unlimited, but spread among partners	Limited to each stockholder's investment
Length of life	Limited by one individual's life span (or until he or she goes out of business)	Limited (partnership is reorganized upon death or withdrawal of any partner)	Unlimited (with ownership of shares readily transferable)

After studying this table, discuss which form of organization would be best for our "Build-a-City" company. Remember that there is no single right answer. Depending on the circumstances, however, some answers will be better than others. Be sure that you consider all possibilities before you make your decision.

agree on methods and policies to be used in operating a business.

As we mentioned in our discussion of single proprietorships, there are two other serious drawbacks you must consider. Both single proprietorships and partnerships are subject to *unlimited liability* and *limited life*. Unlimited liability would become important to you if your business were deteriorating and you found that you owed a great deal more money to your creditors than your debtors owed to you. If you thought you could not reverse the downward trend of your business and if your creditors threatened legal action, you would probably want to dissolve your business. Unlimited liability makes this difficult. Not only are the *assets* (those things that have market value) of your business subject to loss, but your personal property could also be taken to pay your debts. In the case of a partnership, each partner would be subject to this same kind of liability. Your business, instead of being a means of supporting you, could become a hazard capable of wiping out all your savings.

"Limited life" means that the business will end if one of the partners leaves the company. In such an event, a new partnership agreement must be drawn up. The same would apply if one partner died or if the owner of a single proprietorship died. The business and the owners are coexistent.

Once the decision is made to form a partnership, a competent attorney should be hired to draw up the articles of partnership. This is a necessary legal document, or *contract,* that will specify the rights and duties of all partners. With all the effort you have put into the business, you do not want to leave anything to chance.

About 9 percent of all firms in our country are partnerships. Of these, small businesses account for the largest number. Except for some professional firms—such as law, investment, accounting, and medical partnerships—the million- and multimillion-dollar firms stay away from both single proprietorships and partnerships.

The Corporation

A third type of business organization is the corporation. It is usually more difficult to organize than the other two forms. First you must go to a lawyer, who draws up the necessary papers asking the state for the powers you will need to establish your business. The lawyer submits these papers to the state government, which will grant you a charter. The charter gives you the right to do business; it also makes that business a legal person, separate from you before the law. Separating yourself from the business is an important advantage. It means that your business now has *limited liability:* you and other stockholders can lose only the money you have put into the business, and not your personal possessions. Let us suppose that a purchaser of your product was injured because of a defective part in the "Build-a-City" set he bought. The purchaser who decided to sue for damages sustained would not sue you or any stockholders as persons, but instead would file suit against the corporation.

Unlike the single proprietorship and partnership, the corporation has *perpetual life*. No matter how many of its stockholders die, the corporation will continue to exist. Such continuity is of particular value to businesses with heavy fixed costs and capital investment.

Probably the greatest advantage of a corporate form of business organization is its great ability to raise capital. After the corporation is chartered, a primary consideration will be approximately how much money your business needs and how much it is currently worth. Let us assume that you evaluate your present business at $300,000. You would like an additional $700,000 to expand your facilities and have some money to take care of your operating expenses in the transitional stage of your business. To raise this additional money you issue 100,000 shares of stock. You retain 30,000 shares and attempt to sell the remaining 70,000. A share of stock represents ownership. In your particular case, each share of stock will represent one-hundred-thousandth ownership of the proposed corporation. If each share of stock were sold for $10 a share, the corporation would now be worth $1 million. You would have the $300,000 business, plus the $700,000 in cash from the sale of your stock which could be used to meet expansion and operation costs.

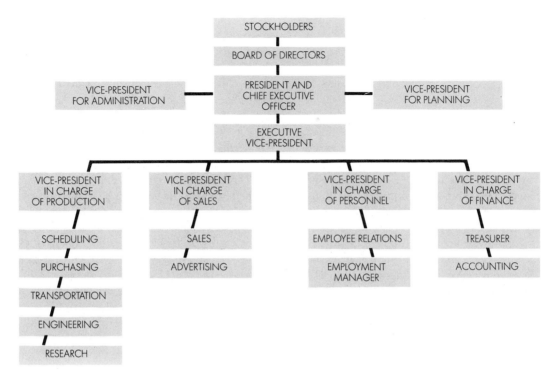

Figure 4–2   Structure of a typical corporation
In the typical corporation, the stockholders elect the board of directors. The
board of directors sets general policy, makes decisions on declaring dividends,
and elects the officers. The officers carry out day-to-day operations and
administer policy.

 The greatest advantage of a corporation is
its ability to raise capital.

Selling Stock

How can you sell your stock? You might think
immediately of the New York Stock Exchange.
You may already be somewhat familiar with this
famous stock exchange and the trading of millions
of shares of stock there every business day. After
checking, you would soon find that only very large,
long-established companies worth many millions
of dollars can be listed on the New York Stock
Exchange, or even on the smaller exchanges located
throughout the country.

A second possibility is to try to sell the stock
yourself. Initially the idea might sound appealing
as you think of a few people who might be able
to buy stock. However, $700,000 is a great deal

of money, and you soon realize that you have neither the time nor the ability to raise the money
through personal sales of stock. After talking this
problem over with a business acquaintance, you
learn about investment bankers. This possibility
sounds like it might be your answer.

The Investment Banker

An investment banker is in the business of selling
securities. Although many people put their money
in savings accounts in order to receive interest,
others are not satisfied with the interest that a bank
pays. They think their money will bring a greater
return if it is invested in some business. They may
not want to organize a business themselves, but
they are willing to take a chance on a business
that is already operating. Thus they buy *bonds* or
stock.

When people buy bonds, they are lending money. When people buy shares of stock in a business, they become owners and share in the returns; however, they do not have to worry about day-to-day management. They may buy shares in a big corporation through a stock exchange, or they may go to investment bankers or stockbrokers to see what stock is available. There is a bigger risk involved in buying stock in a small company than in investing in a large, well-established firm. Yet there is also the chance of a bigger return on the money invested in a new organization. Many businesses that depend on making money with money frequently go to investment banks and buy stock in a growing company.

You decide to go to an *investment bank* and discuss the prospect of its selling your stock. The investment bank is responsible for examining your business and deciding whether the business has a reasonably good chance of growing. If the investment banker thinks it has a chance, he or she will agree to try to sell the stock.

Let us assume that the investment bank is willing to sell your stock. You inform its representative that you want to get $10 a share. The bank will then try to sell your stock for as much as possible. If the stocks sell for $11 a share, the bank keeps the $1 and you receive $10.

What happens if the bank cannot sell the 70,000 shares you have offered for sale? In this case you get back the unsold shares and have to work with the capital you raised, or try to borrow additional capital. Large, well-established businesses may arrange with the investment bank to have it *underwrite* the stock. This means that if the investment bank cannot sell all the stock, it will still pay the business the agreed amount for all the stock. Naturally, this is a better arrangement for the entrepreneur, but there is no way to force the investment bank to make such an agreement.

Transferring Ownership

People can buy or sell their ownership in the corporation quite easily. They do so by putting their stock up for sale. Suppose you decided on the corporate form for your business, and the business has expanded just as you planned. The value of

your business has doubled, so it is now approximately $2 million. Because there are still 100,000 shares, each share should be worth about double its original price. Some of the owners think their stock will not increase further in value and want to sell it. Others admire the rapid expansion of the company and would like to "buy in." The bigger corporations handle this type of exchange by having the sale of their stocks take place in the stock market.

However, the owners of "Build-a-City" stock wishing to sell would either try to arrange the sale themselves or try to have a brokerage house do so. A *stockbroker* is in the business of buying and selling shares of stock for others. Sale of our stock would be an *over-the-counter* sale because the stock is not listed on a stock exchange. The broker differs from the investment banker in that the broker sells stock that is already owned, rather than new issues. Buyers of stock or securities are provided some indirect safeguards by regulation through the Securities and Exchange Commission, an agency of the federal government.

 To invest is to provide new funds for capital. To buy existing stock is to transfer ownership.

Perpetual Life

If the owner of stock in a corporation dies, ownership of the stock passes to the heirs. The corporation continues as though nothing had happened. This characteristic of a corporation, known as perpetual life, is possible because a corporation is considered a person in the eyes of the law. It can sue and be sued without the owners' becoming involved beyond the possible fluctuation of the value of their stock. However, the officers of the corporation, who might also be the owners, may be held responsible for certain acts of the corporation as specified by law. Limited liability provides an important safeguard to owners of shares of stock in the corporation; their personal responsibility and financial liability are limited to the value of the stock they own.

Disadvantages of a Corporation

Before you become too impressed with the advantages of a corporation and make a hasty decision to choose this form of organization, you should consider its disadvantages. Besides having to pay a corporation income tax, you will have to consider that the corporation may fall out of your control. You own 30 percent of the stock in your business—30,000 shares of a total of 100,000. In practically none of the large corporations in this country does any single person own as much as 30 percent of the stock. Such a large block would almost certainly mean control, because most stockholders are not interested in controlling policy and give their proxy (right to vote) to the directors of the corporation. Because your corporation would be a small one with few shares of stock, there is a real possibility that several stockholders might get together to vote you out.

You can try to avoid this difficulty in several ways. One method of keeping control would be to limit your expansion so that you always own over 50 percent of the stock. However, such a move may not give you the money you need to develop as you have planned. An alternative is to try to sell a different kind of stock, one that does not carry voting rights.

The stock we have been referring to so far is known as *common* stock, and each share carries with it the right to one vote on matters concerning the control of the company. Holders of common stock take a chance when they invest their money, because *dividends,* the money paid to the owners of this stock, are paid only after the corporation has taken care of all its other obligations. If the corporation makes a big profit, common stockholders do well; but if business is poor, there may be no dividends. In addition, the value of the stock, which reflects the earning power of the business, may drop and discourage future buying.

Preferred Stock

Preferred stock is a different type of stock that involves less risk but also fewer rights than common stock. Although preferred stock represents ownership, it can better be called a second-class ownership. Rarely does it carry the right to vote. The corporation has an obligation to pay its preferred stockholders a stated dividend before it pays anything to common stockholders. Therefore, if the corporation earns only a small profit, preferred stockholders will get their dividends and the chances are that common stockholders will not receive any dividends. On the other hand, a large profit will not give owners of preferred stock any additional reward, whereas common stockholders may receive substantial dividends on their shares.

If you are able to sell preferred stock rather than common stock to raise the capital you need, you will be sure of maintaining control. However, you will probably find that those who buy preferred stock are not willing to take great risks, and therefore they will favor large corporations that have been in business for years and have a long record of paying dividends. Still less risk is found in *cumulative preferred stock;* a corporation that fails to pay dividends for one or several years will have to pay accumulated dividends to holders of this kind of stock when profits are made.

Selling Bonds

You might also try selling bonds to raise money. A bond does not represent partial ownership of a corporation, but stands for a loan of a specified amount, often $1,000. The loan of $1,000 is referred to as the *principal*. The bondholder receives a specified rate of interest, usually every six months, on the principal invested. Whether or not the business makes money, the corporation must pay interest to bondholders or risk being sued. At the date of maturity, the company is obligated to pay the principal to the bondholder. Bondholders run the least risk of losing their money, but they usually receive the least return on their investment if the corporation makes a substantial profit.

It would be nice if you could sell bonds in your new business. But if a person is worried about taking a risk, why would he or she put money into a new company? After considering the possible alternatives, you decide to ask an investment banker to sell the common stock necessary to raise the money you need.

 Stock represents ownership; bonds are loans.

C Evolution and Concentration of Business

Industrial Revolution Changes Methods of Production

In addition to looking at the classical model and going through the steps of organizing a business unit within the framework of this theory, we must consider the historical force that brought about a change in the real world that was not completely foreseen by such classical economists as Adam Smith.

One of the most important revolutions in the history of mankind was the Industrial Revolution, which occurred after 1750 in western Europe and then in the United States. During the Industrial Revolution, water, steam, and later electricity were harnessed to run new and complex machines. This in turn brought about great changes in the production and distribution of goods, involving different uses of the factors of production.

Fixed and Variable Costs

One change was a greater demand for capital because business firms' costs tended to increase. These costs may be divided into two categories, *fixed costs* and *variable costs*. Fixed costs are those expenses that do not change with changes in production or sales. They pertain only to the short run, because all costs may fluctuate in the long run. The owner of the hardware store on Main Street pays the landlord $800 a month in rent. This amount stands whether sales are $10,000 a month or $50,000 a month. These fixed costs are the overhead.

Expenses that change with the volume of business are known as variable costs. As sales go up, variable costs also go up. The hardware store owner will have to hire additional employees if business gets significantly better. What other examples of variable costs can you think of?

Competition under New Circumstances

After the Civil War, the maturation of the American Industrial Revolution and the spread of a fine system of transportation gave U.S. business a huge market. Producers in Boston could easily sell to buyers in St. Louis. What happened, however, when the national demand for a product declined? Producers of that article did everything in their power to keep sales high in order to pay their fixed costs. This usually meant cutting prices to keep their own customers and also attract some of their competitors' customers. When their competitors followed their example, the battle to obtain a bigger portion of the market led to price wars, or "cutthroat competition." Prices fell even below the cost of production. Why? Because business people who had spent staggering amounts of money developing their businesses could no longer afford to move. They would rather lose money for a short time in the hope either that business for the whole industry would improve or that some of their competitors would falter.

There were some economists who thought that this fierce competition during a slowdown in business was beneficial in the long run. The weaker, less efficient businesses would not survive, and consumers would be left with the strongest, most efficient business people to serve them. Some economists still believe that this so-called *social Darwinism* is best for the economy. Critics of social Darwinism point out that with fewer business opportunities and greater requirements for capital, competition is bound to be lessened. With fewer producers, it is easy for producers to get together and agree on a price that is higher than it would be if the market were free, with the price more affected by supply and demand.

Changes in Production Cause Concentration of Business

If we examine the development of U.S. industry, we find that those industries subject to high fixed costs have moved through the stages previously described. As the cost of machinery, research, and factories increased, it became difficult for new firms to enter the market. In the 1870s and 1880s, as the impact of the American Industrial Revolution made itself felt, the average size of the busi-

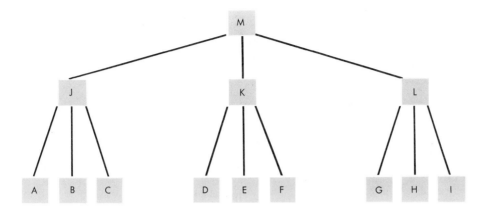

Figure 4–3   A small holding company
Companies A through I are producing companies. Companies J, K, and L are first-level holding companies, and Company M is a second-level holding company.

ness unit increased. It was at this time that the corporation became common, for, as we have discovered, it was the kind of business organization that was best suited to raising large amounts of capital. Prior to 1875 a special act of the legislature was needed to grant a charter; passage of general incorporation acts simplified that process. When business conditions declined, fierce competition developed, and often only the strongest firms survived. These price wars were often disastrous for small businesses and costly for the giants of industry, at least in the short run.

Price Fixing and Combinations

Some leaders of U.S. industry reasoned that cooperation and agreement served their interests better than competition. What would happen, do you think, if all firms in an industry agreed to charge a particular price? If this price were higher than the prices of a competitive market, profits of each producer would increase. This technique, known as *price fixing,* forces consumers to pay a higher price than they would in a competitive market. Another technique producers use is to divide the market among themselves, with each producer having the exclusive right to sell in a particular portion of the market. These methods did not work well in the 1880s or 1890s because the agreements were not committed to legal documents. At a time in our history identified with "rugged individual-

ism," when faith and trust were not relied on, too many business people hedged on their agreements whenever it was possible to make more money. These oral agreements were known as *loose combinations* because they were not binding on the participants.

In time, more formal agreements known as *closed combinations* developed. One type of closed combination was a *trust.* The owners of the producing companies would surrender their common stock and voting control in their own companies to a board of trustees of a new company. In turn, the owners of the producing companies were given the equivalent of their stock in trust certificates. The new company then controlled the entire market and was usually able to make a large profit because of the high prices resulting from the absence of competition. The profit was then divided, and the owners of the trust certificates received dividends.

 Rising fixed costs encourage increased size and concentration of business.

Holding Companies

Another form of closed combination corporation that became popular after trusts started to disappear was the *holding company.* Such a company gains control by buying up enough stock of other companies to control them. Figure 4–3 shows

Table 4–2 Large corporate mergers in the United States, 1981–1985

Buyer	Company Bought	Dollars (billions)	Year
Chevron	Gulf Oil	13.3	1984
Texaco	Getty Oil	10.1	1984
DuPont	Conoco	7.4	1981
U.S. Steel	Marathon Oil	6.5	1981
General Electric	RCA	6.3	1985
Kohlberg, Kravis, Roberts (buyout)	Beatrice Co.	6.2	1985
Philip Morris	General Foods	5.8	1985
Mobil Oil	Superior Oil	5.7	1984
Santa Fe Railroad	Southern Pacific	5.2	1983
General Motors	Hughes Aircraft	5.1	1985
Allied Corporation	Signal Companies	5.0	1985
R. J. Reynolds	Nabisco	4.9	1985
INA	Connecticut General	4.3	1981
Elf Aquitaine	Texasgulf	4.2	1981
Occidental Petroleum	Cities Service	4.0	1982

how such a company can gain control of a large industrial empire with relatively little capital. Companies A through I are producing companies, each worth $100 million. Company J buys enough stock to control Companies A, B, and C. Company K does the same to D, E, and F; and Company L, to G, H, and I. Companies J, K, and L are holding companies. They are created not to produce but only to hold stock of other companies for the purpose of controlling them. For less than $450 million these holding companies control a $900 million industrial empire.

Company M, a higher-level holding company, is formed to gain control of Companies J, K, and L. Company M can now control the $900 million empire for less than $230 million. If any of the producing companies or first-level holding companies have preferred stock, Company M needs far less capital for control. Having holding companies at additional levels can also reduce the capital needed for control. Control can almost always be achieved with far less than 50 percent ownership because many stockholders have no interest in voting.

Before the passage of the Public Utility Holding Company Act of 1935, huge holding companies existed. The Associated Gas and Electric Company, a billion-dollar establishment, was controlled by a promoter who owned about $100,000 of voting stock. Samuel Insull and his associates in a giant utility holding company were able to control their producing companies with far less than 1 percent of the stated value of securities of their producing companies.

Mergers

The most common kind of consolidation today is the *merger.* A merger occurs when two or more companies get together to form one company.

With the deregulation of natural gas, the nation's 20 interstate pipeline companies became fearful of cutthroat competition. Some felt that they could increase their efficiency and improve their market flexibility by merging. In 1985 Internorth of Omaha paid $2.3 billion for Houston Natural Gas Corporation, thereby gaining control of the world's longest pipeline (37,000 miles). The system connected markets from coast to coast and raised sales to $10 billion. Will the consumers reap the benefits of this greater efficiency, or will this vast market power allow Internorth to raise prices?

On occasion, mergers have occurred between smaller companies in an industry dominated by a few giant firms. These smaller companies claim that they need to merge to become more efficient and effective in competing against the biggest corporations. They maintain that such action increases competition instead of reducing it. The Antitrust Division of the Justice Department has not always agreed with them.

Four major waves of mergers have taken place in this country. The first started in 1887, just prior to the passage of the Sherman Antitrust Act, and ended in 1904. It involved such giants as United States Steel and Standard Oil trying to create monopolies in their industries. From the end of World War I until the 1930s, large firms swallowed smaller firms to create oligopolies. The monopoly has no chance and the oligopoly little chance of succeeding today under present antitrust policy.

The third major merger movement began in the 1960s, reached a peak in 1969, and then gradually declined. Many of the acquisitions involved giant firms in one industry buying up large companies in totally unrelated industries. Such mergers are called conglomerate mergers. A classic example is Mobil Oil Corporation's purchase of

"I just figured it out. It seems we're merging with ourselves." (Source: Paul Peter Porges, *Saturday Review,* September 5, 1970. Copyright 1970 Saturday Review, Inc.)

the huge retail chain Montgomery Ward & Company.

Mergers in the last ten years were in the thousands. More important is the value of the transactions, which has risen sharply. The number of mergers and acquisitions shown in Figure 4–4 apply only to those valued at $100 million or more. The petroleum industry had mergers and acquisitions valued at close to $80 billion between 1981 and 1984. Other industries experiencing large takeovers were banking and finance, insurance, mining and minerals, and processed foods.

NUMBER OF MERGERS AND ACQUISITIONS VALUED AT $100 MILLION OR MORE VS. THE NUMBER OF JUSTICE DEPARTMENT CIVIL ACTIONS INVOLVING MERGERS AND THE NUMBER OF JUSTICE DEPARTMENT CRIMINAL ACTIONS AGAINST PRICE FIXING

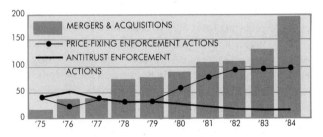

Figure 4–4 Policing the unfair consequences of mergers
The Reagan Administration feels that much of our antitrust policy is out of date and should be revised. Enforcement actions have slackened, and competing firms have been encouraged to work together to improve our nation's technology. Many feel this change is necessary if we are to compete in the world market with countries that largely ignore antitrust action. Sources: W. T. Grimm & Co. (merger data) and the Department of Justice as printed in N.Y. *Times,* Sunday, Nov. 10, 1985. Business Section, p. 1.

CONTROVERSY IN OUR TIMES

Mergers and Acquisitions

In the years 1984 and 1985 approximately 5,000 deals were struck in which one corporation merged with or acquired another. These transactions, involving about $235 billion, were viewed by some as desirable and good for the economy, whereas others warned of the dire consequences of this merger mania. Horizontal mergers involving competitors are likely to be considered illegal by the Antitrust Division of the Justice Department. Vertical mergers, in which one company buys another company in the production process, may be permitted, particularly if it can be shown that such an action will increase efficiency. Conglomerate mergers involving unlike businesses are likely to be approved. But are these popular mergers good for the economy?

Pro

There are firms that are content to make a modest profit and accept their share of the market. This attitude generates little enthusiasm to increase efficiency, expand markets, or improve quality. Stocks in such companies will sell for less than they should. A dynamic firm interested in expanding and looking for companies with growth potential will offer stockholders a higher than market price on their shares, an immediate benefit to those who sell. The acquiring firm will bring in aggressive management to increase sales, improve efficiency, provide capital for research and development, and modernize technology and marketing methods. Usually the firm that is taken over is in desperate need of reorganization and the acquisition is a way to speed up the process. Who benefits? Stockholders make more money, consumers get better products, greater sales increase employment, and no one is hurt. After all, good management techniques are just as valid

in one business as in another. The many examples of successful mergers include that of Nabisco and Standard Brands and that of Allied and Bendix.

Con

The record shows that mergers have not been all that successful. The number of divestitures, in which firms already acquired are released, has jumped to over one-third the number of mergers, and many of the conglomerates that remain have had to absorb the losses from their new additions out of their own profits. Leading conglomerates such as ITT, Beatrice, and Gulf & Western have been selling many of the businesses that they acquired earlier. Mobil Oil Corporation acquired Marcor Incorporated, the parent company of Montgomery Ward & Co. and Container Corporation of America, in 1976. It invested over $600 million to improve Ward's performance and yet received only $17 million in net profits as of 1984.

Mergers and acquisitions frequently get off on the wrong foot by costing too much. Costs are particularly likely to escalate when several acquiring firms fight to take over a company. Paying an amount that is in excess of real value (that is, above what a fair market return might be on the investment) is like buying watered stock. It takes years for the expenditure to pay for itself, if it ever does so.

Mergers are frequently made with little study. Growth is assumed when the industry may actually be in decline. Major management errors are (1) acquiring a corporation that is totally different from the parent, (2) assuming that management of the company bought will stay on, and (3) acquiring a corporation that is too big to han-

CONTROVERSY IN OUR TIMES

dle. Coca-Cola made the first mistake when it entered the wine business. Schlumberger made the second mistake when it bought Fairchild for a high price, only to witness the departure of Fairchild's management, which had a different philosophy about running a business.

The winners in a merger are usually the people involved in negotiating the transaction and, in the short run, the management of the acquiring corporation. Most frequently the shareholders of the acquiring firm lose, as do the consumers of the broad range of products of the conglomerate

because they have to pay for the costly and poorly planned reorganization.

Consensus

Most economists agree that good mergers require careful planning and involve firms producing similar products and having like management philosophies. Costly take-overs should be analyzed before the transactions begin so that the acquiring company is not swept into an uncontrollable buying attitude.

Reaction to Combinations

Interfering with the trading of goods and services is contrary to the model Adam Smith and other classical economists designed. Obstructions to the market, such as monopolies, loose combinations, trusts, holding companies, and oligopolies, brought protests from many U.S. citizens. They wanted the government to do something to ensure competition and help keep prices low. In 1890, Congress passed the Sherman Antitrust Act, which outlaws monopolies and any attempts to form monopolies, as well as combinations and conspiracies in restraint of trade. Because the Sherman Act contained no definitions, did not indicate the meaning of *restraint,* and did not clearly state whether labor as well as capital was to be included, much of its meaning remained for the courts to interpret.

 Antitrust policy in the United States encourages competition. Most countries are not so strict.

In 1914, Congress passed the Clayton Act, in which purposes and meanings were spelled out. Among other things, it prohibited *interlocking directorates* in competing companies, discriminatory price cutting, tying contracts (contracts that force buyers to purchase items they may not want),

and the formation of holding companies. In the same year, Congress created the Federal Trade Commission to help enforce the antitrust acts. A strong effort was made to keep the market free and competitive. In subsequent years, other laws were passed and the Supreme Court handed down rulings about how much competition should exist. With few exceptions, our government has expressed its approval of competition. Has this government policy worked?

Natural Monopolies

There appears to be little disagreement among economists regarding the formation of natural monopolies. In some industries it is not economical to have competition. These industries—utilities and transportation, for instance—are usually characterized by extremely high fixed costs. Consider how costly it would be to have three different sets of railroad tracks running side by side from New York to Chicago for three competing companies. Consider the inefficiency and inconvenience of having many competing regional and local telephone companies, each with its own telephone poles, telephone books, and dial systems. Such industries are called *natural monopolies,* and an appropriate level of government grants such businesses franchises giving them exclusive rights to do business in a given area. If there is no competition, you may ask, how are we protected? The federal government has set up commissions, such as the Interstate Commerce Commission, to regulate those industries that engage in interstate commerce and to protect consumers. State and local governments also have commissions that regulate natural monopolies under their jurisdiction. If a company wants to increase its rate (price), it must get permission from the commission in charge. If a company does not present a good reason for raising rates, such as failing to earn a fair return on its investment, chances are slight that such increases will be granted.

Multinational Corporations in a Global Economy

With the great expansion of world trade after World War II, giant U.S. corporations that had established an increasing share of their sales in other countries started to develop subsidiaries in these other nations. These firms with international investments soon became known as multinational corporations. U.S.-based corporations such as Exxon, General Electric, ITT, Raytheon, General Motors, IBM, Westinghouse, and Ford started the trend. First they built plants abroad, partly to avoid the high cost of U.S. labor and partly to ward off foreign competition. Thus General Motors, Ford, and Chrysler made cars in Europe to be sold in both Europe and the United States. A second approach U.S. firms used was to invest some of their surplus capital in foreign corporations.

In the late 1960s, other nations that had accumulated surplus capital and had expanded their sales volume in the United States started to follow this pattern. Japanese corporations, particularly those in electronics, started

assembly plants in the United States and then began investing in land and raw materials. Auto firms in West Germany and Japan built assembly plants in the United States. Perhaps most significant were the large investments made by Middle Eastern oil-producing nations in established corporations in West Germany, Great Britain, France, and the United States.

Over one-quarter of the income of the larger multinationals was produced by their foreign affiliates. For petroleum products, income from abroad exceeded 50 percent of total income; for office and computing machines, foreign income constituted 45 percent of total income. Countries with the largest investments in U.S. firms were Canada, Great Britain, The Netherlands, Germany, France, and Japan.

Those who support multinationals argue that by producing in the least-cost area, multinationals make their products available to consumers at a lower price than if they confined their production to

one country. Furthermore, they speed up the spread of technology, which helps the economic progress of poorer countries. Although employment may be reduced in some industries in the United States because of multinationals, it is increased in areas where we are more efficient.

Critics point out that multinationals export U.S. jobs when they produce abroad. In addition, they hurt the nation as a whole by shifting some of their taxes out of this country. They also show some of the worst aspects of imperialism by exploiting cheap foreign labor and sometimes interfering with the foreign policy of their host.

There is little doubt that multinationals are here to stay, that they can exert a positive force by increasing competition and keeping costs low, and that they reduce the differential in technology between rich and poor countries. However, the self-interest of multinationals can interfere with the national interest. Should nations place greater control on multinationals to curb their power, or can we rely on the free market and the impact of public opinion to provide such control? This question may not be settled before the 1990s.

Regulation has come under increasing criticism of late because it protects the inefficient firm by providing a fair return on investment. The regulatory bodies, which are frequently made up of former managers from the industry, are often more concerned with the interests of the industry than those of consumers. Rules issued by the various commissions and boards have become so complex that good management practices have become almost impossible. Finally, allowing more competition in such regulated industries as the airlines has demonstrated the advantages of competition to both consumers and the industry, as evidenced by the reduction in airline fares and greater utilization of the airlines' equipment for lower unit costs.

D Can Small Business Survive?

Defining the Problem

The American Dream

Ben Chase was employed as a butcher in a grocery chain store for ten years. He knew his trade well, worked hard, saved whatever he could, and dreamed of starting a business of his own. His wife, Gertrude, also had a job and added her savings to her husband's. In 1970 they heard of a small slaughtering and meat-packing establishment that was for sale in a rural area. With their own savings, a loan from a relative, and a loan from a bank, they bought their own business.

Ben and Gertrude worked hard, sometimes more than 65 hours a week. They were good managers, and they knew how to deal with the farmers and the meat distributors. Their business grew. They had made enough contacts with farmers to ensure a continuing supply, and they had no difficulty in selling everything they could produce. Now semiretired, they own a business worth a million dollars. They have lived the American dream.

A Different Story

When George Morris returned from military service, he got a job in a men's clothing store. He worked for two years learning many aspects of the business. At the end of that time he made the decision to go into business for himself. For $20,000, he bought a rundown store in a poor business location. His own savings and a loan from his parents covered $10,000 of the cost; he borrowed the additional $10,000 from a bank.

George knew that the price of the business was low because much of the merchandise was out of style. However, he believed that as he sold these outdated goods (he had no capital to buy new merchandise and had not established a credit rating yet), he would be able to replace them with the stylish clothing people wanted. He hoped that by marking down the prices on what he had, he could soon clear out his old stock. He also counted on patronage from his many friends.

Two months after George opened his store, a new men's clothing store, part of a chain, opened three blocks away. Now George's stock of suits that had but a short time ago been in style could not be sold for even a third of its original cost. George did not take in even enough money to pay his rent and his note at the bank. Most of his merchandise was valueless. By the end of one year, George Morris was bankrupt, his store just another among the statistics of business failures.

In 1984 there were 700,000 new businesses. What new entrepreneurs fail to realize, or choose to ignore, is that the average life expectancy of a business is less than five years, that about 40 percent of all retail businesses last less than two years, and that many businesses that do survive pay their owners less than they could earn by working for someone else. If we define small businesses as those firms employing fewer than 50 persons, then 96 percent of all businesses are small (see Figure 4–5). Yet the importance of small businesses in the nation's economy, together with the uncertainty of operations of many small firms, raises a question as to whether small businesses will continue to be important in our economy.

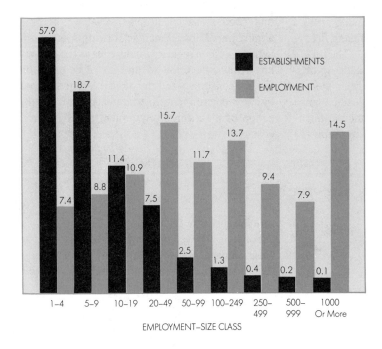

Figure 4–5   Percent distribution of employment and establishments by employment-size class

Although small businesses (employing less than 50) make up 96 percent of all establishments, they employ only 43 percent of the private work force. (Source: Department of Commerce, Bureau of the Census.)

Changes in Business

Until the Civil War, almost all business in our country was small by any definition. Big business appeared first in transportation and manufacturing, where high fixed costs made large-scale operations the only efficient method of production.

Increase in Size

One of the clearest examples of the change in business size is found in merchandising. In the eighteenth and nineteenth centuries the country store, or general store, owned by a proprietor or by several partners, was a symbol of business enterprise. By 1900, however, the pattern of ownership had begun to change as the department store and chain store appeared. Chain stores could buy in huge quantities and save on per-unit costs; if sales lagged in one store, merchandise could easily be transferred to another. Mail-order houses also cut into the trade of the general store. Soon

automobiles made it possible for people to shop outside their own neighborhoods. Advertising in mass media gave large stores the advantage of a big market. Today these large businesses—and, more recently, discount houses—pose a seemingly overwhelming threat to small business.

Problems of Small Business

We have seen that small businesses like George Morris's carry a high risk of failure. Between 1945 and 1959, the average number of business failures per year was 4,000, involving liabilities of $169 million per year. In the period 1960–69, the most prosperous period in our nation's history, the average number of business failures annually was 15,000, with over $1 billion in liabilities per year. During the 1982 recession, 572 business failed in one week; 313,000 businesses failed in 1983. Some specific industries in which small business was most important, such as construction, had significantly higher failure rates.

Advantages of Small Business

If those of you who look to small business as the opportunity for the fulfillment of the American dream are discouraged by the statistics given here, there are other figures that tell a different story. There are 8 million small businesses in this country. More businesses are born each year than die, and the number of small businesses is increasing at a faster rate than is our population.

If small businesses can continue to grow in number and size, they must have some benefits to offset the many handicaps. Small companies do have an advantage in certain kinds of business. Their scale of operations is particularly well suited to the making and retailing of highly specialized products, of articles that are subject to frequent and drastic style changes, and of items requiring craftsmanship as opposed to standardization. Professional and service establishments—such as barbershops, specialty stores, and shops producing special equipment or parts involving much hand labor—are also usually best organized as small firms. The supplying of components to big business by subcontractors is an established practice that is growing in popularity each year. New products are as likely to come from small firms as from large ones, particularly in cases where demand is uncertain and where no specialized machinery has been developed.

 Eighty percent of small businesses are in service and distribution industries.

Small firms are more mobile and can move in and out of business in response to fluctuations in the demand for their goods and services, with less effect on the economy. They can change their production or sales more easily, and they can perform functions in the economy that big business cannot and does not want to do. For these reasons small businesses not only need to remain, but will remain.

Some observers have referred to the decade of the 1980s as the most entrepreneurial in our history. This period gave rise to a group of young, upwardly mobile people known as "yuppies." President Reagan, addressing young Americans, said: "Why not set out with your friends on an adventure and start your own business?" The record shows that they have.

Pros and Cons of Starting a Business

The fact that the number of U.S. business establishments is increasing indicates that, to many people, business constitutes opportunity. Though some businesses fail, as we have seen, others go on to become prosperous concerns.

Benefits

In reality, hope for material gain is only one of the reasons people go into business. Among other objectives and considerations are the following:

1. People think self-employment will permit a greater degree of personal independence and freedom of action than is possible in large organizations.
2. They think they will have a greater opportunity to try out their own ideas, because the bureaucratic aspects of big business often make such ventures difficult or impossible within the framework of a larger organization.
3. They think they can make the American dream come true. There are enough cases of success to make it a possibility, even if the risk is great.
4. Owners look forward to reaping all the benefits from their own labors. They will not have to share with others what they have created and developed under a single proprietorship.
5. There is greater community recognition in being in business for oneself, as long as one is successful.

Disadvantages

Along with the potential benefits of going into business, there are certain definite disadvantages:

1. When one works for someone else, paychecks are regular, hours are usually shorter, and there is no financial risk of losing one's savings or of being unable to repay borrowed money.

2. The responsibilities of owning a business are considerable. Decisions have to be made often, and on their outcome may rest the fate of the business.
3. The regulations and restrictions made by all levels of government concerning business are usually irksome and sometimes costly.
4. Fringe benefits are frequently broader for employees than for employers.
5. Working for a very large business can offer more opportunity for advancement than working for oneself.

Why Do Businesses Fail?

Numerous studies have been made in an attempt to determine why businesses in general, and small businesses in particular, fail. A very small number of failures, less than 10 percent, are caused by such factors as poor health, fraud, disaster, neglect, and marital difficulties. Studies indicate that poor management and insufficient capital are the main causes of business failures.

Too many people go into business without sufficient training and knowledge to cope with the many demands of business. It may seem simple to open a filling station or a grocery store, but using one of these facilities as a customer is quite a different matter from running one as a successful business venture.

Another cause of business failure is lack of capital. Typically, owners of small businesses start out using all their own savings and borrowing as much as they can; still they often have too little money to carry them through the first critical year, when sales are likely to be small. Banks are not eager to lend money to new and unproved firms. When they do, interest rates are likely to be high. Suppliers are seldom willing to advance much merchandise or raw materials until good credit ratings have been built. With little capital, few new firms are able to take advantage of the practice of discounting their bills, whereby a small percentage is deducted from a bill paid within a specified period of time. They may not have the money or the credit to take advantage of bargains they find. A business with sufficient capital has

inherent advantages, and it is most often big corporations that have sufficient capital.

Lack of capital is frequently found to be responsible for other failures. When a downturn in the economy occurs, the big business with adequate capital available can more easily subsist until conditions improve. Inadequate capital can lead to poor accounting records because satisfactory employees cannot be hired. The absence of ready, accurate information on sales or inventory can lead to inefficient operation.

Other Causes of Failure

Additional causes for failure include:

1. Too low a volume of business to cover fixed costs.
2. Overexpansion and overbuying during a business boom.
3. A general inability to control inventory.
4. Poor location, including proximity to competing big business.
5. Lack of specialized knowledge. Owners of small businesses are seldom experts in all phases of business operation. They have to perform so many different functions that they can seldom become masters of any of them. They may often wish they had never gone into business "on their own."

What Can Be Done to Help Small Business?

Small businesses have many difficulties, and many do not operate as efficiently as they might. Therefore, they may waste our limited resources.

We have seen that managerial incompetence and insufficient capital are the two chief problems of small business, accounting for most of their failures. The government has taken steps to provide assistance in both these problem areas.

Small Business Administration

Although there are many agencies—private, local, and state—that help business, the largest and most important agency devoted exclusively to small business is the Small Business Administration

(SBA). This agency, established by Congress in 1953, carries on the following activities:

1. It makes information on management available to small business firms. Pamphlets on such subjects as factory construction, production techniques, and marketing are published periodically as aids to small manufacturers. For people in marketing there is material on sales training, location appraisal, personnel management, profit planning, and similar technical subjects.
2. It helps to provide access to capital and credit at reasonable rates. In addition to making its own loans, the SBA supervises small-business investment companies that have been set up under special legislation to furnish capital.
3. It helps obtain a fair share of government contracts for small businesses.
4. It provides loans to small businesses that have suffered from disasters such as fire, floods, and storms.

Other Government Aid

The federal government gives added help to small business by making the corporate tax lower for the first $25,000 and gradually higher for larger profits. Unincorporated businesses—and most small businesses are unincorporated—do not pay a corporation income tax. State and local governments often give small businesses a tax advantage, although this is frequently offset by special inducements made by communities to encourage big business to move into their area.

Local and state governments, and even geographic regions, have organized development and credit corporations to help business. State departments of commerce offer numerous services to business persons. State universities frequently set up bureaus and research facilities which they make available to business.

Self-Help

Chambers of commerce, retail merchants' associations, and various other trade organizations offer many services to business people. Less publicized but just as important are the cooperatives that have been organized by small business firms to give them the buying power of large companies. The National Retail Grocers Association is made up of regional cooperatives. Money put in by independent grocers is used to buy a warehouse and trucks and to employ workers who buy, store, and distribute merchandise to the individual stores. By banding together on their purchases, the independent grocers have acquired the same buying power as huge chain stores have. This eliminates at least one advantage that big business usually has over small firms.

Conclusion

Small business has a very important role in our economy, but a question remains as to whether it is receiving a fair share of the pie. Much of small business is marginal business—what is left over from big business. Part of the problem of small business stems from the economics of size, but equally important are problems that can be solved through better management techniques. Some help has come from government and some from the efforts of business persons themselves. There is evidence to indicate that additional help may be needed.

Chapter Highlights

1. About two-thirds of the value of our goods and services results from decisions made by private enterprise. An even greater percentage of our gross national product (GNP) is produced by our businesses.
2. Sometimes a business firm is called an enterprise. Those who organize the enterprise are called entrepreneurs.

3. Collecting and organizing the factors of production are essential functions of business management.

4. Goods used to make other goods (tools) are called capital goods. Goods used directly by consumers to satisfy their needs are called consumer goods.

5. Interest is money paid for the use of money; rent, for the use of natural resources; and wages, for labor performed. Profit is money received for risks taken in organizing a business and operating it efficiently.

6. A business can be organized as a single proprietorship, a partnership, or a corporation. Each type of organization has advantages and disadvantages.

7. Unlimited liability and limited life are two serious drawbacks of both the single proprietorship and the partnership, in comparison to the corporation.

8. The biggest advantage of a corporate form of business organization is greater ability to raise capital. Ownership in a corporation is easily transferable.

9. An investment banker is in the business of selling new issues of securities.

10. Common stock is characterized by voting rights and risk; preferred stock usually carries a stated dividend and has no voting rights.

11. Bonds represent a loan rather than ownership. A corporation must pay interest to bondholders or risk being sued.

12. The Industrial Revolution was the result of applying water and steam power to the operation of machinery, largely replacing human power.

13. Fixed costs are those expenses that do not change, regardless of the volume of sales. These costs have become more important since the Industrial Revolution.

14. Variable costs are those directly related to the volume of a particular business.

15. The cost of machinery, research, and factories makes it difficult for new firms to enter an industry. Price fixing occurs when a group of firms agrees to charge the same price.

16. A trust is a closed combination in which producing companies exchange their control and stock for trust certificates. These certificates do not carry voting rights. A trust generally forces people to pay higher prices. Holding companies are another form of closed combination corporations.

17. The most prevalent type of consolidation today is the merger. When an enterprise acquires a firm in an unrelated industry, the firm resulting from the merger is called a conglomerate.

18. The national government attempted to solve the problem of business combinations by passing the Sherman Antitrust Act (1890), the Clayton Act (1914), and the Federal Trade Commission Act (1914). Additional legislation has been passed since.

19. The recent wave of corporate acquisitions has resulted in a contro-

versy over the benefits and costs of such acquisitions to the economy. The transactions have involved multibillion-dollar firms being bought out by other giants, sometimes smaller and sometimes larger than the firm being acquired.

20. Corporations with major investments abroad are known as multinationals. Expansion has been by foreign-owned firms in the United States as well as by U.S. firms in other countries. Controversy exists over whether multinationals have a positive or a negative influence on the economy.

21. Evidence shows that the number of business failures has been increasing and that small business prospers less than big business. The chief reasons for business failures are managerial incompetence and insufficient capital.

22. Small business has an important role in the economy. More businesses start each year than fail. Small business is a proving ground for ideas and resources. It increases competition; it is more flexible and mobile, and so can adjust to changes and special demands; and it is associated with our democratic ideals.

23. To help small business solve its problems, Congress set up the Small Business Administration. This agency provides information on running a business, helps in financing, makes loans for disaster relief, and aids in obtaining government contracts.

24. Other aids to small business are lower tax rates; local, state, and regional development corporations; trade associations; and buying cooperatives.

Study Aids

Key Terms and Names

GNP	holding company	investment bank
single proprietorship	conglomerates	common stock
capital goods	variable costs	bonds
chamber of commerce	fixed costs	social Darwinism
interest	loose combinations	trusts
wages	corporation	merger
factors of production	partnership	natural monopoly
limited life	consumer goods	dividend
cumulative preferred stock	rent	closed combinations
cutthroat competition	profit	multinational corporation
price fixing	liability	
Sherman Antitrust Act	Federal Trade Commission	Interstate Commerce
Clayton Act	Small Business Administration	Commission

Questions

1. Imagine you are a business person starting a new enterprise.
   (a) What forms of organization are available to you?
   (b) What factors will determine your choice of organization?
   (c) What are the advantages and disadvantages of each kind of organization?

2. What form of business organization would you recommend for each of the following? Why?
   (a) Physician
   (b) Appliance manufacturer
   (c) Restaurant
   (d) Grocery store
   (e) Wheat farmer
   (f) Barbershop
   (g) Automobile repair shop
   (h) Steel mill

3. What is the difference among common stock, preferred stock, and bonds? What considerations should affect an individual's decisions as to which of these securities to purchase?

4. Since the Industrial Revolution, most large businesses have turned to the corporate form of organization.
   (a) Explain why the corporate form gained in popularity.
   (b) Describe the structure of a modern corporation.
   (c) Explain the functions of stockholders, the board of directors, officers, and creditors in controlling a corporation.

5. Business has found different ways to gain advantage in a competitive market.
   (a) What are the methods businesses in the United States have used throughout history to control the market?
   (b) Explain the essential differences in these methods.
   (c) What is the most common method of market control today?

6. The new wave of mergers has involved giants with giants, sometimes combining diversified industries.
   (a) What are the advantages and disadvantages of conglomerate mergers for the economy?
   (b) Are the advantages and disadvantages different for firms producing similar products?
   (c) Would you buy stock in an acquiring firm? Why?

7. Multinational firms have become more common among both U.S. firms abroad and foreign-owned firms here.
   (a) How do such firms help or hurt the host country? The country of origin?
   (b) What would your attitude be toward multinationals if you were a stockholder? A worker? A lawyer in the Antitrust Division of the Justice Department?

8. One of the continuing debates of our economy concerns the relative merits of small business and big business.
   (a) What is the definition of "small business"?
   (b) If you started your own small business, what problems would you face?
   (c) What has the government done to help small business?
   (d) Why could it be said: "Managerial skill, research, and a strong bank balance might have prevented many failures"?

9. We may question whether small business is the backbone of our economy, but we cannot question the need for its services.
   (a) Draw up a balance sheet of the advantages and the disadvantages of both a small business and a large business.
   (b) Explain why a very small percentage of our business organizations employ the largest percentage of workers.

Problems

1. To check the growing power of business, the federal government has found it necessary to establish certain controls on business.
   (a) Trace the growth of federal controls over business by means of a chronological table listing the chief regulatory agencies and the laws restricting corporations.
   (b) What circumstances caused the various changes in government policy?

(c) What present business practices might require additional controls?

2. Select four different types of businesses and use the criteria suggested in the chapter to determine whether each would be more efficient as a small or a big business. How might those businesses most suitable for small-scale operations perform if they were decentralized operations of a big business?

3. Trace the successful take-over of one giant firm by another.

   (a) What resistance did the acquiring company experience?

   (b) Who benefited? Who lost?

Costs, Prices, and Output in Competitive Markets

In Chapter 2 we saw how the forces of demand and supply in a free market can influence the price of a good or service and how they can affect the allocation of our resources. In analyzing the supply side of the market, we examined some of the factors that help to determine the quantity of goods produced for sale. (See the discussion of the law of increasing costs, for example.) In Chapter 4 we looked at several ways to organize a business and discussed the advantages and disadvantages of each. Using graphs as visual aids, we examined changes in supply and demand and the extremely important concept of elasticity. You should be sure you understand all of this material before proceeding with Chapter 5.

Naturally, the business person in a free economy is seeking profit. The intelligent executive will not be satisfied, however, simply with the knowledge that the firm is making a profit. He or she will invariably want to make the greatest profit possible—to *maximize* profits. If, on the other hand, the firm should be forced to operate at a loss for a time, it will certainly attempt to incur the least loss possible— to *minimize* losses. Whether a firm exists in a perfectly or imperfectly competitive market, it will try to maximize profits or minimize losses. In this chapter, we shall see how this can be done. We shall examine the firm's different types of costs, how costs may change over a period of time, and how the firm adjusts to these changes.

Chapter Objectives

After completing this chapter, you should be able to:

- Define *profit* and distinguish between the economist's definition and the accountant's definition of profit.
- Define the following basic concepts: fixed costs, variable costs, marginal costs, average total cost, the law of diminishing returns, and economies and diseconomies of scale.
- Distinguish among decreasing, increasing, and constant cost situations and give an example of each.
- Define the conditions that produce pure competition.
- Describe and define the demand curve, marginal revenue curve, and most profitable point of operation for perfectly competitive firms.
- Define and distinguish between the short run and the long run and describe the impact of time on price and supply under both of these conditions.

A Fixed, Variable, and Total Costs

Although we gave some consideration to various costs in Chapter 4, we shall elaborate on these important concepts here.

When the business person wishes to determine whether or not the firm is making a profit, he or she asks two questions: How much money am I taking in? How much is it costing me to produce my output? In more technical terms, *total revenues* (*TR,* the total amount received for the sale of goods or services) are compared with *total costs* (*TC*). The profit (or loss) is simply the difference between the two. If a firm's total revenues are $600,000 during a certain period and its total costs of production are $570,000, then it follows that the firm's profit is $30,000, or the difference between total revenues and total costs. The formula is simply Profit = *TR* − *TC*. Obviously, if total costs exceed total revenues, the firm is operating at a loss. (We sometimes refer to losses as *negative profits*.)

 Profit is the amount of money left after a firm has paid all costs.

A word of warning is in order. The economist does not always compute profits in the same fashion as does the business manager or the accountant. A business manager may make the mistake of thinking of costs solely in terms of the amount of money paid out for labor, raw materials, transportation, fuel, and the like. These are indeed costs, and the economist refers to them as *explicit costs*. But the economist also considers the *implicit costs*—the value of productive resources that the owner supplies personally. For example, suppose the owner of a small store owns the land and the building housing the store. This owner does not pay rent in the sense of spending money each month to pay for the use of the land. But the owner could be renting the land to someone else for, say, $1,000. The economist will consider $1,000 to be an implicit cost and will add this sum to the actual money payments (explicit costs) the storeowner makes to others. Similarly, the value of any labor the owner performs will be considered part of the costs. Thus, if the business person claims a profit of $30,000, the economist may advise that in reality a portion of that amount is not profit at all if no deduction has been made for the value of any self labor performed, the rental value of land personally owned, and the like. These are fine points, however. For the rest of this chapter we shall assume that all costs of doing business are accurately computed according to the theories of an economist.

Fixed Costs

All costs can be classified as either *fixed* or *variable*. In the short run, the firm can use only its existing facilities to increase its output. It cannot add to its plant because there is not sufficient time to do so. During the short run, there are several important costs that are fixed. (In the long run, all costs can change. We shall deal with this fact later in this chapter.) *Fixed costs do not change when the firm changes its level of output.* That is, the firm may produce nothing, it may produce 1 unit, or it may produce 10,000 units, but its fixed costs remain unchanged. Fixed costs include such items as interest on debts of the firm, payments for rent, insurance premiums, taxes on real property owned by the firm, part of the depreciation of the firm's building and equipment, and salaries paid to important executives. These are payments that must be made even though the firm is not producing a single unit of output. The bondholders expect to receive their interest payments on time, the insurance company demands its premiums, and so on. As Figure 5–1 shows, the total fixed costs remain the same, regardless of output.

 Fixed costs: any costs that remain the same, regardless of how much the firm is producing.

Average Fixed Costs

Average fixed cost, AFC, declines, however, as the firm increases its output. Average fixed cost is determined simply by dividing total fixed costs, *TFC,* by the quantity being produced: $AFC = TFC/Q$. The *AFC* curve is also shown in Figure 5–1. Note that during the particular period under consideration, the firm has fixed costs totaling $2,000, as shown by the horizontal solid line *TFC*. If this firm produces 2 units of output, the average fixed cost *AFC* drops to $1,000 (*TFC* of $2,000 divided by *Q* of 2.) When the firm increases its output to 4 units, the fixed costs are spread over a larger number of items, so *AFC* becomes $500. When the firm is producing 10 units, *AFC* is only $200. Clearly, if a firm had nothing but fixed costs, the more it produced, the lower its unit cost (average total cost) would be. In such a case, a firm could continually reduce its average cost simply by increasing production to the limit its productive resources permitted. In reality, however, the firm is also confronted by variable costs.

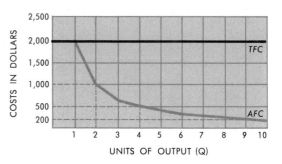

Figure 5–1   Total fixed costs and average fixed costs

The line labeled *TFC* shows the firm's total fixed costs, $2,000. Regardless of the level of output, the total fixed costs remain the same. The curve marked *AFC* shows the firm's average fixed costs at 1 to 10 units of output. Explain why the *AFC* curve will always slope downward.

Variable Costs

Variable costs increase as the firm increases its output. Similarly, variable costs decline if the firm reduces its level of output. All costs that are not fixed are variable. When a firm increases its output, it must acquire more productive resources, such as additional workers and raw materials. More fuel or power will be needed in the plant, and there will be additional transportation costs. Some of the maintenance costs will rise as the firm's plant and equipment are used more intensively. Wages and other variable costs, then, will tend to rise as the firm increases its output and to fall as the firm reduces its output. *Total variable costs, TVC,* will keep rising as the firm increases its output. (This will be illustrated by Figure 5–3 on p. 110.)

 Variable costs: any costs that rise as the firm produces more and fall as the firm produces less.

Average Variable Cost and the Law of Diminishing Returns

Average variable cost is another matter. *Average variable cost, AVC,* is found by dividing total variable cost by the firm's output: $AVC = TVC/Q$. Although average fixed cost declines continually as the firm increases its output, average variable cost does not. At first, average variable cost usually declines as the firm's output increases. After reaching a minimum, however, average variable

cost begins to rise. The *AVC* curve, then, will have the general shape of the letter U. This phenomenon is explained by the *law of diminishing returns,* also called the *law of diminishing marginal productivity.* This law states that *as more and more units of a variable factor of production*

The Concept of Margin

Marginal analysis is one of the most important techniques used in economics. The word "margin" in this context means extra or additional. The *marginal product,* for example, is the additional output we get

when we hire one more worker (or install one more machine). The new worker is our marginal unit of labor. In marginal analysis we examine small changes in quantities. These small changes,

although they are usually part of a much larger picture, can provide very useful information.

The graphs below are based Table 5–1. The first graph shows the firm's total output; the second shows the small changes that occur when we add another unit of labor. Note that even after the point of diminishing returns has been reached (at worker 4), output is still rising (but not quite as steeply). After this point, workers 5, 6, and 7 are still adding to total output, but they are adding *less* than the previous worker (4). Marginal analysis would make management aware of this situation. It is not until the newest worker (8) actually reduces output that the *total* output curve begins to decline. Marginal costs should also be studied. If the firm is operating more than one plant, for instance, and decides to increase production of an item, the plant with the lowest marginal cost should be the first to increase output. Thus, marginal analysis can help management make wise decisions.

We shall use the concept of margin again, not only in relation to a business firm or a labor situation, but also in relation to our total economy. In Chapter 12 we shall see how slight changes in savings and consumption can cause profound changes in the economy as a whole.

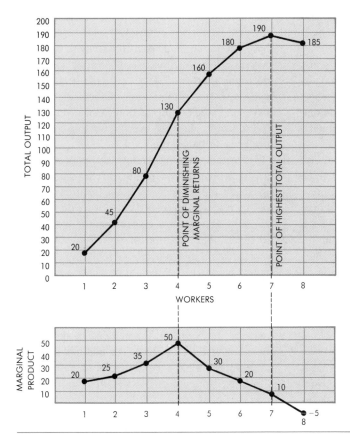

(labor, for example) *are added to a fixed factor of production* (such as capital equipment), *eventually a point will be reached at which the output accounted for by each additional unit of the variable factor will start to decline.* A simple example will help to make this idea clear.

Assume that we are setting up a small factory to produce our "Build-a-City" games. Our fixed factor of production (capital, in this case) is made up of four machines. Machine number one is an electric saw used to cut the wood to the proper size and shape. Machine number two is a sander, which smooths the rough edges of the pieces. The third machine clamps the pieces together to form the parts of the set. The fourth machine is a paint sprayer used to paint the parts. At first, we hire only one worker for our factory. This one person must operate all four machines and perform each step in the production process. He produces 20 sets a day.

We soon realize that we are not operating at our most efficient point. The worker is not able to become a specialist in any one job, for he must go from one machine to another. Because only one machine can be in operation at a time, three machines must be idle while the fourth is in operation. So we decide to hire another worker. Labor, of course, is the variable factor of production that we shall be adding to the fixed factor (capital). Now, with two workers in our plant, we have greater efficiency. One person operates machines one and number two; the other operates machines three and four. Now we can have two machines running at the same time, and each worker can become more adept at handling certain machines. As a result, we experience a marked increase in output. Our total output rises to 45 sets a day. The additional output accounted for by the addition of another worker is called the *marginal product.* The marginal product resulting from hiring the second worker is 25—the difference between our total output when we had one worker and our total output after we hired the second worker.

The success of this move leads us to try adding still another person to our labor force. Now we can have three machines operating at once, and further specialization becomes possible. Total output rises to 80 sets. The marginal product is

35 (the difference between 45 and 80). The addition of the third worker has resulted in an increase of 35 units in our total output. It should be understood, however, that the increase in the marginal product is *not* accounted for by any superiority on the part of the new worker. We assume that the workers are of equal ability. The increase stems from a more efficient combination of labor and capital.

When a fourth worker joins our labor force, total output rises to 130 sets a day. The marginal product is 50, or the difference between 80 and 130. Now we have one worker for each machine. Each worker becomes a specialist in a particular phase of the operation, and all four machines can be running at once. Up to this point, we have been experiencing *increasing returns.* Each time we added a new worker, our output increased more than it had when we added the previous worker. Average output per worker has been rising—from an average of 20 sets per person when we had only one worker to 32.5 per person when our labor force reached four workers. Our total variable costs have been rising; our payroll rose with each new worker. However, the *average* variable cost has been going down. The benefits of specialization and the better combination of labor and capital have increased our production so that average cost has dropped. Thus, the average variable cost curve has been sloping downward.

But this situation cannot last. Suppose we add a fifth worker to our plant, to relieve the others for lunch and coffee breaks. We find that our total output rises to 160 units a day, for we do not have to shut down our machines when the workers go to lunch. The addition of the fifth worker has increased our total output, but it has not increased output as much as the addition of the fourth person. Indeed, the marginal product is now only 30. *Now we are at the point of diminishing returns.* A sixth worker might also be useful, increasing our total output to 180. The marginal product would now be only 20, however. The addition of a seventh worker might account for an increase of only 10 units, bringing our total output to 190. The average output per worker has been declining since the fifth worker—and the average variable cost is *rising.* If we go on adding workers, we shall reach a point where the marginal worker adds nothing to our total output. The "crowding effect" might occur, meaning that we have so many workers in relation to our machines that they are getting in each other's way and thus are reducing efficiency and lowering our output. The addition of worker number eight, then, might result in a marginal output that is negative—by hiring this worker we might actually reduce our output instead of increasing it. Table 5–1 summarizes the situation.

Obviously, a business person must be aware of the law of diminishing returns if the firm is to operate efficiently. (We shall have occasion to refer to this law again in Chapter 7, in terms of its influence on wage rates.)

Total Cost

Total cost is the sum of total fixed cost and total variable cost. When a firm increases its output, total cost tends to rise. Fixed cost remains unchanged, naturally, but total cost will be pulled up by the rise in total variable cost with the rise in output. As Figure 5–2 demonstrates, *average total cost* can be found by dividing total cost by output, $ATC = TC/Q$, or by adding average fixed cost to average variable cost, $ATC = AFC + AVC$.

The average fixed cost curve *AFC*, such as the one in Figure 5–1, slopes steadily downward

Table 5–1 An illustration of the law of diminishing returns

Machines	Workers	Total output	Approxi- mate average output	Marginal product
4	0	0	0	0
4	1	20	20	20
4	2	45	22.5	25
4	3	80	26.6	35
4	4	130	32.5	50
Point of diminishing returns				
4	5	160	32	30
4	6	180	30	20
4	7	190	27.1	10
4	8	185	23.1	−5

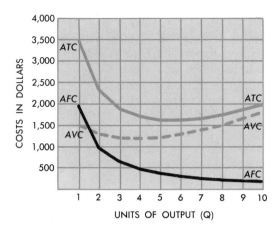

Figure 5–2   Average cost curves
The average fixed cost curve *AFC* is the same as the one in Figure 5–1. The dotted line shows average variable cost, *AVC*. Note that the *AVC* curve drops at first and then rises as a result of the law of diminishing returns. The colored curve indicates average total cost, *ATC*, the sum of the other two costs. Explain why this curve declines and then rises, but does not rise as steeply as the *AVC* curve.

because average fixed cost declines as output rises. Average variable cost, on the other hand, reflects the law of diminishing returns. Average costs drop at first because the firm is combining the variable factors with the fixed factors more efficiently. We can see in Figure 5–2 that when 2 units are being produced, the average variable cost is $1,300. When output rises to 3 units, the curve shows us that average variable cost drops to $1,200. Eventually, we find that new variable factors, although adding to the firm's total output, add less and less at each step. In other words, each new factor we acquire accounts for a smaller addition to total output than the factor that immediately preceded it. This is why the average variable cost curve slopes upward after the output level of 4 units. When 7 units are being produced, the average variable cost is $1,400. At an output level of 10 units, the *AVC* is $1,800.

Average Total Cost

The colored-line curve in Figure 5–2 shows *average total cost, ATC*. This is the sum of the *AFC* and *AVC* curves. For example, at an output level of 1 unit, we can see that *AFC* is $2,000 and *AVC* is $1,500. Their sum is $3,500, as shown by the starting point of our *ATC* curve. When 4 units are being produced, *AFC* is $500 and *AVC* is $1,200. Average total cost *ATC* at this point, of course, is $1,700. When we produce 10 units, *ATC* is $2,000, because *AFC* is $200 and *AVC* is $1,800. Note that the *ATC* curve has the same general U shape as the *AVC* curve. It drops sharply at the beginning because both *AFC* and *AVC* are dropping. It does not level off as soon as the *AVC* curve does, because it is being pulled downward by the declining *AFC* curve. Eventually, it is pulled up by the rising *AVC* curve. Its ascent is not as steep as that of the *AVC* curve, however, because it is partially offset by the *AFC* curve, which is still declining.

 Average total cost: the total cost of production divided by the number of items produced—also called the cost per unit of output, or unit cost.

In Figure 5–3 we show total costs for the same firm as was considered in the previous graphs. The colored horizontal line marked *TFC* shows total fixed cost, $2,000. Again, it is clear that total fixed cost remains the same regardless of the level of output. By adding the total variable cost to the total fixed cost at every level of output, we get the ascending line that indicates our total cost. The *distance* between the *TFC* line and the *TC* line shows us the variable cost at each level of output. At an output level of 8 units, for example, the distance between the *TFC* line and the *TC* line represents $12,000—the total variable cost at that level of output. Referring to Figure 5–2, you will note that the average variable cost at an output level of 8 units is $1,500. Total variable cost is obtained by multiplying $1,500 by eight (*AVC* times *Q*), which gives us our figure of $12,000. To this we add the $2,000 total fixed cost to find that total cost is $14,000 at that level of output.

You can see the relation between the *ATC* curve in Figure 5–2 and the *TC* line in Figure 5–3 at any level of output by cross-checking to see that *TC* = *ATC* × *Q*. For instance, in Figure 5–2, *ATC* is $2,000 at 10 units of output. Multiplying $2,000 by 10, we get the total cost of $20,000, which appears in Figure 5–3.

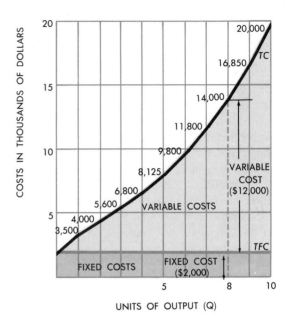

Figure 5–3 Total cost

The ascending line indicates what our total cost of production, *TC*, would be at every level of output. Total cost is the sum of total fixed cost ($2,000) and total variable cost. The dark-shaded rectangle represents total fixed cost. The light-shaded area shows total variable cost at each level of output. How can you determine *average* total cost, *average* fixed cost, and *average* variable cost from this graph?

Marginal Cost

You should have a thorough understanding of the preceding information before tackling marginal cost. *Marginal cost* can be defined as the *additional* cost of one more unit of production. Suppose, for example, that a firm has been producing 2 units of output at a total cost of $4,600. It then decides to produce an additional unit, raising total cost to $5,600—$1,000 more than total cost at an output level of 2 units. The $1,000, then, is the marginal cost—the extra cost of producing an additional unit of output.

 Marginal cost: the extra cost of producing another unit of output.

For clarity, let us carry this process one step

further. The firm decides to increase its output to 4 units and finds that total cost rises to $6,800. The difference between total cost at this level of output and total cost at the previous level is $1,200 ($6,800 minus $5,600). The marginal cost, then, is $1,200.

Marginal cost can also be defined as the *variable cost of the last unit produced*. We saw that the average variable cost curve *AVC* declines for a time and then swings upward. This movement was explained by the law of diminishing returns. Because marginal cost is *a part of* the firm's variable cost, its behavior is explained in the same way.

Using the information contained in Figure 5–3, we have constructed Table 5–2. Table 5–2 shows total fixed cost, total variable cost, total cost, and marginal cost at each level of output. Note that the marginal cost is simply the difference between the total cost figure at one level of output and the total cost figure at the immediately preceding level of output.

Note that the total cost figure in Table 5–2 was obtained by adding total fixed cost and total variable cost at each level of output. Note also that marginal cost declines at first and then begins to rise after a certain level of output (4 units, in this case). Refer to Figure 5–4 for a graphic picture of the same information.

Table 5–2   The determination of marginal cost

Total output	Total fixed cost	Total variable cost	Total cost	Marginal cost
0	$2,000	$ 0	$ 2,000	$ 0
1	2,000	1,500	3,500	1,500
2	2,000	2,600	4,600	1,100
3	2,000	3,600	5,600	1,000
4	2,000	4,800	6,800	1,200
5	2,000	6,125	8,125	1,325
6	2,000	7,800	9,800	1,675
7	2,000	9,800	11,800	2,000
8	2,000	12,000	14,000	2,200
9	2,000	14,850	16,850	2,850
10	2,000	18,000	20,000	3,150

Figure 5–4 shows marginal cost in relation to average total cost and average variable cost. The *ATC* and *AVC* curves are identical to those in Figure 5–2. Notice that the *AVC* and *ATC* curves begin to rise as soon as they are crossed by the marginal cost curve, *MC*. This rise occurs because marginal cost is a part of average variable cost and average total cost. Let us use an analogy. Suppose that you have been keeping a record of your test scores, and that the average is 80. Now you receive a score of 90 on your economics

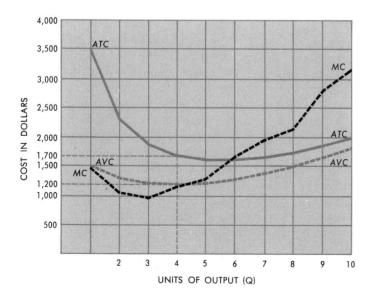

Figure 5–4   Marginal cost
The *ATC* and *AVC* curves are identical to those in Figure 5–2. The broken line, representing marginal cost (the additional cost of the last unit of output), declines at first, then rises. Marginal cost is part of *AVC* and *ATC*. Why do the *ATC* and *AVC* curves begin to rise as soon as the *MC* curve crosses them?

examination, and you add this to your previous scores. What will happen to your average score? Obviously, it will rise. If you had received a score of 70, your average would fall. Because marginal cost is added to the other costs, when the marginal cost figure is greater than the average total cost and average variable cost, those cost figures must begin to rise. (The mathematical rule that applies here states that whenever a number added to a series of numbers is *less than* their average, the average must *decline;* whenever a number added to a series of numbers is *larger than* their average, the average must *rise.*)

Knowledge of marginal cost is extremely important to the firm because it helps the firm to decide whether to increase or decrease output. Marginal cost is the cost that the firm can control most directly. Because marginal cost is the cost that is incurred by producing one more unit, it is the cost that can be eliminated simply by reducing total production by one unit. When a firm increases production, it naturally wants to know how much additional cost will be involved. Marginal cost indicates just how much more the firm must pay out when it produces one more unit. This cannot be learned from average cost figures alone. Examine Figure 5–4 again, for example, and note that average total cost, *ATC,* at 4 units of output is $1,700. Marginal cost at that level, however, is only $1,200. The firm would be making a serious mistake if it assumed that by increasing its output from 3 to 4 units it would add another $1,700 to its total costs. By examining its marginal cost, the firm could see that increasing output to 4 units adds only $1,200. As we shall see shortly, the firm should know marginal cost in order to maximize its profit or minimize its loss.

Costs over the Long Run

Over the long run, all costs are variable. Taxes, interest rates, and other costs that are fixed in the short run can change. In the long-run period, there is time for the industry to build new plants, and there is time for new firms to enter the industry. Costs may decrease, stay constant, or increase in the long run.

Decreasing Costs and Economies of Scale

If unit costs fall as output rises, the firm is experiencing *decreasing costs*. When an industry is new, it often lacks skilled labor and has not yet developed efficient methods of production. As time goes on, better machines are invented, production techniques are improved, and workers become more skilled. Greater specialization becomes possible as new firms enter the industry. The improvement in efficiency leads to lower unit costs of production. The industry supply curve may actually slope downward—an exception to the law of supply. When a decrease in costs makes it possible to sell the product at lower prices, the public often benefits. A study of U.S. economic history will show that the average consumer today enjoys many goods and services that were considered luxury items for the rich a few decades ago. This drop in the price of consumer items can be explained, in part, by the fact that some industries experienced decreasing unit costs as they increased their output.

The size of a firm can also affect costs. In some industries, large firms have lower unit costs of production than small firms. The principle that explains this situation is called *economies of scale*. As firms enlarge their plants, their unit costs decline because of mass production and other factors, such as the following:

1. *Specialization* is possible in a large firm. With many workers in the labor force, each person can be assigned a small but specialized task. Each worker becomes highly skilled and extremely efficient because he or she can concentrate on doing only one operation. In a small plant, one worker is often responsible for many tasks and is thus unable to develop skill or dexterity at any one of them. The principle of specialization also applies to management. The executive in the small firm may be responsible for personnel, production planning, selling, accounting, and several other functions. In the large firm, on the other hand, executives can hire specialists who have been trained in each of these fields, and greater efficiency results.

2. The *principle of factor substitution* can often be better implemented in a large firm. Earlier, in discussing the law of diminishing returns, we saw how one factor of production (labor) was related to another factor of production (capital). We found that in our imaginary firm there was *one point* at which labor was combined most efficiently with capital (machines). Because large firms have more machines and a larger number of workers, they are better able to experiment with various combinations of these two factors in order to find out which "mix" results in the greatest output. Some firms conduct controlled experiments in which they leave one part of a plant as it is, while in another part of the plant they try various combinations of labor and capital to see which combination brings the greatest output at the least unit cost. The principle of factor substitution also applies to other factors of production. The large firm, for example, can try substituting aluminum for steel, to see whether costs are reduced and profits increased. Small firms often lack the resources to engage in this type of experimentation. In many cases they must guess correctly the first time or go out of business.

3. *Better equipment* can be purchased by the large firm. Many modern machines are too costly for small firms, or are not suitable for use in small-scale enterprises. For example, it might be wasteful for the small firm to obtain an expensive computer because its use in the small business would be limited. The large firm, on the other hand, has many uses for the computer and so could get maximum utility from the machine. The very nature of some industries makes it necessary to have large plants. Steel, aluminum, motor vehicles, railroad equipment, and ocean-going vessels are but a few of the products requiring large plants and costly capital equipment.

4. *Research* is costly and difficult for the small firm, but can be carried on by large businesses. In a recent year, three large U.S. firms spent a total of nearly $6 billion on research and development. Through research, the large firm develops new and better products, improves production methods, and reduces costs. The large firm finds uses for materials the small firm has to discard because it does not have sufficient resources to develop by-products.

5. *Marketing advantages* often come with large size. In the *factor market,* where firms are hiring labor, buying raw materials, obtaining capital goods, and borrowing money for investment, the large firm usually has a competitive advantage. It may get a discount from a supplier because it buys in larger quantity. By offering greater stability and security than the small firm, the large firm often attracts better workers. Because the large firm can ship its goods in great bulk, it may pay lower rates per unit. When borrowing money, the large firm often pays the prime rate. This is the lowest interest rate that commercial banks charge, the rate paid by the largest and most stable borrowers. If the large firm wants to raise capital by selling securities, it usually has a much better chance of finding buyers than does the small business. A big business can finance nationwide advertising campaigns on a large scale to broaden the market for its products.

6. *Stability* is likely to be a feature of large businesses. That is, they are less vulnerable than small firms when recession or depression strikes the nation. While small firms are collapsing by the thousands, a large company may take huge losses on one part of its operation, but survive because other parts are profitable. The famous failure of Ford's Edsel car, for instance, was compensated for by the success of other models. A large company may even be able to operate for long periods at a loss, whereas small firms frequently survive almost on a day-to-day basis.

Constant Costs

Thus far, we have discussed situations leading to decreasing costs. It is also possible for an industry to experience *constant costs*. A constant-cost situation is one in which the cost per unit of output remains the same even though output is rising.

The supply curve for the industry in such a case is horizontal. An increase in demand might not result in higher prices in a competitive market, for the industry could expand its output to meet the greater demand without experiencing higher unit costs. This might be the case if raw material, labor, and other factors of production were so abundant that the industry could obtain more of them without increasing the unit cost of production. Much depends on the nature and size of the industry compared with its factors of production. For example, the manufacturers of paper clips could probably increase the output of their product many times over without causing a shortage of the metal used, and thus without increasing the unit cost of output.

There are few (if any) industries that can enjoy decreasing costs or constant costs forever. For a time, an industry may be characterized by decreasing costs. Industries with high fixed costs, such as railroads, telephone companies, and firms producing electric power, have been decreasing-cost industries. (Refer to Figure 5–1 for a partial explanation of this.) A constant-cost situation is likely to be a temporary phenomenon.

Increasing Costs and Diseconomies of Scale

Eventually, an industry will experience *increasing costs*. Most businesses in the United States today, especially in industries that are well established, are experiencing increasing costs. As output rises, the unit cost of production rises. The supply curve slopes upward. As an industry expands, it may have to bid against other industries for existing supplies of labor, raw materials, and capital. The result of this bidding may be higher wage rates, higher prices for materials, and higher interest rates, which naturally raise the average cost of producing the product. Industries that depend heavily on natural resources are often faced with increasing costs as they expand their output. Fishing fleets must go farther out to sea to bring in larger catches. Lumbermen must go deeper into the forests to obtain more timber. Miners often have to dig deeper, tap ores of lower quality, and

use more expensive equipment to expand their output. Thus their costs rise.

 Optimum size: the size at which a firm can be operated most efficiently.

Earlier, we pointed out that a firm may enjoy *economies of scale* as it becomes larger. It is also possible, however, for a firm to exceed its optimum size. A firm can go beyond the size where it would have the lowest unit costs. If a firm becomes too large to be operated efficiently, it will experience *diseconomies of scale*. In other words, its unit cost of production will rise. When a firm becomes too vast to be managed in an orderly manner, the average total cost curve may rise. If a firm is too big, managers may lose touch with workers, with other managerial personnel, and with many important aspects of the production operation. Vital decisions get delayed if they must be made by a top executive who is already occupied with too many problems. A firm producing hundreds of different products can lose track of the cost of producing each one, the market for each product, and so on.

It is difficult to say just what the optimum size of a firm is. The optimum size may be much greater in some industries than in others. To give an extreme example, a firm producing automobiles has a greater optimum size than a firm offering a personalized service such as haircuts. Little would be gained by having a barbershop staffed by hundreds of barbers. An automobile company, on the other hand, requires huge capital equipment, assembly lines, and a great many workers. Some large firms have attempted to meet the problem of diseconomies of scale by decentralizing. One large auto company, for instance, has a number of divisions that enjoy a great deal of autonomy. In fact, the divisions compete with one another. Some economists feel that the U.S. steel industry is suffering from diseconomies of scale and could operate much more efficiently if the huge firms that compose the industry would decentralize. In any event, diseconomies of scale can help to explain the rising supply curve over the long run.

B Output and Price in Competitive Markets

In reality, it is difficult to find a market that meets the definition of pure competition. To be classified as purely competitive a market must have a great many sellers who are acting independently. There must be no collusion among them, new firms must be able to enter or leave the industry at will, and there must be no interference with the market forces that affect supply, demand, and price. The product must be standardized, so that the buyer may substitute the product of one firm for the product of another. (For instance, the wheat produced by farmer Burns must be no different than the wheat produced by farmer Chase.)

If the market is competitive, each firm is such a small part of the industry that it cannot affect the market price. That is to say, the individual firm can greatly increase its production or reduce its production without causing a change in the market price. If farmer Burns doubles the amount of wheat he raises and puts it on the market, his action will not cause the supply curve to shift to the right because his output is such a tiny part of the total output of wheat in the country. There will be no change in the market price if farmer Burns doubles or even triples his production of wheat. Also, in pure competition, the factors of production can be shifted from one firm to another. The seed, the workers, the fertilizer, and the machinery used on Burns's farm could be used just as well on Chase's farm. Since the firm is unable to affect the existing market price, it must adjust to it. With the market price fixed (in the short run, anyway), the firm will attempt to maximize its profits or minimize its losses by adjusting output. In this section, we shall explore how a single firm in pure competition attempts to maximize its profits, how the industry as a whole adjusts to changes in the market price, and how economists evaluate pure competition. Even though pure competition is rare, some market situations (for example, certain agricultural industries) come close to being purely competitive. The model of pure competition enables us to compare the real life situation with the ideal— the "is" with the "ought to be."

Profits in the Short Run

You may recall that in the short run the firm does not have time to add to its plant. Thus, any adjustment that the firm wants to make will have to be done by adding or subtracting *variable* factors of production, such as raw materials and labor. Because the firm is too small a part of the industry to affect the market price by its actions, an increase or decrease in its output will not change the market price. What the firm will do, then, is attempt to produce at the point where its profits will be greatest or its losses minimized. There are several important factors that it must take into account.

First, *the demand curve for the individual firm in pure competition is perfectly elastic*. (See Section B in Chapter 2 for a discussion of elasticity.) A perfectly elastic demand curve is horizontal, indicating that the quantity sold at the going market price will range from zero to infinity. For the individual firm, this means that it can sell everything it can produce at the current market price. The demand curve for the industry as a whole, however, is a downward-sloping curve. If the whole industry increases its output, the extra output can be sold only at a lower market price. Figure 5–5 illustrates these points.

Graph (A) in Figure 5–5 shows the demand curve for the entire industry. It shows that the industry can sell 20,000 units of output at a price of $20 per unit (point *x* on the curve.) If 100,000 units are produced, the price of the product must drop to $10 for the market to be cleared (point *y* on the curve). If the industry raises its output to 200,000 units, it must accept a price of $2 to sell its entire output (point *z*). Let us assume that the market price is $10 for the period we are considering. The demand curve for an individual firm in the industry is indicated by Graph (B) in Figure 5–5. The graph shows that the individual firm can increase its output from 0 to 20 units without affecting price. Indeed, the firm's output makes up much less than 1 percent of the industry's total output. It can double its production (say, from 5

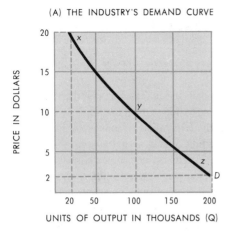

(A) THE INDUSTRY'S DEMAND CURVE

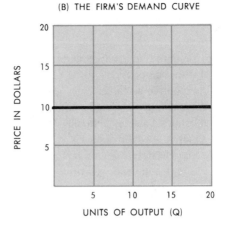

(B) THE FIRM'S DEMAND CURVE

Figure 5–5   Demand curves in pure competition

Graph (A) shows the demand curve for an entire industry in pure competition.
Graph (B) shows the demand curve for the individual firm. If the industry as a
whole increases its output, it must accept a lower price per unit to clear the
market, but if an individual firm increases its output, there will be no effect on
market price. If the demand curve in Graph (B) *did* slope downward, would pure
competition still exist? Why, or why not? If there were a supply curve in Graph
(A), at what point would it cross the demand curve?

to 10 units) and sell the additional output at the
going market price of $10. For the individual firm,
increasing output is like dumping a pail of water
into the ocean—it is such a small addition to the
total that it will not cause a tidal wave (or even a
ripple) on some foreign shore.

Shutdown Point

A firm compares total revenue with total cost to
see what its profit or loss is. At this point, you
might wonder why a firm would continue to operate if it were taking a loss. Remember that there
are fixed costs and variable costs. The fixed costs
must be paid anyway, even if the firm is producing
nothing. Suppose that a firm's *total cost* is $300,000
at a certain level of output, with $200,000 made
up of variable costs (such as labor and raw material) and $100,000 made up of fixed costs (such
as interest payments, taxes, and rent). If the firm's
total revenue is $240,000, it is clearly taking a
loss. The difference between total revenue and
total cost in this case is $60,000—this is its loss.
But notice that the total revenue of $240,000 pays
all of the firm's variable costs ($200,000) and also

pays $40,000 of its fixed cost. If the firm were to
shut down, on the other hand, its loss would total
$100,000—the amount of the fixed cost. Thus,
as long as a firm can cover all of its variable cost
by remaining in operation, it will do so. *Its shut-
down point will be where total revenue no longer
covers total variable cost.* For instance, if the firm's
total revenue drops to $190,000, it clearly cannot
cover its variable cost of $200,000 and is better
off shutting down altogether. If it shuts down, it
will be losing $100,000 (the total fixed cost); if
it remains in operation, it will be losing $110,000
(the difference between the total cost of $300,000
and the total revenue of $190,000). *The shutdown
point can also be defined as the point at which
the price is equal to the average variable cost.*
Can you explain why?

Most Profitable Point

Of course, a firm cannot go on operating at a loss
forever. Many firms will operate at a loss temporarily, however, hoping that conditions will
improve. The decision to operate while suffering
a loss will be based on the possibility of covering

all variable costs. Whether a firm is enjoying a profit or suffering a loss, however, it will try to operate at a level that maximizes profit or minimizes loss. Now we shall see how a firm determines this level of output.

Marginal Cost and Marginal Revenue—Profit Indices

To determine the level of output that will give it the greatest profit or the least loss, a firm must be concerned with its marginal cost and its marginal revenue. As we saw in Table 5–2 and in Figure 5–4, *marginal cost is the amount that each extra unit of output adds to the total cost. Marginal revenue is the amount that each additional unit of output adds to the total revenue.* Suppose that a firm has been producing 100 units of output and selling each unit for $10. Its total revenue would be $1,000 (price, $10, times quantity, 100). When the firm increases its output to 101 units, it finds that total revenue rises to $1,010. The marginal revenue in this case is $10. *For the firm in pure competition, marginal revenue is the same as market price.* Remember, the individual firm in pure competition can sell all it produces at the existing market price. Refer again to Figure 5–5, Graph (B). Note that the firm can sell any additional output for the market price of $10 per unit. The demand curve for the individual firm in pure competition, then, is also that firm's marginal revenue curve.

In the short run, the firm does not have to worry about its marginal revenue, because it can sell each additional unit at the going market price. It *does* have to be concerned about its costs, however. Marginal cost (as shown by Table 5–2 and Figure 5–4) will change. Although marginal cost may drop as the firm increases production and approaches the point of greatest efficiency, eventually it begins to rise. *As long as marginal revenue is greater than marginal cost, the firm will find an advantage in increasing its production.* For example, let us say that a firm can increase its output by adding another person to its labor force. After the new worker is hired, the firm finds that its total revenue increases by $60 a day—this is the marginal revenue. If the firm is paying the worker a daily wage of $50, it did the right

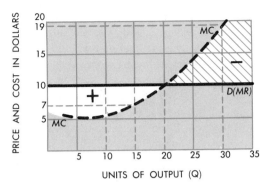

Figure 5–6 Marginal cost and marginal revenue

For the firm in pure competition, the marginal revenue curve *MR* is the same as the demand curve *D*. The firm can sell all its output at the market price of $10 per unit. Ten dollars is the amount that will be added to total revenue when an extra unit is sold. The marginal cost curve *MC* shows the amount that will be added to total cost by each additional unit of output. Any firm improves its profit position by producing up to the point at which the curves intersect. Does this graph show whether the firm is making a profit? Explain.

thing by hiring her. The new worker added only $50 to the firm's total cost, but accounted for an addition of $60 to its total revenue.

Figure 5–6 depicts a situation in which the firm in a purely competitive market can sell its output for the price of $10 per unit. We see that the firm's demand curve is horizontal (perfectly elastic), which means that an increase in the firm's output will *not* cause a reduction in the market price. The firm's demand curve is also its marginal revenue curve, *MR,* which shows that each additional unit the firm produces and sells will add an additional $10 to its total revenue. The broken-line curve is the firm's marginal cost curve. Assume that the firm has been producing 9 units and then decides to produce a tenth. The tenth unit will add $10 to the firm's total revenue, as indicated by the demand or marginal revenue curve, and $5 to the firm's total cost, as indicated by the marginal cost curve. (Proceed upward from 10 on the horizontal axis to the *MC* curve, then move to the left to the vertical axis.) Certainly, it would be advantageous for the firm to produce the tenth unit, for this will add $10 to revenue but only $5 to cost.

Will the firm benefit by producing at a level of 15 units? Indeed it will. The *MR* line shows that producing the fifteenth unit will add $10 to its revenue, whereas the *MC* curve shows that it will add only $7 to total cost. In fact, by increasing its output at any point to the left of the intersection of the curves, the firm will improve its profit position. If the nineteenth unit adds $9.99 to the firm's cost, the firm will still benefit by producing it, for that nineteenth unit adds $10 to total revenue. Now look at the situation in which the firm produces 30 units. The thirtieth unit would add $10 to total revenue, but it would add $19 to total cost. Producing at this level would be foolish, and the firm would benefit by reducing output. At any point to the right of the intersection of the *MC* and *MR* curves, the firm is reducing its profits (or aggravating its losses). The rule,

then, is that *the most profitable point for any firm is the point at which marginal cost equals marginal revenue*. The plus sign on the graph suggests that the firm can improve its profit position by increasing its output up to the point where *MC* crosses *MR*. The minus sign on the graph suggests that the firm will reduce its profits or increase its losses if it produces beyond the point of intersection. This rule for profit maximization applies to firms in all kinds of markets and not just firms in pure competition. Again, profits will be maximized (or losses minimized) where marginal cost equals marginal revenue. (In Figure 5–6, profits are maximized at an output level of 20 units.)

Maximizing Profits

To prove that profits are maximized where marginal cost equals marginal revenue, carefully study

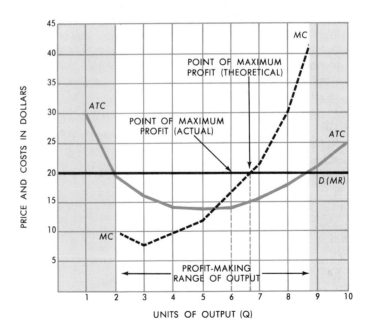

Figure 5–7   The firm's profit position
The horizontal line, indicating a market price of $20, is the firm's demand and marginal revenue curve. The firm can operate at a profit wherever the *ATC* curve is below this line. As long as the firm produces more than 2 units and fewer than 9, it will make a profit. To *maximize* its profit, it will produce as close as possible to the point at which *MC* crosses *MR*, but not beyond this point. In this case, an output of 6 units will yield the greatest possible profit, for this is as close as the firm can come to equating marginal cost with marginal revenue. Compute the firm's profits for several different points to see why this is so.

Figure 5–7. The firm's demand curve and marginal revenue curve are represented by the horizontal line. The going market price is $20, as this curve shows, and every time the firm sells one more unit of output it will increase its total revenue by $20. The colored-line curve represents the firm's average total cost; the heavy broken-line curve represents marginal cost. Notice first that the average total cost curve ATC is *below* the demand (marginal revenue) curve over a wide range of outputs. *Wherever the ATC curve is below the demand and marginal revenue curve, the firm will make a profit.* In other words, where the ATC curve is below the D curve, the *cost* of producing each unit is *less than* the price obtained for that unit.

Let us examine several possible levels of output to see where the firm can make its greatest profit. If the firm produces only one unit of output, its total cost will be $30 (ATC of $30 times Q of 1). When the firm sells that unit for only $20, however, it will take a loss of $10. If it produces 2 units, its total revenue will be $40 (P × Q) and its total cost will be $40 (ATC × Q). At this point, the firm will just break even. At 3 units of output, the firm will take in $60 and its total cost will be $48 (ATC of $16 times Q of 3). Its profit will then be $12. If the firm produces 5 units, its total revenue will be $100 and its total cost will be $70—a profit of $30.

Now, we have maintained that the most profitable point will be where the MC curve crosses the MR curve. For any quantity beyond this inter-section, the firm will be losing profits. In Figure 5–7, the MC curve crosses the MR curve somewhere between 6 and 7. To see whether the rule is valid, we shall calculate the firm's profit position at 6 units and at 7 units. At an output of 7 units, the firm's total revenue will be $140, its total cost will be $108.50 (ATC of $15.50 times Q of 7), and its profit will be $31.50. At an output of 6 units, however, the firm's total revenue will be $120, its total cost will be $87 (ATC of $14.50 times Q of 6), and its profit will be $33. Although the firm in this example can make profits over a wide range, its most profitable point is an output level of 6. Try computing the firm's profit position at 8 units (where ATC is $17.50) and see what you get. At an output level of 9, the firm would lose money, for we see that the ATC curve is *above* the D curve. At 10 units, the firm would be losing even more, for ATC at that point is $24 and marginal revenue is only $20. Our rule seems to be proved, then, that the firm can maximize its profits by producing up to the point where marginal cost equals marginal revenue. (In Figure 5–7 the actual most profitable quantity falls short of the exact theoretical quantity because we must deal with whole units of output.) Table 5–3 shows the firm's profit position at various levels of output.

Minimizing Losses

Having proved that the firm can maximize profits by producing a quantity as close as possible to the point at which MC equals MR but not beyond, let us test the rule again to see whether it applies to

Table 5–3 The firm's profit position

Q	P (MR)	TR (P × Q)	ATC	TC (ATC × Q)	Profit or loss
1	$20	$ 20	$30.00	$ 30.00	—$10.00 (loss)
2	20	40	20.00	40.00	breaks even
3	20	60	16.00	48.00	12.00
4	20	80	14.50	58.00	22.00
5	20	100	14.00	70.00	30.00
6	20	120	14.50	87.00	33.00 (max. profit)
7	20	140	15.50	108.50	31.50
8	20	160	17.50	140.00	20.00
9	20	180	20.50	184.50	— 4.50 (loss)
10	20	200	24.00	240.00	— 40.00 (loss)

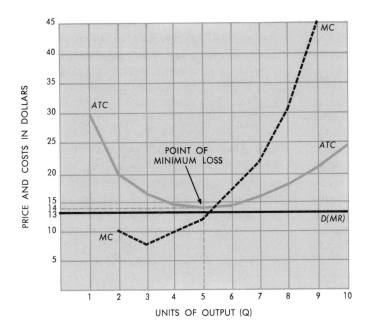

Figure 5-8 The firm's loss position

The MC and ATC curves are identical to those in Figure 5-7, but the D curve has shifted downward. The firm must accept $13 as the going price for its output. With the ATC curve above the D curve at every point, the firm must operate at a loss. It will minimize its loss by operating as close as possible to the point where MC crosses MR. In this case, the firm will minimize its loss by producing 5 units of output. To test this rule, compute the firm's losses at several other levels of output.

minimizing losses. Study Figure 5-8. The cost curves are identical to those in Figure 5-7, but the demand and marginal revenue curve has shifted downward. The market price is now only $13. We can see that the ATC is *above* the market price at *every* level of output. Thus the firm cannot possible operate at a profit. Because the firm can have no effect on the market price, it must try to adjust output to the point at which losses will be minimized.

In Figure 5-8, the firm can come closest to equating marginal cost with marginal revenue at an output of 5 units. Here, the firm will have a total revenue of $65 (P of $13 times Q of 5). Total cost will be $70 (ATC of $14 times Q of 5). The loss of only $5 is less than that at any other quantity. If the firm produces 6 units, for example, it will go beyond the point where MC equals MR. Its total revenue will be $78 (P of $13 times Q of 6), total cost will be $87 (ATC of $14.50 times Q of 6), and the loss will be $9. Table 5-4 shows the firm's losses at various levels of output.

By now, the importance of knowing marginal cost should be very clear. Any firm can maximize its profit or minimize its loss by producing a quantity up to the point where marginal cost equals

Table 5-4   The Firm's Loss Position

Q	P(MR)	TR(P × Q)	ATC	TC(ATC × Q)	Loss
1	$13	$ 13	$30.00	$ 30.00	$ 17.00
2	13	26	20.00	40.00	14.00
3	13	39	16.00	48.00	9.00
4	13	52	14.50	58.00	6.00
5	13	65	14.00	70.00	5.00 (least loss)
6	13	78	14.50	87.00	9.00
7	13	91	15.50	108.50	17.50
8	13	104	17.50	140.00	36.00
9	13	117	20.50	184.50	67.50
10	13	130	24.00	240.00	110.00

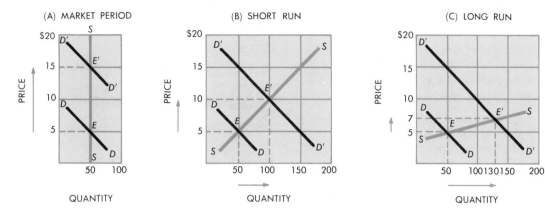

Figure 5–9   Effects of time on supply and price in the industry as a whole

In each graph, the supply curve represents the sum of the supply curves of all firms in the industry, and the demand curves represent the sum of all firms' demand curves. In each graph, the demand schedule has shifted upward by the same magnitude. During the market period (A), supply cannot be increased. The upward shift in demand from DD to D′D′ results in a price increase from $5 to $15. In the short-run period (B), firms in the industry can increase output by producing more intensively in their existing plants. The quantity offered for sale rises from 50 to 100 units. The new equilibrium price is $10. In the long-run period (C), existing firms have time to build new plants, and new firms enter the industry. The quantity offered for sale rises from 50 to 130 units, and price rises from $5 to $7. What would happen to price if this were a *decreasing-cost* industry, with a downward-sloping S curve?

marginal revenue. This rule will also apply to firms in imperfect competition.

How Does Time Influence Supply?

So far we have been considering primarily factors critical in the short-run period. Now we shall examine those factors that bring about long-run equilibrium in perfectly competitive markets.

In analyzing a market situation, time is an extremely important consideration. Some industries can increase supply quickly in response to an increase in price—for example, a manufacturing industry with much idle capacity, plenty of labor, and a productive process that is easily speeded up. Other industries need a long lapse of time before they can respond to rising prices by increasing output. For example, if the public should suddenly double its demand for peaches, the fruit growers could not respond immediately, because

it takes years for fruit trees to grow to suitable size. The time periods necessary to implement change will differ, then, depending on the industry.

It is convenient in analyzing a market situation to identify three time periods—the market (or momentary) period, the short-run period, and the long-run period.

Supply in the Market Period

The *market period* in any industry is a period of time so short that the seller cannot increase supply. The corresponding supply curve for the industry (the sum of the supply curves for each firm) is perfectly inelastic (vertical), as shown in Graph (A) of Figure 5–9. Suppose that a new product becomes an overnight success. The demand for the product is very great, but the sellers have no way of increasing their supply quickly; they can only sell from their existing stocks until the industry is able to increase production. Let us consider an interesting example: a blackout occurred over vast parts of the northeastern United States in 1965. Electrical power failed, and people needed light. There was a sudden demand for candles, but sellers had limited supplies, so candles that had been selling for a few cents commanded a price of $2 or $3.

 Market period: a time so short that sellers cannot increase the supply—also called the momentary period.

Supply in the Short-Run Period

The *short-run period* is long enough to permit changes in the production rates in existing plants, but not long enough for the building of new plants. If demand increases, the industry can hire more workers and use its existing plant and machinery more intensively to increase output and put more goods into the market. The corresponding supply curve for the industry slopes upward to the right [see Graph (B) in Figure 5–9]. Supply is no longer perfectly inelastic. It might be relatively elastic or relatively inelastic, depending on the particular situation. However, supply in the short-run period will certainly be more elastic than the supply during the market period.

 Short-run period: a period of time long enough for existing firms to increase their output with their existing plants, but not long enough for new plants to be built.

Supply in the Long-Run Period

The *long-run period* is long enough for existing firms to build new plants and for new firms to enter the industry. In a growing economy, existing firms that feel there will be a strong demand for their products for many years to come will build new plants, buy new machines, and use their productive resources to the fullest. Other business people, seeing that profits are being made in the industry, will be attracted to it and will start new firms. Now the supply curve for the industry (which is the sum of the supply curves of all the firms in the industry) will slope upward, farther to the right than the short-run supply curve. As Graph (C) in Figure 5–9 indicates, supply is likely to be very elastic—even perfectly elastic. (For the curve to be perfectly elastic, the industry must be increas-

ing the supply of the product just enough to meet changes in demand without affecting the market price.)

 Long-run period: a period of time that allows for the entry of new firms or the building of new plants by existing firms in an industry.

Profits in the Long Run

If an industry is enjoying good profits, the profit position of a typical firm will be like the one shown in Figure 5–7. However, because there is no barrier to the entry of new firms in a competitive market situation, new firms will be attracted to a profitable industry. Let us suppose that many new firms appear on the scene and greatly increase the supply of the industry's product. Assuming there is no change in the market demand schedule, the market price will be forced down because of the industry's increase in supply. Figure 5–8 can be used to illustrate how this situation affects a typical firm in the industry. The firm finds that the market price has dropped (from $20 to $13, in this example). As Figure 5–8 shows, the firm now operates at a loss, because the new market price is not high enough to cover its costs at any level of output. When losses rather than profits are the typical pattern, firms will begin to *leave* the industry, thus reducing the industry's total output. When fewer goods appear on the market, price will again be forced upward.

Long-Run Equilibrium

Where does all this end? In theory, at least, it ends in *long-run equilibrium*—the industry settles at a point where the typical firm neither makes profits nor suffers losses. The firm's long-run equilibrium position is depicted graphically in Figure 5–10. In our analysis of Figures 5–7 and 5–8, we established that the firm can maximize profits or minimize losses only for the condition $MC = MR$. We do not need actual figures in Figure 5–10, therefore, to see that the firm's best level of output in the long run is that point at which marginal cost equals marginal revenue.

Study Figure 5–10, noting that *MC* crosses

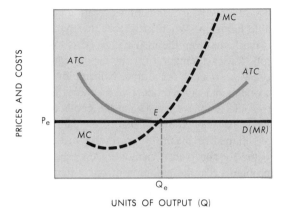

Figure 5–10   The firm's long-run equilibrium position

When the typical firm in pure competition is in long-run equilibrium, price, *ATC*, *MC*, and *MR* are equal. The firm is producing Q_e units of output, for at that level *MC* crosses *MR*. The firm would suffer a loss by producing at any other level, for it is clear that *ATC* is above price at any other point. In what way would this situation be changed if the *D* curve remained the same, but if improvements in technology reduced the firm's average total cost?

MR at level of output Q_e. It should be clear that if the firm operates at any other level of output it will incur a loss. If the firm produces fewer than Q_e units of output, it will suffer a loss because average total cost, *ATC*, will be *above* the demand curve (the market price) at every point to the left of Q_e. If it produces more than Q_e units of output, it will also operate at a loss. Again, *ATC* is above price at every level of output greater than Q_e. It seems, then, that at Q_e units of output the firm is just breaking even. It is barely covering its costs, for *ATC* at that point just equals price. At the equilibrium point *E,* then, *ATC* equals price and equals marginal cost.

Normal Profit

By now you are probably asking, "Why should a firm continue to operate in this industry if it just barely covers its costs?" The answer lies in our definition of *profit.* Earlier, we defined profit as the difference between total revenue and total cost. Wages, rents, the price of raw materials, and other items were included in the total cost figure. How-

ever, *normal profit* is also considered to be a part of the total cost. By *normal profit,* we mean *the minimum amount that is necessary to keep the owner in the industry.* When the typical firm is in equilibrium, as in Figure 5–10, it is making just enough of a profit to keep in business. If the firm were making less, it would go out of business.

Pure Profit

If the typical firm is making more than necessary to keep the owner in business, it is making pure profit. *Pure profit* (or economic profit), then, *is an amount above that necessary to keep the owner in the industry.* It is *not* considered part of total cost. Pure profit is the residual (the "left-overs") after all costs (including normal profit) have been met. When pure profits are being made, other firms will enter the industry. Normal profits are not high enough to induce other firms to enter, nor are they low enough to force existing firms to leave.

Evaluation of Pure Competition

Advantages of Pure Competition

Some economists feel that the situation we have described is ideal. A glance at Figure 5–10 will reveal that the firm in long-run equilibrium in a purely competitive market is producing at the most efficient point—the very bottom of the *ATC* curve. Resources are being used as efficiently as possible. The price is as low as possible, for it just covers all costs (including a modest normal profit as the reward for the entrepreneur). Indeed, the consumer is getting the product at cost.

> Pure competition: a situation in which there are so many firms producing an identical product that no single seller can affect the price. It is easy for new firms to enter the industry, everyone is well informed, and there is no collusion.

The firm that fails to use its productive resources with maximum efficiency will not survive in this market. Again, Figure 5–10 shows that if the typical firm operates at a level where the average total cost is above the minimum point possible, it will suffer losses and will eventually be forced to leave the field. Because firms must use those productive resources that give the greatest possible return for the lowest possible cost, society benefits from maximum efficiency. There is no waste.

In pure competition, the product is standardized, and thus no money is spent for advertising. The consumer will not pay a high price that reflects the cost of advertising the product. The producers will respond to the consumer's demands. The consumer who desires more of a product will offer a higher price, and the existing firms will make pure profits for a while. This will attract new firms to the industry, the quantity supplied will increase, and the price will be held in check. It will even be possible, in the long run, for the consumer to get more of the item at the original price. Therefore, consumer demand will help to determine what will be produced and how the industry will allocate the factors of production. When consumers have obtained enough of the product, or if some other item should appeal to them instead, they will reduce their purchases or offer a lower price. Firms will then leave the industry (for they are taking losses) and enter an industry that is producing a more popular product. Once again, therefore, productive resources will be reallocated in accordance with the wishes of the consumer.

Social Costs of Pure Competition

Some economists would maintain that even if pure competition worked in real life as it does in theory, it would not always be the best or most efficient system. The firm in pure competition may be forced to operate at its most efficient point in the long run, but it is often too small to pay for the research that leads to developing new products and better technology. If the firm can just barely cover its costs, it can hardly devote much of its revenue to research and development. Large firms, on the other hand, that are not operating in perfectly competitive markets do compete in another sense—in developing new products, improving production methods, and lowering costs.

The equilibrium of which we spoke does not usually last very long. New adjustments always become necessary, sometimes creating considerable hardship. When losses become typical and drive firms from the industry, workers lose their jobs (at least temporarily) and capital equipment ceases to operate for a time. Nonemployment of workers and other productive resources is a loss to society, for we are denied the goods and services that they would normally be creating.

If the firm in pure competition is in a constant battle for survival, it cannot be concerned about problems like the pollution of our water and air or the wasteful exploitation of our other natural resources. A firm that is just barely covering its costs cannot install air-pollution-control devices on its smokestacks or purify the water that it has used in the productive process before returning that water to its original source. Some large firms in imperfectly competitive markets, on the other hand, do spend considerable sums to avoid polluting air and water. (Of course, many such firms are also prime polluters of air and water.) Because society as a whole suffers from air and water pollution and from the wasteful exploitation of our natural resources, there are *social costs* that were not taken into account when we spoke of the great efficiency of pure competition.

In pure competition, prices act as signals to businesses, for they reflect the effective demand of the consumer. If the price of a certain product rises, businesses will devote more of their resources to producing that item and less to producing an item that commands a lower price (assuming that production costs are comparable). By *effective demand,* we mean wishes or desires supported by ability to pay. The profit-motivated business in pure competition must be concerned only with effective demand. It cannot concern itself with the needs or wishes of people who cannot pay for what they want. As a result, resources may be devoted to producing yachts and other luxury items, while millions of poor persons live in dilapidated dwellings because they cannot pay for decent housing. Some of our leading economists argue that we are devoting too much of our output to luxury items and too little to schools, better roads, hospitals, and other things that do not usually yield profits.

Finally, it is argued, pure competition does not provide the public with a wide choice of consumer goods. The product in a purely competitive market is standardized. Most consumers prefer to have a wide choice of products. It would be disastrous, in the eyes of the U.S. consumer, if all people had to wear identical clothes or drive identical cars. Some of the imperfectly competitive markets, then, offer a wide range of choices to the consumer.

In summary, although it is difficult to find a purely competitive market in the United States today, the model of pure competition does provide a useful yardstick against which we can measure the realities of our economic life.

Chapter Highlights

1. Profit is the difference between total cost (including implicit cost) and total revenue. Most (if not all) business firms attempt to maximize profits and minimize losses.

2. Total fixed costs (such as interest on a firm's debts) do not change with the level of output, at least in the short run. Average fixed cost declines as output rises. Variable costs (such as wages) do change as a firm's level of output changes. Average variable cost tends to decline at first and then rise because of the law of diminishing returns.

3. According to the law of diminishing returns, if we keep adding a variable factor of production to a fixed factor of production, we eventually reach a point where the output accounted for by each additional unit of the variable factor will decline.

4. Total cost is the sum of fixed and variable costs. Total cost rises as output rises. Average total cost is total cost divided by the quantity produced. Average total cost can also be found by adding average fixed cost and average variable cost.

5. Marginal cost is the additional cost of producing an extra unit of output. It is the variable cost of the last unit produced. Marginal cost tends to decline at first and then rise because of the law of diminishing returns. As soon as the marginal cost curve crosses the average total cost and average variable cost curves, those curves begin to rise. Marginal cost is very important, for it is the cost the firm can control most directly.

6. In the long run, all costs are variable. There is time to build new plants, and new firms may enter the industry. Long-run costs may be decreasing, constant, or increasing.

7. In pure competition, the individual firm is such a small part of the industry that it cannot affect the market price by increasing or decreasing its output. Its demand curve is perfectly elastic, and its marginal revenue curve is identical to the demand curve. Marginal revenue is the same as price for the firm in pure competition.

8. A firm in either a perfectly competitive market or an imperfectly competitive market can maximize its profit or minimize its loss by producing to the point at which marginal cost equals marginal revenue.

9. During the market period, there is no time to increase supply. In the short-run period, supply can be increased by using an existing plant more intensively. In the long-run period, new plants can be built and new firms may enter or leave the industry.

10. In theory, pure competition gives us the product at cost, and typical firms eventually settle at a point of maximum efficiency. Innovations and technological advances often come from firms in imperfectly competitive markets, however.

Study Aids

Key Terms

total revenue	marginal product	perfectly elastic demand curve
total cost	marginal cost	shutdown point
profit	marginal revenue	long-run equilibrium
loss	decreasing cost	market period
explicit cost	constant cost	short-run period
implicit cost	increasing cost	long-run period
fixed cost	economies of scale	normal profit
variable cost	diseconomies of scale	pure profit
law of diminishing returns	principle of factor substitution	imperfectly competitive market

Questions

1. Explain the difference between fixed costs and variable costs and give examples of each as they apply to a firm in your area. Why do average fixed costs fall, whereas average variable costs fall and then rise?

2. Explain the law of diminishing returns, using as an example a potato farmer who makes no change in the amount of land or capital equipment used but keeps adding workers. What is the significance of this law to all producers?

3. Why does the *ATC* curve tend to resemble the *AVC* rather than the *AFC* curve?

4. Why must the *AVC* and *ATC* curves begin to rise as soon as the *MC* curve crosses them?

5. Under what conditions might an industry experience decreasing costs? Constant costs? Increasing costs?

6. Give at least four reasons why economies of scale might occur in an industry.

7. What are the characteristics of a purely competitive market? Why is the demand curve for the individual firm in pure competition perfectly elastic?

8. Explain why a firm will sometimes continue to operate at a loss.

9. Explain how a firm maximizes its profit or minimizes its loss.

10. Describe the possible effects of time on supply, citing examples from an actual industry to illustrate each time period.

11. How is long-run equilibrium established in a purely competitive market? How does long-run equilibrium affect the typical firm?

12. What are arguments for and against pure competition? Do you think that most industry should be purely competitive? Why? Why not?

Problems

1. The *MC, ATC,* and *AVC* curves in the graph at the top of p. 127 are for a firm in equilibrium. The firm is operating in a purely competitive market. Which price will the firm charge—P_1, P_2, or P_3? Why? Why would the firm *not* charge the prices you rejected?

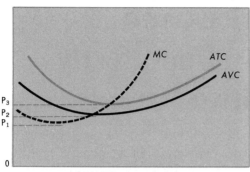

QUANTITY OF OUTPUT

Assuming that you are correct in your selection, study the other two graphs and set forth the conditions that would have had to prevail during the energy crisis of early 1974 for each of those other graphs to have explained the price increase.

4. In 1981, the market price of a certain type of crude oil was $34.10. By 1986, the price had dropped to $13.00. Add a curve (or two) to the graph below to explain the drop in price.

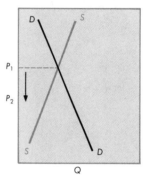

2. If you were asked to add the firm's demand curve to the graph, where would you put it? Why? Why is it *not* necessary to see the demand curve to answer the question regarding which price the firm will charge?

3. In the early months of 1974, gasoline prices rose sharply in the United States, as indicated by the movement from P_1 to P_2 in the three graphs shown below. Learn what you can about the "energy crisis" of 1974 and decide what graph—A, B, or C—best explains the sharp rise in prices. Explain why you selected that particular graph.

GRAPH A   GRAPH B   GRAPH C

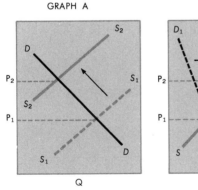

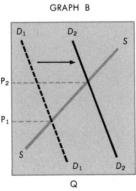

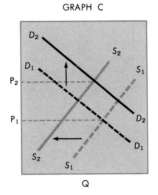

Costs, Prices, and Output in Imperfectly Competitive Markets

In Chapter 5 we described the various kinds of costs a firm must meet, illustrated the law of diminishing returns, and showed how a firm maximizes profits or minimizes losses by producing at the point where its marginal cost equals its marginal revenue. Although these principles were applied to firms in purely or perfectly competitive market situations, they also apply to firms in markets that cannot be described as perfectly competitive. You should be sure you understand the material in Chapter 5 fully before reading further, for in applying those concepts to firms that are not in perfectly competitive markets we face a more complex picture.

Because in real life one rarely finds perfect competition, you might wonder why we spent so much space analyzing perfect competition in such detail. First, since the graphic analysis of perfectly competitive situations is simpler than that of imperfectly competitive situations; this approach allows you to grasp the basic concepts before tackling the more complex graphs in this chapter. Second, it permits you to compare imperfectly competitive markets with perfectly competitive markets and decide which are preferable.

Chapter Objectives   After completing this chapter, you should be able to:

- Define monopoly, oligopoly, and monopolistic competition.
- Explain why the demand curve for imperfectly competitive firms slopes downward.
- Show why the marginal revenue curve for the imperfectly competitive firm lies below the demand curve.
- Confirm that the imperfectly competitive firm can maximize profits or minimize losses by producing at the point where marginal cost equals marginal revenue.
- Explain the theory of the "kinked" demand curve for the oligopoly firm.
- Compare monopoly, oligopoly, and monopolistic competition with perfect competition.

A Monopoly

If a single seller in a market can affect the market price by increasing or decreasing output, the market is imperfectly competitive. Monopoly, oligopoly, and monopolistic competition are terms used to describe such markets. (Some economists use the term "imperfect competition" to refer only to monopolistic competition, but we apply the term to monopoly and oligopoly as well.)

 Imperfect competition: any market situation other than pure or perfect competition.

If there is only one firm selling a product and there is no close substitute for that product, the firm can be called a monopoly. Although there are in the United States huge business combinations that act like monopolies, it is difficult today to find a good example of a pure monopoly. The problem is often one of definition. If we narrowly define the market by limiting it to a single town, we might say that the person who owns the only pharmacy in that town has a monopoly. If we broaden the definition to include all the pharmacies in the county, however, we cannot say that a monopoly exists. Public utilities and other natural monopolies are special cases, which we discussed earlier. Most U.S. industries today fall somewhere between the two extremes of pure competition and pure monopoly, but it will be simpler to analyze these markets if we start by assuming that pure monopolies exist.

 Monopoly: a market situation in which there is only one seller of a particular product.

We found that the demand curve for a firm in pure competition is perfectly elastic (horizontal), but that the demand curve for the whole industry slopes downward. This implies that if the industry as a whole increased its output, it would have to accept a lower market price to sell the additional output. The individual firm, on the other hand, is such a small part of the total picture that it can increase its output to the limit of its capabilities without affecting the market price—thus the horizontal demand curve for the individual firm.

Demand, Marginal Revenue, and Marginal Cost

The situation is quite different for the monopoly firm. By definition, *the monopoly firm is the whole industry*. The demand curve for the industry is the same as the demand curve for the firm, and it slopes downward. Even the monopoly firm is unable to control demand (although it might be able to influence demand through advertising). The monopoly firm is faced with the fact, therefore, that if it increases output it must accept a lower price to sell all that it produces. The monop-

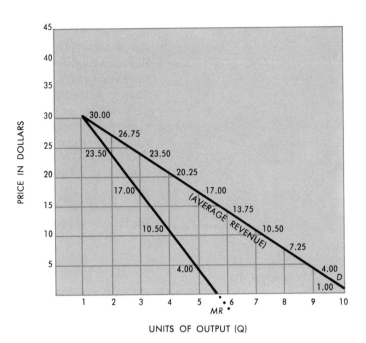

Figure 6–1   The monopolist's demand and marginal revenue

Because the monopoly firm is the only producer, the market price must fall when the firm increases its output. This fall in the market price is indicated by the downward-sloping demand curve. At each point, marginal revenue is below price, as shown by the *MR* curve. What is the significance of the fact that the *MR* curve eventually goes below the horizontal axis?

oly firm can establish any price it chooses, and then sell whatever the consumer will purchase at that price. On the other hand, it can decide how much to produce and then sell its output at whatever price will clear the market. The monopolist must always remember, however, that if output is increased, the price will fall; if it is reduced, the price will rise.

Price alone, however, will not tell the monopolist how to make the greatest profit. Like the producer in perfect competition, the monopolist must be aware of marginal revenue and marginal cost. In pure competition, the firm's marginal revenue is the same as the market price. Thus the firm's horizontal demand curve can represent its *MR* as well as its price. In the case of the monopoly firm, however, marginal revenue will *not* be the same as price. Every time the monopolist increases output, the market price will fall, as the downward-sloping demand curve indicates. For the monopolist (and for other firms in imperfectly competitive markets), *marginal revenue is below price*. As the monopolist increases output, the amount added to total revenue by the last unit produced will be *less than* the amount added by the previous unit produced. Study Figure 6–1 to see why this is so.

The upper line in Figure 6–1 is the monopolist's demand curve. It shows that the price is $30 when 1 unit is produced. The price drops to $17 when 5 units are produced, and to $1 when 10 units are produced. When the monopolist sells 1 unit, total revenue ($P \times Q$) is $30. When output is increased to 2 units, the price drops to $26.75 per unit, for a total revenue of $53.50 ($P$ of $26.75 times Q of 2). The *marginal revenue* (the addition to total revenue resulting from the sale of an additional unit of output) is $23.50. Remember that marginal revenue is the difference between total revenue when only 1 unit is produced and total revenue when 2 units are produced.

At 3 units of output, price is $23.50 and total revenue becomes $70.50. This is $17 more than the firm was taking in before, so marginal revenue is $17. At 5 units of output, the price is $17, total revenue is $85 (5 times $17), and marginal revenue is only $4. Table 6–1 summarizes the situation.

The information in Table 6–1 can be checked with Figure 6–1. Note, too, that if the monopolist produces 6 units, the sixth unit adds nothing to total revenue—it results in a *drop* in total revenue. (Marginal revenue would be negative—*minus* $2.50—and total revenue would begin to decline.)

Table 6–1 The monopolist's price, total revenue, and marginal revenue

Q	P	Total revenue (P × Q)	Marginal revenue
1	$30.00	$30.00	$30.00
2	26.75	53.50	23.50
3	23.50	70.50	17.00
4	20.25	81.00	10.50
5	17.00	85.00	4.00
6	13.75	82.50	−2.50

Most Profitable Point

Price-output adjustment is the same for the monopolist as for the firm in pure competition; it pays each to produce up to the point at which marginal revenue equals marginal cost. As long as producing one more unit adds more revenue than cost, the monopolist can increase profit by producing the additional unit. The difference is that for the monopolist the marginal revenue schedule is not the same as the demand (average revenue) schedule. In pure competition, the demand schedule does not change when a firm increases its output, but in a monopoly the demand curve declines with increased output. Our analyses of

Figures 5–7 and 5–8 showed that the firm can maximize its profit or minimize its loss by producing at the point where *MC* equals *MR* (or as close to that point as possible, without going beyond it). We stated that the same rule applies to firms in imperfect competition. Let us test the rule just one more time by studying Figure 6–2.

First, note that the monopolist can make a profit over a wide range of outputs. The average total cost (*ATC* curve) is below price (the *D* curve) when the firm is producing more than 1 unit and less than 6. In this case, the firm can make a profit by producing any quantity from 2 to 5 units. Marginal cost equals marginal revenue at about 4 units of output, however. It is here that the *MC* curve (the broken line) crosses the *MR* curve (the solid line). The firm's total revenue is $81 at this point (*P* of $20.25 times *Q* of 4). The *ATC* curve shows us that average total cost at this point is $14.50. Total cost, then, is $58 (*ATC* of $14.50 times *Q* of four). Profit is $23, the difference between total revenue and total cost.

Suppose the firm produces 5 units at a price of $17. Here total revenue is $85, total cost is $70, and the firm's profit is only $15. At 3 units of output, total revenue would be $70.50 (*P* of $23.50 times *Q* of 3), total cost would be $48

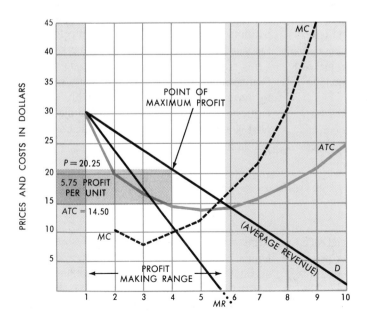

Figure 6–2 The monopolist's costs, prices, and profits

Although the monopolist can make a profit at any point where the *ATC* curve lies below the *D* curve, profit is maximized by producing up to the point at which *MC* crosses *MR* (4 units of output, in this case). The shaded area indicates profit. At 4 units of output, price is $5.75 above average total cost. Total profit is $23.00— $5.75 times *Q* of 4. To test the rule that the firm can maximize profit at the point where *MC* equals *MR*, compute the firm's profits at other levels of output.

Table 6–2   The monopolist's profit position

Q	P	Total revenue ($P \times Q$)	Total cost ($ATC \times Q$)	Profit or loss
1	$30.00	$30.00	$30.00	breaks even
2	26.75	53.50	40.00	$13.50
3	23.50	70.50	48.00	22.50
4	20.25	81.00	58.00	23.00 (max. profit)
5	17.00	85.00	70.00	15.00
6	13.75	82.50	87.00	4.50 (loss)

(*ATC* of $16 times *Q* of 3), and profit would be $22.50. Obviously, the firm maximizes its profit by producing at the point where marginal cost equals marginal revenue. Table 6–2 summarizes the situation.

The same principle would apply if the monopolist were operating at a loss. The loss would be minimized by producing up to the point at which *MC* equals *MR*.

Disadvantages of Monopoly

Why do so many economists object to monopolies? A careful study of Figure 6–2 compared with Figure 5–10 should reveal some of the reasons. In pure competition, there is a very efficient allocation of productive resources in the long run. The typical firm is producing at the lowest point on its average total cost curve as shown in Figure 5–10, and the price per unit is just high enough to cover the costs of production. The firm makes no pure profit. Compare this with the monopolist's situation.

As Figure 6–2 shows, the monopolist is producing at a point (4 units of output) where the average total cost curve (*ATC*) is *not* at its lowest point. The plant is not being used with maximum efficiency. (This would be at an output of 5, the lowest point on the *ATC* curve.) By producing 4 units, the monopolist maximizes profits. A pure profit of $5.75 per unit is made by the monopolist. Whereas a buyer would be getting the product at cost in a purely competitive market, in the monopoly market the buyer pays more than it cost to produce the product. The consumer gets fewer products and pays a higher price.

The monopolist does not use as many productive resources as could be used. (Firms in imperfectly competitive markets often operate below capacity.) Factors of production that could be employed in the monopoly firms are left to be used elsewhere, where perhaps they are used less efficiently. It is also charged that monopolies aggravate inequalities in incomes. The monopoly firm gets a higher price than the firm in pure competition, even if the firm in pure competition has the same production costs. The owners of large firms are usually people of wealth, so the high profits obtained because of monopoly power go to those who are already comfortably situated. Critics of monopoly power claim that the monopolist is enriched at the expense of the consuming public in general.

B Oligopoly

When there are few sellers in an industry and each seller is large enough to affect the market price, an oligopoly exists. The individual firm in an oligopoly market, however, must be aware of the possible effects of its own actions on the other firms in the industry. Many big industries in the United States are oligopolies; that is, a few firms account for most of the industry's output. An oligopoly is indicated by a high *ratio of concentration*. One common measure is the *market ratio of concentration,* which gives the percentage of total production or sales accounted for by the four largest firms in the industry. There may be hundreds of firms in an industry, creating the impression that competition prevails; but if a few giants account for most of the industry's output, shipments, or sales, the industry would be classified as an oligopoly. Table 6–3 provides some criteria for evaluating the market situation.

 Oligopoly: an industry dominated by a few producers or sellers.

It is hard to generalize about oligopolies except to say that all oligopoly markets are dominated by a few sellers and that the sellers must recognize their interdependence. Some oligopolies are huge industries with a national or international market. The automobile industry is an oligopoly, for example, and so are the petroleum refining and steel industries. In a recent year, the total sales of a single firm in the petroleum industry were over $100 billion. The power of relatively few huge corporations is indicated by the fact that 200 large corporations account for over 60 percent of all assets in manufacturing.

In the oligopolies of some industries, the product is not standardized. There is a difference, for example, between the automobiles produced by Ford and those produced by General Motors. In other oligopolies, product standardization is common. Steel of a certain type is much the same, regardless of which firm produces it. Although we usually think of oligopolies as huge industries that have a profound impact on the national or even on the world economy, some are relatively small. Thus, if there are only a few dairies in a particular region, an oligopoly exists in the market for dairy products in that area. Many oligopolies, however, are the type of business in which large-scale production is required and it is difficult for a small firm to enter the industry.

Demand, Marginal Revenue, and Marginal Cost

In any event, one of the most important facts about an oligopoly is that an individual firm cannot change its price without affecting the other firms in the industry. The demand curve for the industry is downward-sloping, and the demand curve for each firm is downward-sloping. An individual firm's curve is not identical to the curve for the industry, however. The individual firm will probably not achieve a lasting gain by cutting the price.

Table 6–3 Criteria for evaluating market conditions

Type of market	Number of sellers	Type of product	Ease of entry
Pure competition	Very many	Standardized	Very easy
Monopolistic competition	Many	Differentiated	Fairly easy
Oligopoly	Few	Some standardized (steel); some differentiated (autos)	Difficult
Monopoly	One	Standardized	Very difficult or impossible*

*If another seller entered this market, a monopoly would no longer exist. One more seller would make the market a "duopoly"; three or more sellers would make it an oligopoly or one of the other types of markets.

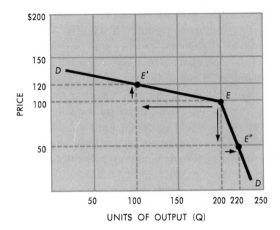

Figure 6–3   The "kinked" demand curve of an oligopoly firm

When an individual firm in an oligopoly market attempts a price increase while its competitors hold the line, it can expect a more-than-proportional decline in sales. In this case, the price is increased from $100 to $120, and sales drop from 200 to 100 units. When the firm tries to lower the price from $100 to $50, it experiences a less-than-proportional rise in sales because its competitors also reduce their prices.

The immediate result might be a large gain in sales at the expense of its competitors, but this gain will be temporary. Its rivals can quickly cut their prices and win back their former customers. Price cutting, then, can bring lower profits or losses to all firms in the industry.

If an individual firm raises its price and the other firms continue to sell at the original market price, that individual firm will lose customers; its sales will decline sharply. For these reasons, the individual firm in an oligopoly rarely raises or lowers the price.

Examine Figure 6–3, which depicts the "kinked" demand curve for an oligopolistic firm. Assume that the going unit price in this oligopolistic market is $100 and that the firm in question sells 200 units. (See point E.) Its total revenue is $20,000. Now it tries raising its price to $120. The competitors continue to sell the same product for $100, however, so our firm's sales drop from 200 to 100. (See point E'.) Its total revenue falls to $12,000. When the oligopoly firm raises the

price unilaterally, demand tends to be *elastic*—the percentage drop in sales is greater than the percentage increase in price. Now suppose that this firm attempts to undercut the competition by dropping its price to $50. But the competitors reduce their prices accordingly, or perhaps sell for even less. Thus the firm's sales rise, but only to 220 units. (See point E".)

Our firm's total revenues are now only $11,000 (price of $50 times quantity of 220). Thus, when the oligopoly firm attempts a price reduction, the demand for its output tends to be *inelastic*—the percentage increase in sales is less than the percentage drop in price.

Deriving the "Kinked" Demand Curve

Let us now consider the derivation of the "kinked" demand curve. Examine Figure 6–4. The heavy curve labeled D_I is the demand curve for the entire industry. The color curve, labeled D_F, is the demand curve for the single firm; note that it is

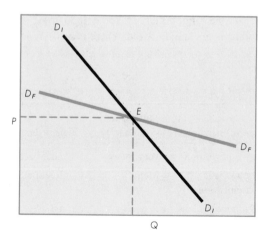

Figure 6–4   Derivation of the "kinked" demand curve

The curve D_I is the demand curve for the whole industry. The curve D_F is the demand curve for a single firm in the industry in an oligopoly market situation. Point E indicates where price and output will be. The "kinked" demand curve for an oligopoly firm will start at D_F, extend to point E, and on down to D_I.

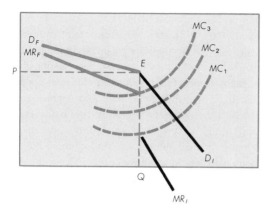

Figure 6–5   Demand, marginal revenue, and marginal cost curves in an oligopoly situation

The "kinked" curve is the same as that illustrated in Figure 6–4. MR_F is the marginal revenue curve derived from demand curve D_F. MR_I is the marginal revenue curve derived from curve D_I. Curve D_F prevails if the firm tries to gain an advantage over its rivals by raising its price. Curve D_I prevails if the firm tries to gain an advantage by reducing its price. Marginal cost can range from MC_1 to MC_3 with no change in the firm's price or output.

crosses the marginal revenue curve (MR)? Remember, in the imperfectly competitive firm the marginal revenue curve will be below the demand curve, as we saw in Figure 6–1. Because we now have *two* demand curves to contend with, where will the marginal revenue curve be? As Figure 6–5 shows, we actually have a break in the marginal revenue curve. The curve MR_F is derived from the demand curve D_F—the single firm's demand curve. The curve MR_I is derived from demand curve D_I—the entire industry's demand curve. The marginal cost curve (MC) can actually be at the top of the MR_I curve (see MC_1), at the bottom of the MR_F curve (see MC_3), or at any point in between (such as MC_2). Thus the firm's marginal cost can vary over a wide range with no change in output or price.

Price

Prices in an oligopoly are often quite rigid, changing only when all the firms in the industry change at the same time. The monopoly firm and the firm in pure competition, if they know their demand schedules, can tell what will happen to the price if they change their output. The monopoly firm does not have to worry about what competitors will do, as there are no competitors. The firm in pure competition knows it can change its output without affecting the price. The oligopoly firm, however, can never be quite certain about what its rivals will do. It is less able to predict what its demand schedule will be and what marginal revenue will be. It is not so easy to find that level of output for which marginal revenue equals marginal cost.

The fear of a destructive "price war" that will hurt everyone in the industry usually prevents price competition in an oligopoly. There is sometimes a tacit agreement whereby everyone watches the "price leader" and charges whatever it charges. The usual result is that the price will be above the point where the ATC curve is at its minimum. The oligopoly firm often makes pure profits and fails to produce at its most efficient point. The price will generally be higher than it would be in pure

much more elastic than the D_I curve. If the firm could reduce its price without its competitors' responding, then that firm could greatly increase its sales by reducing its price below P. Because the others *will* respond, however, the firm is confronted by the industry demand curve, D_I. Its own demand curve applies if it tries to raise its price above P, but the industry's demand curve applies if it tries to drop its price *below P*. Thus we find the "kinked" curve, which starts at point D_F near the vertical axis, goes to the "kink," point E, and then extends down curve D_I.

> "Kinked" demand curve: the demand curve for a firm in an oligopoly—a curve showing that others in the industry will *not* follow suit if the firm raises its price, but *will* follow suit if it lowers its price. That is, demand is elastic if the firm raises its price, but is inelastic if the firm lowers its price.

But what about the rule that firms produce at the point where their marginal cost curve (MC)

competition, but lower than it would be if a pure monopoly existed. (Some firms in an oligopoly do better than others. Recently, one firm in the auto industry failed to pay dividends, whereas other auto firms were making profits.) If the firms in an oligopoly face the same (or very similar) cost and demand situations, they will probably act jointly (engage in collusion) to maximize their joint profits. In such a case Figure 6–2 (describing a pure monopoly) will apply.

There are elements of competition in an oligopoly. It is always possible that new firms will enter the industry if high profits are being enjoyed.[1] Nonprice competition, in the form of attempts to provide a higher-quality product, better services to customers, or advertising, may exist. Individual firms may develop better productive techniques or better products in an attempt to earn

high profits without touching off a disastrous price war. Oligopoly firms have often acted together in a way that has harmed the public and violated the antitrust laws, but they have also been responsible for many improvements in technology and products that have ultimately benefited society as a whole. The oligopoly probably produces fewer goods, employs fewer factors of production, operates at a less efficient point, and charges higher prices than would a purely competitive industry. It is quite possible, however, that some industries would perform no better as purely competitive industries than they do as oligopolies. It is hard to imagine thousands of small steel mills operating efficiently, for the steel industry is one in which economies are achieved through large-scale production. A few economists (such as J. M. Clark) have argued that a degree of monopoly is preferable to cutthroat competition in certain industries. In recent years, however, some U.S. oligopolies have faced intense competition from foreign industries.

[1]Where massive amounts of capital are required (as in steel and auto production), entry of new firms is unlikely.

Can Cartels Always Raise Prices?

A cartel, loosely defined, is a group of producers who "attempt to control the price of a commodity by regulating its supply." Several such producer associations were formed by third-world (poor) nations in the 1970s, and they caused the prices of such commodities as oil, cocoa, and tin to rise. Between 1980 and 1985, however, prices of several commodities dropped, and some of the cartels began to disintegrate. Members of the International Cocoa Agreement were no longer able to support world cocoa

prices because large crops raised the supply and put downward pressure on prices. Indeed, the soaring prices of the 1970s encouraged producers to increase their output, thus contributing to the glut of the mid-1980s. It should be noted, however, that prices would probably have dropped even further if it were not for the existence of the cartels.

(Source: Adapted from James Sterngold, "A Time of Crisis for Cartels," *The New York Times*, December 3, 1985, pp. D1 and D7.)

C Monopolistic Competition

Monopolistic competition has many of the characteristics of pure competition. Firms in the industry are many, and entry of new firms into the industry is often very easy. It is difficult for the firms to act in concert because there are so many and they may not recognize their interdependence. Each firm accounts for only a small part of the industry's total output, with the result that the individual firm has little control over market price. A single firm's actions may have little effect on the industry as a whole, although its influence can be greater than that of the firm in pure competition. A chief difference between monopolistic competition and pure competition is that product differentiation exists in the former. There is some sort of difference between the products of the competing firms. The difference can be in styling (as in women's garments), quality, color, packaging of the product, or merely brand name. However slight these differences may be, they do suffice to remove the industry from the realm of pure competition. The product of one firm can be a close substitute for the product of another firm, but the individual firm *does* have an element of monopolistic control over its own product. Thus a single firm can cause a slight change in the market price if it changes its output. A certain amount of price competition may be found, but there will also be nonprice competition in the form of advertising, services, and packaging.

> Monopolistic competition: a situation in which there are many sellers of an item and it is easy for others to enter the field, but the products of the firms are not identical and an individual firm may be able to influence the price. This type of market is very common in the United States.

Demand, Marginal Revenue, and Marginal Cost

The demand curve for an individual firm in monopolistic competition is not the same as the demand curve for the industry. A firm's demand curve will not be perfectly elastic, as in pure competition, but will likely be highly elastic. Certainly it will be much more elastic than the demand curve of a pure monopolist. If the individual firm reduces its price, it will increase its sales by a considerable amount, for its product is very similar to the products of its competitors. If the individual firm raises its price, on the other hand, it will lose sales, for its customers can easily obtain good substitutes. The few customers it retains may be accounted for by such factors as preference for the firm's packaging, brand-name loyalty, habit, and the like.

Like the monopoly firm, the firm in monopolistic competition will find that its marginal revenue curve lies below the demand curve. If the firm increases its output, it must expect to sell at a lower price. Again, this means that the amount added to the total revenue by each additional unit sold will be less than the amount added by the preceding unit. Figure 6–6 shows the firm's demand and marginal revenue curves. The entire industry's demand curve, of course, would be much steeper (less elastic).

In Figure 6–6 we have dispensed with the figures on the axes. It should no longer be necessary to prove to the reader that the firm's most profitable level of output is where MC crosses MR. The curve MC crosses MR at output Q_e on the horizontal axis. The demand curve shows that price at that point will be P_e. Note that the demand curve is tangent to the ATC curve in this case. This means that the firm is making no *pure* (or economic) profit. Average total cost just equals price at Q_e units of output, so the firm is just covering its costs. This need not always be the case.

In the short run, the typical firm in the monopolistically competitive market may enjoy pure profits. The ATC curve would then be *below* the demand curve, as in Figure 5–7 and Figure 6–2. But it is easy for new firms to enter the industry; business people would be attracted to the field by these high profits. As with pure com-

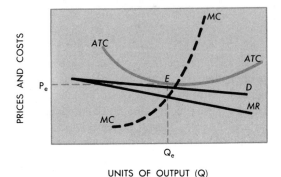

UNITS OF OUTPUT (Q)

Figure 6–6   Price-output adjustment of the firm in monopolistic competition

The typical firm in monopolistic competition has a highly (but not perfectly) elastic demand curve. Like the monopoly firm, it must accept a lower price if it increases its output. To maximize its profit, the firm produces to the point at which $MC = MR$. The price P_e is slightly higher and the quantity Q_e is slightly less than would be the case in pure competition. Note that the firm is not producing at its most efficient point, which would be at the very bottom of the ATC curve. How would this diagram change if demand for the industry's product increased?

petition, too many firms might enter, increasing the total supply and forcing the market price down. Now the ATC curve for the typical firm would be *above* the demand curve at all points. Losses would become typical in the industry, and firms would begin to leave. Eventually, things would settle at a point where the demand curve is tangent to the ATC curve, as is shown in Figure 6–6.

The firm is making no pure profit, but just covering its cost (which includes the *normal profit* necessary to keep the owner in the industry). A long-run equilibrium exists; the normal profit is not high enough to induce other entrepreneurs to enter the industry nor low enough to force existing firms to leave. Although this situation seems very similar to pure competition, further study of Figure 6–6 will show that the presence of an element of monopoly power *does* have an effect.

When long-run equilibrium exists, the typical firm in *pure competition* produces at the minimum point on its average total cost curve. In Figure 6–6 the firm is producing slightly to the left of that point. Thus it is not producing at its most

efficient point. Total output is slightly below what it would be in pure competition. The price is a bit higher than it would be in pure competition also. The firm cannot operate at any other point, however, without suffering losses. To make normal profits and to prevent losses, the firm is forced to produce at a level of output lower than its point of greatest efficiency. Thus, cost and price are higher than they would be in a purely competitive market. The consumer pays for these economic wastes.

On the other hand, the firm in monopolistic competition must often try to improve the product or offer better service so that it can compete with its rivals. It will also advertise in the hope of increasing its share of the total market. The consumer may derive some benefit from a wider variety of styles or differences in quality that result from monopolistic competition. One of the best examples of monopolistic competition is in the women's garment industry,[2] where slight differences in styling are important to the consumer. There is more choice in monopolistic competition than in pure competition, where the product is completely standardized. The public may benefit from improvements in the product. The consumer ultimately bears the cost of advertising, however, and although advertising plays a useful role in our economy, many economists charge that too much is spent on it. Finally, critics of monopolistic competition charge that oligopolies can develop from such competition, as the weaker firms fall by the wayside and the few remaining strong firms capture increasingly large shares of the market.

An International Perspective

The picture we have painted of imperfectly competitive markets is somewhat simplified. For example, in discussing the monopoly we have been assuming that one firm, with one plant, produces one product instead of assuming that a firm may have many plants and produce many products. Another assumption we have made is that we are

[2]The ratio of concentration in the women's dress industry is only 19—that is, the four largest firms account for only 19% of the value of shipments in the industry.

in a closed economy—U.S. firms produce only for a U.S. market. In reality, of course, markets are often international in scope, and the ownership of many firms has become international as well.

As we mentioned in Chapter 4, many corporations are now international (or multinational) companies with offices and plants in dozens of other countries. Many are owned, at least in part, by foreigners.[3] Some corporations are forming "joint ventures" with foreign firms. For example, General Motors has formed a joint venture with Toyota to manufacture Corolla-based Chevrolets. Can we say, then, that the ratio of concentration for the U.S. automobile industry is 93? The automobile industry has become, in fact, an international oligopoly. By 1982 the Japanese had captured nearly 25 percent of the automobile market in the United States. Hundreds of thousands of foreign cars are being built in the United States, either in plants owned by foreign firms or in facilities owned jointly by U.S. and foreign manufacturers.

Production is often international as well. Parts may be manufactured in one country, assembled in a second, and packaged in a third. In the electronics industry, for instance, circuits have been printed on silicon wafers in California, then shipped to Asia to be cut into tiny chips and bonded to circuit boards, then sent back to the United States to be assembled into calculators. Thus, the problems of studying market situations and production costs are becoming more difficult. Nevertheless, the models presented in this chapter can be used as analytical tools. Each case must be judged on its own merits. In some instances the power of a U.S. oligopoly may be lessened by foreign competition; in other cases the phenomenon of the multinational corporation or the joint venture may make an oligopoly even stronger.

---

[3] Direct foreign investment in the United States exceeds $60 billion. (Direct investment means that a foreign firm owns 10 percent or more of a U.S. company.)

REVIEW MODEL

Long-Run Equilibrium

■ Although we have examined long-run equilibrium before, let us review the basic principles. Assume that Graphs A, B, and C depict the situation of a typical firm in an industry. Perfect competition prevails. Thus in each graph the firm's demand (and marginal revenue) curve is perfectly horizontal. The firm must accept whatever price exists in the market—it cannot affect market price by its own actions alone. An increase or decrease in the individual firm's output will have no effect on the market price. If output changes for the industry as a whole, there will be a change in price. This is reflected by the fact that the firm's demand (and marginal revenue) curve is different in each of the three graphs.

In Graph A, the firm is making pure profits. Average total cost (the *ATC* curve) is below the market price over a wide range of output. The firm can make above-normal profits by producing more than Q_a or less than Q_b units of output. (At what point will the firm produce to *maximize* its profit?)

When pure profits prevail in an industry, other firms enter the field. This increases the industry's total output and—other things being equal—brings a reduction in the market price. The new situation is shown in Graph B. Here the firm's average total cost and marginal cost curves have not changed, but the market price has dropped from P_p to P_l. It is now impossible for the firm to make a profit, because its average total cost is *above* the market price at all points. The best the firm can do is to minimize its loss. (At what point will it produce to do this?)

Because the typical firm in the industry is operating at a loss, many firms leave the field. These departures cause a reduction in supply and a rise in the market price. Finally we arrive at the price (P_e) in Graph C. Again, the firm's *ATC* and *MC* curves have not changed. Now the price the firm is receiving for its product just equals the cost of producing that product, where the average total cost is at its lowest point. The firm must produce Q_e units of output, for it is here that the firm's marginal cost just equals the price. If the firm produces at any other level of output, it will surely incur a loss. The price it is now receiving just covers the production costs, including "normal" profit—a profit just high enough to keep the firm in the field but not high enough to attract other firms into the industry. The firm is in long-run equilibrium. It is producing at its most efficient point (the bottom of the *ATC* curve), and the buyer is in effect getting the product for what it cost to produce it.

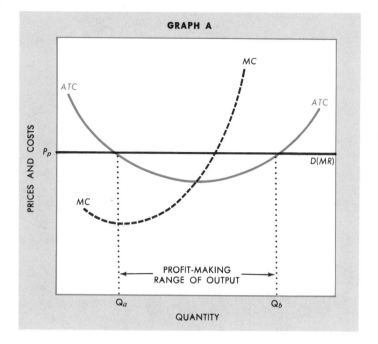

■ The firm in this perfectly competitive industry is making pure profits. The price (P_p for profitmaking price) is above average total cost over a wide range of output. The firm makes a profit as long as it produces more than Q_a units of output and less than Q_b units of output. (Identify the point on the horizontal axis at which the firm will actually produce to maximize its profit.)

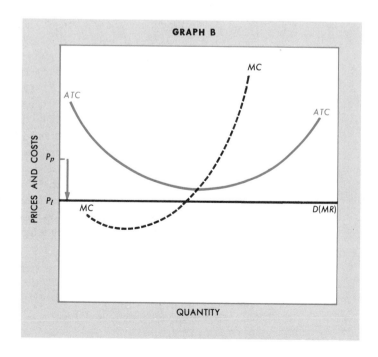

■ Because high profits have attracted other firms into the industry, supply rises and price falls from P_p and P_l (for loss-producing price). Now the typical firm cannot make a profit since the cost of each unit of output (the ATC) is above price (P_l) at all points. (Identify the point at which the firm can minimize its losses.)

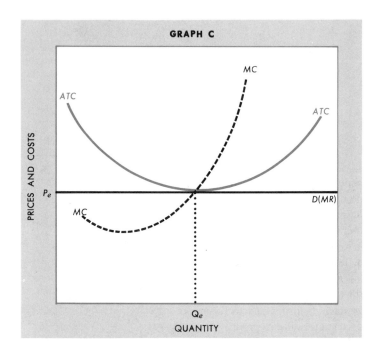

■ With the typical firm taking a loss, there has been a "shake-out" in the industry because many firms have left the field. This reduces supply again, and the *equilibrium price* (P_e) at which the firm just barely covers the unit cost is finally reached. There are no pure profits, and the firm's "normal" profit is just high enough to keep it in the field but not high enough to attract new competitors. The firm is producing at its most efficient point (the lowest point on the *ATC* curve).

■ Now we have a situation that is somewhat more complex because the firm we are analyzing is not in a perfectly competitive market situation. Monopolistic competition prevails. Note that in Graph D the firm's demand curve *D* slopes downward. It must accept a lower price for its product if it increases its output. Its marginal revenue *MR* is not the same as price (the *D* curve). The firm is doing well, however, for the *ATC* curve is below the *D* curve over a wide range. As long as it produces more than Q_1 units and less than Q_3 units, the firm makes a profit. It maximizes its profits by producing Q_2 units of output. (Why?) The firm is enjoying pure profits—profits higher than those needed to keep it in the industry. What price is the firm receiving for its product, P_a or P_b? Why?

But the situation will change because there are many producers of the product in question. The only difference, perhaps, is that the manufacturers use different brand names and different packaging. It is fairly easy for new firms to enter the industry. Attracted by the high profits being made by existing firms, new companies enter the field. Assume that the average total cost, *ATC,* and marginal cost, *MC,* for the firm in Graph D remain the same. Because of the entry of new firms, however, the quantity of goods available for sale rises and the market price drops. See Graph E. Our firm's *D* and *MR* curves drop. By producing at Q_e units of output, our firm just barely covers its costs (which include a modest normal profit), and it receives a lower price (P_e) than before.

Draw curves of your own to show what will happen if the firm's average total cost rises while *D* remains the same, and if *D* drops even further while *ATC* remains the same.

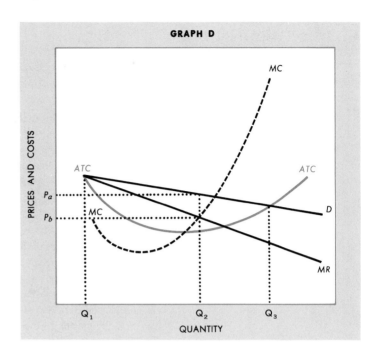

■   This firm in a monopolistically competitive market is making pure profits because its *ATC* curve is below its demand curve over a wide range of output—between Q_1 and Q_3. Why does it limit production to Q_2 units of output? Why not produce more— say, Q_3 units? Assume that this situation is typical of firms in the industry. Why does this situation tend to induce new companies to enter the field? How will the new firms change the picture?

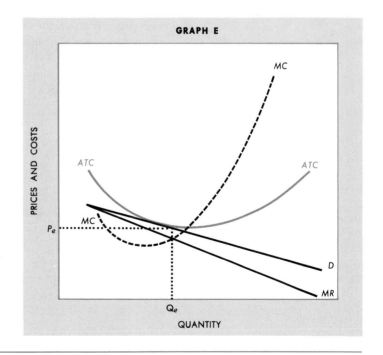

■   The firm is no longer making pure, or above-normal, profits. By producing at Q_e units of output, it just covers its costs. Yet this situation differs from the situation of the firm in perfect competition. Compare this graph with Graph C. Why does the firm in perfect competition (Graph C) produce at its most efficient point (the bottom of its *ATC* curve), whereas the firm in Graph E fails to do so? Why does the *D* curve slope downward in Graphs D and E but not in Graphs A, B, and C? Why is the *MR* curve the same as the *D* curve in Graphs A, B, and C but not in Graphs D and E?

Chapter Highlights

1. A monopoly exists when there is only one firm selling a product and there is no close substitute for that product. Pure monopolies are rare, however.

2. An oligopoly exists when there are a few sellers in an industry, each large enough to affect the market price.

3. Monopolistic competition is similar to pure competition in that there are many firms producing a product and entry into the industry is fairly easy. There is some product differentiation, however, and an individual firm can cause a change in the market price by changing its output.

4. In imperfectly competitive situations (monopoly, oligopoly, and monopolistic competition), a firm's marginal revenue will be less than its price, or average revenue. A firm's demand curve will slope downward.

5. Monopolists tend to use fewer resources than they could, produce fewer goods, and earn above-normal profits.

6. Many large industries in the United States are oligopolies. An oligopoly exists where there is a high *ratio of concentration*—the four largest firms in an industry produce or sell 50 percent or more of the industry's total output.

7. Although the firms in an oligopoly may compete through advertising or developing new techniques and better products, they rarely engage in price competition for fear of a "price war" that will hurt them all.

8. Firms in imperfect competition (monopolies, oligopolies, and monopolistically competitive firms) probably produce less than they could, with the result that the market price is higher than it would be in pure competition. These firms fail to produce at their most efficient points—the minimum point on the average total cost curve.

9. Many oligopolies are now international in scope, and some large U.S. firms have formed joint ventures with large foreign companies.

Study Aids

Key Terms

imperfect competition
monopoly
oligopoly
monopolistic competition
ratio of concentration

market ratio of concentration
"kinked" demand curve
"price war"
"price leader"
product differentiation

nonprice competition
brand-name loyalty
joint venture
multinational corporation

Questions

1. Define the terms monopoly, oligopoly, and monopolistic competition.

2. Why is it difficult to find an example of a pure monopoly in our economy?

3. Why does the demand curve for a firm in imperfect competition slope downward? What is the significance of this phenomenon?

4. Why does a monopoly firm fail to produce at the minimum point on its average total cost curve?

5. Explain the statement "Firms in an oligopoly must recognize their interdependence."

6. Compare monopolistic competition with pure competition and pure monopoly.

7. Explain the ratio of concentration and how it is measured.

8. Using graphs, show why the demand curve for a firm in an oligopoly market is "kinked."

9. Why is there a "break" in the oligopolist's marginal revenue curve?

10. What are some of the benefits claimed for oligopolies?

11. Explain why a firm in monopolistic competition can make only "normal" profits and yet not be producing at its most efficient point (the bottom of its *ATC* curve).

12. What are some benefits the consumer might derive from the existence of monopolistic competition?

13. How have large foreign corporations affected the market power of U.S. oligopolies?

Problems

1. Study different industries in your area and classify them according to whether they are purely competitive, monopolistic, oligopolistic, or monopolistically competitive. Be prepared to defend your classification by indicating how you have defined the market in each case, the ratio of concentration in each case, profits in each industry, and so on.

2. Locate an article about an antitrust case in a recent issue of a business magazine such as *Fortune* or *Business Week* or on the financial pages of a recent newspaper. Make a study of this case. On what grounds is the firm (or firms) being accused of destroying competition? What economic aspects of the case lend support to the accusation? What aspects tend to weaken the accusation?

3. Graph A following shows the demand and marginal revenue curves for an oligopoly firm.

Graph B shows the demand and marginal revenue curves for the entire industry. Using graph paper (and different colors for each curve), draw these graphs on the same scale—superimpose the curves in Graph B on Graph A. With a dotted line, identify the firm's demand curve if we assume that the other firms in the industry will respond to its attempt to cut prices. With a dashed line, identify the marginal revenue curve. What is the significance of the fact that the *MR* curve in Graph B goes below the horizontal axis? On the graphs as you have redrawn them, locate the price that will be charged and the quantity that will be produced. Mark the range over which the marginal cost curve can shift with no change in price or output.

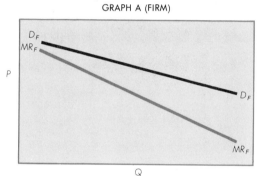

GRAPH A (FIRM)

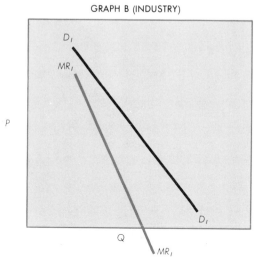

GRAPH B (INDUSTRY)

Labor:
Its Uses and
Rewards

The production of goods results from putting factors of production together to turn out the materials and services society wants. We have just seen how business represents supply when it goes to the market with goods and services, and how it represents demand when it goes to the market for the factors of production. In this chapter we will concentrate on the market concerned with the factors of production—in particular with the factor of labor.

In addition to representing human value, labor represents, in dollars, our most valuable resource. Because resources are limited, we must choose how they are allocated. Just as prices, which result from the interaction of supply and demand, help in allocating our production, wages (the price for labor) help in allocating our supply of labor. Many factors influence the demand and supply of labor. Some of these factors interfere with the mechanism of the classical model of capitalism. It is pertinent now to look at the causes and the consequences of changes in the status of labor, with particular attention to the roles of government and labor unions.

Chapter Objectives

When you have completed this chapter, you should be able to:

- Define labor as a factor of production.
- Describe the composition of the U.S. labor force and identify current trends in participation rates by such groups as women and young people.
- Define productivity and discuss its relation to wages and standard of living.
- Describe how wage rates are determined under the classical model of capitalism.
- Explain the impact of unions and minimum wage laws on wage rates.
- Suggest at least two factors that could lead to unionism.
- Explain the causes of friction in labor-management relations and list the main weapons each side uses in dealing with the other.
- Identify some of the new approaches to work and discuss their possible implications.

A The Role of Labor in Production

What Is Labor?

Labor is one of the four factors of production. Its responsibility is to take natural resources and man-made instruments of production and fashion them into products that businesses want for sale to consumers. Labor is human effort used in creating value to satisfy wants. The value that labor creates varies from country to country, region to region, and job to job. For examples of wage and earnings differentials, see Table 7–1. Value from labor can be increased by providing tools (capital) and skills (education) for workers to use. The human effort, shaped by the skills necessary for production, is what businesses bid for when they seek labor's services in the market for the factors of production.

You should not think of labor involving only physical effort. The role of labor has changed as manufactured energy has been substituted for human energy in the production of goods.

Managers who receive salaries and people who are self-employed must also be considered labor. The economist considers that self-employed people in effect pay themselves a wage or salary, because if they performed the same work for someone else, they would be paid.

 Labor: all human effort that is used to produce goods and services.

Unique Qualities of Labor

The foregoing description of labor places it in the classical model without differentiating it from the other factors of production. Actually, labor has at least two characteristics that make it unique. First, labor cannot be separated from human beings. This means that, as a factor of production, labor has feelings and is capable of independent action. Second, labor has the means of buying back the goods and services produced. Machines are not sensitive to the surroundings in which they are used, and if they are not used today, they can frequently make up for the lost output at some other time. The same may be said about most natural resources. Moreover, none of the other factors is also a consumer.

The supply of labor tends to be inelastic, particularly for a short period. This is more true of skilled labor than of unskilled labor, since several years may be needed to develop the talent necessary to perform skilled work acceptably. Another factor contributing to the inelasticity of labor is

Table 7–1   Wage and earnings differentials: What is labor worth?

Industry Differentials

Labor is worth more (on the average) in some industries than in others. In the mid-1980s, the average annual earnings of employees in each of five industries were as follows:

Mining	$28,518
Transportation	23,434
Construction	21,835
Manufacturing	21,075
Finance, Insurance, Real Estate	18,921

(Includes executive pay, bonuses, tips, and payments in kind.)

Regional Differentials

Labor is worth more in some geographic locations than in others. In the mid-1980s, the average hourly earnings of electricians engaged in maintenance jobs in each of four cities were as follows:

San Francisco, California	$14.09
Chicago, Illinois	13.56
Newark, New Jersey	12.59
Jackson, Mississippi	11.33

Job Differentials

Labor is worth more in some jobs than in others. The average weekly earnings in each of five occupations within one broad industrial classification in the mid-1980s were as follows:

Secretaries	$387.00
Stenographers	336.50
Accounting clerks	305.50
Typists	264.50
File clerks	228.00

(In Houston, Texas, May 1984.)

Sex Differentials

Male labor is worth more than female labor. In spite of legislation that prohibits wage differences based on sex, women often receive less than men do for performing essentially the same jobs. Great caution must be used in interpreting sex differential figures and other data suggesting discrimination based on sex, race, ethnic group, etc. Such factors as training, experience, and seniority may account for part of the wage or salary differential. Even after all these variables have been taken into account, however, we find clear evidence of discrimination. During one recent year, the median earnings of women were well below those of comparably employed men in many fields. Female earnings represented the following percentages of male earnings in the following areas:

Field or job	Female earnings as percentage of male earnings
Professional and technical	64%
Managers and administrators	58%
Clerical workers	62%
Sales workers	50%

(For full-time year-round workers.)

Sources: U.S. Departments of Labor and Commerce.

the low degree of mobility of the worker. Returning to our satellite computer, we find that it may suggest offering the worker more dollars than he or she is currently earning to induce him or her to move from one section of the country to another. However, workers may prefer to remain where they are because they have established roots in the community.

Another difference between labor and the other factors of production is illustrated by the backward-sloping labor supply curve shown in Figure 7–1. The law of supply tells us that more items will be offered for sale as the price rises. The wage rate is the "price" of labor. As Figure 7–1

shows, more hours of labor are offered for sale as the wage rate rises, because more people enter the labor market to earn that higher wage or because existing workers agree to work overtime. The *substitution effect* is being felt; more people are willing to substitute work for leisure at the higher wage rates. At point *T*, however, a strange thing occurs. As the wage rate goes above $20, *fewer* hours of labor are offered for sale. Now the labor market is experiencing the *income effect*. Because of the higher wage rate, workers can work fewer hours and still enjoy a good level of living and meet their needs and wants. They are willing to trade-off the extra pay for more leisure. (The letter

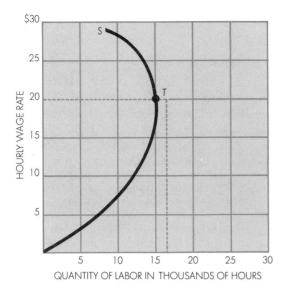

Figure 7–1 The backward-sloping labor supply curve

As the wage rate rises from zero to $20, more hours of labor are offered for sale by workers. At wage rates above $20 (the trade-off point), fewer hours of labor are offered for sale because workers would rather enjoy more leisure than extra income.

T is used to indicate that this is a trade-off on the labor supply curve.) Psychological and cultural factors are important in determining whether a particular worker will exhibit the substitution effect or the income effect. We would not expect the other factors of production to have backward-sloping supply curves. Thus, labor *is* different, and we must take the differences into account in trying to analyze labor in our economy.

Characteristics of the U.S. Labor Force

Of the more than 240 million people in the United States, over 118 million were counted as members of the labor force in 1986. Although this represents only about 49 percent of our total population, a closer look reveals that about 77 percent of the people in the prime working age group (ages 25–54) are in the civilian labor force. About 94 percent of men in the 25–54 age group are in the labor force, and nearly 70 percent of the women in that age group are in the work force.

Women are becoming increasingly important in the labor force. By the 1980s over 42 percent of all workers were women, compared with only about 31 percent in 1953. It is estimated that by 1990 45 percent of the labor force will be women.

The U.S. labor force grew rapidly from World War II to the mid-1980s. Some economists believe that the influx of women and young people into the work force in the late 1970s and early 1980s explains in part the high rates in unemployment. By the mid-1980s, however, the labor force had absorbed people born during the postwar "baby boom." Between 1985 and 1995 the percentage of women between the ages of 16 and 54 in the labor

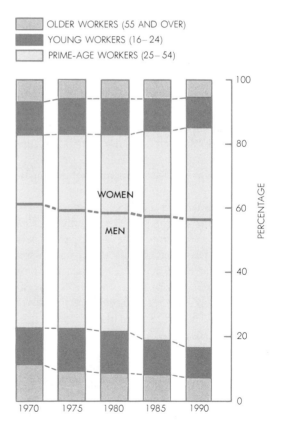

Figure 7–2 Distribution of the civilian labor force

Note the increasing importance of women in the labor force; the greatest growth has been and will be in the prime age group (25–54 years of age). (Source: U.S. Bureau of Labor Statistics.)

force is expected to continue to rise, while the percentage of men in that age group in the work force will probably decline slightly or remain stable. Between 1985 and 1995 about two-thirds of the growth in employment will be accounted for by women. Their labor force participation rates in the 16–54 age group will not exceed those of men, but will come close.

The impact of women in the labor force goes beyond the mere number of new entrants. Many women are entering fields formerly considered to be "masculine." For example, in 1972 only 4 percent of all lawyers were women; now the figure is over 15 percent. Women still holding the traditionally female jobs are demanding pay equity with men. *Comparable worth* is one of the most controversial issues of recent times. Supporters of comparable worth won a key case in the state of Washington, where beauticians working in state institutions were being paid less than barbers. Job analysts have found other disparities between male and female wages for jobs that they considered to be comparable in terms of training, skill, difficulty, and responsibility. For instance, a male mechanic in Washington was receiving $1,462 per month, whereas a female medical-record analyst was receiving only $892 a month. Several states have established commissions to study job classification systems in an effort to identify wage rates that reflect such criteria as training, experience, and responsibility rather than male-female differences. Opponents of comparable worth assert that there is no objective way to compare the worth of two different jobs, that comparable worth schemes will destroy free enterprise, and that wages ought to be determined by market forces.

The "dependency ratio"—the ratio of nonworkers to workers—provides important information about the U.S. labor force. In 1982 the dependency ratio was about 113. That is, for every 100 people in the labor force there were 113 nonworkers those 100 had to support. By 1985 the ratio was about 111 because the number of teenagers (age 13–19) declined and the number of children (those under 13) grew at a slow rate.

The percentage of older persons in the labor force (age 55 and over) has been declining and will probably continue to decline during the late 1980s.

Productivity

Generally, the U.S. labor force is characterized by high productivity. Output per worker-hour has been high because of a well-trained and well-educated labor force, sophisticated technology, ample supplies of capital (tools, machines, factories, and so forth), and managerial efficiency.

 Productivity: output per some unit of input, such as output per hour of labor.

This high productivity has enabled the United States to provide a high level of living for its citizens, to outproduce most other nations and yet have a smaller percentage of the population in the work force, and to support a growing number of retired persons. Table 7–2 gives some evidence of the high level of living U.S. citizens enjoy. In comparison with many other countries, the United States achieves greater output with fewer workers. In agriculture, for example, the USSR has employed eight times as many workers and still achieved lower yields per acre.

Other industrial nations, however, have been experiencing greater average annual percentage changes in output per worker-hour in recent years. Between 1970 and 1980, the productivity increase in manufacturing was greater in Japan, The Netherlands, France, Germany, and Italy than in the United States. The increase in Japan was 102 percent compared with only 28 percent in the United States. The United States experienced a decline in productivity growth between 1977 and 1982. There was a healthy 3.5 percent rise in 1984, but this rise was exceeded by the gains in eight other industrial nations.

Although lagging productivity is a matter of concern, the picture is not entirely bleak. In some of the other nations, *unit labor costs* (the labor costs for each unit of output) in manufacturing rose more rapidly than they did in the United States. Indeed, by 1975, total labor costs per hour in Sweden, Norway, Denmark, and Canada had risen above those in the United States. Unit labor costs in the United States rose about 78 percent in the

Table 7–2 Evidences of the high level of living in the United States

The working hours required for the average manufacturing employee to buy specific goods in each of three countries are listed below.

Item	Washington, D.C.	London, England	Moscow, USSR
Large color TV set	86	177	713
Small refrigerator	43	35	208
Man's suit	20	25	68
Weekly food supply for four people	12.5	21.4	42.3
Man's leather shoes	8	11	33

Source: "What's the Difference?" chart produced by the National Federation of Independent Business.

1970–80 period, while labor costs in Britain, Belgium, West Germany, and France increased over 200 percent and labor costs in Japan rose 192 percent. There was little change in unit labor costs in the United States in 1984, but the labor costs in other industrial nations dropped that year because the U.S. dollar rose in value in relation to other currencies. (When the U.S. dollar rises in relation to a foreign currency, U.S. goods and services become more expensive to the holder of foreign currency. Conversely, similar goods and services in that foreign nation become less expensive to holders of U.S. dollars. We shall have more to say about currency values in Chapter 18.)

An interesting way of evaluating a nation's productivity and level of living is to look at the distribution of its labor force among the categories of occupations. The great increase in the number of white-collar occupations and the equally dramatic reduction in the proportion of blue-collar workers and farmers show that we have far less need than formerly for workers to engage in the physical aspects of production and far more need for workers to supply services rather than goods. (See Figures 7–3 and 7–4.) The fact that farm workers made up fewer than 2.5 percent of the labor force in 1985 and blue-collar workers accounted for less than a fourth can be attributed in large measure to high productivity. Increases in output per worker-hour have made it possible for us to meet our needs for food and other physical goods with smaller and smaller percentages

of our labor force devoted to goods-producing industries. Thus a larger percentage of our work force can concentrate on the production of services.

 Services: intangible goods, such as the work of dentists, lawyers, actors, and athletes.

Importance of Capital to Labor Productivity

In underdeveloped countries, most workers must use a large amount of their energy to provide for the physical necessities of life. Without modern equipment (capital) to work with or the skills

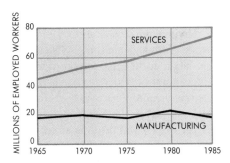

Figure 7–3 Employment trends in goods-producing and service-producing occupations, 1965–1985

In the late 1940s, the number of workers producing services began to exceed the number of workers producing goods. The service-producing industries include transportation and public utilities; finance, insurance, and real estate; wholesale and retail trade; and health. (Source: *Business Week*, July 8, 1985, page 62.)

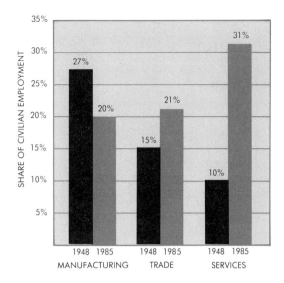

Figure 7–4   Employment trends in three major industrial categories

The percentage of total civilian employment accounted for by manufacturing jobs has declined, whereas that accounted for by trade and service jobs has risen. (Source: U.S. Bureau of Labor Statistics.)

needed to use such tools, few workers can be freed to provide the luxury goods or extra services associated with a high standard of living. With over 35 percent of the USSR's labor force engaged in agriculture and little of the total output available for export, it is easy to see why the USSR has a lower level of living and a lower average productivity than we do. Although the United States uses less land and labor, it uses many more tractors, trucks, grain combines, and other such equipment, and also much more electricity on its farms.

Generally, an increase in the amount of capital available per worker will result in an increase in the output per worker. This relationship applies to service workers as well as to manufacturing employees. Capital investment per worker has soared in many service industries in the last decade, as businesses have purchased new computers, word processors, electronic accounting equipment, telecommunications facilities, and medical testing instruments. Productivity certainly increases with the use of tangible capital items such as these, but improvements in productivity can also be realized by investment in *intangible capital* such as health, education, and better management techniques. Indeed, some economists assert that advances in knowledge and in worker education have contributed more to productivity growth than have increases in tangible capital.

The reduction of the average workweek from 70 hours in 1850 to less than 40 hours today, the fact that today less than 20 cents of the consumer's dollar goes for food as compared with 45 cents in 1901, and the general increase in our level of living are all explained by rising productivity—and rising productivity is explained in large measure by investment in both physical and human capital.

Nations that devote a large percentage of their output to capital investment often show the highest percentage increases in productivity. Between 1962 and 1977 Japan invested 32 percent of its total output in equipment, plants, and the like. Japan's average annual percentage increase in productivity for this period was 8.4 percent. During this same time period the United States devoted only 17.5 percent of its output to capital investment, and the productivity increase averaged only 2.7 percent per year.

In the next section we shall see how productivity affects wages.

B How Wages Are Determined

Wages: Reward for Labor

Wages are the prices paid for human effort. When the price of labor is expressed as payment per hour, per week, or for some other period of time, it is called a *wage rate*. Whether it is called a wage, a salary, or a commission, the payment represents a cost to the employer in return for value created. Payment for labor, in addition to being the most costly factor in production, is the source of about three-fourths of the nation's income. To see how labor earns wages by creating value in the market for the factors of production and then spends these wages in the market for goods and services, refer to the chart of the model in Figure 1–3.

Differences in Wages

When you enter the market as a potential wage earner, you are interested in getting the highest price for the efforts you will perform. If you turn to the "help wanted" section of your newspaper or visit an employment agency, you can get some idea of the wage rate for various jobs. Why is there so much difference in pay for different jobs? Why is it that similar jobs may pay different wages? Wouldn't everyone be better off if all jobs paid more?

Suppose you reverse your role and enter the market as a business person seeking to hire workers. You are now concerned with costs. If you can keep the cost of production down, you can offer your products for sale at a lower price and make a larger profit. Because labor is likely to be your largest cost, you want to employ workers at the lowest possible wage. You will probably ask yourself, What will determine how much I have to pay to get the help I need? How free am I to determine what wages I shall pay? Can higher wages attract labor that can create greater value?

Real Wages and Money Wages

Before we examine what determines wages, we must distinguish between money wages and real wages. The term *money wages* refers to the amount in dollars paid for a given amount of work. The term *real wages* refers to what those dollars will buy in the market for goods and services at a given time. Workers are most interested in real wages. Given a situation in which all who sought employment were working, if most of these workers demanded and received a 10 percent increase in their money wages but did *not* create any additional goods and services, would they be any better off? What would happen to people whose income remained the same?

 Nominal wage: the same as money wage—pay expressed in dollars and cents without regard to purchasing power.

Wages under the Classical Model

We have learned that the laws of supply and demand determine allocation of our resources by interacting to determine price. Here our resource is labor and our price is wages. Let us see how these tools help determine wages.

It is obvious that wages must be related to the value that labor creates. An employer cannot afford to pay workers more than the value they create, for to do so would mean losing money. We must therefore consider labor's productivity. We shall assume that the cost of our other factors of production remains the same and that each worker has equal ability.

Law of Diminishing Returns Influences Wages

Let us use for our illustration the business we started in Chapter 4, "Build-a-City." Our factory has a fixed number of machines, a fixed amount of raw materials coming in each week, and a certain number of hours per week for work. As we start to add workers, we find that even though each worker has the same ability, the value each worker adds to the total product is not the same. At low levels of production, each additional worker adds more to the total value of the product than the preceding worker did; for example, the tenth worker might add $160 to total value whereas the ninth might add only $150. However, we soon see a change. We reach a point where additional units of labor yield decreasing value; for example, the eleventh worker might add $157 to total value and the twelfth worker might add only $154. An increase in the quantities of one factor of production (labor, in this case) in relation to fixed quantities of other factors of production may result in an increase in total output, but eventually the additional output that results from each new addition of that factor will become less and less. This phenomenon is called the *law of diminishing returns*.

Marginal Productivity Related to Wage Rates

Because of the law of diminishing returns, an employer will hire workers up to the point at which the wage received by the last worker equals the value that worker adds to the firm's revenue. We call this principle the *marginal productivity wage theory*. Marginal productivity can be expressed in terms of additional unit output as "marginal physical product," or in terms of money value as "marginal revenue product."

If we keep a record of what each additional worker adds to the value of the total product, we can discover what each worker's marginal productivity is. Figure 7–5 shows the marginal productivity of our workers after the law of diminishing returns has set in. It is also a demand

schedule for labor. Under pure competition, we would hire additional labor as long as the cost to us in wages was not more than the additional value we received.

Maximum Wage

At this point, you might ask why we cannot pay a higher wage, since the value added by workers before the 300th worker is greater than $140. Are these workers being cheated? The answer is *no*. Because every worker in the force of 300 has equal ability and can be interchanged with every other worker, the marginal product of the last worker sets the maximum wage the employer can pay. When a firm is in a purely competitive market where it must meet the competitive market price of other firms, it cannot afford to lose money on any worker.

Here the theory, or model, of marginal productivity has set the pattern for how wages should be determined. Remember, however, that a model is an abstraction of the real world, not the real world itself. Even if we had pure competition, the value added by the last worker could only be estimated by the employer and employee, as neither knows the exact value created by each worker.

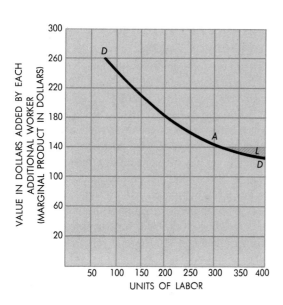

Figure 7–5 Marginal productivity theory applied to labor

Under pure competition, wage rates are determined by marginal productivity. Demand schedule *D* shows the marginal productivity of workers after the law of diminishing returns has set in. With 300 workers *(A)*, the employer can afford to pay $140. The value each additional worker over 300 would create would be less than $140, and the employer would have to either cease hiring or lower wages to the level of the marginal product of the last worker hired. Area *L* is where marginal productivity is below the wage rate ($140).

Effect of Supply and Demand on Wage Rates

The economic tools we have studied can explain the interaction of supply and demand. These tools help explain the equilibrium point for wage rates and the number of workers employed. Figure 7–5 shows the marginal productivity of workers. This is our demand for labor.[1] For a given supply of 300 workers, the equilibrium point for the wage rate is $140 per week. If supply *A* remains the same, how can wages increase? In Figure 7–6 we see that by increasing demand D_2, supply remaining the same (inelastic), we can increase wages to $160 per week. How can demand for the product, and consequently wages, be increased? The

[1] The demand for labor is a derived demand. Consumers do not have a direct demand for auto workers; they demand cars. The auto manufacturers' demand for workers is thus derived from consumers' demand for cars.

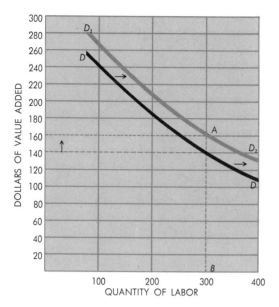

Figure 7–6   Marginal productivity of labor
By increasing demand, with supply of labor remaining the same, wages are increased. Increasing marginal productivity will bring about an increase in demand.

most reliable way would be to increase the productivity of the worker. Our marginal productivity curve, which is our demand curve, would shift upward with greater productivity per worker. Figure 7–7 shows that as output per worker-hour goes up, so do wages.

Factors Affecting the Supply of Labor

The factors affecting the supply of labor are numerous and complex. We can consider only a few of the most important influences. When we seek to hire workers for our "Build-a-City" plant, we shall look for many different kinds of talent. We may need skilled operators of complicated machinery, as well as electricians, plumbers, painters, bookkeepers, salespeople, and unskilled workers. When we enter the labor market, we are seeking particular kinds of labor, not labor generally. Unskilled workers without jobs may want to be employed as machine operators; however, unless they receive specialized training for this

job, they do not count as part of the supply in the market for machine operators.

Skill of the Worker

One of the important problems we face is that we have many different supplies of labor. During recent

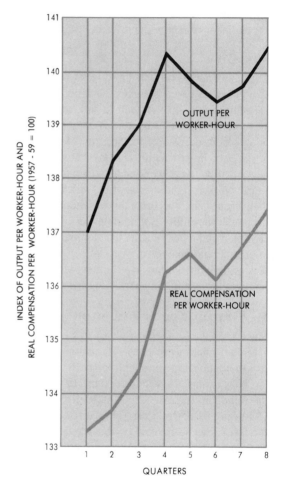

Figure 7–7   Output and compensation per labor-hour
The graph depicts trends in output and real compensation per worker-hour during a recent two-year (eight-quarter) period as compared to the period 1957–59, which has been used as a base. During the first quarter, for example, output per worker-hour was 137, or 37 percent higher than output during the 1957–59 period, while real compensation was about 33.3 percent higher. How is it significant that the two lines tend to follow the same pattern? (Source: U.S. Bureau of Labor Statistics.)

periods we have had high unemployment, but at this same time we have had shortages of engineers, nurses, doctors, and many others whose skills require long periods of training. Unemployment among unskilled workers and among members of minority groups averages two to three times higher than the national rate. Whereas skilled workers can move into the unskilled labor market, unskilled workers have difficulty moving into the skilled labor market without further training.

Mobility

The labor supply is affected by a lack of mobility. Workers who have pleasant associations with a particular job will often tend to stay where they are even though the wage rate is higher in some other place, because of the security of a known position compared with the risk of moving to a new situation. After working for a firm for several years, workers build up seniority, which protects them from being the first laid off when business declines. They may also build up funds in a pension plan and other benefits that companies offer after a certain number of years of service. This lack of mobility is even more limiting when moving involves settling in a new geographic region.

Minimum Wages and Supply

Since 1938 the United States has had laws putting a "floor" under wage rates. The *minimum wage* law the national government passed in that year has been amended several times; the 1977 bill set the minimum wage at $2.90 for 1979, $3.10 for 1980, and $3.35 for 1981. The vast majority of the labor force is covered by this act. Most state governments also have minimum wage laws covering some of the workers not covered by federal statute, but in most cases the state level is below the federal standard.

 Minimum wage: the lowest amount that an employer may legally pay a worker per hour.

Figure 7–8 shows graphically what happens to the supply situation when minimum wage laws exist. Note how the increase in the minimum wage rate decreases the number of workers that employers seek to hire.

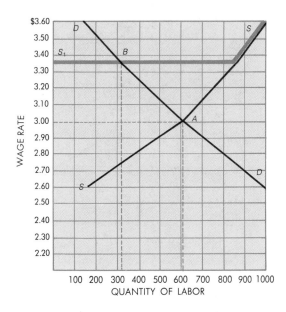

Figure 7–8   Effect of a minimum-wage law
In a free-market situation, the wage rate would tend to settle at $3.00 (point *A*), for here the demand and supply curves for labor intersect. In 1977 a minimum wage law passed, requiring employers to pay $3.35 per hour by 1981 regardless of labor supply conditions. The colored horizontal line at $3.35 depicts this situation. Note that the line crosses the demand curve at point *B*, a quantity of 320, indicating that employers will hire only 320 workers if they must pay the $3.35 rate. (Organized labor disputes this analysis, asserting that past increases in the minimum wage resulted in only a few isolated cases of this sort.)

Economists do not agree on the value of minimum wage laws to labor. Those who argue against these laws point out that such restrictions encourage unemployment. Many employers might want to hire additional workers, but they can do so only if these workers produce at least as much value as they receive. Those who are just entering the labor market or who have very little skill may not be worth the minimum wage rate because they would add less value than they would receive. Because no employer will knowingly hire a worker for more than he or she is worth, the minimum wage law can cause unemployment for those whose productivity is below the general level.

Those who favor the minimum wage law claim

that the lowest-paid wage earners have no one to bargain for them and thus are easily imposed upon by employers. These proponents of the wage law also feel that workers who cannot create sufficient value to be paid the minimum wage rate should not be considered part of the labor force and should qualify for public assistance or training to become more productive. Very low wage rates tend to discourage employers from making their firms more efficient, thus retarding progress. Such rates also tend to reduce incentive among employees.

Labor Unions and Supply of Labor

Labor unions can influence wages by controlling the supply of labor. Some unions, mainly those with highly skilled workers, restrict their membership, thus causing the supply curve to shift to the left. Other unions may be successful in organizing almost all the workers; these unions will try to set a wage rate higher than what it might be under purely competitive conditions. Figure 7–9

shows graphically what happens when union membership is restricted. In such a case, what happens to the number of workers employed? Do you think that this shifting of the supply curve, causing a change in employment, acts as a check on how far unions can raise wages?

Other Factors Influencing Supply

Numerous laws have been passed that have had the effect of reducing the available supply of labor. Although we shall deal with specific labor legislation later, we have listed below some factors that affect the supply:

1. Prohibiting children under a certain age from working reduces the labor force.
2. Providing social security payments allow older members of the labor force to retire.
3. Fixing a standard workweek of 40 hours with a higher wage rate for overtime (more than 40 hours) encourages employers to hire more workers rather than have present workers put in long hours.

Explain what each of the factors listed above does to the supply curve for labor.

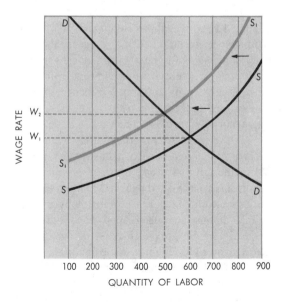

Figure 7–9   Effect of union membership restrictions on wage rates

Unions that restrict their membership can increase the wage rate by shifting the supply curve to the left. What has happened to the number of people employed?

Summary: Wages under the Classical Model

Under conditions of pure competition, where workers and employers act independently and are willing to move from market to market and have a complete knowledge of the labor market, interaction of demand and supply will determine wage rates and the number of workers employed. The additional value that the last worker adds will determine the maximum wage that the employer can pay.

Because conditions of pure competition rarely exist, other factors influencing wages must be considered. Markets with a single large employer, unions, and government laws bring about changes in demand and supply which in turn change both the equilibrium point for wage rates and the quantity of labor from what they might be under conditions of pure competition.

C A Sketch of the Labor Movement

Early History of Unionism

Unions as we think of them today had their start with the Industrial Revolution and the factory system in eighteenth-century England. When workers stopped doing their jobs in their own homes, raising their own food, and using their own tools, they became increasingly dependent on their employers. Independent artisans became factory hands whose jobs required little skill, and thus they were in a poor bargaining position. Employers could get all the help they needed, pay low wages, and give little thought to unpleasant or dangerous working conditions.

 Union: an employees' organization that attempts to represent, protect, and promote the interests of workers.

Early unions in the United States were small, strictly local, and temporary. The government did not recognize them as legal bargaining agents for workers, the courts were hostile to them, and they were often prosecuted as illegal conspiracies. Even after the courts decided that unions were not illegal conspiracies, union methods (such as strikes) were often considered illegal.

After the Civil War, efforts to form *national unions* were more successful. The founding in 1881 of the American Federation of Labor, or AFL (originally called the Federation of Organized Trades and Labor Unions), is considered the real beginning of the modern U.S. labor movement. Under the leadership of Samuel Gompers, the AFL brought independent unions together in a federation, adopted a businesslike approach to union management, and disavowed direct political action, violence, and radicalism. The AFL adhered to "pure and simple unionism," promoting higher pay, shorter working days, and better conditions. Unlike some earlier unions, the AFL did not expend its energies in the support of causes that did not directly affect workers.

The AFL favored *craft organization*. Under this system skilled workers in the same field (such as plumbers) belong to the same union. The different craft unions could affiliate with the AFL while maintaining much of their local autonomy. Skilled workers tend to be scarcer and therefore have more "clout" in dealing with management. Employers who realized that acceptance of unions was inevitable favored the AFL because it seemed to be less of a threat than other organizations that espoused radical ideas, political action, and government involvement. By 1920, about 10 percent of the labor force belonged to AFL unions.

Unions in the Twentieth Century

AFL membership declined during the 1920s for a number of reasons: people blamed unions for rising prices, some business organizations conducted vigorous antiunion campaigns, and government and the courts seemed to favor management. Failure to organize unskilled workers also weakened the union movement. The 1930s, however, brought legislation favorable to labor, such as the Wagner Act of 1935, which recognized labor's right to bargain collectively. The National Labor Relations Board (NLRB) was set up to supervise union elections, certify the legal bargaining agent for the workers, investigate contract violations, prevent management from interfering with the organization or management of unions, and prevent employers from discriminating against unionized workers.

In the mid-1930s the Congress of Industrial Organizations (CIO) was established. Unlike the AFL, the CIO stressed *industrial organization*. Under this system all workers in an industry belong to the same union regardless of their jobs or skills. (Craft unions are also called *horizontal*, and industrial unions are called *vertical*. The cartoon shows why.) The CIO won some important strikes and succeeded in organizing the workers in the vital steel and auto industries. The Roosevelt administration was generally favorable toward labor, and union membership grew rapidly.

After World War II, however, there was another wave of antiunion sentiment resulting from a large number of strikes that inconvenienced the public.

Craft unions are sometimes called horizontal because they include workers with the same or similar skills, no matter what industry they work in. Industrial unions may be called vertical, since all workers in an industry, no matter what their skill, are in the same union.

The Taft-Hartley Act of 1947 was passed, extending the protections of the Wagner Act to management as well as to labor. Workers could no longer be forced to join unions or to strike, unions could no longer refuse to bargain with management, and strikes to enforce union recognition were banned. Unions could now be sued by workers, employers, or other unions; and the *closed shop* (wherein only union members may be hired) was outlawed. States were authorized to outlaw the *union shop* (wherein workers must join a union after being hired). Unions were required to give 60-day notice that a change of contract was desired before they could go on strike. A means of delaying work stoppages that might affect the national health or safety was established. The Taft-Hartley Act did not prove to be the "slave labor law" that unions had feared, but neither did it end the labor problems that businesses faced. In 1955 the AFL and CIO merged, creating a union with a combined membership of 16 million. Life is not always harmonious within this "house of labor," however, and many workers belong to independent unions outside the AFL-CIO.

Recent History

When congressional investigations uncovered corruption and undemocratic practices in some unions, the Landrum-Griffin Act of 1959 was passed. Also known as the Labor-Management Reporting and Disclosure Act, this law spells out the democratic procedures that unions must adopt, imposes harsh punishment for embezzlement of union funds, and places restrictions on the use of picketing and boycotts in certain instances (such as to extort a bribe from an employer). In recent years, unions and their leaders have been declining in popularity, but public opinion polls show that the same is true of business people, public officials, educators, and many others. Union membership rose from about 15 million to 20 million between 1950 and 1970, but as a *percentage* of total nonagricultural employment it declined.

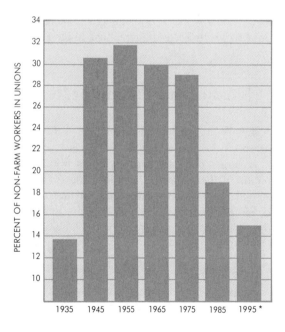

Figure 7–10 Percent of nonfarm work force belonging to unions in the United States
Union membership soared in the 1930s and 1940s. After 1975, however, the percentage of the work force belonging to unions dropped sharply. Unions found it difficult to organize such growth industries as high technology and financial services. (Source: *Business Week,* July 8, 1985, page 72.)
*Estimated.

Between 1980 and 1985 union membership dropped from 20.1 million to 17.3 million—from 23 percent to less than 19 percent of the nonfarm work force.

Unions have made some important gains, however. For example, after long years of frustration in attempting to unionize farm workers, the AFL-CIO United Farm Workers Organizing Committee obtained a model contract with a large fruit company in California in 1967. Resistance to unions has been strongest in the Southeast, but between 1964 and 1970 membership rose by 36 percent in eight southeastern states, as compared with only 15 percent in the nation as a whole. The supply of labor has become tighter as more industry has moved to the South, there has been a decline in the number of communities relying on a single firm or plant, blacks and young workers have been receptive to union organization, and southern politicians have become less hostile toward unions. White-collar workers, often thought to be hard to organize, have been joining unions in increasing numbers. During a recent decade, the percent of white-collar workers in unions nearly doubled. Professional persons such as teachers, professors, concert artists, engineers, and scientists have been looking with greater favor on union organization. Government workers not only have been flocking to join unions but also have been demonstrating great militancy. Between 1960 and 1974, the number of employees of federal, state, and local governments belonging to unions more than doubled.

In summary, in assessing the importance of unions in the United States, it is necessary to consider not only the percentage of the labor force belonging to labor organizations (and the percentage is low in comparison with that of many other industrial nations), but also the fact that strong unions exist in key industries and that many occupations once considered "immune" to unionization are becoming organized and militant. The extent to which the U.S. labor force will be unionized remains to be seen.

D Labor-Management Relations: Focus for Conflict

Although labor and management both profit from prosperity because a "big pie" allows everyone to have larger portions, conflicts about the distribution of the pie arise. Each side tries to make sure that its position and demands will prevail. To do so, both management and labor use methods they consider necessary to "win."

Weapons Used by Management

In addition to the methods previously described, management has also used the following devices.

Company unions were set up by management to discourage or prevent workers from joining an existing union or starting a union of their own. These unions were largely dominated by management.

Yellow-dog contracts required that workers promise not to join a union as a condition of employment.

Blacklists containing the names of union organizers were circulated among employers to prevent these organizers from getting jobs.

By closing the business, or threatening to close it, the employer could exert great pressure on workers. Such an employer's strike is called a *lockout*.

Frequently, the issuance of a temporary *injunction*—a court order restraining some person or group from particular actions—was enough to break a strike. Employers would request judges to issue injunctions to prevent unions from striking or picketing, claiming such action threatened their property.

All these devices have been declared illegal or have been sufficiently limited in use as to be ineffective. Recently, however, employers have found new ways of weakening union power. The use of *contingent workers* has increased. These are part-time, temporary, or freelance workers who are less likely to be unionized and who do not receive pensions, health benefits, or vacation pay.

In 1985 it was estimated that over 29 million people were contingent workers. Many employers have established *two-tier wage agreements* wherein newer workers get lower rates of pay than older workers doing the same jobs. This may cause animosity among workers and resentment toward the union. (About one-third of the union-management contracts in force in 1985 included two-tier agreements.) Some firms have attempted to annul labor contracts by filing for reorganization under Chapter 11 of the Bankruptcy Code. In 1984, Congress placed limits on this practice by requiring that a bankruptcy judge must find the annulment necessary for the reorganization to work. Judges have supported the unions in several cases, but management has prevailed in others.

Weapons Used by Unions

The heart of unionism is collective bargaining, in which union officials negotiate with management to secure such benefits as higher wages, shorter hours, improved working conditions, longer vacations and sick leaves, and better retirement benefits. Only by uniting do members of unions feel they can compete successfully with management. The union seeks to be recognized as the bargaining agent in the making of contracts. A contract is a legal agreement between labor and management covering conditions of work and labor relations for a specific period of time. To represent the workers most effectively, the union tries to enlist all the workers in the company. It does this by one of the following means, listed in order of preference:

The *closed shop* makes it a requirement of employment that the worker be a member of the union. By limiting membership, the union can control the supply of workers. This practice is now illegal.

The *union shop* allows the employer to hire anyone, but the new worker must join the union within a specified period.

The *agency shop* requires all workers to pay dues to the union because the union acts as their agent in bargaining, but workers are not required to join the union.

The union may ask the employer for a *check-off* agreement, whereby the employer deducts union dues from the employee's paycheck.

Two variations of the preceding conditions have developed within recent years. The *maintenance-of-membership shop* requires workers to continue their membership in the union for the duration of the contract. If they are not members, they do not have to join. The *preferential shop* has an agreement with management that union members will be hired in preference to nonunion workers as long as union members are available. In opposition to these arrangements, many employers prefer an *open shop,* wherein management does not recognize any union as a bargaining agent for its employees.

The *strike* is a work stoppage organized by labor. It is most likely to be used at the time of expiration of an existing labor contract. If the stoppage is not sanctioned by the union, it is called a *wildcat strike.* Without the power to strike, unions would be in an extremely weak bargaining position. When a strike occurs, the employer not only is faced with loss of income but also is likely to lose some customers permanently. In addition, fixed costs, which in some cases may be substantial, continue.

Strikes are very costly for workers also. Although the union often compensates workers for loss of pay by providing strike benefits and some states give unemployment benefits, a prolonged strike will force most workers to dip into their savings or to borrow money. Even when a strike results in the workers' winning most of their demands, it may take years to make up the lost income. The inevitable loss of income has led some to believe that a long strike is never worthwhile. Others point out that the threat of a strike would be ineffective if strikes did not take place.

Because strikes cause inconveniences to the public and receive much newspaper coverage, many people get a false impression of their number and severity. Typically, in a year less than one-half of 1 percent of days of work is lost because of strikes, considerably less than the amount of time lost because of accidents, illness, and absenteeism.

Picketing is an activity carried on by unions during a strike. By placing picket lines around a business, the workers hope to prevent nonunion workers (scabs) from taking their jobs. They also try to persuade customers to avoid doing business with the company.

A *boycott* is a refusal by a union to patronize a business with which it is having a dispute. A *secondary boycott,* now illegal, occurs when the union also refuses to deal with anybody using the goods of the employer with whom they are at odds.

A *union label* signifies that the product was made by union workers. Organized labor has tried to persuade consumers to buy only goods with such labels.

A *slowdown* occurs when workers purposely reduce the speed at which they work, increasing the cost of production.

Political action is an important method by which labor has sought to accomplish its aims. Financial contributions, together with posters and sound trucks, are used to help candidates who are "friends of labor." Although it is highly debatable whether the unions have much control over their members when they go to the polls, few politicians, particularly from highly industrialized states, are willing to risk the antagonism of organized labor.

"Pension power" is one of the newer weapons. Employee pension funds total many billions (nearly $700 billion in 1984), and unions are attempting to have a strong voice in how the funds will be invested. Unions oppose investments in firms that are known for antiunion activities. This weapon was used effectively to organize workers in a large textile company. Threats to withdraw pension accounts from a large bank that dealt with this company and the "blacklisting" of other firms related to the textile company helped to end the company's resistance to recognizing the union. Of course, management is resisting union efforts to share in the control of pension funds.

The *corporate campaign* is one of the most recently developed union tactics. Here, unions use public relations methods and various legal maneuvers to put pressure on a company through its stockholders or creditors. As owners of some of the firm's stock, employees can conduct proxy fights, speak up at annual stockholder meetings, nominate candidates for the board of directors, or threaten to support another corporation that is trying to gain control of the company. The boards of directors of some major corporations now include union representatives.

The *employee buyout* is perhaps the most unusual development. Workers have actually purchased companies (usually firms that are in financial difficulty) in order to protect their jobs. They will then accept lower wage rates, give up some of their benefits, and work harder to improve productivity. Several of these experiments have been quite successful, but a few have failed. (Ironically, in one case the workers went on strike against their own company!)

Resolving Conflicts

Collective bargaining, with little or no outside interference, is the method of conflict resolution both labor and management prefer. Of course, some firms would prefer not to have to deal with unions at all. When workers in a company are not union members (or perhaps are members of some union but have no union contract), a union organizer will usually approach them and try to induce them to accept the union as their bargaining agent. The organizer will assure them of such things as higher wages, better working conditions, greater job security, and better fringe benefits (such as insurance and vacations). Management may try to convince the workers that they can get these things without a union contract, but the organizer will warn the workers that benefits can be assured only if they are acquired by contractual right and are not subject to the employer's whim. If the workers vote to accept union representation, the NLRB will declare the union to be the sole bargaining agent and the firm will have to accept it.

 Collective bargaining: an arrangement whereby an organization (usually a union) speaks for all workers in a particular category when dealing with management.

In spite of the impression the news media often create, most labor-management differences are settled peacefully around the bargaining table. A typical contract will specify that the company should recognize the union as exclusive bargaining agent for the type of employees specified, ban discrimination against union members, define what constitutes a workday or workweek, provide for lunch and relief periods, set forth the conditions and rates for overtime work, indicate the wage rates for the various types of jobs covered, list the holidays to be recognized as nonworking days, set the terms for vacations, and spell out seniority and security provisions. Procedures for handling grievances will be detailed, along with conditions under which a worker can be disciplined or discharged. There may also be provisions for the health and safety of the employees, apprenticeship and training, sick leave, insurance, retirement benefits, severance pay, and leaves of absence. The union will agree not to strike, and the company will agree not to have a lockout for the duration of the contract. No matter how detailed and well planned a union contract is, it cannot cover every possible problem that might arise. Indeed, disputes often occur over the meaning of various parts of the contract itself. When labor and management have reached an impasse, there are several possible ways of solving the problem.

Methods of Reaching Agreement

Conciliation, mediation, and arbitration are means of settling disputes. Some people use the term *conciliation* to refer to attempts at peaceful settlement through direct conference between employer and employees (or their representatives) without the assistance of outsiders. Others use the term to mean the intervention by a third party who attempts informally to bring the two sides together. This third party, or mediator, may suggest the terms of a settlement, but has no power to compel either side to settle.

Mediation is often used synonymously with conciliation, as defined in the second instance above. Others consider mediation to be more formal than conciliation. Mediation often involves a commission before which the two parties appear with their attorneys. In any event, the mediator may investigate the situation and suggest solutions, but cannot force the parties to accept any solution. Good mediators are usually persons trained in labor law and economics; in their role as "industrial diplomats," they must be strictly objective and impartial.

If mediation fails, the disputants may decide on *voluntary arbitration*. They must both agree to have a third party enter the case and to accept his or her decision. (Some union contracts spell out the conditions under which the parties will resort to arbitration. For example, it may be decided that the arbitrator's authority will be limited to interpretation of the terms of the contract.)

Compulsory arbitration exists when the government directly or indirectly compels the parties to submit their differences to an impartial outsider for adjudication. Compulsory arbitration has been used in Australia, New Zealand, and France. Kansas, in 1920, set up a court of industrial relations as part of a system of compulsory arbitration for certain industries. Both management and labor opposed the system, for both preferred free collective bargaining to government decree.[2] The U.S. Supreme Court in 1923 declared unconstitutional the Kansas court's power to fix wages in industries that are not public utilities, and in 1925 held that the fixing of hours of work through compulsory arbitration by a state agency infringes on the liberty of contract and rights of property guaranteed by the Fourteenth Amendment's due process clause. The Kansas legislature then abolished the court. During wartime emergencies and disputes posing a threat to the public health or safety, the federal government has sometimes taken actions that have had the effect of compulsory arbitration.

Labor and management both realize that industrial peace is important for an industry and for the economy in general. Once a contract has been signed, differences that arise are usually settled through an orderly and peaceful procedure. Strikes capture the headlines, but the vast majority of cases are settled quietly and peacefully. After a union becomes established in an industry, management often accepts it with good grace. Contracts set forth the responsibilities as well as the rights of labor, peace is virtually assured for the

---

[2] "With compulsory arbitration you're over a barrel," said the late Michael Quill, president of the Transport Workers Union. (On WNBC-TV, January 7, 1961.) A natural enemy of Mr. Quill, the National Association of Manufacturers, stated, "Compulsory arbitration . . . leads inevitably to a totalitarian state." (In *NAM News*, January 4, 1947.)

duration of the agreement (three years, often), and it may be much easier to deal with one person or committee representing all the workers than with each individual.

The Classical Model and Labor Today

The classical model is no longer the exclusive guide in determining wage policy. The number of persons employed in jobs where individual workers can draw up separate contracts with their employers has been reduced considerably in all fields and to almost nothing in our mass-production industries. Organized labor, though it makes up less than 19 percent of our labor force, has a definite influence on wage rates of *unorganized* workers. State and federal legislation on minimum wage rates, maximum hours, child-labor, and conditions of work have brought about changes in the supply and demand curves as applied to labor.

Industrywide Bargaining

Sitting around a bargaining table today, one might find representatives of the workers on one side and those of a great corporation on the other. The contract will probably apply not only to the workers of the corporation concerned but also to labor throughout the particular industry. Negotiating labor contracts that will set a pattern for workers in an entire industry is known as *industrywide bargaining*. In recent years some companies have become disenchanted with this practice, but it is still common.

Settlements in key industries frequently set a pattern for settlements in other mass-production industries. New kinds of agreements often become widely accepted, too—agreements in which wage increases are based on an estimate of increases in productivity per worker, on an *escalator clause* that provides workers with automatic increases and decreases related to fluctuations in the cost of living or profits. Any benefit gained in one contract will probably be applied to other contracts. Even the wages of those not organized are eventually affected.

Classical Model Still Important

Although the evidence presented here indicates a change from the classical model, we have not departed entirely from that model. The productivity of labor is, in the long run, the main factor in determining real wage rates. Although unions may limit the supply of labor available, causing wages to rise, higher wages can come only from increased productivity.

Suppose that a strong union is able to bargain for an increase of 5 percent in wages when productivity has gone up only 3 percent. Such a change will increase the cost of production per unit and force the employer to cut into profits or raise prices. In industries where there is little competition, the additional cost will probably be passed on to the consumer. In competitive industries, prices will rise eventually because of the additional purchasing power in the hands of the workers, who are also consumers. However, in the interim some of the weakest firms will be forced out of business. Under these conditions, unemployment will probably rise, thereby causing wages to fall.

If prices rise 2 percent to pay for the additional cost, the 5 percent increase in wages will bring about an increase in purchasing power of only 3 percent, the same as the increase in productivity. Some critics of labor use the illustration just given as proof that labor is responsible for what is called a *cost-push* inflation. They maintain that wage increases that are in excess of increased productivity have raised costs and forced prices up. Defenders of labor reply that the cost of additional wages should come from excessively high profits. Some critics of industry go a step further and say that business welcomes the opportunity to give a wage increase, because such action permits them to raise prices even more than enough to pay for the additional cost of labor, making profits larger than before.

Recently, the pressures of competition have actually forced wages to drop in some unionized industries. Indeed, the term *givebacks* has become common, as some major unions have agreed to wage reductions and the loss of some fringe benefits in the hope of preventing layoffs. One reason for the increased competition is that foreign businesses have captured substantial shares of the U.S. market in such industries as automobile manufacturing. Another reason is that the recession of 1981–82 brought high unemployment rates and the threat of bankruptcy in several important fields—air transportation and building construction, for example. It appears that the market mechanism is still an influence, even in situations where huge oligopolies and powerful unions exist.

Do Unions Raise Wages?

The debate on the influence of unions in raising wages will undoubtedly continue. We do know

that monopoly power in both industry and labor has brought about changes in the supply and demand for labor. We also know that labor as a whole cannot long receive wages in excess of the value it produces, and that probably some government regulation is necessary to make sure that no segment of the economy disrupts the development of the economy as a whole. We can all agree that if we can make the pie (the total goods and services produced) grow faster than the population that will consume it, everyone can have a bigger portion. A highly skilled labor force, characterized by a high degree of productivity, has been one of our country's chief assets in achieving a high standard of living.

E New Approaches to Work

Work Dissatisfaction

In recent years many studies have been made of the extent to which U.S. workers are satisfied with their jobs. The results of several of these studies suggest that between 10 and 19 percent of our workers are dissatisfied. Perhaps this is a remarkably small percentage. But it still means that over 10 million people are unhappy with their jobs. Job dissatisfaction is large enough a problem to cause concern to many employers, union officials, sociologists, and others.

There are several probable causes of worker dissatisfaction. The type of job held appears to be a factor. One study concluded that white-collar workers are generally more satisfied with their jobs than are blue-collar workers. For example, 93 percent of the university professors polled stated that they would choose similar work again, but only 16 percent of the unskilled auto workers would select the same type of employment. Other factors revealed by a number of researchers are monotony, lack of stimulus, work roles that are too narrow, feelings of powerlessness, lack of identification with the company, poor communication channels with management, rigid work rules and

requirements, lack of opportunities to advance to better jobs, feelings that the company is indifferent, the manufacture of useless or even harmful products, isolation of the workers from their colleagues, lack of opportunities to contribute something personal and unique to work, fear that automation will cost the worker his or her job (fear that a machine will replace human labor), low levels of responsibility, compulsory retirement policies, and low pay. Dissatisfaction was particularly strong among young, well-educated workers, young blacks, and women in the labor force.

Being unhappy with one's job causes low productivity, high absenteeism, high worker turnover, wildcat strikes, poor-quality products, and even industrial sabotage, according to a study for the U.S. Department of Health and Human Services. Job dissatisfaction was also found to be linked to mental and physical illnesses (such as heart disease), alcohol and drug abuse, delinquency, violent behavior, and suicide. The discontented workers also tend to have negative attitudes toward society, the employer, and even their union. (They are less likely to be active in union affairs, and they see their unions as "doing nothing" to help them.)

Programs for Improving Worker Satisfaction

Although some observers have questioned the validity of the research done on worker dissatisfaction, arguing that the problems could be solved by achieving the traditional trade-union goals of higher wages, better working conditions, and more job security, many experiments with new approaches to work have been launched.

Profit-sharing is not a new idea; indeed, it continues to be mentioned as one way of making workers feel they are part of the company. (By 1958 there were at least 25,000 U.S. firms sharing their profits with their employees. By 1986, 10 million workers were enrolled in employee stock ownership plans.) Profit-sharing can take many forms. The *universal cash plan* (which existed in the United States as early as 1797 in a small glass factory) involves distributing to all workers a share of the firm's profits at least once a year. According to Peter F. Drucker, a leading management specialist, this type of plan tends to work only in very small firms and has not had the desired effect of greatly increasing worker productivity. Such a plan might even damage relations with the workers if profits are small or if the firm is operating at a loss.

Another version is the *qualified profit-sharing pension plan,* in which the firm's payments into the employees' pension fund fluctuate with the company's earnings. This type of plan has been used primarily with executive-level employees, however, and has as its major purpose saving taxes rather than stimulating worker productivity or ensuring industrial peace. In the *profit-sharing benefit plan,* the employer's payments for such benefits as insurance vary with the level of profits. In effect, the employee may also share in the firm's losses, and this plan appears to have done little to end worker discontent.

In any event, there are two serious problems with profit-sharing plans. First, they rarely survive during bad times when there are no profits to share. Second, they create a dilemma for union leaders who feel that all members doing the same work should receive the same pay and benefits. For instance, suppose that one automobile man-

ufacturer is making good profits while a competing firm is operating at a loss. The workers in the former firm receive higher pay or benefits than those in the latter firm, even though they are doing the same work and belong to the same union.

Flexible work schedules are being tried by some employers. Each worker must put in a given number of hours each month but may start work at any time within a certain time band (such as between 7 A.M. and 10 A.M.) and may leave at any time within another time band. Workers may not even have to follow the same work schedule each day; they may be able to vary their schedules to suit their needs for time off. The benefits of flexible work schedules are that workers can choose the hours when they work best, avoid rush hours when commuting, take care of personal business during the work day, and so on. Being able to select one's own working hours may boost morale, cut down on tardiness, reduce absenteeism, and give the worker a feeling of responsibility. On the other hand, "flexi-time" is not suitable for every firm. If John Jones must work at the same time as Mary Smith in order to get a particular job done but Mary's preferences for a schedule differ from John's, conflicts can arise. If a given number of workers must be on duty at a certain time to serve a firm's customers but most workers want those hours off, the scheme may prove to be unworkable.

The *compressed workweek* enables workers to put in a four-day workweek by working ten hours each day. Thus they still work forty hours a week but have three days off instead of two. It is estimated that about 1 percent of U.S. workers are on these compressed schedules, and many firms report that production has increased and costs have declined as a result. There has been opposition from unions, however, possibly because they fought for years to win the eight-hour day with premium rates for overtime. Some fear that the ten-hour day could result in worker fatigue and a consequent increase in illnesses and injuries.

Joint-production committees have been established in a number of firms. These are formal advisory bodies designed to improve production and working conditions. Although they are created by the union and management through collective bargaining, they do not usually deal with negotiable issues (such as wages, fringe benefits, and grievances) but limit themselves to issues not covered in union-management contracts. One of the earliest joint committees was set up by the Baltimore and Ohio Railroad in 1923, and it resulted in workers' submitting thousands of suggestions that helped to improve productivity, reduce grievances, stabilize employment, raise wages (somewhat), and improve working conditions. In addition to joint-production committees at the plant level, there have been industrywide committees and even community-level committees. (Perhaps the best example of a community-level effort is the committee that was established in Jamestown, New York, in 1972. It brought together labor leaders, business executives, and community representatives to end the loss of plants and jobs attributed to a "bad labor-relations climate." As a result, strikes and grievances were reduced, and several plants were saved from liquidation.) At the plant level, teams of supervisors and hourly workers have been formed to overcome bottlenecks in production, and "work teams" have been established in which employees help to set production standards and determine policies relating to overtime, work-break periods, layoffs, and leaves of absence.

Of course, there is considerable variation in the way in which these plans work. In one small company in Michigan, the workers elect their representatives to work with management. Increases in productivity are then shared by everyone from top company officers to the lowest-paid employee. In another firm all the employees in a given department work as a group. Thus there is great "peer pressure" to perform well, because the earnings of the workers rise if the department increases its productivity. Some employees have been given the freedom to rearrange their tasks, determine the pace and the sequence of their various operations, and establish their own rules. To reduce monotony, a worker may be allowed to assemble an entire product (or a substantial part of it, such as an engine) instead of simply turning the same bolt hour after hour or doing some other boring and repetitive task.

Quality circles, which have been particularly successful in Japan, are being tried by a number of U.S. firms. A quality circle is a group of workers who meet periodically to discuss production problems and propose solutions. Quality circle meetings give workers a voice in how their jobs are to be done and an opportunity to confer with management. Participation is voluntary (and on company time), and it improves morale by giving workers a feeling of creative involvement. Productivity rises, absenteeism declines, and better labor-management relations can result. Some companies are also attempting to end the adversary relationship with labor and promote cooperation instead. For example, recently a steel company agreed not to close its Ohio plant in return for an agreement by the union that there would be no strike for at least eleven years. Several firms are experimenting with plans to offer workers job security in return for labor peace. In Japan, workers are usually intensively loyal to the company, and the company offers them lifetime security. They are not threatened by increases in productivity because they will not lose their jobs as a result of introduction of better methods (such as the use of robots) and because they will share in the benefits of productivity. This system helps to explain why Japanese auto workers have been about twice as productive as U.S. auto workers, while hourly labor costs have been only about 41 percent as high.

In mid-1985, General Motors and the United Auto Workers Union reached a new agreement that went far beyond quality circles. It included *co-determination*—an arrangement whereby the union will have veto power over management decisions at all levels. Workers will receive salaries instead of hourly wages, plus bonuses related to profits and output. Most will have lifetime job guarantees. Teams made up of from 6 to 15 workers will elect a "counselor" and will be responsible for meeting budgets and production schedules, for reducing absenteeism, and for handling safety and health problems. The teams will determine workers' job assignments, allocate resources, and do short-range planning. The workers' salaries will be below the prevailing industry rate; however, there will be fewer job categories, the company will be able to move workers from job to job to a greater extent than in the past, and shop stewards who have traditionally been paid by the

CONTROVERSY IN OUR TIMES

The Workers' Role in Management

Traditionally, it has been the workers' role to work and management's role to manage. Managers have planned and directed the firm's operations with little thought to consulting the labor force. Managers have rarely felt compelled to obtain the workers' opinions or to explain their decisions to their employees. At most, companies have provided "suggestion boxes" in which workers could place ideas for improving procedures. In recent years, however, many management specialists have been arguing that workers are more than sellers of labor—they have a vital stake in the company and may be able to make significant contributions to its management. Furthermore, major company decisions profoundly affect workers and their dependents. This is particularly true of plant closings, which may put thousands on the unemployment lines. Should workers, then, play a stronger role in management?

Pro

Workers should have a role in management. At the very least, the labor force should be informed of major policy decisions. (A common complaint among rank-and-file workers is the lack of information about company policies and actions.) Between 1980 and 1985 about five million workers were the victims of plant closings and permanent layoffs, often with no warning. At least 90 days' notice ought to be given in such instances so that workers have time to adjust. Management should consult workers before closing a plant, because the workers might be able to suggest ways of improving productivity and reducing costs and might be willing to make concessions that will help keep the plant operating.

It should become a general practice to include workers in some managerial decision making. There ought to be representatives of the workers on the firm's board of directors or other major policymaking groups. If rank-and-file workers are given a voice in the planning and management of the work flow, they will help to make improvements, their morale will rise, and their productivity will increase. As a further incentive, they must be given a share in the company's profits. This can be done through employee stock-ownership plans, bonuses, or rewards for efficiency and productivity. Finally, when a plant can no longer operate at a profit, the workers should be given the opportunity to purchase the plant and run it themselves.

Con

In today's dynamic economy, companies face intense competition at home and from foreign firms. Management has become very complex, and managers must react very quickly to changing conditions in domestic and world markets. However skilled and well-intentioned they might be, workers are not trained to cope with modern managerial problems. The need to consult with worker representatives could cause delays and even enable competitors to learn of company plans that ought to be kept confidential.

As for notifying employees of plant closings, it must be realized that business has as much right to close a plant as it has to open one. Delaying a plant closing in one place might delay a plant opening elsewhere. A company might miss out on a good opportunity and nullify some of the potential gains of moving its operation from one place to another, thus giving an advantage to a competitor. Being required to report plans for a plant closing might make it difficult for the firm to sell the plant, to refinance its debts, to attract new investments, or to save itself from a merger with another company. Also, the closing of an

CONTROVERSY IN OUR TIMES

inefficient operation would be delayed, thus aggravating the problem by forcing the company to continue to operate at a loss.

Some sort of employee profit-sharing plan might be acceptable if it would serve to raise morale and productivity, but such plans go sour when the firm operates at a loss. In short, employees want to share the profits but do not want to share the burden of losses. Furthermore, any such plan must not permit employee control or enable the workers and their unions to use the plan to favor another corporation that is attempting a take-over. (The employee stockholders could make a deal with the other corporation, offering to vote in favor of a merger in exchange for promises of higher wages and benefits.)

Consensus

The old "adversary approach" to labor-management relations is counterproductive. Our economy is facing strong competition from abroad and cannot afford costly labor battles that hurt everyone involved, including the consumer. Management must treat workers as intelligent human beings rather than as simple tools of production. Unions and workers must learn that it is in their best interests to cooperate with management and raise productivity. They might insist on having a stronger voice in management, but it is doubtful that they can replace well-trained and experienced managers.

company while doing full-time union work will now have to work a shift. This agreement applies to General Motors' new Saturn plant; it will not necessarily be adopted by other plants. Certainly, however, the plan will be scrutinized carefully by both management and labor elsewhere.

Are the New Approaches Successful?

Perhaps it is too early to say whether or not these new approaches to work are successful. One firm that has been using *participatory management* for approximately thirty years reports that productivity has increased and that it has been able to increase wages substantially. Some firms have reported productivity increases as high as 66 percent and reductions in unit labor costs of as much as 47 percent. Higher wages resulting from these experiments have reportedly induced workers to improve their performance even further.

Critics, on the other hand, have raised serious questions about these claims and even about the research on worker dissatisfaction. William Gomberg, professor of management and industrial relations at the Wharton School of Finance, fears

that the sensational productivity gains may be short-lived. After the novelty of the new work situation has worn off, production may return to "normal." He charges that in one successful experiment the workers were very carefully screened in advance, and that there is no evidence that success in this situation would be repeated elsewhere. Others assert that efforts to make work more interesting cannot substitute for the traditional union goals of higher pay, better job security, and more generous fringe benefits.

In conclusion, it appears that "the jury is still out" on the question of new approaches to worker satisfaction. More and better research (particularly long-range research and experimentation) is needed before we can say with confidence that the new approaches to work are achieving the desired effects.

Effects of International Developments

Developments in other parts of the world are having profound effects on U.S. management and labor. We have already noted some of these effects in other parts of this chapter. Several European nations have "imported" workers from countries with a surplus of labor, thus reducing their own production costs and making themselves more competitive with the United States. (Their labor supply curves have been shifted to the right by the use of foreign workers.)

One response of U.S. management has been to become tougher in dealing with U.S. unions. Some firms have departed from industrywide bargaining because they feel they can do better by going "one-on-one" with unions. Thus, the workers in one steel mill may receive lower wages and fewer benefits than those in another mill. Other firms have become more conciliatory and have adopted some of the paternalistic practices found in Japanese firms. Another response of U.S. firms has been to have some components of their products (such as automobile parts) manufactured in a country where labor costs are lower.

Unions have also been forced to make adjustments. They have even had to learn to deal with foreign employers who are building plants in the United States. Some major unions are beginning to join with management in seeking ways to improve worker productivity. Multinational corporations have created problems for unions. One leading U.S. union has been planning meetings with foreign unions to work out global strategies for organizing the employees of huge multinational firms.

Chapter Highlights

1. Labor is one of the four factors of production. It represents human effort used in creating value. This value varies with the skill and tools of the worker.

2. Labor differs from the other factors of production because it can act on its own initiative and because it buys back what it helps to produce.

3. The U.S. labor force is highly skilled, and an increasing proportion is engaged in white-collar jobs.

4. Wages are prices management pays for human effort. Wages, which provide income for the worker, are the most costly factor of production.

5. *Money wages* refer to the amount of money paid for a given amount of work. *Real wages* refer to the buying power of that money.

6. The demand schedule for labor is determined by the marginal productivity of workers.

7. Under conditions of pure competition, wage rates and the quantity of labor demanded are determined by the interaction of demand and supply. Minimum wage laws and unions change the supply curve, and at certain levels tend to reduce the number of workers hired.

8. Labor unions are organized to improve the bargaining position of workers. The history of organized labor has moved like a pendulum, with progress made from 1898 to 1904, 1914 to 1920, and 1933 to 1947. The periods before, in between, and after were characterized by unfriendly courts, unfavorable legislation, and conflicts with employers.

9. The American Federation of Labor and the Congress of Industrial Organizations were the main labor organizations to formulate U.S. labor policy.

10. Unions can be organized along both craft and industrial lines.

11. The federal government gave its official endorsement to unions in the Wagner Act. The Taft-Hartley Act attempted to balance the power of unions and management.

12. Collective bargaining is the heart of unionism. Conciliation, mediation, and arbitration are methods of reaching agreement.

13. Because of concern over worker dissatisfaction, employers have been experimenting with new approaches to work by establishing profit-sharing plans, allowing employees to set their own work schedules, and giving workers a voice in some of the managerial decisions.

14. Such international developments as intense foreign competition and the growth of multinational firms have forced labor and management to change their policies.

Study Aids

Key Terms and Names

labor
labor force
wage rate
real wages
injunction
closed shop
collective bargaining
craft union
substitution effect
income effect
check-off agreement
industrial union
company union
money wages
law of diminishing returns
contingent workers
corporate campaign
co-determination
universal cash plan

marginal productivity wage theory
yellow-dog contract
blacklist
lockout
union shop
maintenance-of-membership shop
wildcat strike
picketing
slowdown
mobility of labor
minimum wage
demand for labor
open shop
preferential shop
qualified profit-sharing pension plan
profit-sharing benefit plan

participatory management
boycott
conciliation
compulsory arbitration
automation
profit-sharing
flexible work schedules
compressed workweek
mediation
voluntary arbitration
escalator clause
joint-production committee
"pension power"
givebacks
quality circles
two-tier wage agreement
employee buyout
industrywide bargaining

Landrum-Griffin Act
AFL
CIO

Taft-Hartley Act
Wagner Act

National Labor Relations Board

Questions

1. Labor is one of the integral parts of the productive process, yet it is sometimes called a "unique" or "peculiar" factor. What differentiates it from the other three factors—natural resources, capital, and entrepreneurship?

2. Explain why a profile of the labor force would show that the vast majority of workers are in the 20–65 age group and a very low percentage are in the younger and older age groups.

3. Labor has been called a "commodity," subject to the law of demand and supply in the marketplace. Do you agree? Why or why not?

4. To ensure maximum profit, an employer will be guided by the following factors in hiring new workers and in setting wages: labor's productivity, its marginal productivity, and its supply and skills. Explain how each factor influences wage payments.

5. Explain why the percentage of our labor force engaged in the physical aspects of production has declined since 1900.

6. Using the analytical tools of economics you have learned thus far, give the arguments for and against the minimum wage.

7. What factors besides minimum wages and unions influence the supply of labor?

8. Draw an imaginary supply and demand graph for labor, labeling wage rates and numbers of workers. Show what happens when output per worker-hour increases. Explain the changes.

9. What big factors impeded the growth of the labor movement in the United States? What encouraged its growth?

10. What weapons has management used against labor, and what weapons has labor used against management? Evaluate the effectiveness of each method in resolving labor-management disputes.

11. Why has organized labor sometimes referred to the Wagner Act as the "Magna Carta of the labor movement"? What were the objectives of the Taft-Hartley Act with regard to the unions?

12. "In spite of many factors interfering with the classical model's approach to wage determination, the theory it offers is still important in explaining wage rates." Explain the meaning of this statement.

13. What are some possible causes of worker dissatisfaction?

14. What are some of the new approaches to work designed to improve employee morale, and what are some of the arguments for and against each approach?

15. How have international events forced U.S. employers and unions to change their policies?

Problems

1. Turn to the "Help Wanted" section of a newspaper. List in descending order the wages paid for different jobs. Explain the reasons for the differences in wages offered. Explain why you might not seek the highest-paying job.

2. Why does elasticity in demand for labor affect the power of a union in influencing wages? Would that influence you in seeking a job?

3. In a brief essay, justify the demands of labor for the following:
   (a) An increase in wages coupled with a guarantee that prices of the article will remain the same.
   (b) A share in the profits of industry without a direct contribution to the risks.
   Now draw up the notes for a speech of rebuttal by the head of a large corporation.

4. What are the arguments against compulsory arbitration as put forth by unions? By management? Present the argument of the public in support of compulsory arbitration of big labor disputes.

5. Examine the accompanying graphs on p. 173 and decide which of the three applies to each of the following actions undertaken by a labor union. Explain your choice and tell why other graphs do not apply.
   (a) Along with most other unions, the union in question succeeds in inducing Congress and the president to restrict immigration.
   (b) The union works with management to improve labor productivity, thus enabling the firm to lower the price of the product.
   (c) The union succeeds in getting stronger child-labor laws so that employers have much greater difficulty in hiring minors.
   (d) The union joins management in financing a highly successful advertising campaign for the firm's products.
   (e) The union convinces Congress and the president that household workers should receive at least $3.50 per hour.

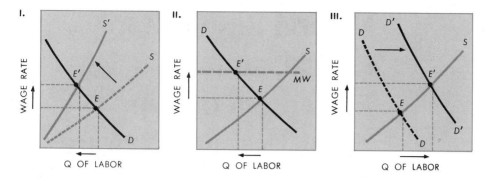

Three tactics for raising wages
I. Reducing the supply of labor.
II. Setting a minimum or standard wage.
III. Increasing the demand for labor.

6. Prepare a list of arguments for and against each of the following plans:
   (a) Giving employees a share of the profits.
   (b) Permitting workers to set their own work schedules.
   (c) Letting committees of employees decide how a product is to be produced, how work roles are to be allocated, and how productivity can be increased.

Natural Resources, Capital, and Entrepreneurship: Their Uses and Rewards

Although labor is extremely important in producing the goods and services we want, there would be no products without the other three factors: natural resources, capital, and entrepreneurship. We are concerned here with what contribution each of these factors makes to the production process, how a business enterprise acquires the right amount of each, and what rewards accrue to each. Because the supply of all factors of production is limited, how we allocate these resources to produce what consumers want is still our central problem. As with labor, rewards must be based on what each unit of a factor contributes to the total value of the product. We shall return to our classical model of pure competition to determine resource allocation and to study conditions that deviate from it. At the end of this chapter, there is a step-by-step review of how the factors of production get priced.

Because land is what nature has provided, why should we have to pay for it? Should it be nationalized? Should an individual have to pay a higher interest rate than a big corporation? Should business be allowed to make as large a profit as it can?

Chapter Objectives

When you have completed this chapter, you should be able to:

- Give a working definition of the production function.
- Discuss how the theory of marginal productivity helps a business to select the most efficient combination of production factors for a given level of output.
- Define and distinguish between *economic rent* and *land rent*.
- Explain the relation between interest as payment for loanable funds and as payment for capital.
- Apply supply and demand analysis to interest rates.
- Define and distinguish among *gross profits*, *net profits*, and *economic profits*, and present the case for profits under capitalism.
- Criticize the distribution of income among the factors of production under capitalism.

 # Production and Distribution Characteristics of the Factors of Production

Selecting the Best Combination of Factors

Production is the process of combining certain amounts of four ingredients—natural resources (such as land), labor, capital, and entrepreneurship—to make the goods and supply the services we want. The business owner goes to the market for the factors of production knowing that the firm wants to produce certain kinds of goods in certain amounts and that to do so, it needs certain quantities of each of the factors of production. The owner should have some idea of the value of the products the firm will make and offer for sale in the consumer market. This value cannot be certain, since prices may change, but a logical estimate is in order. The firm wants to buy the best combination of the factors of production to produce the goods. Determining how many units of each factor to use so that cost will be lowest and revenue highest is the key to success in business. It is also the answer to our basic question of allocating our limited resources to yield the greatest return in consumer satisfaction. This principle is illustrated in Table 8–1, which shows that changing the combination of units put into production yields a different value for output (same cost but

more revenue). We assume that each input unit, regardless of which factor of production is considered, costs the same. In this example we increase our output by reducing our labor and entrepreneurship inputs and increasing our capital inputs.

Table 8–1 Input-output analysis of factors of production

	Units	
Natural resources	6	
Labor	60	Yields 100,000 units of production
Capital	8	
Entrepreneurship	26	
	100	

	Units	
Natural resources	6	
Labor	58	Yields 110,000 units of production
Capital	12	
Entrepreneurship	24	
	100	

Altering the composition of the factors of production can increase efficiency. The problem for the business person is to add units of each factor only so long as the cost for each unit (the marginal cost) is less than the value that the unit can add (the marginal revenue product).

Each additional unit of production creates additional value, known as the marginal product. As long as the costs of additional units that we add (inputs) are no more than the value of the additional value created (output), we can continue to add factors to expand production. The business person will expand production, requiring additional factors of production, up to the point where marginal cost equals marginal revenue. Because each factor of production reaches the point of diminishing returns at a different level, we shall have to decide which factors will be the most profitable to add. When output (the value of goods and services produced) is increased without increasing input (the cost of the productive factors), *productivity* is increased. Productivity also rises when output can remain the same with less input. Increasing our productivity, referred to as *output per hour,* is the best way to raise our standard of living.

Dividing Return among the Factors

Many people think of distribution as moving goods from the initial producer to the final consumer. The economist has a special meaning for distribution, relating primarily to the problem *For whom. Distribution*—or, more accurately, *functional distribution*—concerns who, or what groups, will get what portion of the value or income created. Another way of stating the problem is, How do we divide the pie? The size of the portion each factor receives is the reward for the value each has contributed; more simply, the value that each factor contributes is determined by the demand and supply for each factor in the market.

Although we measure the value that each factor receives in dollars, we call the reward that each receives by a different name. Labor receives wages; natural resources, rent; capital, interest; and the

The Marginalists and Neoclassical Analysis

The Industrial Revolution brought with it a host of social and economic problems that caused great discontent in Europe during the nineteenth century. Not satisfied with the answers the classical economists provided, people turned to new methods, such as socialism, trade unionism, and government intervention, to find solutions.

Some economists were unwilling to accept either popular alternatives to laissez-faire or certain aspects of classical economic thinking. These men—including W. Stanley Jevons and Alfred Marshall of England; Karl Menger, Friedrich von Wieser, and Eugen Böhm-Bawerk of Austria; John Bates Clark of the United States; Herman Heinrich Gossen of Germany; and Léon Walras of France—developed a new approach, the marginalist or neoclassical school.

Marginalism focuses on resource allocation. How can limited factors of production be used to satisfy the most needs? Like the classical economists, marginalists set their theories within a laissez-faire environment and oppose interference with the free market. They concentrate on microeconomics—the analysis of the single firm, the individual producer and consumer, and the formation of price for a single good. Their early theory starts with marginal utility as it relates to demand, and later spreads to cover marginal cost on the supply side. Marginalists advocate using the concept of marginal productivity to account for the payment to each of the factors of production and to determine how a business can maximize profits. Emphasis is on the yield from each unit added, since this return influences the decision to buy or sell more.

Marginalism is still important, although its use has been modified by more recent theories. The most significant of these theories is the macroeconomic approach of Keynes and his followers.

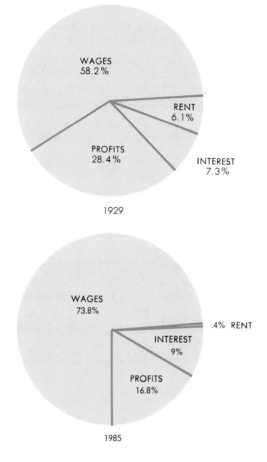

Figure 8–1   Distribution of national income among factors of production
The figure for profits combines corporate profits before taxes and the income of unincorporated enterprises. (Source: U.S. Department of Commerce.)

entrepreneur, profits. Figure 8–1 shows the portion each factor received in 1929 and in 1985. Remember that the pie in 1985 was far larger than the pie in 1929, so all factors did receive more.

Marginal Productivity Applied to the Factors

The *theory of marginal productivity* is based on the law of diminishing returns. You recall that as we add more workers beyond a certain point, each additional worker adds a lesser amount to the total

value of our production than did the preceding worker. This means that it is wise for us to keep adding workers only up to the point where the marginal revenue product (the value added by hiring one more worker) just equals marginal cost (the addition to total cost accounted for by that additional worker). If we go beyond that point, we are paying the new worker more than the value that he or she adds to our total revenues. Figure 8–2 shows this situation graphically.

 Businesses try to increase factors of production up to the point where marginal cost equals marginal revenue product.

This same theory is applied to the other factors of production. The same pattern of decreasing yields will emerge as units of either land or capital are added. When the last additional unit costs more than the value that unit creates, profits

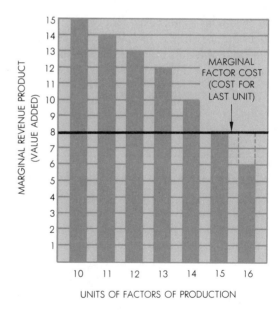

Figure 8–2   Most efficient production
It will pay the business person to continue adding units of factors of production as long as the value created by the last unit (the marginal revenue product) is not less than the cost of hiring the last unit (the marginal factor cost). Using a sixteenth unit in this case would result in a loss. Where should the producer stop adding units of factors of production if the cost goes up to 10?

are bound to be less. The producer should stop adding factors of production before this, when the marginal cost for resources and the marginal product—the added value obtained from the resources—equal each other.

To refine our understanding of the theory of marginal productivity, we must differentiate between marginal physical product and marginal revenue product. The former refers to the physical units added by the last additional factor, whereas the latter refers to the dollar value added. Because business people and owners of the factors of production are interested in making the most dollars and because of certain technical issues that need not concern us, we shall use marginal revenue product in our discussion of marginal productivity.

Importance of the Right Combination of Factors

In conditions approaching pure competition, the incentive for business people to seek new combinations of factors of production to reduce costs and increase profits ensures that the economy, and

ultimately society, will progress. The development of new machinery that costs less than the workers it replaces frees the displaced workers to seek jobs where their marginal productivity will be higher, given that there are jobs for the displaced workers and that they are willing to move to another place for work. As we have seen, there is reason to question whether these assumptions about job opportunities and labor mobility are correct.

 Introducing new technology may require changing the combination of factors.

Firms that operate under conditions of imperfect competition must also consider their costs. However, because such firms have some control over supply and thereby can keep their prices higher than they could under pure competition, they can afford to be less efficient. The poorly managed business operating under conditions of partial monopoly can conceal wasteful use of limited resources under the cover of higher prices. The consumer must pay the difference in order to offset the potential loss of profit resulting from such waste.

B Natural Resources and Rent

Natural resources (land, for example) are ingredients that nature provides, which we use in production. These resources are different from the other factors of production primarily because their supply is fixed. Our nation must be considered very fortunate to have such an abundance and variety of resources, although in the last few years we have been made aware of the limitations of our supply of natural resources.

The Nature of Rent

When you hear the term *rent*, you most likely think of a tenant paying a certain amount of money

per month to use property owned by a landlord. That tenant may be a family renting an apartment, a business person renting a store, or a salesperson renting a car. When used in this way, *rent* means the price paid for the use of some durable good such as land, buildings, equipment, or even all three. Economists, however, have a more exact definition for *rent*. *Economic rent* is the price paid for unimproved land or other natural resources. It is the price paid for any factor of production that cannot be reproduced. Economic rent is subject to the same laws of supply and demand as all other factors of production; however, because the supply of natural resources is assumed to be fixed, the supply curve is perfectly inelastic.[1] This means that the price of rent is determined by demand. In our discussion we shall use *land* in its common usage, recognizing that all natural resources may be treated in a similar manner.

Why Do We Pay Rent?

Some of you may wonder why rent should be paid when nature, rather than people, has provided the natural resources. Why should anyone receive payment for something given to all of us? To find the answer to this question we must return to our basic question of allocating limited resources to meet unlimited wants. With the supply of land and other natural resources inelastic, many business people and consumers will seek to own or use this fixed supply for their own benefit. But who should rightfully get it? Obviously, it should be the person who needs it most. How do we tell who has the greatest need? The classical economist would answer that it should be offered to the person who is willing to pay the most, because we determine value in our economic system by price. Let us illustrate this idea by using the case of our "Build-a-City" business. After considering the advantages of several possible locations, we shall examine in detail the merits of the last location for three possible customers.

 Rent helps allocate land to its most valuable use.

The Right Location

We should like to find for our "Build-a-City" plant a location that is reasonably close to our source of supply for labor, for wood, and for inexpensive transportation to our consumer markets. The rent

for land in the heart of the metropolitan area is costly. Retail stores that depend on gathering thousands of consumers are all bidding to get locations accessible to customers. With the supply of land so limited and the demand so great, the rent (the price for the use of the land) is very high. Since we do not need thousands of customers to come to our plant, paying the high rent for this location would be a waste of money.

We cannot locate our plant in the residential section of the city because of zoning laws and "economic laws." It would make little sense for us to pay the cost charged to those seeking to rent or build apartments or homes in this residential area. Besides, the smoke and noise from our factory would create ill will toward our company and would not be tolerated.

Five miles outside the city on an important highway is a piece of land for sale. It is large enough for our plant and for parking spaces for our employees. Very few residential dwellings are located there. Most of the surrounding area is now being used for farming. Public transportation is available for employees, since a bus from the city goes by the site every half hour. Our supply trucks can avoid costly delays in city traffic, and a railroad feeder line is less than two miles away. Those competing with us for the land are farmers and land speculators who foresee the expansion of suburbs, perhaps ten years from now. Our productivity per acre is far greater than that of the farmer, and land speculators cannot afford to pay money out for ten years without receiving any income, merely in the hope that they can get a high price at some time in the future. We can afford to rent the land at a slightly higher price than either the farmer or the land speculators will pay, because we can get the highest return from it. Our limited resources of land are thus finding their greatest value to society. Figure 8–3 shows this relation graphically.

Because the land speculators are the only other entity bidding against us and they believe their potential marginal productivity is much less than ours, we are able to secure the land for slightly more than $400. If another manufacturer had been bidding against us, we might have had to go up

[1]Most economists use the term rent for any payment made for a factor of production that is fixed or has an inelastic supply curve. Therefore the earnings of superstars in entertainment and athletics may be considered economic rent.

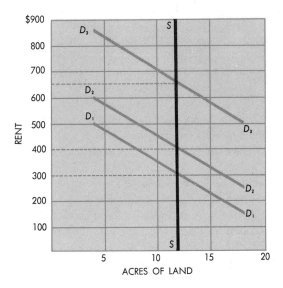

Figure 8–3   Price determination of land
Because the marginal revenue product of our business D_3 is higher than the marginal revenue product of the farmer D_1 and of the speculator D_2, we shall be able to rent the land. Explain why we shall not have to pay our full marginal revenue product for rent ($650) in the example shown here.

their costs remained the same, then the economic rent would be $40,000.

Even before you began to study economics, you may have heard the terms *marginal, submarginal,* and *supramarginal* applied to land. These terms have a very specific meaning in economics. *Marginal land* refers to land for which the cost of producing income from it is equal to that income. With no surplus, it is no-rent land. *Submarginal land* describes land for which the cost of producing income from it is greater than the value of the income. This is wasteful use of our resources. *Supramarginal land* is land for which the cost of producing income from it is less than the value of that income. Land that is submarginal at one time may become marginal or even supramarginal when the demand for the products produced from it increases, causing prices to rise and income to go up. During the world food crisis in the early and mid-1970s, when the demand for U.S. food increased, land that had been submarginal and hence not used was brought under cultivation. The higher prices for food increased the income that could be derived from this land beyond the cost of production.

to our full marginal revenue product of $650. Thus the land in this case does not reach its full marginal revenue product.

Determining Economic Rent

David Ricardo, one of the great classical economists, explained rent as the return arising from differences in the productivity of land. Rent can be figured as the difference between the income derived from using the land and the cost of producing that income. If the cost to a farm family of producing $100,000 worth of wheat is $80,000, including payment to themselves for their labor and their initiative and enterprise, then the economic rent would be $20,000. The farmers must pay themselves for their labor and the capital they use at the same rate as if they were working and using their capital for someone else. If they used more productive land so the yield per acre was greater and their wheat was worth $120,000 while

Cost of Natural Resources

In the mid-1970s the cost of some natural resources rose dramatically and awakened the world to the limitations of supply. The cost for the raw materials necessary for any economy, but particularly for industrialized nations, skyrocketed in 1974, in some instances more than 100 percent. A combination of factors altered market conditions.

On the demand side, the higher income in industrialized countries shifted the demand curve upward and to the right, and bidding between nations became more competitive. The most notable case was competitive bidding for petroleum. Even the multinational oil companies, representing an oligopsony (a few large buyers), lost control of the price they paid for crude. On the supply side, Middle-Eastern oil producers, members of the Organization for Petroleum Exporting Countries (OPEC), created a successful combination of restricted production and higher prices. The effects

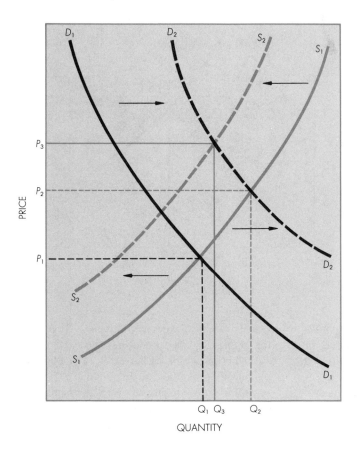

Figure 8–4 Changes in demand and supply for oil between 1960 and 1974

Actual price changes were even greater than those shown.

of this combination on the world economy were traumatic.

We have defined natural resources or land as having a fixed supply. How can we then say that the supply of oil can be shifted? The amount of oil in the ground, in shale rock, coal tars, or wherever it may be found in its natural state, is fixed. We have not located all of it, but fossil fuels take so very long to be formed that we consider them nonreproducible. When we extract the oil, work has been applied and the oil becomes capital to help us further our production.

Now let us return to our analysis of what happened to the cost of oil. Figure 8–4 shows the changes in the demand and supply of oil. D_1 represents demand and S_1 supply during the 1960s. The equilibrium price is P_1, and the quantity sold is Q_1.

As technology spread, the demand for oil grew. This change in demand is reflected by a shift to the right, from D_1 to D_2. However, the supply curve for oil did not change; it is still S_1. The new equilibrium price is where the new demand, D_2, intersects the existing supply curve, S_1. Equilibrium price has moved up to P_2, and the quantity sold clearing the market is Q_2, a significant increase.

In 1973 the Middle-Eastern oil producers, having organized a cartel, imposed an embargo and restricted supply. The effect of this restricted supply is shown by a shift of the supply curve, representing a decrease, from S_1 to S_2. What happened to the equilibrium price? To the quantity sold?

Let us now look at the market structure for oil from 1979 to 1982. The official price for a

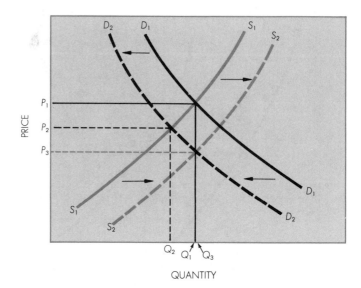

Figure 8–5 Why the price of crude oil has fluctuated

Many circumstances changed between 1979–1982, causing shifts in both supply and demand and therefore different equilibrium prices and quantities exchanged.

barrel of Arabian light crude moved from approximately $12 in 1979 to $34 at the beginning of 1982. This sharp increase in price with an expected increase in profit caused oil companies to intensify their search for oil. New explorations in Alaska, Canada, Mexico, the North Sea, and other areas, coupled with the reopening of wells that were previously too costly to operate, reduced the world's dependence on OPEC. Oil supplies from OPEC dropped from 70 percent to less than 50 percent. Domestic output increased sufficiently to allow a reduction in imports from 50 percent to less than 30 percent. During this same time period the high cost of oil caused consumers to (a) shift to other fuels, (b) develop and use more efficient machines, and (c) adopt new habits, such as turning thermostats down in the winter and up in the summer. A worldwide recession also caused a decline in the use of oil. Daily demand dropped from 65.11 million barrels in 1979 to 57 million barrels in 1982, a decline of 12.5 percent. Figure 8–5 shows what happened in 1982.

Q_1 represents the quantity of oil that members of OPEC *agreed to* at their meeting early in 1982. There was a surplus of oil in the world that was driving prices below their officially agreed on OPEC price. Pressured by Saudi Arabia, the largest oil producer, member countries agreed to limit supplies to Q_1. Demand for oil was esti-

mated to follow the demand curve D_1. By restricting supply to Q_1, the producers expected to realize a fixed price of $34 per barrel, P_1, given the supply curve S_1 and the demand curve D_1.

OPEC failed to take several major factors into consideration when setting a fixed price. Demand for oil actually declined for all of the reasons stated above, including a worldwide recession that was deeper and longer than anticipated. This decrease in demand forced the demand curve to shift to the left from D_1 to D_2, bringing the new equilibrium price down to P_2. While OPEC kept the official price at $34, member countries were actually selling their oil at $30 a barrel and below—where S_1 and D_2 intersect. The new equilibrium price was P_2, and the new quantity sold was Q_2.

Many oil-producing countries, in anticipation of high oil revenues, borrowed huge sums of money for their economic development. For example, Mexico had a foreign debt of $80 billion. To meet their repayment commitments, these countries frequently increased their production, thus producing a new short-term supply curve, which is shown by the shifting of the supply curve to the right, from S_1 to S_2. The new equilibrium price was P_3, and quantity increased from Q_2 to Q_3 (same as Q_1, but at a considerably lower price).

The early months of 1986 saw the collapse of OPEC's power to control the market. The glut of oil brought prices below $13 a barrel. However, this was a mixed blessing. As the lower prices filtered throughout the economy, costs were reduced and purchasing power shifted from oil-producing to oil-importing nations. The United States and other nations whose governments and private banks had lent huge sums of money to such nations as Mexico were in danger of not being repaid. Just as important in the long run was the abandonment of projects to find oil substitutes. Investments in methods to get oil from shale rock and coal tar and in research on substitute forms of energy dropped—a course of action we may regret in the future.

C Capital and Interest

Competition for Use of Loanable Funds

One definition of capital is a "man-made instrument of production." We should expect interest to be the payment or reward to the owners of capital for the part their money plays in obtaining the means of production. When we think of interest, however, we are more likely to think of it as payment to those who lend money from those who borrow money.

In our economy, business, consumers, and the various levels of government all borrow money and pay for its use. In borrowing, they compete with one another for the use of loanable funds.

Business Pays for Use of Capital

When we consider production from the point of view of management, we must first decide what to produce and then determine what natural resources and labor are needed to make these goods. An increase in production is most frequently achieved by putting tools (machinery) into the hands of workers to make them more productive. How will workers get these tools?

Let us first explain in a very simple way how the tools can be obtained, assuming that this is the only business in our society. Under our present system of production, we produce $1,000 worth of goods per day. We now take 20 percent of our workers and shift their efforts into the manufacture of tools of production. This reduces the value of the items we are producing for consumption to $800 a day. After 10 days we have sacrificed $2,000, but we have also completed the machines we need to produce more goods. These machines, which represent added capital, were obtained by the company by sacrificing present output of goods. Is it worth it? Only if the value of our production has increased sufficiently to pay back the $2,000 we have lost plus some value in addition. If additional value is achieved, it is the result of the increased capital (tools) we added to production. This capital, like the other factors of production, must be paid for.

In our complex society today, we define interest as the price paid for using money or loanable funds. Business people who wish to increase the size of a store (adding capital) or to buy machinery for a factory (also adding capital) borrow money. They expect to be able to increase business enough to pay back the principal (the amount of money borrowed) and the interest (the price for borrowing the funds) and still have money left over. The money they borrow comes from those who have saved some of their income instead of spending it all on consumer items. This in turn frees workers who might have been producing consumer goods to engage in the production of capital goods. Furthermore, those people who have money saved are now able to lend it for the production of capital goods and thus to receive interest as their reward for sacrificing their present desires to consume. We can now see the relation between interest as payment for loanable funds and as payment for capital.

 Interest rates will influence the allocation of loanable funds.

Consumers Pay for Use of Loanable Funds

Consumers as well as business people borrow money. Total short- and intermediate-term consumer credit outstanding amounted to more than $668 billion by the end of 1985. The reasons for consumer borrowing are many, but in each case borrowers induce lenders to forgo the use of funds by offering interest. Some loans may be looked on as investments, as in the case of money borrowed for a college education. Some may be used to take care of an unexpected crisis. Some are for the purchase of goods that are costly but that are used for many years (durable goods). The demand for loanable funds by consumers competes with the demand for loanable funds by business people. In each case the borrower pays interest for the use of the lender's capital.

Government Pays for Use of Loanable Funds

The federal, state, and local governments also need to borrow money. Sometimes this money is borrowed to pay for important capital improvements, such as road construction; sometimes it is used to meet an unforeseen emergency, such as a flood; and, in the case of the federal government, it is used to finance a planned deficit in order to help overcome a depression. (The impact of the huge federal deficits in the mid-1980s will be discussed in Chapter 15.) State and local governments often compete with others seeking to borrow, and this competition causes interest rates to rise. The federal government helps the smaller units of government to borrow funds by allowing the interest on their bonds to be tax-free.

Determining Interest Rates

Interest is stated as a rate of return for money borrowed, whether for business, consumer, or government use. The rate of interest specifies how many dollars the borrower has to pay for every $100 borrowed for one year. It tells the lender how many dollars he or she will receive for each $100 lent for that year. A business that borrows $5,000 from a bank at 10 percent must pay back

$5,500 at the end of one year. The practice of having the interest paid in advance, so that the borrower receives principal minus interest, is called *discounting*.

Stating interest as a rate rather than as an absolute figure ($500 in the above example) allows the borrower to make a comparison with others borrowing different amounts. A business borrowing $10,000 for one year with $900 interest is thus paying more dollars in interest than the borrower in our example above, but is paying a lower interest rate (9 percent).

The examples used above assume that the borrower has the use of the entire principal for the full year. If payments are made on the principal before the end of the full term of the loan (many small loans are repaid monthly), the interest is higher. This is because interest is being paid on the full amount ($5,000) when some of the principal has already been repaid. The truth-in-lending act made it mandatory that all lending institutions state the true, or annual, interest rate to be paid by the customer.

There are many factors that cause interest rates to vary:

1. The supply of loanable funds and demand for them.
2. The difference in the risk of repayment.
3. The duration (long-term loans generally command higher interest rates).
4. The cost of administering the loan (short-term loans are far more costly when figured as a percentage of the loan).
5. The ability to shop around for the best "buy."

Pure Interest

Economists frequently speak of "the" interest rates as though the factors just mentioned did not exist and every borrower paid the same rate. They are referring to "pure" interest, which is the rate paid to use money without the factors mentioned above taken into consideration. The rate of interest for long-term U.S. government bonds is usually cited as the closest approximation of pure interest, because the factors mentioned previously, except for the first, are almost eliminated.

Real Versus Nominal Interest Rates

Suppose you borrowed $1,000 for one year at 15 percent in 1980. In 1984 you went back to the bank, but this time they charged you only 12 percent for your $1,000 loan. Which was the better interest rate for you?

In 1980 inflation was 13.5 percent. That means that you had to earn $1,135 that year in order to buy the same goods that $1,000 bought one year earlier. Since inflation eroded 13.5 percent of your purchasing power, or the money you paid back to the bank, your real interest rate was 1.5 percent (15 − 13.5 = 1.5), although your nominal interest rate was 15 percent. In 1985 the rate of inflation was 3.6 percent. What was your real interest rate? (Just subtract the annual inflationary rate from your nominal interest rate to find your real interest rate.)

 The expectation of the inflationary rate will influence the setting of nominal interest rates.

The Demand for Loanable Funds

Demand for loanable funds refers to the amount of dollars that people will borrow for a given time at different rates of interest. These demands come most often from the money requirements of business people, consumers, and governments. If we define interest as the price paid for loanable funds, we can rightfully expect the reappearance of our familiar demand and supply model.

Demand of Business

What determines the shape of a demand curve for loanable funds? Once again the law of diminishing returns appears, with the result that the marginal revenue product of money causes the demand curve to slope downward. The first $1,000 that we borrow to improve the looks of a store or add to the productive capacity of a factory will generally yield a bigger return than the next $1,000. The second $1,000 will usually yield a bigger return than the third $1,000, and so on. Borrowers in business must try to determine potential earnings above the additional cost of adding units of capital and then compare that figure with the cost of the interest. They can afford to borrow up to the point at which the interest for the last amount borrowed (marginal cost for loanable funds) equals the amount they can earn above their costs on the last unit bought with the borrowed money (marginal revenue product). Thus if they borrow an additional $10,000 and must pay $1,000 for its use for a year, they should foresee earning more than this amount from the use of this money; otherwise it will not pay them to borrow these funds. Here, as with wage rates and rent, we see how the theory of the marginal revenue product determines the demand. Because the money is usually spent on items that last many years, business people are forced to estimate what the long-term yield will be on each unit of capital they buy.

Demand of the Consumer

Most of the money that consumers borrow is not used in production; it is used to satisfy the needs of the borrower. It is, therefore, subject to the law of diminishing marginal utility. Thus the demand curve is similar to the downward-sloping one applicable to the business person. Demand for meeting emergencies is very inelastic; for durable consumer goods such as automobiles, more elastic; and for luxury items, most elastic.

Demand of Government

The federal government's demand curve for most loanable funds is inelastic, because until recently much of the national government's debt came about during such emergencies as wars and recessions, when it was impractical to cover all expenditures through taxes. The demand curve of state and local governments is more elastic.

The Supply of Loanable Funds

The supply of loanable funds refers to the amount of dollars that lenders will offer for a given time at different rates of interest. The sources of loanable funds are personal savings, business savings, and lending by commercial banks.

Most personal savings come from families whose incomes are in the top 10 percent in the nation. These people are more likely to save because they can buy the things they need and still have money left over. Much of our saving is for particular purposes, such as a college education, a house, or protection in case of loss of income.

Most business saving finds its way back into business to support its growth. Particularly since World War II, companies have shown a tendency to use money from profits to support expansion, rather than paying it all out in dividends or borrowing money in the open market. Although such businesses are not contributing to the market for loanable funds, they keep existing supplies of loanable funds at a higher level by satisfying or reducing their own needs. When not using their savings, they sometimes make these funds available to other businesses.

When commercial banks make loans available to borrowers, they are extending credit. This credit is a primary source of loanable funds needed by businesses as well as by consumers. (These functions will be explained more fully when we discuss banking in Chapter 14.)

Not all savings are available as loanable funds. Some individuals and businesses may decide that they prefer to keep their savings in a form in which it is not available to borrowers. Their decision to hold their money rather than make it available is determined by their *liquidity preference,* the desire to keep savings in the form of ready cash. It should be recognized that keeping savings in cash during periods of rising prices is equivalent to losing purchasing power.

Amount of Loanable Funds

What determines the amount of loanable funds? Although economists do not completely agree, most recognize that higher interest rates will cause some savers to transfer some of their money from a highly liquid condition (cash) to loanable funds (interest-bearing securities). Modern economic theory places great emphasis on the relation of savings to the general economic well-being of the nation (national income). People tend to save more as income rises. Greater savings provide more money for loanable funds. We can conclude that the supply curve of loanable funds slopes upward, unlike the demand curve for loanable funds and

like most of the supply curves we have been discussing.

Interaction of Demand and Supply of Loanable Funds

Interest rates, like the other factors of production, are determined by the interaction of demand and supply. For a given demand for loanable funds and a given supply, interest rates will be at the point where supply and demand curves meet.

According to classical theory, in the free marketplace interest exercises a significant influence in regulating the economy. Loanable funds will be steered into those businesses that can afford to pay the highest interest rates. These are the same businesses that have the highest marginal revenue product and are producing the things that the consumer wants most. High consumer demand, supply remaining equal, means high prices. High prices will induce business persons to expand their capital facilities, even if they must borrow at high interest rates. This will result in an increase in the production of goods consumers want. It will usually bring higher profits also.

Another regulatory function that interest is supposed to have is keeping savings and investment in balance. When business conditions are poor, more loanable funds will be available (supply) than businesses and consumers want (demand). Interest rates will go down to a point where many businesses will find it profitable to borrow. This will help stimulate the economy. If business conditions are rising so fast that there arises a threat of inflation and a shortage of loanable funds, the interest rates will rise enough to discourage marginal producers from expanding.

In the mid-1970s interest rates began to soar. This was a reflection of a deliberate policy by the Federal Reserve Board to keep the supply of loanable funds from growing too rapidly, which would be inflationary (see Chapters 13 and 14). In the 1980s high interest rates discouraged consumers from borrowing for purchases that would involve long-term commitments, such as homes. Even businesses, which try to pass along the extra costs for borrowing in the form of higher prices to consumers, hesitated to borrow when rates exceeded 20 percent.

 Lower interest rates can trigger a business expansion.

How Free Is the Market for Loanable Funds?

Until the 1930s, the price for loanable funds was largely determined by demand and supply in a free market. As the government has become increasingly involved with the total economy, the lending market has become much less free. The government, by borrowing large sums of money, influences the interest rates set by the Federal Reserve Bank. Government support for certain kinds of loans—to housing, small business, and farmers—and its powers to tax and spend also affect a very large portion of the market. Because of this government influence, most economists refer to the price for loanable funds as an *administered price,* subject to modification by individuals. Some economists believe that the federal government has gone too far in trying to control the money market. Others think it is the duty of the government to control the money market to help keep the economy prosperous and the country "healthy."

D Entrepreneurship and Profits

What Is Profit?

Entrepreneurship is directly responsible for initiating production. The business person (entrepreneur) takes a cue from consumers in deciding what they want—or, in the case of a new product, what they might want. The business person who believes that a business can be organized by assembling the other three factors of production into an efficient producing unit and selling a product so that revenue will be greater than cost will go ahead. The expectation of making a profit is the incentive.

Profit means different things to different people. According to some public opinion polls, many people are not sure what it is, but they are sure it is too large and represents too much of the consumer's dollar. Workers may look at profit as an unfairly large payment to the entrepreneur that deprives them of a higher wage. The business person thinks of profit as the difference between total revenue and total cost. During negotiations before the settlement of the second baseball strike in August, 1985, the Players' Association claimed the owners had made profits of $91 million, an accounting firm said owner profits were $43 million, and the owners insisted they had lost $9 million. The truth was that all three were correct.

The disparity in the figures was due to the fact that each group was defining profit differently. Let us now see if we can develop a more exact definition of what profit is.

Gross profit is the difference between what a business firm sells its product for and what it costs to produce that product. The merchant buys $200,000 worth of merchandise during the year and sells it for $270,000. His gross profit is $70,000. The percentage difference between his cost and the selling price is 35 percent, and he calls this markup.

Net profit is what the business person has left after paying expenses—rent, wages, and interest—and setting aside money to allow for the loss due to depreciation (wearing out) of capital. Our merchant has to subtract from his gross profit his payments for rent ($6,000), wages ($20,000), interest on money borrowed ($1,000), repairs and upkeep ($1,000), taxes ($1,000), electricity and other expenses ($1,000). Expenses for operating the business come to $30,000. Gross profit is $70,000, and net profit is $40,000.

Economists have a narrower definition of what constitutes profit. They are concerned with payment for all the resources that have gone into production, whether they come from outside the business, like those listed above, or from inside the business. Costs that come from the outside are *explicit costs*. Those costs within the firm are *implicit costs*. Economists point out that our merchant has not paid himself a wage (some prefer the term "salary") or interest on his own capital invested in the business. If he worked for someone else for the same hours and with the same skill, he would be paid a going market wage for his effort. Likewise, if he took money out of the business and placed it in securities involving similar risks, he would receive dividends. Because economists are concerned with allocation of resources and their efficient use, they must think in terms of *opportunity costs* (sometimes called *alternative costs*)—the value that could be produced if these implicit factors were used in producing other things. If the merchant could get a job paying $30,000 a year and earn 8 percent, or $3,200, on an investment of $40,000 of capital, economists would insist that he subtract an additional $33,200 from his net profit. *Economic* (or *pure*) *profit* is what is left after all explicit and implicit costs for wages, rent, and interest are paid. It is possible to have a loss instead of a profit. What is the economic, or pure, profit of our merchant?

 Accountants and economists define profits differently.

Why Should There Be Profits?

Because our merchant has been paid for his labor and for interest on his capital, why should he receive profits also? Probably the most important justification for profits is that the expectation of profits acts as a motivating force to get people to:

1. Start businesses to produce goods and services that consumers want.
2. Think up new or better products to attract customers (innovation) and assume the risks of production.
3. Improve the efficiency of production so as to use fewer resources at lower cost.
4. Provide funds for improving and expanding of the firm.

To see how the expectation of profits might influence business decisions, let us return to our own business venture, "Build-a-City." Why did we wish to start a business at all? We all had jobs that gave us a living wage. In addition, available statistics showed that an average of 600 businesses fail in the nation each week. Why look for trouble? We took the chance because we felt we could be one of the small number of firms that succeed in making large profits, more than we could earn in our present jobs. It may be the profit motive that caused us to think about a new product that consumers would want, or it may be that we thought about the new product first and then decided that the idea could be put into action, thus providing us with a profit. In either event, society benefits by the motivation that profits give to producing new and better products. The economist Joseph Schumpeter believed that much of society's progress could be attributed to the influence of the profit motive on new ideas in business.

With our business operating successfully, we now look for ways to improve it. We try plastic as a substitute for wood, which has become increasingly expensive. We try new machines and hire more workers instead of paying overtime. These reduced costs may lead to additional profits. In a less favorable situation, where competing producers have lowered costs and taken away some of our business, we might have to find methods of reducing our costs to make any profit at all. In either event the motivation of profits benefits us as well as society.

Suppose our business does well enough that we want to expand our productive capacity. We shall have to obtain additional funds. We can borrow the money by selling bonds or by obtaining a loan from the bank. However, if interest rates are high, we may want to finance expansion ourselves. Instead of taking our profits out of the business and enjoying a higher standard of living now, we use these profits to pay for expansion. Because of implicit costs, we must decide whether our profits will yield more invested in our own business or invested in something else. We may consider reducing our risks by diversifying—putting our profits in other kinds of enterprises. What influences will determine what we do?

What Are the Sources of Economic Profit?

If we lived in a society that had pure competition and a static economy within which no changes ever took place in products, efficiency, consumer preferences, and sources of supply, we would have no economic profit. With all knowledge complete, all factors would receive their marginal revenue product and the market price would leave no surplus for economic profit.

 Under pure competition there would be no economic profit in the long run.

The real world we live in is not static. It is changing constantly—and in many different directions. Our economy rarely sees pure competition at work. Therefore, economic profit does exist. When profit is made because of innovations, inventions, or efficiency—all of which allow a firm to have a temporary advantage—it may be regarded as a just reward. Sometimes profit results from pure chance, such as a big change in supply and/or demand that makes existing inventories much more valuable. Sometimes profit is made by not paying the factors of production their full marginal revenue product. These sources of economic profit stem primarily from dynamic aspects in society and cannot be easily avoided. They are usually temporary and rarely hurt the economy.

Effect of Competition on Profit

Profit in the long run can easily result from differing degrees of imperfect competition. Under strong competitive conditions, an industry that is making high profits will attract additional firms into the field, causing prices to decline. If, however, barriers such as patents are placed in the way of new firms entering the field, profits may continue to be high. If a business concern is able to restrict supplies (shift the supply curve to the left), prices will be artificially high and yield higher profits. This was the motive behind the cut in the production of crude by some of the largest oil-producing countries. A study of the profits of various industries in the United States showed that

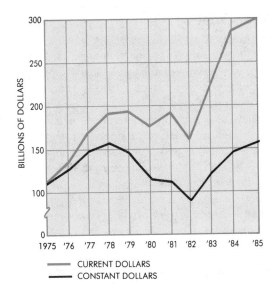

Figure 8–6 A look at corporate profits

The graph shows corporate profits after adjustments have been made for inventory valuation and capital consumption. Note the fluctuations. The changes in profits are less severe in constant dollars than in current dollars. (Source: Department of Commerce, Bureau of Economic Analysis.)

those that were most competitive—textiles and clothing—had the smallest profits, whereas those that were most like monopolies and oligopolies—electrical equipment—had the largest profits.

Patents and Copyrights

There are two special cases we should recognize in which government action endorses monopoly and thereby interferes with a competitive market in determining price. To encourage inventions and new ideas, the government issues *patents* to inventors. Upon receiving approval from the United States Patent Office of their patent applications, inventors have a monopoly on their inventions for seventeen years. *Copyrights* on the publication of literary productions are issued to authors or publishers and remain in effect until fifty years after the death of the author. The monopoly prices allow for higher profits, but these profits are the rewards for furthering progress.

Franchises

A *franchise* is a license that some governmental authority grants to a business, giving it the exclusive monopoly to perform a particular service in a given area.[2] A franchise is usually granted to a natural monopoly because it is in the interest of society to prevent duplication of service. Under the franchise, government regulates prices, and profit is a major consideration in determining those prices. Public utilities are perhaps the best example of government franchises. In such cases, the franchise grants an exclusive monopoly to perform a particular service. Prices are regulated, usually in relation to profit.

How Large Should Profits Be?

The debate on the size of profits seems to be a never-ending one. Although our classical model of pure competition calls for no economic (pure) profits in the long run, it does allow for temporary profits. Such profits help to allocate resources where society thinks they are needed most, and also motivate business to operate efficiently and provide new and better products. Actually it is the expectation of making profits that causes business firms to take risks, to innovate, and to increase their efficiency. However, if businesses did not make profits, there would be no expectation, and thus no motivation to produce.

Because perfect competition is rare, the amount of profits is partly determined by the degree of imperfect competition. Monopolistic practices may yield excessively high profits, causing con-

sumers to pay more for the product than they would under competitive conditions. These higher prices may also protect inefficient operation and interfere with the allocation of resources. Very high profits in an industry have frequently brought governmental investigations by Congress, the Justice Department, and various regulatory agencies.

Businesses that involve great risk have to offer opportunities for substantial rewards to provide incentive for investors. Those businesses that are quite stable can attract firms without offering such high rewards. When the conditions of supply and demand that characterize pure competition are too distorted by interference with a relatively free market or by special circumstances such as war, some government action is called for. A tax beyond the normal corporation profits tax, known as the *excess profits tax,* was in operation during World War II. Enactment of this tax is an example of government action to protect the consumer. Such action can result in corporate inefficiency, however, because incentives for cutting costs are reduced.

Fluctuations in after-tax profits for all business corporations have tended to reflect closely general business conditions. The variation in profit from industry to industry shows how competition can act in limiting profits.

 Critics of capitalism fail to see the role of profits in allocating resources.

Perhaps the only answer we can safely give to the question of size of profits is that profits should be as large as necessary to attract enough businesses to provide an adequate supply of the goods and services that consumers want at prices they are willing to pay.

[2]The term also applies when a manufacturer gives a distributor the right to handle his or her products.

E The Problem: Does the Classical Model Distribute Income Fairly to the Factors of Production?

You should now understand how the various factors of production are paid. Our model calls for each factor to be used to that point at which marginal factor cost and marginal revenue product are

equal. If all businesses operate in this way, the business person will realize the greatest possible profit and society will benefit from the most efficient allocation of limited resources.

There are many critics of this theory. Most of the opposition has focused on the concern that one factor of production might receive too large a portion of the pie at the expense of other factors. Some critics have suggested eliminating the classical model entirely on the grounds that the assumptions it makes, such as a purely competitive market, are no longer applicable. Others have suggested altering the model. Consider the alternatives before reaching a tentative conclusion. Keep in mind the total productive process and also the role of functional distribution to the factors of production.

Critics Who Oppose the Model

The best-known critic of capitalism was Karl Marx. (We have already looked at some Marxist thinking in Chapter 3.) His theory of the value of labor is pertinent to our present discussion of the fair distribution of income to the factors of production.

Marx's Theory of the Value of Labor

All wealth, said Marx, is the result of the labor that is put into its creation. Natural resources have no value unless people use them. Capital is a product of human labor. The income landowners and investors receive is unearned because they are contributing nothing to the value of the product. What the capitalist receives in the form of rent, interest, and profit is surplus value that rightfully belongs to the worker. The worker is exploited and the capitalist is the exploiter, and society becomes two hostile groups. The capitalist accumulates more and more capital, but the worker does not have the purchasing power to buy back the goods he or she produces. This situation leads to declining demand and periodic depressions. Eventually a revolution will take place, and labor will then receive full value for its product.

According to Marxian theory, the United States, with its predominantly private-enterprise economy, should see labor receiving a progressively smaller and smaller share of the national income and landlords, investors, and entrepreneurs receiving an increasingly larger share. Figure 8–1 shows, however, that wages have been the only reward that has increased greatly as a percentage of the national income.

If the market with its pricing mechanism does not determine answers to the allocation of resources—the *What, How,* and *For whom*—then what will? Is a central planning board, as in communism, in a better position to make decisions than is the market, where the consumer is the decision maker?

Henry George and the Single Tax Movement

Another well-known critic, who focused on only a portion of the classical model, was U.S. writer Henry George. In his famous book *Progress and Poverty,* published in 1879, George advocated a plan that caused such interest that over a million copies of his book were sold.

George reasoned that although the supply of land in the world is fixed, the number of people using it is increasing. With the increase in its use, the value of the land increases. Thus land on the edge of a city increases in value as the population of the city spills over into the suburbs. Owners of the land are now able to collect a higher rent than before, even though they didn't earn it. Because they did not make the land or improve the land, what they receive in rent is an unearned increment.

George believed that the receipt by landlords of pure, or economic, rent was the cause of all poverty. If this rent were taxed at 100 percent, all society would share in the value that nature and the movement of population made possible. He said that the income from such a tax would be sufficient to finance all government activity and permit the abolition of all other taxes. Because of this basic premise, the idea was called the Single Tax Plan. The money saved by eliminating other taxes could then be used in production.

There are a number of obvious shortcomings to George's theory, such as the fact that rent provides less than 1 percent of national income and therefore is inadequate for our government's revenue needs. However, some underdeveloped and developing countries are giving serious consideration to his ideas. The nationalizing of all wealth below the surface is extremely important to Mexico with its newly discovered oil deposits.

Critics Who Accept the Model with Modifications

Throughout our study of economics, we have referred to the world that "is" and the world that "ought to be." So far, the ought-to-be world has largely been our classical model operating under market conditions of pure competition. In Part Three we shall introduce another model. However, among those who accept most of the classical model are those who feel the world that "is" is so far from the original model that new methods should be applied to the functional distribution of income. These new methods would either revive the intent of the classical economist who sought an efficient and fair method of distribution or recognize the importance of other values in our Western heritage.

The Need to Limit Unearned Interest

We have justified payment of interest as a reward for saving instead of consuming and as a necessary condition if the economy is to have sufficient funds to buy the capital needed for its growth. We cannot expect people to make funds available without some reward. Criticism of our present system of distribution of rewards for loanable funds is concentrated on those people who receive interest from inherited wealth.

The right to hand down property—including loanable funds—is part of our entire concept of private property. Very few people in our country would question the right of individuals to bequeath to their heirs enough wealth for them to live decently and to have the means to get a good start in life.

However, many have questioned the fairness of allowing heirs to live on accumulated fortunes without earning anything themselves. To prevent what may be called "unearned interest" and the perpetuation of a "moneyed class," states have passed *inheritance taxes* (on those receiving) and the federal government has imposed *estate* and *gift taxes* (on the estate or giver). These taxes have been aimed primarily at gift estates above $600,000. Because there are various "loopholes" in the inheritance laws, few people have protested.

Some economic historians claim that it was through the accumulation of huge fortunes that we were able to have enough loanable funds in this country to support our economic growth. With high taxes on accumulated wealth, we may dry up our sources of loanable funds unless the government steps in to supply whatever funds are necessary for our capital expansion. Would we be better off if the government made decisions on where loanable funds should go?

Considering an Answer

How free do we want our economy to be? Do the economically strong factors of production receive greater rewards than the weaker factors? To what extent should rewards be based on the degree of service to society? What problems can a planned economy have in distributing its shares to be factors of production? Will the market be destroyed as the principal method of allocating resources? If government made the decisions, would those decisions be more equitable? How may your values influence your decision?

Pricing the Factors of Production

Following is a step-by-step review of the demand and supply forces interacting in the market for the factors of production. Here business represents demand seeking to buy additional units of natural resources, labor, or capital in a competitive market. The owner of the factors represents supply. Under pure competition, the cost of buying an additional unit is set by the market. Because land is assumed to be fixed, it has an inelastic supply and is not applicable to this example.

■ The marginal revenue product *MRP* is the value in dollars that each additional factor adds. As units of a factor are added, each additional factor will probably add greater value to production than did the previous unit, until the law of diminishing returns sets in. At what point does the law of diminishing returns start?

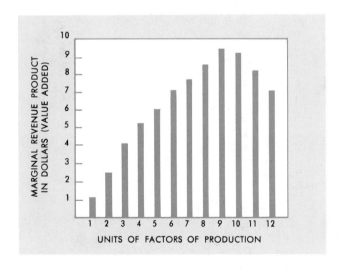

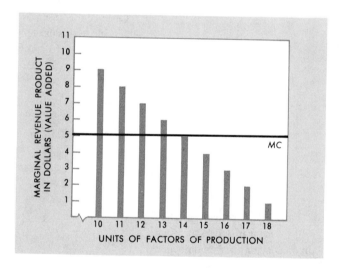

■ Under pure competition, interacting supply and demand set the cost for each factor of production. The equilibrium price is $5. This means that at a price of $5 the individual firm can buy as many units of the factor of production as it wishes.

MRP	Units	MC
$9	10	$5
8	11	5
7	12	5
6	13	5
5	14	5
4	15	5
3	16	5
2	17	5
1	18	5

■ Above on the left is a schedule for an individual firm operating in an industry characterized by the first two graphs. The graph above on the right depicts the same data. The marginal revenue product *MRP* is the demand by that firm for buying additional units. Marginal cost *MC* represents the supply of the factors for that firm. The cost is set in the market; the individual business is too small to alter it (pure competition). How many units of the factor will the firm buy? Equilibrium is where demand *MRP* intersects supply *MC* for that firm.

  If the firm bought a fifteenth unit, the cost for that unit, *MC*, would be $5, whereas the value added to production, *MRP*, would be $4. Therefore, the firm would lose money on that unit. Why does the firm hire the fourteenth unit? The firm will not know whether it will make money, break even, or lose money until the fourteenth unit is bought.

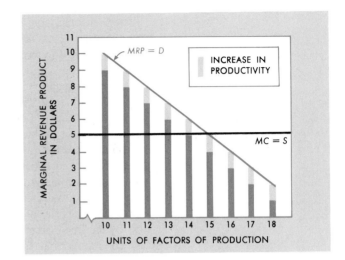

■ How many units of factors of production would the firm buy if productivity increased?

If the owners of the factors of production move into a monopoly position and raise their rates by $2 (MC) without any increase in productivity, how will the firm react?

Chapter Highlights

1. Dividing the income received from production among the factors of production is called functional distribution.

2. The interaction of demand and supply will determine the price for each factor of production.

3. Additional units of factors of production will be added up to the point where the marginal revenue product and the marginal factor cost are equal.

4. Getting the right combination of factors can improve the efficiency of production.

5. Rent is most commonly defined as the price paid for the use of some durable good. Economic rent is the price paid for the use of natural resources or any other factor that cannot be increased or decreased in response to price changes.

6. In contrast to the other factors, land and most other natural resources are assumed to have a fixed supply, which is shown by an inelastic supply curve.

7. Although some critics question the justification of paying rent, such payment helps allocate natural resources efficiently.

8. In the mid-1970s the cost for some natural resources rose sharply as producers tried to form oligopolies, or international cartels.

9. The Organization of Petroleum Exporting Countries (OPEC) successfully controlled the supply and therefore the price of oil in the 1970s. Oil-importing nations responded in the 1980s with changes in demand and the development of oil substitutes.

10. Interest is the price paid for the use of loanable funds. Because of the use that is made of borrowed money, it can also be said that interest is payment for the use of capital.

11. Business people, consumers, and governments borrow money and pay interest.

12. Interest is stated in terms of a rate of return. Rates vary because of the demand and supply of loanable funds, risk, time, administrative costs, and competition in the market. Real interest is the nominal rate minus the inflationary rate.

13. Demand for loanable funds is subject to the influence of the marginal revenue product for businesses and diminishing marginal utility for consumers; it is inelastic for the federal government.

14. The supply of loanable funds comes primarily from individuals in the highest income group and from business itself. Higher interest rates will tend to decrease the liquidity preference of people.

15. Since 1930 the price of loanable funds has been determined less and less by the free market, as government has increased its borrowing and control over interest rates.

16. Profit means something different to the public, the business firm, and the economist. The economist, who is interested in payments to all factors of production, must consider both explicit and implicit costs before figuring economic profit—what is left over after all other factors have been paid.

17. Profit serves our economy well when it is used as an incentive for entrepreneurs to make products the consumer wants, to increase business efficiency, and to stimulate progress. Economic profits are eliminated in a static economy with pure competition. Profit from imperfect competition represents inefficient use of the factors of production.

Study Aids

Key Terms

functional distribution	franchise	gross profit
productivity	liquidity preference	economic profit
marginal cost	administered price	net profit
marginal revenue product	production function	explicit costs
theory of marginal productivity	loanable funds	implicit costs
economic rent	interest	alternative costs
submarginal land	real interest	patent
single tax	principal	excess profits tax
copyright	discounting	surplus value

Questions

1. Allocating the various factors of production and distributing rewards to them are basic problems of a business enterprise.
   (a) What determines how a firm's revenues will be divided among the factors of production?
   (b) What might induce a business firm to change the way in which it combines the factors of production?
2. Explain the relation between demand for land and determination of rent.
3. Using the classical view of rent, explain why

payments of rent for land differ with varying degrees of productivity.

4. Explain the changes in the market for oil in the early 1980s.

5. Interest, like rent, represents payment for use—in this case, use of loanable funds.

   (a) Explain how paying interest for the use of money can be justified.

   (b) What factors determine the rate charged?

   (c) How has activity of the federal government influenced the rates of interest?

6. Interest differs in some respects from the payments made to the other factors of production.

   (a) Explain the reasons for variation in the demand for loanable funds on the part of the individual consumer, the business organization, and federal and local governments.

   (b) How may changes in interest rates help regulate the economy?

   (c) Why is it important to project the inflationary rate in evaluating interest rates?

7. Interpretations of the word *profit* differ according to the individual's point of view. Explain the meaning of the term *profit* to the business owner, the public, and the economist.

8. What is the role of profit in a free economy? What are the arguments in favor of profit? Against?

Problems

1. Henry George was among those suggesting modification of the classical model of capitalism.

   (a) Explain the basic ideas of the single tax advocated by Henry George.

   (b) What effect would the application of his theory have on land development today?

   (c) What are the main objections to his theory?

2. The meaning of *fair profit* is different for producer and consumer, and varies from one industry to another.

   (a) Study the information available on some of the cases in the petroleum industry and present the arguments of the producer and the consumer concerning prices and profits.

   (b) Study some of the requests of public utilities (railroad, telephone, electric companies) for rate changes and indicate the factors these utilities use to determine a base rate.

3. Functional distribution in the classical tradition has been distorted by such factors as wage and price controls, excess profits taxes, profit-sharing plans, rent controls, and the guaranteed annual wage. Explain how any of these factors would alter the normal allocation of resources. Then take any two of these factors and examine industries or periods in which they altered the traditional market mechanism. Did the changes you predicted take place?

Government and Its Developing Role In the Economy

Although the classical model depends on the market, with price instead of government allocating resources of the nation, no one would deny that government has become increasingly important in answering many basic economic questions. In this chapter, we will consider the government's relationship to the economy in the classical model of pure competition, its relationship to today's economy, and the practical application of public finance. We will consider both regulation and production by government.

Government, like business, pays out money and is paid for its activities. How government prepares its budget, what outlays are included in that budget, and what taxes government imposes are issues that affect everyone in the nation. We will examine some of the principles used as guides in attacking many of the controversial problems concerning government and the economy.

This chapter presents some of the most difficult matters every citizen has to face. Almost everyone wants to see better schools, universally available medical care, and good roads; but are you as a taxpayer willing to help pay for them? Are you motivated to work longer hours if you can keep only two-thirds of that extra income? If government is short of revenue, should it tax or borrow? If taxes have to be increased, how do you separate self-interest from the public good?

Chapter Objectives

When you complete this chapter, you should be able to:

- Explain how the classical economic model views government in terms of the four conditions government is expected to establish and maintain.
- Discuss four principles that can be used to decide on the extent of desirable government involvement in the economy.
- Discuss how both the legislative and the executive branches of government should participate in preparing a budget.
- List at least two main types of expenditures by each level of government that are peculiar to that level.
- Present a case for or against any tax, based on the characteristics of a fair tax.
- Evaluate the income, sales, and property taxes.
- Suggest how each level of government might improve its tax structure.
- Compare the public expenditures and revenues of other countries with our own.
- Determine when government borrowing might be more appropriate than taxing.

A The Nature of Government's Role in the Economy

Government's Role in the Classical Model

The classical model is frequently referred to as the private or free enterprise system, because it places its emphasis on the individual decisions of the consumer and of the business person, made without interference by the government. This means there must be a free flow of goods and services as ordered by the consumer and a free market for the factors of production to be hired or bought by the business person. However, certain conditions must exist in order for the market mechanism to function, and providing this type of environment may require some minimal government action.

Pillars of Capitalism

Private property, the right of the individual to exercise reasonable control over things owned, provides an important incentive for producing.

Related to this right is *freedom of contract,* allowing individuals to enter into agreements resulting in the production and distribution of goods and services. *Economic freedom*—guaranteeing the individual the right to move within the economy to any job desired, to buy or sell property, and to start a business—permits the economy to change. *Competition* assures efficiency of production and safeguards the consumer.

 In the classical model, government's role in the economy is largely restricted to safeguarding the pillars of capitalism.

The four conditions just described are the pillars of the classical model and must be present if the system is to function smoothly. In the classical model it is the work of the government to see that these conditions exist, that the nation is protected internally (the police and fire departments) and externally (the armed forces), and that the life, liberty, and property of all within its boundaries are safeguarded.

Capitalism, Government, and Our Business

Let us consider for a moment the importance of the requisites of capitalism in connection with our theoretical business, "Build-a-City." When we incorporated, we went to the state government to obtain a charter. Having a charter gave us status as a separate entity before the law. Economic freedom allowed us to enter into this business and gave us the assurance that what we earned was ours (taxes excluded). If our property were not protected from thieves, fire, and foreign invasion, we would have little incentive to work hard, save, and build a larger plant. If we could not be sure of the enforcement of contracts, we would be gambling every time we filled a big order for a customer. Refusal on the part of the customer to meet contractual obligations could mean our ruin. In each of these areas, we depend on government not to perform the economic functions but to assure an environment where economic functions can be carried out.

Historical Role of Government in the U.S. Economy

Although great restraint is placed on government action in our "ought-to-be" world, a brief look at what government has done so far shows how we have moved from the classical theory. Let us examine some of the beliefs developed about government's activity in our economy and the resulting changes in its practices.

Government as a Help to Business

Because business is responsible for organizing our factors of production and producing our wealth, anything that government can do to aid business will help the entire economy. Alexander Hamilton in his "Report on Manufactures," supporting tariffs as a protection to industry, and Henry Clay with his American System, favoring protective tariffs and a "home market" for U.S. products, believed that the country would benefit if business thrived. Protective tariffs, land grants to railroads, strong patent laws, and guarantees on certain business loans are examples of government intervention on behalf of business.

Government Intervention to Enforce Competition

The passage of antitrust laws—the Sherman and Clayton Acts—was received with mixed feelings by classical economists. Some claimed it was proper for the government to maintain competition to ensure the survival of capitalism. Others argued that such laws represented needless government interference. They said that to break up trusts was to penalize the most efficient and would only reduce incentive.

Government as a Help to Weak Economic Groups

Because business was strong and had advantages at the market for buying the factors of production, many thought that government should step in and help weak groups. This idea resulted in the exemption of labor from the antitrust laws and in such aids to labor as minimum wage and maximum hour laws. Price supports for agricultural products, another example of interference with the free market price, represented a further attempt to aid weak economic groups.

The government has increasingly protected the consumer. Most recently this protection has been extended to include protection of the environment from pollutants. (Government protection is discussed more fully in Chapters 10 and 17.)

Government as a Producer in the Absence of Business Venture

Although most consumer needs are met by business, some are not. When unfulfilled needs exist, it is usually because business produces to make a profit and only indirectly seeks to fill needs. Originally, there was no profit to be made in producing electric power in the Tennessee Valley; under these conditions private enterprise had no incentive to risk an investment that appeared to have little chance of returning a profit. The federal government, which has no need to show a profit but is obliged to consider the needs of its citizens, moved in to fill the void. In the case of atomic energy, private enterprise did not have the resources to develop so costly an industry. Some utilities at the local level and social security at the national level are other cases in which the government is a direct producer.

Government as a Stabilizer

When the market mechanism of the classical model fails to do its job, Keynesian economics calls for the government to supplement the forces of supply and demand. It does this by using the budget to create surpluses and deficits (fiscal policy) and by exercising control over the money supply (monetary policy). These tactics are occasionally reinforced by "jawboning," or temporary wage-price controls. (Part Three will develop these ideas in some detail.)

 Government's increasing involvement in the economy has evolved to meet unforeseen problems.

How Deeply Should Government Be Involved in the Economy?

One of the primary controversies today concerns the degree of government involvement in the economy. Most U.S. citizens, accepting the free enterprise system, agree that government should take whatever steps are necessary to preserve the pillars of capitalism. Protecting property, ensuring enforcement of contracts, and assuring economic freedom require government involvement. Most citizens agree that the government must have the right to protect the consumer from monopolistic power, but sharp differences of opinion exist concerning government regulation of the market. Even greater differences of opinion exist about what government should produce. Although there is a broader area of agreement than disagreement among U.S. citizens, many political campaigns have been, and undoubtedly will continue to be, waged over government's role in the economy.

Principles Guiding Government Action in the Economy

Both tradition and theory have provided us with the following principles, which many economists believe should guide us in deciding how deeply the government should become involved in the economy:

1. Government should remain outside the economy so long as private enterprise is meeting the people's needs. When these needs are not met and there appears to be little chance of their being met by business, government must step in. In launching communication satellites, government went into partnership with business, doing what private enterprise alone could not do. Controversy has long existed over the adequacy of private enterprise to meet the health needs of all citizens. Despite the passage of Medicare, Medicaid, and other bills expanding medical coverage, debate still continues on the extent to which government should be in this field. The market is much preferred as an allocator of resources, but there are times when government involvement may be called for.

2. When government does furnish a service or product, it should do so through existing facilities and capacities of business. The government uses military equipment, but business builds most of this equipment on contract with the government. There is little controversy when the government orders private enterprise to build the equipment necessary for sending a person to the moon or for supplying our armed forces. In contrast, controversy does exist over the ownership of atomic energy power plants that supply power for communities.

3. If government must furnish a service, that service should be supplied at the local or state level, if possible. There is little controversy over local support of public schools, but some controversy still exists over the degree of federal involvement in education.

4. Services that do not lend themselves to a market economy but which citizens agree are necessary for the society as a whole are handled by government. All of us recognize the need for national defense, but what price should each citizen pay for it? In this connection, that the state has the power of com-

pulsion is important. Those who do not feel the need for national defense must still share in the cost. Government support of the arts is a subject of controversy because not all citizens agree that it is a necessity and because generous gifts by families and foundations have made the problem less critical.

Differing Influences of Citizens and Consumers on the Economy

Although people are usually both citizens and consumers, the influence of these two groups on the economy is not equal. A look at the differences in their influence gives us added bases for comparing the decision-making process of private and public sectors of the economy.

1. A citizen is able to influence the public sector of the economy by casting one vote. Theoretically, each citizen's vote counts the same as every other citizen's, although it must be recognized that money can affect this voting. A consumer, by spending dollars in certain ways, helps to determine what will be produced in the private sector. The rich person, by spending many more dollars, has a far greater influence, although this is balanced by the fact that there are many more people of modest means than people of wealth.

2. A citizen has little influence on the specific expenditures in the public sector, because representatives cannot run on a platform listing how all public revenues will be spent. Special elections for specific projects, such as school bond issues, are the exception. The consumer can carefully consider each purchase, weighing the potential satisfaction against all other possibilities.

3. Citizens frequently organize themselves into political groups to increase their influence over the public economy. Only rarely have consumers organized to effect a change in the private sector.

In considering whether some aspect of the economy is better suited for the public or the pri-

 # The Institutionalists and Reform

One of the outstanding contributions of the United States to economic thinking was the development of the institutionalist approach to economics. Thorstein B. Veblen (1857–1929), John R. Commons (1862–1944), and Wesley C. Mitchell (1874–1948) were the three dominant figures of this school.

Unhappy with the many social and economic ills of the early part of the twentieth century, these men were not satisfied with the laissez-faire approach of the classi-

cal and neoclassical economists. Studying the environment, they disclosed the existence of widespread poverty, depressions, growing monopolies, and government favoritism toward business. In such circumstances, they were unwilling to trust society to the "magic" of economic laws that were supposed to correct all imbalances and bring about a "harmony of interests."

In place of the theorizing of the orthodox economists and the socialism they found unacceptable

because of its militancy and its conflict with the established order, the institutionalists sought social reform through greater participation of the government in the economy. Let the government act as an umpire between competing economic groups and interfere when extreme imbalances in the distribution of income develop! Let the government provide social security, reform credit institutions, and enforce protection for weak economic groups!

Many of the reforms the institutionalists advocated have become an integral part of our social and economic system. Few deny the importance of the institutionalists to the development of our present-day economic institutions in the United States.

vate sector, we should weigh our influence as citizens and as consumers. Abraham Lincoln's words might be used as a guide: "The legitimate object of government is to do for the community of people whatever they need to have done, but cannot do at all or cannot do so well for themselves in their separate individual capacities."

The Growth of Public Expenditures

In 1929 expenditures for all levels of government were $10.3 billion. That amount represented 10 percent of the GNP, which is the total value produced in the economy. Fifty-five years later expenditures in inflated dollars had climbed to $1,258 billion, which was one-third of the GNP. Federal spending rose from 3 to 23 percent, while state and local expenditures as a percentage of GNP rose more modestly, from 7 to 10 percent.

Our nation's recent experience of growing government expenditures in real dollars is not different from that of other mature industrialized nations. In Sweden, a socialist country, government expenditures are 51 percent of GNP; in West Germany, a capitalist country, they are 37 percent. Why are these percentages rising?

Appraisal of the Increase

There is little doubt that U.S. voters started to rebel against higher taxes to support higher expenditures. This rebellion began at the state level in the mid-1970s and helped to give Ronald Reagan a sweeping victory, since he advocated cutting spending and reducing taxes. In spite of these promises, all the Reagan Administration was able to do was to slow the increase in government expenditures.

Since the administration of Franklin D. Roosevelt, government has increasingly been taking on responsibilities for individuals that formerly were handled by families and private charities. Senator Ernest Fritz Hollings explained this situation well:

A veteran returning from Korea went to college on the GI Bill; bought his house with an FHA loan; saw his kids born in a VA hospital; started a busi-

ness with an SBA loan; got electricity from TVA and, later, water from an EPA project. His parents retired to a farm on social security, got electricity from REA and soil testing from USDA. When the father became ill, the family was saved from financial ruin by Medicare and a life was saved with a drug developed through NIH. His kids participated in the school lunch program, learned physics from teachers trained in an NSF program, and went through college with guaranteed student loans. He drove to work on the interstate and moored his boat in a channel dredged by Army engineers. When floods hit, he took Amtrak to Washington to apply for disaster relief, and spent some time in the Smithsonian museums. Then one day he wrote his congressman an angry letter asking the government to get off his back and complaining about paying taxes for all those programs created for ungrateful people.[1]

The number of people receiving benefits is an impressive indicator of the impact of government payments. To cite just the largest programs, there are 38 million people on social security, 29 million on Medicare, 23 million on Medicaid, 23 million in the school-lunch program, 21 million in the food-stamp program, and 12 million eligible for aid to families with dependent children.

From 1934 payments for individuals expanded rapidly until 1980. Under President Reagan's administration, however, payments to individuals plateaued, while expenditures for national defense and net interest increased. Attempts to sharply cut programs in human services met with strong opposition in Congress. When the economy was growing rapidly (4.2 percent from 1960 to 1973), additional revenues flowed into the treasury without increasing the tax rates. However, during the last 10 years, real economic growth dropped to an annual rate significantly below 3 percent. With little willingness on the part of the government to cut programs, a slowdown in the growth of real revenues, and more than a tripling of interest in real dollars because of the huge budget deficits, expenditures as a percentage of GNP continued to climb throughout the 1980s.

[1] Excerpt from a speech given to the National Black Caucus of State Legislators, Hilton Head, South Carolina, December 4, 1982.

Increased Government Regulation

Along with the growth in services provided by government, the growth in regulatory agencies and in laws regulating the private sector has greatly increased the function of government in the economy. Antitrust legislation, labor legislation, banking legislation, and the creation of the Federal Trade Commission, the Interstate Commerce Commission, the Securities and Exchange Commission, and the Federal Communications Commission illustrate how far we have departed from laissez-faire. Administrative and compliance requirements by the Department of Energy, the Environmental Protection Agency, and the Occupational Health and Safety Administration have added approximately $100 billion to the cost of doing business. These additional costs are passed on to the consumer in the form of higher prices.

 The pendulum swings regularly for and against government regulation.

A major conflict exists between those who place a premium on a healthy environment both now and for future generations and those who feel we have sacrificed our economic well-being for uncertain future outcomes. This problem will be discussed more fully in Chapter 16. Somewhat less controversial is the new trend toward encouraging competition in industries that are subject to government regulation. The promotion of competition among the airlines cut costs to the consumer and sometimes benefited the carriers as well. This approach is expected to be repeated in other regulated industries.

B The Nature of Government Expenditures

Planning for Spending: Mechanics of Preparing a Budget

Although differences exist in the budget procedures of different levels of government and of different state and local governments, the mechanics of budget making usually follow a certain pattern. The chief executive (president, governor, mayor) instructs the administrative heads to prepare estimates of their departments' needs as much as 18 months in advance of actual expenditures. The administrative heads consult their staffs, review their past budgets, and evaluate the demand for new or expanded activities within their departments. They submit an estimate of their needs, sometimes asking for more than they expect to receive since they know it is easier to cut down than to obtain additional appropriations. The chief executive consults the budget director and finds that proposed expenditures add up to a sum far beyond the government revenue expected. This means that unless the budget is reduced, additional taxes must be requested—not always a popular move with the electorate. Because adminis-

trative heads are responsible for the operation of their departments, the chief executive usually allows them to make the necessary adjustments. The chief executive then receives the revised estimates, and either accepts them or, if the total request still seems too high, makes final reductions after consultation with the administrative heads and close associates.

Legislature Approves Budgets

The budget, usually a thick document resembling the telephone directory of a large city, is submitted to the legislative branch, which must give final approval. Until recently, Congress distributed sections of the budget to appropriate committees, where parochial political interests were expressed with almost no attention to total revenue and expenditures. The Ways and Means Committee in the House of Representatives and the Finance Committee in the Senate reviewed the appropriations ceilings, ironed out differences between the two houses, and submitted important bills for final legislation. Congress did not have the expertise that the president had, and what emerged was more

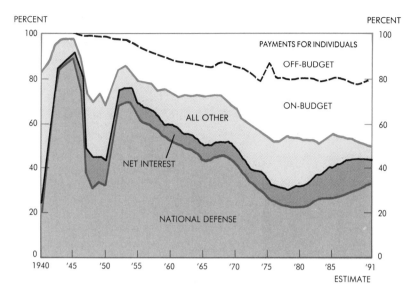

Figure 9–1   Percentage composition of federal government outlays

Under the Reagan Administration, expenditures as a percentage of total outlays show increases in national defense and net interest and decreases in payment for individuals. Off-budget are federal entities that are owned and controlled by the federal government but have been excluded from the budget totals. (Source: Office of Management and Budget.)

of a consensus of political forces than the budget that would best serve the nation.

Congress has responded to this problem by setting up its own Congressional Office of the Budget to provide the needed experts. Various committees go over the president's budget, authorizing overall goals for spending and estimating receipts for each of the revenue categories. After establishing priorities, goals, and ceilings and engaging in debate and amendment, Congress passes concurrent resolutions that have the force of law. Only then does Congress deal with appropriation bills. This new system provides a more coordinated approach to budgeting.

State and local governments still follow the older pattern in which the chief executive proposes the budget and the legislature appropriates, with little coordination between the two parties. Rarely does the chief executive get all he or she asks for. The budget that finally emerges is usually a compromise of many forces.

What Governments Spend For

As you have seen, almost all spending is carried on at the three main levels of government—federal, state, and local. Some similarities exist in the nature and procedures of spending at all levels. However, the three levels of government differ significantly in what they spend their money on.

Federal Expenditures

Figure 9–1 shows the changes that have taken place in federal expenditures. The most significant shifts have come in national defense, human services, and net interest. In 1970 national defense accounted for 41.8 percent of the federal budget and 8.4 percent of the GNP. By 1984 military spending had dropped to 26.7 percent of the budget and 6.4 percent of the GNP, whereas spending for human resources and net interest had grown. In 1970 human services expenditures were 38.5

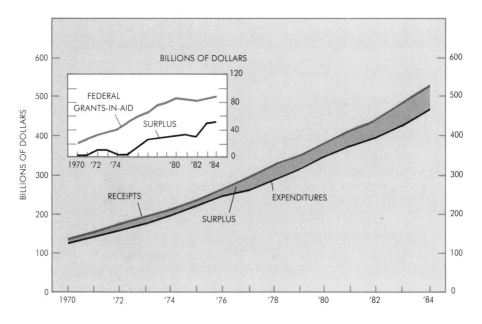

Figure 9–2 State and local government finances, 1970 to 1984

(Source: Chart prepared by U.S. Bureau of the Census.)

percent of the budget and 7.8 percent of the GNP. By 1984 these figures had increased to 50.7 and 12.1 percent, respectively. Net interest climbed from 7.3 and 1.5 percent, respectively, to 13 and 3.1 percent in 1984. Since defense, human resources, and interest accounted for nearly 90 percent of the 1984 budget, you can see that significant cuts can come only in these three areas.

President Reagan did reverse the trend of the late 1970s toward allocating a declining percentage of public funds to the military, and he halted the percentage growth in welfare, but these changes were minor in comparison to the increase in the interest payments on government-borrowed funds.

 The percentage of public expenditures for human services has been increasing since the 1930s.

State and Local Expenditures

From 1970 to 1984, expenditures by all state and local governments increased only slightly less rapidly than those of the federal government. But in the same period the combined state and local government revenues showed a surplus over expenditures for all but three years, and the deficit totaled a mere $1.5 billion. In contrast, the federal government was in deficit for all but two years. This situation is explained in part by the increasing size of federal grants-in-aid, shown in the inset of Figure 9–2. President Reagan has sought to reverse this trend by calling for a "new federalism," which would require a realignment of fiscal responsibilities, with greater involvement for human services being turned over to state and local governments. Federal grants-in-aid were cut sharply when revenues slowed, reflecting the recession. Surpluses in state and local governments are quickly disappearing.

Figure 9–3 shows that education, public welfare, highways, health and hospitals, and protection account for almost three-fourths of all expenditures. The portion devoted to education has declined somewhat as a result of declining enrollments. During periods of recession, spending for public welfare tends to increase and expenditure for highways tends to decline.

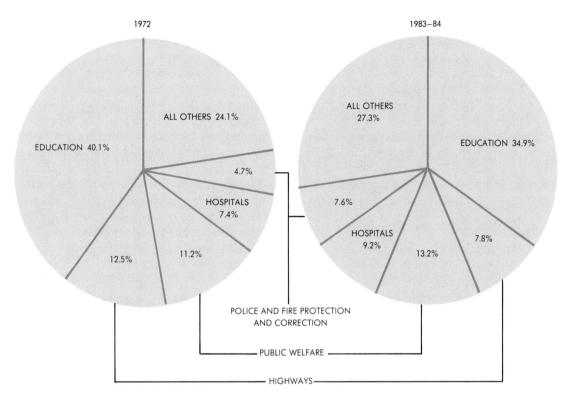

Figure 9–3   Combined state and local direct expenditures, 1972 and 1983–84.
(Source: U.S. Bureau of the Census.)

C   The Nature of Government Revenue

Sources of Government Income

Governments finance their expenditures from a variety of sources, including taxes, receipts from other levels of government, earnings from government enterprises, fines, and fees. Although taxes are by far the biggest source of government income, receipts from other levels of government are important. The federal government gives grants to states on a matching basis for welfare and health, and most recently has extended this policy to local governments for fighting poverty. State governments give funds to local governments, frequently on a per capita basis. New York State distributes over half of every revenue dollar to local units of government.

Money collected from public agencies, often called "authorities," is a very important source of revenue, particularly at the local and state levels. The same is true for fees, licenses, and fines.

Why Must Governments Tax?

Because all levels of government in our country account for one-third of our gross national product and employ close to one out of every six workers (including members of the armed forces), clearly these governments represent the largest buyers in both the market for goods and services and the market for factors of production. When governments hire about 16 percent of all workers, they are taking these workers away from possible jobs they might have in the private sector. These workers are producing something (usually services) that the society, acting as citizens rather than consumers, has decided it needs. This production is determined by our elected government to be more valuable to the nation than that which would result if these workers were employed in the private sector. We get the factors of production to work for government rather than private enterprise by offering sufficient dollars. Where does the government get the money to pay these dollars? The easiest and most obvious way to answer this question is to refer to the sources of government revenue previously listed. However, such an answer ignores the relation of government activity to the total economy.

Before we consider this topic further, we should observe that in our nation only the federal government may legally print money to pay its bills. During the Civil War the government printed greenbacks to cover much of its expenses. A few changes in existing laws would allow the federal government to do the same thing today. If it did so, it could eliminate taxes and people would have more money to spend in the private sector for the many things they want but cannot now afford. This sounds wonderful, but as you probably suspect, there is an important flaw. The problem here is that we are thinking of wealth in terms of money instead of in terms of goods and services.

You will recall that our basic economic problem is limited resources to fill unlimited wants, which forces us to make choices. If we use all our factors of production most efficiently and total production is 100 units, all within the private sector, no resources will be left to produce units of production in the government sector. If we decide we need 30 units of production in the government sector, we can get those units only by increasing our resources (which in this instance we cannot do) or by taking factors of production away from the private sector. By printing money to pay for production, the government increases the dollar demand without increasing the supply of production. This results in price increases, as shown in Figure 2–9, the graph for supply and demand.

 Taxes serve to reallocate resources from the private to the public sector.

In contrast, by taxing, the government takes away from people money they might otherwise spend in the private sector. This loss of purchasing power reduces the demand for units of production in the private sector, freeing units of production (which are now unemployed), and thus allows for a transfer of the factors of production from the private to the public sector. If payments by government and private enterprise are the same, a 30 percent tax reduces the potential demand of people in the private sector market by 30 percent. Units of production in the economy can now be divided, 70 units produced by private enterprise and 30 units produced by government. By taxing, government diverts the factors of production from the private sector to the public sector without threatening stable prices.

What Determines a Fair Tax?

Few people think of taxes as payment for certain services received by government. The main reason for not thinking in these terms is that it is difficult for us to put a price tag on the specific benefits we receive from government. Supply and demand may determine the price of consumer goods such as clothing, and they may even suggest the proper allocation of resources between education and defense. However, they do not delineate how much you, as a taxpayer, should pay for such services as fire or police protection. This is another matter entirely, which in turn brings up the question of what principles should be used in determining tax assessment.

Benefits Received

The oldest principle determining a fair tax is *benefits received*. This principle, which differs little from the basic principle applied to purchases in the private sector, asks the taxpayer to pay the government according to the benefits he or she derives from government. Although it is logical to tax gasoline to pay for roads that cars, buses, and trucks use, we could hardly expect people on welfare to pay a tax that will be used in welfare payments. And determining the benefits each citizen derives from a collective service such as defense or police and fire protection would be a complex problem.

Ability to Pay

Most people in our society believe that those who have the greatest wealth or the highest income should pay the most taxes, regardless of the benefits they get from government. The reasoning behind this principle is that as a taxpayer's wealth or income increases, his or her ability to pay taxes increases even faster. According to the theory of diminishing marginal utility (Chapter 2), parting with the last dollar of a $30,000 income will involve far less sacrifice than parting with the last dollar of a $15,000 income. Although very few people suggest that all taxpayers should make equal sacrifices, the practical needs of raising revenue without causing undue hardship make this principle acceptable without testifying to its absolute fairness.

Determining the fairest principle to use for a just tax is a matter of values rather than of economic science and is determined in the political process. Nevertheless, U.S. citizens have apparently accepted to a certain extent the principle of *ability to pay,* and our U.S. tax system reflects this acceptance.

Other Factors in Evaluating Taxes

Many other factors, in addition to fairness, must be considered before a tax is levied. From the government's standpoint, the total revenue that a tax yields is a primary consideration. Local and state governments must find taxes that provide a fairly predictable and steady income. The federal government needs a tax program flexible enough to help the economy during changes in business activity. Consideration must be given to the cost of collecting a tax, since high costs incurred in administering a tax may make it uneconomical for both the taxpayer and the government.

Effect on Production

Another important consideration in evaluating a tax is how the tax affects production. One of the most frequent arguments against a high income tax is that it destroys the incentive of business people and employees to work harder and more efficiently. Although evidence can be found both to prove and to disprove that taxes affect initiative, few economists deny that at some point such an effect could become real.

Effect on Specific Goods

Taxes can significantly influence the sale of specific goods or services. A lower sales tax on low-nicotine and low-tar cigarettes than on regular cigarettes caused shifts in the sales of the different types of cigarettes. Manufacturers responded to the changes in consumer preferences by altering production. A cabaret tax could force the proprietor of a restaurant to eliminate entertainment. Using your knowledge of demand and supply curves, tell what happens to the quantity purchased when a tax forces the price up. Does it matter whether the demand is elastic or inelastic? For an illustration of the effect of an excise tax, see the Review Model in Chapter 2.

Reflection of Values

It is far easier for lawmakers to place a tax on tobacco and liquor than on almost any other commodity. It is easy to get the impression that society is saying, "If you smoke and drink, you will have to pay for your indulgence in more ways than one." However, those who believe high taxes can discourage people from buying cigarettes or liquor underestimate how inelastic the demand for these products is.

Convenience

Before World War II, when the federal income tax was relatively low, income taxpayers generally made payments once a year. Today, most families would find such an arrangement almost catastrophic. The burden of paying taxes is made more tolerable through the withholding of a predetermined amount from each paycheck or through arrangements to pay four times a year. Simplicity of directions for payment is also important.

Shifting the Burden

A tax placed on one person or group can be *shifted* to someone else. A manufacturer may shift the tax placed on him or her to the retailer. The retailer, in turn, may shift the tax to the ultimate consumer. It is important to determine the *incidence* of the

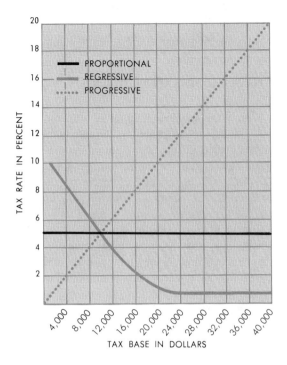

Figure 9–4   Evaluating the ability-to-pay principle

Taxes evaluated according to the ability-to-pay principle may be classified as progressive, proportional, or regressive, depending on the relation of the tax rate to the tax base.

tax—that is, where it finally comes to rest and where shifting is no longer possible. Taxes can be shifted backward to the initial producer as well as forward to the consumer. The effects of shifting can be more far-reaching than a mere price increase. The increase in price can cause sales to decline, eventually resulting in loss of jobs. A good tax establishes the incidence where the tax makers intended it.

Evaluating Ability to Pay

In evaluating a tax for fairness according to the ability-to-pay principle, economists have frequently used one particular criterion: that taxes should be judged on the relation the tax rate has to the tax base. A *tax rate* is the percentage that

is taxed. The *tax base* is the subject on which the tax is levied. If the tax rate increases as the tax base increases, the tax is *progressive*. If the tax rate remains the same, regardless of the base, the tax is *proportional*. If the tax rate decreases as the base increases, the tax is *regressive*. Figure 9–4 shows these relationships graphically.

Consider an income tax as an example. A regressive tax would be one that called for, say, the first $2,000 of income to be taxed at 10 percent, the next $2,000 of income at 8 percent, the next $2,000 at 6 percent, the next $2,000 at 4 percent, the next $2,000 at 2 percent, and all additional income at 1 percent. With this tax rate, a person with a taxable income of $10,000 would pay $600, or 6 percent of income, while a person with a taxable income of $20,000 would pay $700, or 3.5 percent of income. A proportional tax would call for a uniform rate, say 5 percent. Then our person with the lower income would pay $500, while our higher income recipient would pay $1,000.

A progressive income tax might call for 1 percent on the first $2,000 of taxable income, 2 percent on the next $2,000, 3 percent on the next, continuing with an increase of 1 percent in the tax rate on each additional $2,000 of income up to $90,000. In this case our first person would pay $300, or 3 percent, and our second taxpayer would pay $1,100, or 5.5 percent.

The regressive tax places the greatest burden on low-income groups, whereas the progressive tax falls most heavily on high-income groups. Few taxes are deliberately designed to be regressive. This would be bad politics and would run counter to our sense of justice. However, any tax in which every taxpayer pays the same number of dollars, regardless of income or tax base, is very regressive. A motor vehicle operator's license is an example. A retail sales tax of 3 percent on all purchases appears to be proportional, but is in effect regressive. This is because the low-income groups spend a greater proportion of their income (frequently all of it) than the high-income groups; thus the spending of those with high incomes is less affected by the sales tax. Many economists believe that in determining ability to pay, it is better to consider income than amount spent.

D The Federal Tax System

Tax Revenues: Progressive or Regressive

As Table 9–1 shows, our federal government secures revenue from a wide variety of sources. It is obvious that *individual income* and *social-insurance taxes* are the largest sources of revenue. Together these taxes provide 81 percent of federal revenues. During the 1960s the corporation income tax contributed over 20 percent of revenues. In an attempt to stimulate business, President Reagan lowered corporation tax rates; this action reduced corporate revenues to less than 10 percent.[1] A very small portion of our total revenue comes from estate and gift taxes and from customs collections, which were a big source of revenue in the nineteenth century. A larger share comes from federal *excise taxes,* which are sales taxes placed on specific goods and services, such as alcohol, tobacco, gasoline, motor vehicles, jewelry, and admissions to places of entertainment. These taxes are frequently the result of the treasury's constant efforts to raise new revenue without causing too much political backlash.

Except for income taxes and estate and gift taxes, federal taxes are regressive. Taxes on commodities and services are not based on the buyer's income. Although people with high incomes probably spend more than others for jewelry, furs, and admission to expensive places of entertainment, this factor is outweighed by the large percentage of income that people in lower income groups must spend for such necessities as gasoline, automobiles, and appliances. The latter have also been most affected by the rise in federal excise taxes. Social security payments may seem to be proportional to income. However, because they are based on a maximum tax base, income above that figure is not taxed. The regressive effect of social security taxes is lessened when benefits are considered.

"First dollar I ever earned—after taxes." Don Orenek, *Look* Magazine, November 3, 1964, © 1964. Reprinted by permission.

Taxes on the transfer of estates and on sizable gifts have been collected by the federal government since 1916. The great majority of people never need concern themselves with estate taxes, since the tax base does not start until amounts above $600,000 are reached.[2] The rates are highly progressive, reflecting the strong sentiment against an aristocracy of wealth. Taxes on large gifts are used to discourage the evasion of estate taxes by making transfers before death.

Income Taxes: Significant Source of Revenue

Those who favor the ability-to-pay principle of taxation usually consider net income of individuals or businesses the fairest tax base. Although there is broad support for taxing net income at a progressive rate, considerable controversy exists over what to consider net income, what deductions to allow, and the extent to which corporations should be taxed. A few examples will illus-

---

[1] All tax reform proposals being discussed in Congress in 1986 call for reversing this trend. If passed, revenues from corporate taxes would increase while those from personal income would decline.

[2] No limit on spouse.

Table 9–1 Budget receipts by source and budget outlays by agency, 1984–90 (in billions of dollars)

	1984 actual	Estimate					
		1985	1986	1987	1988	1989	1990
Budget receipts by source:							
Individual income taxes	296.2	329.7	358.9	392.5	433.6	475.5	512.6
Corporation income taxes	56.9	66.4	74.1	87.5	99.0	106.7	112.5
Social insurance taxes and contributions	241.7	268.4	289.4	309.5	346.5	376.5	409.1
Excise taxes	37.4	37.0	35.0	35.0	33.6	33.1	33.5
Estate and gift taxes	6.0	5.6	5.3	5.0	4.7	4.7	5.1
Customs duties	11.4	11.8	12.3	12.8	13.4	14.0	14.7
Miscellaneous receipts	17.0	18.0	18.6	19.5	19.6	19.5	20.1
Total budget receipts	**666.5**	**736.9**	**793.7**	**861.7**	**950.4**	**1,029.9**	**1,107.7**
Budget outlays by agency:							
Legislative branch[1]	1.6	1.8	1.8	1.7	1.7	1.7	1.8
The Judiciary	.9	1.0	1.1	1.2	1.2	1.3	1.3
Executive Office of the President	.1	.1	.1	.1	.1	.1	.1
Funds appropriated to the President	8.5	11.1	12.1	12.4	12.0	11.6	10.8
Agriculture	37.5	45.1	38.5	37.0	36.3	32.8	32.8
Commerce[2]	1.9	2.1	2.0	1.9	1.9	1.9	2.4
Defense—Military[3]	220.8	246.3	277.5	312.3	348.6	382.3	418.3
Defense—Civil	19.5	19.0	20.3	21.1	22.5	23.7	24.9
Education	15.5	17.4	16.9	16.0	15.7	15.8	16.1
Energy	10.6	11.0	9.3	10.2	11.0	11.5	12.0
Health and Human Services	292.3	318.5	330.3	350.2	374.6	398.6	423.7
Housing and Urban Development	16.5	28.9	15.4	14.3	13.8	13.6	14.1
Interior	4.9	5.0	4.4	4.2	4.2	4.2	4.2
Justice	3.2	3.9	4.0	4.0	3.9	4.0	4.0
Labor	24.5	23.5	22.8	22.6	22.8	23.1	23.4
State	2.4	2.7	3.3	3.3	3.4	3.3	3.4
Transportation	23.9	26.2	25.1	23.9	23.4	23.6	23.6
Treasury[2]	148.3	176.7	181.0	190.6	200.5	193.6	187.8
Environmental Protection Agency	4.1	4.4	4.6	4.6	4.6	4.4	4.0
General Services Administration	.2	.4	.1	.2	*	.2	.3
National Aeronautics and Space Administration	7.0	7.3	7.8	7.8	7.9	8.6	9.3
Office of Personnel Management	22.6	23.6	24.8	26.0	27.3	28.5	29.8
Small Business Administration[2]	.3	.7	.1	—	—	—	—
Veterans Administration	25.6	26.8	26.7	26.8	27.4	27.7	28.1
Other agencies[4]	11.3	12.3	10.8	8.0	6.3	5.0	4.0
Allowances[5]	—	1.1	.4	.7	1.8	2.9	4.0
Undistributed offsetting receipts	− 52.3	− 57.9	− 67.6	− 74.5	− 78.3	− 86.5	− 94.0
Total budget outlays	**851.8**	**959.1**	**973.7**	**1,026.6**	**1,094.8**	**1,137.4**	**1,190.0**
Budget surplus or deficit(−)	− 185.3	− 222.2	− 180.0	− 164.9	− 144.4	− 107.5	− 82.4

*$50 million or less.

[1]Includes allowance for 10 percent reduction beginning in 1986 (Executive recommendation).

[2]Reflects proposed abolishment of the Small Business Administration on December 31, 1985 and transfer of activities to the Departments of Commerce and Treasury.

[3]Includes allowances for civilian and military pay raises for Department of Defense.

[4]For all years includes amounts for the National Archives and Records Administration for activities formerly included in the General Services Administration.

[5]Includes allowances for civilian agency pay, military pay raises for the Coast Guard, and contingencies.

Note.—Beginning in 1985, the budget reflects establishment of a military retirement trust fund. Amounts for 1984 are shown on a comparable basis.

trate the difficulty of determining what is fair for all and yet will provide adequate income.

What Constitutes Income?

Should food that farmers grow to feed their own families be counted as income? Should payment in kind, such as commodities given to a lawyer by a client, be counted as income? Should fringe benefits, generous at some companies and meager at others, go untaxed? Why should homeowners be allowed to deduct real estate taxes from income, whereas tenants who pay these taxes to landlords in rent are allowed no such deduction? Is it fair to apply the standard exemption to an infant as well as to an adult? Should a person such as a baseball player or an actor, who earns a high income during a short productive period, be asked to pay at the same rate as a person whose income is more evenly earned throughout his or her working life? Should profits reinvested in a business be taxed in the same manner as distributed dividends? Many of these questions have been answered in recent legislation, but serious controversy still exists, particularly whenever stories come out about millionnaires who pay no income tax.

The selection by Congress of deductible items reflects society's values and goals. Without contributions to charities and other nonprofit agencies, many worthwhile enterprises would cease. It is clear that we do not want that to happen. When savings were considered inadequate to provide money for investment, people were encouraged to buy individual retirement accounts (IRAs) up to $2,000 per worker per year, deferring tax payments on that income until retirement. At retirement their income would probably be lower and would be taxed at a lower percentage. To encourage people to take risks in enterprises, the gain when stocks appreciate and are sold is taxed at a lower rate than if that money were earned as straight income. The deduction of state and local taxes is based on the principle that no one should pay taxes on taxes. Interest on home mortgages is deductible because the government wants to encourage people to buy homes.

Each deduction means the government will receive less revenue. However, by accepting a lesser amount the government is supporting a cause

Table 9–2 Personal income tax rate schedule for married taxpayers filing joint returns and qualifying widows and widowers (December 31, 1985)

Use this schedule if you checked **Filing Status Box 2 or 5** on Form 1040—

If the amount on Form 1040, line 37 is: Over—	But not over—	Enter on Form 1040, line 38	of the amount over—
$0	$3,540	—0—	
3,540	5,720	...... 11%	$3,540
5,720	7,910	$239.80 + 12%	5,720
7,910	12,390	502.60 + 14%	7,910
12,390	16,650	1,129.80 + 16%	12,390
16,650	21,020	1,811.40 + 18%	16,650
21,020	25,600	2,598.00 + 22%	21,020
25,600	31,120	3,605.60 + 25%	25,600
31,120	36,630	4,985.60 + 28%	31,120
36,630	47,670	6,528.40 + 33%	36,630
47,670	62,450	10,171.60 + 38%	47,670
62,450	89,090	15,788.00 + 42%	62,450
89,090	113,860	26,976.80 + 45%	89,090
113,860	169,020	38,123.30 + 49%	113,860
169,020	....	65,151.70 + 50%	169,020

Source: U.S. Treasury Department, Internal Revenue Service. The personal income tax is designed to be progressive. Can you think of ways in which people with high incomes can avoid its progressive intent?

or goal that it considers important. The question in each case hinges on the trade-off between what benefits might be gained in the private sector of the economy and what costs the lost revenue might impose on the public sector. Will the benefits of an energy credit given for insulating your house do more to further the national interest than would direct government expenditure of the lost tax revenue?

Attempts to correct the alleged inequities in the income tax system have been going on for years. These attempts will be discussed in Section F, Evaluating the U.S. Tax System.

Corporation Income Tax

Business corporations, like individuals, must pay taxes on their income. In 1966 the corporation income tax provided 23 percent of all government receipts. By 1983 the figure had dropped to 6.2 percent, but by 1987 it is expected to climb to 10.2 percent.

The corporation income tax is often criticized as double taxation. Not only must the company pay taxes on its profits, but individual shareholders must also pay personal income taxes on dividends paid by the company. The principle of ability to pay is ignored in taxing dividend income. The small stockholder has been given some relief by the provision allowing taxpayers to deduct the first $100 they receive in dividends from their personal income ($200 for married couples filing joint returns). In addition, money that is gained from the increase in the value of stock sold at least six months after its purchase is considered a capital gain. The law allows the seller of such stock to pay a lower tax rate on the capital gain. However, gains from stock owned for less than six months are taxed at the rate of regular income.

Many business people have complained—probably with some justification—that high corporate taxes interfere with their opportunities to reinvest their profits in their businesses. Such interference can hinder the growth and modernization of businesses. Some industrial nations that have expanded rapidly in the last 15 years have far lower taxes on corporations than the United States does. Many economists believe that low corporation taxes have been a help in this business expansion.

A corporation income tax is based on a corporation's annual income after it has paid its expenses. Dividends to stockholders are not included as expenses. Recent changes in the tax law have reduced the rates in order to encourage business investment in research and new capital equipment. The new rates are more progressive, increasing from 15 percent on the first $25,000 of taxable income to 46 percent on all taxable income above $100,000. (These rates are likely to change in 1987.) The incidence of the tax tends to fall on the stockholders in highly competitive business because shifting the tax to the consumer would raise prices and cut down on sales. In oligopolies, where prices can be largely determined by the producers, it is the customers who frequently must bear the tax burden.

Social Insurance Taxes

Payments by the government to support old-age retirement, Medicare, workers' compensation, and unemployment insurance are supported by payroll taxes. These social insurance taxes are paid for by employer and employee. When they were first started in 1935, payments were small and constituted a very small part of total revenue. By 1960 social insurance taxes had risen to 18 percent of revenues, and the government estimates that they will reach 36 percent by 1987. Tax rates have increased to 14.3 percent and will be applied to a tax base (income) of approximately $43,000 in 1987. Both the rate and the base will continue to rise. Some workers find that their contribution to social security is higher than their income tax payment.

At first glance, our social-insurance system seems to be regressive because the income above the tax base is exempt. However, the benefits received from the tax revenue are very progressive. Studies have shown the benefits to be more progressive than the tax costs are regressive.

 Federal taxes are slightly progressive.

E State and Local Government Revenue

Most state constitutions require the governor to submit a balanced budget and the legislature to pass one that is in balance. Since 1968 the states have shown a surplus of receipts over expenditures. In 1984 this surplus amounted to $52 bil- lion. It is not surprising that President Reagan, having run budget deficits of nearly $200 billion for three successive years, told state governors that they should start assuming some of the duties of the federal government and that grants-in-aid to state and local governments would be reduced. Return to Figure 9–2 to see the growth of receipts and expenditures, the accumulated surplus, and how federal grants-in-aid helped these governments accumulate their surpluses.

Much of the federal money is given on a matching basis. Therefore, if a state pays its recipients generous public-assistance grants, as California and New York do, it is likely to receive higher per capita dollars. The average payment per person in the United States in 1984 was $323. The lowest was $216 in Texas, and the highest was $833 in Wyoming. New York's was $488.

As we analyze state and local revenue, it is important to remember that individual income taxes are the most progressive of all taxes, sales and property taxes the most regressive, and corporation taxes lie somewhere in between. Since the federal tax structure is the most progressive and the tax structure of the state is next and that of local governments is least progressive, the current tendency toward having revenue filter down from the highest to the lowest level of government is leading to a fairer assignment of taxes according to ability to pay.

State Tax Systems

The largest single source of state tax collection, accounting for 31 percent, is the general retail *sales tax*.[3] Most states that have a sales tax impose it on all purchases, although there is a growing tendency to exempt food and medicine in order to ease the burden such a tax imposes on people with low incomes. Some items carry state excise taxes in addition to general sales taxes, federal excise taxes, and, on occasion, local taxes. If we remove all taxes from cigarettes, the price becomes almost unrecognizable. Excise taxes are popular with legislators because they are easily hidden and less likely to antagonize voters. Collection of excise taxes is relatively simple, involving either the use of periodic sales reports to determine the amount to be taxed or sales to the manufacturer or distributor of revenue stamps. In highly competitive industries, the incidence must fall on the con-

[3]This does not include federal revenues.

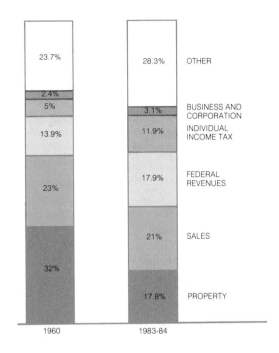

Figure 9–5 Changes in sources for combined state and local government revenues

With increases in the relative share contributed by the individual income tax, federal revenues, and business and corporation taxes, state and local government revenues become somewhat less regressive. From 1980 to 1982–83 the percentage of revenue received in revenue sharing from the federal government declined significantly. However, note that the figures used here differ from those in the text because state and local governments are combined. (Source: Department of Commerce, Bureau of the Census.)

sumer, because the producer does not have enough economic profit to absorb the additional cost. In less competitive areas, the burden is either shared with or shifted to the consumer, so that the tax does not cut too heavily into profits.

The general retail sales tax places the incidence directly on the consumer, but it would not be accurate to assume that the producer is unaffected. Higher prices to the consumer result in fewer sales, thereby affecting everyone. Although it is easy to collect and the burden seems light because the consumer (taxpayer) pays only a small amount at a time, the retail sales tax is very regressive and evasion is not difficult. Families with an income below $10,000 will probably spend all of their income. With the exception of rent, their entire income may be subject to this tax. Families with an income of $50,000 will probably spend only part of their income. The part that they do not spend will not be affected by the sales tax.

Evaluating the Sales Tax

Since over 90 percent of all states collect general sales taxes and many local governments have turned to this method to help raise revenue, attempts have been made to lessen the regressive features of this tax. Many states have exempted food. If medicine, fuel, and utilities are also exempted, the general sales tax becomes slightly progressive at low-income levels, proportional at middle-income levels, and regressive only at upper-income levels. Families with low incomes spend the largest portion of their income on rent and food. As income rises, a larger percentage of income is spent for other items, thereby increasing the percentage of income taxed. However, the percentage of income that can be saved in the higher income brackets increases so rapidly that the regressive features of the tax remain, even with the exemptions mentioned.

An increasing number of economists have suggested that all necessities should be exempted from excise and general retail sales taxes and that the same taxes should be raised substantially on luxuries. Following this suggestion would allow these taxes to conform to the ability-to-pay principle. The difficulty with such a procedure lies in determining what constitutes necessities and luxuries. People with low incomes spend a greater percentage of their income on tobacco, for instance, than people in the upper levels of income do. What would be the problem with exempting clothing? Although there may be some items that everyone considers luxuries, such as expensive jewelry, furs, and limousines, the amount of revenue yielded by a tax on these items would be too small to meet the needs of government.

Other State Taxes

Gasoline taxes and fees collected for drivers' licenses and automobile registrations are good examples of taxes based on the benefits-received principle. Some states earmark all such revenues for road construction to ensure that those who use the highways will get what they pay for. Because drivers also benefit from other state services, it is doubtful whether putting receipts in the general revenue fund would make much of a difference in benefits received.

In 1985 all but six states had some form of individual income tax. Although state income tax rates are far lower than federal tax rates, some states' income taxes, such as West Virginia's, are very progressive. In West Virginia rates range from 2.1 to 13 percent and account for much of the state's income. Illinois, in contrast, has a proportional tax of 2.5 percent, accounting for only a small portion of the state's income.

Tax receipts from corporate income, inheritance and gift taxes, and property taxes account for the remainder of state tax revenue. The first two are progressive taxes, whereas the vanishing state property tax is regressive. Inheritance taxes differ from federal estate taxes in that they are placed on the receiver rather than on what is given.

The lottery has become an increasingly popular source of state income. To make the lottery more acceptable morally, states frequently earmark receipts for education. Since, like all gambling, it is totally voluntary and is not a necessity, it must be judged as a consumer expenditure, not a tax.

Local Tax Systems

Property taxes are the oldest and most widely used source of revenue for local governments. These taxes account for 75 percent of all tax revenues raised at the local level and for about 25 percent of all revenue received by local governments, including payments from state and national government sources. Property taxes are divided into two categories—real estate taxes on land and personal property taxes on such items as securities, furniture, and cars.

One of the chief reasons property taxes have remained an important source of revenue is that it is a relatively simple matter to have them yield

"The city cut our budget." (Source: Leonard Herman, *Saturday Review,* December 26, 1970. Copyright 1970, Saturday Review Inc.)

the revenue needed by the government. If a school district needs to raise $2 million to finance its annual operation and the property that it can tax is *assessed* at $100 million, officials set the tax rate at 2 percent of the assessed valuation. If expenses go up the following year to $2.5 million, then the tax rate is merely raised to 2.5 percent.

Evaluating Property Taxes

Administration of property taxes has often been so inefficient and unfair that some people feel this tax should not be allowed to persist. Appraising the true value of property, particularly personal property, is very difficult even for experts, and assessors are not necessarily chosen or elected because they are experts. Not all people report all their property, and there is a strong tendency to undervalue that which is reported. The assessor cannot be expected to be an expert appraiser of all things as well as a detective and still manage to remain on speaking terms with other members of the community. Because it is common practice to underestimate the value of property, the honest citizen is severely penalized.

Determining the value of real estate is not quite so difficult as appraising personal property, but it is doubtful that many communities achieve great accuracy in their assessments. Real estate

values have climbed faster than assessments, and changes in neighborhoods have brought about changes in the value of properties. When property is sold, the value can be determined; but little real property is sold often enough to keep pace with changing values. Local governments find it easier to obtain the extra revenue they need by raising tax rates rather than antagonize voters by reassessing properties to increase the tax base.

At one time, ownership of property was a fairly good criterion of ability to pay. As our nation has become more industrialized, salaries and profits have become more important indicators of a taxpayer's ability to pay. A small family does not need as big a house as a large family. Assuming that each family has the same income and builds a house of similar quality, the bigger house of the large family will be assessed for more, although the smaller family may have a greater ability to pay. Inexpensive property tends to be overassessed in comparison with high-priced property. Wealthy people are more likely to have influence with assessors or to threaten court action because of overassessment. Tenants usually have property taxes shifted to them as part of their rent.

Several general characteristics of the property tax have emerged from our discussion. It is (1) regressive to a considerable degree, (2) capable of being shifted to tenants and, in the case of factories, to consumers, (3) easily evaded, and (4) not susceptible to efficient administration. Although the property tax reflects the benefit principle by funding police and fire protection and certain other local services, it is frequently used to support such general services as education. Although the federal government is prohibited from using the property tax and state governments are turning to other sources of revenue, it probably will remain the main source of revenue for local governments unless court actions require a change.

 State and local taxes tend to be more regressive than proportional.

Other Local Revenues

The sales tax is becoming more popular with local governments as they are finding the need for more revenue but at the same time are meeting greater resistance to raising the property tax. Additional revenue is obtained from fees, permits, receipts from parking meters, and municipal businesses. A relatively new but increasingly important tax that several cities now use is a tax on wages and salaries of all persons working within the city. Although this *payroll tax* ignores income from interest and profits, it does force suburbanites who work in the city and use its facilities to share in the costs of operating the city. Who would be likely to favor such a tax?

F Evaluating the U.S. Tax System

Appraising Current Practices

A tax system should encourage efficient and full use of a nation's productive capacities without hindering allocation of resources according to the wishes of consumers. It should yield the revenue needed to finance whatever government operations its citizens decide on without disturbing economic growth and stability. The tax burden should fall according to a principle or principles that society accepts as fair to all.

Although few would disagree in theory with using these criteria for evaluation, strong disagreement arises when specific taxes are measured against them. There is general agreement that the ability-to-pay principle, tempered by benefits received, should determine how the tax burden should be distributed. There is less agreement on what tax base should be used in determining ability to pay. Avoiding the use of *good* or *bad,* since such terms involve value judgments and not economic conclusions, let us see what generalizations we can develop about the U.S. tax system:

1. The final incidence of many taxes at all levels of government is not where lawmakers intended.
2. Excise and business taxes ultimately affect allocation of resources according to the wishes of consumers. This happens because people act in one manner as citizens voting for services in the public sector and in another manner as consumers shopping in the private sector.
3. Business taxes affect the economic growth of some businesses, particularly small businesses, in which capital may be hard to obtain.
4. Many taxes are ill conceived and are merely politically expedient devices to raise additional revenue with minimum voter protest.
5. Tradition, the high yield in revenue, government needs, and inertia are responsible for the continued existence of certain taxes that fail to meet most of the criteria for a good tax. One example of such a tax is the property tax.
6. Federal taxes are mildly progressive because of the importance of the personal income tax.
7. State and local taxes are slightly regressive because of general retail sales and property taxes.
8. Most economists agree that taxes as a whole are mildly progressive among all families except the poorest and the wealthiest. Most poor families pay regressively, whereas most wealthy families pay more progressively.
9. Federal taxes are considered to be not merely producers of revenue but also important instruments for economic growth and stability. (This use of taxes will be discussed further in Part Three.)
10. Many economists think that the U.S. tax structure, although better than the tax systems in most other industrial countries, is too much of a hodgepodge as a result of considerations of political expediency, and that considerable improvement could be made by simplifying and reorganizing it into a more uniform system.

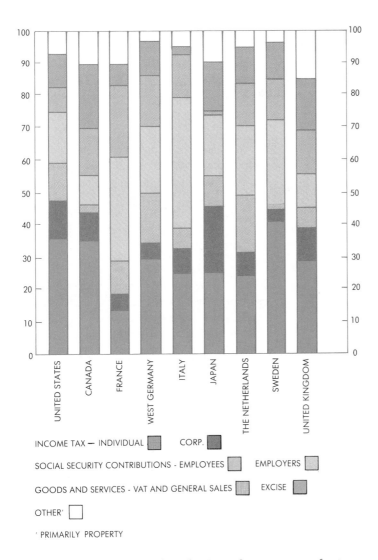

Figure 9–6 Percentage distribution of tax revenues by type of tax for selected countries
(Source: O.E.C.D.)

Taxes at the present time reduce purchases in the private sector of the economy by one-third. It is doubtful that this percentage will decrease. As both a consumer and a citizen, you should be concerned about an equitable tax structure. Since our tax laws are changed frequently, it is important for you to become aware of the directions of possible changes so that you can prepare for them.

Taxes in Other Countries

With deficits growing larger, our federal government has been looking for other sources of revenue. The first observation that any investigator makes when comparing revenue sources in this country with those of other mature industrial countries is that many other countries collect

CONTROVERSY IN OUR TIMES

Reagan's Tax Reform Proposal[1]

Every administration and every Congress has tax reform as a high priority. No one pushed for a change in our tax structure more than President Reagan. In 1985 he said, "…we ought to take our current tax system out and string it up. It's been tried and found unfair, unworkable and unproductive." The plan he has suggested has two parts. First there would be only 3 tax brackets—15, 25, and 35 percent—the latter for incomes above $70,000. At present there are 14 tax brackets ranging from 11 to 50 percent. President Reagan's plan also increases personal exemptions from $1,040 to $2,000. Obviously these actions alone would reduce revenues significantly, hardly a sensible outcome when deficits have increased each year. However, the second part of the plan increases the tax base, or the amount that is taxed. Numerous deductions would be eliminated, such as most employees' business and entertainment expenses and some travel expenses. The large deduction for state and local taxes would also be disallowed; the Treasury estimates that this step alone would raise $150 billion over five years. Eliminating interest payments other than those for first-home mortgages, including workers' fringe benefits as income, and eliminating most investment credits are other methods proposed for raising the tax base.

Pro
Supporters of President Reagan's plan point out that his approach flattens the effect of deductions. Currently, deductions taken by the wealthy reduce their tax by 50 percent, whereas deductions taken by people in the lowest income bracket cut their tax by only 11 percent. The effect of eliminating many deductions would be offset by the new lower tax bracket the taxpayer would fall in.

Another appeal of the plan is its alleged simplicity. Surely anyone filling out a long tax form can appreciate any plan that would simplify the procedure. As the plan has been modified, however, some deductions have been returned, adding additional detail.

Con
Criticism of the personal income portion of the Reagan plan stems from the fact that many public finance analysts have shown that the plan would favor the poor and the very rich and would harm the middle class. Others have pointed out that the plan runs counter to American tradition in taxing income twice, the result of eliminating the deductibility of state and local taxes. Since taxes paid on income or property taxes are not part of the taxpayer's income, why should they be taxed?

Consequences
The Treasury has calculated that the individual taxpayer would pay 7 percent less than he or she is currently paying, but corporations would make up the difference.

. After a planned reduction in corporate taxes during Mr. Reagan's first administration, as shown in Figure 9–5, it came as a shock to business to be asked to make up the difference lost by lower revenues from personal income taxes. Businesses would pay 37 percent more than they do under the current law. Although maximum corporate tax rates would decline from 46 to 33 percent,

[1] While both the Senate and House plans for reform differ from the Reagan proposal, each has the same major features discussed here. The one significant exception is that the deductions of state income and local property taxes remain unchanged.

CONTROVERSY IN OUR TIMES

capital gains would be treated as ordinary income after inflation, investment credits would be eliminated, and depreciation would be spread over a longer period of time. Generally the provisions would hurt the older industrial industries such as steel, automobiles, and transportation.

Service industries, including those in the hi-tech field, would benefit from the lower rates.

In the final analysis, the influence of lobbyists rather than the equity and economic viability of the program will probably determine the nature of the taxes we have.

substantial revenue from the value-added tax (VAT). Since 1967 all member states in the European Community have levied the VAT. It is a tax levied at each stage of production and distribution on the increase in the value of the goods and services. In the manufacture of a shirt, for example, the raw-materials supplier, the fabricmaker, the shirtmaker, the wholesale distributor, and the retail store are all taxed in turn on the marginal value each adds to the finished product. To avoid taxing a tax, the government allows each company to subtract the VAT paid in the earlier production stage plus his or her production costs when figuring out the tax base. This procedure prevents compounding of the tax.

Revenue from VAT fluctuates from 8 percent in Luxembourg to 17 percent in France, with the average revenue for the nine countries being 16.6 percent of total revenue collection. If the VAT were applied on top of other federal taxes at 16 percent, it would reduce our deficit by two-thirds.

What are the advantages of the VAT? For one thing, revenues from VAT do not fluctuate nearly as much as do revenues from income taxes. If applied on all goods evenly, the VAT should not influence decisions on investment and consumption. The tax would be easily visible, would be difficult to cheat on, and would allow people to see when taxes were raised.

The most obvious argument against enacting the VAT is that it tends to be regressive; poor families pay a larger percentage of their income in taxes than do wealthy families. This inequity,

based on the principle of ability to pay, could be altered by having different tax rates for necessities and for luxuries, but such a procedure would reduce the efficiency of collections and increase administrative costs.

Most industrial countries collect a far greater percentage of their revenue from taxes on goods and services, including the VAT, than does the United States. The big exception is Japan.

In summary, although the VAT could raise revenue quickly, it is doubtful it will be adopted unless people see problems arising from the deficit and feel the need to raise public money.

Revenues from income taxes, both corporate and individual, are highest in the Scandinavian countries, the United States, Canada, Japan, and the United Kingdom, averaging about 42 percent of total tax revenue. Corporate taxes average about 8 percent, except in Japan, where they are 20 percent of total tax revenue. In France the pattern is very different, with income taxes only contributing 18 percent.

Social security contributions are lowest in Canada (11.3 percent) and highest in Italy (47.2 percent). They are 27.7 percent in the United States. In most countries employers pay the larger share. Figure 9–6 shows the distribution of tax revenues in nine selected countries. The data combine national, state, and local taxes, or the equivalent. Contrast the distribution in France with that in Sweden. Which country do you think is likely to have a more progressive tax structure? How do you explain the differences between the United States and Japan?

G Public Borrowing and the Public Debt

Reasons for Borrowing

It might seem that the most direct way to meet governmental financial obligations would be to tax to the extent necessary to obtain the required revenue. However, there are times when such a procedure is not possible. When governments are unable to meet their financial obligations out of their current revenues, they can make up the difference by borrowing. This borrowing creates a public debt, the size of which is the subject of much controversy. Public borrowing and public debt are frequently compared with the borrowing and debt of businesses and families. Although these kinds of debt do have certain features in common, there are also very significant differences. Failure to recognize these differences has led to much misunderstanding of the nature and significance of our public debt.

There are four main reasons why governments borrow:

1. Short-term adjustments have to be made to correct the imbalance of revenues and expenditures. Because expenditures may be somewhat greater than expected, or tax collections slower or smaller than expected, governments make short-term loans. Expenditures tend to be spread throughout the year, whereas some tax collections are made only annually or semiannually. Short-term loans are relatively easy to finance, and the interest rates are usually lower than those for long-term loans.
2. Financing large public works that will be used over many years usually requires borrowing. Waiting until the government had the money would deprive people of essential services. It is sound financial policy to pay for such projects over no longer a period than that during which the project will furnish services to the people. Some public projects, such as the Tennessee Valley Authority, state turnpikes, and municipal transportation systems, yield revenue from which the loans can be paid back.

3. Unanticipated emergencies cannot be paid for out of current revenues. Wars and natural disasters have added greatly to our public debt.
4. Deliberate spending in excess of current income has been carried out by the federal government as a means of stimulating the economy. (This concept will be explained in Part Three.)

 Borrowing may serve a useful purpose in the economy.

Size of the Public Debt

If someone had predicted 30 years ago that the gross debt of the federal government would go beyond $2 trillion by 1986, those listening would probably have said that in that case we would be on the verge of bankruptcy. The truth is that in spite of the size of the public debt, our federal government's credit is very good. This points out the hazard of long-range predictions.

The term *federal debt* commonly refers to the gross debt, which includes all outstanding obligations of the federal government. Most economists consider the net debt, which includes only the federal obligations held by the public, the more significant statistic, because payments from one government agency to another have a relatively small effect on the economy.

The size of any debt must be considered in relation to the size of income. A family with an income of $50,000 a year can afford to carry a $5,000 debt better than a family with an income of $10,000 can afford to carry a $1,000 debt. In 1945 our net federal debt was $252.5 billion, and our gross national product was $212.3 billion. Debt was 119 percent of GNP. By 1985 the *net* debt had risen to nearly $1.5 trillion, but it represented less than 38 percent of GNP. The *percentage* of our federal debt in relation to our national income had therefore declined.

The *gross* federal debt may be viewed from two perspectives. The color curve in Figure 9–7 shows the debt as a percentage of GNP, measured

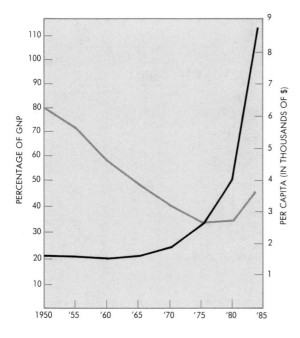

Figure 9–7   Gross federal debt as a percentage of GNP and debt per capita

GNP increased more rapidly than did the federal debt from the end of World War II until the middle 1970s. Since then economic growth has slowed and budget deficits have risen. The colored curve shows gross federal debt as a percentage of GNP, as measured by the left axis. The black line shows federal debt per capita, as measured by the right axis.

by the left vertical axis. The debt as a percentage of GNP reached a low of 36 percent in 1974, climbed slowly until 1980, and then rose sharply. However, from 1950 to 1974 GNP rose much more rapidly than debt, and thus even in 1985 the percentage was lower than it had been in the 1950s and part of the 1960s.

The black curve shows the gross federal debt per capita. In 1970 every person in our country owed close to $2,000 on the federal debt. By 1985 this amount had climbed to over $9,000 per capita. If you computed the amount for a family of four, it would be a pretty staggering figure.

Ownership of the Federal Debt

Most of our public debt, unlike debt in many other countries, is held internally. This means that U.S. citizens owe this money to themselves. Table 9–3 shows who holds the federal government securities. An internal debt is paid when the government takes some of its revenue, paid by citizens, and meets its obligations on bonds and notes held by other citizens, or in some instances by the same citizens. This procedure has frequently been

characterized as taking money out of one pocket and putting it into another pocket. This interpretation must be qualified by pointing out that frequently the pockets do not belong to the same people. In other words, paying off an internally held debt does not mean reduction in the total wealth, but frequently it does result in redistribution of the wealth.

An externally held debt is one that is owed to a foreign country. In this case, the people of one country must take out of their pockets money that will go into the pockets of people in a different country. Externally held debts are similar to private debts in terms of the sacrifices involved in repayment. The percentage of our total debt held by foreigners has been increasing rapidly since 1970. If this trend continues, it could negatively affect our living standards, as has been the case in England.

Consequences of a Public Debt

Let us consider some of the fears associated with our growing debt to see whether, according to economists, they are justified.

Table 9–3   Ownership of U.S. government securities, September, 1985

	Billions of dollars	Percentage of total
U.S. government agencies and trust funds	315.2	17.3
Federal reserve banks	169.7	9.3
Commercial banks	196.9	10.8
Foreign and international	210.2	11.5
Corporations	56.5	3.1
State and local governments*	190.1	10.4
Individuals	151.3	8.3
Miscellaneous purchases†	533.2	29.3
Total	1,823.1	100.0

Source: U.S. Treasury Department, *Monthly Statement of the Public Debt of the United States*

*Estimate

†Savings and loan associations, dealers and brokers, corporate pension funds, and nonprofit institutions.

Can We Go Bankrupt?

Many economists believe that since the federal government has the power to tax or print money, it need never go bankrupt. Just as important, however, is the credit rating of its securities as reflected by the relatively low interest rates.

Some governments have gone bankrupt, but their financial failure was due to declining GNP in relation to public debt. This unfavorable ratio caused a lack of confidence in the government's ability to meet its financial obligations in money that had reasonably stable purchasing power.

Will Future Generations Bear the Burden of the Present Debt?

Wars, which contributed significantly to the large size of the debt, imposed most of their burdens on those who were living at the time. The real economic sacrifice came when productive factors were turned to making armaments instead of making goods and services people of that generation wanted and would have produced had there been peace. The goods and services that might have been produced can never be realized. Why? Because the resources that would have made them were making other things, primarily armaments.

Future generations bear the burden of using their productive resources to repair what has been destroyed. They are also handicapped by not inheriting the additional supply of capital goods that each generation adds to help each succeeding generation. In weighing these costs we must consider whether this is too high a price to pay for the preservation of freedom.

Is the Interest on the National Debt a Burden?

In 1960 interest on the national debt amounted to 9.3 percent of federal outlays. By 1986 interest had risen to 15 percent and was the third largest federal outlay. Although the decline in interest rates starting in 1983 helped keep payments down, the continuing deficit eliminated much of the benefit. When one realizes that the federal government must pay nearly 15 cents of each dollar collected for interest, the burden seems awesome.

Huge interest payments limit the flexibility in adjusting the government's expenditures to what normally would be different priorities. However, the interest must be paid. If the debt stood still, the problem would be less serious, but it does not—it keeps growing.

Do Government Securities Use Up Savings That Private Enterprise Needs for Expansion?

The federal budget deficit jumped from $50 billion in 1980 to $150 billion in 1983, pushing our public debt over the $1 trillion mark. The government was forced to borrow huge sums of money for which it had to compete with the private sector. Since the demand for money (savings) rose and the supply of money was increased very slowly by the Federal Reserve Bank (see Chapter 14), interest rates climbed sharply.

Interestingly, high interest rates led foreign investors to put their money in U.S. securities. In other words, a significant portion of our debt came to be supported by investors from other countries. If real interest rates drop, this source of funds will disappear, forcing the government to borrow from our domestic savings pool. Such borrowing will "crowd out" loanable funds for private investment.

Can Increasing the Debt Be Inflationary?

If the government sought to pay its obligations by printing money, inflation would be the consequence. More money would be competing for the same amount of goods, causing prices to rise. Large-scale government borrowing at a time when all our productive resources are being used is also highly inflationary. Although government officials are aware of these dangers, the politics of the budget may interfere with sound economic policy.

Some Concluding Observations

A few years ago most economists were not so worried about the debt as they are today. So long as economic growth was vigorous, revenues would increase. When the economy slowed, a deficit could be used to stimulate greater activity. However, the huge deficits of the eighties showed that we expected more from our government than our resources could provide. Groups with diverse interests wanted to make no sacrifices and the federal budget got out of control, generating huge deficits.

In Part III we will return to this problem. At that point we will be better equipped to consider one of the most serious economic problems of this decade.

As 1985 was drawing to a close, Congress recognized its inability to cope with the ever-growing federal budget deficit and enacted the Gramm-Rudman-Hollings Balanced Budget and Emergency Deficit Reduction Act. This act calls for a procedure allowing the President to reduce categories of expenditures, such as defense spending and revenue sharing, by certain percentages if Congress does not make the hard decisions. The law clearly grew out of the public's concern about the growing deficit and Congress's inability to find a solution that was politically acceptable. The overwhelming majority of economists, meeting at a session of the American Economic Association in New York City at the time of the act's passage, were opposed to Gramm-Rudman-Hollings on the grounds that it could eliminate Congress's ability to respond to the public needs, reduce the flexibility of their actions, and ignore the government's responsibility to frame economic policy to meet other economic goals such as high employment, stable prices, and economic growth.[5] In 1986 the full impact of the act began to register as the law had to be implemented. Enactment of Gramm-Rudman-Hollings illustrates how political and economic objectives can conflict.

[5] A recent Supreme Court ruling declared sections to be unconstitutional. Modifications are being made to retain the intent: budget deficit reduction.

Chapter Highlights

1. The classical model calls for minimum government interference in the economy to allow allocation of resources according to consumer

preferences. It is the responsibility of government to provide an environment favorable for the market economy by preserving the pillars of capitalism: private property, freedom of contract, economic freedom, and competition.

2. In the U.S. economy government has become more active in seeking to satisfy the needs of the people. How deeply involved government should be in the economy is controversial, although tradition and theory have provided guiding principles.

3. Citizens and consumers may be the same people, but they affect the economy in different ways.

4. Public expenditures of federal, state, and local governments have increased enormously in the last 30 years, although inflationary prices and military expenditures account for a substantial part of this increase. An additional factor contributing to increasing expenditures has been our demand for more and better services, particularly in education and welfare.

5. Government budgets are prepared by chief executives and their administrative staffs, but they require legislative approval. Political considerations affect their preparation and passage.

6. The main source of government revenue is taxes. Government imposes taxes to move resources from the private to the public sector without jeopardizing prices.

7. Taxes can be evaluated according to the principles of benefits received or ability to pay, their revenue yield, their effect on production and allocation of resources, their convenience to the taxpayer, and their incidence. A tax can be judged progressive, proportional, or regressive, depending on the relation of the tax rate to the tax base.

8. The largest portion of federal revenue comes from income taxes, both personal and corporation, and from social-insurance contributions.

9. State revenue is obtained mainly from sales taxes, gasoline taxes, income taxes, business taxes, fees, and grants from the federal government.

10. Property taxes and federal and state grants are the main sources of revenue for local governments.

11. Controversy exists about local financing, particularly the property tax.

12. Federal taxes are mildly progressive, whereas state and local taxes are mildly regressive. Much could be done to improve our tax system.

13. The public debt stems from government borrowing to make up the difference between revenue and expenditures. The tremendous increase in the size of the debt has caused concern and controversy.

14. A major portion of the federal debt is the result of international conflicts.

15. Although a large public debt can have adverse consequences, as long as its growth is accompanied by increases in the gross national product and it is managed carefully, it can be a useful tool. Sharp increases in the public debt in the eighties have made it a serious problem.

Study Aids

Key Terms

pillars of capitalism	progressive tax	regressive tax
tax shifting	proportional tax	ability-to-pay principle
incidence of the tax	sales tax	tax rate
taxable income	evasion	tax base
personal property tax	public debt	revenue sharing
avoidance	internal debt	estate tax
double taxation	excise tax	federal debt
benefits-received principle	payroll tax	value-added tax (VAT)

Gramm-Rudman-Hollings Balanced Budget and Emergency Deficit Reduction Act

Questions

1. The classical model of capitalism forms the basis of the U.S. economic system.
   (a) Describe the four basic pillars of the capitalist system.
   (b) What must the government do to ensure an environment favorable for the proper functioning of the capitalist system, even though such action is contrary to the original system?
2. Throughout our nation's history, the federal government has aided business development in many ways.
   (a) Describe the various methods that the government has used to help business.
   (b) Why has government action in the economy increased? Is this good or bad? Why?
3. As the economic strength of part of the business sector increased, the relation of government to business changed.
   (a) Describe the steps taken to ensure competition.
   (b) How did the government help weak sectors of the economy?
   (c) How did the government take over some of the functions of the business community? Why did the government do this?
4. Different levels of government have different functions and require different resources.
   (a) What are the major functions of each level of government?

   (b) How do the different levels of government differ in the way they raise revenues?
   (c) What is the purpose of shifting resources (funds) from one level of government to another?
5. According to the criteria you have learned for evaluating taxes, what are the principal weaknesses in the U.S. tax system? Looking at Figure 9–6, determine which countries you think would have the most progressive/regressive taxes, assuming that their tax bases and tax rates are similar to ours?
6. In what ways would you change our federal tax structure? Identify your objectives and how you would reach them.
7. Would you favor a value-added tax? Why?
8. When the government needs additional funds, why does it often borrow money rather than print it or raise taxes?
9. What are the major concerns with sharply increasing our public debt?

Problems

1. Throughout our nation's history, government has increased its activity in the economy.
   (a) Make a time line of the economic development of the United States, listing the highlights of the opposing forces, aids to business, and controls over business.
   (b) How do these actions reflect a change in

philosophy about government participation in the economic scene?

(c) Does the added activity of the government indicate a possible weakening of our capitalist system?

2. Obtain a copy of your most recent state or city budget. What have been the effects of federal revenue sharing?

3. Study the most recent federal income tax form and instruction booklet. Make a critical evaluation of the tax, explaining why you consider certain portions to be fair or unfair.

4. Study the fiscal situation of your local government. What are its chief needs? Are the current means of raising revenues adequate? If not, what changes could be made to improve the system?

The Consumer's Role in the U.S. Economy

The purpose of production is primarily to satisfy consumer wants. In theory, consumers provide answers to the questions of what to produce and how to allocate the resources needed for production. However, consumers' choices are limited in many ways—by their individual incomes, by imperfect competition, and by psychological and social pressures that influence their demands. The needs of consumers in poor countries differ from the needs of consumers in rich countries like our own.

In this chapter we shall see what part consumers play in the classical models and what forces in our society have placed limits on consumer power. We shall then consider whether consumers need protection and, if so, what kind of protection. Particular attention will be given to inequality of income, demand creation, and consumer credit.

You might keep the following questions in mind as you read this chapter: How much free choice do I have when I go to the market? Can my behavior really influence the producer? Do I have the necessary information to make wise choices, or do I need help?

Chapter Objectives

After completing this chapter, you should be able to:

■ Define consumer sovereignty according to Adam Smith's classical model and discuss the factors that limit consumer sovereignty in the U.S. economy.
■ Define and describe the Lorenz curve.
■ Make a case for and against advertising in our economy.
■ Discuss the advantages and disadvantages of credit to the consumer.
■ Decide whether the U.S. consumer is in need of more protection than is now offered.

A Consumer Sovereignty

The Consumer's Role in the Classical Model

Adam Smith, the chief architect of the classical model, used the principle of *consumer sovereignty* as the foundation of his entire system. He wrote, "Consumption is the sole end and purpose of all production," and he had no sympathy with systems that favored the producers. Consumers go to the market to buy the goods and services they want. Business listens and sets production according to consumer preferences. The question *What* is answered by consumers. In answering the *What*, the consumers are also influencing the allocation of resources.

Because consumers, individually and collectively, have limited resources (incomes) and unlimited wants, they have to make choices. In making choices they seek to maximize their total satisfaction. Because consumers know best what will provide them with the greatest satisfaction, there should be no restraints on the consumers' right to register demands except where they may harm others. The idea that the individual, rather than the collective society, should determine the *What* is fundamental to the classical tradition. The reasoning behind this idea is that if each individual can maximize his or her satisfaction, then the entire society will do the same.

Many economists believe that time and experience have made clear a flaw in this last argument; that flaw is referred to as the "fallacy of composition." They believe that what is true for the individual is *not* necessarily true for all society. Conversely, what is true for the society as a whole is not necessarily true for every individual within it.

Defining Needs

If consumers are to determine individually the *What*, they do so by deciding what their needs and wants are. The individual consumer's identification of his or her own needs, if performed without any qualifications, can present problems. Some people have little experience and poor judgment in shopping. Money is sometimes spent on gambling, drinking, and lavish entertainment at the expense of necessities for self and family. In an affluent society like ours, wants are sometimes created as businesses seek to boost sales. Frequent style changes are used to create quick obsolescence of goods, and advertising influences wants that are in no way related to survival or even physical comfort.

 Should consumers be protected in the marketplace by government agencies?

Some people believe that in a society where needs go far beyond physical survival, consumers should have protection from themselves and others. Others think that consumers identify only their selfish, short-run needs and give little thought to the collective good of the society. Such critics point to the failure to approve school bond issues at a time when purchases of luxuries are increasing.

Before doing away with consumer sovereignty, it might be wise to consider whom you will allow to decide the *What*. Undoubtedly consumers make errors, but they also learn from their mistakes. What group would you trust more?

Limitations on Consumer Sovereignty

In a mature, predominantly private-enterprise economy like our own, three factors limit the consumer's sovereignty and ability to satisfy individual needs completely: (1) distribution of personal income, (2) demand creation by business, and (3) imperfect competition. These conditions all have the effect of placing limits on the consumer. Each factor deserves our consideration.

Distribution of Personal Income

A family's consumption depends on its income, its savings, and its credit. Of the three, income is the most important. It is the main factor in determining what the other two will be. Because spending is usually adjusted to current income and expectations of future income, we need to know the characteristics of personal income to understand the consumer better.

Critics of capitalism usually concede that total wealth and total income in the United States are high. They admit that average income is high, but they say this statistic does not give a true picture of how people are actually living, because the great concentration of wealth among a few distorts the average. How true is this statement?

In Chapter 17 we will take a close look at poverty, its characteristics, and how to deal with it. Here we are concerned only with income distribution and how it may influence consumer spending.

Distribution of Family Income

Table 10–1 on p. 232 shows the changes that have taken place from 1967 to 1984 in median income for all families, as well as for whites, blacks, and those of Spanish origin. The median is the midpoint between highest and lowest when incomes are ranked. The median income in constant 1984 dollars is the more significant statistic, as it does not reflect the impact of inflation.

Note that U.S. families reached their highest income in 1973, as measured in constant dollars. By 1982 income had declined by about 10 percent. In 1984 median income of blacks was only 57 percent and of hispanics only 72 percent that of white families.

Lorenz Curve

One method of determining inequality of income distribution is through the *Lorenz curve*. On the horizontal axis of Figure 10–1 we find the percentage of family units, and on the vertical axis the percentage of total personal income. If income were distributed with absolute equality, 20 percent of the family units would have 20 percent of the income, 40 percent of the family units would have

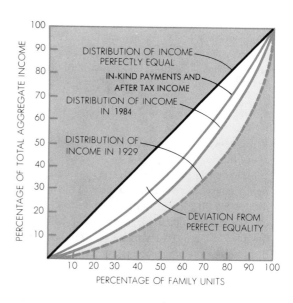

Figure 10–1 Lorenz curves of family personal income of consumer units

The 45° line shows what perfect equality of distribution would look like. The Lorenz curve shows the degree of inequality in the distribution of personal income. (Source: U.S. Department of Commerce, Bureau of the Census)

Table 10–1 Money income of households—median household income in current and constant (1984) dollars, by race and Spanish origin of householder: 1967 to 1984

Year	Median income in current dollars (dol.)				Median income in constant (1984) dollars (dol.)				Annual percent change of median income of all households	
	All households[1]	White	Black	Spanish origin[2]	All households[1]	White	Black	Spanish origin[2]	Current dollars	Constant dollars
1967	7,143	7,449	4,325	(NA)	22,222	23,174	13,455	(NA)	(x)	(x)
1970	8,734	9,097	5,537	(NA)	23,363	24,334	14,811	(NA)	6.9[3]	1.7[3]
1971	9,028	9,443	5,578	(NA)	23,154	24,219	14,306	(NA)	3.4	−.9
1972	9,697	10,173	5,938	7,677	24,076	25,258	14,743	19,061	7.4	4.0
1973	10,512	11,017	6,485	8,144	24,570	25,750	15,158	19,035	8.4	2.1
1974	11,197	11,710	6,964	8,906	23,584	24,665	14,668	18,759	6.5	−4.0
1975	11,800	12,340	7,408	8,865	22,773	23,815	14,297	17,109	5.4	−3.4
1976	12,686	13,289	7,902	9,569	23,147	24,248	14,418	17,460	7.5	1.6
1977	13,572	14,272	8,422	10,647	23,263	24,463	14,436	18,249	7.0	.5
1978	15,064	15,660	9,411	11,803	23,984	24,933	14,983	18,792	11.0	3.1
1979	16,461	17,259	10,133	13,042	23,556	24,698	14,500	18,663	9.3	−1.8
1980	17,710	18,684	10,764	13,651	22,324	23,552	13,568	17,208	7.6	−5.2
1981	19,074	20,153	11,309	15,300	21,784	23,016	12,916	17,474	7.7	−2.4
1982	20,171	21,117	11,968	15,178	21,706	22,724	12,879	16,333	5.8	−.4
1983	20,873	21,886	12,443	15,776	21,761	22,818	12,973	16,447	3.5	.3
1984	22,415	23,647	13,471	16,992	22,415	23,647	13,471	16,992	7.4	3.0

NA Not available.   X Not applicable.

[1] Includes other races not shown separately.   [2] Persons of Spanish origin may be of any race.   [3] Change from 1967.

Source of tables 741 and 742: U.S. Bureau of the Census, *Current Population Reports*, series P–60, No. 149, and unpublished data.

40 percent of the income, and we should eventually have a diagonal line.

However, because the lowest 20 percent of family units receive only 4.7 percent of the income, the lowest 40 percent only 15.7 percent, and so on, we find the income curve dropping below the diagonal. Figure 10–1 shows the Lorenz curve of distribution of personal income for the United States for 1929 and for 1984. That the distribution curve in 1984 is closer to the diagonal line of perfect equality indicates a trend toward more equal distribution of personal income. Although too little evidence is available for us to draw firm conclusions, it appears that industrialized countries with more mixed economies than ours—such as Sweden, Israel, and Australia—have a more nearly

equal distribution of personal income than do less developed countries, where greater inequality seems to prevail.

Dividing Personal Income

Distribution of personal income is a matter of individual values that the citizens of each country must decide for themselves. Socialists in Western Europe and in this country have advocated government ownership of basic industries and greater services by government as a means of creating a more nearly equal standard of living. However, the general rise in personal income, with even the lowest incomes more nearly adequate than in former years, and the rapid increase in government expenditures for income security have greatly reduced the appeal of the socialist argument in our country.

Income Differences and the Existence of Poverty

Although there has been a trend toward equalization of income, inequality still exists.

There can be little doubt that this inequality has a significant effect on kind and quantity of consumer purchases and, through the vicious cycle of poverty, on income and credit for spending. Differences exist between geographic regions, with the middle Atlantic, north central, and far western states having higher personal incomes than the mountain and southern states. However, the economic gains made in the South in the last few years have narrowed these differences. We noted earlier the substantial differences in income among occupations, but even within occupations there are large variations due to differences of ability and discrimination. Minority groups and women in particular are hurt when they go to the marketplace to sell their factors, and they are equally hurt when they go to the production market to seek credit or purchase homes. Those in the lowest fifth of income received have their consumer sovereignty reduced not only by having fewer dollars but by such factors as the markets they buy in, the credit they need, and the information and power they need for effective shopping.

 Poor people have fewer alternative markets to shop.

Impact of Inflation

The voices of the poor, complaining about merchants who charged excessively high prices, were weak and almost unheard until 1969. Then, when many saw prices rising faster than earnings, numerous homemakers took to the picket lines. The consumer movement, which can be traced back to the New Deal, was given another big push. This time, however, almost everyone seemed involved because almost everyone was being hurt in some way.

Few economists would attribute the major cause of inflation to any sudden change in the pricing practices of business or greater disregard for the consumers. Interest in consumer protection—and, consequently, the amount of consumer protection legislation—started growing sharply under President Kennedy, when prices were relatively stable. This interest has increased as inflation has affected the low- and middle-income classes. The movement took hold largely through the efforts of Ralph Nader, with his investigation into the automobile industry. The concern and efforts of two well-known, articulate women, Betty Furness and Bess Myerson, gave the movement national coverage. The legislation and enforcement that have emerged are probably more important for those with smaller incomes, not only because their dollars have greater marginal utility than those of higher income groups, but also because they have fewer opportunities to protect themselves as consumers.

B   Relation of Demand Creation to Consumer Spending

How Personal Income Is Spent

In an economy as wealthy as our own, less than half of the average consumer's income is spent on food, clothing, and shelter. Although poor countries concern themselves with producing enough to provide the bare necessities of life for their people, business in our country devotes much energy to stimulating consumer demand for things

that consumers could get along without and, in some instances, would not have thought about if no effort had been made to whet their appetite.

Countless individual variations may be found in the ways families spend money. Each family tries to maximize its satisfactions with the income it has available. Because needs and tastes differ, budgets also differ. Speaking generally, poor fam-

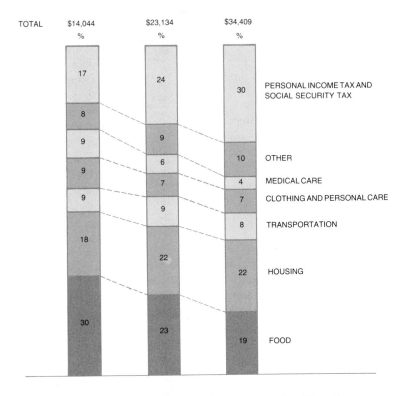

Figure 10–2   Urban budgets for four-person families, three income levels (Autumn, 1981)

As personal income increases, the percentage spent for food, clothing and personal needs, and medical care declines, while the percentage spent for taxes and housing increases. (Source: Current Population Census, Department of Commerce, 1982)

ilies spend most of their income on food, housing, and medical care and very little on recreation. As income rises, expenditures for recreation, education, and household equipment increase rapidly. Money spent for food, housing, and clothing must not be thought of as covering only necessities. Eating in fine restaurants, living in homes with central air conditioning, and owning clothes for formal affairs are a far cry from meeting the needs for survival. On the other hand, we must be careful when we use the word *necessity*. The clothing needed by a teacher is different from the clothing needed by a factory worker, although their incomes may be the same. The junior executive may have a difficult time explaining to a $16,000-a-year employee that he or she cannot make ends

meet even with a $35,000-a-year income. However, some things that are necessities to the executive would be luxuries to other people.

The United States Department of Commerce has analyzed the personal consumption expenditures in the United States for 1981.[1] This analysis is shown in Figure 10–2. It is very difficult to place certain expenditures in such a simplified distribution. The cost of food includes charges for any processing that reduces homemaker preparation time. Beverages and tobacco are included as food. Many appliances are included under hous-

[1]The Bureau of Labor Statistics announced in the spring of 1982 that it could no longer provide expenditure data because of cuts in its budget.

ing. Durable goods—those items that do not need to be replaced after each use and that last for a considerable time—make up an increasing percentage of total budgets. Because consumers can make automobiles, appliances, and other durable goods last an extra year or more, the demand for these products fluctuates considerably. Those businesses connected with the production and sale of durable goods must create demand in the mind of the consumer, if none already exists.

 The level of income is a big factor in determining how households spend their money.

Advertising: Key to Demand Creation

Thorstein Veblen, an economist and sociologist at the University of Chicago at the beginning of the twentieth century, studied the spending habits of people in the United States. He observed that consumers at all income levels tried to demonstrate their superiority through extravagant purchases. He called buying expensive things for show *conspicuous consumption*. Today we often refer to this practice as "keeping up with the Joneses." Read the advertisements for luxury cars and note their appeal to social status. When an advertisement says, "Move up to——," the implication is that you will enjoy more prestige. In some circles a mink coat means that the wearer "has arrived." Paintings, jewelry, and even collections of books are bought because the "best" people have these things. The assumption is that purchasing these prestige items will make you one of the best people.

Built-in Obsolescence

Automobile and appliance manufacturers may work hard to improve their product; at the same time, they know that style changes, along with new gadgets, will be sufficient to spur consumers to consider their present car obsolete and buy a new one. This built-in obsolescence puts pressure, primarily of a social nature, on consumers to trade in a product still in good condition for a new one. The entire structure of the market in several fields is based on "trade-ins" and "moving up." The

greatest appeal of this strategy is to the middle class and the newly rich, both characterized by social and economic mobility, to whom status symbols are visible evidence of progress. People at the lower economic levels cannot afford to play this "game," whereas those long established at the upper economic level do not have to play it.

The Case for Advertising

Changes in hair styling and clothing, colors for decorating, and even packaging give a "new look." The consumer is bombarded by all the media of mass communication—in 1984 by over $88 billion worth of advertising, three times the amount spent in 1975. The advertising agencies, using information psychologists have provided on the suggestibility of humans, have used advertising to limit consumer sovereignty; they have thereby placed a powerful weapon in the hands of the producer. This change has somewhat altered the consumer's position from what is called for in the classical model, but this is not necessarily a disadvantage. A mature capitalistic economy must at various times stimulate consumer demand in order to avoid a depression. This stimulus to consumer demand can come from government; it can also come from business. Advertising is business's way of stimulating consumer demand. If that demand is allowed to decline, production will fall off and so will jobs, because the income that businesses need to pay their labor will no longer be available.

As a means of providing information to the consumer, advertising can be looked on both favorably and unfavorably. Proponents point out the need for advertising to acquaint the public with the existence of new products and improvements in older products. How does the business firm let the public know that it has something special to sell? If we want to sell our "Build-a-City" sets, we can send salespersons to retailers and leave it to the retailers to initiate sales of our sets. However, let us suppose that retailers are not advertising or that they hesitate to take on a new and untried product. By advertising, we go directly to consumers to inform them of our game and create a demand. Consumers can then request that retailers have "Build-a-City" sets in stock.

The Case Against Advertising

Critics of advertising point out that the great expense of advertising can be met only by large, established firms. Introducing a new product requires more money than a small producer can afford. Big advertising campaigns, aimed at *product differentiation,* lead the public to think that only the name brands can be trusted, since they are the only ones that have "zing" in them. This belief leads to imperfect competition, limiting consumer choices.

Other criticisms of advertising are that it is a waste of money, because no real value is added to the product; it distorts values; and it creates consumer demand for such products as tobacco, beer, and patent medicines. Testimony taken before a Senate investigating committee revealed that the drug industry spends more on advertising than it does on research. Critics also question the real value to consumers of the information given in advertisements.

Advertising as a Part of Our Economy

Many of the criticisms of advertising are undoubtedly true for particular cases, but they need not be so for advertising in general. There is a need for the advertising industry, as for many other segments of our economy, to take stock of its code of ethics. The government has already taken steps to control certain kinds of advertisements through the Food and Drug Administration. Self-policing by business will prevent additional government controls.

In an economy where more than half of consumer purchases are for things not necessary for survival, creation of demand through advertising may be an important means of keeping business on an even level. There is little likelihood of a decline in the importance of advertising.

Relation of Imperfect Competition to Demand Creation

Consumers' choices are limited and impeded by markets with less than pure competition. When new firms find it difficult to introduce their products into the market either because they are not allowed to enter the market or because they are not able to let the consumer know about their product, progress is stifled and the consumer must take what the few large firms have to offer.

Although imperfect competition has hurt consumers by limiting their choice of products, the spread of large discount stores has probably kept retail prices from increasing even faster than they have. However, this benefit to consumers has been at the expense of owners of small businesses.

C Consumer Credit: A Factor in Demand

Consumer Savings

Personal savings and *consumer credit* have an important effect on consumption. Because saving is the opposite of consuming, an increase in one will, for a given income, result in a decrease in the other. Consumer credit allows the consumer to expand consumption without having to gear buying strictly to savings and income. In a mature economy like our own, demand creation is important. It is doubtful whether demand could be expanded without consumer credit.

What Determines Savings

Consumer saving usually varies according to income. When income rises, families are able to increase the percentage of income saved. Savings for all families in our country fluctuate with the national income, increasing as income increases. During the Depression of the 1930s, savings dropped so low that in 1932 and 1933 people actually spent more than they received in income, which resulted in dissavings. During World War II, when incomes went up but consumer goods were in short supply, savings amounted to over 20 percent of take-home pay. Savings averaged 6.8 percent of take-home pay in the 1970s, but dropped to 4.6 percent in 1985. Deviations in this percentage reflect changes in business conditions and price levels.

What Constitutes Savings

By savings we do not mean merely the money deposited in a savings bank, stored in a vault, or hidden under a mattress. Money paid on a life insurance policy, used to buy stocks or bonds, or even to make mortgage payments that go beyond interest and depreciation is considered in the same category. Most families like to have a reserve of some kind. Savings provide a buffer for emergencies and give the family additional security.

How Savings Are Held

In considering where to put savings, the consumer should consider *safety; liquidity,* or how quickly and easily savings can be converted to cash; *rate of interest;* and *stability of value,* or how the savings will *fluctuate* with prices. Usually no one form of savings can be strong on all these characteristics. Deposits in savings accounts provide safety and liquidity, but they usually yield a relatively low return, and they do not give protection against sharp price rises. Stocks are not so safe, particularly if the owner does not have a long period of time to convert them into cash. Until the 1970s, stocks were more likely to yield a higher rate of return and give better protection against inflation than other forms of savings. Many investors still feel that good common stocks are the best hedge against inflation for long-term investments. Most consumer economists recommend diversifying savings so that changing conditions will never place the family in too difficult a position. However, each family has to determine how its own interests will be served.

 Savings include more than money in the bank.

Factors Influencing Savings

The most important single factor affecting the amount of savings is the general health of the economy. When their income goes up, people will spend more, but they are likely to save even a higher percentage of their income than previously. The prosperity of the late 1960s and early 1970s caused savings as a percent of disposable personal income to increase from an average of 5.8 percent to 7.2 percent. In the period from 1977 to 1983, a sluggish period, the rate of savings dropped to 6 percent.

Another factor affecting savings is the change in price levels. From 1979 to 1981 prices increased by nearly 40 percent. Consumers were likely to "buy now" rather than wait, because buying later would mean paying higher prices. Higher consumption meant less savings.

The extension of credit facilities through *MasterCard, VISA, American Express,* and other credit cards has allowed people to spend more conveniently. This convenient credit has resulted in higher rates of consumption and, conversely, lower rates of savings.

President Reagan tried to reverse this trend by inducing people to save. The one-time, tax-free interest account and the Individual Retirement Account (IRA), which permits income tax payments on savings of up to $2,000 per worker to be deferred until retirement, did little to increase personal savings.

The ratio of personal savings to disposable income is far higher among the Japanese and German consumers than among their U.S. counterparts.

Changes in Consumer Spending and Consumer Credit

The opposite of savings is spending. Therefore the factors that bring about changes in savings result in equal but inverse changes in consumption, or spending.

Consumers may increase their current spending by using present income (thereby saving less) or by using past savings, or they may borrow money and reduce their future savings by paying back loans. The two largest consumer items are homes and automobiles. Few people are able to pay for these items out of savings or current income.

Mortgage debt for residential housing in 1984 reached $2 trillion, or 56 percent of our GNP. Installment credit for automobiles reached $172 billion, or nearly 38 percent of all installment credit granted.

Sales of houses and cars are highly sensitive to interest rates. From 1981 to 1985 interest rates declined approximately 20 percent. This decline stimulated sales of both homes and cars and resulted in sharp increases in mortgage and installment credit.

The largest portion of nonmortgage consumer credit is installment credit, which differs from other consumer credit in that the seller is allowed to repossess the article purchased if the buyer defaults on payment. This practice involves greater risks with respect to repayment because the article purchased loses value as it is used. More than a third of installment credit is granted for automobile purchases. Noninstallment credit includes charge accounts, service credit, and single-payment loans. Credit in all of these categories is 3 to 7 times greater than it was 20 years ago.

How Credit Affects the Consumer

Availability of credit has led to new patterns of consumer spending. Credit has the appearance of extending the range of choices open to the consumer. However, many people question whether credit always permits the consumer to exercise choice most effectively.

Advantages

One of the great difficulties most young married couples encounter is that their needs are greatest when their incomes are lowest. When the breadwinner has a beginning job, furnishing an apartment, buying a car, and meeting the costs of raising young children present an overwhelming problem. A family needs a washing machine more when children are young than when they have

grown up and left home. Why wait and save for the washer when it can be paid for in regular installments while it is being used? Many families must purchase durable goods such as automobiles and appliances by means of installment buying or not at all.

Businesses are as concerned about the availability of consumer credit as consumers are. They know that a drop in consumer credit can bring significant drops in consumer purchases. Credit frees consumers from waiting until they have enough savings to make their purchases.

Some Dangers

There are serious disadvantages to credit. Buying on credit involves extra costs. Interest rates vary, but enough cases have been reported of total interest costs being greater than the original price of the purchase to serve as a warning to those who borrow. Stores that grant credit are hard pressed to compete in price with stores that demand immediate payment for goods.

 When credit is used wisely, it can enhance a household's living standards without being extravagant or dangerous.

Another danger is that credit lures people into buying things they may not need. Many people are tempted to exceed their financial means when they look only at the amount of the down payment and the size of each month's payment. "No money down and three years to pay" and "For pennies a day you can own a new——" are catch phrases that get too many U.S. families into debt over their heads. Consumers can help themselves by

1. Determining what the cost of the credit will be in addition to the original cash price.
2. Deciding whether their income is sufficient to cover the payments without too many other sacrifices.
3. Shopping for credit as they would for other purchases.
4. Reading all the print in credit contracts.

D   Protecting Consumers

As we sketched the design of the classical model, we learned that all the people concerned—business persons, labor, owners of other factors of production, and consumers—were expected to act independently. Because the system is organized to provide benefits to consumers, competition rather than cooperation among those within each group was considered essential. We have already pointed out how each of the interest groups has sought collective action to protect itself from others. Although labor and management have organized to guard their special interests, the interests of the individual consumer have frequently been neglected. Consumer cooperatives, private consumer agencies, and government all provide some protection for the consumer. The question remains as to whether the interests of consumers are adequately protected by present practices. There are three basic issues we must consider:

1. Why do consumers need protection?
2. What protection is now available to them?
3. Do consumers need more protection?

Why Do Consumers Need Protection?

Before the Industrial Revolution, the consumers' task of making choices and judging quality was a relatively simple one. Little of the merchandise offered for sale was packaged, so they could see what they were buying; and it was reasonably easy to judge the quality of the few simple items offered for sale. In some instances, if consumers did not like what they saw, they went home and made the article.

Today consumers find themselves surrounded by hordes of products packaged in multicolored wrappings in every conceivable shape and size, all claiming to do the best job. The technical information necessary to determine quality is well beyond the knowledge of the average consumer. Claims and counterclaims, giveaways, coupons, packaging, and trademarks lend chaos

to confusion. Determining what is the best appliance, the best fabric, or even the best canned food frequently turns out to be impossible. And errors made in judging quality and performance may be costly. In most instances the cost is money, performance, or satisfaction; but in some instances it may be health and safety. A poorly wired electrical appliance or a dangerous drug can produce a disaster for the consumer.

Freedom of consumer choice is frequently limited by manufacturers. We have mentioned demand creation and advertising as methods of reducing sovereignty for consumers and transferring it to producers. This tendency has gone so far that some marketing specialists have changed their goal from giving consumers what they want to making consumers want what they have to offer them. Misleading advertising, imperfect competition, buying by habit, the use of only brand names, and the unorganized position of consumers in contrast to other groups in our economy have made the need for some kind of consumer protection vital.

What Protection Do Consumers Now Have?

Although the original objective of the classical model was to benefit consumers, later influences have interfered with the realization of that aim. We have seen that some groups concerned with the factors of production, such as labor and management, organized to protect their interests. Organizing for protection became important for consumers, too, especially as created demand and "easy credit" made their situation more complicated.

Consumers get protection from both private and public sources. Consumer cooperative stores have been set up throughout the country for the purpose of getting good merchandise at reasonable prices. Members of the cooperative provide the funds to start and maintain the business; merchandise is sold at market prices, but "profits" are returned to members according to their purchases. A nationally famous private research foundation, Consumers Union, tests and rates products. Their results are made known in their periodicals, which accept no advertising. Many producers and retailers set standards and stand behind their sales with an offer to return the customers' money if they are not satisfied. Better business bureaus and chambers of commerce help consumers by searching for frauds that cheat the public. Finally, in the private sector, Ralph Nader's name has become synonymous with protecting consumer safety and the environment.

All levels of government have been involved in consumer protection for many years. At the state and local level, there are regulatory agencies in the fields of water purity, sanitation, food handling, building inspection, accuracy of scales, financial institutions, credit agencies, and many other areas. At the federal level, the Food and Drug Administration, the Federal Trade Commission, the Bureau of Standards, and the Department of Agriculture are among the 400 departments, divisions, and agencies administering over 1,000 programs related to consumers.

Do Consumers Need More Protection?

A good case can be made for increasing consumer protection even though much has been done. Budgets for testing and disseminating information have been small, and those consumers who need protection most—the poor—rarely know where to go to seek relief. Yet a number of economists feel that too much protection may work against consumers' best interests.

Meeting rigid standards adds heavily to the cost of a product and will increase prices. Some restrictions discourage producers from developing new products, particularly in the drug industry. The growing number of regulations creates an uncertainty that causes delay in production, increases the threat of damage suits, and discourages new business from entering the field, which might increase competition.

Although we have come a long way from the classical approach of *caveat emptor* (let the buyer beware), finding a proper balance between freedom and security is not easy.

Chapter Highlights

1. The classical model assumes that the objective of production is consumption. Consumers determine what the production shall be by registering their wants in the market.
2. Needs of consumers differ. In wealthy nations, a great deal of production is for goods and services not needed for survival.
3. Consumer sovereignty is limited by the distribution of personal income, the creation of demand by business, and imperfect competition.
4. A family's consumption depends on income, savings, and credit. Income is the most important factor. The Lorenz curve, used for measuring distribution of income, shows family unit incomes to be quite unequal. However, incomes tend to be more nearly equal today than they were in the 1930s.
5. Recent inflation has hurt all groups and helped stimulate consumer activity. The lower income groups benefit most from government consumer action because they have few alternatives in the market.
6. In our economy efforts are made, largely through advertising, to create demand among consumers. Some controversy exists about the

benefits of demand creation, particularly for products that are not necessities.

7. Imperfect competition limits consumer choices and efficient use of resources.

8. Consumer savings can be kept in a variety of ways, each having advantages or disadvantages in terms of safety, liquidity, interest, and stability of value.

9. Consumer credit, which has increased rapidly, allows consumers to use products while they pay for them. Credit can help consumers and business if used wisely.

10. Controversy exists as to how far the government should go in attempting to protect the consumer and to supervise business.

Study Aids

Key Terms and Names

caveat emptor	consumer sovereignty	consumer credit
Lorenz curve	installment credit	conspicuous consumption
durable goods	consumer cooperatives	built-in obsolescence
personal income	public assistance	product differentiation

Ralph Nader	Thorstein Veblen	Consumers Union

Questions

1. Evaluate the theory of consumer sovereignty associated with classical capitalism. To what extent does the consumer really guide and direct the U.S. economy?

2. Given the value we place on political equality, the great inequalities of an economic system based on unlimited competition for profit may seem inconsistent. What is the essential difference between equality of opportunity and equality of income?

3. How does income relate to spending for necessities, spending for nonessentials, and personal savings?

4. Explain the following statements and evaluate the truth of each:
   (a) Advertising serves as the lifeblood of production for consumption through demand creation.
   (b) Advertising may lead to waste and excessive cost.

5. Describe how savings and credit function in consumer spending.

6. What are the main factors the consumer should consider when determining the form of personal savings?

7. How can buying on credit benefit the consumer? The seller? In what ways may credit buying harm the consumer?

8. Consumers have found it necessary to protect their interests.
   (a) Explain the reasons for the development of laws for consumer protection.
   (b) Defend the continued use of laws to protect the consumer.
   (c) What steps have consumers taken to help themselves?
   (d) What public and private agencies are available to provide help?

Problems

1. Study the trends in consumer spending and saving. Data can be found in *Business Conditions Digest, Survey of Current Business, Statistical Abstracts*, and *Business Week*. What

percentage of personal income is the consumer saving today? Is this percentage different from that of 5 or 10 years ago? If so, what explains the difference? Include data on consumer credit trends in your study.

2. Explain the meaning of the phrase *caveat emptor.* To what extent does it express the philosophy of present marketing and consumption? What recent legislation has been designed to increase consumer protection? How would you evaluate the effectiveness of this legislation?

3. Select three products that consumers frequently buy. Check the ratings of the various brands of each product in *Consumer Reports.* Is it true that "you get what you pay for"?

4. Find the range of interest rates for both personal and business loans. Explain why there are such significant differences.

PART

III

The U.S. Economy As a Whole

Measuring the Nation's Economy

This chapter will introduce you to modern macroeconomics, the study of the economy as a whole. You will learn what tools the economist uses in evaluating the basic state of the economy. Just as the physician measures the health of a patient by checking many factors, so the economist looks at many indicators to judge whether the economic machine is working properly. When the reports are in, the economist, like the physician, can diagnose and prescribe. Foremost among these tools is a different model to explain the working of our economic system.

The model we will examine in Part Three is known by many names—"national income determination," "welfare capitalism," "the Keynesian model," and other intriguing titles. Whatever you call it, you should recognize that this model is consistent with what we have described as a mixed capitalistic system. It differs from the classical model in that it approaches the economy from the aggregate, or national, standpoint rather than from the standpoint of the individual firm or institution. It modifies and adds to rather than replaces the classical tradition. It is not a different economic system in the sense that socialism and feudalism are different from capitalism. Some economists think of this model as an extension of classical capitalism designed to meet conditions of today's world.

As you read this chapter, you will find economic terms that are used regularly on the front page and the financial pages of your newspaper. Although the concepts may be somewhat distant to you at first, you should ask yourself how these measurements and tools might apply to you personally. In the world of production, how can you prepare yourself if business activity is declining? Will you be better off in an upturn? As you read this chapter, you can begin to speculate an answer to these and other questions related to the economy as a whole.

Chapter Objectives

When you have completed this chapter, you should be able to:

- Define GNP and be conversant with the three alternative methods for calculating it.
- Provide a working definition of MEW, compare MEW with GNP, and discuss the usefulness of each as a measure of our national economic welfare.
- Define NNP, NI, PI, and DPI.
- Define and distinguish among leading indicators, lagging indicators, and composite indicators, and explain why a business person might be interested in each.
- Identify and describe each of the four phases of a business cycle.
- Discuss the possible causes of business cycles.

A National Income Accounting

The National Economy

When people interested in business gather, conversation frequently turns to economic conditions. Although attention may be focused primarily on local conditions, broader questions will be raised concerning such topics as unemployment, prices, inventories, the stock market, steel production, and automobile and department store sales. Although such conversation may clarify some issues, evaluating overall economic conditions for a country as large and complex as ours is not a simple task. One segment of our economy may be growing at a time when another segment is declining. Some producers may be more prosper-

Although the growing number and accuracy of measurements provide the economist with more workable data for forecasting, the evaluation and interpretation of such data are often the subject of controversy.

ous than ever at a time when most business people are complaining of losses. You may be surprised to learn that a few businesses, such as gold mining, did well during the Great Depression of the 1930s. On the other hand, during its most prosperous times our nation has had more than six hundred business failures a week. However, business persons know that no matter how well they may be doing at present, they will, in all probability, eventually feel the general trend of the economy. To decide wisely about their own businesses, they must know the economy as a whole. How can we determine the direction of economic trends and evaluate their movement?

Keeping Our Records

In order to evaluate the past and project future progress, we must have data concerning many types of activity. It is as essential for a nation to keep records of its economy as it is for a physician to keep careful records of his or her patients. Not until 1929 did the United States Departments of Commerce and Labor start to keep accurate measurements of the nation's economy. Table 11–1 shows some of the primary economic indicators used in determining the level of business activity.

Economists know that collecting data on particular segments of the economy is comparatively easy. However, for detailed analysis, certain

Table 11–1   Primary economic indicators

	1984	1985[1]	Percentage of Change
Unemployment rate (issued in monthly percentage of labor force)	7.5%	7.1%	− 5.3
Industrial production index (monthly, base of 1967 = 100)	121.8	124.5	+ 2.2
Gross national product (GNP, 1982 dollars)	3,492.0	3,573.5	+ 2.3
Producer price index, Finished goods (monthly, base of 1967 = 100)	291.1	293.8	+ .9
Consumer price index (monthly, base of 1967 = 100)	311.1	322.2	+ 3.6
Personal income (in billions)	3,111.9	3294.2	+ 5.9
Consumer installment credit (monthly, in billions)	557.9	667.9[2]	+19.7
N.Y. Stock Exchange (weekly)	94.85	120.2	+26.7
Raw steel (monthly, thousands of net tons)	1,547	1,700	+ 9.9
Electric power (millions of kilowatt hours)	52,261	52,092	− .3
Freight car loadings (billions of ton-miles)	16.9	17.9	+ 5.9

[1] Fourth quarter, or December, preliminary.

[2] November to November.

Source: *Survey of Current Business,* Department of Commerce, February 1985. A variety of measurements are used in studying economic development and predicting the direction of trends. How would you assess the movement of the economy?

statistics are of special value—those concerned with the overall view. We do not want to see only the trees; we want to see the forest, too. In economics, we call the study of the economy as a whole *macroeconomics*. This approach differs from the approach of Part Two, where we engaged in a detailed study of individual factors of the economy—*microeconomics*.

Gross National Product: The Basic Measure

When reading reports of the nation's economic condition in a newspaper or magazine, you are very likely to encounter the term *gross national product,* or simply GNP. GNP is the measure most often used to determine how well the economy is faring; government and business alike use it to determine their future policies and plans. What does GNP include? If the retail prices of all the goods and services produced during the year were added up, the figure arrived at would be the gross national product for that year.

Methods of Figuring GNP

There are three different approaches to determining gross national product. All three will yield the same answer, because each is doing the same thing—measuring the total value of goods and services produced in the nation during the year. The first approach has already been described: totaling up the final market price or retail value of all production. This approach is easy to understand because it follows exactly the definition of GNP—the value of the nation's production, or product, before anything is subtracted from the total. Shortly we shall subtract items from GNP, and the word *gross* will be replaced.

The Expenditure Approach to GNP

It is also possible to look at GNP from the point of view of goods and services bought rather than produced. This method is called the expenditures approach; it involves recording who is buying the

goods and services in the marketplace. There are four categories of buyers: (1) individuals buying as households, (2) government, (3) businesses, and (4) foreign purchasers, which we shall call "foreign investment." Figure 11–1 shows the expenditures of each of these buyers.

About two-thirds of all expenditures in the marketplace are for consumer goods and services and are made by families buying to satisfy their needs. These consumer items include durable goods, such as washing machines and cars; nondurable goods, such as food and gasoline; and services, such as entertainment and medical treatment. Economists call these household purchases *personal consumption expenditures.*

The second largest buyer in the marketplace is government. Government at all levels accounts for over one-fifth of total expenditures. Most items on federal, state, and local government budgets are included. The main exceptions are expenditures by publicly owned businesses that sell to the people—for example, the post office and some transportation systems and utilities. Such expenditures are included under personal consumption.

Investment expenditures made by business account for most of the remaining purchases. Under this category are all purchases of capital goods (such as machinery and equipment), all construction (including homes), and the differences between inventories at the beginning of the year and at the end of the year. If total inventories were to decline during a particular year, it would mean that more goods were used than were produced, and the difference would have to be subtracted from the total investment expenditures. If there were surplus inventories, the additional value of goods would have to be added.

The final and smallest item tallied in the expenditure approach is net foreign investment. The total for this category is calculated by adding together all the expenditures made by foreign countries in the United States and subtracting from that amount the total of all U.S. purchases made abroad. In 1985 the total was a negative $75 billion because our consumers bought more foreign goods and services than foreigners bought from us. For now we will include net foreign investment under investment, recognizing that because

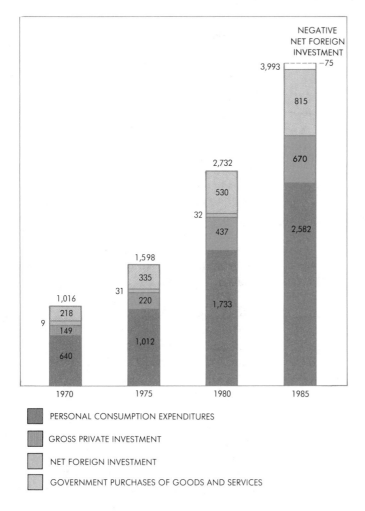

Figure 11–1   Gross national product and its components

Source: U.S. Department of Commerce, Office of Business Economics.

it is a negative number it is actually reducing the size of investment. We will return to this subject in Chapter 18.

 Personal consumption expenditures, *C*, plus investment, *I*, plus government expenditures, *G*, equals aggregate income, GNP.

Although the logic of the expenditure approach is clear, you may question how the total value of production and the total value of expenditures can be the same when some of the product is not sold.

It is true that some of the production is not sold to the ultimate consumer; but if we regard this production as part of the inventory bought by other producers, then it is clear that the totals of the expenditure approach and the production approach should be equal.

The Income Approach to GNP

The third method of determining GNP is by analyzing income. Because the factors of production are responsible for the making of goods and services, it is possible to determine GNP by adding

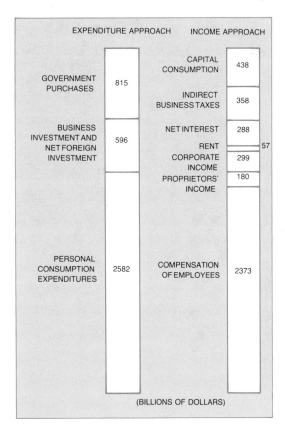

Figure 11–2   Two views of the GNP, 1985
Source: U.S. Department of Commerce, Office of Business
Economics.

up all the payments made to those involved in this production. The sum of all wages, salaries, interest, rent, and profits, plus indirect business taxes and capital consumption, must be calculated. The resulting total represents the payments, or income, side of the goods and services produced. This figure is most frequently referred to as *gross national income* because it deals with income instead of production. However, the gross national income should equal the gross national product.

Whether the production, the expenditure, or the income approach is used, the same total is reached—the gross value of what the nation produced for the year. Remember that product refers to the value of production, whether produced or bought, and income refers to the payment for that

production. Figure 11–2 shows a comparison of the expenditure and income approaches.

 GNP is equal to (1) the final market price of a nation's production in a given year, or (2) $C + I + G$, or (3) national income + capital consumption + indirect taxes.

Common Errors in Computing GNP

In computing GNP, it is easy to make two types of errors: (1) double counting and (2) counting transfer payments as value created. Unless corrected, these mistakes will result in a distorted picture of economic conditions, preventing an accurate accounting and evaluation of actual production.

Double Counting

One of the problems in determining GNP using the production method is how to avoid double counting. You will remember that in our first definition of GNP we were careful to refer to value as the final market price, or retail price. An example, illustrated in Table 11–2, will make the reason for this distinction obvious.

When a farmer sells his cattle to a slaughterhouse, he receives payment for his product. The slaughterhouse sells the meat at a higher price to a wholesale distributor. The wholesale distributor sells the meat at a higher price to retail stores, which in turn sell the meat to consumers at a still higher price. Each of the above—the farmer, the slaughterer, the distributor, and the retailer—has

Table 11–2   An illustration of double counting

	Correct Method		Double Counting
	Price Received	Value Added	
Farmer	$1,000	$1,000	$1,000
Slaughterer	1,200	200	1,200
Distributor	1,500	300	1,500
Retailer	2,000	500	2,000
		$2,000	$5,700

contributed value to the final product. We must add the value that each has contributed when calculating GNP. However, we must *not* add the total price received by each. If we do so, we shall have added the farmer's contribution four times, the slaughterer's three times, and the wholesale distributor's twice. Doing so would be *double counting*. We must remember to count only the value added by each step of production and not the total value paid by each of those involved in the various stages of production.

As you can see from Table 11–2, the value the product actually added to society's wealth is $2,000, not $5,700. The value created in each stage of production must be added only once.

Transfer Payments

Another kind of double counting may occur when GNP is figured on the income side. Should the money that Aunt Harriet gave you for a graduation gift be added to your income when GNP is figured? If you do add it, you will be double counting. You did not create value; Aunt Harriet did. Therefore, Aunt Harriet will have to include in her income the gift she gave you. What you received was a *transfer payment;* the value was not created by you. Social security benefits are another type of transfer payment. Value is created during work-ing years, and during those years it counts as income for GNP. However, the value created to pay for social security is not received until payment is made during retirement. This payment at retirement is a transfer payment, because the value you created in the past and added to the GNP at that time is being returned to you to use.

Other Weaknesses

There are other weaknesses also inherent in determining gross national product. Economics tends to be a cold, unemotional, and frequently undiscriminating discipline. When GNP is computed, we consider value only in terms of dollars and cents. In the present context, only when the product or service is actually offered for sale on the market does it have value. This means that one of the most valuable contributors in our society, the housewife and mother, is not given credit for contributing to GNP. If she does the same work for someone else and is paid for it, the amount of her paycheck is included in GNP. The same may be said of that great U.S. institution known as "do-it-yourself." Steps built by someone in your family, or even by a neighbor, do not count as part of GNP unless some payment is made. Volunteer work is never considered as part of GNP because volunteers are not paid for their labor.

The Underground Economy

Recent studies have estimated that between 5 and 15 percent of income is not being recorded. Because of this underground economy, our actual production is $200 to $600 billion dollars higher than the GNP government statisticians report. Also, since our local, state, and federal governments are not collecting sales, individual, and corporate income taxes on unre-ported income, they have to charge us honest taxpayers an extra $25 to $70 billion.

What is the underground economy? It is the income of all those engaged in illegal activities such as the sale of drugs, prostitution, and collection of protection money. It is the unreported earnings of those who "moonlight," collect unemployment insurance while working part-time, babysit, conduct businesses that deliver to particular areas in order to avoid sales tax payments, or those who barter to exchange goods or services. This income escapes being counted as GNP and thus is not taxed.

There are some who claim the problem has grown more serious because taxes have gotten higher, and the motivation to cheat is greater.

Do you believe that an additional tax cut would bring about a decrease in such unethical behavior?

Another problem in evaluating GNP—one that some experts consider a big weakness—is the failure to distinguish between the billions of dollars spent on luxuries and the billions of dollars spent on education, steel mills, and other goods and services associated with the strength and productivity of a nation. These critics may have a valid argument if GNP is used for comparing the military potential of nations (for example, the United States and the USSR). However, the criticism does not actually apply to the GNP as a measuring device, but rather to its use in measuring something it was never meant to measure, such as military strength.

MEW—Measure of Economic Welfare

In the last fifteen years, economics has come under increasing criticism for ignoring the quality of life in favor of the market value of goods and services. Not only does GNP fail to consider the valuable contributions of those who produce without pay, but just as important, it fails to subtract the cost of cleaning up the water and the air and of treating other pollution resulting from production. The cost of national defense, police protection, and urban congestion does not, according to some, really add to the economic welfare of the nation.

In 1972, two well-known economists, William Nordhaus and James Tobin, proposed a new measurement for evaluating standard of living, called Measure of Economic Welfare (MEW).[1] This measurement is a modified version of the GNP based on the premise that the purpose of economic activity is consumption, not production. Therefore, certain costs resulting from production, primarily pollution, are subtracted from GNP. Services such as police protection, for which budgets are increasing rapidly, do not reflect more welfare. On the other hand, the value that "do-it-yourself" householders, houseworkers, volunteers in the Red Cross, religious and civic club members, and so on create is added to GNP because

our standard of living, or welfare, is greatly improved by these combined efforts.

Criticism of MEW centers on the assumption that consumption and welfare are the same. Because MEW ignores how income is distributed, it can measure only collective happiness. Criticism also focuses on the crude estimates of value placed on production not previously counted. It is doubtful that GNP will be replaced as the basic macroeconomic measurement for many years; but the effort to find other indices for evaluation should be encouraged, because new indices will provide us with additional perspectives for planning.

GNP as a Basis for Comparison

Because gross national product is a measure of the real wealth of a nation—the value of all its goods and services—we may wish to consider how our country's annual GNP has grown and how it compares with the GNP of other nations. Any time such comparisons are made, a standard measuring device must be used. Therefore, when we compare the GNP of our country at different times, we must be sure that the dollars we are measuring are constant dollars (that is, that they purchase equal amounts of goods and services). When we compare our GNP with the GNP of another country, we must equate another unit of currency—an English pound, a French franc, or an Italian lira—with our dollar. The attempt in either case is to keep the units of measure equivalent.

 GNP is sometimes used to compare nations in ways it cannot and should not be.

Fluctuations in GNP

Until 1929 the United States Departments of Commerce and Labor did not keep records of the gross national product and other similar measurements, thus tracing the growth of our nation's GNP is complicated. However, studies made by the National Bureau of Economic Research give a fairly accurate picture and show some patterns of growth of the GNP. Our annual production of wealth (GNP) increased five times from 1929 to 1985, whereas our population did not quite double during the

[1] William Nordhaus and James Tobin have replaced MEW with the label net economic welfare (NEW) and have modified the concepts slightly.

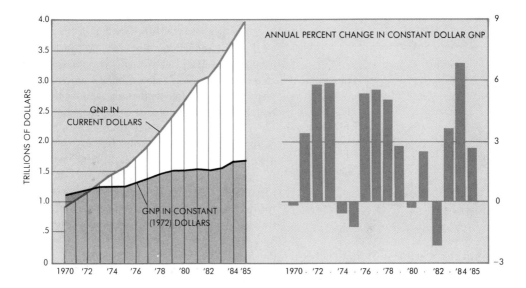

Figure 11–3   Comparison of GNP in constant (1972) and current dollars

Why is GNP in constant (1972) dollars higher than GNP in current dollars up to 1972 and lower than GNP in current dollars thereafter? (Source: U.S. Bureau of the Census. Data from U.S. Bureau of Economic Analysis.)

same period. This means that the production of real wealth per person during this period increased almost three times. Figure 11–3 shows our economic growth from 1970 to 1985. Growth averaged about 4 percent in the 1950s and 1960s, slowed to 3 percent in the 1970s, and declined to 2.8 percent in the first half of the 1980s. Although the general trend is upward, important fluctuations appear.

Our GNP Compared with GNP of Other Countries

When we compare the GNP of the United States with that of other countries of the world, it becomes obvious why a famous economist referred to the United States as the "affluent society." Table 11–3 shows the relative position of several selected countries in terms of GNP. Note that these statistics place the USSR in second position, far behind the United States in total value of goods and services. If Japan's remarkable economic growth continues, Japan may overtake the USSR by 1990.

If the GNP of each of these countries is divided by the total population of that country, the resulting amount represents *per capita output*, which provides a measure of the total value per person in each of the countries listed. Table 11–4 gives this information. Occasionally per capita output is used to determine the relative standard of living

Table 11–3   Gross national product for selected countries, 1984 (billions of dollars)

Country	GNP
United States	$3,663
USSR	1,843
Japan	1,298
West Germany	738
France	618
United Kingdom	542
Italy	385
Canada	289

Source: Department of Commerce, International Monetary Fund, O.C.E.D., 1984.

Table 11–4 Per capita output for selected countries, 1983

Country	Amount
United States	$14,110
West Germany	11,430
Canada	12,310
France	10,500
Japan	10,120
United Kingdom	9,200
Italy	6,400
USSR	5,991

Source: World Development Report, 1985, World Bank.

of people in particular countries. Such conclusions are not very reliable, because they fail to take into consideration the vast inequality of wealth within a country. However, we can note that the output per U.S. worker is considerably higher than that of the British, Italian, and Soviet worker. These statistics emphasize how remarkably productive our economy is.

Other Measurements

Although gross national product is the most frequently used measurement of our national economy, several other measurements closely related to GNP are very important. As we move from GNP through four additional measurements, you will come to better understand the production, expenditure, and income approaches. You may find it helpful to remember that *product* emphasizes the value of what is produced and *income* emphasizes the payment to those producing.

Net National Product

One weakness of GNP as a measure of total output is that it fails to take into account the loss in value of capital goods that takes place as output is produced. Because machinery depreciates as it is used, part of the production of society must be devoted merely to replacing the value of the capital goods used up in the production process during that year. For example, a farmer has a tractor that he estimates is capable of 10 years' operation in helping to produce his crops. He recognizes that each year

he must set aside a portion of the money received from the crops to pay for the value of his tractor used up in production. If he does not, he will be fooling himself as to how much real value he has created. When the tractor breaks down completely 10 years after its first use, the farmer will be faced with the total cost of replacement.

Gross national product gives an exaggerated picture of output, just as the farmer received a distorted view of his income. In both instances, failure to consider the capital that was consumed (depreciated) in the process of producing accounted for the error. This error can be corrected by subtracting from the GNP *capital consumption,* that part of the capital goods depreciated during production. The remainder gives a more accurate picture of the actual value of output for the year. That truer value is called *net national product,* or *NNP.*

National Income

Although we have explained GNP from the output, the expenditure, and the income approaches, GNP and NNP traditionally are determined through the output approach, as the word *product* suggests. *National income (NI),* on the other hand, measures the income side. National income is defined as the total earned income of all the factors of production—namely, profits, interest, rent, wages, and other compensation for labor. National income does not equal GNP because the factors of production do not receive payment for either capital consumption allowances or indirect business taxes, both of which are included in GNP. The money put aside for capital consumption is for replacement and thus is not counted as income. Indirect taxes include sales taxes, property taxes, and excise taxes that are paid by businesses directly to the government and so reduce the income left to pay for the factors of production. Three-fourths of national income goes for wages, salaries, and other forms of compensation to employees.

Personal Income

Whereas national income shows the income that the factors of production earn, *personal income (PI)* measures the income that individuals or households receive. Corporation profits are included in national income because they are

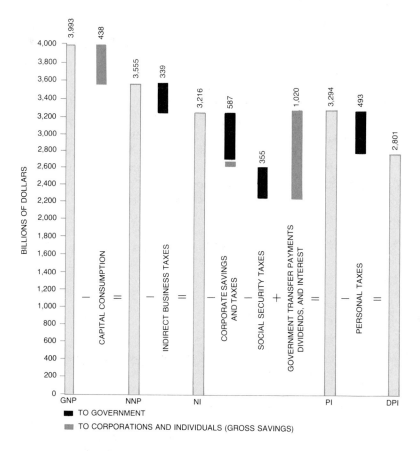

BILLIONS OF DOLLARS

GNP — CAPITAL CONSUMPTION = NNP — INDIRECT BUSINESS TAXES = NI — CORPORATE SAVINGS AND TAXES — SOCIAL SECURITY TAXES + GOVERNMENT TRANSFER PAYMENTS DIVIDENDS, AND INTEREST = PI — PERSONAL TAXES = DPI

■ TO GOVERNMENT
■ TO CORPORATIONS AND INDIVIDUALS (GROSS SAVINGS)

Figure 11–4   Measurements of the nation's income
Source: U.S. Department of Commerce.

earned. Out of these profits, however, corporation profit taxes must be paid to government, and some money must be put into the business for expansion. Only that part of profits distributed as dividends goes to the individual; therefore, out of corporation profits only dividends count as personal income. The factors of production earn money for social security and unemployment insurance contributions, but this money goes to government (which is not a factor of production), not to individuals. It is therefore part of national income but not part of personal income.

On the other hand, money received by individuals when they collect social security or unemployment compensation is not money earned but money *received*. Interest received on government bonds is also in this category, because much of the money received from the sale of bonds went to pay for war production and that production no longer furnishes a service to the economy.

Disposable Personal Income

The money people receive as personal income may be either spent or saved. However, not all spending is completely voluntary. A significant portion of our income goes to pay personal taxes. Most workers never receive the money they pay in personal taxes, because it is withheld from their paychecks. The money that individuals are left with after they have met their tax obligations is *disposable personal income* (DPI). Disposable income can be divided between personal consumption expenditures and personal savings.

It is important to remember that personal saving is what is left after spending. It is quite possible to have a minus saving, or a dissaving. How can this occur?

Figure 11–4 on p. 255 shows how to calculate each of the five measurements of the economy we have discussed. With this information, we can summarize the various measures of our national income as follows:

1. *Gross national product* (GNP) is the retail price of goods and services produced during a given period, usually a year.

2. *Net national product* (*NNP*) is the gross national product minus the capital consumed in producing GNP.
3. *National income* (*NI*) is NNP minus indirect business taxes (not considered payment for production), or the total payments earned by factors of production.
4. *Personal income* (*PI*) is NI minus corporation savings and taxes and social security payments (taxes) plus transfer payments and government interest, or the income that is received by individuals.
5. *Disposable personal income* (*DPI*) is PI minus personal taxes, or the sum of personal consumption expenditures and personal savings.

B Measuring Business Activity

In our economic system, business has the primary responsibility for production. In the measurements already studied, government has occupied a very significant place, receiving income (usually from taxes) and spending money. However, even when government receives and spends, a significant portion of the transactions are done through business. (In Chapter 12 we shall be concerned with the relation between government and business in terms of the general trend of the economy.) Since business activity is vital to the nation's economy, we shall now discuss some of the ways used to measure it.

Every business person is interested in knowing both how his or her particular business is faring in comparison with other businesses and what the general business climate is. On the basis of this information, the owner can make plans for the business. There are two broad categories of *indicators* to turn to for information: representative and composite.

Economic Indicators

Economists, like physicians, look for indicators to see how the economy is doing and, still better, to forecast where it will be going. Some indicators

are considered representative because they actually involve or reflect activity in other businesses. The production of steel and electricity or railroad car loadings reflects a broad spectrum of business activity. More important are the composite indicators, which combine a number of representative indicators. In many instances composite indicators provide a more accurate diagnosis and forecast.

Leading Indicators

Every month the Department of Commerce publishes the *Business Conditions Digest,* which charts indicators in three groups: leading, coincident, and lagging. Leading indicators are economic variables that rise or fall before other variables, including GNP. The Department of Commerce identifies twelve leading indicators from which it computes a composite that is helpful in forecasting. These leading indicators are

1. Average workweek for production workers in manufacturing
2. Layoff rate in manufacturing
3. New orders for consumer goods and materials
4. Vendor performance measured as a percent of companies reporting slower deliveries
5. Net business formation

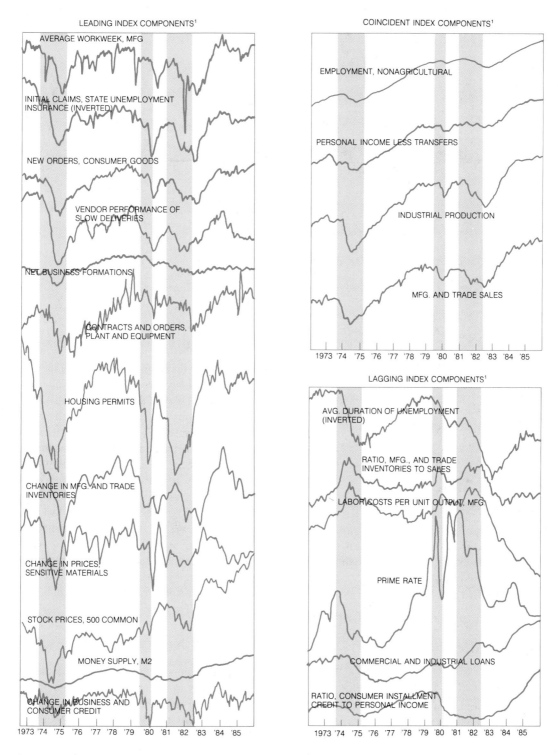

LEADING INDEX COMPONENTS[1]

AVERAGE WORKWEEK, MFG

INITIAL CLAIMS, STATE UNEMPLOYMENT
INSURANCE (INVERTED)

NEW ORDERS, CONSUMER GOODS

VENDOR PERFORMANCE OF
SLOW DELIVERIES

NET BUSINESS FORMATIONS

CONTRACTS AND ORDERS,
PLANT AND EQUIPMENT

HOUSING PERMITS

CHANGE IN MFG. AND TRADE
INVENTORIES

CHANGE IN PRICES,
SENSITIVE MATERIALS

STOCK PRICES, 500 COMMON

MONEY SUPPLY, M2

CHANGE IN BUSINESS AND
CONSUMER CREDIT

1973 '74 '75 '76 '77 '78 '79 '80 '81 '82 '83 '84 '85

COINCIDENT INDEX COMPONENTS[1]

EMPLOYMENT, NONAGRICULTURAL

PERSONAL INCOME LESS TRANSFERS

INDUSTRIAL PRODUCTION

MFG. AND TRADE SALES

1973 '74 '75 '76 '77 '78 '79 '80 '81 '82 '83 '84 '85

LAGGING INDEX COMPONENTS[1]

AVG. DURATION OF UNEMPLOYMENT
(INVERTED)

RATIO, MFG., AND TRADE
INVENTORIES TO SALES

LABOR COSTS PER UNIT OUTPUT, MFG

PRIME RATE

COMMERCIAL AND INDUSTRIAL LOANS

RATIO, CONSUMER INSTALLMENT
CREDIT TO PERSONAL INCOME

1973 '74 '75 '76 '77 '78 '79 '80 '81 '82 '83 '84 '85

[1]ALL OF THE FIGURES CITED ABOVE ARE IN PERCENTAGE CHANGES, INDEXES OR CONSTANT DOLLARS.

Figure 11–5 Leading, coincident, and lagging business indicators
Economists use leading indicators in forecasting business activity. Coincident indicators help explain the present state of
the economy; lagging indicators usually follow the rise and fall of GNP. The shaded bands represent recessions. (Source:
U.S. Department of Commerce, *Business Conditions Digest.*)

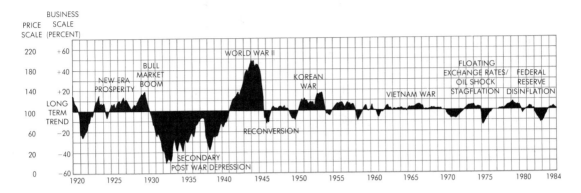

Figure 11–6   Fluctuations in the U.S. economy

The pattern of general business activity can be determined by combining several indicators into a composite. (Source: Courtesy AmeriTrust Company, Cleveland, Ohio.)

6. Contracts and orders for plant and equipment
7. New building permits for private housing units
8. Net change in inventories on hand and on order
9. Change in sensitive prices
10. Change in total liquid assets
11. Stock prices
12. Money supply

Coincident Indicators

These are four primary coincident indicators which run parallel with the GNP:

1. Employees on nonagricultural payrolls
2. Personal income minus transfer payments
3. Industrial production
4. Manufacturing and trade sales

These indicators run parallel with the GNP.

Lagging Indicators

Six lagging indicators, which follow business activity by about three months, are

1. Average duration of unemployment
2. Manufacturing and trade inventories
3. Labor cost per unit of output in manufacturing
4. Average prime interest rate charged by banks
5. Commercial and industrial loans outstanding
6. Ratio of consumer installment debt to personal income

Composite Business Indicators

Rather than rely on the measurement of one segment of the economy, even if that single indicator is representative, economists have put several different phases of our business activity together into a general, or composite, indicator. Many banks and universities make composites of indicators to show business fluctuations. One of the most widely used composites is put out by the AmeriTrust Company of Cleveland. This composite reflects the fluctuation of business activity back to 1790. It must rely on several different measurements for the earlier years, because data used for some of our modern measurements are not available or are unsuitable. Figure 11–6 shows the changes in U.S. business activity from 1920 to 1984 and indicates the key reasons for these changes.

Forecasting Methods

Sophisticated computers now enable economists to use hundreds of different components of the economy in their calculations. Using econometric models, they make forecasts for the total economy and for individual segments. The early optimism that many people showed about econometric models when they first became widespread about fifteen years ago has not been justified, because our economy is far too complex and subject to many sudden changes. Nevertheless, techniques are improving, and the forecasts we have help those responsible for stabilizing the economy.

The Survey Research Center of the University of Michigan and the U.S. Department of Commerce use opinion polling. The former makes quarterly surveys on consumer intentions to buy; the latter polls businesses to determine their plans for capital goods expenditures. The statistics from both polls are useful in forecasting.

Changes in Business Activity

A word of caution must be given about interpreting measurements of our nation's economy. There are three types of changes in business activity: seasonal, trend, and cyclical. In evaluating and forecasting business activity, the effect of these changes—particularly of business cycles—must be considered.

Seasonal Fluctuations

Nature causes some seasonal variations by providing a more favorable environment for certain kinds of production, such as construction, at one time of the year than at others. People cause some seasonal variations in business activity; in these, tradition often plays a part, as with gift giving at Christmas. Economists allow for these differences. A chart may indicate an upturn in retail sales in January, although dollar sales were actually higher in the preceding month.

Trends

Trend changes refer to extended time periods and indicate the long-range direction of the economy. Figure 11–6 shows more business activity in 1923 than in 1960. This does not mean that more business was done or more goods were produced in 1923 than in 1960. During those 37 years our capacity to do business and to produce increased tremendously. However, our business activity in 1923 in relation to our potential in that year was greater than our business activity in 1960 as compared with our potential that year. Figure 11–7 shows how trend is taken into consideration when business activity is measured.

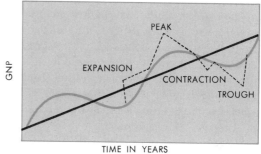

PHASES OF THE BUSINESS CYCLE

IN MEASURING BUSINESS ACTIVITY, NORMAL GROWTH RATE MUST BE TAKEN INTO CONSIDERATION. PHASES OF A SINGLE BUSINESS CYCLE ARE INDICATED.

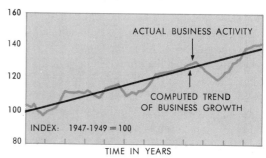

THE INDEX OF BUSINESS ACTIVITY MAY BE MEASURED AGAINST THE TREND OF BUSINESS GROWTH.

Figure 11–7   Measuring business activity
Trend is a factor that must be considered in measuring business activity.

Business Cycles

The fluctuations that we have seen in all the measurements of our economy have been observed and studied by economists for many years. These ups and downs of the many phases of business activity deviate from what we might expect the normal increase in our economy to be; and though these fluctuations do not show a perfect rhythm, we can discern patterns. These patterns of movement are called *business cycles.*

Economists have noted four phases in a business cycle. The upswing is usually referred to as *expansion,* or *recovery;* the uppermost point is the *peak,* or *prosperity;* the downswing is *contraction,* or *recession;* and the low point is the *trough.* A recession is defined as a decline in the real GNP (constant dollars) for two successive quarters. If a recession is severe and long, as in the early 1930s, it is called a depression. The first graph in Figure 11–7 shows these four phases labeled with the terms we shall use: *expansion, peak, contraction,* and *trough.*

Recovery is associated with increases in demand, which are reflected in production, employment, prices, and payments to the factors of production. During a period of recovery all measurements of business activity will not rise at the same rate. Prices will tend to rise more slowly than production, and interest rates and retail sales may not increase at all in the early stages. However, for the great majority of indicators the general tendency will be to move upward during recovery. When most indicators reach a high or near-high point, we are in the prosperity phase. Capital goods, such as machinery, will usually be on the decline by the time retail sales hit their peak, but the composite picture will reflect optimism.

An examination of Figure 11–6 shows that prosperous periods do not continue indefinitely. In the recession phase, some of the leading indicators—such as average hours worked, durable goods, construction, and steel—go down, and such coincident indicators as employment, industrial production, and freight car loadings also decline. When most of the indicators hit low points, a pessimistic outlook such as we associate with a depression becomes prevalent.

 Business cycles are studied with the hope that by having more information about cycles we will be able to reduce the extremes of peaks and troughs.

Studies reveal that the average length of a major cycle is slightly more than four years. However, the variations in the length of time and the severity of the cycles are great, so these statistics are not very useful for analyzing any one particular cycle.

Theories about the Causes of Business Cycles

If we were to make a systematic study of the theories concerning the causes of business cycles, we should soon find ourselves overwhelmed. The number of theories seems to be almost as great as the number of students studying the problem. However, because most of the differences are in emphasis, we can arrange these theories in categories. The most common way to classify them is according to whether the causes they suggest are external or internal.

External Causes of Cycles

Theories based on external causes attribute fluctuations to forces that exist and operate outside the economic system. The best-known forces are those that relate to weather, war, population growth, innovation, and political events.

Innovations

One example of a theory based on external causes is the *innovation theory,* developed principally by the late Harvard professor Joseph Schumpeter. According to Schumpeter, new ideas and processes are introduced in clusters, whether they are new methods of doing business (supermarkets), new machines (computers), new products (televisions), or the opening up of new sources of raw materials (gold rush). Although these inventions and discoveries may be made during a contraction of the economy, it is not until a few daring innovators put money into developing them that a wave of investments develops. These investments lead to an expansion of the economy, stimulating production and income. However, the wave will finally run its course, leading in time to recession and depression. During the slowdown, new ideas and processes will be developed, but they will have to wait for enterprising people or firms to introduce them.

Some inventions, such as the steam engine and the automobile, have led to numerous other inventions and have resulted in tremendous investments in these areas. Other innovations have resulted in only minor investments. This is particularly true of fads, such as miniature golf and Frisbees. What other innovations affecting business activity can you think of?

Internal Causes of Cycles

Theories based on internal causes relate fluctuations to factors within the economy itself. As the economy expands, forces are generated that will, at a certain level, work to bring about a contraction. Likewise, as a recession reaches the point of a depression, forces within the economy reverse the cycle. Examples of internal causes are underconsumption, overinvestment, psychological factors, and monetary causes.

Monetary Theory

An example of a theory based on internal causes is the monetary theory of the cycle, developed primarily by English economist R. G. Hawtrey. The amount of money banks have available for investment varies considerably. At the beginning of a revival, banks have plenty of money available and interest rates are low. The low interest rates and the availability of bank loans encourage business firms to borrow and to expand their operations. As more and more firms do so, the availability of money declines and the interest rate increases. Prosperity is soon reached, but by that time the banks no longer have money to lend out and interest rates are prohibitive for all but a few. Investments then decline, and spending and employment are thus reduced. Some signs of a contraction are visible. The decline continues, finally becoming a recession. However, as the decline progresses, the supply of money that banks have available for credit starts to increase, causing interest rates to drop. Soon the easy access to low-cost loans makes investment opportunities too attractive for businesses to pass up. Expansion will once again take place.

There is no doubt that the monetary theory explains a great deal about business fluctuations, and, as we shall see in Chapter 14, proper action can do much to counter the direction of the business cycle. However, there have been times when bank credit was available and interest rates were low but businesses did not respond. Likewise, a shortage of money, with business persons bidding interest rates up, has frequently failed to dampen enthusiasm in a period of expansion.

The Importance of Interacting Factors

Most economists believe that business cycles are caused by many interacting factors, and that no single formula is sufficient to explain the complex set of reactions that actually takes place. Further-

Cartoon printed by permission of the artist, Derek (Dirk) Thompson.

more, analysts stress the differences between one business cycle and another and usually consider the primary causes to be different for each cycle. The labels of the composite index in Figure 11–6 indicate the causes of the principal fluctuations in the U.S. economy in the twentieth century. Do they suggest any consistent pattern of causes for the various cycles?

The greatest fluctuations tend to occur in the areas of investment and capital goods, which react to such external causes as wars, technological changes, and increases in population. Any additional investment due to external causes will set in motion a series of internal factors, which in turn will tend to magnify the effects of the external causes. Additional machinery means more jobs. More jobs lead to bigger paychecks. Bigger paychecks increase the demand for goods and services. However, even with optimism running high, the amount of capital goods will reach a saturation point and investment will begin to decline, leading to a shift in the cycle.

  No single theory explains all business cycles.

Although investment appears basic, it can be changed by external factors, or it can be influenced by the levels of income or production. Those who believe investment takes place in response to the growth of income and production, instead of the reverse, adhere to the *acceleration principle*. According to this view, a high level of income is not enough to keep the economy moving upward because the machinery in operation and the amount of merchandise in stores have been pushed to a high level, equal to what is needed. If no additional *growth* takes place, the only new machines and merchandise required are replacements for those that become worn out or sold. Therefore, an increase in the demand for automobiles will cause automobile producers to buy new machines to manufacture the automobiles. However, once they have enough machines for this high level of automobile production, the only new machines they will need are replacements for those that are worn out. Producers of the machinery needed to make automobiles can maintain a high level of production only when there is a growing demand for automobiles, not a sustained high demand. Table 11–5 shows how a recession can start when sales merely level off rather than take a definite turn downward.

Anticipating Fluctuation

If business persons are to operate successfully, they must anticipate the fluctuations of the business cycle and gear their production accordingly. In order to do this, they frequently employ economists to determine the direction in which the economy seems to be moving. The government also employs a large staff of economists who track the business cycle and try to predict its direction.

Table 11–5   Business fluctuation explained by the acceleration principle

	Output of "Build-a-City" Sets	Machines Used in Production	New Machine Purchased		
			Replacement	Expansion	Total
1975–80	100,000	5	1	0	1
1976–81	120,000	6	1	1	2
1977–82	140,000	7	1	1	2
1978–83	160,000	8	1	1	2
1979–84	160,000	8	1	0	1

Merely sustaining consumer production at high level, as shown for 1984, is not enough to keep producers of capital goods at the same level of production. Producers of machinery must have a growing market at the consumer level if they are to avoid contraction of business. The same principle holds true for the wholesalers supplying retailers with merchandise.

Using evidence from their studies, these specialists make recommendations in an effort to reduce the extremes of the cycle and to maintain stability in the economy.

Attempts to predict the ups and downs of the business cycle have too often been unsuccessful. Leading indicators—such as industrial stock prices, residential construction, steel production, and new orders for durable goods—have been of some help, but they have also been misleading at times. Just as jokes are made about errors in predicting the daily weather, so criticism is aimed at economists when their carefully planned projections fail. Despite occasional mistakes, the weather forecaster keeps trying, and so does the economist.

Each is employing new methods that will lead eventually to more accurate forecasting.

In this chapter we have seen a variety of means for measuring the national economy. We have also observed the wide range of fluctuation occurring in the economy. This instability of the economy has been the main problem facing economists in the twentieth century. Recessions and depressions have meant unemployment, lower wages, reduced or vanished profits, losses and bankruptcy for business firms, smaller revenue for government, and a stifling of vitality and growth for the economy. In Chapter 12, we shall examine methods of stabilizing the economy using a different model of capitalism developed about 50 years ago.

Chapter Highlights

1. The study of the economy as a whole is called macroeconomics, in contrast to the study of individual units, or microeconomics.

2. Gross national product (GNP) is the total retail value of all the goods and services produced during a year.

3. There are three methods used to determine gross national product: the product (or output) approach, the expenditure approach, and the income approach.

4. The product approach uses as its base the sum of goods and services produced. The expenditure approach determines GNP by totaling spending in the marketplace. The buyers are divided into four categories—individuals buying as households, government, businesses, and foreign purchasers. The income approach arrives at gross national income (GNI) and refers to total payments made to those involved in production in addition to capital consumption and indirect business taxes. The gross national income is equal to gross national production.

5. In determining GNP, economists count the value produced for the market. As a result, labor that is not rewarded by wages or payment cannot be considered part of GNP.

6. Dissatisfaction with what GNP measures and what it does not measure has brought a new but not yet widely accepted index, measure of economic welfare (MEW).

7. Net national product (NNP) measures the value of goods and services added to the nation and is determined by subtracting from GNP the value of the capital consumed in producing it.

8. National income (NI) measures income rather than product and is the total earned income of all the factors of production. It is NNP minus indirect business taxes.

9.   Personal income (PI) is the income received by individuals before they pay their personal taxes. It is determined by subtracting social security payments and corporation savings and taxes from national income and adding transfer payments and government interest.

10.   Disposable personal income (DPI) refers to the total value of personal consumption expenditures and personal savings. It is determined by subtracting personal taxes from personal income.

11.   Economic indicators help economists evaluate business activity. Both representative and composite indicators may be leading, coincident, or lagging with respect to economic activity.

12.   There are three kinds of variation in business activity: seasonal, trend, and cyclical.

13.   There are four phases to a business cycle: expansion, peak, contraction, and trough.

14.   The average length of a full business cycle is slightly more than four years.

15.   External causes of business cycles refer to forces outside the economic system. The causes most frequently referred to are those that relate to weather, war, population growth, innovation, and political events.

16.   Internal causes of business cycles refer to factors within the economic system. These include overinvestment, psychological factors, and monetary causes.

17.   Although investment (capital goods) shows the greatest fluctuation over the business cycle, many interacting factors contribute to the overall cycle. No simple formula is sufficient to explain all reactions.

18.   It is important for the health of the economy to be able to interpret trends, predict business activity, and prescribe policy in order to reduce the extremes of the business cycle.

Study Aids

Key Terms and Names

GNP (gross national product)
NNP (net national product)
NI (national income)
PI (personal income)
DPI (disposable personal income)
MEW (measure of economic welfare)

personal consumption expenditures
capital consumption
external and internal theories
acceleration principle
macroeconomics
microeconomics
double counting

transfer payments
business cycle
representative indicators
composite indicators
leading indicators
coincident indicators
lagging indicators

Joseph Schumpeter

R. G. Hawtrey

Questions

1. What is the basic difference between macro and micro approaches to the study of economics? What is the importance of each?
2. One of the tools used to compare the economic strength of nations is the GNP.
   (a) What methods may be used to arrive at GNP?
   (b) What errors may occur in computing GNP?
   (c) Why is it important to use constant dollars in calculating GNP?
3. What other methods and measures are available to judge the strength of the national economy?
4. How are GNP, NNP, NI, PI, and DPI determined? What is the unique feature of each? What is the use of each?
5. The state of health of the business community may be judged by various indicators. How may this evaluation be made over a long period? What dangers are inherent in forecasting?
6. Cyclical variations are a constant threat to economic stability.
   (a) What is meant by the business cycle?
   (b) What are the various component phases of the business cycle?
   (c) Describe the external and internal forces responsible for fluctuation in business activities.
   (d) Why is it important for a business person to make a successful prediction of business trends?

Problems

1. Every month the U.S. Department of Commerce publishes the *Business Conditions Digest*. Look at the leading indicators charted in this publication and evaluate their predictive value.
2. What effects would a recession or depression probably have on each of the following: (a) a food-processing company, (b) a firm producing machine tools, (c) a commercial bank, (d) the owner of common stocks, (e) the owner of bonds, and (f) a personal finance company? Check in *Survey of Current Business* to see if your predictions are accurate.
3. Using the *Statistical Abstract,* prepare a series of graphs showing the following for the years 1975 to 1985. What conclusions can be drawn from your material?
   (a) GNP
   (b) Personal income
   (c) Disposable personal income
   (d) National income
4. Business cycles have had a significant influence on our country's economic development. Use Figure 11–6 to answer the following questions.
   (a) What were the causes of the main variations in business activity before 1933?
   (b) What explains the long period of prosperity that typified much of the 1960s?
   (c) How would you contrast the 1980s with the 1960s?

National Income Analysis: A Different Model

In the United States, we have the resources and the science and technology needed to ensure enough production to meet our basic needs for survival, with many luxuries in addition. Unfortunately, our system has frequently operated far below its potential level of output. When workers are unemployed and resources are not used, our economic system is falling short of optimal performance.

Economists set up models of economic systems in the hope that these models will guide us in making full and efficient use of our productive resources. Most economists set as a goal the operation of our economy at a full-employment level without inflation. In this chapter, we will examine a different model that shows how the level of our national income is determined and how this income can be changed in an effort to sustain full employment without inflation. We will compare this Keynesian model with the classical model, both within the framework of our mixed capitalist system, to see how each model is designed to achieve the goal of full employment without inflation.

As you read this chapter, you should consider whether our country could have another depression similar to that of the 1930s. Can we rely on the market forces to regulate the economy or do we need more government involvement?

Chapter Objectives	When you have completed this chapter, you should be able to:

- List the conditions necessary to produce equilibrium at the full-employment level without inflation in the classical model.
- Identify the weaknesses of the classical model.
- Using the 45° line as an analytical tool, describe and discuss the relation between aggregate income and aggregate demand.
- Using the 45° line as an analytical tool, discuss the Keynesian view of government's role in maintaining full-employment equilibrium.
- Define the multiplier effect and discuss its relation to government economic policy decisions.

A Full Employment Without Inflation: The Classical Answer

Identifying Our Goals

In Part Two we mentioned that economists develop theories and prepare models to show how an economic system should work in answering the important questions of allocation. We showed how, in our market economy, the price system allocates resources; we also found that some of our resources, such as labor, may not always be fully used. People in our country are increasingly in agreement on the desirability of setting as a goal for our economy a level of production that would provide jobs for everyone who wants to work. When production is below this level, our economy faces a decrease in demand and a general contraction. On the other hand, when production goals are set at a level beyond what our resources can achieve, the result is inflation, not additional production. For example, employers collectively do not obtain additional labor by bidding against each other for the services of workers, as workers are merely shifted from one industry to another.

Most economists believe that a *full-employment economy* (one in which everyone in the working force who wants to work can find a job) without inflation is an appropriate goal for all countries. Maintaining this condition involves smoothing out the peaks and troughs of the business cycle so that stability and economic growth are consistent with the increase in resources for production. The problem may be stated this way: How can our system yield a GNP large enough to sustain a full-employment economy without causing inflation? Figure 12–1 shows our nation's economic record from 1968 to 1985.

GNP and Full Employment

When economists refer to a "full-employment GNP," they mean that the economy is producing enough goods and services (GNP) to employ all those in the labor force who wish to work. If some of the working force remains unemployed when the GNP is at $4 trillion, additional production of goods and services is required to raise the level of employment. Increasing the GNP to $4.1 trillion might provide the jobs necessary to reduce unemployment. It is important to recognize that a small percentage of unemployment is accepted as normal. Because there are always some people in the process of moving into or out of the labor force or perhaps moving from one job to another, unemployment at or below 4 percent of the labor force has traditionally been considered full employment.

There is some disagreement among economists as to what unemployment rate should be considered the full-employment level. Some European countries have unemployment rates lower than that of the United States, but the percentage of adults in their labor forces is lower than ours. Many economists consider an unemployment rate of 5 to 6 percent more appropriate for the United States, because our labor force has been growing at an unprecedented rate. New entrants are primarily women and young workers who tradition-

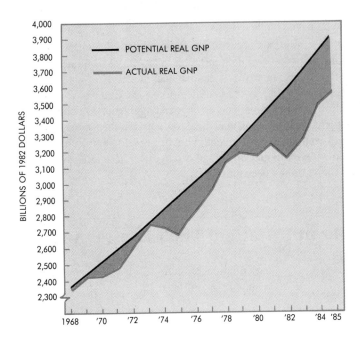

Figure 12–1   GNP: potential and actual performances
Assuming real economic growth of 3 percent per year, the U.S. economy
performed well below its potential for most of the period from 1970 to 1985.
(Source: Department of Commerce.)

ally have higher rates of unemployment. Economists frequently use the natural rate of
unemployment instead of a percentage rate to
describe full employment. The natural rate of
unemployment is the rate below which inflation
will be triggered. We will use a rate of 4 percent,
recognizing that it is controversial.[1]

 The key goal is to achieve full employment
without inflation.

Determining GNP: The Classical View

Although considerable agreement exists on the
desirability of a full-employment economy, differences remain regarding the method by which
this condition could, and should, be achieved.

The classical, or laissez-faire, economists take

the general position that the economy should
operate without interference with the laws of supply and demand, and that government should be
involved in the economy as little as possible. Under
these conditions, they believe, flexibility of prices,
wages, and interest rates will keep our economy
producing at a level high enough to sustain full
employment without inflation. Although there
might be times when external causes would bring
about production above or below a level of full
employment without inflation, such deviations
would be temporary. A closer look at the classical
economist's position, using tools from the previous chapter on national income measurement,
will help clarify how gross national product is
determined.

Figure 12–2 is designed to help you understand how the gross national product is determined. It will be most helpful if you refer to it as
you proceed from step to step in the explanation
that follows. Figure 12–2 is divided into four
parts, (*a*) to (*d*); in the following explanation we

[1] The Humphrey-Hawkins Act (passed in 1978) set a 4 percent
unemployment rate as a preferred economic goal.

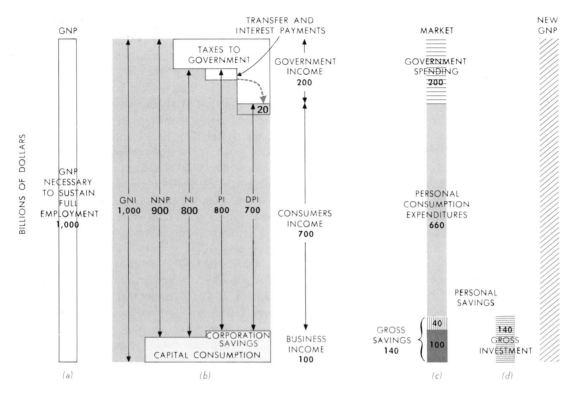

Figure 12–2   Determination of GNP
Gross national product will remain at the full-employment level if government
spending equals government revenue and business invests all the money saved.

will progress from the left side, (a), to the right
side, (d).

Full-Employment Level (a)

The full-employment level is the amount of goods
and services we need to produce to employ at least
96 percent of our labor force (at or below the 4
percent unemployment rate). This amount increases
each year as productive capacity grows. As the
labor force becomes larger and more skilled and
as the use of equipment and other resources
becomes more efficient, it will be necessary to
have an ever-increasing gross national product to
sustain full employment.

Economists can estimate the GNP needed to
achieve a full-employment level (as in Figure 12–2)
without inflation. In Figure 12–2, we set GNP at
$1 trillion because this figure is easy to work with.

Gross National Income (GNI) (b)

Gross national income is equal to gross national
product, but GNI measures the dollars received
for producing whereas GNP measures the retail
value of the product. In (b) we see how the $1
trillion GNI is distributed. As we move from left
to right, from gross national income to disposable
personal income, income is divided among three
groups: consumers, business, and government.

As shown at the top of the chart, $220 billion
goes to government, mainly in the form of taxes.
However, of this amount, $20 billion is returned
to individuals as transfer and interest payments.
This leaves government with $200 billion. At the
bottom, $100 billion is put aside by all businesses
for capital consumption and by corporations for
savings. Consumers retain $700 billion in dispos-
able personal income (including the $20 billion

from transfer and interest payments indicated by the arrow on the graph). The right-hand side of (b) shows what the economy looks like before consumers go to the market to spend. Our $1 trillion gross national income is now divided into $700 billion for consumers, $200 billion for government and $100 billion for business.

Expenditures in the Market (c)

In (c) we see GNP (the product side) and the expenditures made for goods and services by those now in possession of the dollars (GNI). Keep in mind that the two are equal. If all GNI ($1 trillion) is spent, all the goods and services ($1 trillion) will be sold.

To simplify the explanation, let us visualize production as taking place throughout a single year but expenditures as taking place only at the end of the year, when annual production is complete. Imagine for that end-of-year occasion a giant market with the entire $1 trillion GNP for sale and with government, consumers, and business there to buy.

In (c) we observe that government is spending exactly the same amount as it has received (excluding the money it has taken in and returned for transfer and interest payments). It has taken money from businesses and individuals in the form of taxes and has then spent it in the market. This would be one of those rare cases in which government balanced the budget—a situation that our classical economist would doubtless approve of!

Next, consumers go to the market. Consumers have $700 billion to spend—their income after taxes plus the transfer and interest payments from government (DPI). However, we see that their personal consumption expenditures amount to only $660 billion; $40 billion is placed in personal savings. If this $40 billion is not spent by someone, $40 worth of production will remain unsold.

Now it is businesses' turn to buy. They find it necessary to replace used equipment and inventories for the production of goods and services for the next year. When businesses go to the marketplace to buy, they do not make purchases to satisfy their needs as consumers. Instead, they buy to produce or distribute goods and services to other producers, to distributors, or to the consumer. Thus, instead of calling their purchases "consumption expenditures," we call them *investments* (that which is used to further production).

In (b) we can see that business people put aside a total of $100 billion for capital consumption and corporate savings. In (c) we have added to this $100 billion the $40 billion that consumers have saved, for a total of $140 billion in *gross savings*. The $140 billion in gross savings means there must be $140 billion worth of production left unsold in the market. It is crucial to know what will happen to this gross savings.

If business people invest the total amount of gross savings ($140 billion), they will use up the remainder of GNP. Note in (c) of Figure 12–2 that gross savings and gross investment are the same. That part of income that had not previously been spent (gross savings) has now been used to buy up the remaining production through investment. This means that in our example all the goods and services on the market have been purchased, because all government income has already been spent, as well as most of the income received by the various factors of production, which has been used for personal consumption expenditures. As our imaginary year ends, all the gross national income has been used to purchase all the gross national product. What do you think will be the size of next year's GNP?

 Aggregate demand is made up of personal consumption expenditures, business investment, and government spending.

The New GNP (d)

Business, which provides the bulk of the GNP, has in the past produced and sold output worth $1 trillion. It is not likely that businesses will try to reduce production. Because everything produced has been sold, why should business consider producing less? Lower production would mean that the price tags for all production would add up to less than $1 trillion. It would also mean that less than $1 trillion would be paid in income (GNI).

Why wouldn't companies try to produce more than in the past year? They might try, but if they did so they would immediately encounter problems, such as a shortage of workers. (At present, we are assuming that no additional workers or other productive resources are being added to the working force.) You will remember that GNP has been set at a full-employment level. If businesses seek to get more workers by raising wages, these workers will have to come from some other industry. The additional production in one industry will be offset by a decline in the production in another. As businesses compete with one another for scarce workers and resources, wages will rise. However, because total production will be no greater, we shall have a demand greater than supply. Prices will rise. The new GNP will *look* bigger because the prices of goods and services will be higher and income will be greater because workers will be getting more wages. (Other factors of production will also have larger income.) However, although this new GNP will be higher in terms of dollars, it will be the same as the old GNP in terms of goods and services. In other words, if we try to move the GNP higher when production is already at a full-employment level and when capacity to produce is not being increased, the result will be inflation. Inflation can be avoided only if the capacity to produce is increased by adding more workers, more efficient machines, or both.

We can conclude that if the economy is operating at a full-employment level and businesses invest the same amount as is saved, the gross national product will continue at the same high and desirable level.

Investment and Saving

What if investment does not equal savings? Certainly business cannot always be expected to invest the same amount as gross savings. Since saving (the opposite of spending) and investment seem to be the keys to determining the new GNP, let us see what happens when they are not equal. Figure 12–3 shows the two possibilities: in (a) gross investment is less than gross savings, and in (b) it is more than gross savings.

Savings Larger than Investment

Let us suppose that business firms have a gloomy outlook for the next year. Some production remains,

even after both government and consumers have been to the market. Business persons, looking at the remaining production, sense that there has been less buying than they hoped for (more savings), or they think that people, having bought so much in the previous year, might cut back on their spending in the next year. Under either of these circumstances, businesses will be less likely to invest very much money for next year's production. They may buy fewer machines or let inventories in their stores decline. If enough businesses do this, total investment will add up to less than total savings, and there will be goods and services left in the market. Companies will then cut back their production because the supply of production is greater than the demand. They will employ fewer resources. Some workers will have to be let go, some machinery will be idle, and marginal firms will be forced out of business. As a result of these changes, the new GNP will be lower. The decline in production will cause a drop in employment—below the level of full employment. It appears from this illustration that when savings exceed investment, GNP will decline. This condition is illustrated in Figure 12–3(a).

 When savings, S, is larger than ($>$) investment, I, then the aggregate income, Y, will fall ($\downarrow$).

Investment Larger than Savings

What would happen if businesses invested more than the amount saved? Let us suppose that businesses come to the market expecting purchases in the new year to be larger than they were in the past year. As they start buying the remaining production, they soon realize that there is a greater demand for production that there is supply for production. You might reasonably wonder how this is possible when the income side and the production side are supposed to be the same. The answer is that the money businesses use for investment comes from savings, but not necessarily from savings confined to last year. Besides, banks can extend the credit necessary to provide money to businesses, with the result that current investment can exceed current savings.

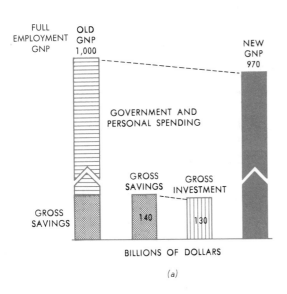

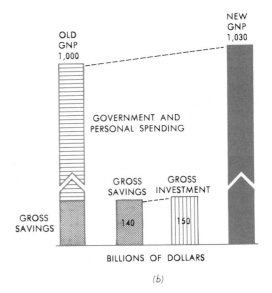

Figure 12–3   Relation of investment to savings in determining the new GNP

In (a), gross savings, $140 billion, is larger than gross investment, $130 billion, causing the new GNP to fall ($S > I \rightarrow$ GNP $\downarrow$). In (b), gross investment, $150 billion, is larger than gross savings, $140 billion, causing the new GNP to rise ($I > S \rightarrow$ GNP $\uparrow$). In both (a) and (b), the difference between savings and investment is $10 billion, but the change from the old to the new GNP is $30 billion. This is because of the multiplier effect, which will be explained on pages 288–289.

In (a), the new GNP declines in real terms; less goods and services are produced. In (b), the rise in the new GNP is only in dollar terms—inflation—because the old GNP of $1,000 billion was already at the full-employment level. Can you determine what the multiplier is?

 When savings is less than investment, the aggregate income will rise so long as all resources are not used, $S < I \rightarrow Y \uparrow$.

If investment does become greater than savings, and if *aggregate demand* (the expenditures of government, consumers, and business) exceeds the aggregate supply of current production, the GNP will increase. However, because we are already operating at a full-employment level, as shown in Figure 12–2, the increase of investment over savings will lead to inflation. Inflation occurs because the demand for production exceeds the capacity to produce, causing prices to rise. Figure 12–3 (b) shows what happens to GNP when investment is larger than savings in a full-employment economy. Real GNP stays at the same level;

the increase in GNP above the full-employment line is only inflation.

 Aggregate demand and aggregate supply should be in balance for full employment without inflation.

Changing Interest Rates

According to classical theory, the two conditions pictured in Figure 12–3 would be only temporary. Two factors would act to correct these situations: interest rates and wage-price flexibility. Let us see what effect these factors might have.

If businesses invested an amount less than savings [Figure 12–3(a)], the GNP would fall below the level of full employment. This economic decline would result in a decline in the interest rates on savings as well as a decline in rates for those who wished to borrow money for investment. With more money available from savings than investors wish to borrow, the laws of supply and demand would bring about a reduction in interest. The new low rates of interest would soon provide the necessary corrections in the economy. Because high interest is an inducement for saving, the lower interest would produce more spending and less saving. Previously, the high interest rates may have discouraged business firms from investing. Now lower rates for loans would encourage businesses to borrow in order to increase their inventories or buy new machines. With lower interest rates stimulating consumer spending and business investment, savings and investment would soon be in balance and the GNP would once again be at the full-employment level.

Wage-Price Flexibility

What if the changing interest rates did not produce all the results desired? The classical theorist would expect flexibility in wages and prices to do the rest of the job. With GNP still below the full-employment level, the surplus labor resulting from this decline would bring about a reduction in wages. The lowering of wages would cut down the cost of production, allowing businesses to reduce prices on their goods. These lower prices would lead to increased sales, encouraging employers to hire additional workers. On the income side, the factors of production would receive less in dollars (lower wages, lower profits) because prices would have declined. However, costs on the product side would also amount to less because of the lower prices there. The dollar amount of the GNP might be lower and the sum of the price tags might be lower, *but the all-important sum of goods and services would be at the level of a full-employment economy.* When prices and income both decline the same amount, the real GNP (that is, the goods and services produced and consumed) will not be reduced. In time wages and prices will adjust downward, leading to a new dollar figure (perhaps $960 billion) for the full-employment GNP.

According to classical theory, interest rates

Before unemployment insurance, expanded government welfare, and assistance under the antipoverty program became available, the unemployed often suffered great hardship. Conditions became acute during periods of recession and depression. (Source: United Press International.)

and wage-price flexibility also exert a corrective influence when investment is greater than savings. What might the stages of this self-regulating process be?

> Classical theory assumes that the market, operating through changing interest rates and flexible wages and prices, will produce equilibrium at full employment without inflation.

Are There Errors in the Classical Theory?

The classical economist described the capitalistic system as a successfully self-regulating system that would always come to rest—that is, reach a state of equilibrium—at the full-employment level without inflation. According to classical theory, this result is manifested because of flexibility both in the interest rate for savings and investment and in wages and prices.

In opposition to classical beliefs, however, many economists contend that events have shown that the theoretical readjustment does not always take place. Small rises and declines in the business cycle could be explained as temporary maladjustments that correct themselves; some of the larger peaks and troughs could be explained by external causes such as wars. But one important economic occurrence that cannot be explained so easily is the Great Depression of the 1930s. During those years, many of the economists who followed the classical tradition, as well as some of the political leaders and business persons who accepted the classical theories, believed that "prosperity was just around the corner." They said that if we would just wait a little longer, the natural self-regulating factors that make the market economy an excellent system would correct the terrible imbalances that were producing a shrinking GNP and contributing to even greater unemployment.

Although these people may have been willing to wait for the corrective effort to occur, a majority of the American people apparently were not. With the growing demand for other solutions, the time was ripe for the introduction of a new economic model, or at least a modification of the old one. There was a pressing need to explain why self-regulation was not doing the job required and to recommend action for relief.

B The Model with Government Excluded

John Maynard Keynes and the "New Economics"

Politically, the change in our economic policy is associated with the New Deal and Franklin D. Roosevelt; in economics it is associated with an English economist, John Maynard Keynes (pronounced *kānz*). As the originator of a new model, Keynes was responsible for bringing about a revolution in economic thinking. In the course of this revolution, many economists turned from classical theory to the "new economics," based largely on Keynes's theories. According to the new ideas, a mature capitalist economy is not always able to maintain itself at a full-employment level without inflation. The reason the economy does not maintain this desirable level is that the two key items in self-regulation—changing interest rates and wage-price flexibility—are not sufficiently effective.

Does Interest Regulate Savings and Investment?

The classical economist reasons that consumers will deprive themselves of some goods and services if they have sufficient incentive to do so. To understand the flaws in this reasoning, ask yourself these questions: Would you take your savings out of a bank and spend it if interest rates declined? Is high interest the incentive that makes you save? Although a surplus of savings is going to lower the interest rate and allow businesses to borrow at lower rates of interest, would you, if you were in business, increase your investment when people are spending less, even if you could borrow at lower rates?

Now let us consider some further questions. Suppose that the economy was already at a full-employment GNP and that businesses were investing in excess of savings (an inflationary situation). With a shortage of savings, interest rates would rise, thus encouraging people to save and discouraging business from investing. Would you, as a business person, refuse to invest because of higher interest rates at a time when people are buying more and prices seem to be rising, particularly when you know that rising prices will make it easier for you, a debtor, to pay back your loan?

If your answer to each of these questions is yes, you have a tendency to agree with the classical theorists. Recent history, however, shows that business often behaves differently.

Challenges to the Classical Theory

If interest rates are not the key in determining savings and investment, what is? Modern economists have discovered that saving and investing are seldom, if ever, carried on by the same people. In reality, much of existing savings come from families that may be motivated to put money aside for expected spending or for financial security. Studies reveal that savings are closely tied to the level of national income. The higher the national income, the greater the amount of savings.[2] As for investment, the most significant factor in its determination is the amount of profit that businesses *expect* to make. Although interest rates can

---

[2] A recent Nobel Laureate in economics, Franco Modigliani, believes that economic growth rather than income determines savings. Japan and Italy, which have higher growth rates than the United States, also have higher savings rates.

be and sometimes are factors in determining profits, business people will more likely react to rising or falling sales expectations. Few businesses increase their inventories or plant equipment when the economy is contracting, even though interest rates may be low.

The theory of self-correction through wage-price flexibility is also subject to strong criticism. Many differences exist between the classical model and the actual functioning of the economy. A downswing in the economy will undoubtedly exert pressure for some decline in wages and prices, but that decline is likely to be very limited. The cost of labor is actually prevented from declining significantly. This inflexibility of wages is due primarily to two factors: minimum wage laws and the power of organized labor in maintaining wage levels.

The movement of prices is equally "sticky." Many of the products we buy come from industries in which prices are administered (determined

---

 # John Maynard Keynes and the "New Economics"

John Maynard Keynes (1883–1946), more than any other economist in the twentieth century, is responsible for modifying classical thinking in the industrial nations of the West. During the 1930s, the United States and the nations of Western Europe were mired in the Great Depression. As the inoperativeness of the self-correcting mechanism of classical economics became apparent, the need for new solutions to the problem became more acute.

The first significant contribution to a solution of the problem came from the Swedish economists, particularly Professor Gunnar Myrdal, who used the aggre-

gate, or macroeconomic, approach. Their analysis of the relation between savings, investment, and income was very similar to Keynes's conclusion of his monumental work *The General Theory of Employment, Interest, and Money,* published in 1936. Keynes emphasized the correlation between national income and employment. He showed that income was determined by consumption, investment, and government spending. Consumption changes with income (as savings do), but income is influenced mainly by the amount of investment. Because investment is the least stable of the three items

determining income and because it may not be adequate to maintain a national income sufficient to achieve full employment, the government should intervene to promote full employment. Government can intervene through the use of appropriate monetary and fiscal policies.

Economists today recognize that Keynes's approach had certain weaknesses. His model was oriented to the short run and was basically static; insufficient attention was paid to economic growth. Furthermore, Keynes did not recognize that in the long run people's spending habits change, adapting to the higher levels of income. Nevertheless, Keynes's contributions to economic theory are regarded by most economists as the most significant of this century.

"Confound it, Merriwell! Do you mean that all this time you've been talking micro while we've been talking macro?" Drawing by Lorenz; © 1982 The New Yorker Magazine, Inc.

by the conscious price policy of the seller). Other prices may also be influenced by price fixing or by regulation by government or business. As a result, recessions do not usually bring any significant decline in prices. Certainly there is not enough decline in price to result in any significant increase in purchasing power. Therefore, instead of the predicted reduction in wages and prices because of a downswing, we find fewer workers employed and prices declining so slightly that increased buying is unlikely. As a result, little self-correction takes place.

Keynes questioned whether the market alone could make the necessary corrections.

Consumption, Savings, and Income

If traditional capitalism, contrary to theory, does not have a feature of self-correction, what can be done to create a full-employment economy without inflation? As you have already learned, the GNP level depends on the relation between savings and investment. Having explored the criticisms of the classical interpretation of these key factors, let us see what Keynes and other modern

economists learned about these factors that might be useful in developing a new model for our economy—one that would remain within the broad framework of capitalism.

When we speak of savings we are also speaking about consumption, given the complementary nature of savings and consumption. What we do not save we spend, and what we do not spend we save. Therefore, our discussion of savings is also a discussion of consumption. For the present, a consideration of government is omitted because we are assuming that government income and expenditure will be exactly equal. In Figure 12–2, we used the figure of $1 trillion to represent a full-employment GNP without inflation. Because government income and expenditure amounted to $200 billion, the full-employment noninflationary GNP for the private sector (including both consumers and business) was $800 billion.

When we examine national income statistics, we find a very strong and direct relation between consumption and GNP. As any of the five main national income measurements (GNI, NNP, NI, PI, DPI) go up, the amount of consumption also increases. Figure 12–4 shows consumption and disposable personal income for a 14-year period. Note that consumption increased by almost the same percentage as disposable personal income

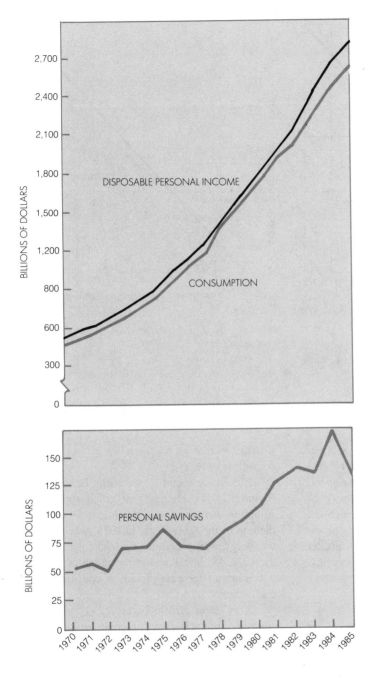

Figure 12–4 Disposable personal income influences the level of consumption

Usually, as disposable personal income increases, so does consumption. (Source: U.S. Department of Commerce estimates.)

did. During this period, consumption was approximately 92 to 95 percent of DPI.

In 1982, DPI was close to $2.17 trillion and consumption was $2.03 trillion. Where was the $141 billion that was not spent? It must have been in personal savings—that part of the DPI that was not consumed. If we measured savings for the last ten years, we would find that, like consumption, it too has been remarkably constant.

In 1933 in the depths of the Great Depression, consumption was greater than DPI. How can we spend more than we earn? As we have seen,

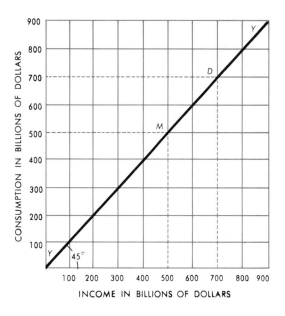

Figure 12–5   A new tool: the 45° line

Using the 45°-line approach, a new tool, we can better understand the theory of income analysis. The dashed lines plotted at points *M* and *D* on the line *Y* show consumption equal to income.

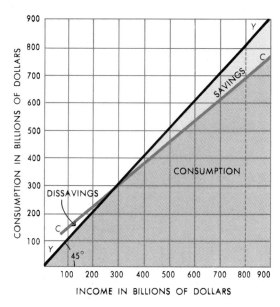

Figure 12–6   Schedule of consumption and savings

The 45° line *Y* measures levels of income. The consumption line *C* measures what spending is likely to be at different levels of income. The difference between income *Y* and consumption *C* is savings *S*.

we do so by borrowing, by using savings accumulated in earlier years, or by buying on credit.

People at very low levels of income spend more than they earn. As income increases, consumption and income come into balance. Soon income surpasses consumption and savings grows. The greater the aggregate income (DPI), the greater the consumption, but also the greater the savings.

A New Economic Tool: The 45° Line

A useful economic tool for relating income, savings, and consumption is the 45° line, shown in Figure 12–5. On the graph, *the horizontal axis measures income and the vertical axis measures consumption.* Line *Y* is a diagonal, 45°. Any point along the 45° line is equally distant from the horizontal (income) axis and the vertical (consumption) axis. Point *M* on the 45° line in Figure 12–5 shows income and consumption to be the same.

It indicates that we are spending *all* our income, regardless of its size.

But do we spend all we earn? Look back at Figure 12–4. Although that graph shows consumption increasing with income, it never shows them to be the same. Only in 1933, when income was very low, was consumption more than income. Thus the 45° line *Y* shows the range of incomes but is not an accurate picture of consumption at each level of income.

Now let us turn to Figure 12–6. Here consumption for each level of income is plotted. The consumption line *C* is lower than the income line (45° line, or *Y*) above $300 billion of income. The lightly shaded area between consumption and income is savings. As you continue to learn about this model, the usefulness of national income determination will become evident.

 Consumption + savings = income. Savings is indicated by the space between the *Y* and the *C* lines.

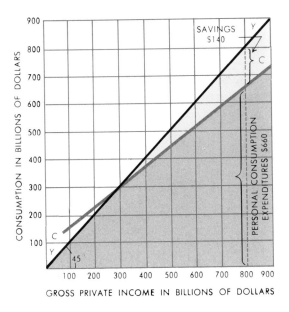

Figure 12–7   Schedule of propensity to consume

The propensity to save increases as income increases.

Propensity to Consume and Save

Although prices, consumer credit, availability of goods, and fluctuations in purchases of durable goods are all considered factors in determining consumption, most modern economists agree that income is the single most important factor. In Figure 12–7 the 45° line is used to analyze income. In Figure 12–2, $1 trillion represented the GNP needed for full employment without inflation, with $800 billion of this amount in the private sector. With that same amount for the private sector, Figure 12–7 shows that $660 billion of gross private income will be spent by individuals in the market and $140 billion will be gross savings. Why will gross private income be spent in this way? Economists have discovered that people tend to spend and to save certain proportions at particular levels of income. The tendency to spend a certain amount at a certain level of income is called the *propensity to consume*. The tendency to save a certain amount at a certain level of income is called the *propensity to save*. With an aggregate private income of $800 billion, the propensity to consume will be $660

billion and the propensity to save will be $140 billion.

In order to sustain an $800 billion gross private income with gross savings at $140 billion, how much gross investment is needed? If the new GNP (or, in this case, the new gross private income) is to equal the old gross private income, gross investment must equal gross savings. A gross investment of less than $140 billion will mean less production and therefore less employment and a lowering of our gross private income. A gross investment greater than $140 billion can only cause inflation, because we are already producing at full employment.

Determination of Income

Figure 12–8 shows what will happen if gross private investment is only $100 billion (*b*), $40 billion less than gross savings. Then, at the market (*c*), with $660 billion of personal consumption expenditures and $100 billion of investment, $40 billion of goods and services will be left over (or not produced). The new gross private income will be insufficient to sustain full employment. However, the gross private income does not drop to $760 billion; our diagram shows it dropping to $700 billion (*e*). This is due to the *multiplier effect,* which in this case is 2½. Briefly, the multiplier effect means that any change in spending or investment, either public or private, brings about a greater change in income. This is shown in (*d*). In our example, $40 billion of additional investment by business will increase income by $100 billion. Thus, the multiplier is 2½. What would happen in the preceding example if all things remained the same except that there was a gross investment of $120 billion? (More will be said about the multiplier later in this chapter.)

Using the 45° Line to Determine Income

Let us consider once again the example explained in Figure 12–8, but this time let us see how it looks when we use the diagram with the 45° line.

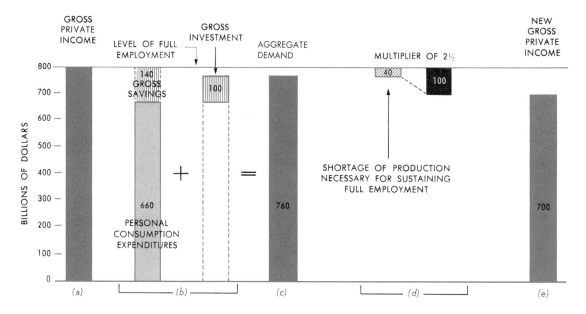

Figure 12–8   Determining gross private income

When gross private investment is less than private savings ($40 billion less), the new gross private income will decline by an amount ($100 billion) greater than this difference because of the multiplier effect. Since the full-employment level without inflation is $800 billion in Figure 12–8, the new gross private income shows the economy in a recession.

This combination is shown in Figure 12–9. You will recall that the 45° line indicates income and that line *C* is the actual consumption line, or the propensity to consume (the tendency to spend certain amounts at various levels of income). Move to the right along the horizontal axis, which measures gross private income, until $800 billion is reached. The solid vertical line shows what the propensity to consume will be and what the propensity to save will be at the gross private income level of $800 billion. You can see that it is the same as that found in Figure 12–7.

When Savings Are Larger than Investment

Let us see what happens to the gross private income when only $100 billion is invested and $140 billion is saved. The *C* line shows the consumer in the market. The business firm also goes to the market, so its "purchases" (investment *I*) must be

added to the personal consumption expenditures *C*. This is done by adding $100 billion, the investment, to personal consumption expenditures, as shown by the line *C* + *I* (consumption plus investment). Line *C* rises because consumption increases with income. Line *C* + *I* is parallel to line *C* because investment has been fixed at $100 billion, regardless of income. We can now find the new gross private income. Locate the point where the *C* + *I* line crosses the 45° line (our income line). This intersection, indicated by the arrow labeled "New GPI," is at $700 billion, the new gross private income.

New Income Means New Consumption

In Figure 12–9, you can see that the new GPI is lower than the old GPI. Total personal consumption expenditures have dropped to $600 billion. This drop occurs because consumption is deter-

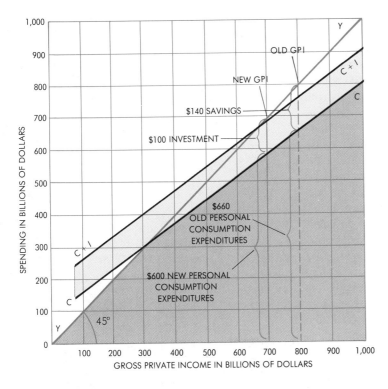

Figure 12–9   Determining gross private income using the 45° line

In this graph we see the same example as in Figure 12–8, but this time we use the 45° line as a tool for analysis.

mined mainly by income. What happens to savings when income has been reduced to $700 billion? Because personal consumption expenditures are now $600 billion and because what is not spent is saved, we know that savings will drop to $100 billion. The level of spending and the level of savings have both decreased as income has fallen.

When Investment Is Larger than Savings

Using the 45°-line diagram in Figure 12–9, we can determine what gross private income will be when investment is increased to $150 billion. We shall position the $C + I$ line $150 billion above the C line, instead of $100 billion above it. The new GPI will be at the point at which the $C + I$ line crosses the 45° line, Y. What will personal consumption expenditures be? How much will savings be? Will this new gross private income be good for the economy?

By now you should recognize that if we know

the nation's propensity to consume (that is, the consumption, or C, line) and we know what gross investment is, we can determine what gross private income will be. Once again we are able to see the importance of the relation of consumption, as well as investment, to savings.

Let us leave our diagrams and statistics for a moment and consider in a very general way what these illustrations mean. A contracting economy (reducing GPI from $800 billion to $700 billion) results when retail stores do not fill up with merchandise and manufacturers do not increase production or invest enough to use up the savings available. Because fewer workers are needed, income declines. When this happens, consumption also drops, and so does the ability to save. The diagrams and statistics shown here tell an unemotional story. For a more personal view of how a contracting economy may hurt people, talk with someone whose income has been lowered or who has been removed from a job because of a decline in business activity.

Fluctuating Investment and Income

We have seen what economic reactions take place when gross private income drops to $700 billion, $100 billion below the level needed for full employment. Now let us consider what can be done to expand income back to the $800-billion level. We cannot afford to wait for the possible readjustment that may occur (due to a drop in the wage-price level or to changing interest rates on savings and investment) to bring about the necessary expansion. What other means are available for achieving a readjustment? Might consumers be persuaded to spend more at the market? During the 1957–58 recession, President Eisenhower urged the U.S. public to buy more in an effort to stimulate business. Unfortunately his efforts did not work.

Although it is true that both personal consumption expenditures and gross investment determine aggregate income, the variation in investment is far greater than the variation in consumption, as shown in Table 12–1. The decline in investment is accompanied by a slowdown in the increase of the GNP.

Although not all economists agree, most of them would list the amount of business investment as a greater factor in determining aggregate income than the more stable consumption by householders. Therefore, to raise aggregate income in order to attain full employment, it is important to get business firms to increase their investments. Referring to the diagram with the 45°

Table 12–1   Fluctuation of investments and personal consumption expenditures (in billions of 1972 dollars)

	Personal Consumption Expenditures	Gross Private Domestic Investment	Gross National Product
1973	768	200	1,254
1974	763	184	1,246
1975	779	162	1,232
1976	823	177	1,298
1977	864	201	1,370
1978	903	237	1,439
1979	927	236	1,479
1980	931	208	1,474
1981	948	226	1,502
1982	957	197	1,476
1983	1,009	221	1,535
1984	1,067	290	1,639

Source: U.S. Department of Commerce, Office of Business Economics.

Gross private domestic investment fluctuated far more than personal consumption expenditures. Compare the rise and fall of investment with GNP. Lines are drawn under recession years.

line, we may say that the problem is to raise the $C + I$ line so that it will intersect the 45° line at $800 billion or whatever the full-employment level may be. Before we try to determine how to increase investment, let us return to the market to consider the actions of another important buyer—government.

The Model with Government Included

Until now, we have been able to omit government from consideration because we were proceeding on the assumption that the government was balancing its budget, keeping expenditures equal to revenues. Actually, we know that this has rarely happened in recent times, particularly at the federal level. In the years since 1960, budget surpluses have occurred only twice. What have been

the effects of the unbalanced budget on the economy?

The Unbalanced Budget

In Chapter 9, you learned that the federal government is less restricted than families, businesses, or local and state governments with respect to keeping its budget balanced. The U.S. government not only may borrow money, but also may actually print money to pay its bills, as it did during the Civil War. However, such a great power, if not used wisely, might well destroy the nation's economy. The German government after World War I tried such a tactic as a way out of its difficulties, and devastating inflation was the result. The Republic of China during and immediately after World War II followed the German example, with similar results. Our own government has, in general, avoided such extreme measures to protect us from the hardships of uncontrolled inflation resulting from the indiscriminate printing of money. However, the unbalanced budget has numerous effects as it increases the national debt.

Our working model in Figure 12–2 shows that when government goes to the marketplace, it purchases $200 billion worth of goods and services, one-fifth of all goods and services bought and usually more than the total bought by businesses through gross private investment. This sizable purchase requires the employment of a large portion of our work force. To pay for these goods and services, the government collects revenue, chiefly in the form of taxes, from almost everyone. Paying taxes to the government limits people's spending for tangibles such as automobiles and for intangibles such as vacations. However, it does supply U.S. citizens with collective benefits such as schools, roads, and defense against foreign invasion. We have in our economy a long tradition of free enterprise, preferring to have individual households make independent decisions as to what and how much they want of the goods and services available. However, as our society has become more complex and as people have become more interdependent, the demands and expenses of government have increased.

Growing Federal Expenditures

We know that government participation in the economy has increased (see Chapter 9). Our immediate concern is the significance to the economy of increased government expenditure and control when the government's budget is not balanced. How does this governmental activity affect the national economy under differing employment conditions?

Determining Income with Government Included

Income Below Full Employment

Let us assume, as we did in Figure 12–2, that $1 trillion of GNP is required to achieve a full-employment economy. Let us further assume that private consumption and investment add up to $800 billion, with $200 billion still awaiting collection by the government. What would happen if government collected this $200 billion but spent only $160 billion? Figure 12–10 on p. 284 provides an answer. Instead of falling only $40 billion below the $1 trillion full-employment GNP level, the economy has declined $100 billion, due again to the multiplier effect. By spending less than was collected, the government has left goods and services unpurchased in the marketplace. As unsold stocks of merchandise accumulate, business firms are likely to plan to reduce production below the previous year's level, because this outstanding surplus may lead to reduced prices and profits. Curtailing production will reduce the GNP below the level of full employment. Aggregate demand is $40 billion below the level of full employment without inflation. It would require an increase of $40 billion in consumption, investment, government spending, or a combination of all three to bring aggregate demand up to a level of full employment. This insufficiency in the amount of aggregate demand is called the *deflationary gap*.

Income Above Full Employment

In contrast to the preceding example, let us assume that this time government takes in $200 billion and spends $240 billion (the private sector of the economy remains the same). Adding together private consumption, investment, and government spending brings the aggregate demand for goods and services to $1.04 trillion, which is above the full-employment product of $1 trillion. With the demand for goods and services above the supply and the economy already operating at the full-

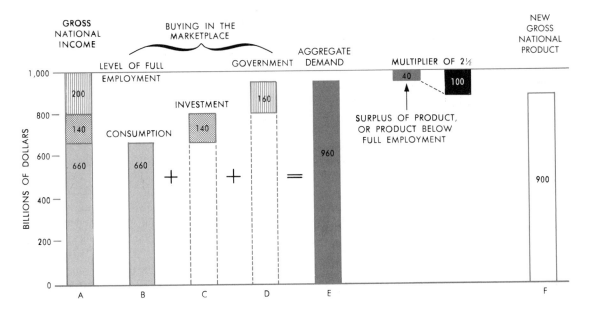

Figure 12–10   Income determination when aggregate demand is too low

If aggregate demand in the private sector of the economy is sufficient to sustain full employment but the government collects more in revenue than it spends, the GNP will decline by a multiple of the difference between government income and government expenditures. The new aggregate income will not be sufficient to maintain the economy at a level of full employment, causing a deflationary gap.

employment level, inflation will result. Figure 12–11 demonstrates this situation, with the multiplier compounding the effect by 2½. The new GNP is $1.1 trillion, $100 billion above full employment and therefore inflationary. If we reduce aggregate demand by a total of $40 billion by cutting consumption, investment, government expenditures, or a combination of all three, we should achieve our desired goal of full employment without inflation. We call this excessive $40 billion of aggregate demand the *inflationary gap*.

Income Determination with the 45° Line

Let us see how the information on income determination, shown in Figures 12–10 and 12–11, looks when combined with the diagram of the 45° line.

 National income is determined by $C + I + G = Y$.

Income Below Full Employment

Figure 12–12 shows aggregate income falling $100 billion below the full-employment income of $1 trillion, just as it did in Figure 12–10. Our aggregate income Y is determined by taking consumption C plus investment I plus government spending G; aggregate income is found at the point at which the $C + I + G$ line crosses the 45° line (Y line), which is at $900 billion. Income will be below the full-employment level because $40 billion worth of goods and services have *not* been purchased by consumers, businesses, government, or any combination of them. Because of this surplus of goods, businesses in general will reduce production, realizing an income of $100

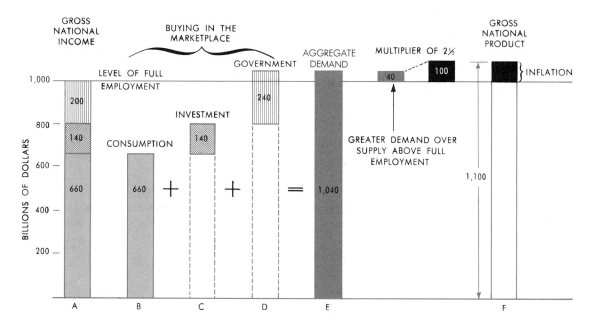

Figure 12–11 Income determination when aggregate demand is too high

If aggregate demand on the private sector of the economy is sufficient to sustain full employment but government spends more than it collects, the GNP will rise by a multiple of the difference between government income and government expenditures. The aggregate demand (total spending) is greater than the capacity of the economy to produce, resulting in an inflationary gap.

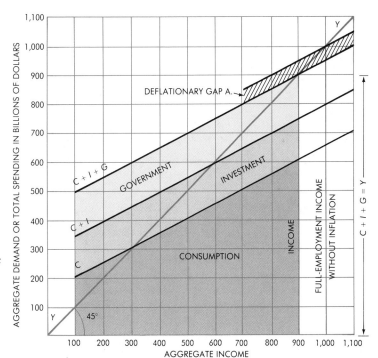

Figure 12–12 Income determination using the 45° line—underemployment

Aggregate income is determined at the point at which aggregate demand—consumption plus investment plus government spending—intersects the 45° line. $C + I + G$ must be increased by $40 billion ($A$) to reach a full-employment income. A is the deflationary gap.

billion less (the multiplier effect) than $1 trillion, the full-employment level. An increase in $C + I + G$ of $40 billion, represented by the striped area (A) above the $C + I + G$ line, would provide the demand for goods and services needed for full employment.

Income Above Full Employment

Figure 12–13 shows what happens when aggregate demand, $C + I + G$, is greater than full-employment income (note Figure 12–11 also). The $C + I + G$ line crosses the Y line at $1.1 trillion, $100 billion above full-employment income. Under these circumstances, the demand for goods and services is greater than can be supplied with the existing labor force. Business firms, in their desire to fill the greater demand, bid against one another to obtain workers and other resources, causing prices to rise. Production will be at the $1 trillion level, or full employment; however, because of rising prices, the goods and services will carry a total market price of $1.1 trillion. This new full-employment level is not desirable because it is inflationary. If $C + I + G$ (aggregate demand) can be reduced by $40 billion, supply and demand will reach an equilibrium level at the previous full-employment income, $1 trillion. In Figure 12–13, line $C + I + G$ must be lowered by the amount shown in the striped area (B), $40 billion, so that it crosses the Y line at $1 trillion, the noninflationary full-employment level.

 A deflationary gap calls for stimulating C, I, or G. An inflationary gap calls for reducing aggregate demand.

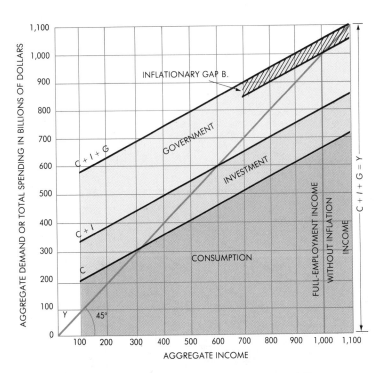

Figure 12–13 Income determination using the 45° line—inflation

Aggregate demand is greater than what a full-employment income can supply, causing an inflation. $C + I + G$ must be reduced by $40 billion (B) to reduce aggregate income to the full-employment level. B is the inflationary gap.

Equilibrium

By now it is clear that the relation between savings and investment is critical in maintaining GNP at full employment. Let us look further at the interaction between savings and investments.

Think of savings as all production not bought by consumers, C. Savings is represented on our 45°-line diagram by the space between the C line and the 45° line. Think of investment as made up of private I (business) and public G (government). Investment is represented by the space between the C line and the $C + I + G$ line. These areas are marked in Figure 12–14. With these revised definitions, it is clear that if savings are greater than investment (government and business are not buying all the production remaining after consumer purchasing), the aggregate income will fall.

An amount of savings larger than public and private investment produces a declining aggregate income ($S > I$ = declining Y). By contrast, if investment is larger than savings (government and business demand more production than is left by consumers at the market), income will rise ($I > S$ = rising Y). Under these conditions, aggregate income will be at the point at which savings and investment are exactly the same. That is the *equilibrium point,* shown at E in Figure 12–14. It is also the point at which our $C + I + G$ line crosses the 45° line, because at that point $S = I$.

You will recall that a big disagreement exists between classical and Keynesian economists over where equilibrium will be achieved. The classical economist maintains that if the economy is free from any restraints in the operation of the market (supply and demand operate under pure compe-

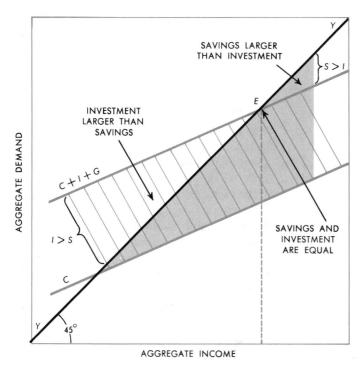

Figure 12–14   Determining aggregate income using savings and investment

Aggregate income is at that point at which investment (private and public) and savings (gross savings and taxes) equal each other. This is shown at point E, equilibrium (where the $C + I + G$ line crosses the Y line). When $I > S$, income will rise. When $S > I$, income will decline.

tition), equilibrium will be at the full-employment level without inflation. The new model, used by Keynesian economists, indicates that equilibrium can be and frequently is at a point below full employment, because investment is smaller than savings.

Achieving Full Employment Without Inflation

Most economists and policymakers believe that one of our chief economic goals should be achieving a full-employment economy without inflation. Using our new tools for analysis, we can phrase this goal as having the $C + I + G$ line intersect the Y line at an income level high enough to support full employment but not so high as to cause inflation. According to Keynesian theory, it should be possible for government to assist in achieving the goal of full employment without inflation by means of public policy. (Chapter 14 will present a further consideration of the policies mentioned here.)

When $C + I + G$ is too low (below $1 trillion in our examples), a policy providing for corrective measures to increase aggregate demand should be put into effect if full employment is to be maintained. Since 1961 many federal budgets have had planned deficits, raising aggregate demand. Economists differ on priorities: Should the increases be made by reducing personal taxes, thereby stimulating C; by cutting corporate taxes, thereby encouraging greater I; or by having additional government expenditures, whether for schools, the defense program, or a new river project? There is much disagreement about which policy is best. Any of these tactics—and many others also—can be used to raise aggregate demand, $C + I + G$, to full-employment income.

When aggregate demand is above the full-employment income level, a policy for lowering it is needed if inflation is to be prevented. Such a measure would be the opposite of one of those previously suggested. Raising taxes, cutting government expenditures, or discouraging business investment will help to lower the $C + I + G$ line,

making it possible to achieve the goal of full employment without inflation.

The Multiplier Effect

At several places we have noted the importance of the multiplier effect in magnifying changes. To understand the causes and effects of the multiplier, we must consider it in more detail. Return first to Figure 12–12. The $C + I + G$ line crosses the 45° line at $900 billion. If we add $40 billion of government purchases, the $C + I + G$ line moves upward so that it crosses the 45° line at $1 trillion, a gain of $100 billion. Additional purchases of $40 billion bring about an increase of $100 billion of aggregate income, showing graphically the multiplier effect. The same effect can be brought about by increases in consumer spending or business investment, because an increase in the amount spent by any one purchaser or combination of purchasers in the marketplace raises the $C + I + G$ line and raises aggregate income by some multiple of the additional purchase.

Why the Multiplier Effect?

You are probably wondering why there is a multiplier effect. To find an answer, let us suppose that government spends $40 billion more than it collected or that business increases its investment by that amount. Assuming that prices remain constant and that we are operating our economy at a level below full employment, the injection of this new investment or government spending does not create a demand for goods and services in excess of our ability to produce them. The bulk of the $40 billion will probably be received by suppliers of goods. They will spend part of it and save part of it. The part they spend will be received by workers and other suppliers—in general, by people who will in turn spend part of it and save part. Employees receiving additional wages and business firms receiving additional profits will take part of their money to the market to spend and will save the rest. The effect of the additional $40 billion of spending on the nation's economy as a whole will far exceed that basic figure because it will continue to be spent, though in an ever-decreasing amount. Because part of the $40 billion is spent many times, the total effect is far greater than the original amount.

 The multiplier effect will increase the impact of expenditures on income.

Determining the Multiplier

We need to know in advance what the amount of the multiplier will be, if we are to predict change accurately. Earlier we explained people's spending habits as a propensity to consume—the tendency to spend a certain amount of their income at a particular level of income. When income and spending increase, so does the ability to save and the amount saved. If we add $40 billion of income to the economy through investment or additional government spending, what portion of this amount will be spent? If 60 percent, or $24 billion, is spent, we can say that three-fifths of the *additional* income is the new propensity to consume. You recall that we refer to the last unit in production as "marginal." Because we are not speaking about what fraction of total income is spent but only what fraction of the additional unit, we refer to this three-fifths as *marginal propensity to consume*. Sixteen billion dollars of the $40 billion of additional income is saved. That means that two-fifths of this additional income is saved. The *mar-*

ginal propensity to save is two-fifths. Marginal propensity to consume (three-fifths, or $24 billion)—plus marginal propensity to save (two-fifths, or $16 billion) must equal one (the total amount of new income added). If you know the marginal propensity to save, you can easily figure out the marginal propensity to consume ($1 - \frac{2}{5} = \frac{3}{5}$). To find the multiplier, merely invert the marginal propensity to save ($\frac{2}{5}$ becomes $\frac{5}{2}$, or $2\frac{1}{2}$). If you know the marginal propensity to consume, you can calculate the marginal propensity to save. Subtract the marginal propensity to consume from 1 and then invert the fraction to get the multiplier ($1 - \frac{3}{5} = \frac{2}{5}$; invert to $\frac{5}{2}$, or $2\frac{1}{2}$). What would the multiplier be if the marginal propensity to consume were three-fourths? What will be the increase in aggregate income if business persons invest $20 billion more and the marginal propensity to consume is five-sixths?

 The marginal propensity to consume, MPC, plus the marginal propensity to save, MPS, equals 1. The multiplier is the reciprocal of MPS.

Before continuing, review the step-by-step development of the Keynesian model at the end of this chapter. If you do not understand any step, turn back to the appropriate place in this chapter for a more complete explanation. Much of the remaining material in the book is based on an understanding of this model.

When private investment is not sufficient to stimulate a full-employment level of spending, government may provide the needed help. Can government supply too much stimulation to the economy?

Some Needed Corrections

In explaining how to determine aggregate income, we have taken some liberties. Oversimplifying can lead to a distortion if we fail to make the proper corrections. You will recall our assumption that although production takes place throughout the year, payment for that production and the spending of income received took place only once during the year—at the end. Our diagrams may be accurate for the past but not for determining income for the future. Although government and business draw up budgets for the year and many consumers also plan their expenditures, we know that both

---

The Paradox of Thrift

The fallacy of composition implies that what is good for the individual is good for all. The paradox of thrift suggests that what may make good economic sense for the individual household may not make good economic sense for the economy as a whole. In times of recession the average household is likely to try to increase its savings out of fear of a decline in wages or profits or even a total loss of wages or a family business. The family reasons that the additional savings will pro-

tect the household if income is reduced or cut off. But what happens if most households follow this policy of thrift?

Since savings is the opposite of consumption, an *increase in savings* results in a *decrease in consumption*. Such a decrease reduces aggregate demand and decreases aggregate income. You can follow these steps in the figure. The planned increase in savings is shown by the movement of the savings line from SS to $S'S'$. This movement brings a corresponding drop in aggregate demand from $C + I + G$ to $C' + I' + G'$. The old equilibrium is where $C + I + G$ crosses the diagonal line Y at an aggregate income of OQ. With increased savings and decreased aggregate demand, the new equilibrium is where $C' + I' + G'$ crosses Y at OQ'. Note that the decline in aggregate demand brings about a far greater decline in aggregate income as a result of the multiplier effect.

What happens to savings? Remember that the level of national income is the major factor in determining savings. Because of the lower level of income, the amount of actual savings may turn out to be no greater than it would have been if consumers had not tried to be thrifty.

The Paradox of Thrift   If enough individual households try to increase savings when resources are not all utilized, the effect will be a reduction in national income and actual savings will be no higher than before.

income and expenditures are subject to an almost infinite number of changes. If consumers become excited about a product, as they did about automobiles in 1984, they will increase their purchases. This in turn may increase investment in the middle of the year. More profits and wages increase both income and the revenue that government receives from income taxes.

Adding Foreign Investment

We also took the liberty of leaving out of our income determination equation the impact of international trade. More accurate is the equation $C + I + G + (X - U) = Y$, where X = exports and U = imports. Until the 1980s net exports rarely changed the aggregate demand by more than 1 percent. This condition changed when our country's balance of trade became negative in ever-increasing amounts. Our imports kept rising faster than our exports for reasons that will be explained in some detail in Chapter 18. In the mid-1980s

the net investment in foreign trade has had a negative effect on our GNP.

Economists analyze accumulated data; with this information they project plans and make forecasts. They sometimes make mistakes, because economics is not an exact science. For example, government economists overestimated income for 1985 by a considerable margin. Too many variables either cannot be controlled or are not measured with sufficient accuracy. People tend to be fickle on the production line and in the marketplace. This does not mean that analysis, projection, and planning are a waste; we are far better off making educated guesses and trying to control conditions than gambling on the unknown. With the development of more and more measurements of the economy like those described in Chapter 11, and with data available at more frequent intervals, it is expected that economic analysis will become more exact.

Chapter Highlights

1. The classical model expects that a full-employment economy without inflation can be achieved merely by allowing the natural laws of supply and demand to operate and by keeping government out of the economy as much as possible.

2. According to the classical model, temporary dislocations in the economy are corrected by changes in interest rates and fluctuations in wages and prices.

3. Large business fluctuations—particularly the long-lasting big depression of the 1930s—led to a new economic model.

4. John Maynard Keynes, an English economist, developed this new economic model well within the capitalistic system. He thought that insufficient attention was being paid to maintaining a full-employment economy. Because interest and wage-and-price flexibility did not stimulate demand sufficiently, the government became responsible for setting policies to accomplish this purpose.

5. The aggregate income of the nation is determined by adding personal consumption expenditures, business investment, and government spending ($C + I + G$ = income).

6. According to the Keynesian model, when consumption plus investment plus government expenditures does not add up to enough production of goods and services to employ everyone who wishes to work, policies must be set up to increase spending. This increase in

spending can be brought about by raising government expenditures over government income (deficit spending), by encouraging businesses to invest more, or by using other economic policies. Personal consumption expenditures change primarily with income and are not altered so easily.

7. When consumption plus investment plus government spending adds up to an amount that exceeds what we are capable of producing, inflation will occur. Policies that discourage personal consumption expenditures, business investment, or government spending are needed to curb inflation.

8. People tend to spend particular amounts of their income at different income levels. The tendency to spend certain amounts of income at certain income levels is known as the *propensity to consume*. The tendency to save certain amounts of income at certain income levels is known as the *propensity to save*.

9. The amount of *additional* income that people tend to spend is known as the *marginal propensity to consume*. The amount of *additional* income that people tend to save is known as the *marginal propensity to save*. The marginal propensity to consume and the marginal propensity to save add up to one.

10. The multiplier effect makes it unnecessary to increase or decrease aggregate spending ($C + I + G$) by the full amount in order to bring that spending up or down to the level of full employment without inflation. Because of the multiplier effect, the increase or decrease in aggregate income is more than the amount of spending added or subtracted. The reciprocal of the marginal propensity to save (MPS) is used to calculate the multiplier effect.

Study Aids

Key Terms

gross national income	propensity to save	marginal propensity to save
full-employment economy	propensity to consume	Keynesian model
balanced budget	45° line	inflationary gap
multiplier effect	deficit spending	deflationary gap
investments	equilibrium point	aggregate income
$C + I + G = Y$	marginal propensity to consume	aggregate demand

Questions

1. How does the classical economist answer the following questions?
   (a) How will full employment without inflation be achieved?
   (b) What accounts for our failure to achieve the level of full employment without inflation?

2. The theories of John Maynard Keynes have had a significant impact on economic thinking. In what ways did he disagree with the classical economists?

3. What do most economists consider to be the principal factor in determining investment? Using the 45°-line diagram, explain why

aggregate income will be at both the intersection of the $C + I + G$ line and the 45° line and the point at which savings and investment (both public and private) are equal.

4. If investment is larger than savings, what will probably happen to income? Why will such a change take place? Under what conditions is it likely to be harmful to the economy?

5. If the full-employment level without inflation is estimated to be $1 trillion and if aggregate demand ($C + I + G$) is equal to only $970 billion, what amount of additional spending is needed to raise aggregate demand to the full-employment level? Assume the multiplier to be 3.

6. Assume that the government decides to stimulate the economy by reducing taxes, increasing its spending, or both. How will the marginal propensity to consume (MPC) and the multiplier enter into the consideration of how much to cut taxes and how much to spend? Which income groups will receive the most immediate benefits of these government actions?

7. If most Americans suddenly increased their savings, what would be the probable effects on the economy? When would increased savings be considered good for the economy? When would it be considered bad?

8. What factors might nullify the government's efforts to stimulate the economy during a recession or to control inflation during a period of prosperity?

Problems

1. You are a member of the Council of Economic Advisors. Your estimates indicate that the economy is short of a full-employment level by $150 billion. The marginal propensity to save is one-fourth. Prices appear relatively stable. Unemployment is at 6 percent. Prepare a staff paper for the president giving:
   (a) The several options for achieving full employment.
   (b) Your personal recommendation and your reasons for it.

2. Using the conditions described in Problem 1, write another paper from the standpoint of your membership in one of the following:
   (a) A labor union.
   (b) A consumer group.
   (c) A giant corporation.

3. In the mid-1960s, when the Vietnamese war was escalating, President Johnson declared that in the United States we could have "both guns and butter."
   (a) What did he mean?
   (b) What were the consequences?
   (c) What do you think his motivation was?

4. During the 1970s and 1980s, inflation was just as serious a problem as unemployment. Using both the classical and Keynesian approaches, explain why it is more difficult to curb rising prices than rising unemployment.

REVIEW MODEL

National Income Determination

This is a review exercise in the functioning of the Keynesian model. The purpose of this exercise is to show how our aggregate income is determined and how policy decisions can bring about changes in that income.

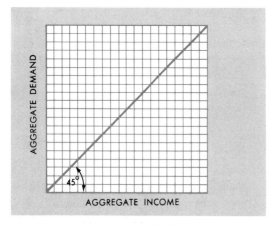

■ On our graph, the vertical axis measures aggregate demand (spending) and the horizontal axis measures our aggregate income. A diagonal line, 45°, implies total spending of income regardless of size.

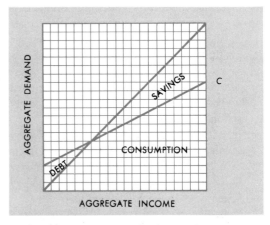

■ We know that consumers do not spend all their income; they save more as their income increases. Line C shows consumer spending rising as income rises. What consumers do not spend, they save. The area between the 45° line and the consumption line represents savings (or debt).

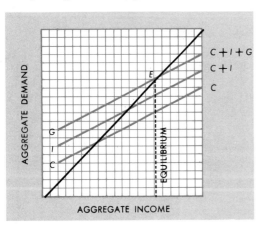

■ In addition to consumer spending, we have business investment I and government spending G. Total spending, or aggregate demand, is represented by the sum of consumption C, investment I, and government spending G. Aggregate income, or equilibrium, can be determined by locating the point at which the $C + I + G$ line crosses the 45° line. This approach relates to the formula for income determination: $C + I + G = Y$(income).

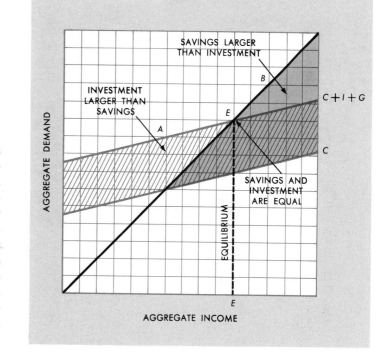

■ Aggregate income will be in equilibrium when investment (public *G* and private *I*) equals savings. At *A*, investment is larger than savings (demand greater than supply encourages expansion), and aggregate income will rise. At *B*, savings is larger than investment (supply is larger than demand), and aggregate income will decline. At *E*, investment and savings equal each other (equilibrium), and aggregate income will thus remain unchanged.

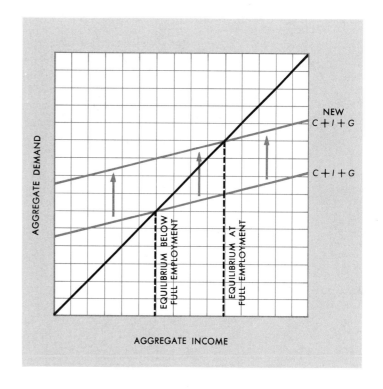

■ Keynesian economics calls for economic policy to bring the equilibrium point up to full employment without inflation. This is represented graphically by raising the *C* + *I* + *G* line (total spending), which originally crossed the 45° line below full employment. The new aggregate demand is now sufficient to sustain full employment without causing inflation.

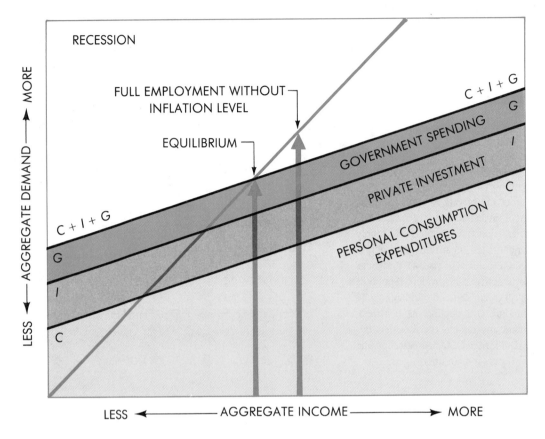

■ You see here a graphic representation of the economy in equilibrium below the full-employment level. Personal consumption *C* ▭ , business investment *I* ▭ , and government spending *G* ▭ add up to total spending, or aggregate demand. The *C* + *I* + *G* line crosses the 45° line at equilibrium below full employment. Savings and investment are equal at this point. The economy is not making full use of its resources. It is producing below its capacity because aggregate demand is not sufficient to support full employment.

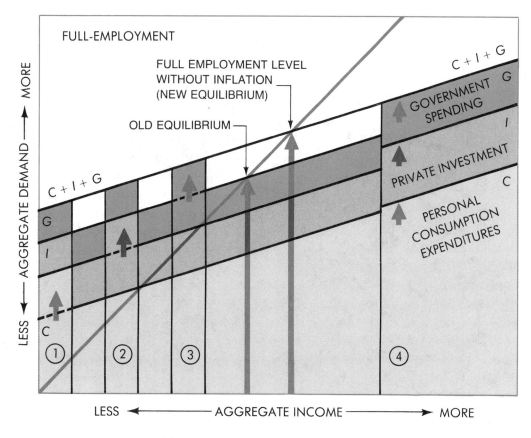

The economy can be stimulated to a new equilibrium at the full-employment level without inflation through various policy decisions:

1. Personal consumption expenditures *C* can be increased by decreasing taxes, thereby providing the consumer with more buying power. This is shown graphically in bar 1, where *C* ▭ moves upward, thereby raising the *C* + *I* + *G* line so that it crosses the 45° line at full employment.

2. Investment by business *I* can be increased by cutting business taxes, reducing interest rates for borrowing investment capital, or both. This is shown graphically in bar 2, where *I* ▭ is increased to bring the *C* + *I* + *G* line up to the full-employment level.

3. Government spending *G* can be increased without increasing taxes. This is shown graphically in bar 3, where *G* ▭ is increased to bring the *C* + *I* + *G* line up to the full-employment level.

4. A combination of the above three methods can be used in which *C* ▭ , *I* ▭ , and *G* ▭ are all increased to raise the aggregate demand.

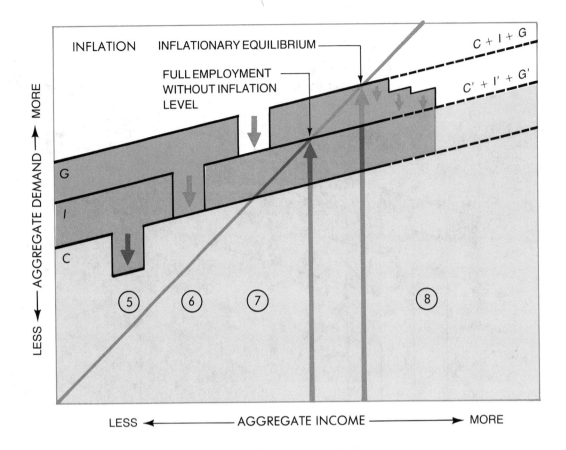

Here is a graphic representation of the economy in equilibrium above the full-employment level. The aggregate demand (total spending) is greater than what the total resources of the nation can produce. Policy calls for reducing aggregate demand, so as to lower the $C + I + G$ line to the level of full employment without inflation, $C' + I' + G'$. This can be accomplished by:

5. Increasing taxes so as to reduce personal consumption expenditures. (This is shown graphically at 5 by a decline in C ▭ and a drop in the $C + I + G$ line to the noninflationary full-employment equilibrium.)

6. Discouraging investment (reducing I ▭ at 6) by raising interest rates, increasing business taxes, or reducing the supply of loanable funds).

7. Reducing government spending (reducing G ▭ at 7) without changing taxes.

8. A combination of the above. (This is shown graphically at 8 by a decline in C, I, G.)

Money and Prices and Their Relation to the Economy

Economic activity is the production, distribution, and consumption of goods and services. In economies with specialization of production, where exchange is necessary, money is essential. Money can be used to stimulate or discourage production, to facilitate distribution and exchange of goods and services, and to measure values. Because money is so enmeshed in people's lives, it has frequently been regarded as an end in itself instead of a means for accomplishing the economic purposes indicated.

Although money is used and sought by virtually everyone, many people are uninformed or mistaken concerning the real nature and function of money in the economy. We will now consider both these aspects of money and the relation between prices and money.

Since inflation has been critical in recent years and may become critical again, in which case everyone will be affected by it, this chapter is one of the most important in this book.

Chapter Objectives

After studying this chapter, you should be able to:

- List the four functions of money and at least three characteristics that money must have in order to perform these functions.
- State and explain Gresham's law.
- Identify the three main components of our money supply.
- Define an index and explain why economists use indices.
- Explain the quantity theory of money, including the role of the money supply, the velocity or turnover of money, and the output of goods and services.
- Define and distinguish between demand-pull and cost-push inflation.
- Make the case for and against indexation and other proposals for dealing with inflation.

A Money: Its Functions and Characteristics

Have you ever examined your paper money closely? See if you can locate a $5, $10, or $20 bill printed before 1964 and marked "Federal Reserve Note" over the portrait. In the upper-left portion above the seal, a statement written in fine print says that the note is *legal tender* and that it "is redeemable in lawful money at the United States Treasury, or at any Federal Reserve Bank." Does this mean that the bill is *not* lawful? At the bottom center the same bill says, "Will pay to the bearer on demand X dollars." Does this mean that your X-dollar bill is *not* X dollars?

Much confusion exists about the real nature of money. Many people believe that money has no value unless it is backed by gold or silver. They think that the Federal Reserve note is only a symbol for money, and that real money is the precious metal backing the note. Some people look on money as wealth and believe that it must have *intrinsic* value.

If we were to study the history of money, we would find that in different places and at different times a variety of things have been used as money. Cattle, shells, beads, tobacco leaves, and various metals—including iron, zinc, bronze, and copper—have all been used as a basis for exchange. The precious metals, particularly silver and gold, have proved most satisfactory for this purpose and have been most commonly used in modern times.

Until early 1968, the United States backed its Federal Reserve notes with 25 percent gold, but this did not mean that citizens could use gold as money or convert paper dollars to gold. Clearly, *it is not what money is but what it does* that is important.

The Functions of Money

Under the simple economic conditions of the past, when most goods and services were produced by the family, necessary exchanges were usually accomplished by bartering goods for goods. Hunters exchanged furs and meat for grain and ammunition. Although the variety of things that our early ancestors produced was remarkable, total production was small because there was no specialization. As specialization developed, it not only increased production but also made the barter system nearly impossible. Although it might be possible for you to pay a doctor or a lawyer with goods or services, what would a giant corporation such as General Motors use to pay its employees? What could it accept in payment for its cars? How would it decide what stockholders should receive? Any economy with specialization of production needs a *medium of exchange*. This is the chief function of money.

 A medium of exchange is anything that is widely accepted in payment for goods and services and in settlement of debts. Money is the most common medium of exchange.

Medium of Exchange

Returning once again to the basic model of our economy at work, we can see clearly how money serves as a medium of exchange. When businesses sell their goods to consumers, they receive payment in the form of money. This money is then used to pay those who created the goods and services. Because consumers are also the owners of the factors of production that created the value, they receive payment in the form of money. Money itself does not satisfy wants, but it simplifies the exchange of the many different forms of value in our society. Owners of the factors of production exchange the value they create by using their labor, land, or capital for money. They prefer to receive payment in money rather than in goods, because the businesses that are using their services may not have the goods they want. If the suppliers of factors of production are given money, they can go to the market for goods and services and, acting as consumers, buy goods and services there. In this way, money becomes the single item that can be used by consumers and businesses for exchanging values.

Measures of Value

A second function of money is as a measure of value. How do we compare the value of a shirt with the value of a seat at a concert? What is the value created by a carpenter who builds a bookcase, or by a cobbler who puts new heels on a pair of shoes? Just as we need measurements for distances, weights, and energy, so we need measurements for the value of things offered at the market. In a barter economy we can speak of a shirt as being worth a seat at a concert, but in a money economy we use a *unit of account* to measure value. In the United States, the dollar is our *measure of value*. Thus the shirt is worth $15, and the seat at the concert is worth $15. All things having value at the market may be measured with the common unit of account, the dollar. The use of such a unit simplifies the exchange of goods.

Store of Value

A third function of money is as a store of value. You may seek to accumulate your wealth or the purchasing power that you have earned, rather than spend it immediately. Money is one form in which savings are accumulated.

Standard of Deferred Payments

The last function of money is as a standard of deferred payments. When you buy something but do not pay for it immediately, your payment is expressed in terms of money to be paid in the future. With the wide use of installment buying, this function of money has become increasingly important.

Characteristics of Money

For money to perform the functions indicated, it should possess special characteristics:

1. Most important of all, it must be *acceptable*. Only when it is accepted as purchasing power in the broadest market can it truly be a medium of exchange.
2. It should be *durable* so that it will not wear out too quickly; or failing this, it should be replaceable at a low cost.
3. It should be *portable* so that carrying it will not be burdensome.
4. It should be *divisible* so that the value of items that are fractions of the unit of account (for example, cents) can be calculated and handled easily.
5. It should be easily *recognizable* so that all will know what it is and what its value is.
6. It must be *homogeneous* so that all similar units have equal value.
7. It should have a high degree of *stability of value;* otherwise people may hoard it, waiting for its value to increase, or spend it immediately, fearing it will lose value.

From Commodity to Paper Money

Commodity money is a useful good that serves as a medium of exchange. Salt, cattle and various metals have been used as money. Commodities have often been used in simple economies as a basis for exchange. When a commodity becomes standardized as money, it usually loses much of its commodity form and takes on instead the aspect of money. When gold and silver were used as money, they became scarcer as ornaments. As economies became more complex and transactions increased, paper money representing units of gold or silver was more often used. This convertible paper money could be redeemed for the gold or silver that it represented. It is much easier to pay several thousand dollars in paper money than in gold or silver. So long as people recognized that they could convert this paper money to gold or silver, they willingly accepted it.

Inflexibility of Gold Supply

One of the chief difficulties in using gold, silver, and other precious metals as the basis for a money system is that as an economy continues to develop and greater value is produced, the amount of money in circulation, serving as a medium of exchange, needs to increase also. However, the supply of precious metals depends more on unpredictable discoveries than on demand. If no new gold is discovered and if no equally acceptable money is added to the money supply, prices will probably decline. This reduction, together with the shortage of money, can have an adverse effect on business.

By reducing the amount of gold or silver that stands in back of convertible paper money or by printing money that cannot be converted, the government can expand the amount of money available to meet the economic needs of the society. By freeing the money supply from the limitations of chance gold discoveries, the government obtains some flexibility in managing the supply of money in circulation.

Dangers Inherent in Commodity Money

There are, however, several dangers in allowing government to change the backing of money or to print inconvertible paper money. If government allows some money to be converted and other money not to be converted, or if it has two kinds of money (as we once did), one of which is backed by a higher-valued amount of metal, an effect known as *Gresham's law* will set in. This law states that when two types of money are in circulation and have equal stated values but different market values in terms of commodity content (the backing of one is worth more than the backing of the other), the less valuable type will drive the other out of circulation. This means that the government must either allow all money to be redeemable with the same metal or allow no money to be redeemable. In 1933, the government ordered that all gold and *gold certificates* be turned over to the U.S. Treasury in exchange for other kinds of money, largely because some people, fearing that other kinds of money would decline in value, had begun to hoard these certificates and coins.[1]

Another danger in a government's printing inconvertible paper money is the irresponsibility with which it may be done. *Fiat money,* which is money that circulates by order of the government, is characteristically used to meet emergencies. The greenbacks issued during the Civil War had behind them only the promise of the government to pay. If money is issued faster than the output of goods increases, prices will rise rapidly and the value of money will fall correspondingly. Metallic backing of money has become less significant as governments have developed a better understanding of the true function of money and have gradually learned to regulate the money supply.[2]

Our Present Money Supply

The three main kinds of money in use can be classified as *fractional currency, paper currency,* and *bank money* (checkable deposits).

Fractional Currency

A very useful but relatively small portion of our money supply is composed of coins valued at less than one dollar. These coins make up less than 3 percent of our total money supply, but they are convenient for making small purchases. Pennies,

---

[1] In late 1974, U.S. citizens were again permitted to buy gold.

[2] President Reagan established a Gold Commission to consider the possibility of returning to a gold standard. In 1982 the Commission, in its final report, rejected this idea, but concluded that gold's role might become more significant at some future time.

nickels, dimes, quarters, and half dollars are called *fractional currency* because they are valued at a fraction of a dollar. There are also one-dollar coins. Most coins are *token money*—the value of the metal is less than the face value of the coin. If the value of the metal in a coin should rise above the face value of the coin, people would withdraw the coins from circulation and melt them down to sell the metal.

Paper Money

From 20 to 25 percent of our money supply is made up of paper currency. The bulk of this money is issued by the Federal Reserve banks and is known as Federal Reserve notes. Silver certificates were issued by the U.S. Treasury from 1878 to 1963. Legislation in 1890, largely in response to the demand of western silver and agrarian interests, required that the Treasury buy silver bullion to back currency and coinage. Because the need for silver as a commodity has greatly increased, legislation was passed in 1963 that dropped the requirement that part of our currency be in silver certificates, and $1 Federal Reserve notes were then printed for the first time.

Bank Money

Over 70 percent of our total money supply (M_1) is made up of bank money, or *checkable deposits*. Most people know this type of money as deposits in their checking accounts.

Because writing checks is convenient and much safer than carrying large amounts of cash, about 90 percent of all transactions are made by check. Checks are a means of transferring ownership of deposits. As long as checks are accepted as a medium of exchange, they can properly be called bank money. (See Table 13–1.)

 Demand deposits can be withdrawn, usually by writing a check, with no advance notice to the bank.

Near-Money

The definition of our money supply given above is a very narrow one. It may surprise you to learn that the definition of money changes from time to

Table 13–1 Composition of the money supply (M_1) in the United States as of mid-1985

Coins, currency, and traveler's checks	28.9%
Checkable deposits:	
Demand deposits	44.1%
Conventional NOW accounts	17.5%
Super-NOW accounts*	9.5%

*Super-NOW accounts are checkable deposits paying unregulated interest rates.

Source: Federal Reserve Bank of New York

time. Narrowly defined, money consists of *transaction balances*—the money held by the public to use for current spending. Such money, usually called M_1, is made up of coins, paper currency, demand deposits and other checkable deposits (such as NOW accounts and share drafts in credit unions), and traveler's checks.

In addition to these items, families and businesses hold large amounts of assets that sometimes act like money even though they fail to meet our narrow definition of money. We shall call such assets *near-money*. Although they cannot be used immediately to buy goods or services, they can be converted to money very easily. These liquid assets include savings accounts at thrift institutions such as savings banks, shares in money market mutual funds, time deposits at commercial banks, and savings bonds. These and other similar assets do not circulate in the way that currency and checks circulate, but they must be considered in analyzing people's spending habits and in assessing the relationship between the money supply and the price level.

There are several measures that include these near-monies—M_2, M_3, and L. L (which stands for liquidity, or overall ability to spend) is the broadest measure; it shows the ability of all sectors of our economy to spend. During one recent period L was nearly six times as great as M_1. You need not learn the components of each of these measures. When we use the term "money" in this text we shall be referring to M_1. (M_1 is included in M_2, M_3, and L. Thus, only the portion of each measure that exceeds M_1 can be called near-money.)

Our Current *M*'s

The technical definitions of the *M*'s, on which this table is based, can be found in the *Federal Reserve Bulletin**

M₁:	1. Currency (including coin) in the hands of the public 2. Traveler's checks 3. Demand deposits (balances in checking accounts) 4. Balances in NOW and super-NOW accounts 5. Balances in accounts with Automatic Transfer Service (ATS) 6. Balances in credit union share draft accounts
M₂: *M₁* plus	1. Savings and small time deposits (less than $100,000) at depository institutions (including MMDAs) 2. Overnight repurchase agreements (RPs)** at commercial banks 3. Certain Eurodollar*** deposits 4. Shares in money market mutual funds held primarily by households and small businesses
M₃: *M₂* plus	1. Large time deposits ($100,000 or more) at depository institutions 2. Repurchase agreements with maturities longer than one day at commercial banks and savings and loan associations 3. Shares in money market mutual funds that are used by large financial institutions and corporations

*The *Federal Reserve Bulletin* is published monthly by the Board of Governors of the Federal Reserve System, Washington, D.C.

**RPs are the sale of securities, with a simultaneous agreement by the seller to repurchase them at an agreed upon price. Large institutions use RPs to invest idle funds for short periods, frequently one day. Because overnight RPs have such a short maturity, they are viewed as money.

***Eurodollars are dollar deposits in banking offices outside the United States.

(Source: Federal Reserve Bank of New York.)

B   The Relation Between Money and Prices

Price Levels and Price Indices

Although some disagreement exists about what effect the supply of money has on the economy, economists generally recognize that a change in the supply of money can influence business activity and price levels. The relation between money, prices, and business activity is explained by the quantity theory of money, or the *equation of exchange*. Before we can examine this relation, however, we must first consider what is meant by the price level and how it is measured.

Price Levels

If you were to look at a newspaper printed in 1933, you would be surprised at the prices prevailing at that time. You might feel envious as you read about the 5-cent bus fare, the loaf of bread or quart of milk for less than 15 cents, and the dinner at a good restaurant for $1. This kind of information about costs provides an indication of *price levels*—the average prices for things purchased during a given period of time. Price levels are extremely important because, when taken together with income, they determine the level of living.

Price levels are also important from a slightly different point of view. If prices are low, money will have greater value, because a given amount of money will buy more goods. In contrast, if prices are high, money will have less value, because the same amount of money will buy fewer goods.

Index Numbers

Price levels are usually measured by index numbers. A *price index* is a device for measuring the changing value of money over a given period. It can also measure the average price of several selected commodities at a given time. Because the prices of the things you buy determine the real value of your money, both definitions of index numbers are appropriate.

How Index Numbers Are Constructed

Economists make use of several different price indices. Each one is designed to measure the price level of a particular market. The two most widely used indices are the Producer Price Index and the Consumer Price Index, both compiled and issued by the Bureau of Labor Statistics of the United States Department of Labor. Industrial production and farm prices are other commonly used indices. We shall use a simplified example of the Consumer Price Index to illustrate the method involved in constructing an index.

We begin by selecting a *base period,* usually a "normal" period—free from wars, big depressions, or other such factors. Recently the U.S. government has been using a single year, 1967, as the base period for the Consumer Price Index, but a longer period can also be used. (Previously,

1957–59 constituted the base period.) We then select a number of common goods and services frequently bought by consumers and assign a relative weight to each item. This weight is determined by the share of the total expenditure accounted for by an item in the budget of the typical urban family. For example, more weight must be assigned to coffee than to shoes because so much more is spent on the former. Next we multiply the price of each item by its weight (relative importance). We then total the figures so obtained for a variety of items to get the cost of a standard "basket" of goods in the base period. The price index for any year is the ratio of the cost of a basket of goods in that year to the cost of the same basket of goods in the base period, times 100.

Suppose that the weighted sum of prices in 1967 equals $2,500. The price index for any subsequent year will be computed in relation to that base. Now, suppose that in 1986 we find the cost of the same basket of goods to be $8,500. To compute the Consumer Price Index (CPI) we use the following formula:

$$\frac{1986 \text{ figure } (8,500)}{1967 \text{ figure } (\$2,500)} \times 100 = \text{CPI } (340)$$

The CPI of 340 indicates that it took $340 in 1986 to buy the same goods and services one could get for only $100 in 1967. In other words, average prices rose by 240 percent, and there was a decrease in the value (purchasing power) of money.

Because the things consumers buy change both in kind and in number, those who figure the price index must from time to time make changes in the items selected and the weights assigned. Changes must be made with great care so that there will be no distortion of the measurement that gives the price level or the index. However, we must remember that the results can be interpreted only as an approximation of actual prices or of the cost of living at a given time.

Figure 13–1 shows changes in consumer and producer prices from 1977 to 1986, with 1967 as the base period. In the 1970s prices were not only rising, but rising at an increasing rate, a fact that greatly alarmed most people in the United States. The failure to take price indices into account can

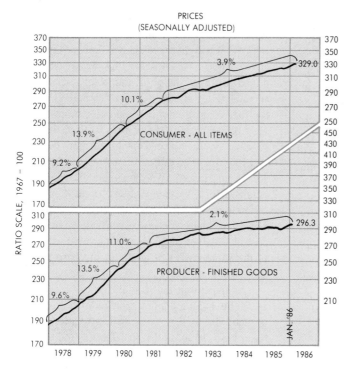

PRICES
(SEASONALLY ADJUSTED)

Figure 13–1   Consumer price index and producer price index

The inflationary spurt that started around 1973 caused many to name inflation as the number one problem in the United States. After 1981 the rate of inflation became more moderate, as shown by the fact that the curves became less steep. (Source: Federal Reserve Bank of St. Louis.)

result in misinterpretation of important figures. For example, during the first five months of 1974, retail sales expressed in dollars rose by 5.5 percent. Actually, however, sales in terms of real goods had *declined* by 5.4 percent. The 5.5 percent "gain" was an illusion created by inflation. Many people had found that although their nominal income in dollars had increased, the *real* income (the goods and services they could purchase with their nominal income) had dropped. A typical U.S. family of four had an after-tax dollar income of $10,976 in 1974 and $21,550 in 1984. However, in terms of the purchasing power of 1974 dollars, the 1984 income was worth only $10,175—$801 less than 1974 income!

Figure 13–2 shows how much (in round numbers) the typical family would need to have in 1984 to maintain its 1974 purchasing power. Over the long run, the average U.S. family has increased its level of living. After adjustment for inflation, the average family of the 1980s is enjoying a much higher real income than the average family in 1949. In the ten-year period 1963–73, the buying power of the typical household rose about one-third. Of course, some people have fallen

behind in the race with inflation; others have kept even or have outrun it. Also, some items in the Consumer Price Index are rising faster than others and some are actually declining, even though the

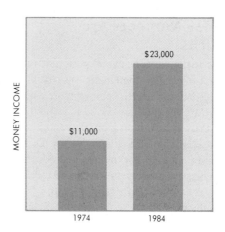

Figure 13–2   Effect of inflation on purchasing power

In 1974 a typical family of four had an income of nearly $11,000, after taxes. In 1984 the family needed a money income of about $23,000 to have the same purchasing power.

weighted average of all items is increasing. (For example, in one recent year prices for medical care rose by 6.2 percent while the prices of home appliances dropped by 1.2 percent.)

Why Are Stable Prices Important?

We have observed the relation of inflation and deflation to GNP and to other measurements of the economy as well as to the goal of full employment. Now we are prepared to consider inflation and deflation in a different context—in relation to money supply and prices. *Inflation* can be defined as an increase in the general price level or a decrease in the value of money. *Deflation* is a decrease in the general price level or an increase in the value of money. Economists generally agree that stable prices are desirable and that inflation and deflation have harmful effects on the economy. There are numerous reasons supporting this conclusion. Let us see how changes in price levels affect various segments of the economy.

 When average prices change little, even though the prices of particular items may rise or fall sharply, we have stable prices.

Borrowing

One economic activity that closely follows changes in price levels is the borrowing of money. A change in the price level between the time money is borrowed and the time it is paid back means that, in effect, the original agreement has been changed. The borrower will repay the lender an amount of purchasing power different from that originally borrowed. If the price level has risen 10 percent, the borrower is paying back dollars that will buy 10 percent less goods and services than this same amount of dollars would have bought originally. Such a change benefits the borrower, or debtor, and harms the lender, or creditor.[3] Deflation also affects both debtor and creditor. How does the impact of deflation differ from that of inflation?

Fixed Incomes

Stable prices are very important to people living on fixed incomes. For such people inflation may

[3] If creditors expect inflation, however, they will try to raise interest rates accordingly.

result in a lower standard of living. Let us look at an actual case. In 1965, an elderly woman retired. Her private pension plus social security benefits at that time totaled $291.00 per month. She was luckier than some people in that her pension was not absolutely fixed. In January 1974, her monthly income totaled $356.40. If we take 1965 as the base period and adjust her 1974 income for inflation, however, we find that her purchasing power in terms of 1965 dollars had dropped to $242.45! She had suffered a loss in buying power of $48.55. Thus, although it seemed that she had obtained a 23 percent gain in income (the gain in her *nominal* income), her *real* income had actually declined by 17 percent. And this happened at a time when the aging woman was becoming less able to take care of herself, required more medical care, and so on. (Recognizing the plight of the elderly, in 1972 the Congress tied social security benefits and taxes to inflation, providing automatic increases in benefits when the cost of living rises and automatic increases in the amount of wages taxed when the benefits are increased.)

Other kinds of fixed income are similarly affected by inflation. A life insurance policy paying the beneficiary $12,000 may have seemed adequate when it was taken out in 1940, but today its real value is less than half the original face value. Rent and wages set in fixed dollars and covering long periods of time are subject to the same loss of purchasing power when the price level moves up, as is interest on bonds.

In contrast to inflation, deflation would increase the purchasing power of the incomes described here. However, the trend in recent years has not been toward deflation. The years since 1940 have witnessed an almost steady increase in prices, and the purchasing power of people on fixed incomes has steadily decreased. (The term "disinflation" came into popular use in 1982 to describe the decline in the rate of inflation.)

Investments

Some people believe that rising prices encourage business persons to invest. If the investing occurs when the economy is producing less than its full-employment capacity, the effect on prices will be slight, because the increased dollars will result in increased production. Additional investment made when the economy is operating at or close to production capacity will accelerate the inflationary pressure, because little or no additional production can follow. Deflation, on the other hand, tends to slow down investment and thereby increase unemployment.

The value of common stock has often risen as fast as or faster than prices, leading many people to believe that stocks represent a good "hedge" against inflation. There is no guarantee of this, however. During the inflation of the late 1960s, stock prices declined. Similarly, in 1974 the composite index of prices on the New York Stock Exchange dropped sharply, whereas the cost of living rose at an annual rate of over 12 percent.[4] Deflation is often accompanied by a decline in common stock values. The market value of preferred stock tends to be more stable.

 Investment is the use of money to make more money, to gain income, or to increase one's capital.

Because the amount of interest on bonds is fixed, bonds have sometimes seemed like good investments during times of deflation. After a bond has been issued and sold, however, its market value *can* change. The value of a bond initially sold for $1,000 might drop to $600 in the bond market. If it is held to maturity, the buyer will get the $1,000. If circumstances force the holder to sell before maturity, however, the holder may receive less than he or she paid for it. There are no simple guidelines for the individual who hopes to guard against inflation or deflation by putting personal savings in stocks and bonds.

The Relation of Money and Price Level

The relation between money and price level is extremely significant in our economy. For a better understanding of how these elements interact, let

us use as an example a simple economic situation in which we eliminate all costs but labor. There are 20 people in our example, and all are employed at a bakery whose only product is bread. Each day 20 loaves of bread are produced. Everyone in the economy works and receives $1 a day. At the end of the working day all are paid $1, and they go directly to the market, which has 20 loaves of bread for sale. What will the price of a loaf of bread be? If bread sold for more than $1, there will be loaves of bread left over and no one to buy them. Supply will be greater than demand and the price will have to come down. If the price is less than $1, the consumers will soon bid the price up, because demand will be greater than supply. At $1 per loaf the market will be cleared.

What will happen if it is decided that the workers are being exploited and are entitled to a raise? The proprietor might perhaps agree to pay everyone $2 a day rather than undergo a work stoppage. To pay the higher wages she must have an additional $20 made available to her, for a total of $40. However, there are still only 20 loaves of bread available per day. The day the raise comes through, workers will rush to buy bread. When workers have $40 to spend and there are only 20 loaves of bread, what will happen to the price of bread? In a short time the increased money (demand) will drive the price up to the equilibrium level, where the market will be cleared. What would happen to the price of a loaf of bread if the proprietor reduced wages to 50 cents a day?

Let us now suppose that the amount of money in the economy remains the same, but production increases to 40 loaves a day. What will happen to the price of a loaf of bread? If prices are to be stable, the money supply must be increased as production increased. Our example shows in a very simplified way how price level is determined by the quantity of money and the quantity of goods and services that are offered for sale.

Velocity of Circulation

Our example may appear unrealistic, because people usually are not paid every day and do not spend immediately exactly what they earn. The fact remains, however, that as people earn, they

[4]For a scholarly study of the value of stocks as inflation hedges, see Frank K. Reilly, *Companies and Common Stocks As Inflation Hedges* (New York: New York University Graduate School of Business Administration, 1975).

also spend. Money circulates in the economy from consumers to producers and back to consumers several times during a year. The rapidity with which money changes hands in this way is called the *velocity of circulation,* or simply *velocity.* A $1 bill that circulates three times, or that has a velocity of 3, has the same economic effect as $3 that circulates once. If we produced 3,000 loaves of bread a year, the price level would react in the same way whether there was a payment of $3,000 with a velocity of 1 or $1,000 with a velocity of 3.

> Velocity is the speed with which money changes hands. If the number of times dollars (on the average) change hands during a year increases from three to six, then velocity has doubled. The use of electronic banking devices increases velocity.

The Equation of Exchange

As we noted earlier, economists use an equation called the equation of exchange to express the relation among money, prices, and business transactions. This equation can be written $MV = PT$ where

M is the money supply (currency + checkable deposits).
V is the velocity of circulation.
P is the general price level (index number).
T is the total business transactions in the economy.

The left-hand side of the equation, MV, represents the total spending for the year. The right-hand side, PT, is the total business for the year. If, as in our previous example, money supply is $1,000, velocity is 3, and we produce and sell 3,000 loaves of bread, the price level can easily be determined. The equation $MV = PT$ is easily converted to

$$P = \frac{MV}{T}$$

or

$$P = \frac{\$1,000 \times 3}{3,000} = \frac{\$3,000}{3,000} = \$1$$

If we double the money supply M but keep velocity V and transactions T the same, we shall have doubled the price level, causing inflation. If we double the number of transactions T but keep M and V constant, we shall have cut the price level in half, causing deflation. It would now appear possible to draw the conclusion that if we want the economy to grow (have a higher GNP) and yet want to maintain stable prices, we must balance an increase in actual production T with an increase in spending MV.

A case taken from U.S. history will demonstrate this conclusion. From your study of U.S. history, you may recall the variable economic circumstances of the farmer in the period from shortly after the Civil War until the turn of the century. During the Civil War our nation's money supply M had increased with the introduction of greenbacks. Although production increases during wars, the supply of civilian goods may not increase and may even be reduced. With money supply high and transactions in the civilian market limited, inflation results and prices are high. Many farmers borrowed money after the Civil War for newly introduced equipment and for the development of new lands. They did so at a time when the price level was high. Although production increased rapidly after the war, the money supply did not (that is, business transactions T grew but money supply times velocity MV did not). This brought about a decline in the price level, particularly for agricultural products. As a result, farmers had to pay back more in terms of purchasing power than they had borrowed.

Farmers sought different ways to decrease deflation. One solution was to increase M in order to generate inflation. Higher prices would mean that fewer bushels would be needed to pay back what was owed. One early suggestion was to increase M by issuing more greenbacks. Later the free and unlimited coinage of silver was urged for the same reason. Although neither of these solutions was adopted, M did eventually increase as a result of changes such as the Sherman Silver Purchase Act (repealed three years after its passage), the discovery of gold in Alaska, and the development of the cyanide process for the more efficient extraction of gold from ore.

Changes in Velocity

The experience of farmers after the Civil War seems to indicate that a change in the amount of money in circulation *causes* a change in the price level. Until recently, most economists believed that velocity remained almost constant. Studies have shown, however, that this is not always true, particularly over short periods of time. An increase in the amount of money may be followed by a decline in velocity, as happened during World War II. In the period since World War II, the quantity of money has often grown at a slower rate than production, but velocity has increased. Over the 30 years following World War II, velocity rose at an average rate of 3.5 percent, generally declining during recessions and rising during business expansions. The overall trend has been upward since 1947, with velocity reaching 7 percent in 1982.[5]

Economists still consider the equation of exchange important in showing the relation of money to prices and business transactions. Much economic policy concerns the control of M as one way of keeping a stable price level and influencing business activity.

Effect of Changes in the Money Supply

The actual effect resulting from a change in the money supply depends largely on whether the economy is operating at a full-employment level. From the end of the 1930s until 1942, there was a sharp increase in our nation's money supply, with a corresponding increase in production. At the beginning of this period, over 9 million people were unemployed and a large part of plant capacity was idle. The additional money stimulated production to a full-employment level. This change took place without any significant corresponding increase in the price level (about 3 points). The

[5] Velocity can vary greatly over short periods. For example, in the first quarter of 1981 velocity rose by 18 percent, which helped to explain a sharp increase in nominal GNP in the face of a very small increase in M_1. Then, velocity fell steeply in 1982, rose sharply in 1984, and took a sharp drop in the first half of 1985.

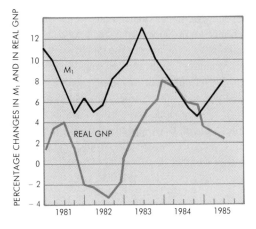

Figure 13–3 Relationship between money supply and real GNP

The black line shows percentage changes in the money supply (M_1). The colored line shows percentage changes in real GNP (the actual output of goods and services). Although the relationship between the two is not perfect, the curves suggest that a rise or fall in the money stock is accompanied, after a lag, by a rise or fall in real GNP. (Source: *The New York Times*, July 18, 1985, page D1, and Federal Reserve Bank of St. Louis, February, 1986.)

increase in the amount of money was matched by an almost equal increase in goods and services, with only a moderate increase in prices. A different effect was evident after the war. About one year after the war ended, the price level rose sharply, by 25 percent in three years. Although the elimination of price controls was a factor in this increase in prices, a more basic cause was the accumulation of money and near-money that could be easily converted into cash and spent for goods. Because our economy was already operating at full capacity, we could not produce all the goods and services consumers and businesses demanded. By bidding against one another, consumers and businesses forced prices to rise. During the 1950s and 1960s, our money supply increased far more slowly than did production. The increase in velocity offset some of the effects of the slow growth of M.

As Figure 13–3 shows, there appears to be a relationship between changes in money supply (M_1) and changes in real GNP. A rise or fall in the money stock will be followed, after a lag, by a rise or fall in real GNP.

Real GNP is the gross national product adjusted to account for changes in average prices. It measures the actual output of the economy.

In a similar fashion, an increase or decrease in the money stock has often been accompanied, after a lag of about two years, by an increase or decrease in the GNP deflator, or *General Price Index*. (The General Price Index includes all items, not just those purchased by consumers.) Again, the relationship is not perfect, but it does suggest that the money supply plays an extremely important role in the direction taken by prices and output in our economy. In the next chapter we shall discuss *monetary policy*—the efforts by the Federal Reserve System to control inflation or to stimulate the economy by influencing the supply of money.

Demand-Pull Inflation

The classical explanation for inflation is called the *demand-pull* theory. This label is used because the theory explains inflation as we have just done—when too much money is pursuing too few goods, demand pulls prices up.

Although the demand-pull theory sounds reasonable as an explanation for much of our inflation, at times it seems to explain nothing. One such time was the period 1956–60, when the price index rose more than 10 points. During these years our economy was operating below full-employment capacity. Though it is true the *M* was increasing at a slower rate than production and some economists thought we had more to fear from unemployment than from inflation, other economists offer a different explanation for the slowdown in business activity at a time when prices were rising.

 A general increase in prices caused by a rise in aggregate demand is called demand-pull inflation.

Cost-Push Inflation

Some economists suggest that there is another kind of inflation, which originates from the supply, or cost, side rather than from the demand side. The year 1956 was a good one for business, and many of the big labor unions negotiated three-year con-

tracts containing very favorable terms. Profits were very high, and businesses expected that by increasing efficiency in production—and if necessary, using some of the expected additional profits—they could absorb costs without raising prices. When a recession struck in 1958, the previously negotiated wage increases put a great pressure on business to pass these increased costs on to the consumer. Economists call this particular kind of inflation *cost-push inflation*[6].

 Cost-push inflation is a general increase in prices caused by a rise in the costs of production or a decrease in aggregate output of goods and services.

In our economy, both big labor unions and giant businesses are able to exert some pressure on the market. Although wages and prices seem to be flexible in their upward motion, unions' potential control over wages and businesses' potential control over prices have often canceled downward pressures. Business blames labor for the "wage-price" spiral, saying that higher wages mean higher costs, which business cannot absorb without a price increase. Labor points to the considerable power of business in controlling prices, frequently pushing prices beyond the point of paying for increased wages. These higher prices reduce the purchasing power of increased wages and cause workers to seek added gains. According to labor, management can afford to pay increases because of higher profits and increased productivity.

Both the demand-pull and the cost-push theories of inflation have a place in explaining rising price levels. Historically, the most severe inflations have been demand-pull. When "creeping inflation," or inflation that takes place slowly over a period of several years, occurs during periods of less than full employment, it can frequently be explained by the cost-push theory.

The "New" Inflation

In 1977 an economics research group called the Exploratory Project for Economic Alternatives issued a report that a new type of inflation had

---

[6]There have also been "supply shocks" such as the oil price increases of the 1970s.

appeared—a type that could not be controlled by conventional economic policies. This inflation is caused by such factors as world weather conditions (for example, bad weather might destroy crops and raise food prices), oil price increases, and wasteful use of oil and other resources. The report pointed out that price increases in four basic necessities—food, housing, health, and energy—accounted for two-thirds of the inflation in consumer prices. (These four items account for about 70 percent of the average family's consumption budget.) Labor costs were not seen as important factors in causing inflation.

Others, however, have found different causes for the inflation of the late 1970s. Some blamed big unions for negotiating large pay increases. Too much spending by the federal government was seen as the major factor by others. Inflationary psychology, which leads consumers to rush to buy new cars, appliances, and houses for fear that prices will rise even more in the future, was also cited as a cause. Other suggested causes of inflation were industry's failure to cut costs and increase productivity and actions by the Federal Reserve that resulted in higher interest rates. Some people felt complex federal regulations (such as pollution controls) caused manufacturing costs to rise.

International Factors

Events outside a country can affect prices within that nation. When the value of the U.S. dollar was declining in the world money markets, imported goods rose in price. People in the United States had to spend more dollars to buy a product made in a nation whose currency had risen in relation to the dollar. Some economists believe that the inflation of 1973–74 was primarily caused by international factors. The rate of inflation rose from only 3 percent in 1972 to 12 percent in 1974. World crude oil prices had quadrupled; there was a great increase in the demand for food, exhausting U.S. surplus supplies; the value of the dollar had depreciated in world markets in the 1971–73 period; and the world's money supply had expanded by 27 percent in 1972–73. A worldwide prosperity had created a demand for nearly all raw materials, thus pulling up their prices. These international factors may explain why U.S. efforts to control domestic inflation by wage and price controls were not very effective.

 # The Problem: How Much Inflation Is Tolerable?

In previous editions of this book we devoted this section to a discussion of the problem of "creeping" inflation—a modest increase of 2 or 3 percent per year in average prices. However, when inflation rates hit double-digit numbers (10 percent or more per year), the argument over creeping inflation seemed almost laughable.

By the mid-1980s, inflation rates were again moderate (2.3 percent in July of 1985 and below 1 percent in early 1986). Yet some argued that average prices should be stable, and that even an inflation rate of 2 or 3 percent caused too much hardship to old people on pensions and others whose money incomes do not rise as fast as average prices. Others felt that modest price increases would help to keep the economy growing, for businesses would be stimulated to keep inventories high and thus would create jobs and income.

As inflation rates of 6 percent or higher became common, many Americans would have gladly settled for the 2 or 3 percent rates that had been debated several years earlier. The basic argument continues, however, over the rate of inflation the nation can tolerate. For example, some have been saying that a 5 percent rate of inflation every year would be acceptable. Opponents argue that this rate is too high. One authority notes that with a 5 percent annual rate of inflation, a worker making $6.00 an hour today would have to make $54.00 an hour 45 years from now to have the same purchasing power—and an item now costing $30 would cost nearly $270 in 45 years. Furthermore, even if a person's money income rises as fast as the rate of inflation, he or she will still lose purchasing power so long as the personal income tax is progressive (tax rates rise as income rises). (Does Figure 13–2 tend to support this argument?)

Is Indexation the Answer to Inflation?

Indexation is one of the proposed means of coping with inflation. With indexation, various payments, such as wages, rents, and interest on bonds and bank deposits, would rise in accordance with increases in a price index. The real purchasing power of one's income would not decline, then, because of inflation. Comprehensive indexing has been practiced in Brazil, Finland, and Israel, and the noted U.S. economist Milton Friedman has supported some sort of indexation in the United States. The concept is not entirely new to us, for in 1948 the General Motors Corporation offered to include in its contract with the United Automobile Workers an "escalator clause." (Escalator clauses are often called COLAs—cost-of-living adjustments.) By 1977 nearly 6 million U.S. workers were covered by escalator clauses. Although these agreements vary widely, they nearly always relate pay increases to the Consumer Price Index. For example, a worker's pay might rise by a penny an hour for each climb of four-tenths of 1 percent in the CPI. Millions of people receiving food stamps and government pensions have also been "protected" through indexation. In the business world, some rates on commercial loans have been geared to changes in the prime rate (the rate banks charge their biggest borrowers on commercial loans), and some long-term contracts for fuel, raw materials, and machinery have called for automatic cost adjustments.

In the eyes of many, indexation seems to be a simple and fair solution to the problem of inflation. If everyone's income payments rise by 10 percent every time average prices rise by 10 percent, then everyone is in the same relative position as before the price increase—or so it would seem. A number of leading economists doubt that indexation would work. There are some difficult practical problems, such as how to index the value of corporate stocks, land, and houses. Then, it is feared, if everyone were protected from inflation by some sort of indexation, the government would

have no incentive to fight price increases. Such outside factors as the OPEC oil embargo could create great inflationary pressures, and even without these "exogenous shocks" we might still have industry and labor trying to run ahead of the general price index. Fearing that general indexation would result in endless inflation, some economists have taken a middle position. They approve of indexing some things, such as government bonds. (Formerly, the owner of a U.S. savings bond would find the interest destroyed by inflation and—adding insult to injury—would have to pay income tax on the interest.)

"Jawboning," Guideposts, and Controls

Presidents have sometimes resorted to persuasion—humorously referred to as "jawboning"—to control inflation. It is doubtful that such efforts have much effect, however, unless they are backed by some sort of "muscle." There have indeed been instances of large industries rescinding price increases and unions holding down wage demands in response to government persuasion. Note that the persuasion has often been backed up by threats of action, however. For example, President Kennedy threatened to bring antitrust action against the steel industry and to reduce government purchases from firms that failed to cooperate with government-suggested price-wage levels. President Johnson brought about a rollback in aluminum and copper prices, but he had threatened to use the government's large stores of aluminum and copper to keep prices in line. (The industries knew that the government could force the market prices down by selling its own supplies.) President Carter's "jawboning" was a combination of moral suasion and threats. Some of the "voluntary" compliance with government requests to rescind price increases has undoubtedly been motivated by fears that direct price-wage controls would follow if industries did not cooperate.

Presidents Kennedy and Johnson attempted to hold down wage increases by establishing guideposts. Wages were to increase no more than 3.2 percent a year—3.2 percent being the average increase in productivity during a five-year period prior to the setting of the guideposts. Prices were fairly stable during the Kennedy-Johnson guidepost period (1962–66). Some credited the guideposts with curbing inflation, but others argued that prices were stable during that period because the economy was operating within its capacity and because the growth in the money supply had not been excessive. In any event, prices rose rapidly after the guidepost policy was dropped.

President Nixon disavowed jawboning, guideposts, or any form of formal controls. In 1971, however, he dramatically announced a temporary freeze on nearly all wages and prices. After the 90-day freeze, a complex policy of controls (which included wage-increase guidelines and "targets" for price increases) was applied for 14 months. This, in turn, was followed by a period of voluntary controls—but these were backed by the president's threat to renew the wage-price regulations. The Nixon Administration also tried "dollar-for-dollar cost pass-throughs" that permitted companies to pass increased production costs along to their customers. By the time Nixon's control program ended (in 1974), however, the CPI was rising at a rate of over 12 percent.

Some economists still favor controls, but many others think they are unworkable or that such direct action is undesirable in a market economy. Thus, just as physicians may disagree on the best treatment for a patient (although strongly agreeing on the diagnosis and the need for action), economists disagree on the best "cure" for a problem like inflation.

The Tax-Based Incomes Policy (TIP) Proposal

One of the newer proposals for curbing inflation is to institute a *tax-based incomes policy* (TIP). There are several variations of the proposal, but the idea is that the government would set a wage-increase guidepost and a TIP tax schedule. If a company granted wage increases above the target figure (say 5 percent), it would be penalized by a tax surcharge. If it held wage increases to a figure below the guidepost, it would be rewarded with a subsidy ("negative tax"). Another plan calls for workers to receive tax rebates when their pay increases fall short of the government's guidepost figure and tax penalties when their pay goes above it. Supporters argue that such schemes would be flexible and that the government would not directly intervene in collective bargaining or in setting prices. Inflation resulting from labor costs would be diminished, and the worker's take-home pay would not be seriously eroded. Opponents point out that there are other causes of price increases besides rising wages, so TIP would deal with only part of the problem; that it would be easy to evade TIP taxes; and that administering the program would be difficult if not impossible.

These are but a few of the proposals for dealing with inflation. In Chapters 14 and 15 we shall examine the use of monetary policy and fiscal policy as weapons against inflation.

Chapter Highlights

1. Many myths about money still exist in popular thinking. One of the most common myths is that money must have intrinsic value, as gold does, to function as money.
2. An economy that has specialization of production needs money as a medium of exchange.
3. Money also functions as a measure of value, a store of value, and a standard of deferred payment.
4. If money is to perform its functions well, it must be durable, portable, divisible, recognizable, homogeneous, stable in value, and, most important, acceptable to the public.

5. As an economy grows and becomes more complex, commodity money will give way to convertible paper money. Eventually inconvertible paper money may become standard, as it did in our economy.

6. As governments become more responsible in controlling money, the need for backing of currency becomes less important.

7. The three principal kinds of money in use today are fractional currency, paper currency, and checkable deposits. Checkable deposits constitute about 71 percent of our money supply.

8. Near-monies are liquid assets that can be easily converted into money. Deposits in savings institutions and U.S. government bonds are important categories of near-monies.

9. Price levels are the average prices paid for goods and services for a given period. Changes in price levels can be measured by index numbers.

10. Inflation is an increase in the general price level or a decrease in the value of money. Deflation is a decrease in the general price level or an increase in the value of money.

11. Stable prices are important in protecting the debtor, the creditor, the investor, and people living on fixed incomes.

12. The relationship of money, price level, and business transactions can be expressed by the equation of exchange: $MV = PT$.

13. Studies have shown that the velocity of money varies and has been a significant factor in the relation of money to prices and business activity.

14. The effects of increasing or decreasing the money supply will vary depending on whether the economy is operating at full employment or at a lower level of employment.

15. Demand-pull inflation occurs when too much money pursues too few goods. The excess demand results in rising prices.

16. Cost-push inflation is caused by price increases due to escalating costs. This situation can develop when wages increase faster than output per labor-hour or when prices rise faster than wages, which then forces workers to seek higher wages.

17. Inflation has also been blamed on bad weather, oil price increases, "inflationary psychology," failure to increase productivity, the wasting of resources, costly federal regulations on business, high interest rates, and international factors.

18. Opinions differ on the amount of inflation that is "tolerable" and on the possible effectiveness of such anti-inflation tactics as indexation, "jawboning," price-wage controls, and the tax-based incomes policy.

Study Aids

Key Terms

medium of exchange	greenbacks	commodity money
Gresham's law	silver certificates	liquid assets
Federal Reserve notes	currency	price level

price index	transaction balances	guideposts
inflation	near-money	creeping inflation
GNP deflator	fiat money	indexation
Consumer Price Index	equation of exchange	escalator clauses
measure of value	M_1, M_2, M_3, L	COLAs
velocity of circulation	unit of account	"jawboning"
intrinsic value	paper currency	tax-based incomes policy (TIP)
wage-price spiral	index numbers	bank money (checkable
base period	deflation	deposits)
deferred payments	demand-pull inflation	token money
fractional currency	cost-push inflation	

Questions

1. Money serves many purposes in a nation's economy. List and explain the chief functions of money.
2. What are the specific characteristics of money?
3. Government policies on money supply and price levels make it possible to reduce the more extreme effects of inflation and deflation.
   (a) What are some actions that the government can take to influence price levels and the supply of money?
   (b) What are the potential dangers of each of these actions?
4. Recently, some leading economists proposed that gold no longer be used as a means of payment among nations. What characteristics should a new "international currency" have?
5. Explain the possible effects of deflation and inflation on the following:
   (a) a pensioner
   (b) a lender of money
   (c) an owner of common stock
   (d) an owner of fixed-rent property
   (e) a union wage policy committee
   (f) a civil service employee
6. Explain the statement "The business and consumer segments of our economy can plan most effectively if assured of price stability over a period of time."
7. Evaluate the following statements:
   (a) "Full employment without inflation is the underlying strength of our economy."
   (b) "Wage increases need not be inflationary."
   (c) "A mild inflation helps to promote economic growth and prosperity."
   (d) "Inflation in one nation can be 'exported' to other nations."

Problems

1. Obtain the most recent data available on the U.S. money supply. What percentage of the money supply is made up of coins, of paper currency, of checkable deposits? Why do bank deposits make up the largest percentage? How does each type of money meet the criteria of good money?
2. Why was the 25 percent gold backing removed from Federal Reserve notes in 1968? What effect, if any, did this action have on the value of the dollar? Explain. What principles of money are illustrated by this event?
3. Make a brief survey of the history of money in the United States. What forms of money have been used? What events led to the adoption of each (such as U.S. notes)? How successful was each form of money as a medium of exchange?
4. Select 5 commodities and 5 services available to the consumer both in 1925 and at present.
   (a) Assign an appropriate cost to every item for each date. Make a total of the costs for each date.
   (b) Create an index number for each item, using 1925 as a base of 100. When your lists are complete, compare the prices for each item at the different dates. What conclusions can you draw?
   (c) Explain some of the reasons for the use of the index numbers.
   (d) What weaknesses are inherent in the use of index numbers?

5. Because of the delicate balance between inflation and stability in our economy, a change in wage rates is particularly significant.
   (a) Select any one of the major labor contracts negotiated in the last two years and explain how the wage agreement might affect prices.
   (b) Assume you are the representative of the public in a labor dispute. What arguments would you use to make both union and management negotiators realize that a purely selfish approach would hurt them both?

6. Consider the following situation. A few years ago, a woman put $1,000 in a savings account. To date, the interest on this account totals $305. Adjusting this principal plus interest for inflation, we find that inflation has wiped out the gain—the purchasing power of the total in her account ($1,305) is no greater than the purchasing power of the original $1,000. Now suppose that indexation had been applied to her situation, and that her account now totaled $1,531. Expressed in constant dollars, her account would equal $1,175. There would have been a real gain in purchasing power. Should such accounts be indexed? If so, should indexing be required by law or should it be a matter of choice on the part of the parties concerned? If you approve of indexation in this case, do you also approve of it for all other things? If you owe someone money, would you be willing to increase your interest payments so that the creditor suffered no loss because of inflation? Would making all payments subject to indexing solve the problem of inflation or would it simply feed the inflationary flames? Why? Discuss the reasoning behind your answer.

7. Assume that inflation is soaring at a rate of about 13 percent and the unemployment rate is well over 7 percent. One economist urges that we avoid general tax increases and tighter money (higher interest rates) for fear of making unemployment even worse. Another replies that the unemployment rate is really deceptive because the rate for married men is only 2.5 percent. He notes that the high overall rate is being pulled up by a very high unemployment rate among teenagers who are not supporting families. Thus, he says, if we take actions that do indeed increase the unemployment rate these actions will not cause extreme hardship to most working people. Assume the second economist's figures are correct. Which economist would you agree with? Why?

8. As interest rates reached their highest point in a hundred years, an economist stated: "The Federal Reserve should tighten money even further so that the interest rate goes higher. This will make it harder for businesses to obtain loans and to invest. Business investment pours money into the economy; and since we are now in a serious inflation, we need to discourage investment. With less money going into the economy there will be less demand, and prices will be checked or even reduced." A business person replied: "Nonsense. Interest is one of the costs of doing business. The high interest rates we pay on loans cause us to raise our prices, since we must cover all costs. Furthermore, if we borrow money for investment purposes now, we shall be adding to our productive capacity by acquiring new plants and equipment. Thus, in the future we'll produce more goods, and by putting more goods on the market we add to supply and—in the long run—help force prices down." Which person is "right"? Why?

9. Construct your own "personal price index," using the techniques described in this chapter for preparing a weighted price index. List your expenditures for food, shelter, transportation, clothes, personal care, medical care, entertainment, and other items you commonly purchase. Weight the items in accordance with the percentage of your total expenditures that each item represents. Is the total for your "basket of goods" close to the national average? Are you in a better or worse position than the national Consumer Price Index indicates? (Suppose you had also included the taxes you pay, such as the personal income tax and social security tax—how would this change your personal price index?)

Banking, Money Creation, and the Federal Reserve

In the previous chapter we considered the importance of money to the national economy. Here we are concerned with financial institutions that deal with money and credit. Through these institutions the money that people save is made available to those who need it for investment or purchases. Like all resources, money must be carefully allocated in the right amounts, to the right places, and at the right times to further the production of the goods and services that consumers want.

Controlling the supply of money as a means of influencing business activity and price levels is important for the well-being of the entire economy. Our banking system is influenced by the Federal Reserve, which makes monetary policy decisions that influence the supply of money in the United States. Again, we shall introduce tools to help us analyze what kind of policy decisions should be made. In Chapter 11 we considered fiscal policy, or how the budget can be regulated to influence aggregate demand. In this chapter we concentrate on how the money supply can be controlled to help achieve our economic goal of full employment without inflation. Finally, in Chapter 15 we shall put monetary and fiscal policy together to show how modern economics can contribute to a healthy economy.

Chapter Objectives   On completing this chapter, you should be able to:

■ List and explain the functions of the various types of banking institutions.

■ Show how the banking system helps to create money.

■ Describe the Federal Reserve System and explain its functions.

■ Discuss the advantages and disadvantages of the principal "weapons" of the Federal Reserve.

■ Briefly describe Milton Friedman's "monetarist" theory.

■ Give arguments for and against monetary policy as an effective means of achieving our economic goals.

A Kinds of Financial Institutions

Banks and Their Functions

Many people think of a "financial institution" or "bank" primarily as a convenient place to deposit valuables, particularly money, for protection against the hazards of theft and fire. Actually, many different kinds of businesses can be called banks or financial institutions.[1] Although each of these serves a particular purpose, they all have one activity in common—collecting money from a source that does not need it immediately and channeling it to others that do need it immediately. Thus these various financial institutions are intermediaries in the flow of money throughout the economy. In addition to this general activity, financial institutions carry on many specialized functions.

 As defined by the Bank Holding Act, a bank is an institution that accepts demand deposits and makes commercial loans.

Depositories

The earliest banks were mere depositories for safekeeping valuables. Centuries ago, many people deposited their gold in the vaults of goldsmith shops and withdrew it as needed. So that such a bank could meet its expenses, depositors paid a fee to have their money stored. Later, as these banks issued notes payable in gold, bookkeeping and the balance sheet became important tools for keeping accurate records.

Lending

With many businesses and individuals wanting to borrow money and with funds lying idle in bank vaults, banks naturally turned to the business of lending money. Depositors were told that if they would permit the bank to use their money for lending, they would not have to pay a storage fee. Under certain conditions they could even receive payment (interest) for the use of their money. The banks could afford these arrangements because they loaned the money out at a rate of interest higher than that which they paid to the depositors.

Money Creation

In the course of lending money, bankers discovered that the total amount of money they had on deposit fluctuated very little. Although individuals might alter the size of their accounts considerably from day to day, the total of all deposits in a particular bank remained fairly constant, because withdrawals by some people were usually balanced by deposits by others. This discovery allowed bankers to use most of the money on deposit for loans with little fear of a shortage of funds, even when some depositors wished to withdraw their money.

Using this knowledge, *commercial banks* today are in effect able to create money by using funds

---

[1] The federal Bank Holding Act defines a bank as an institution that accepts demand deposits and makes commercial loans. Therefore, in the financial industry, savings institutions and savings and loan associations are often called "thrifts" instead of "banks."

from *demand deposits* as the basis for additional deposits, in the form of loans extended to borrowers. This ability to create money is very important to individual banks and to the economy as a whole. Let us see how banks create money, recognizing that our example holds true for the banking system as a whole and not any single commercial bank.

Assume that there is a very small nation with only one bank—a monopoly bank. The bank has a total of $100,000 in cash on deposit. Its depositors have checkbooks and can withdraw their money at any time simply by writing checks. Those receiving the checks usually deposit them in their own accounts at this bank. Most of the cash never leaves the vault; in fact, no more than 5 percent of the cash is ever out of the bank at any one time. Playing it safe, the bank decides always to keep at least 10 percent of the cash on hand to meet any demand for cash that depositors might make. In short, it has established a *reserve requirement* of 10 percent. The bank places $10,000 in reserve (10 percent of its demand deposits) and makes the remaining $90,000 available for loans.

Needing some new machinery, the Ace Construction Co. applies for a $90,000 loan. Certain that the new machinery will increase Ace's business and revenues and that the loan will be repaid in a short time, the bank approves the loan. Ace gives its *promissory note* (IOU) to the bank, and the bank simply credits Ace's account with $90,000. Ace does not want the cash: it is quite content to use checks. In making this loan, the bank has created credit in the form of a demand deposit, which Ace can draw upon by writing checks. The bank has taken Ace's promissory note and converted it into money (checks serve as money). The nation's money supply has risen by $90,000. How can this be? Shouldn't there be something behind the paper that is used as money? In this case, it would be incorrect to say that there is nothing behind this new $90,000 in checkbook money, because in effect the assets and good reputation of Ace are behind it. The bank's deposits increase to $190,000—the original $100,000 in cash plus the $90,000 in credit. Of course, the bank's reserves must now rise to $19,000, which is 10 percent of its total deposits.

Must the bank now stop this business, or can it go further? If Ace withdrew the cash and the recipient (the manufacturer of machinery) decided to keep the cash in its vault instead of the bank's, indeed the bank could go no further. But this is highly unlikely. The manufacturer, Bulldozers Inc., deposits the money in its own account in the bank. All the bank must do now is deduct $19,000 from the original $100,000 (a simple bookkeeping operation), for this is the amount it has to keep in reserve against total demand deposits. This leaves $81,000 ($100,000 minus $19,000) available for lending.

Assume that the entire $81,000 is loaned to Carey's Department Store, which plans to add a gardening center to its existing facilities. Carey's gets a deposit of $81,000, so total demand deposits rise to $271,000. Remember that these deposits serve as money—$100,000 of which has cash behind it, and the rest of which is backed by the credit of Ace and Carey's. When Carey's writes a check for $81,000 to pay Dempsey Builders for constructing the new gardening center, Dempsey in turn deposits the check with the bank. The bank has lost no cash whatsoever. Its reserve, of course, is now $27,100, which is 10 percent of total demand deposits. Deducting this $27,100 from the original $100,000 leaves the bank with $72,900 available for lending.

Can this cycle go on forever? No—eventually the bank will have made loans of $900,000. At that point its total deposits will be $1,000,000 (the original $100,000 plus $900,000 in loans). The bank must stop here, because it has to keep a 10 percent reserve. The original $100,000 in cash is now 10 percent of total deposits. With no excess reserves, the bank does not dare make further loans. But notice that the economy now has a money supply of $1,000,000. This checkbook money has $100,000 in cash and $900,000 in credit and business property behind it. The bank has created $900,000 in new money.

Fortunately, it is not necessary to go through this tedious step-by-step process to find out how much in demand deposits the commercial banking system can create. All we need to do is multiply our original $100,000 by the reciprocal of the reserve requirement. In this example the reserve requirement was 10 percent, or $\frac{1}{10}$. The reciprocal of $\frac{1}{10}$ is $\frac{10}{1}$, or simply 10. By multiplying \$100,000 by 10, we find that \$1,000,000 in demand deposits can result from a mere \$100,000 in cash. If the reserve requirement had been 20 percent ($\frac{1}{5}$), how much in demand deposits could have resulted from the same amount of cash?

The procedure outlined above is unrealistic, because in reality there are thousands of commercial banks. In real life, no single bank can bring about the deposit expansion we described. If we think of the entire commercial banking system as one huge bank, however, the procedure (although overly simple) works pretty much as we have indicated. Later in this chapter we shall repeat the process to show how it works when many banks are involved.

Other Financial Institutions and Their Functions

In addition to commercial banks, many other types of financial institutions exist in our economy. They are designed to meet the different requirements people have for their savings. Each of these institutions tends to have a particular function and to serve a certain kind of depositor.

Savings Institutions

There are three main forms of savings institutions: *mutual savings banks, savings and loan* (or building and loan) *associations,* and *savings departments* in commercial banks.[2] These institutions take the money for which people have no immediate need and place it in personal savings deposits. Savings institutions may request that depositors give notice of intent to withdraw funds, although they do not often do so. Because of this requirement, savings accounts are called *time deposits* so as to distinguish them from demand deposits (checking accounts), from which money may be withdrawn at the depositors' will.

 Thrifts are institutions, such as savings banks and savings and loan associations, that perform some, but not all, banking

functions. They originated primarily to serve individuals and small savers as opposed to business firms.

The distinction between savings accounts and checking accounts is breaking down, however. In 1972 some mutual savings banks in Massachusetts and New Hampshire began to issue NOW accounts (NOW means *negotiable order of withdrawal*). People may withdraw funds from their savings accounts by writing a NOW, which is much the same as writing a check. In effect, then, the NOW accounts are interest-bearing checking accounts. The banks that first issued NOW accounts were state-chartered institutions. The NOW accounts, of course, gave them a competitive advantage over savings institutions under federal regulatory jurisdiction. In 1973, a federal law was passed authorizing all depository institutions in those two states (except for credit unions) to offer NOW accounts; and in 1980 the same privilege was granted to institutions in the rest of the country. In 1978, the Federal Reserve gave commercial banks the right to offer their customers ATS—*automatic transfer service*. With ATS, people can keep funds in interest-bearing savings accounts and have the bank shift money from their savings accounts to their checking accounts. The U.S. League of Savings Associations charged that ATS violated a federal law prohibiting commercial banks from paying interest on checking accounts, but a federal court decision did not sustain this argument. Technically, the customer's savings account is separate from his or her checking account, but the practical result is the same as if interest were being paid on the checking account. As we noted in Chapter 13, NOW accounts, ATS accounts, and credit union share drafts are considered to be part of our money supply (M_1). Share drafts are like checking accounts that pay interest on minimum account balances.

Most of the savings in thrift institutions comes from people of modest means who expect to receive interest on their money but are unwilling to take much risk. Mutual savings banks invest their deposits in mortgages, government bonds, and securities that involve little risk. Savings and loan associations concentrate primarily on home mort-

[2]Credit unions are also quite important. See the next section.

gages. Under a law passed by Congress in 1980 (the Depository Institutions Deregulation and Monetary Control Act), the thrift institutions were given powers traditionally limited to commercial banks. In addition to legalizing NOW accounts nationwide, this law authorized savings banks to offer demand deposits to business customers, allowed savings and loan associations to offer consumer loans and to issue credit cards, permitted credit unions to make real estate loans, and enabled savings banks to grant commercial, corporate, and business loans. These and other provisions of the law helped to break down some of the differences between commercial banks and thrift institutions.

Nevertheless, the early 1980s were a time of serious problems for the thrift institutions. To attract deposits, they were forced to offer high interest rates. Because the rates they were paying were often higher than the rates they were receiving on old mortgage loans, hundreds began to lose money. The government encouraged mergers to prevent failures, and in 1982 the Federal Reserve Board, for the first time, allowed a commercial bank holding company to acquire a savings and loan association.

Personal Trusts

Trust companies and the trust departments of commercial banks invest the funds of people with financial security who want to provide income for their families. In 1980 the federally chartered savings and loan associations were also given trust-fiduciary powers.

The money deposited in these institutions is invested in many different types of securities providing an assured return; speculative securities are usually avoided. These personal trusts must not be confused with industrial trusts (Chapter 4).

Insurance Companies

The purpose of *insurance companies* is to allow people to pool their resources in order to minimize the risk associated with accident, sickness, death, and other unpredictable circumstances. Although the money these companies collect must be paid

out at some time, they control huge sums of money, most of which is placed in long-term investments. A large portion is put into bonds and mortgages, although significant investments, strictly regulated, are made in real estate and stocks.

Consumer Credit Institutions

A tremendous increase in consumer credit has taken place in recent years. Consumers borrow from small finance companies, credit unions, sales finance companies, and the small-loan departments of commercial banks. Most finance companies do not obtain their loanable funds from the public. Instead they frequently turn to other financial institutions, from which they borrow at rates lower than those at which their clients can borrow. For example, Ford and General Motors have set up finance companies to aid their dealers in selling cars. *Credit unions* are set up on a cooperative basis for a particular group, such as civil service employees, workers in a large company, or people who live in a housing development. Members of a credit union can put their savings into the credit union and receive shares for these deposits. Each share earns interest for the contributor. Members can borrow at comparatively low rates of interest.

Other Financial Sources

For long-term capital investment large businesses frequently require an amount of money beyond the resources of most commercial banks. Such firms may decide to raise the money by issuing bonds or stocks. Investment banks or, less often, brokerage houses may be asked to manage the sale of these new securities.

The federal government, too, has become a primary source of loans in many fields. Through a variety of agencies the federal government assists farmers, home owners, small businesses, and smaller units of government. In many instances, the government does not lend the money itself, but merely insures payment to the private banker of a certain percentage of the loan. This practice has made borrowing possible for many families and businesses to which loans might otherwise not be available.

B Commercial Banks and the Creation of Money

Organizing and Operating a Bank

Commercial banks have been unique among financial institutions because of their ability to create money. (As we have stated, however, NOW accounts in savings banks and share drafts in credit unions are now considered to be part of our money supply, M_1.) Demand deposits (checking accounts) make up a major part of our money supply. The ability of these banks to maintain and create demand deposits by loans and investments influences the supply of money in our economy.

We previously set up an imaginary business in order to understand business organization and some of its problems. Let us now do the same with a commercial bank, having as our objective an understanding of how these banks affect our economy.

Organizing a Bank

Banking is a business in which the main product offered for sale is money. As in other businesses, the incentive in banking is to earn profits. Because commercial banks hold the bulk of checkable deposits, we shall focus on these institutions.

We begin by calling a meeting of people interested in using their money to organize a commercial bank. We decide how much capital will be needed and whether we wish to function as a state or a national bank. Both state governments and the federal government have laws regulating banks under their authority. Having agreed that we shall raise $300,000 in capital, enough for us to qualify as a commercial bank in a city of our size (40,000), we decide to petition the state banking authority to issue a charter. We become a corporation under the name The Felix Bank, and we start to sell stock in our company.

As we begin operations, we set up a *balance sheet*—a statement showing *assets, liabilities,* and *net worth*. Assets equal liabilities (the claims of nonowners against the firm) plus net worth (the claims that the owners have against our assets). Having sold $300,000 worth of stock in our bank, we have on hand $300,000 in cash and we have outstanding capital stock worth $300,000. The cash is an asset of the bank. (Cash held by a bank is called *vault cash*.) Note, however, that the stock outstanding represents claims the stockowners have against our assets. Our balance sheet is as follows:

Assets	
Cash	$300,000

Liabilities and Net Worth	
Capital stock	$300,000

A board of directors has been appointed, which in turn appoints a president and bank officers. A building costing $200,000 is purchased and furnished with $60,000 worth of equipment. The value of our assets has *not* changed, but those assets now have a different composition. The balance sheet reflects this as follows:

Assets	
Cash	$40,000
Property	$260,000

Liabilities and Net Worth	
Capital stock	$300,000

The balance sheet is still in balance and always will be. People begin to deposit money in our bank, and soon we have a total of $100,000 in *demand deposits*. These are checking accounts, and the depositors can draw out part or all of their funds at any time simply by writing checks. Thus the demand deposits are claims against our bank's assets and must be added to the liabilities side of the balance sheet. The cash we received from the depositors, however, is considered an asset and is added to the assets side. Note the effect on the balance sheet.

Assets	
Cash	$140,000
Property	$260,000

Liabilities and Net Worth	
Capital stock	$300,000
Demand deposits	$100,000

Assets still equal liabilities and net worth. Have any other changes occurred? The amount of checkbook money, or demand deposits, has increased. However, because the amount of currency in circulation has dropped by the same amount ($100,000), and because currency that is held by a bank is not counted as part of the nation's money supply, the total money supply has not increased. If the reverse occurs (that is, if someone withdraws cash from the bank), our deposit liabilities will decrease and currency in circulation will increase by the same amount. (What will this do to the balance sheet?)

Now suppose we decide to join the Federal Reserve System (the Fed). State-chartered banks may join if they wish to. (If we had been chartered by the United States Comptroller of the Currency as a national bank, we would have been required to join the Federal Reserve System.) We must keep a *reserve deposit* in the Federal Reserve Bank. The amount we have to deposit with the Federal Reserve Bank will be a certain percentage of our demand deposits. If the *reserve requirement* is 10 percent, we shall have to keep $10,000 on deposit with the Federal Reserve Bank. If the requirement is 14 percent, we shall have to have $14,000 in our reserve account with the Fed. (Actually, vault cash can also be counted as part of our reserves, but banks rarely keep more than 2 percent of their deposits in cash.)

Let us assume that our bank is required to meet a 10-percent reserve requirement. (Let us also forget about vault cash. We would be foolish to keep much cash on hand, because vault cash earns no interest and cash withdrawals are usually matched by new cash deposits anyway.) We must therefore deposit $10,000 with the Federal Reserve Bank—10 percent of the $100,000 in demand deposits in our bank.

The $10,000 is the bare minimum we must have with the Federal Reserve Bank, and we are quite certain that we shall acquire new deposits in the near future, so we might as well send even more money to the Federal Reserve. Indeed, we decide to go all the way and deposit the entire $140,000 in cash listed on the balance sheet above. The new balance sheet is as follows:

Assets	
Cash	$0[3]
Property	$260,000
Reserve account	$140,000

Liabilities and Net Worth	
Capital stock	$300,000
Demand deposits	$100,000

We have met our legal requirement, and we have *excess reserves*. That is, we have $130,000 more than we are required to have in our reserve account. (The reserve of $130,000 is an asset for us and a liability for the Federal Reserve Bank.) This will save us the trouble of sending additional reserves to the Fed every time our deposit liabilities are increased.

We have now reached a vital point in this discussion, because the capability of commercial banks to make loans depends on excess reserves. The ability of the commercial banking system to create money also depends on the amount of reserves. In times past, reserves were regarded as a safety fund to protect depositors from possible losses. These reserves would be drawn on in the event that a bank was confronted with large withdrawals of cash. Under our system, however, the required reserves cannot be used to meet unexpected withdrawals of cash. If all of a bank's depositors suddenly demanded cash at the same time, its legal reserves would not suffice to cover the withdrawals. (It should be noted, however, that when depositors withdraw cash, the bank's deposit liabilities decrease. The amount of required reserves drops, thus releasing some of the bank's reserves.)

The purpose of required reserves is to give the Federal Reserve System a way of controlling the depository institutions. As we shall see, the Fed can use this power to discourage banks from extending too much credit during a period of infla-

---

[3] In reality, of course, we would not deposit all of the cash. We would keep about 1½ to 2 percent of our total assets in cash. Because vault cash can be counted as part of our reserves, however, it will be simpler in this discussion if we assume that all of it has been deposited with the Fed. Thus we won't have to bother adding cash and deposits in the Fed to determine our total reserves.

Federal Deposit Insurance Corporation

Before 1933, and particularly during the period 1929–33, bank failures were not uncommon. If a bank overextended itself in creating credit or if several of its important loans could not be repaid, depositors in the bank would frequently become panicky and begin to make large withdrawals—to make a run on the bank. Because the bank had only a fraction of its deposits backed by currency (fractional reserves as opposed to 100 percent reserves), the bank would soon be unable to meet withdrawals, and most depositors would lose their money. Most frequently a bank merely needed time to improve its cash position by calling in some of its loans and not making additional ones. In 1933

the number of bank failures reached a peak, forcing the federal government to intervene and close the banks temporarily. To help restore the public's confidence in banks and strengthen the banking community, Congress passed legislation setting up the Federal Deposit Insurance Corporation. This corporation, an agency of the federal government, now insures over 90 percent of all mutual savings and commercial bank deposits for up to $100,000 per deposit. The FDIC has built up its insurance fund by charging member institutions one-twelfth of 1 percent of their total deposits.

As a result of the protection provided by the FDIC and through other kinds of supervision, bank

failures have been reduced to a few isolated instances. When deposits are federally insured, people no longer rush to withdraw their money if they become concerned about the financial condition of their bank. The delay gives the banks the necessary time to adjust their cash credit balance, and this action helps to reduce the possibility of bankruptcy. For an example of the value of the FDIC, note that the failure in 1974 of the huge Franklin National Bank did not touch off a panic, and that depositors lost no money as Franklin was taken over by another bank. (Deposits in savings and loan associations are protected in a similar fashion by the Federal Savings and Loan Insurance Corporation. Deposits in credit unions are also insured. Some runs on thrifts occurred in 1985, but these institutions did not have federal deposit insurance.)

---

tion when the economy needs "cooling off," or it can use this power to encourage creation of more credit when the economy needs to be stimulated.

Let us see how the Federal Reserve enters the picture in the daily business of The Felix Bank. Suppose that one of our depositors writes a check for $10,000 to pay for merchandise for her store. She sends the check to the manufacturer, who is located in another city. The manufacturer deposits the check in his account at the Liberty Bank in his city. The Liberty Bank sends the check to the Federal Reserve Bank, thus increasing its reserve account by $10,000. On the Liberty Bank's balance sheet an additional $10,000 is entered on the assets side (in its reserve account) and an additional $10,000 on the liabilities side, because the $10,000 can be withdrawn by the manufacturer upon demand. Meanwhile, the Federal Reserve

Bank reduces the reserve account of The Felix Bank by $10,000. On our balance sheet we decrease the assets side by $10,000 and the liabilities side by the same amount—our reserve account has decreased by $10,000, but so too has the amount of our demand deposits. The balance sheet is now as follows:

Assets
Property	$260,000
Reserve account	$130,000

Liabilities and Net Worth
Capital stock	$300,000
Demand deposits	$90,000

The *legal* or *required* reserve of The Felix Bank is now only $9,000, which is 10 percent of our total demand deposits. (How much do we now have in excess reserves? What is the difference between the amount of excess reserves we now have and the amount we had before? Why is the decline in excess reserves less than the decline in demand deposits?)

In addition to noting what has happened to each bank involved in this simple transaction, give careful thought to what has happened to the commercial banking system as a whole. It is extremely important to realize that although one bank gained deposits and another lost deposits, there has been no loss of deposits for the system as a whole. Similarly, one bank gained reserves and another lost them, but for the system as a whole, there has been no loss. Even in the case of our bank, it is probable that our loss of the $10,000 will soon be balanced by a new deposit. The system is extremely dynamic. Deposits now flow from bank to bank in a never-ending circle. When the system as a whole gains or loses deposits, the economy is affected most importantly.

Creation of Money by the Entire Banking System

If we lend money to the limit permitted by our legal reserve, we risk having an adverse clearing balance (an overdraft) in our account with the Federal Reserve Bank. People with *derivative deposits* (deposits arising from loans we have made to our customers) usually write checks almost immediately on their deposits, far more often than those with *primary deposits* (deposits arising from cash). Thus we might find that our reserves have declined below the legal requirement, as checks drawn on our bank are presented for payment from our account with the Federal Reserve Bank.

The fear of having an adverse clearing balance limits a single bank to using its excess reserves. However, if the banking system is considered in its entirety, we can see that adverse clearing balances for some banks must be matched by favorable clearing balances for other banks. If more money is drawn on our account than we gain from checks deposited with us from other banks, we lose reserves. To understand what happens when the banking system creates money by expansion of demand deposits, let us follow an example through all the steps.

Creating Money by Deposits

Mr. Smith, our imaginary customer, arrives at the First Bank with $1,000 in cash, which he deposits in his checking account. The First Bank, whose demands for loans exceed its ability to grant them, now has additional money to work with. We assume that the Federal Reserve has set the legal reserves at 10 percent. The First Bank sees that Mr. Smith's deposit of $1000 was, at first, covered 100 percent by cash. Since it must keep only 10 percent in reserve, the First Bank realizes it now has $900 in "excess reserves" that it can lend out. The First Bank lends $900 to Mr. A and puts $100 in its reserve account with the Federal Reserve Bank in its district. Mr. A immediately writes a check on his derivative deposit to Mrs. B. Of course, the First Bank still has the $100 of required reserves against the $1,000 deposit liability to Mr. Smith. The bank has taken care of its legal reserve requirement and wants to lend out any excess reserves. (It is foolish to hold excess reserves, because they earn no interest whereas money loaned out does earn interest for the bank.)

Mrs. B deposits Mr. A's check in her own account at the Second Bank. With $900 in a new deposit, the Second Bank puts $90 (10 percent of $900) in reserve and lends the remaining $810 to Mr. C. Mr. C now pays Mrs. D the amount of $810, which Mrs. D deposits in her account in the Third Bank. The Third Bank puts $81 (10 percent of $810) in reserve and loans $729 to Mrs. E. Mrs. E pays the $729 to Mr. F.

Mr. F deposits Mrs. E's check in his account at the Fourth Bank. With the new deposit of $729, the Fourth Bank puts $72.90 in its reserve account at the Fed and loans the remaining $656.10.

This expansion process continues on through the banking system until all of Mr. Smith's $1,000 of currency ends up in the reserves of the banks involved. Through the banking system's process of granting loans, Mr. Smith's $1,000 has been expanded to $10,000 of deposits. (See Figure 14-1.)

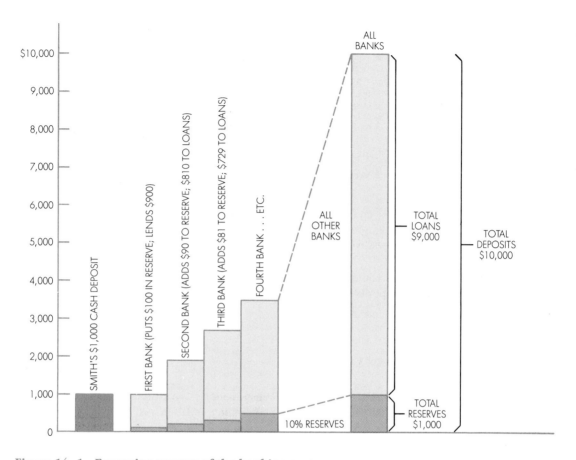

Figure 14–1   Expansion process of the banking system

Mr. Smith's new $1,000 deposit eventually serves as the support for $10,000 of
deposits ($9,000 loans and $1,000 reserves), with a 10-percent reserve
requirement. Note that the effects are cumulative. The bar for Second Bank
includes reserves and loans of First Bank, the bar for Third Bank includes
reserves and loans added by First and Second banks, etc.

We can see in Table 14–1 that, with a 10
percent legal reserve requirement, $1 of reserves
can support $10 of deposits or $9 of loans. Reserve
dollars are frequently called "high-powered" dollars because adding or subtracting reserve dollars
has the ultimate effect of increasing or decreasing
the deposits by many times the value of the reserve
dollars themselves.

You may wonder why the First Bank could
not take Mr. Smith's $1,000 deposit and add it to
its reserve account. In this way, the First Bank
could have expanded its loans to $10,000. This
would be acceptable if those who borrowed the

money left all of it in their accounts or if the First
Bank were the only bank in existence. However,
people who borrow money use it; when their checks
were deposited in other banks, the First Bank would
not have had the reserves or cash to make payments to the other banks.

You may also wonder why banks would create demand deposits, knowing that such deposits
are apt to be withdrawn quickly, and why they
would not want to keep more of those excess
reserves on hand. Remember that the system is
very dynamic. While Mr. A is withdrawing money
from his account at First Bank, Ms. Y is depos-

Table 14–1   An illustration of the creation of money by demand deposits

Banks	Deposits	Reserves (10%)	Loans
First	$ 1,000.00	$ 100.00	$ 900.00
Second	900.00	$ 90.00	810.00
Third	810.00	81.00	729.00
Fourth	729.00	72.90	656.10
All other banks together	6,561.00	656.10	5,904.90
Total	$10,000.00	$1,000.00	$9,000.00

iting money in her account there, and Mr. Z is putting money into a new account at First Bank. The bank need not be worried unless withdrawals consistently exceed deposits.

It is important to understand that the individual banks *cannot* expand their deposits ten times: each bank that lends money no longer has use of the funds. A bank's balance sheet would not show loans and investments larger than nine times its required reserves, or nine-tenths of its deposits. *It is the banking system as a whole that expands our money supply* through the use of demand deposits, as shown by the total in Table 14–1.

C   The Federal Reserve System

With the exception of the First Bank of the United States (1791), the Second Bank of the United States (1816) and the National Banking Acts of 1863 and 1864, our federal government concerned itself less with banking operations than did the governments of other industrial nations during the nineteenth century. This inactivity ended in 1913, when Congress passed the Federal Reserve Act. This legislation, later expanded, created the Federal Reserve System as the central banking institution of the United States. Its purpose: to provide currency, regulate the total amount of money in the economy according to need, and furnish other financial services needed by both public and private sectors of the economy. Our Federal Reserve System differs from the centralized banking systems of most other industrialized nations by being a relatively new institution, more decentralized, and not government-owned. Our nation's monetary policy is in the hands of a small group of appointed specialists who are responsible for serving the interests of the general public, rather than those of the stockholders of any single bank or group of banks, and who must at times act on behalf of the government. As we shall see, mon-

etary policy is an extremely important tool for controlling inflation and stimulating a lagging economy.

 A central bank deals mostly with other banks, extending loans to them, holding their reserves, and helping to supervise them. It usually serves as banker to the government and helps to control the nation's supply of money and credit.

Organization of the Reserve System

By the Federal Reserve Act, our country is divided into twelve districts, each with a Federal Reserve Bank located in one of the big cities in the district. Most of the districts have at least one additional Federal Reserve Bank branch. (See Figure 14–2.)

Federal Reserve Banks

Each Federal Reserve Bank is owned by its member banks. The member banks are required to buy stock in the Federal Reserve Bank but receive none of the powers associated with ownership of a private corporation. They get only a modest div-

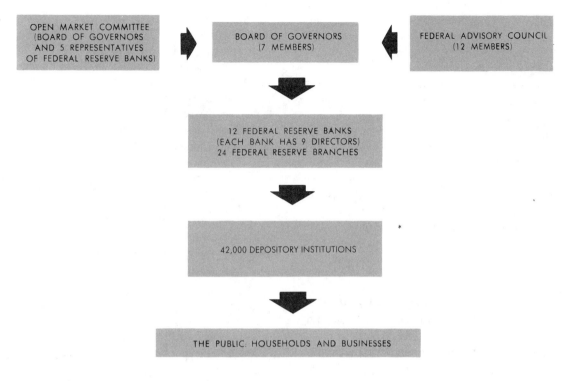

Figure 14-2   Organization of the Federal Reserve system
*Approximate figures, as of early 1986. (Authors' estimates.) (Source: Federal
Reserve System, Board of Governors.)

idend. It must be emphasized that Federal Reserve
banks are not profit-seeking. Money left over after
payment of dividends and operating expenses is
turned over to the U.S. Treasury. Each Federal
Reserve Bank has a board of nine directors, six
chosen by the member banks and three by the
Board of Governors. Only three of the nine directors may be bankers. Thus, the board is expected
to operate in the public's interest. The policy of
each Federal Reserve Bank must conform to the
general policy set by the Board of Governors.

Board of Governors

The final responsibility for the functioning and
policy making of the Federal Reserve System is
with the seven-member Board of Governors, which
oversees the entire system. Members of this Board
are appointed by the president and are confirmed
by the Senate for 14-year terms. These terms are
arranged so that a new appointment is made every

2 years, a provision that minimizes the influence
of pressure groups. Originally organized to coordinate the functions of Federal Reserve banks, the
board has gradually extended its influence over
the entire banking system. Its influence was greatly
increased by the Depository Institutions Deregulation and Monetary Control Act of 1980, which
required that all financial institutions—not just
member banks—post reserves with Federal Reserve
banks. Nonmembers were also given the right to
borrow from Federal Reserve banks.

Federal Open Market Committee

One of the most important functions of the Federal Reserve System is the buying and selling of
government securities. These activities are carried on by the twelve-member Federal Open Market Committee. Seven members of this committee
are the members of the Board of Governors, and
the other five are presidents of Federal Reserve

banks, always including the president of the Federal Reserve Bank of New York.

This committee meets frequently to determine policy on open-market operations, which influence our money supply. The committee gives specific instructions to its agent, the Federal Reserve Bank of New York, regarding the purchase and sale of government securities.

Federal Advisory Council

Each Federal Reserve Bank annually selects from its district some prominent commercial banker to serve on the Federal Advisory Council, which meets in Washington at least four times a year. This council was designed to present the views of bankers to the Board of Governors; its powers are purely advisory.

Member and Nonmember Banks

About 5,600 of the approximately 14,800 commercial banks in the United States were members of the Federal Reserve System in the mid-1980s. Nationally chartered banks are required to join; state-chartered banks may join if they choose to do so and meet certain standards. Member banks are required to comply with the numerous regulations of the Federal Reserve System, including one requiring periodic examinations by bank inspectors of the Federal Reserve. The Federal Reserve System also exerts a strong influence over nonmembers. As we have seen, all depository institutions must adhere to the Fed's reserve requirements.

Services of the Federal Reserve

The Federal Reserve System provides a wide range of services to banks throughout the country. Through these services its influence extends from the highest levels of government down to the local community. We shall examine the activities of the Federal Reserve to analyze how it determines and carries out particular policies.

Holding Reserves of Depository Institutions

The Federal Reserve Bank in each district holds on deposit the legal reserves of banks. Cash in the banks' vaults can also be counted toward these reserves. Any amount held on deposit above the legal reserves (that is, excess reserves) can be drawn on by the banks. Banks try to keep a balance between having sufficient reserves, to avoid falling below legal reserve requirements, and having too large excess reserves, which earn no interest. Many banks frequently borrow from one another to maintain this delicate balance.

 Reserves are the portion of a bank's deposits that must be set aside and may not be used to make loans. The minimum reserve is specified by law.

Providing Currency for Circulation

Currency in our country comes either from the United States Treasury or from the Federal Reserve banks. Federal Reserve notes make up most of our currency. Federal Reserve banks issue this currency to banks as they need it, simply subtracting the amount from the banks' reserve accounts. Although there is always a need for new currency to replace what wears out, public demand for currency increases sharply at certain times of the year, such as during the Christmas season. Federal Reserve banks keep a large supply of currency on hand so that banks can draw on their accounts as the new money is needed.

During February, when business activity normally declines and there is less need for currency, banks frequently find themselves with too much cash available. They then simply redeposit the surplus currency with the Federal Reserve Bank, just as their customers have done with them. This cash is then credited to their reserve accounts.

Providing a Clearinghouse for Checks

With more business being handled by check than by cash transactions, the process of clearing checks is staggering in its volume. Figure 14–3 shows the steps involved from the time a check is written in payment for merchandise until the time it is subtracted from the checking account of the buyer.

Many large cities have *clearinghouses,* where

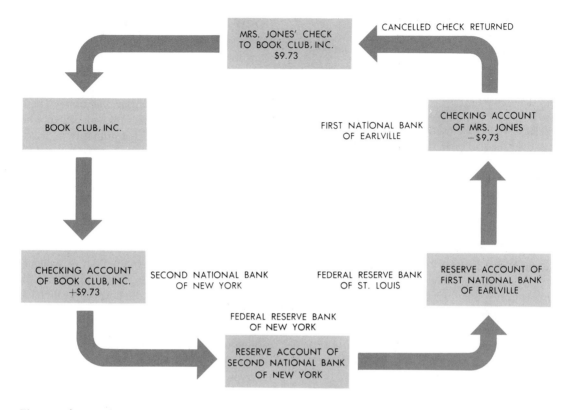

Figure 14–3   The route of a check
One of the services furnished to banks by the Federal Reserve System is the clearing of checks.

representatives of the commercial banks can meet to settle their accounts with other banks in the city. However, checks from out of the city are turned over to the Federal Reserve Bank for collection and crediting to banks' reserve accounts. In the future, electronic data-processing equipment will probably be used more widely to transfer funds, reducing costs and delays.

Serving as Fiscal Agent for the Federal Government

Because the United States Treasury has no bank of its own, the Federal Reserve serves as its fiscal agent. This activity involves keeping most of the government's accounts. Receipts from taxes, the sale of securities, and other collections as well as payments for salaries, redeemed securities, and other expenses are handled through the Federal Reserve System.

 A fiscal agent is a person or institution that handles the funds of another person or institution.

Supervising Member Banks

The authorities of Federal Reserve banks exercise wide supervision over member banks by means of detailed reports on the management, investments, loans, and other activities of the member banks. Periodic inspections, together with those made by the Federal Deposit Insurance Corporation and by the Comptroller of the Currency for national banks or examiners for state banks, help to protect the public, improve banking practices, and maintain the standards of nonmember banks.

Controlling the Supply of Money

The nation's economy is subject to fluctuations, and such fluctuations are accompanied by changes in the price level. There is a relation among the supply of money M, the price level P, and business activity T. As our nation's central bank, the Federal Reserve System exercises considerable influence over the size of M. Through its control over discount rates, open-market operations, and the reserve ratio, the Federal Reserve System can help in the effort to provide a full-employment, non-inflationary economy.

Discount Rate

We know that Federal Reserve banks provide a banking system for private banks. Banks use this system in two main ways—for depositing funds and for borrowing funds. When business firms face a shortage of funds, they go to commercial banks to borrow. When these banks are short of reserves, they can borrow from the Federal Reserve Bank.[4] The Federal Reserve Bank simply credits the commercial bank's reserve account with the amount of the loan.

The rate of interest that the Federal Reserve Bank charges banks for loans is called the *discount rate*. The Reserve Bank can raise or lower that rate with the approval of the Board of Governors. Raising the discount rate to banks will in turn tend to cause them to raise interest rates to their own customers. Lowering the discount rate will tend to allow banks to offer lower interest rates to their customers.

Banks hold highly marketable assets such as short-term U.S. securities. These are *secondary reserves,* and banks sometimes sell these securities to increase their reserves before borrowing from Federal Reserve banks. Although discount rates have a strong influence on all interest rates, they are relatively less effective when banks have large excess reserves or a great many liquid assets.

[4]In 1980 the privilege of borrowing from the Fed was extended to savings banks, savings and loan associations, credit unions, and nonmember commercial banks.

Open-Market Operations

The Federal Reserve System, acting as the fiscal agent for the federal government as well as the chief instrument for controlling the supply of money, buys and sells short-term government securities through *open-market operations*. These purchases and sales are made through dealers who represent investors interested primarily in Treasury bills (three- to six-month loans). Banks often hold such securities as secondary assets and frequently buy and sell them to adjust their own reserve positions.

When the Federal Open Market Committee orders the Federal Reserve Bank of New York, as the agent for the Federal Reserve System, to sell securities, this action has the effect of reducing the reserves of banks, thereby reducing their ability to lend money. Let us see how this result takes place.

The Federal Reserve Bank sells a dealer $1 million worth of these securities. The dealer pays for the bills by drawing a check on a bank. The reserves of the dealer's bank are reduced, and the bank's ability to grant additional loans is reduced. The dealer buys these bills for Company A, which has surplus cash that it does not plan to use for three months. Company A wants to earn interest on this surplus money rather than let it lie idle. To pay the dealer, Company A draws checks on the several banks with which it has accounts. Deposits and reserves are both reduced. Because each reserve dollar supports several times as many deposit dollars, banks are forced to restrict their credit expansion by several times the amount of the loss in reserves. When a bank buys Treasury bills, its reserves are reduced. Because its excess reserves are used up even faster, credit expansion is restricted to an even greater degree.

Suppose the situation is reversed and the Federal Reserve Bank is ordered to buy securities. Company B has Treasury bills it wants to sell. When its dealer sells these bills to the Federal Reserve Bank, Company B receives payment through a check drawn on the Federal Reserve Bank. Company B then deposits this check in its accounts at several banks. These banks then forward their checks to the Federal Reserve Bank for

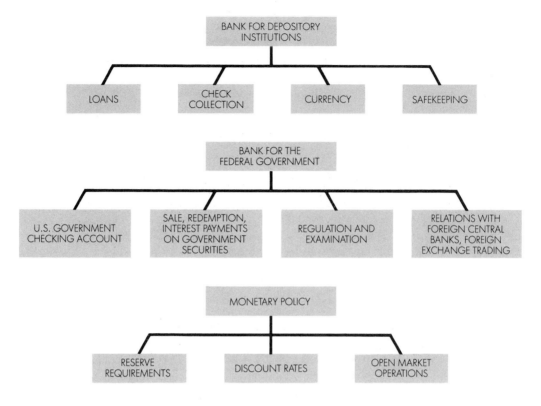

Figure 14–4   Functions of the Federal Reserve system
(Source: Federal Reserve Bank of New York.)

credit to their reserve accounts. Deposits and reserves are increased equally, and because one reserve dollar can support several deposit dollars, the banks now have excess reserves to use for loans. Each dollar added to the reserves allows commercial banks to loan several dollars, creating new demand deposits.

Open-market operations are the *most important* tool of the Federal Reserve System for expanding and contracting the money supply. Unlike the other tools, this one is used on a day-to-day basis and is very flexible.

Reserve Requirements

The Board of Governors of the Federal Reserve has the power to raise or lower the reserve requirements of banks within certain limits. Under the original Federal Reserve Act of 1913, specific

and inflexible reserve requirements were established (ranging from 5 percent for time deposits to 18 percent for demand deposits in member banks in cities classified as Central Reserve Cities). Congress lowered the requirements in 1917, but in 1935 took the very important step of permitting the Federal Reserve to vary the requirements within specified ranges. From time to time, these ranges were changed to enable the Federal Reserve to cope with current problems or in recognition of changing conditions in the economy. In 1972, a significant reform was made—a system of graduated reserve requirements on net demand deposits for all member banks was introduced. For example, in 1980, the reserve requirement was 7 percent on the first $2 million of demand deposits, plus 9.5 percent on the next $8 million, plus 11.75 percent on the next $90 million, plus 12.25 percent on the next $300 million, plus 16.25 percent on everything over $400 million.

Then the Depository Institutions Deregulation and Monetary Control Act of 1980 decreed that *all* depository institutions would be subject to the same reserve requirements. The act imposed a reserve requirement of 3 percent on the first $25 million, and from 8 to 14 percent on deposits in excess of $25 million. (The $25 million figure is to be adjusted each year.) Time deposits that are not transferable and are held by "natural" persons are not subject to reserve requirements. Time deposits that are transferable or are held by corporations or institutions (i.e., "nonpersonal" deposits) have a reserve requirement ranging from zero to 9 percent. This law is regarded as the most important banking act since the 1930s.[5]

Originally, reserve requirements were designed to promote the safety and liquidity of banks, but as many banks failed during the 1920s and 1930s, it became evident that reserves did not perform this function very well. In the event of a bank

[5]For details on reserve requirements and the reasons for changes in the system throughout their history, see "Reserve Requirements" in the April 1974 and May 1974 issues of the *Monthly Review* of the Federal Reserve Bank of Kansas City. For details on the 1980 law, see "The Depository Institutions Deregulation and Monetary Control Act of 1980," in the September/October 1980 issue of *Economic Perspectives* of the Federal Reserve Bank of Chicago.

Friedman and Monetarism

Although many U.S. economists are of the Keynesian school and believe that fiscal policy (such as changes in taxes and government spending) are important factors affecting business activity, there is also interest in and support for the *monetarist theories* of Professor Milton Friedman, formerly of the University of Chicago, and now at Stanford. (The monetarist position is sometimes called the *Chicago School*.) According to Dr. Friedman, the main determinant of employment, prices, and the level of output is the rate at which the Federal Reserve changes the nation's money supply.

The monetarist thesis is that (1) the actions of the Fed dominate the movements of the monetary base*, (2) movements of the monetary base dominate movements of the money supply over the course of the business cycle, and (3) accelerations or decelerations of the money supply are followed by accelerations or decelerations in economic activity. (The money supply is usually defined as currency in circulation plus checkable deposits. Friedman would add time deposits in commercial banks to this definition.) Severe inflations and depressions have been caused primarily by the failure to provide a stable monetary framework, according to Professor Friedman.

Arguing that open-market operations alone would be a sufficient tool for monetary policy, Friedman has proposed that the Fed abandon its practice of changing the discount rate and reserve requirements. The Federal Reserve would simply increase the stock of money at a fixed rate (between 3 percent and 5 percent a year), without regard to the business cycle. This would help to prevent large and rapid price fluctuations and ensure long-run stability in the dollar's purchasing power. If the economy began to slump, the automatic increase in the money supply would help to keep it moving; if inflation set in, the fact that the increase in the money supply was to be kept to a modest rate would help to restrain the rising prices. It would no longer be necessary to tinker with taxes and government spending or attempt to "fine-tune" the economy, and government interference with the free market would be held to a minimum.

*The *monetary base* is the sum of reserves held at the Fed and currency and coin outside the Federal Reserve and the U.S. Treasury. It has been about 38 percent of the size of M_1 in recent years.

failure, the bank's reserves would provide only a portion of the cash needed to protect its creditors. Obviously, because the law requires that a certain percentage of deposits be maintained, those deposits cannot be used to pay depositors. Thus reserve requirements are now seen as a device for controlling bank credit and the supply of money. For example, in 1938 the Fed used its new power to vary reserve requirements to reduce them in order to counter a contraction of credit in the economy and a business slump. Then, as the outbreak of World War II brought a threat of inflation, the Fed raised the reserve requirements to their ceiling levels.

Changing the reserve requirements can be a very powerful tool, and thus it must be done with caution. If the legal reserve requirement is 10 percent, $1 of reserves can support $10 of demand deposits. A 14-percent reserve reduces the number of dollars of demand deposits a reserve dollar will support to a ratio of 1:7. Banks that have plenty of excess reserves can readily adjust as the reserve requirement is raised. However, those banks whose reserves are low will be forced to borrow, to sell securities, or both, to meet the new requirements. If this action is taken when the discount rate is high and when the Reserve banks are not interested in purchasing securities in the open market (providing reserves to banks), the banks may face an economic crisis. These banks will have to curtail their lending operations; this effect is, of course, exactly what the Federal Reserve intends to achieve when it raises the reserve requirements. Reducing reserve requirements creates additional excess reserves, allowing banks to make additional loans. The ability to make more loans should result in an increase in the money supply.

Other Controls Used by the Federal Reserve

In addition to its three principal methods of controlling credit, the Federal Reserve has several minor methods it exercises from time to time. The major methods are aimed at control of the entire supply of money, whereas the minor methods are aimed at particular markets.

Margin Requirements

When people buy stock through a broker, they may pay a part of the purchase price and borrow the rest, using the stock as collateral. The percentage of the total price that must be paid at the time of purchase is called the *margin*. The Board of Governors of the Federal Reserve has the power to determine what the margin will be. When the margin requirement is set at 50 percent, buyers must pay half the amount of their stock purchase and may borrow the remainder. If the board decides there is danger of inflation due to excessive speculation on the exchanges, it may raise the margin requirement. The Board has the power to lower the margin requirement also.

Moral Suasion

The officers of the Federal Reserve banks have frequently tried to persuade bankers to follow policy recommendations by such means as face-to-face talks, letters, and releases to the press. The purpose of this *moral suasion* is to induce banks to be selective in increasing or decreasing credit when it appears that granting credit for certain types of loans might be harmful, although credit for other loans might not be. This technique for regulating credit has had only moderate success, and almost no success when banking has been very competitive.

Temporary Powers

When inflationary pressures have seemed particularly strong, as during World War II and the Korean conflict, Congress has given the Federal Reserve additional powers over credit in selected fields. Because durable goods, such as automobiles and appliances, were in extremely short supply during the war years, the Board of Governors was able to regulate the minimum down payment and limit the period for payment on such purchases. By increasing down payments and reducing the time for payment, they caused the demand for these goods to be reduced and the inflationary pressures to be lessened. As supply of these goods caught

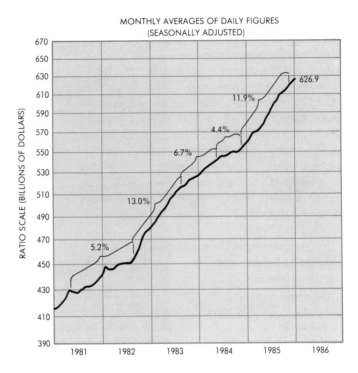

MONTHLY AVERAGES OF DAILY FIGURES
(SEASONALLY ADJUSTED)

Figure 14–5   Changes in the money supply (M_1)

As the economy has grown, so too has the nation's money supply (M_1). Note, however, that the rate of growth varies, and that at times the money supply has actually declined for short periods. The percentages shown are annual rates of change for the periods indicated. (Source: Federal Reserve Bank of St. Louis.)

up with demand, the regulations were allowed to lapse. A similar regulation in the early 1950s accomplished the same purpose in the real estate market.

The Federal Reserve and the Use of Monetary Policy

The most important purpose of the Federal Reserve System is to control the supply of money the nation needs in order to maintain an expanding economy with stable prices. Through the functions of the Federal Reserve, *monetary policy* can be adjusted to allow for the expansion or contraction of demand

deposits according to the needs of the economy. Thus inflation may be met by (1) an increase in the discount rate, (2) sale of securities in the open market by the Federal Reserve, and (3) an increase in the reserve requirements. When particular parts of the economy are severely affected, selective controls can be used. A deflation in the economy would call for the opposite type of monetary policy. The main controls over the supply of money involve changes in the reserves available to the banking system.

The monetary policies of the Federal Reserve System are designed to help control business cycles and promote the objective of a full-employment economy without inflation.

CONTROVERSY IN OUR TIMES

The Independence of the Federal Reserve

The role that a central bank should play has been a controversial issue since the early nineteenth century. Recall, for example, President Andrew Jackson's "war" on the Second Bank of the United States, an institution (chartered in 1816) that performed some of the functions of a central bank. Our current version of a central bank is the Federal Reserve System. The Federal Reserve System (the Fed) has almost always been involved in controversy. It is not owned or controlled by the federal government, but can act independently in setting monetary policy. It exerts a powerful influence over the nation's supply of money and credit. Some people fear this power and go so far as to propose that the Fed be abolished. Many others wish to retain the Fed but to give the president and/or the Congress greater influence over its policies. Others would like to see the Fed have even greater independence and power. The Federal Reserve was established by the Congress to act in the public interest. Should the federal government have more power over the Fed?

Pro

The president should have more power over the Federal Reserve. The fact that the Fed can act independently means that it can nullify actions taken by the administration. The president is elected by the people, to serve all the people. Although members of the Federal Reserve Board of Governors are appointed by the president, their staggered 14-year terms protect them from political pressures. They can ignore the wishes of the president, who is responsible to the people. If the administration were attempting to stimulate our economy during a recession, the Fed could weaken its actions by tightening up on the supply of money and credit. The reverse could also

occur—the Fed could pump money into the economy at a time when the administration's actions were designed to reduce aggregate demand in order to control inflation. At the very least, the president ought to have the power to appoint a new chairperson of the Fed at the start of the president's own term. This and other possible actions to reduce the Fed's independence could assure us of having only one coordinated economic policy at a given time.

Con

The independence of the Fed must be preserved. Actually, the Fed is not totally independent. It does pay attention to political trends, to the wishes of the administration, to the needs of the U.S. Treasury, and to the desires of the people. It often tries to coordinate its monetary policies with the fiscal policies of the administration. The fact that the Fed is able to counter administration politics is a positive factor, because such power enables the Fed to weaken unwise actions taken by a politically motivated president. For example, during an election year a president might try to win votes by overstimulating the economy through federal borrowing, spending, and tax cuts, thus risking inflation. The Fed could counter this action by tightening the supply of money and credit. Through their power of appointment, presidents can already place on the Board of Governors people who agree with their economic philosophies. Currently, the Fed can act very quickly when it spots an economic problem or trend that needs to be corrected. If it were under the thumb of the administration or the Congress, it would become embroiled in lengthy debates over the nature, seriousness, and possible cures for economic problems. Precious time would be

CONTROVERSY IN OUR TIMES

lost, and a small brush fire (such as a rise in the inflation rate) could turn into a conflagration.

Consensus

The Federal Reserve may have made mistakes at times, but it has also earned high praise from many economists. The administration often blames the Fed when things go wrong or when unpleasant medicine must be forced upon the public, and it is just as quick to take the credit when Federal Reserve actions work well. If the

Fed should ever abuse its powers, the Congress can change the laws pertaining to the Federal Reserve in particular and to our banking system in general. Conditions change over time (consider, for example, the growth of international banking), and the Fed's powers can be modified accordingly. Destroying the Fed altogether, or seriously reducing its powers, might bring back some of the problems that existed when we had no strong central bank.

D The Problem: How Effective Is Monetary Policy in Achieving Our Economic Goals?

In 1961, the Commission on Money and Credit, an independent research and policy group supported by several private foundations, issued a report on our nation's financial institutions. As you might expect, there was no agreement on how well our government's monetary policy works. Nevertheless, a consensus was reached on some issues. The report also produced some suggestions for improving our system and some new thinking about what monetary policy can and cannot do.

In presenting some of the arguments for and against the effectiveness of monetary policies, we are not looking for exact answers, because we do not have absolute standards for evaluating these policies. We realize that what may be the best answer in one case may not be in another. What we do hope to achieve by looking at both views is a better understanding of our entire monetary policy and its strengths and weaknesses.

Several qualifications must be made before presenting the two positions. So far we have ignored monetary policy on the international scene, particularly as it concerns balance of payments. Some fear that there is frequently a conflict between what is good monetary policy domestically and

what is good monetary policy internationally. We are also leaving the effect of *fiscal policy* (the use of government's taxing, spending, and borrowing powers to influence business activity and the economy as a whole) for consideration in Chapter 15. Because monetary and fiscal policy are very closely related, it is difficult to distinguish the effects of each one separately. If you will keep in mind that our objective here is limited to evaluating monetary policy, these limitations should not interfere with our partial analysis. You will find the arguments related to ideas discussed earlier in this unit.

Monetary Policy Is Effective

Many economists agree that economic policy should be aimed at a full-employment economy without inflation and with a rate of growth that will provide an increasing standard of living for all. Because money is significant in influencing price levels and business activity, monetary policy, by controlling the money supply, can help substantially in achieving these goals.

Monetary policy can be highly effective in stabilizing prices. By carefully watching and evaluating business conditions and price trends, the Federal Reserve can restrain inflationary and deflationary tendencies before they pose too serious a problem. Although the supply of money changes through the action of individuals—spending, saving, and borrowing—these actions in turn are greatly influenced by limits placed on the availability of money and the interest rates.

When the economy seems to be expanding too rapidly and too many dollars are pursuing too few goods, the Federal Reserve can limit the growth of M by raising the reserve requirements. Or, it can "soak up" money by selling government securities in the open market. Most often it will do the latter.

The result of such action is that demand for loanable funds will become greater than supply, thereby increasing interest rates and forcing some prospective borrowers to postpone their plans for investing or buying. As the amount of demand deposits created through loans is reduced, inflationary pressures can be relieved.

If the economy appears to be entering a recession, more money can be made available through the Federal Reserve's purchase of securities in the open market or through the reduction of reserve requirements. This increase in the supply of money will result in lower interest rates, thus encouraging the marginal borrower to carry out plans for investment or purchase. By encouraging the creation of additional demand deposits through making money available for loans and through reducing interest rates, monetary policy can help to reverse the deflationary tendency that may have developed.

If we assume little change in velocity (V), we can see from the equation of exchange ($MV = PT$) how changing the supply of money can affect both price levels and business transactions. Only if T increases at the same rate as M will P remain unchanged.

Policies that make money available to business firms and reduce interest rates will not in themselves make businesses borrow. Nevertheless, an easy-money policy creates an environment that encourages expansion. The lowering of the discount rate during the recessions of 1954, 1958, 1960, 1971, and 1975 was intended to counteract the slowing down of business activity. In contrast, a policy of tight money was used during the upswings from 1955 to 1957 and in 1959, 1968, 1973, and 1978 to moderate the tendency of business to expand too rapidly. The Fed's tight-money policies of 1981–82 helped to lower the rate of inflation. Using monetary policy to dampen business booms and to offset declines by stimulating business expansion may help us to achieve the economic objectives of full employment without inflation and adequate economic growth.

Finally, monetary policy has an advantage over fiscal policy in that it is much more flexible. When the Board of Governors of the Federal Reserve discovers a trend in the economy, it can act quickly to meet the changing conditions. It does not have to wait for long congressional debates, as is the case with fiscal policy decisions. Monetary policy can be altered quickly according to changing requirements and can be significant in creating economic stability.

Monetary Policy Is Not Effective

Some economists believe that monetary policies will not achieve the goals of our economy. In our economy, total demand includes consumers, government, and business. This aggregate demand determines the level of income of our nation. Monetary policy is primarily directed at business. Consumer spending and savings, except for real estate, are determined mainly by income and are little affected by small changes in interest rates. This is particularly true of installment buying. Government spending is likewise only rarely curtailed because of changing interest rates; moreover, such curtailments have occurred only in the case of state and local governments. Therefore, some conclude that monetary policy is effective only in controlling business investment.

The easy-money policy used to offset a recession is weak because business people do not borrow merely because money is available and interest rates are low. They borrow when they believe that they can earn money as a result of heightened expectations of profits. During a recession, when even existing facilities of a business are not being fully used, it is unrealistic to think that the business firms will add new facilities. The period of the Great Depression pointed out this weakness in monetary policy.

A tight-money policy can be more effective in combating inflation than an easy-money policy can be in dealing with a recession because it can actually "dry up" reserves. However, a tight-money policy also has serious weaknesses.

1. Since World War II, big businesses that are not in price-competitive industries have built up large surpluses of cash by not distributing the bulk of their profits in dividends. They have been able to finance much of their modernization and expansion programs out of these funds without turning to the banks. Interest rates or the availability of reserves has almost no influence on their plans. Even when they do have to borrow, monopolistic firms can pass the higher interest charges on to their customers. Small businesses in competitive industries are hard hit by tight money, and such a policy discriminates against them.[6]

2. Although the Federal Reserve is interested primarily in controlling the supply of money and will therefore effect an increase in interest rates to deal with inflation, the United States Treasury, which uses the Federal Reserve as its fiscal agent, is interested in borrowing money at a lower rate of interest. Although this conflict of interest is not always serious, it was during World War II and in the years immediately following. It could become a serious problem again.

3. Monetary policy is designed to curb a demand-pull inflation by restraining spending. Because a cost-push inflation arises from the supply side, reducing the reserves can actually aggravate the condition. This was illustrated in 1958, which was a year of recession as well as one in which the Consumer Price Index climbed. Tight money discouraged investment and economic expansion at a time when unemployment was growing. Some econo-

mists would argue that the recessions of 1970 and 1958 were similar and for almost the same reasons. And what should the Fed have done in 1974, when prices were soaring while the unemployment rate exceeded 7 percent and there was a decline in the nation's real output of goods and services? Many blamed the Fed's tight-money policies for the serious recession and high unemployment rates of 1981–82. (The Fed received some credit for bringing the rate of inflation down, however.) Some charge that in "curing" one problem the Fed creates others.

4. According to a relatively new theory—the *theory of rational expectations*—attempts to affect economic activity through fiscal and monetary policies will not work unless the policies come as a complete surprise to the public. But people have learned to anticipate actions by the government and the Federal Reserve and to act accordingly, thus offsetting the desired effects of the public policy actions. For example, if labor and management expect the Federal Reserve to take actions that will result in price increases, they will immediately try to raise their own wages and prices to protect themselves from the coming inflation. Thus, instead of bringing about an increase in the output of goods and services through the stimulus of increasing the nation's money supply, the Federal Reserve's actions will cause labor and management to raise wages and prices without a rise in output— and *this* will cause inflation.[7]

5. International factors can weaken the Federal Reserve's actions. Banking is a vast international business, and U.S. banks have many branches in other nations. U.S. banks have been able to obtain funds from the Eurodollar market, a vast pool of U.S. dollars on deposit in foreign banks. The Federal Reserve cannot control this huge worldwide network. On the

---

[6] Some industries are hurt more than others during a period of tight money. An example of a highly sensitive industry is housing construction.

[7] See Chapter 15 for a further discussion of the theory of rational expectations. For a more detailed account of the theory of rational expectations, see the 1977 *Annual Report* of the Federal Reserve Bank of Minneapolis, Minnesota, 55480 (free).

other hand, because the United States is an important world power, actions taken by the Federal Reserve can create problems for other nations. Some have blamed the Federal Reserve for the high interest rates in the United States, charging that these high rates attract money from abroad—money that some of those nations need for their own development. Thus, the Federal Reserve may hesitate to take an action domestically for fear that that action will antagonize our allies.

Considering an Answer

The debate on the effectiveness of monetary policy goes on. It is unlikely that it will ever be resolved; but in searching for answers, we learn more about the kinds of policies that can be used to realize our economic goals.

At this point you might well ask, "If the experts disagree, how can I expect to provide an answer?" Actually, because experts disagree over most of the important controversies, the final decision must be made by others—the citizens—through their support of programs and policies. Indications of broad popular support will generally influence government action and policy.

Consider, for example, the importance of a demand-pull inflation and the problem it continues to pose for the economy. Does making money more easily available at lower interest rates encourage investment? Does monetary policy play favorites, and if so, is this bad for the economy as a whole? These are a few of the questions that you should consider.

Chapter Highlights

1. There are many kinds of financial institutions. All are concerned with collecting money from sources that do not need it immediately and channeling it to potential users.

2. Savings institutions, personal trust companies, insurance companies, consumer credit agencies, investment banks, and commercial banks all serve a particular purpose in channeling funds. The government's influence over lending has become increasingly important.

3. Banks serve as depositories for valuables and as agencies for lending money.

4. The creation of demand deposits by banks is the most important source of money in our economy. Some of the banks' money must be kept in reserve to meet the reserve requirements of the Federal Reserve. Although banks invest some of their money in short-term securities—mainly U.S. Treasury bills—at low interest rates, they usually lend most of their money to businesses and individuals.

5. The Federal Deposit Insurance Corporation was created in 1933 to insure depositors against loss of their money in bank failures.

6. Although a single bank is limited in its ability to create demand deposits, the banking system as a whole can lend several times its reserves, the amount depending on the reserve requirements. A 10-percent reserve requirement (1:10) will allow demand deposits to expand to ten times the size of bank reserves.

7. The Federal Reserve System acts as the central bank for the United States. It is decentralized into twelve districts, each with a Federal Reserve Bank (located in an important city) and its own board of

directors. The entire system is coordinated by the seven-member Board of Governors.

8. The chief function of the Federal Reserve is to regulate the supply of money according to the needs of the economy.

9. The chief tools for controlling the volume of money are:
   (a) Discount rate—the rate of interest banks must pay when they borrow from the Federal Reserve Bank.
   (b) Open-market operations—the purchase and sale of securities, primarily short-term government notes, by the Federal Reserve Bank.
   (c) Reserve requirements—the amount of money banks must keep in reserve in relation to their demand deposits.

10. The Federal Reserve has also been given selective controls over specific markets, such as the purchase of stocks on margin.

11. Monetary policy is the adjustment on the money supply to help achieve our economic goals of full employment without inflation, stable prices, and economic growth.

12. Inflationary tendencies can be offset by reducing the supply of money through such measures as raising the discount rate, selling securities in the open market, or raising the reserve ratio. Recession may be offset by actions opposite to these.

13. There is considerable controversy over how effective monetary policy is in helping to achieve our economic goals.

14. International factors, such as the Eurodollar market, can affect monetary policy.

Study Aids

Key Terms and Names

savings bank
credit union
secondary reserves
legal reserve
discount rate
margin requirement
NOW account
demand deposits
promissory note
share drafts
personal trusts

commercial bank
time deposit
reserve ratio
balance sheet
derivative deposits
member bank
automatic transfer service
   (ATS)
excess reserves
clearinghouse

monetary policy
monetarism
fiscal policy
reserve requirement
tight-money policy
easy-money policy
theory of rational expectations
Eurodollar market
primary deposits
moral suasion

Federal Reserve System
Board of Governors
Depository Institutions
Deregulation and Monetary
Control Act of 1980

Advisory Council
FDIC

Federal Open Market
   Committee
Milton Friedman

Questions

1. What is meant by the statement "The banking system is the intermediary in regulating the flow of money"?
2. Commercial banks and savings banks carry on the major share of the banking in our country.
   (a) What differences exist between these two kinds of banks?
   (b) How does each strengthen the economy of a community?
3. Many economists feel that a system of controls over banks is necessary, even if every single bank is wisely, efficiently, and honestly managed. Why is this so?
4. Why could a district Federal Reserve Bank be called the "bankers' bank"?
5. Explain why banks are required to hold reserves.
6. How does the commercial banking *system* expand the nation's money supply? What is the role of the *individual* bank?
7. The Federal Reserve has a strong influence on our money supply.
   (a) Why are open-market operations called the most important tool of the Federal Reserve System?
   (b) Why are reserve requirements called the most powerful tool of the Federal Reserve System?
   (c) What are the weaknesses of the discount rate as a means of controlling our money supply?
8. Explain why the establishment of the FDIC has created confidence in our banking system among depositors.

Problems

1. Find in a local newspaper, or obtain from the bank at which you do business, a copy of a bank balance sheet. Evaluate the financial condition of the bank, making specific references to liquidity, reserves, loans, types of securities, and the reserve ratio. In what ways does this bank benefit the community?
2. Using graphs, charts, or tables, show how a change in the reserve requirement from 10 to 20 percent would affect an individual commercial bank, the commercial banking system, and the economy as a whole. Use imaginary deposit figures.
3. In the late 1970s nearly 300 foreign banking institutions were operating in the United States—nearly triple the number existing in 1972. Because they were not under Federal Reserve control, they were able to do many things that U.S. banks could not do, such as operate in more than one state. In August of 1978, Congress passed the International Banking Act, forcing these banks to obtain FDIC insurance, keep reserves at the Federal Reserve, and refrain from accepting deposits in new branches outside the state in which they initially operated. Note that many U.S. bankers said they *welcomed* the foreign banks, and many state banking officials were *opposed* to having them come under Federal Reserve supervision.
   (a) To what extent should the Fed control foreign banks operating in the United States?
   (b) Why did U.S. bankers often welcome these foreign banks?
   (c) Why did state banking officials oppose federal regulation of these foreign banks?
   (d) Is the growth of foreign banking in the United States good or bad for our economy?
4. The Federal Reserve is charged with the responsibility for controlling the nation's supply of money and credit, and it can act independently of the president. In December 1964, President Johnson called on the nation's banks to refrain from raising the interest rates on loans. The biggest banks acceded to his request.
   (a) Should they have done so?
   (b) Should the president be prevented by law from acting in this manner?
   (c) Should the Federal Reserve remain independent of the administration?
   (d) If policies clash (as when the Fed wants to tighten up on money but the president wants an easy-money situation), who should prevail?

5. In May 1974, Franklin National Bank, one of the nation's largest commercial banks, found itself in trouble. The bank had suffered large losses ($40 million) in its tradings in foreign exchange, and it announced that no dividends would be paid on either its common or its preferred stock. Within two weeks, the bank's deposits declined by 11 percent ($325 million), and the world of business and banking began to tremble. The sudden collapse of a German bank added to the confusion and worry. Was a bank panic about to begin? The Federal Reserve came forward with a massive rescue operation, arranging loans of over $1 billion for Franklin National. (Later in the year, Franklin National was taken over by European-American Bank. Depositors suffered no losses in the process.)

   (a) Is such action by the Fed justified?

   (b) Suppose that this action had added to total bank reserves at a time when the Fed was trying to control inflation. In such a situation would the Fed be justified in *not* aiding the bank?

6. Study the Depository Institutions Deregulation and Monetary Control Act of 1980. What factors led to the passage of this law? What are its major provisions? Explain each provision. How did the act change our banking system? Why is it considered the most important banking law since the 1930s?

7. In the spring of 1984 it was rumored that a huge bank, Continental Illinois Bank and Trust Company, was in serious trouble. Its depositors (including many foreign investors) began a run on this bank, withdrawing as much as $8 billion a day. Although bank deposits were insured by the FDIC for a maximum of $100,000, federal regulators decided to guarantee every depositor that every cent would be safe. All other general creditors of the bank were also fully protected against loss. In view of the fact that some smaller banks had been allowed to fail (four banks failed just a week earlier), many people criticized this action. Learn as much as you can about the Continental Illinois case (note that the bank was operating at a profit a year later), and discuss the wisdom and fairness of a policy that seemed to favor large banks over small banks.

PART

IV

Contemporary Problems of the U.S. Economy

Formulating Modern Economic Policy

In Parts One and Two, you became acquainted with the classical approach to economics. You learned what many of the tools of this system are, how they work in the marketplace, and how they answer the basic questions of economics. In Part Three, you were introduced to a different model, the Keynesian. You learned to use fiscal and monetary analyses in order to understand our economy better.

In the present chapter we will begin by looking at and in some cases, reviewing our economic goals and the monetary and fiscal tools used to try to achieve them. Underlying our theory is our model of the "ought-to-be world."

In Section C we will turn to the world that is—the performance of our economy in the 1980s. Here we will evaluate whether we have succeeded or failed in meeting our goals: Are the goals realistic or should they be changed? Have we failed in our analysis or in our application of existing tools?

We will then discuss the supply-side economics associated with the Reagan administration. Existing economic theory failed to explain the combination of stagnant growth and inflation that characterized the 1970s. If past solutions did not work, perhaps a new or modified variation of an old approach might be helpful.

In Section D we will examine a relatively new theory, rational expectations, which has already had some effect on economic policy and could have an even greater impact in the future.

Finally, in Section E we will look at what is currently the hottest issue in economics—the federal deficits and public debt—particularly as they affect you and the economy.

Chapter Objectives

When you have completed this chapter, you should be able to:

- Identify the major economic goals.
- Define and distinguish between discretionary and automatic stabilizers.
- Evaluate fiscal and monetary tools in light of our recent economic performance.
- Identify the exogenous and endogenous factors in our environment that bring into question the appropriateness of our goals and the ways we use our economic tools.
- Understand the approach of the supply-siders and what their critics have to say.
- Examine the theory of rational expectations to see what it may contribute to economic policy.
- Reevaluate the federal budget deficits and the public debt and explore what influence they might have on economic performance.

A   Our Nation's Economic Goals

Full Employment

Before the crisis of the 1930s, economists paid little attention to unemployment. Until that time, economic theory had assumed that unemployment was self-correcting and that any tampering with the automatic mechanism of the free market would do more harm than good. J. B. Say, a French economist who was an advocate of the laissez-faire school, formulated an economic theory stating that equilibrium would be achieved at the full-employment level because supply would create its own demand. His reasoning was seldom questioned. Any rise in unemployment was looked on as only a temporary condition. Past experience tended to support this theory, so there was little reason to question it. The attitude toward unemployment changed during the Great Depression of the 1930s, when unemployment rose from about 3 percent in 1929 to more than 24 percent in 1933. Although progress was made in reducing unemployment through the New Deal measures of President Franklin D. Roosevelt, mass unemployment

was a great national concern until the beginning of a war-time economy following our entry into World War II.

Employment Act of 1946

When World War II ended, the hopes of the American people for the future were high. Once again the economy was operating at a full-employment level. With the memory of the economic hardships of the 1930s still deeply implanted in their minds, the majority of the people were not willing to trust laissez-faire exclusively to determine the performance of the economy. Sharing this view, Congress passed the Employment Act of 1946. Although the act does not go so far as to commit the federal government to a full-employment economy, it does charge the government with taking steps to create an environment that will promote maximum employment.

Since the passage of the Employment Act of

1946, monetary and fiscal policy have been aimed at keeping the unemployment rate at 3 to 4 percent. It has been accepted that at that level anyone seeking a job can find one at the level he or she is trained for within a reasonable period of time. It also has been accepted that having 96 or 97 percent of the employment force working would not create so great an aggregate demand on prices or wages as to cause them to rise. In recent years, however, economic conditions have led to the Full Employment and Balanced Growth Act of 1978, better known as the Humphrey-Hawkins Act.

Unlike the older laws, the new act requires the president to set up specific goals annually, and it focuses on price stability, growth, and productivity, as well as the establishment of a target of unemployment of 4 percent for workers aged 16 to 19, and 3 percent for workers 20 years and older. The president is to set annual goals for five years ahead and the administrations' budget is expected to reflect those goals. The act also calls for the Federal Reserve Board to report its monetary goals to Congress twice a year so they may be considered in light of the president's budget. Most economists and policy makers consider the goal of maintaining unemployment at 3 to 4 percent unrealistic. The demographic factors explained in Section C suggest that the natural rate of unemployment, where inflationary pressures would begin, is probably about 6 percent.

Economic Growth

Our nation's wealth, whether measured totally or on a per capita basis, is impressive. This wealth has been due to the annual percentage increase in our GNP, in both constant dollars and per capita terms (divided by our population). From 1870 to World War II, that rate of growth was at about 3 percent per year. In the 1960s it averaged 4.2 percent; in the 1970s, 3.4 percent; and from 1980 to 1985, less than 2 percent.

Before the 1970s most economists accepted 3 percent as a reasonable goal for growth in the GNP. Such a level of growth would permit an economy to function at a full-employment level

without causing more inflation. Such an annual growth rate would permit expansion by enabling business to hire both those persons newly joining the work force and those workers who had been previously displaced by increases in productivity. Continued growth would then be assured by improvements in our technology resulting from new inventions and new methods of producing; the addition of capital goods such as machines, factories, and stores; and greater aggregate demand.

Price Stability

Not until the 1970s did the American people show a concern about inflation during peacetime. High prices were associated with wars, which caused a scarcity of civilian goods and an increase in aggregate demand. In the twenty years from 1950 to 1970, the only years in which prices increased more than 3 percent were 1951, 1957, 1968, and 1969. Only in 1957 were we free from war. The average rate of increase for the sixteen remaining years was only 1.4 percent. However, from 1974 to 1982 the average increase in the Consumer Price Index was 8.4 percent.

Although the Humphrey-Hawkins Act specifies as a national objective "reasonable price stability" and suggests the need to improve government policies to deal with inflation through a coordinated approach including the Federal Reserve System, it does not specify a target rate for price increases. A 3-percent rate, which might have been obtainable in 1972, appeared unrealistic in the early 1980s. However, three factors brought about disinflation—a drop in the rise in prices to only 3 to 4 percent from 1983 to 1985. First, the serious recessions of 1980 and 1982 reduced aggregate demand significantly, causing the inflation rate to drop from the double-digit rates of 1980 and 1981 to 6.1 percent in 1982. Second, the increasing value of our dollar in relation to most currencies of the world allowed us to import such foreign products as automobiles, clothing, and electronic equipment at bargain prices. Finally, the vigorous anti-inflationary actions taken by the Federal Reserve reduced borrowing demands by both business and consumers.

Productivity

So far we have confined ourselves to goals that are macroeconomic. But you will recall that we concentrated on microeconomics in Parts One and Two with the emphasis on efficiency. The problem of *How* to produce has as its aim maximizing output for fixed inputs. The ratio of output to input is called efficiency or, when expressed in output per work hour, *productivity.* Increasing efficiency is a microeconomic goal when applied to individual producing units. However, it becomes a macroeconomic goal when applied to the economy as a whole, as viewed from the perspective of a production possibility curve (see Section B in Chapter 1) showing what the national economy is capable of producing. Because national economic policy has a major bearing on productivity, both approaches must be used.

You will recall that in Chapter 7 (on labor) we mentioned that real wage increases, as contrasted to inflationary hikes, come about through increases in workers' productivity. If output per work hour increases at 3 percent per year, then, assuming we maintain our employment level, workers could have 3 percent wage increases without putting pressure on prices. Although fluctuations in other aspects of the economy may make annual increases of 3 percent very difficult to achieve, an annual average at this level over a five-year period is considered a desirable goal.

The 1978 act recognized the slowdown in productivity and emphasized the need for government policy that would encourage capital formation and increased investment in technology, which are the key elements for increasing output per work hour. In the 1983 Annual Report of the Council of Economic Advisers, increasing productivity was identified as an important approach to fighting inflation. Productivity in the business sector increased 3.6 percent the following year. We shall have more to say on this subject in Section C.

Other Goals

An assumption that has been and still is basic to our economic policy is that it is important to establish or maintain a competitive market. We already have shown that we have strayed far from our free market model in the form of administered prices and wages. Yet we have vacillated in how vigorously we enforce our antitrust laws. Since 1978 a spirited movement has been under way to increase competition, particularly in government-regulated industries such as the airlines and trucking. More important has been the increase in competition brought about by the expansion of international trade and the increase in the number of new businesses entering the market. Whether the recent merger movement, primarily involving conglomerates, will counter these trends cannot be judged at this point.

An important goal to many is the fair distribution of income. Just as it is important to have the national economy—the "pie"—grow bigger, it is also important that the pie, whatever its size, be divided in a way that society approves.

Many people would include as an objective having a highly decentralized market. Others might emphasize protecting weak economic groups, such as small business and the farmer. Maximizing the freedom of both consumer and producer would be placed high on many lists. Others would stress equal economic opportunities for everyone. There is also the goal of free trade among nations, which many economists, including Adam Smith, have urged (Chapter 18). A popular goal in the mid-1980s has been balancing the federal budget. This topic will be discussed in Section E.

 Economic goals may conflict with each other, requiring policy makers to set priorities.

The goals of economics are decided not by the economist but by society as a whole. Because economic goals involve value judgments and different goals may stress conflicting values, the citizens and the government in a democratic nation are responsible for determining what goals to pursue and what priority these objectives should have. When citizens, through their elected representatives, decide what goals to pursue, the economist can suggest the tools to use to achieve the objectives.

B The Keynesian Approach to Economic Policy

Having examined the broad objectives of our economy and some of the tools used to carry out fiscal and monetary policies, we are now ready to put these tools to work to achieve our economic objectives. Specifically, we want to determine how we can use the tools modern economics has developed to formulate fiscal and monetary policies that will provide full employment, satisfactory economic growth, and price stability without undue fluctuation in the business cycle. At times in this survey, reference to the review of the Keynesian model in Chapter 12 may be helpful. Meeting some of our other goals will be considered in Section C.

Discretionary and Automatic Stabilizers

The tools we have identified with monetary and fiscal policies are used to stabilize the economy; that is, they are designed to reverse the direction of the business cycle when the economy appears to be expanding or contracting too rapidly. Thus modern macro-economic policy is used to reduce the severity of the fluctuations in the business cycle by *countercyclical* (reversing the direction of the cycle) action. The tools by which this is accomplished are known as *stabilizers*.

Discretionary Stabilizers

Any economic tool used for countercyclical action on the decision of designated officials is known as a *discretionary stabilizer*. When several tools used to compensate for the economic fluctuations are brought into action by some governmental authority or authorities, the program is called *discretionary policy*. At present all our monetary tools, such as the discount rate and open-market operations, are discretionary because action must be initiated by the Board of Governors or the Open Market Committee. A tax cut is an example of a discretionary fiscal policy.

Automatic Stabilizers

Discretionary policy, if it is to work efficiently, depends on accurate forecasting. Taking appropriate countercyclical action to combat a predicted drop in business activity can be harmful if the forecast turns out to be wrong. Consider what would happen in a home without modern heating controls if, after all the fires were banked, a severe cold spell suddenly arrived instead of the predicted warm spell. In economics, automatic stabilizers are used to mitigate the difficulties of forecasting. *Automatic stabilizers* are tools that work against the cycle of their own accord without any action required of a public official, just as the thermostat of the modern heating unit in our home automatically maintains the temperature inside at the required level, regardless of changes in the temperature outside. One example of an automatic stabilizer is the federal income tax. When income rises, not only does the payment in dollars to the government go up, but also the ratio of payment to income rises. When income declines, tax payments are reduced in proportion even faster. This result occurs because the progressive feature of the income tax arranges personal incomes according to level, or bracket, each of which has its own tax rate. An upswing in business would cause people to pay higher taxes and curb some of their purchasing power. A downswing would result in smaller tax payments, leaving people with proportionately more money to spend. In a similar manner, unemployment insurance acts as an automatic stabilizer.

 Many economists consider the market to be the best automatic stabilizer.

Fiscal Policies and Their Effects

Modern fiscal policy calls for public spending and public taxation to help achieve the economic goals of full employment, economic growth, price sta-

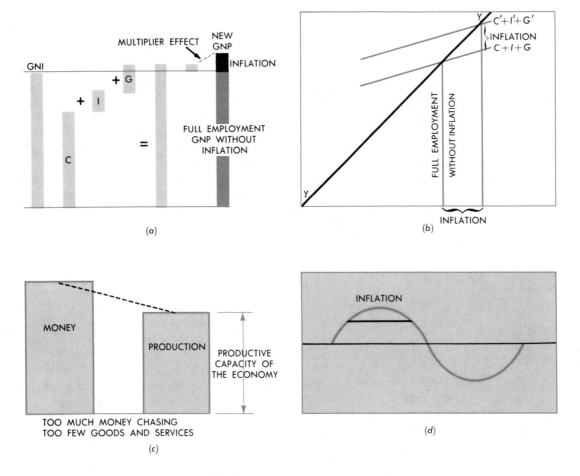

Figure 15–1   The economy in inflation

Several views of the economy in an inflation are shown here. In (a) and (b), the
models for income analysis (C + I + G = Y) show an aggregate demand
greater than the full-employment capacity of the economy. In (c), too much
money is chasing too few goods and services. In (d), the business cycle is shown
at an inflationary peak.

bility, and little cyclical fluctuation. Counter-cyclical action calls for inflations to be dealt with by budgets that will produce a government surplus and recessions to be treated through budgetary deficits. Government, as the largest single revenue receiver and spender in the nation, is thus in a strategic position to raise or lower aggregate demand in the economy. It can do this by altering tax rates, by changing its spending program, or by a combination of both methods. Figure 15–1 uses several models to show our economy in an

inflationary boom. Let us see what fiscal policy can do to reverse the cyclical trend.

Taxes as a Tool

When the government taxes the people, it decreases their disposable personal income and thereby also reduces personal consumption expenditures C. By increasing taxes, the government can reduce C even further. By decreasing taxes, it can increase C.

In Figure 15–1, we see that the aggregate

demand—consumption plus investment plus government spending $(C + I + G)$—is greater than what the economy can produce, resulting in an inflation. Modern fiscal policy calls for reducing aggregate demand to eliminate the inflationary forces. By increasing taxes and making sure there is no corresponding increase in investment or government spending, the government can decrease aggregate demand. On our models this effect is depicted as reducing C and keeping I and G the same, so that $C + I + G$ is equal to full employment without inflation.

Discretionary Tax Policy

When the government economists sense a strong inflationary trend, they may suggest that legislation be passed to increase taxes. Excise taxes may be raised on a large number of goods and services, or they may be specifically directed at those goods and services likely to be most in demand but short in supply. The personal income tax can be increased generally or selectively. If inflationary forces are very strong as a result of shortages in civilian goods, as they were during World War II, the rate increases might be placed on the lowest income group. These people tend to spend all their income, and therefore the tax effect of lowering personal consumption C would be maximized. People in the upper income groups save a substantial portion of their income; raising their taxes would probably reduce their savings more than their expenditures. A recession calls for policies opposite to those just described, in order to increase C. We must realize that in either situation good economics may have to give way to good politics in determining proper action.

Taxes can also be altered to change the size of business investment. Rarely (primarily only during a war period) are attempts made to discourage investment, because an increase in I usually results in an increase in supply, the productive capacity of the economy, as well as the demand side. I can be stimulated by allowing businesses to deduct their new investments from their gross profits (depreciation allowance) faster than previously. A reduction in the corporation income tax will also stimulate I.

Taxes as Stabilizers

Probably our most important automatic tax stabilizers are the progressive personal income tax and the corporation income tax. We have already seen that an increase in the national income will bring a proportionately larger increase in tax receipts without any action by Congress or the president. This has the effect of slowing down the increase in C and consequently decreasing aggregate demand. Similarly, a reduction in national income will bring about a proportionate reduction in tax receipts, with a smaller reduction in disposable personal income. If the difference between the lowest and highest tax rates in our personal income tax is reduced, the automatic stabilizing effect drops considerably (see Chapter 9). A single tax bracket or a flat tax would reduce the effect still further.

Some of our other tax programs also have a stabilizing effect. For example, during periods of low unemployment the taxes that support our unemployment compensation program flow into the reserve fund much faster than money is paid out. If the business cycle should reverse itself and unemployment increase, payments would be made faster than money would flow into the fund, thus creating a countercyclical effect. The same results occur in the case of social security payments.

Government Spending

Unless the taxing tool is used in conjunction with government spending, fiscal policy cannot be planned effectively. Raising C by means of a tax cut can be offset by reducing government spending G. Likewise, reducing C by means of a tax increase can reduce aggregate demand in the private sector. However, a corresponding increase in government spending will increase aggregate demand in the public sector and neutralize the overall effect. Although the methods cited will bring about a change in the allocation of resources between the public and private sectors, it is only through the creation of budgetary deficits and surpluses that we actually change the aggregate demand. Assuming that government revenue remains constant or nearly constant, let us see

"Annual income Twenty pounds, annual expenditure Nineteen Nineteen six, result happiness. Annual income Twenty pounds, annual expenditure Twenty pounds ought and six, result misery"—Mr. Micawber's advice to David Copperfield. Mr. Micawber's advice may still be appropriate for the family, but many would doubt its applicability to government. What is good for the family may not be good for the economy as a whole because savings, when not invested, can be a drag on the economy. If private enterprise does not invest these funds, then government may develop policy that will put them to work. What policy is best for any particular time may be highly controversial.

how government spending changes aggregate demand and modifies the business cycle.

Government Purchases

In Chapter 9 we saw that a very significant portion of government expenditure is used for the purchase of goods and services. Expenditures for defense, our space program, and a variety of public works projects involving the construction of highways, dams, and public parks are extremely important in meeting specific needs. They also are important in accounting for a significant part of aggregate demand.

Just as it is traditional to expect a government to prepare a budget listing the things it wishes to furnish its citizens, it is also characteristic of the Keynesian approach to think of government expenditures as a tool for regulating the aggregate demand in order to achieve full employment without inflation. During an inflation, modern fiscal policy might be aimed at trying to reduce government spending G. Under such circumstances, only the most important government projects would be approved, and an attempt would be made to cut all unnecessary spending out of the budget. A

recession would call for an increase in G. Those projects that would be delayed under an inflationary condition would now be started. Older projects already under way might be expanded. The purpose of the additional expenditures is not merely to secure additional goods and services for the nation but also to increase the G element with the intention of stimulating the economy.

Government spending G is somewhat slower in affecting the aggregate demand than are changes in taxes, because time is required to start government projects. And once the projects are under way, it is difficult to stop them, even if the economy has moved out of recession and toward inflation. Government programs do have an advantage over a tax cut, however, because they guarantee that the funds will be spent at least once. This tends to increase the multiplier effect. They also provide for direct employment and usually help the durable goods industries, which are often hardest hit by recessions.

Transfer Payments

In addition to the automatic stabilizers financed by specific taxes for certain transfer payments, such as social security and unemployment insurance, the government frequently provides money out of general tax funds for direct payments to groups that are hardest hit by a recession. Money is given to states to permit them, whenever their jobless rate remains high for an extended period, to increase the length of time during which unemployment compensation is paid. By the parity system, farmers receive payment from the government if they have huge crop surpluses. Grants and loans given to students provide opportunities to increase the skills of the working force as well as reduce the number of potentially unemployed workers that join the labor force each year.

Countercyclical Budgets

Preparing federal budgets with a view to countering the movement of the business cycle has gained much support among economists since the end of World War II. The prolonged upswing and the sharp increase in our economic growth rate following the tax cut of 1964 won over many people whose main concern previously was balancing the budget. The argument used to support passage of this tax cut was aimed partly at critics of this type of fiscal policy. Its adherents pointed out that only by increasing the tax base could we really hope to balance the budget. Reducing taxes would increase the national income sufficiently that the drop in the tax rate would be more than offset by the bigger incomes that would be taxed. Most economists agree that the tax cut accomplished what it was designed to do. The economic upswing was prolonged, the economic growth rate was bettered, government revenues were increased, and prices were kept reasonably stable. The unemployment rate was reduced to 3.7 percent by early 1966. With increased government spending for the Vietnam conflict, the problem concerning tax policy was reversed. The question then became, Should we increase taxes to reduce aggregate demand in order to avoid an inflation?

Most economists today reject the idea that a budget deficit is necessarily expansionary and will move the economy toward full employment. They argue that deficits resulting from a sluggish economy that reduces government revenue to below government expenditure would actually produce

a budget surplus before the level of full employment was reached. They reason that as the GNP increases, tax collections rise even faster, and so the budget would be balanced at some GNP level below full employment. A budget surplus before full employment was reached would start the contracting effect.

In order to evaluate the government's fiscal policy—that is, whether the budget will be inflationary or deflationary (stimulate expansion or contraction)—the full-employment budget concept is used. The economist asks: If the economy were to operate at a full-employment level throughout the year, would the federal budget produce a surplus or a deficit? As pointed out previously, this approach was used successfully in 1964–65.

 Fiscal policy can take many forms, with different consequences for different economic groups.

Problems in Fiscal Policy

To achieve the desired effect, fiscal policy must be correctly timed. Applying economic tools too soon may convert a newly begun upswing into a recession. Applying the tools very late, which is more likely to happen, reduces some of the effectiveness of the policy and may cause an inflation.

It is very difficult to take the appropriate action at precisely the right time. It is difficult to predict the course of business activity. Because the various parts of our economy do not move in the same direction simultaneously, determining the best indicators (see Chapter 11) is extremely difficult.

Political considerations are significant in slowing down the initiation of appropriate fiscal policy. If taxes are to be raised, what taxes should be selected for change? Congressional representatives must consider which of their constituents will raise the greatest objections, as well as which tax would be best for the economy. If an increase in expenditure is called for, which state or congressional district will be most favored with appropriations? Historically, Congress has tended to act very slowly in response to economic changes; when it has finally acted, the action has frequently been too late or too little to be effective.

Fiscal activities of state and local governments tend to reinforce the trend of the business cycle. When the cycle moves upward, their incomes increase and so do their expenditures. Falling incomes reduce their revenues, and they respond by cutting their budgets. Raising taxes during recessions and lowering them during inflation is quite common and only aggravates the unfavorable condition. During the deep recession of 1982, cities and states tried to hold down their expenditures, frequently doing so by reducing the number of public employees. Such actions only aggravated the downturn. Constitutional and statutory requirements for balanced budgets sometimes cause governments to act in this way.

Appropriations for defense constitute, directly and indirectly, a significant portion of our federal budget. Unfortunately for the economy, our defense requirements are not necessarily countercyclical to our business activity, and thus efforts to avoid economic fluctuations may be hampered.

Inflationary forces of the cost-push type result from the efforts of pressure groups trying, rightly or wrongly, to improve their relative economic position. Such inflationary forces are somewhat immune from the stabilizers we have mentioned. Pressures from the president or from public opinion have provided some restraint in the past, but we have no assurance that this informal method will be successful in the future. Having the Council of Economic Advisers announce the percentage increase in productivity for the previous year and ask businesses to use this figure as a guide for wage negotiations may lessen the effect of the cost-push type of inflation—if their advice is followed, that is.

Monetary Policies and Their Effects

Modern economic policy calls for the use of monetary policy as well as fiscal policy to achieve our economic goals. Through control of the supply of money and of interest rates, the aggregate demand can be influenced to move upward or downward so as to create greater economic stability. In (a) and (b) of Figure 15–1, the $C + I + G$ must be reduced, and in (c) the supply of money must be contracted. Monetary policy works primarily on investment I, and so our discussion will begin with policy that mainly influences the size of I.

The Federal Reserve can increase or decrease the supply of money M by its open-market operations and by changing discount rates and reserve requirements. Interest rates are determined by the supply and demand for loanable funds. Through the combined use of these tools, monetary policy can be used to influence the size of I. Paul Volcker, Chairman of the Federal Reserve Board of Governors, showed the power of the Fed in helping to bring down the inflationary rate in the early 1980s.

Effects on Investment (I)

If the economy appears to be entering an inflationary spiral, the Board of Governors of the Federal Reserve will decide to take appropriate action. They will call together the Open Market Committee and give instructions to the Federal Reserve Bank in New York to sell government securities in order to reduce the excess reserves of the member banks. This action will limit the money that member banks have for the granting of loans. The board may also decide to raise the discount rate to discourage member banks from borrowing from the Federal Reserve banks. The board probably will delay changing the reserve requirements, hoping that the course of action already outlined will be enough to tighten credit and stop the increase in prices. The fact that they need to initiate action shows that monetary policy is discretionary rather than automatic.

As the supply of M is reduced, the supply curve shifts to the left, increasing the interest rate. Increasing the discount rate will also raise interest rates. Because business will borrow only when they think they can earn more on what they have borrowed than what they must pay in interest, those with a low marginal productivity for loanable funds (those who expect to make little on what they borrow) will postpone borrowing. Figure 15–2 shows how higher interest will reduce I.

To combat a recession, an opposite action would be taken. The discount rate might be lowered, the Federal Reserve Bank might buy secu-

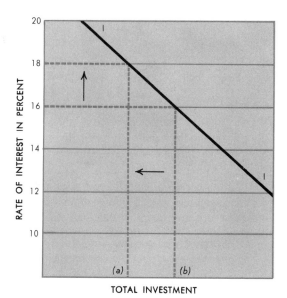

Figure 15–2 Controlling business fluctuations through changing interest rates

Increasing the interest rate (↑) reduces investment (←) from (*b*) to (*a*), lowering aggregate demand and reducing inflationary tendencies. Reduction of interest rates can be used to increase investment and fight recessions. Until recently lowering interest rates was considered more controversial than increasing them.

rities, and the reserve requirements might be lowered. The increased supply of *M* would lower interest rates, and investments would, as a result, increase from (*a*) to (*b*) in the model shown in Figure 15–2.

The example we have used here assumes investment is generally responsive to interest rates. Most economists do not accept this principle for low interest rates when the economy is functioning in low gear. (Their objections to this theory were presented in Chapter 12.)

Effects on Consumers (*C*)

As pointed out earlier, interest rates influence consumer expenditures for durable goods. Those high-priced items that most households purchase by borrowing are most affected. High interest rates lower sales of homes, cars, and appliances. When buying durable goods that require monthly pay-

ments, consumers view lower interest rates as merchandise on sale.

Evaluation of Monetary Policy

Monetary policy is more effective in controlling booms than in controlling recessions, because demand-pull inflation can be curbed by restricting the supply of loanable funds. In a recession the supply of *M* may be increased and interest rates lowered, but there is no way of forcing business firms to invest. The old cliché "You can lead a horse to water but you can't make him drink" describes the problem monetary policy faces in dealing with a contracting economy.

Monetary policy is far more flexible than discretionary fiscal policy and can be changed more quickly, although there is usually a time lag before the new credit policy takes effect. People who look with the most favor on monetary policy as an instrument for control point out that it is neutral in that it does not discriminate against any particular borrower. Critics disagree with this argu-

Source: Tom Darcy, *Newsday.*

ment. They point out that the large, well-established corporations supply the funds for their own financing by using their undistributed profits or by issuing new stock, so small and expanding companies that must finance expansion by bank loans are hardest hit when credit controls are tightened.

 Monetary policy is likely to be more neutral and flexible than fiscal policy.

Another argument against the use of policies affecting the long-term growth rate of the economy is that tightening credit may discourage investment in capital goods. Increasing capital

goods should increase the productive capacity of the economy. Although it may be temporarily desirable to reduce inflationary pressures by reducing M, we may also be slowing down the long-range growth potential of the production side. Such an effect would be undesirable.

In addition, some industries that depend heavily on credit are hit far harder by a tight-money policy than are others. The housing industry suffered one of its sharpest setbacks in 1980 to 1982 as a result of high interest rates and the decline of money in savings institutions that do most of their business providing loans for home mortgages.

C Performance: An Evaluation of Our Models

At this stage in your study it appears as if the economist has developed a clear-cut course of action for fighting inflation or recession. Unfortunately, the world that is turns out to be far more complex than the world that ought to be. In 1965 the economist appeared to be "king of the hill." By the 1980s the public was questioning whether the economist had any solutions for a world caught up in a severe recession on the one hand and rampant inflation on the other.

A quick look at the performance of our economy in both periods as well as our economic goals shows the magnitude of the problems.

	1964–66	Goals	1980–82
Average unemployment	4.5%	4%	8.1%
Average economic growth	5.5	3	0
Average price rise	2%	3%	10.0%

During the 1964–66 period we exceeded two out of our three major goals and were close to our target for unemployment. In the early 1980s we missed all our targets by a wide margin. The country had a combination of recession and infla-

tion, frequently called *stagflation,* similar to that of the period 1974–75. Professor A. W. Phillips of the London School of Economics and many other economists felt there was a clear trade-off between unemployment rates and wage rates. Indeed, Phillips showed that relationship in Great Britain from 1861 to 1957. Figure 15–3 shows a similar curve for the United States for the period 1953 to 1964.[1] However, Figure 15–3 also shows points for more recent years. The new, less regular curve reflects shifts upward and to the right. Note that the points for 1975, 1980, and 1982 are significantly out of the trend line. This deviation can be explained in part by the sudden impact of the two sharp increases in the price of petroleum for the two earlier years and the serious recession and disinflation that many economists feel was brought on by the extreme anti-inflationary monetary policy taken by the Fed. Is the idea of a trade-off between unemployment rates and inflation (or wage rates) faulty or is there some reason why it has not occurred? Consider the impact of the following factors, which are largely exogenous.

---

[1]Percentage increase in prices is substituted for wage rates because it is a better measure of inflation.

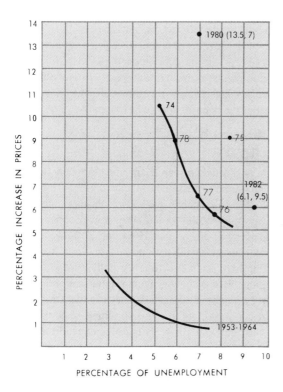

Figure 15–3 The Phillips curve

The trade-off between unemployment and prices between 1953 to 1964 is quite easily seen. There is little doubt that the curve shifted to the right in the 1970s. For example, note that in the earlier period we could expect to have an inflation rate of only 1 percent with an unemployment rate of 6 percent (6 on the horizontal axis; 1 on the vertical). During the 1970s, however, we would have 9 percent rate of inflation with the 6 percent unemployment rate.

Inflationary Factors

Most economic historians place the beginning of The Great Inflation with President Lyndon Johnson's attempt to fight the war against poverty at the same time he was escalating the war in Vietnam. President Johnson merely assumed that there was enough slack in the economy with new technology, capital investment, and workers to increase our aggregate supply. The inflationary rate averaged 1.24 percent from 1960 to 1964. From 1965 to 1969 it rose every year, starting with 1.7 percent and ending at 5.4 percent. The inflation rate fell below 5.4 percent only twice in the 1970s.

From 1972 to 1974, a drought caused a worldwide shortage of food. Prices on food rose nearly 40 percent in the United States during this period and more than that in many other countries. More dramatic was the beginning of the oil embargo in 1973–74 by the Organization of Petroleum Export Countries. Some economists estimated that higher oil prices added approximately 3 percent to the wholesale price index. Later, in 1978–79, the Iranian Crisis caused energy prices to double in just two years. The cost of energy rose 240 percent from 1973 to 1981, when an oil glut finally caused energy prices to stabilize. For countries that had to import all their oil, the price shock was even greater. The increase in energy prices may be viewed as cost-push inflation (Chapter 13).

Demographic Factors

In the decade of the 1960s, 11.1 million people were added to the labor force. However, the 1970s saw the work force swell by 22.2 million. This figure does not include the very large but unknown number of illegal aliens who came into this country, usually to work for wages below the minimum set by law. How does this factor affect inflation?

In the 1960s an economic growth rate of nearly 4.5 percent would have been required to create the additional 1.05 million jobs needed annually to achieve a national goal of full employment, i.e., 96 percent of our labor force working. In the 1970s 2.1 million jobs would need to have been created to achieve full employment, requiring a growth rate of nearly 9 percent. Yet the economy expanded at less than 3 percent. For the first part of 1980, the figures were even gloomier.

As we saw in our study of Keynesian analysis, an economy operating below full employment should use monetary and fiscal policies to stimulate aggregate demand in order to achieve a full-employment level of aggregate income. According to Keynesian theory, such measures should not result in inflation so long as there is unused capacity to produce, e.g., idle or only partially used plants and unemployed workers seeking jobs.

During the 1970s the accumulated deficit of the federal government amounted to $451.2 billion, surely as large a stimulus as fiscal advocates would suggest. To satisfy the monetary advocates, the money stock, M_1, increased at an annual rate of 6.6 percent. Real interest rates, the prime rate minus inflation, were very low, less than 2 percent. These stimulants, both fiscal and monetary, should have provided sufficient aggregate demand for the United States to reach full employment in normal times. However, the annual growth in the labor force outran the growth in the economy. Why?

Declining Productivity

Output per work hour is the measurement used to determine productivity. If we can increase output with the same amount of input or reduce input and achieve the same output, we increase productivity. Increasing our productivity over the years has been a major factor in raising our standard of living. U.S. productivity gains were the envy of the rest of the world until they began to slow down in the 1970s. From 1946 to 1967, output per hour increased in the private business economy an average of 3.2 percent. From 1973 to 1982 it not only dropped to below 1 percent but was lower than that of many other industrialized countries. With the labor force growing and productivity remaining almost stagnant, it was not surprising that real earnings (what wages would buy) of non-agricultural workers actually declined from 1973 to 1982 by 16 percent.

There are five major factors that account for our nation's poor performance: (1) increasing government regulation and the cost of compliance, (2) inadequate investment in research and development, (3) insufficient capital formation to provide better tools and plants for our workers, (4) the entry into the work force of large numbers of inexperienced workers in the 1970s and (5) the huge increase in the price of energy.

Government Regulation

The effects of government regulations designed to reduce pollution, increase safety, and protect minorities from job discrimination are not included in our GNP. Although most people would agree with the desired social outcomes of these regulations, the cost of compliance has been estimated to be in the neighborhood of $100 billion. All studies show that regulation is costly, but most policy makers now recommend that in designing rules the benefits should be compared to the costs.

Research and Development (R&D)

It is through research and development that we get our new ideas on how to increase productivity. In 1964 we spent 4 percent of our total output on R&D. Spending for R&D has now dropped to 2.7 percent of our output. However, not only has the percentage of GNP in new technology dropped, but there is also a difference in the type of investment. Because of stringent regulations and a poor return on investment, industry is concentrating its research dollars in low-risk, small-scale projects with quick payoffs. Therefore, expenditures for basic research, measured in constant dollars, have actually declined since 1968.

Although recent budgets have shown an increase in R&D expenditures, most of these expenditures are for defense research. Our non-defense R&D expenditures are less than those of Japan and West Germany. The U.S. leadership in technology is being seriously threatened.

Capital Formation

Research and development provides the ideas, but capital formation—new machines, factories, and so forth—translates those ideas into practice. The U.S. record in this area, so important for increasing productivity, is dismal by almost any standard.

The growth rate of the ratio of our capital investment to our labor force was 3 percent from 1947 to 1967. From 1974 to 1983 it dropped to 1 percent.

Recently there has been some improvement in investment, following changes in our tax laws.[2] Changes such as lowering corporation taxes and allowing businesses to depreciate their investment in new capital have stimulated new investment.

---

[2]The tax bill debated in Congress in mid-1986 favored depreciation benefits for high-tech industries but not for heavy industries such as steel.

Less Experienced Workers

From the middle of the 1960s until the mid-1980s, the swell of new job entrants into the labor force changed the composition of the work force. The Council of Economic Advisers calculated that these young and inexperienced workers reduced the annual rate of growth by about 0.35 percent. The decline of our birth rate in the 1960s, resulting in the entry of fewer young workers into the job market in the mid-1980s, and the accumulation of experience by earlier entrants, including women, have started to reverse this trend.

Unemployment

There are four basic types of unemployment: frictional, seasonal, cyclical, and structural. *Frictional* unemployment causes the least problems and may even be looked upon favorably by economists. It is the ever-present movement of workers from one job to another. It results from the facts that some people are retiring while others are moving into the labor force, that some industries are declining while others are expanding, that some people are being promoted and others are replacing them. It is the sign of a dynamic economy responding to normal changes.

Seasonal unemployment is a way of life for many workers. Construction workers in the North, sales clerks, and resort workers are subject to changes in employment demand. *Cyclical* unemployment corresponds closely to the rise and fall of the business cycle. As we have seen, we can try to stabilize the economy with an economic growth rate that will allow us to adjust to changes in the size of the labor force by using fiscal and monetary policies to reduce unemployment.

The most serious problem in our time is *structural* unemployment. This type of unemployment results from changes in the demand for certain types of labor in the economy. Such changes are caused by the introduction of labor-saving machines, the importation of more competitive foreign goods, the decline of certain industries or changes in consumer preferences.

The unemployment rate during the latter part of 1982 averaged over 10 percent. However, the unemployment rate for unskilled and semiskilled workers was more than double that rate. At the same time there were serious shortages of computer specialists, nurses, engineers, and some types of teachers. What happens if monetary and fiscal policies are used to stimulate the economy and jobs? Additional upward pressure is put on wages in labor markets where shortages exist, and there is little noticeable reduction in the unemployment rates in markets with labor surpluses.

What is the effect on wage rates of having many labor markets? In markets where employment is high, wages will rise. But will wages decrease in markets experiencing high unemployment rates? The classical economist would expect a decline in wages to stimulate employment. We have noted, however, that wages tend to be sticky in a downward direction. The general wage rate is thus likely to increase without any significant increase in employment. Unless our labor force can be trained in broad skills that will permit workers to shift from declining to expanding markets quickly, unemployment is likely to remain high.

Price Increases in Energy

As we observed in Chapter 8, the price of oil escalated in the 1970s, with subsequent increases in the price of other forms of energy such as natural gas and coal. Because energy is needed in almost all production including services (for example, to heat offices and run cars), the basic cost had to be passed on to the consumer. The impact, a cost-push inflator, rippled throughout the economy. The supply curve shifted to the left. The first shock wave hit in the mid-1970s, and the second wave followed in the early 1980s.

With higher energy prices and many new workers entering the labor force, many businesses found it cheaper to employ more labor than to buy new machines. This shifted our capital-labor ratio. These factors contributed significantly to the slowdown in productivity. Many other mature industrial nations that had to import almost all their energy found their productivity increases sliding even more than that of the United States. The sharp decline in oil prices in 1986 should shift the supply curve to the right somewhat and help stimulate productivity gains.

Global Perspective

With the exception of Japan, other industrial countries are having an even more difficult time trying to achieve their economic goals. Some have experimented with our new approaches. Margaret Thatcher has pushed the supply-side approach, as has Canada. France, under socialist president Francois Mitterrand, has lessened government involvement, as has Germany. But what has been the result? Using data from the Organization of Economic Co-operation, economists at the Morgan Guaranty Trust Company estimated that the gap between what nations could produce and what they did produce in 1985 was approximately $500 billion.[3] Although the United States was responsible for 40 percent of this total, the gap was actually larger in Germany, France, and the United Kingdom. Canada's unemployment rate was higher than ours, and even Japan's performance was sluggish compared to that of a few years ago. Europe's

[3]Reported in *Newsweek*, January 27, 1986, p. 47.

poor economic performance has been attributed to high wages and the exporting of capital to the United States because of high interest rates. In Japan, high consumer savings has placed a slight damper on its growth.

Success or Failure?

The preceding review of the U.S. economy's performance in the 1970s and 1980s seems to indicate failure. Not only did we not meet our goals for full employment, economic growth, price stability, and productivity, but our performance was less impressive than it had been in the 1960s. Was our failure due to poor policy decisions or inadequate tools? Did we misinterpret the data, not have enough data, or use poor timing in applying appropriate action? Have changes in our environment been so significant as to make our economic goals unrealistic? Do we need a new model to explain our performance, and, if so, do we need new tools to better achieve our objectives?

D | Reaganomics: Supply-Side and Rational Expectations

The economic problems of the 1970s, particularly the combination of recession and inflation, seemed to defy existing economic theories and solutions. To explain recent developments, a set of economic principles emerged which came to be known as supply-side economics. During the political campaign of 1980 and after his election, President Reagan made supply-side economics a topic of conversation. Because of the partisan nature of the controversy, the collection of economic ideas and specific legislative proposals is sometimes called "Reaganomics."

Two Views of Supply-Side Economics

Classical and Keynesian economists have different views of aggregate demand and aggregate supply; these views are illustrated in Figures 15–4

and 15–5. You will recall that the classical economist believed in Say's law, that supply creates its own demand. Therefore, if the forces of demand and supply are allowed to work, aggregate income will reach an equilibrium level at full employment without inflation, Y_{FE}. Aggregate income may also be called output or aggregate supply. Figure 15–4 shows the classical view, in which aggregate supply, *AS*, is a vertical line at the full-employment level of output (income). This is true only in the short run, since improved technology and more labor will move the *AS* line to the right. Where aggregate demand, *AD*, crosses aggregate supply, *AS*, is the equilibrium level for price, P_e. If the price were at P_1, causing output to be less than Y_{FE}, flexible wages and prices would soon bring the economy back to equilibrium. Conversely, if prices were temporarily too low, at P_2, the market would soon make the necessary corrections, pushing wages and prices to P_e.

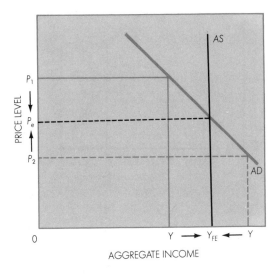

Figure 15–4   The classical view of aggregate demand and supply

The classical economist believes that in the short run, aggregate supply, *AS*, is inelastic and at full employment, Y_{FE}. The price level will be at equilibrium, P_e, where *AS* and *AD* meet. If prices rise to P_1, surplus labor will cause wages to decline, stimulating new jobs. *Y* will shift to the right, reaching Y_{FE}, and prices will return to P_e. Lower prices will create a shortage of labor, pushing wage rates up and causing prices to return to P_e.

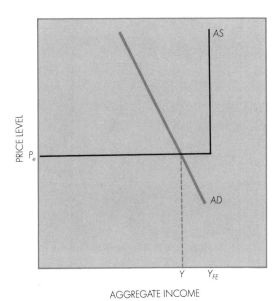

Figure 15–5   The Keynesian view of aggregate demand and supply

Keynesians believe that equilibrium will tend to be below full employment output, *Y*, rather than at Y_{FE}. Since wages and prices tend to be sticky below full employment, aggregate supply, *AS*, is elastic until full employment income is reached.

The Keynesian view is shown in Figure 15–5. You may recall from Chapter 12 and the beginning of this chapter that Keynes did not accept Say's law. He felt that aggregate income (supply) did not normally move to the full-employment level because wages and prices were not very flexible, particularly in their downward movement. In Figure 15–5 we see *AS* as completely elastic until the full-employment level is reached, when it becomes totally inelastic. Regardless of how low aggregate supply (income) is, prices will remain at P_e. With aggregate demand, *AD*, intersecting aggregate supply, *AS*, below full employment, Y_{FE}, the economy is in a recession. Monetary or fiscal stimulation is needed to shift aggregate demand, *AD*, to the right. This action is shown in Figure 15–6, where full employment is reached. Now, however, the intersection of *AD* and *AS* is at the inelastic portion of aggregate supply, forcing prices to rise to P_1.

But why couldn't aggregate demand be increased only to the point where the elastic and inelastic lines of *AS* meet? For the answer we have to recall that in the 1970s over 2 million new workers were joining the labor force each year. With the nation committed to an unemployment rate of 4 percent, more and more aggregate demand was required. At the same time capital became much more expensive because of the increased price of energy and the largely unskilled nature of the new workers. What was needed most was an increase in aggregate supply (supply side) rather than an increase in aggregate demand (Keynesian).

The Supply-Side Position

Figure 15–7 shows what supply-siders want to do. Like the classical economists, they believe that supply creates its own demand. However, the aggregate supply must expand to take care of the

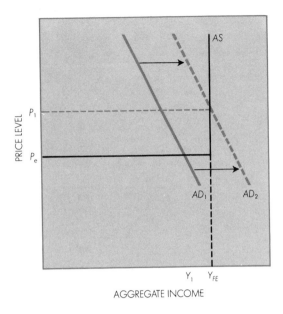

Figure 15–6   Supply-siders' explanation of stagflation

Stimulating aggregate demand from AD_1 to AD_2 in order to achieve full employment pushes prices up to P_1.

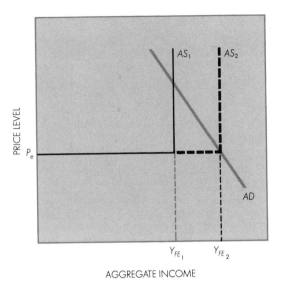

Figure 15–7   Supply-siders' solution to stagflation

Supply-siders believe that by stimulating aggregate supply through tax cuts, increased savings that reduce interest rates, greater investment in new plants and equipment, and increased productivity, full employment can be reached without raising the price level.

growing supply of labor, technology, and investment in new plants. Therefore it is necessary to establish policy that will increase the nation's capacity to produce, shifting AS to the right to AS_2. Now aggregate demand and aggregate supply intersect at the same equilibrium price but with higher income/employment levels. Full employment is reached, but without inflation, as AD intersects AS_2 at Y_{FE2}.

According to supply-siders, the essential difference between the Keynesians who established policy in the 1970s and themselves is that the former concentrate on consumers and businesses purchasing goods and services, or aggregate demand, while they are concerned with the economy's ability to produce the goods and services, or aggregate supply. Their program centers around cutting tax rates and increasing savings and investment. Let us follow their logic.

1. A reduction in the personal income tax rates will have the same effect as an increase in wage rates. It will increase the incentive of individuals to save because their return on savings (or other assets) will increase.

2. Increasing savings, the supply of loanable funds, will lower interest rates and increase investment.

3. Permitting businesses to write off their depreciation faster will give them higher after-tax returns and thus encourage them to increase their capital formation (new equipment and buildings). Cutting corporate taxes will provide a similar stimulant to invest.

4. Placing newer equipment in the hands of labor will increase productivity, which will keep costs down.

5. Changing the balance between the public and private sectors of the economy in favor of the latter will reduce inflationary pressures. Since productivity in the private sector increases faster than productivity in the public sector, the transfer of resources will permit more goods and services and a more balanced growth.

6. Lower tax rates will reduce demands for higher wages because workers' takehome pay will be greater, their disposable income will not evaporate because the inflation rate will be slowed, and their consumption and output will increase.
7. Overregulation by government stifles invention and investment and adds to the cost of production.
8. International trade will increase because the inflation rate will be slowed and thus foreign currency will buy more in the United States.

The Laffer Curve

In 1974 Professor Arthur Laffer, an economist at the University of Southern California, developed a graph that he claimed showed how a reduction in income tax rates could lead to an increase in total tax revenues. The now-famous Laffer curve shown in Figure 15–8 shows that very high tax rates reduce the incentive for people to work because it leaves them with increasingly smaller increments of money. Let us examine this curve more closely.

Our two variables are tax rates and tax revenues. At a 0-percent tax rate there is no tax revenue. At a 100-percent tax rate there also is no tax revenue. (At such a rate you would refuse to work, since everything you earned would be turned over to the government.) If tax rates are reduced anywhere in the upper portion of the curve *A–B*, tax revenues will be increased. Tax reduction in the *B–C* section will reduce revenue. Obviously Laffer and the supply-siders believe our tax rates are above *B*. Many economists disagree; they feel the United States has not reached the tax rate that would reduce incentive, income, and government revenue.

Reducing Taxes

A major step was taken in implementing supply-side economics when Congress passed the Economic Recovery Tax Act of 1981. On October 1, 1981, a 5-percent reduction was made in taxes on wages and salaries. An additional 10 percent was applied on July 1, 1982, and 10 percent again a

year after that. The top individual tax rate for income earned from interest and dividends was reduced from 70 to 50 percent, and the tax rate on long-term capital gains for individuals was cut from 28 to 20 percent.

In order to encourage savings, the act provided for All Savers Certificates. These certificates permitted individuals to receive up to $1,000 in tax-free interest income ($2,000 for couples filing jointly) for one year. A more permanent incentive is the individual retirement account (IRA), through which one can defer tax payments on up to $2,000 of income ($4,000 for couples filing jointly) until sometime after age 59.

To encourage investment, businesses were permitted to depreciate new buildings in 15 years and new equipment in 3 to 5 years. In both cases the time period had formerly been considerably longer.

One other major change was to index personal income tax rates to reflect cost-of-living increases. This feature prevents the government from increasing its revenues merely as a result of inflation rather than for the more rational reason of higher real income.

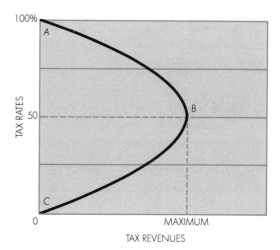

Figure 15–8   The Laffer curve
The Laffer curve shows the relationship between tax rates and tax revenues. Reducing rates from *A* to *B* increases tax revenues.

The Role of Monetary Policy

Most supply-siders abhor the loose-money policy of the Federal Reserve in the 1970s. The rapid increase in the money supply was considered a major factor in accelerating the inflationary pressures. The Reagan program for economic recovery involves a slow and steady growth in the money supply. Indeed, President Reagan praised Chairman Volcker's vigorous anti-inflationary position, which slowed down the growth in the money supply and forced interest rates up to unprecedented levels.

With much of President Reagan's program in place by the end of 1981, his administration began projecting that the recession would soon turn around. However, the recession continued and intensified throughout 1982. Unemployment rose as the industrial production index, GNP, investment, and the index of leading indicators for the first three quarters declined. The only good news was the significant decline in the inflationary rate.

Donald Regan, then Secretary of the Treasury, announced publicly that the excessively high interest rates caused by the Fed's tight-money policy were interfering with President Reagan's economic recovery and expansionary fiscal policy program. Particularly hard hit were the automobile and construction industries which are most susceptible to interest rates. Regan hoped the Fed could ease the tight controls.

Finally, in September, 1982, when the unemployment rate was announced to be 10.1 percent and the inflationary rate had slowed to 2.5 percent, Volcker gave signals to the financial market that he would expand the money supply somewhat faster. This expansion in turn would reduce interest rates and stimulate investment and purchases of automobiles and construction. The stock market reacted quickly and positively, while the rest of the economy showed a very slow response. Were consumers and businesses waiting for still further declines in interest rates? How long does a coordinated supply-side program take? One thing was quite clear. Supply-side economics did not offer a quick panacea to problems that had been accumulating for many years.

Supply-Side Economics Works: Pro

It is clear from the performance of the U.S. economy in the 1970s that the nation was not meeting its goals. Inflationary rates were rising, chronic high unemployment was getting worse, economic growth had slowed to almost a standstill. After 20 years of tinkering with aggregate demand in Keynesian fashion without success, the country was ready to try something new—supply-side economics. Instead of increasing aggregate demand, economic policy would focus on increasing aggregate supply.

The heart of the Reagan program for economic recovery is to reduce tax rates, which will increase savings. The increased savings will reduce interest rates and thereby stimulate investment. This new investment, or capital formation, will increase productivity by increasing both our efficiency and our capacity to produce. A greater supply of goods produced more efficiently will help keep prices from rising. Since workers will retain more of their earnings, there will be less pressure for wage increases. Workers' consumption and output will rise, increasing economic growth.

Critics refer to the Reagan program as the "trickle-down theory," associated with President Hoover. They view the tax cuts as offering the major share of benefits to the rich and to business and leaving the "leftovers" to trickle down to the middle class and the poor. This criticism distorts the real meaning of the supply-side approach. Obviously the marginal propensity to save is far greater for people in the upper income levels. Cutting their taxes will increase savings and stimulate investment. This in turn will increase aggregate supply and improve productivity. More jobs will be created without putting pressure on prices because we will have a greater capacity to produce.

Tax cuts that primarily benefit the poor and middle classes will increase consumption, or aggregate demand, without increasing supply. This is because the marginal propensity to consume is highest for the poor. The additional aggregate demand without additional aggregate supply will cause prices to rise.

The built-in mechanisms for inflation, such

as automatic wage increases that reflect price rises and escalation of government programs that are politically popular, cannot be changed quickly. They took years to develop, and it will take years to bring them under control.

Nevertheless, let the record speak for itself. Inflation was double digit when President Reagan came into office, and it has returned to the level of the 1960s. Economic growth rose sharply from 1980 to 1985 with only an interruption in 1982. Employment has risen by eight million jobs; interest rates are down by more than 50 percent; and the country has avoided a downturn for four years. While the huge deficits are regrettable, defense needs made military spending a necessity, and Congress refused to cut spending.

In a report of the House Republican Conference in 1984, Congressman Jack Kemp said, "Most supply-side economists unambiguously predicted in 1981 that a capital gains tax cut would cause a stock market surge, would bolster the venture capital industry, and would increase public stock offerings enough to generate more tax revenues as well as create more small businesses and more jobs. All four predictions—predictions that populist Republican supply-siders were willing to make—have now been realized. If this is failure, we need more of it!"

Supply-Side Economics Is a Fad: Con

There is almost nothing new in supply-side economics. It is classical and neoclassical economics repackaged. The market is assumed to be sufficiently flexible that it will allocate resources in the most efficient way. Therefore, if we reduce government's involvement in the economy, putting more of our resources in the private sector, the interaction of demand and supply will result in better productivity and more stable prices. Nonsense!

The market is far from flexible. The recent merger movement has concentrated business power into fewer hands, and organized labor is not about to let wages move downward in order to create more jobs. The market is not dead, but it needs prodding by government.

The real stimulant that will revive the economy will come when we recognize that neglect of the public sector has gone on for so long as to threaten the very infrastructure of our nation. The assumption of supply-siders that resources are more effectively used in the private sector has forced federal, state, and local governments to patch roads and bridges, and has allowed our cities to decay and our educational institutions to compromise their programs. It is this type of neglect that can damage our economy more permanently.[4]

Increasing spending in selected areas in the public sector will encourage the private sector to invest in more productive equipment, since the U.S. government does very little of its own construction.

The supply-siders' approach is primarily aimed at increasing capacity and *efficiency* in the production of goods. President Reagan and supply-siders promised an increase in savings and instead the savings rate has dropped from 7.5 percent in 1980 to below 5 percent. Growth was projected to remain at 4 to 5 percent and it is one-half that. Unemployment is actually higher than under the Carter administration; the promised balanced budget is in deficit by $200 billion; the debt is over $2 trillion; and the balance of international accounts is over $100 billion a year. Worst of all, poverty has grown rapidly among the young. Both an ardent Democrat, Senator Daniel Patrick Moynihan of New York, and Dr. Herbert Stein, Chief Economist for President Nixon, as well as the Conservative American Enterprise Institute, agreed in July, 1986, that there is a vast difference between the claims and the performance of the Reagan programs and that after almost six years nothing has changed.[5] What is needed more is *effectiveness:* putting our resources to work to accomplish our goals. Efficiency is getting the biggest return for our inputs. A service-oriented society that already can provide a decent standard of living for all may have to shift its values. Let the market

[4]In April 1983 a 5-cent surcharge was put on each gallon of gasoline. The revenue is used to pay for repair of bridges and roads.

[5]*New York Times*, Business Section, Sunday, July 27, 1986, p. 8.

do its work when it can, but when it doesn't, the government should intervene.

Most economists today point out that although inflation has slowed and unemployment has dropped, it has been at a cost of doubling our debt to $2 trillion during Reagan's administration. Savings are very low, contrary to supply-siders' predictions, and we now have a glut in many parts of the economy. Is this success?

The Theory of Rational Expectations

Professors Robert Lucas of Chicago and Thomas Sargent of Minnesota presented a macroeconomic viewpoint—the theory of rational expectations—that gained acceptance by President Reagan and some of his advisors. This theory is based on the assumption that people take both past and current information into account when formulating their expectations about the future. Since most people are more sophisticated about the economy and economic policy today than they were in the past, they use this information in making decisions. If, for example, the government announces that it will take some time to control inflation, consumers are likely to spend more now, even on items they may not need immediately. This is because waiting would mean spending even more later. The additional spending will only accelerate the inflationary rate. Such behavior may have exacerbated the high inflation in 1980–81.

In contrast, the severe recession in 1982 may have been made worse and lasted longer because both consumers and businesses saw the interest rates declining. Consumers delayed large expenditures for which borrowing was required and business held back on new investment for equipment and inventories, hoping to cut costs even more by waiting for interest rates to decline fur-

ther. These actions may have delayed the recovery.

The effects of such anticipatory action on active macroeconomic policy, whether monetary or fiscal, could be devastating. If, as the supporters of the theory of rational expectations claim, individuals adjust to anticipated policy, that policy will have no effect on output. Like those who accept the classical and neoclassical position, advocates of the theory of rational expectations believe that the flexible market will make the proper adjustments and any policy measures by government can only harm the economy. The *Economic Report of the President* of 1982 made the argument for less government involvement and greater reliance on the market to solve our economic problems.

Critics point out that the evidence does not support the position that wages and prices will adjust, at least not in the short run. Therefore, they believe some government policy is needed to precipitate or direct change. They further criticize the assumption that people have sophisticated knowledge about what economic policy is and how to deal with it in their own best interest. Do you feel you know enough at this time to anticipate the trend of the economy and react appropriately? How do you feel about your government's doing something by doing nothing?

Reaching a Conclusion

The arguments given are only a few of those used by both sides. Obviously trial and error will teach us a great deal. So will the changing dynamics of the world we live in. Probably our own positions are a product of our own value systems, which change as our position in life changes.

Economists have learned much but they have more to learn than they already know. The road ahead is less dangerous if we know the road we have already traveled.

E Deficits and Debts

The year 1985 was a memorable one in U.S. economic history. In that year our nation's public debt reached $2 trillion, we became a debtor nation for

the first time in over 60 years, our federal budget deficit went beyond $200 billion, our merchandise trade deficit was extended to $118 billion, personal savings dropped to its lowest level, and consumer borrowing rose to its highest level. One economist called Uncle Sam a "Credit Junkie" and noted that from 1982 to 1986 Uncle Sam spent nearly $500 million a day more than he took in.[6] What does this debt mean to each of us? To our economy? Will our credit evaporate? These are the top-priority problems facing the United States in the late 1980s. It is likely these problems will concern the American people into the 1990s.

Clarifying Our Terms

In this section, we will refer to several different debt or deficit situations. Because many people confuse these situations, clarification is in order.

When we refer to the federal *deficit,* we mean the amount by which the federal government's spending exceeded its revenues in a given year. The government usually borrows money to make up the difference, and this borrowing leads to the federal *public debt.* The public debt is the debt that piles up over the years as annual deficits continue to occur. Thus, a deficit of $200 billion this year will add to the long-term debt which has been building up for many years and which in 1985 totaled $2 trillion. The public debt is the amount that the government owes. Most of this debt is owed to U.S. citizens (banks, business firms, individuals, and even government agencies). Only about 11 percent of this debt is owed to foreign investors, who have purchased U.S. government securities.

 Federal deficits increase the public debt.

The deficit and debt we have just described must not be confused with the deficits in our balance of trade and payments or with our position as a net-debtor or net-creditor nation. As will be explained in Chapter 18, we have a *deficit in our balance of payments* when the total flow of payments from foreigners to Americans is less than the total flow of payments from Americans to for-

[6]Larry L. Hungerfore, "Who Made Uncle Sam a Credit Junkie?" *Winston-Salem Journal,* May 25, 1985.

eigners. Our balance-of-payments situation is measured at least once a year.

In referring to the United States as a net-debtor or net-creditor nation, we are again considering the long term. This time, however, we are concerned with where our nation *as a whole* stands in relation to the rest of the world, not with the federal government's debt alone. Until World War I, the United States had always been a debtor nation. The value of the goods and services we imported often exceeded the value of the goods we sold to foreigners, and foreigners were investing far more in the United States than Americans were investing in other countries. Thus, we had to pay interest and dividends to investors abroad. During World War I the situation was reversed. The war-torn nations of Europe needed U.S. goods, so our exports more than doubled, while the value of the goods we imported declined. By 1919 we had become a creditor nation—foreign nations owed more to the United States than the United States owed to them. This net credit position continued until 1985, at which time the United States once again became a net-debtor nation. The value of our imports greatly exceeded the value of our exports, and foreigners were investing heavily in U.S. securities, largely because of the relatively high interest rates here.

 Once again, we have become a net-debtor nation because we owe more to foreign nations than they owe us.

The Impact of Deficits and Debt

In Chapter 9, Section G, you learned a great deal about public deficits and public debts. That was before you learned how to use macroeconomic tools and concepts to analyze their impact on the economy as a whole. Now you might want to review the main reasons why government borrows and the several perceptions about the size of the debt, who owns it, and what some of the consequences of a large public debt might be. This will allow you to examine whether we should be concerned with the deficits and debt and what we might do about them, if indeed something should be done.

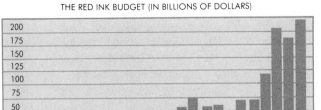

Figure 15–9 Federal budget deficits and surpluses
Federal budget deficits from 1980 to 1985 are greater than all the deficits before 1980.

Deficits

Traditionally deficits are large during wartime, when financing a total war effort out of current output would cause too great a strain politically and economically. However, large deficits also occur during recessions, when business activity declines, causing government revenues to fall even more. Such a deficit, we have seen, can be the goal of a fiscal policy designed to stimulate the economy to full employment and thereby bring with it greater public income.

With the implementation of supply-side economics, taxes were cut dramatically. The desired stimulation of the economy did not take hold until late in 1983. From 1981 to 1983 the deficit increased 163 percent. The increase in business activity did not provide sufficient revenue to reduce the deficit significantly, and it rose even more in 1985. Although Reagan and Representative Jack Kemp, an advocate of tax reduction, felt that the stimulating effect on the economy would be great enough to reduce the deficits, the record shows otherwise.

The Debt

The impact of growing deficits has caused the federal debt to double, from $1 trillion in 1981 to $2 trillion in 1985. What is a trillion? A trillion seconds ago (32,000 years ago) humankind was emerging from its cave dwelling. Figure 15–10 shows the percentage annual increase in our fed-

eral debt and its cumulative size. But what does this huge debt mean to you? To our economy?

Nothing dramatic happened when our federal debt reached $2 trillion, but lurking in the background were ominous signs. Most economists urged Congress and the president to "bite the bullet" by planning a gradual reduction of the deficits. Our representatives, realizing what a hot political issue the deficit and debt had become, passed the Gramm-Rudman-Hollings Deficit Reduction Act to reduce the deficit over a five-year period so the budget would be balanced by 1991.[7]

How serious is the problem of our federal debt? In Chapter 9 we pointed out that if our debt was owed to ourselves, completely repaying it would mean a reallocation of funds, with some citizens gaining and other citizens losing. However, the aggregate flow of funds would remain in the country. This is no longer the case. Let us see why.

The deficits and debt usually are paid for out of savings. When consumers, businesses, and other governments do not spend all their income, these savings are made available to borrowers in the credit market. These funds are distributed by our price system. Supply of and demand for savings will determine interest rates. Because the federal

[7]The Supreme Court declared sections of this Act unconstitutional. However, new legislation to meet the court's objections was introduced immediately. Regardless of the constitutional outcome, the fundamental question is whether the nation can or should operate under such rigid constraints.

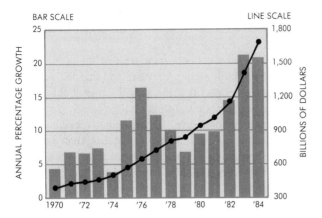

BAR SCALE — 25, 20, 15, 10, 5, 0 (ANNUAL PERCENTAGE GROWTH)
LINE SCALE — 1,800, 1,500, 1,200, 900, 600, 300 (BILLIONS OF DOLLARS)

1970 '72 '74 '76 '78 '80 '82 '84

Figure 15–10   A large and growing federal debt

The bar graph shows the percentage increase in the Federal debt from the preceding year. The black line, corresponding to the scale on the right, shows the size of the debt.

government has had to borrow so much of these funds, there has been less and less left for other borrowers. This "crowding out" has caused real interest rates (nominal interest minus inflation) to rise. The high rate of real interest has attracted foreign capital, which means that when we pay investors back we have an actual flow of resources from our country. The outflow of resources lowers our standard of living, and the high demand for U.S. currency increases the value of the dollar in relation to other currencies. The increase in value

of the U.S. dollar, which makes U.S. products more expensive and foreign imports cheaper, takes away jobs here. This point will be discussed more completely in Chapter 18. Another factor is that our debt service has risen from 10 percent of our federal budget in 1980 to about 15 percent in 1986.

The Federal Reserve influences the money supply to support a full-employment, non-inflationary economy. With the deficit increasing rapidly, the Fed might be tempted to boost the money supply with newly created funds. If new money

DURING GEORGE BUSH'S EIGHT HOURS AS ACTING PRESIDENT, THE DEFICIT INCREASED $200 MILLION.   — NEWS ITEM

Get Well

DEFICIT

were used to finance the new debt, we would say the debt had been monetized. But more money without additional production leads to inflation.

Conclusion

Let us return to our original questions about the impact of deficits and the debt on you and the economy. Some have suggested eliminating the deficit immediately by raising taxes and cutting expenditures. Such a program might prove to be a disaster. Most of our government expenditures are commitments, and there is very little room for discretionary cuts. Raising taxes by the magnitude necessary to eliminate the deficit would bring on a recession or worse.

Most economists agree that the problem has been building up for years and that the negative effects described above will come about slowly, affecting our standard of living both personally and in aggregate. This gradual erosion of our economy can be more devastating than a sudden shockwave. People are moved to act when facing the latter situation, but are complacent in the former.

Chapter Highlights

1. Our economic goals include full employment, adequate economic growth, price stability, and productivity. By the Employment Act of 1946 and more recently the Full Employment and Balanced Growth Act of 1978 (Humphrey-Hawkins Act), the federal government accepted far more responsibility for establishing an economic climate consistent with our economic goals than the classical economist might have wished.

2. Other economic goals include efficient use of resources, fair distribution of income, freedom for the consumer and producer, equal opportunities for all, and freer trade.

3. The tools of fiscal and monetary policies can be used to help achieve our economic goals. These tools are designed to raise or lower aggregate demand to produce a countercyclical action.

4. Automatic stabilizers, such as the personal income tax and unemployment insurance, lessen the effects of the business cycle without the need for direct action by any agency of government.

5. Discretionary policy requires deliberate action. Altering government spending or taxes to produce a budgetary surplus or deficit is an example of a discretionary fiscal policy.

6. Altering taxes compensates for the expansion or contraction of the economy more quickly, but altering government spending is more likely to result in a greater multiplier effect.

7. Monetary policy is more flexible than fiscal policy. If the supply of M is altered and interest rates are changed, investment and consumer expenditures can be changed. Monetary policy is more effective in fighting an inflation than in fighting a recession.

8. An evaluation of the performance of the U.S. economy in the 1970s and early 1980s shows that we failed to meet our economic goals; we had a better record in meeting our targets in the 1960s. However, the economic performance of most industrial nations over the last decade was even poorer than that of the United States.

9. The Phillips curve, which shows the trade-offs between wage rates (or percentage increases in prices) and unemployment rates, lost much of its pattern after 1963. It did, however, move generally upward and to the right.

10. Many inflationary factors operating outside the economy, including the oil embargo, food shortages due to drought, and demographic factors, forced price levels up but had no positive effect on employment rates.

11. Productivity declined primarily because of increased government regulations, inadequate investment in research and development, insufficient capital formation, and the entry of large numbers of inexperienced workers into the work force.

12. Increasing aggregate demand no longer created more jobs because workers could not easily move from one type of job to another. Instead, shortages were created in some fields, causing wages to rise, while other labor markets had surpluses.

13. Supply-side economics provides a set of principles that its supporters believe will deal successfully with stagnant growth, high unemployment, and inflation.

14. Keynesians believe that a cut in the tax rates will increase consumption. Supply-siders feel that the greater disposable income will yield greater savings. Greater savings in turn will reduce interest rates, stimulating capital formation and raising productivity. This process will create more jobs and reduce inflation.

15. Supply-siders also believe in reducing the public sector, minimizing government regulation, and using tight money to fight inflation.

16. The Laffer curve is a hypothetical model that shows that higher tax rates can reduce government revenues. Laffer's supporters, including President Reagan, believe that cutting tax rates now will increase government revenues.

17. The Economic Recovery Act of 1981 implemented President Reagan's supply-side program by cutting taxes on personal income, interest, dividends, and capital gains and providing for faster depreciation on new capital formation.

18. Supporters of supply-side economics say their program needs time to work after years of following misguided Keynesian demand-side programs. Critics point out supply-side failures and suggest alternatives, including massive government expenditures, to improve our infrastructure, effectiveness, and growth.

19. The theory of rational expectations says that people take past and current information into consideration when formulating their future expectations. Supporters of this theory believe that the government should take no action because any action could exacerbate problems; the market will make the proper adjustments.

20. The growth of the federal budget deficits and debt is viewed by most economists as posing a potential danger to the economy. The external holding of much of the debt, higher interest rates due to the crowding out effect, and inflationary pressures could hurt our economic performance.

Study Aids

Key Terms and Names

economic growth
automatic stabilizers
productivity
theory of rational expectations
effectiveness
frictional unemployment
structural unemployment
deficit
price stability

countercyclical policy
full-employment budget
capital formation
Phillips curve
crowding out
discretionary stabilizer
discretionary policy
stagflation
growth rate

demographic factors
research and development
   (R&D)
supply-side
demand-side
Laffer curve
public debt

Council of Economic Advisers
Employment Act of 1946
J. B. Say

Humphrey-Hawkins Act
Paul Volcker
Employment Recovery Tax Act
   of 1981

Questions

1. The ideas of Keynes led to new economic policies for our nation.
   (a) Explain the reasons for the Employment Act of 1946.
   (b) How does the Humphrey-Hawkins Act differ in approach from the 1946 act?
2. Considering that we are the wealthiest nation in the world, is our continued economic growth important?
3. Economists tend to agree on broad economic goals, although they may differ on the means of achieving them.
   (a) What are the main economic goals of the United States?
   (b) How are our economic goals determined?
4. Several tools are available for influencing the pattern of business cycles.
   (a) Explain the difference between automatic and discretionary stabilizers.
   (b) Give several examples to illustrate each type of stabilizer.
   (c) What are the dangers in using hasty discretionary action to bring about countercyclical activity?

5. Explain why an annually balanced budget is at variance with modern economic theory.
6. How may political considerations interfere with appropriate fiscal policy?
7. Explain the following statement: "Monetary policy is more flexible than fiscal policy."
8. How would you evaluate the performance of the U.S. economy with regard to
   (a) how well it meets our economic goals.
   (b) how well it adjusts to changes in the environment.
   (c) its most significant weaknesses.
9. What are the key elements of productivity? How may improved productivity help to achieve other economic goals?
10. Is the trade-off analysis implied in the Phillips curve helpful in explaining our economy in the 1970s and 1980s? Why or why not?
11. How well does the theory of rational expectations explain your own economic behavior?
12. If there are truly many labor markets, how may you protect yourself from future economic downturns?

13. What do the critics of supply-side mean when they say that supply-side economics is merely repackaged classical economics?
14. Is there a trade-off between effective and efficient economic policy?
15. Will future generations have to bear the burden of our debt? In what way?
16. Explain how deficits can harm our economic performance.

Problems

1. Explain the differences between Keynesian and supply-side economics. Contrast the tax packages for each.
2. Using a U.S. history book, identify all the tax cuts passed by the federal government since 1960. Then turn to the Economic Report of the President, *Statistical Abstracts,* or the *Federal Reserve Bulletin* to find the percentage changes in personal consumption expenditures and savings for the years following the cuts. Does the evidence give you a clue as to whether the Keynesians or supply-siders are right?
3. Compare the performance of our economy during the last 10 years with the performance of the economies of any two of the following countries: West Germany, Japan, France, Canada.
4. What are the economic difficulties in attempting to reduce the deficit rapidly? Consider both tax increases and expenditure cuts.

The Environment and Energy

A U.S. senator once referred to the waterways of the Ohio valley as "a vast floating garbage can." At times the atmosphere over our metropolitan areas has high concentrations of sulfur dioxide, carbon monoxide, and particulate matter. Acid rain (probably caused by sulfuric pollutants from coal-fired power plants, smelters, and motor vehicles) is causing billions of dollars in damage to lakes, trees, and buildings. The pollution problems in this country are duplicated in Japan, Italy, Greece, the USSR and Sweden. There are numerous reports of serious illness and even death caused by pollution from raw sewage, poisonous industrial wastes, and emissions from the internal combustion engine. Between 1980 and 1986, at least 135 Americans were killed by toxic chemicals.

Pollution has bothered conservationists for decades. It is now of sufficient intensity to concern the public. Economists have turned their attention to the causes, costs, and possible cures for pollution. On the other hand, however, economists are also concerned about economic growth, and environmentalists often assert that economic growth is accompanied by pollution of the air, contamination of the water supplies, and destruction of wildlife habitats. To complicate the issue, energy, which is essential to life and to the preservation of the standard of living we most desire, has become increasingly expensive. Unfortunately, to increase our energy supplies we must often aggravate the pollution problem. In this chapter we shall examine these issues and try to provide insight into the dimensions of the pollution problem and how it might be analyzed.

Chapter Objectives

When you have completed this chapter, you should be able to:

- Explain some of the problems involved in measuring the quality of life.
- Explain why a social or external cost, such as pollution, is more difficult to measure than an internal cost.
- List the major factors in the increase in pollution and provide an example of the effect of each.
- Discuss the feasibility of using internalization of costs, negative incentives, taxes, and direct government controls as tools for controlling pollution.
- Provide an example of how efforts to control pollution can affect resource allocation.
- Discuss the apparent impact of recent government actions to control pollution.
- Use laws of supply and demand to explain the energy problem.
- Show how and why trade-offs are involved in the problems of pollution and energy supply.

A The Quality of Life

Resources for the Future, Inc., a non-profit organization, conducted a public-opinion survey to determine the attitudes of the American people toward the quality of life. People were asked: "All in all, compared with ten years ago, do you feel the quality of life in this country has grown worse, improved, or stayed the same?" Of those surveyed, 41 percent felt that the quality of life had grown worse; 39 percent said it had improved; 16 percent thought it had stayed the same; and the rest had no opinion.[1]

The quality of life depends on human security, safety, comfort, and other factors relating to health, pleasure, and happiness.

What are some of the problems that people see as being destructive of our quality of life? A survey taken by National Opinion Research Center suggests that crime, drugs, environmental pollution, urban problems, and racial issues are some

of the causes of concern. (This is inferred from the fact that many people felt the government was spending too little on these problems.)[2] In Chapter 11, we briefly discussed the MEW (measure of economic welfare) and noted that the GNP as currently measured fails to account for some of the negative factors that tend to accompany economic activity. In this chapter we will give more detailed consideration to some of the factors that affect the quality of life.

Measuring the Quality of Life

A yardstick must be accurate if it is to serve its intended purpose. We have been using the GNP as a yardstick of our economic well-being and growth, although it has the weaknesses already noted. Now we shall briefly examine other criticisms of the GNP as a measurement tool.

It has been charged, with considerable justification, that the GNP does not measure happi-

[1] Robert Cameron Mitchell, "The Public Speaks Again: A New Environmental Survey," *Resources*, September-November 1978, p. 2.

[2] *Ibid.*, p. 3.

ness or overall social conditions that have an impact on real standards of living. The concept of "happiness" does not lend itself to quantification—it cannot be measured objectively. Measures of economic growth do not accurately convey the quality of life. Indeed, economic growth has bad aspects as well as good. Pollution is one example of an undesirable effect associated with economic growth. Thus growth involves some costs that are not easily measurable. Nevertheless, attempts are being made to develop "measures of pleasantness," or measures of the quality of life. Consideration is given to such factors as rates of economic growth (as traditionally measured), population density, population per physician, rate of infant mortality, rates of suicide and murder, number of automobile accidents, number of students in colleges, percentage of dwellings with bathrooms, and rates of ownership of TV sets and telephones. A nation receives a score in each category on the basis of its percentage above or below the average for all other countries (*above* for the pleasant factors, and *below* for the unpleasant ones). The United States would get a high positive score for education but a high negative score for its murder rate.

These measures may help us evaluate relative living standards, but they contain as many flaws as the GNP (if not more). For example, high population density is considered a negative factor. Yet one of the areas in New York City with the highest population density is not a slum but an area occupied by affluent people living in luxurious high-rise apartments. A country with a large desert area might have a low population density, but be very poor. On the population density factor, then, such a country would get an unrealistically high positive score. An impoverished nation with few automobiles would have a good score on automobile accidents. Measures such as these have to be used with even greater caution than the GNP.

Many value judgments and subjective factors enter into efforts to measure the quality of life. For example, in their MEW formulation, Nordhaus and Tobin exclude defense and police expenditures on the ground that they do not directly improve the consumer's well-being. Others argue, however, that these expenditures indirectly contribute to our well-being and thus should be taken into account. Nordhaus and Tobin subtract the "disamenities of urbanization," such as costs associated with traffic congestion, pollution, and crime. The costs of some aspects of these problems can be measured fairly easily. For example, we can add up such costs of crime as those involved in maintaining a police force and criminal courts, buying burglar alarms, replacing goods lost through theft, and the like. But how can we measure fear—the fear that people have of walking the streets at night? This is a subjective factor, and the fear that one person feels may not be as intense as that of another, even though they live in the same area. Nordhaus and Tobin suggest that the difference in incomes between those living in large cities and those living in small towns and rural areas gives us an indication of the costs of urban disamenities. The higher income received by the city dweller is the "disamenity premium" that helps to compensate for the unpleasant aspects of urban life. This is a crude measure, of course, because it fails to account for the fact that some people prefer city life and for the many other elements that enter into wage differentials.

 Disamenities are things that are disagreeable or unpleasant.

In spite of the many problems of measurement, economists will undoubtedly continue to develop *social indicators* as measures of the quality of life. Otherwise, economic statistics might be misinterpreted. For example, we might assume that the quality of health in the United States is higher than that in other nations because we spend a higher percentage of our GNP for health care than do other countries. We find, however, that life expectancy is greater and infant mortality rates are lower in some other countries where a *smaller* percent of GNP is devoted to health. The development of measures of the quality of life will help us in setting goals and in determining the costs and benefits related to those goals. Now we shall examine two issues that definitely affect our quality of life and directly affect each other—pollution and energy.

B Pollution Versus Growth

It is extremely difficult to ascertain in money terms the damage pollution causes. According to J. H. Dales, pollution costs are the sum of public expenditures to avoid pollution damage, private expenditures to avoid such damage, and the welfare damage of pollution.[3] By *welfare damage,* Dales means the monetary equivalent of pollution damage that is not prevented. We shall first concern ourselves with welfare damage.

Pollution Damage

Because of air pollution, houses must be painted more often, clothes must be laundered more frequently (incidentally contributing to water pollution), and crops are damaged. In several states, air pollution is now costing farmers more in crop damage than the combined effects of wind, cold, and ice. Farming in some parts of the United States has been halted by pollution from autos and factories. For example, farming has been largely eliminated in the Niagara Falls region of upstate New York because of the increase in the number of chemical factories there. (Naturally, the estimated costs of the loss of these farms and their output must be weighed against the gains received through the presence of the chemical firms.)

Health officials estimate that several thousand people die each year because of air pollution. Heart and respiratory diseases are aggravated by small changes in day-to-day pollution, and thus pollution hastens the deaths of many city residents. Estimates have been made of the costs in terms of expenditures for medical care and output lost because of worker illness, but we cannot measure the pain, anguish, and other human suffering that also result. (In lawsuits for damages, however, dollar values are put on such factors as these.) The public tends to become concerned when dramatic episodes occur, such as a thermal inversion. Hundreds have died during thermal inversions. A

"Finish your soup, dear, before it gets dirty."
(Source: Alden Erikson, *Look* Magazine, June 13, 1967.)

thermal inversion occurs when a layer of warm air forms over an area, trapping the cooler air beneath it. Smoke and other pollutants that would normally move up and disperse over a wide area are trapped below, forming a thick haze, or smog. Table 16–1 gives the death toll from several thermal inversions.

It is often considered important to place a

Table 16–1 Death toll from thermal inversions

Date	Place	Deaths*
1930	Meuse Valley, Belgium	63
1948	Donora, Pennsylvania	26
1952	London, England	4,000
1953	New York City	200
1956	London, England	1,000
1962	London, England	300
1963	New York City	400
1966	New York City	80

*Deaths occurring daily in urban areas as a result of continuing air pollution are not included—only those deaths "in excess of normal." The deaths are for human beings only. In the Donora episode, 800 animals were also killed by the polluted air.

[3] J. H. Dales, *Pollution, Property and Prices* (Toronto: University of Toronto, 1968).

dollar figure on the damage done by pollution so that the public can be given an indication of the benefit to be derived from correcting it. Taxpayers would be less likely to complain about an additional dollar on their tax bill if they were aware that the dollar would be used to eliminate a pollutant that is doing $1.50 worth of damage to property or health. Although an overall figure on pollution damage is hard to come by, conservative estimates place that figure in the billions. It is sometimes possible to determine the cost of pollution damage in specific instances. For example, profits in Connecticut's clam industry dropped from about $48 million in the 1920s to about $1.5 million by the 1970s. (The $48 million was actually about $20 million in the prices of the 1920s. We have inflated the 1920 figure to equate 1920 prices with more recent prices.) This reduction in profit was largely due to pollution and destruction of marshes.

In a recent 20-year period nearly 700,000 acres of our coastal estuaries were lost because of pollution coming from chemical factories, petroleum refineries, pulp mills, and pesticide factories concentrated in the coastal states. California has lost 67 percent of her estuarine habitat; half of Connecticut's tidal marshes have been obliterated. The value of an estuarine acre off the coast may exceed $60,000, based on the potential harvest of shellfish and bait worms. This gives us at least a rough idea of the damage caused by pollution of the estuaries. These and other figures on water pollution damage fail to take into account such factors as the destruction of the natural beauty of a waterway and the loss of its recreational value.

Other evidences of pollution are unsightly junkyards, rubbish littering the side of a road, and waste materials found in parks or other public and private places. Abandoned automobiles alone constitute a serious problem in some areas. Big cities often spend millions of dollars over and above their regular garbage collection costs to clean up trash—and help pollute the air by burning it in their incinerators! The *opportunity cost principle* suggests that the *real cost* would include the educational facilities, health clinics, roads, or other goods and services the citizens could be enjoying if money were not spent on the cleanup.

More difficult still is the problem of measuring the damage caused by noise pollution. The market value of a house in a neighborhood adjacent to an airport is less than the value of a similar house in a quiet area. This value difference can be measured fairly precisely, but there is no way to measure the damage done by the fact that one's sleep is disturbed or that one's nerves become frayed by the noise of the aircraft.

Pollution as a Social Cost

Pollution is generally considered a *social cost*— a cost borne by the people as a whole rather than by the producer or consumer whose economic activities brought it about. In large measure, pollution can also be called an *external cost*. If a firm pours wastes into a stream instead of disposing of them in a manner that does no harm to the public, the cost of the waste disposal has been shifted to society as a whole and thus becomes a social, or external, cost that those who suffer from the pollution bear. If a firm installs facilities for the harmless disposal of its wastes, the costs of these facilities are considered *internal costs* and are included with the other costs of production. Unit costs might indeed rise, and the firm might pass the additional costs on to its customers. Shareholders might bear some of the added cost in that their dividends might be decreased. In any event, the producers and the consumers of the product would be carrying the burden of waste disposal instead of the public at large. Although more and more industries are trying to cut down on pollution of air and water, the costs of pollution and waste disposal are still largely social costs.

> The pleasure you get from looking at the rose garden of your neighbor would be a *positive externality,* because the garden costs you nothing. Having your sleep disturbed by your neighbor's noisy lawnmower would be a *negative externality.*

Social costs are said to be outside the price system. This helps to explain the difficulty of measuring pollution costs. Waste material that a firm dumps into a river is not bought and sold in the marketplace. If it were, it would be an easy matter to measure its value in dollars and cents. The value would be included in the gross national product. The plant's accountant does not assign a cost to the wastes that the firm is pouring into the stream. Of course, there may be some charges for using sewer systems, putting filters on furnaces, collecting trash, and other activities related to the waste material.

Wastes create a cost for someone, and any part of this cost not borne by the manufacturer is an external, or social, cost. Social cost can be either direct or indirect. People who have to repaint their houses every year because of the damage done by smoke emanating from a nearby factory are directly bearing part of the cost of air pollution. The cost of repainting would be a direct cost. Society bears some cost collectively, as in the case of a tax increase to build sewage treatment plants. This tax increase would be considered an indirect social cost.

The problem of accurately measuring the cost of pollution damage will not be solved easily. We can produce figures on the cost of cleaning up a polluted lake, the price of a new sewage treatment plant, and even crop damage resulting from air pollution. We can estimate the additional cost of building maintenance necessitated by the effects of smoke and harmful gases in the air. The costs of illness and death related to pollution are not so easily ascertained, however. The incidence of lung ailments rises in areas of heavy air pollution, but it is hard to say how much of the cost of treating them can be attributed to air pollution as opposed to other causative factors. And as yet we have devised no way to place a money value on the effect that pollution has on our esthetic values. A once-beautiful stream now clogged with filth has become an eyesore, but we do not know how to measure the esthetic deterioration that has occurred.

Causes of Pollution

We have mentioned many of the primary causes of pollution. Industry usually gets the lion's share of the blame, but farmers, individuals, and even government itself contribute to the problem. Some see pollution as a natural consequence of our economic growth and development. It is no coinci-

dence that the waste produced in the United States is growing at about the same rate as the GNP. Few economists propose that economic growth be halted as a means of controlling pollution. Instead, they tend to concentrate on some of the following specific causes.

As the population increases, more waste will accumulate, our natural resources will be exploited at an increasing rate, and there will be increasing demands for the production that in itself contributes to the problem. Unrestricted population growth and the rapid expansion of technology and industry are cited by many as the main overall causative factors in our environmental crisis. Even if the population remained static, however, the pollution problem would still be serious.

We must look beyond the simple fact of overall population growth to realize its effects on the environment. More people means more demand for more production—production that is bound to increase waste and pollution. The urban portion of the population has grown rapidly. In rural areas where there is a small population, waste and pollution are often more tolerable because they can be spread over the countryside.

Population congestion aggravates air pollution. An increase in the number of automobiles produced and sold is usually seen as a good sign for the economy. But it also means that more fumes enter the air. (In the process of producing more cars, waste accumulation and water and air pollution will also increase.) More smoke will enter the air from a greater number of home heating systems. Studies have shown that death rates from lung cancer (per 100,000 of population) are twice as high in large cities (population over one million) as in rural areas. As more people attempt to use a public good, such as water or air, the quality of that good in terms of the service it renders to each individual deteriorates. Water, air, and public land (such as public beaches or parks) are limited in supply—in technical terms, the supply curve for these goods is inelastic. For a time, more users can be accommodated with little or no deterioration in the quality of the goods. Each good has a "threshold," however. When the threshold has been reached, *interference effects* become obvious and the individual derives less satisfaction from the public good. Deterioration in quality then increases disproportionately.

> A public good is something useful that cannot be divided among members of society. There is no basis for pricing goods like police protection and national defense in a private market, so they are provided by government.

Although technological advances have helped make our economy grow and have helped us enjoy a high standard of living, they have also contributed to pollution. For example, the rapidly growing chemical industry has produced hundreds of new compounds, many of which are toxic. The highly publicized "death" of Lake Erie was brought about in large measure by the fact that 7 million pounds of chemicals were being dumped into it daily, robbing the lake of its life-supporting oxygen. Other industries dump wood bark, chips, sawdust, oil, blood, manure, and mineral wastes into our water. Acid drainage from coal mines helped to make the waterways of the Ohio Valley what authorities referred to as a cesspool, an open sewer, and a "vast floating garbage can." The Cuyahoga River has been so clogged with oil and sludge that it has actually been a fire hazard! An estimated 70 percent of industrial thermal pollution is caused by the steam-generated electrical power industry. With a growing population and more industry, more electric power plants are appearing all the time, and more are needed. Some authorities are alarmed at this trend, asserting that thermal pollution is destroying fish and plant life in our waterways.

Into our waters go poisonous insecticides, fertilizers, and the drainage from dairy barns, pigpens, and manure heaps. Furthermore, through poor conservation, farmers, ranchers, and lumbermen have helped to create pollution problems. As private developers (and even some government agencies) convert farm land and forest areas to industrial, commercial, and housing sites, they too often destroy trees and other greenery. To a certain extent, trees and other plants help control air pollution. The green leaves attract and hold pollutant-laden dust particles, which are subsequently washed into the soil, where they may eventually disintegrate into basic soil elements. Many farmers are unable to afford the costs of good conservation practices, with the result that the social costs of poor conservation have been enormous.

Few individuals realize the extent to which they contribute to the waste and pollution of our waters. Consumers contribute to air pollution by improperly maintaining home heating systems, burning leaves and rubbish, and using automobiles extensively. The individual who is careless in discarding trash, the home gardener who employs poisonous insecticides and herbicides, and the homemaker who uses detergents instead of soap and plastic instead of biodegradable containers all contribute to the environmental problem.

Ironically, government itself often contributes to pollution. In a congested city, sewage treatment plants and incinerators for waste disposal may partially solve one aspect of the problem, but these facilities are simultaneously helping to pollute the air. The federal government has had problems with the disposal of atomic wastes and poisonous gases.

In addition to the steady and somewhat predictable pollution caused by industries, farms, and municipal sewage disposal, we are also faced with sporadic and accidental incidents. These incidents may be highly dramatic, as in the case of the wreck of the huge oil tanker *Amoco Cadiz* off the coast of France in 1978. Thousands of tons of oil poured into the sea, polluting the fisheries and 125 miles of the Brittany coast. Or they may be little known, such as the problem caused when a plant technician opened the wrong valve and poured 6,000 gallons of poisonous aniline into the Kanawha River. Unfortunately, the unpublicized accidents are very numerous. There were 550 such incidents in the Ohio Valley alone during a three-year period. Between 1980 and 1985 there were at least 7,000 accidents involving toxic chemicals.

Thus the causes of pollution are many and varied. Some are economic, arising out of the productive process and related to the conditions of a market system that encourages an ever-increasing output of goods and services. Some are related to daily living, such as the waste from millions of human beings that enters our water supply in the form of toilet, bath, dish, and laundry water. The finger of blame can point in many directions.

Controlling Pollution

Before we can take steps to control pollution, we must know what is causing it, how much it is costing society, what steps are feasible for controlling it, and how much it will cost to control it. Unfortunately, we do not have easy answers to any of these questions.

Often, not only the amount but the nature of the pollutants entering our waterways undergoes change. Each pollutant has to be factored out separately and tested to determine its effects on the water. As yet there is no efficient way to monitor phosphate concentrations in sewage water, and these concentrations can change rapidly during a day. (Phosphates are the oxidized form of phosphorus present in household detergents, and their presence in sewage varies, depending on the time of day people do their washing.) If phosphate concentrations cannot be measured rapidly, it is difficult to determine what quantity of chemicals to add to the water to eliminate the phosphates. One authority fears that it is even possible to pollute the water by adding excessive chemicals to "unpollute" it. The nitrogen in sewage can be eliminated by letting it flow through large cooling towers. When exposed to air, this nitrogen is eliminated in the form of ammonia gas—thus a water pollutant becomes converted into an air pollutant!

One thing is certain. The cost of dealing with pollution will be enormous. The automobile has been a primary factor in air pollution, and federal projections show that without controls, air pollution by automobiles will increase. Even the United Automobile Workers union once urged federal action that would have banished the internal combustion engine from automobiles. The UAW, along with several conservation groups, also urged that pollution-control devices be installed and that the manufacturers be required to keep these devices in repair without cost to the auto owner. Installation of these devices in used as well as new cars was advocated. Few economists oppose the idea of having pollution-control devices in cars, but most seriously doubt that this can be done at no cost. The question is—who pays the cost?

Industry in the United States has been increasing its antipollution efforts. One study estimated that corporate investment to meet clean air goals established by legislation would average $9.5 billion annually. It was also estimated, however, that meeting the pollution standards would result in over $16 billion saved in health-related costs alone. In addition, there would be a reduction in damage to property, crops, and wildlife. The cost for antipollution efforts in particular industries is very high. In one recent year, the paper industry (which has been a big polluter) devoted nearly 24 percent of its capital budget to pollution control and worker safety. The steel industry devoted 23 percent of its capital budget to pollution control; the nonferrous metal industry, 21 percent; and the chemical industry, 12.5 percent.

Some industries are in a better position than others to pass these costs on to the consumers. Elasticity of demand often determines how much of the cost can be passed on. If demand is relatively inelastic, as is the case for many of the necessities of life, price can be increased without a correspondingly great decline in sales. If demand is relatively elastic, the percentage drop in sales will exceed the percentage increase in price, resulting in lower total revenues for the firm. Some firms might be forced to curtail operations (this has already happened in some cases) or even to close down altogether.

Pollution control, then, can bring about a reallocation of resources. Suppose, for example, that substantial increases in the prices of motor vehicles and gasoline bring about a sharp decline in auto sales. Auto workers might lose their jobs, many gasoline stations might go bankrupt, the sales of auto accessories and tires might drop, and so on. Many people whose livelihoods directly or indirectly depend on the automobile would suffer, at least temporarily, until they shifted to new occupations. Thus some of the cost of controlling pollution would press heavily upon them. Those who had ceased to be motor vehicle owners would shift to public transportation, increasing the demand in that sector. Because many public transportation facilities, such as commuter railroads, are already obsolete and inadequate, there would be urgent need for new investment here. Undoubtedly a substantial amount of the cost would ultimately fall on the taxpayer. So, once again, the general public would bear the cost. Because demand for the services provided by public transportation facilities is often inelastic, the consumer would also probably feel the pinch in the form of a fare increase. (When New York City subway fares were increased by 50 percent in 1970, the number of riders dropped by only about 5 percent, indicating a highly inelastic situation.) A disproportionate share of the burden of a fare increase would be assumed by the low-income consumer, since its effects would be *regressive*. The working person who earns $200 a week and finds her transportation cost rising by $2 per week is paying an extra 1 percent of her pay each week. The $800-a-week executive riding the same train is paying only one-fourth of 1 percent extra.

These are but a few of the possible allocation effects. Many more could be considered (an entire book could be devoted to them), such as the possibility that greater overall efficiency might ultimately occur if more people would ride commuter trains instead of driving their cars on our congested highways. Here we are simply trying to point out the importance of carrying out careful economic analyses before deceptively simple solutions are adopted.

 The passing on to the consumer of a tax levied on an industry that causes pollution is an example of an allocation effect.

Several ways have been suggested to make the polluter bear the costs of clean-up. One proposal is that effluent or emission fees be imposed on the creators of pollution. This scheme represents an attempt to rely largely on the market sys-

tem. The fees would serve as *negative incentives,* inducing polluters to keep such pollutants as harmful smokestack emissions below specified levels. Those who discharge noxious fumes into the air or sewage into the water would pay a fee based on the emission of smoke per hour or the amount of sewage effluent. The polluter would be induced to keep emissions as low as possible and perhaps even to try to find ways of filtering the emissions to recapture usable chemicals. Recently, a large chemical company reported that an investment of $3 million in air pollution control was yielding $100,000 a year in recovered chemicals. Distillery wastes can be dried and used for cattle fodder, vanillin and alcohol can be made from sulfite wastes, and molasses can be made from citrus peelings. Thus, by *recycling* or reclaiming waste products, at least some of the costs of pollution control could be defrayed. Those in favor of effluent fees assert that such fees would provide the incentive to find uses for waste products and to develop more efficient methods of reducing pollution. Opponents fear that large firms would simply see the fees as "licenses to contaminate," and small firms might have to shut down (thus reducing competition and possibly encouraging monopoly or oligopoly in the industry) because of added costs.

Some feel that government should use its taxing power to control pollution. Suggestions have included higher taxes on leaded gasoline, a disposal tax on all goods that require disposal within 10 years of origin, and a tax on packaging that would about equal the cost of disposing of the packaging. One economist proposed an excise tax on automobiles high enough to pay the cost of getting rid of junked cars. (He acknowledged that this would probably be a "mild deterrent" to the use of autos and implied that such a deterrent would be a good thing.) Others point out that these schemes would place the burden on the consumer, resulting in a shift of the market toward low-pollution commodities that might be inferior to commodities the consumer actually prefers.

Many people favor direct governmental controls and regulations. Some states have enacted very rigorous comprehensive pollution laws, but action by one state can mean little if other states fail to adopt similar plans. Waterways, air currents, and winds do not stop at state lines. Thus the citizens of one state may often bear the cost of pollution perpetrated by another state. Unified control by the federal government might seem to be the logical answer, but fear and distrust of federal authority is endemic in the United States. As one Chamber of Commerce representative once put it, "We should not have to run to Washington every time we want to flush the toilet."[4] One way around this problem is to form regional compacts in which several states cooperate.

Actually, federal action to control pollution is not new. In 1899, Congress passed the Refuse Act, permitting private citizens to bring to the attention of federal attorneys information about the discharge of refuse into navigable waters. The law provided for fines of from $500 to $2,500 a day and 30-day jail sentences, and stipulated that the citizen who reports the polluter may receive half the fines collected.

Other early laws were the Public Health Service Act of 1912, which authorized research on water pollution, and the Oil Pollution Act of 1924, which attempted to control oil discharges in coastal waters only. The modern history of federal action began with Public Law 845 in 1948. This law stated that national policy was "to recognize, preserve and protect the primary responsibilities and rights of the states in preventing and controlling water pollution," although it offered federal technical aid and grants of money. Interstate compacts were encouraged. Subsequent legislation (including Public Law 660 in 1956, the amendments of 1961, the Water Quality Act of 1965, and the Clean Waters Restoration Act of 1966) broadened the base of federal involvement, strengthened enforcement provisions, authorized more funds for sewage treatment plants and research, established quality standards for interstate waters, and made it unlawful to discharge oil into U.S. territorial waters.

The federal government did not begin to act against air pollution until the passage of the Air Pollution Act of 1955, which authorized expenditures for research and aid to state and local governments. Under the Clean Air Act of 1963 and its amendments, more funds for grants and research were provided, the federal government was empowered to take action to abate interstate air pollution, and the secretary of health, education and welfare was authorized to set standards controlling emissions from new motor vehicles. The Air Quality Act of 1967 (amended in 1970) established air quality regions and enabled the secretary of HEW to approve quality standards adopted in those regions. More money was provided for research on controlling pollution from the combustion of coal, oil, and gasoline.

The 1970s brought a marked increase in interest in pollution. Public Law 91-224 (1970) tightened controls over pollution of waters by oil and sewage from vessels and discharges from mines, and established controls over thermal pollution from atomic power plants. The federal government moved against states as well as private companies accused of polluting waterways. The Federal Environmental Protection Agency (EPA) was established in December 1970. The EPA set clean air standards for cities, but many big cities complained that it was impossible to meet those standards by the deadline. A tough water pollution law was passed in 1972, requiring every company that discharges waste into any waterway to apply for a permit. Companies must inform the EPA of the amount and nature of their pollutants, meet state water quality standards, and install the "best available" control technology. This law also established an impossible goal—complete elimination (zero discharge) of water pollution by 1985.

Some industries have complained that pollution control is adding to their costs and thus aggravating inflation, but many are working to develop such products as safer pesticides, motors that will not pollute the air, and incinerators that will dispose of solid waste without creating pollution. We will have more to say about pollution control in the final section of this chapter.

---

[4]Hearings of Committee on Rivers and Harbors, House of Representatives, 79th Cong., 1st Sess., November 1945, p. 183.

C The Energy Problem

Most U.S. citizens have vivid memories of the energy crisis that came in the form of the Arab oil embargo of 1973–74. As Figure 16–1 shows, oil prices soared from less than $3 to nearly $35 a barrel between 1973 and 1980. Consumers felt the effects directly through gasoline shortages, rising gasoline prices (see Figure 16–2), and increased costs of home heating fuel. Because goods and services require energy for their production, many other consumer items also increased in price as the cost of energy rose. Many people felt the cause was merely a "plot" by the oil companies to raise profits, and many sought quick and easy solutions, such as the use of solar energy. Experts on energy, however, believed a serious problem did exist.

In spite of recent oil "gluts" and falling prices, many authorities warn that it would be a mistake to assume that we no longer have an energy problem. Oil supplies are expected to tighten in the years ahead, making it possible for OPEC (the Organization of Petroleum Exporting Countries) to raise prices once again. In 1985 OPEC was providing about 40 percent of the world's oil supply; it is projected that by the year 2000 OPEC will be the source of 52 percent. It is expected that there will be a steady rise in world energy demand between now and the end of the century, with the developing nations, in particular, increasing their use of energy.

Although steps have been taken to conserve energy and to find new sources, many believe that the federal government has moved too slowly in establishing a workable energy policy. Some fear that people in the United States will return to their wasteful habits, as they are lulled into compla-

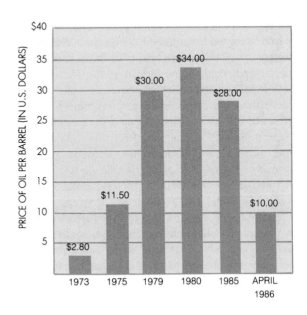

Figure 16–1   Oil prices
The effect of the Arab oil embargo of 1973–74 is shown by the sharp increase in price between 1973 and 1975. The drop in price after 1980 is explained, in part, by the success of conservation efforts in reducing demand, and the recession of 1981–82.

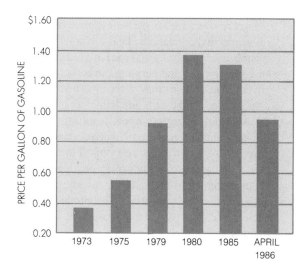

Figure 16–2   Gasoline prices

This graph depicts one aspect of the energy problem—gasoline prices in a typical city in the Northeast for the same years as in Figure 16–1. Although consumers tend to be well aware of gasoline prices, they do not always realize that the costs of many other items change because of changes in fuel prices. Indeed, a drop in oil prices should help to reduce inflation.

cency by falling fuel prices. It is estimated that motorists waste billions of gallons of gasoline each year by failing to keep their automobiles in good repair and by violating the speed laws. Our energy consumption as a percent of gross national product is much higher than that of other leading industrial nations. There are many reasons for this high energy consumption, of course, but we can ill afford to waste energy. We shall deal with some of the basic elements of the problem and discuss several proposals for dealing with it.

Energy Supply

Simply defined, energy is the ability to do work. Energy can take many forms. It can be chemical, as in such carbon-bearing substances as food and the fossil fuels. It can be physical, as in the nuclear structure of matter. It may depend upon position, as in water situated on a high plateau or behind a dam. For *potential* energy to become *kinetic* (active) energy, something must be placed in motion. There are many kinds of "flowing" energy, such as heat, light, electricity and sound; and there are various ways to change energy from one type to another and to use it to accomplish some sort of work. The energy flow itself may satisfy some needs, as is the case in our use of wind, waterfalls, tides, or sunlight to produce heat or do work. We have relied most heavily on stored chemical energy, however, and the amounts stored are limited. Over the long run, as economic activity has increased, the use of energy has increased also. Our increasing usage has caused a decline in both the quantity and quality of energy available.

In the process of adding to the supply of one good, we reduce the supply of another. For example, to make steel we use (destroy) a certain amount of oil. If we move steel bars to market in a truck, we burn gasoline—and it is estimated that a motor vehicle uses only about 15 percent of the chemical energy in the gasoline; the rest is wasted.[5] Remember, too, that in producing the gasoline we used energy and wasted about 20 percent of the energy in the original crude oil in the process. Indeed, energy is so essential to everything in modern life that some have proposed that we treat it, along with labor and capital, as a separate factor of production. It is clear, in any event, that we cannot afford to waste energy—however we choose to define "waste."

Because energy comes in a variety of forms, there are many units of measurement. There is also considerable variation in the units employed to express energy usage. The problem of measurement is beyond the scope of this book, and we will resort to the use of tons of coal, barrels of oil, or cubic feet of gas. During the 1970s, oil reserves in the United States dropped from about 40 billion barrels to less than 30 billion, and average daily production of oil in the United States dropped also. This decline occurred in spite of a great increase in oil drilling and the rise of OPEC oil prices. Proved reserves of natural gas dropped from 290 trillion cubic feet in 1970 to 200 in 1979; the United States was adding to those reserves only half the amount being used each year. Note that we are referring only to *proved* reserves— only the recoverable portion of oil and gas, as opposed to resources that cannot be recovered. The output of natural gas in the United States is expected to decline by 1 percent a year between now and the year 2000.

The conversion of underground resources into useful energy supplies requires investment. Indeed, it also requires the use of energy. For investors to take the risk of financing the exploration and development of energy resources, there must be some expectation that the return will exceed the cost, and that the return will be at least as great as it would be if the investor had put the money

elsewhere. Because tax measures, price controls, environmental regulations, land-use policies, and controls over energy imports can have heavy effects on costs, prices, and earnings, uncertainty over government policies may deter investment. Foreign sources can be very unreliable, as shown by the Arab oil embargo of a few years ago and the Iranian political crisis in 1979. Recent new discoveries, such as the discovery of oil in Mexico, can by no means solve our supply problem. What about switching to other sources of energy, such as nuclear or solar energy? The production of nuclear energy is very capital-intensive. A large initial investment would have to be made, accompanied by an enormous expenditure of energy. Thus we cannot hope to resolve an energy crisis in the fossil-fuel industry through a high rate of nuclear reactor construction, at least not in the short run. Similarly, a rapid conversion to solar energy is uneconomical at the present time. In short, there are no easy answers to the energy supply problem.

Energy Demand

The long-run trend has been for energy use to increase as economic activity increases. Economic growth and population growth require that more and more fuel be used simply to sustain the country's life-support system. In the production process, energy is used in three ways—to heat or cool the work space, to transform an input (such as iron ore) to some other form (iron), and to provide power for workers (such as for electric power tools). In addition, households use energy for light, heat, cooling, cooking, and refrigeration. Transportation accounts for some 25 percent of energy use in the United States.

The demand for energy tends to be highly inelastic. This is shown graphically in Figure 16–3. An increase in the price of energy will result in a less-than-proportional decline in sales. Of course, there has been a close relationship between energy use and economic growth. Between the end of World War II and the mid-1960s, energy use in the United States increased at a rate of about 3.5 percent annually—which means that energy use was doubling every 20 years. The rate rose to 4.5

---

[5]*Waste* is a subjective term. It is possible to compute the minimum amount of energy required to produce a given product and then estimate the "efficiency" of energy use. From the technological point of view, we could say that if 80 percent of the original energy in a fuel ends up as mechanical work in a machine and the rest is dissipated into the atmosphere, we have "wasted" 20 percent. However, 100 percent efficiency in this sense is impossible.

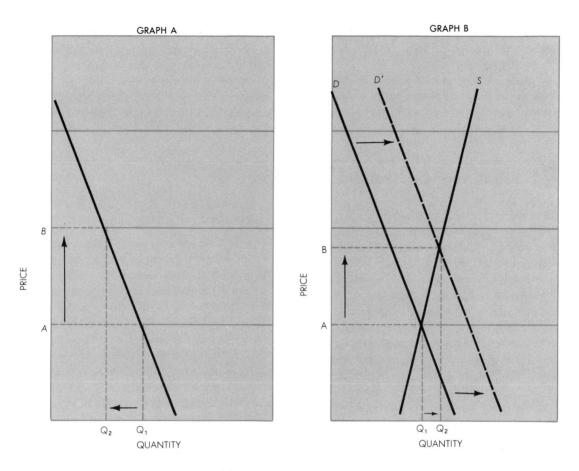

Figure 16–3   The inelastic demand for energy
The demand for energy is highly inelastic. As graph A shows, a rise in price results in a less-than-proportional drop in the amount sold. In the late 1970s it was estimated that for every 1 percent increase in price there would be a drop of only .35 percent in energy sales. In some specific situations the coefficient of elasticity is even lower. For example, in Britain a 250 percent rise in gasoline price brought only a 4 percent drop in consumption. Supply is also highly inelastic. Graph B shows that an increase in demand will bring about a small increase in the quantity offered for sale but a large increase in price.

percent annually in the mid-1960s; at that rate, usage would double every 15 years. These increases were more rapid than the growth in our population. With only 6 percent of the world's population and land area, the United States was consuming 33 percent of the world's energy. Other industrial nations were using, per capita, only a fraction of the energy that the United States was using. Before 1973, world energy consumption was rising faster than the rate of economic growth.

Following the dramatic rise in oil prices in 1973–74, however, energy consumption dropped somewhat, there was an effort to reduce waste, and the ratio of energy growth to economic growth changed from more than one to less than one. In the United States, the demand for petroleum products increased by only 1.4 percent in 1978, as compared with 6.9 percent in 1976. Between 1978 and 1982 the overall per-capita energy use in this country dropped by 20 percent. Indeed, some feel that OPEC actually "did us a favor" by raising prices, for this forced us to reduce waste and improve efficiency.

Although conservation policies in the industralized countries are having a positive effect, the developing nations are continuing to consume energy at rates faster than their GNP growth. This is because they are moving from the status of agrarian economies to that of industrial nations. In any event, the world will continue to need more and more energy in the future. It is unrealistic to expect a sharp decline in the demand for energy.

D What Are the Trade-Offs?

Remember, the basic problem of economics is *scarcity*—we do not have all the productive resources we would need to satisfy all human wants. Given this fact, we must be aware of the trade-offs involved in any decision. The *real cost* of having more of product X is that we must give up the opportunity to have more of product Y. There is a conflict in goals. Most economists favor economic growth. A growing economy (an increase in real output per capita) is desired, not simply to give everyone more luxuries, but to meet the needs of the poor for better housing, more adequate medical care, and better nutrition. Growth will also enable us to give more assistance to the developing nations, maintain our own economic and military strength, provide jobs for new entrants into the labor force, and cope with some of our other pressing problems. On the other hand, the environmentalist is apt to point to the fact that growth is accompanied by more pollution, greater demands on scarce energy supplies, and increased exploitation of nonrenewable natural resources. Because economists do not want to breathe polluted air or drink contaminated water, and because many leading environmentalists know that zero economic growth would mean great hardship, the two sides are not always poles apart. Some sort of accommodation must be reached, and each side must ask itself: "What am I willing to give up (trade off) to achieve my goal?" This section will not tell you what we *ought* to do, but it *will* point out some of the trade-offs, or real costs, involved in choosing one goal rather than another.

 A trade-off involves accepting less of one thing in order to have more of something else.

Cost-Benefit Analysis

Suppose there are three possible ways of reducing the air pollution caused by a particular industry. An economist using cost-benefit analysis would attempt to estimate the benefit to be derived from each possible course of action and the cost of taking each action. The solution yielding the greatest benefit for the lowest cost would then be chosen. This procedure can be a fairly simple matter if we narrowly define costs and benefits and if we confine ourselves to a very specific situation. For example, one paper mill has found that it spends $100 a day to operate a purification facility, and that it recovers $500 a day in reusable chemicals as a result. Another study revealed that the typical junked automobile can produce $56 worth of marketable metal products at a processing cost of $51. An engineering firm did a feasibility study for the aluminum industry and concluded that a $15 million investment in a plant to recycle trash into reusable aluminum, other metals, glass, paper fiber, sand, and so on could be operated at a profit. In these cases, the benefits clearly outweigh the costs. But this will not always be true. One large oil company got back only 10 cents for every dollar expended on attempts to recover such chemicals as sulfur and sulfuric acid. One trash recycling plant in Delaware reported that it cost $60 to extract a ton of steel from scrap at a time when the processing of a ton from iron ore cost only $13.50. And the public, while giving lip service to pollution control, has not shown a tendency to expend much effort to help. When the steel industry established 80 recycling centers around the country to which citizens could take used cans, less than one can was collected for every 1,000 cans sold annually.

Many of the real costs of pollution are not easily measured, however. The physical discomfort caused by smog and the esthetic deterioration resulting from litter or unsightly industrial facilities cannot be expressed conveniently in money terms. Nevertheless, efforts must be made to consider all the real costs and real benefits when pollution-control measures are evaluated.

Pollution Trade-Offs

Some of the trade-offs associated with pollution control were noted in Section B when we discussed the possible effects of various proposals to control environmental damage. We shall discuss a few others here. One of the trade-offs is that we must accept higher prices if we are to have less pollution. To comply with government regulations, industry must invest in pollution-control equipment or in other ways add to production costs. It is generally agreed that pollution-control costs add to the rate of inflation, although there is disagreement on how much. One study made in 1979 suggested that air and water pollution programs would add only three-tenths of 1 percentage point a year to the Consumer Price Index through 1986. However, the Director of the Council on Wage and Price Stability, Barry Bosworth, contended that pollution regulations would add as much as 1.5 percentage points to the inflation rate. In any event, it is clear that the closer we come to a pollution-free environment, the greater will be the cost. Study Figure 16–4 to see why this is so.

The costs of pollution-control equipment installed by industry are usually passed along to the consumer in the form of higher prices for products. Government programs to control pollution or to clean up and repair past damage are paid for by the taxpayer. Another trade-off, then, is that we must give up the opportunity to have lower tax rates in order to have a cleaner environment. Many cities, already beset with serious economic problems, have been unable to meet federal standards. For example, in the late 1970s, of 105 urban areas with populations greater than 200,000,

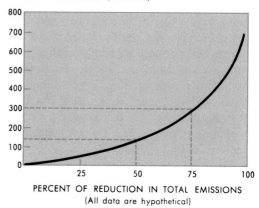

EXTRA COST OF CARS WITH EMISSION CONTROLS (DOLLARS)

PERCENT OF REDUCTION IN TOTAL EMISSIONS
(All data are hypothetical)

Figure 16–4 The cost of reducing pollution from automobiles
Assume that the data in the accompanying graph accurately show the extra cost per car of emission-control equipment. (The real-life situation is not very different.) The curve shows that if we decide to reduce the harmful air-polluting emissions by 50 percent, we shall have to pay less than $200 extra per car. Stopping 75 percent of the emissions will cost us $300 extra per car. As we approach 100 percent, the extra price per car soars. Indeed, stopping the last 1 percent will cost us more than stopping the first 40 percent did. This same phenomenon applies to many pollution-control situations (perhaps to all). An analysis of one manufacturing firm's pollution-control possibilities revealed that removing the last 1 percent of the plant's emissions would cost *ten* times as much as removing the entire first 99 percent! Recognizing that zero pollution is impossible in many cases because of the acceleration in costs as shown above, at what point would you stop? What economic factors would you take into account in reaching your decision?

only 3 were meeting smog standards. Cities might have to increase taxes or deprive their citizens of certain services in order to reduce pollution, However, the cost of *not* reducing pollution is *also* heavy. It has been estimated that in New York City alone pollution does over $1 billion worth of damage to health and property each year.

In some cases an increase in unemployment, already a serious problem in the United States, is one of the costs of a cleaner environment. It was in recognition of this fact that the Environmental Protection Agency offered to make exceptions to its effluent guidelines for steel companies that might be forced to shut down plants and lay off workers because of the cost of meeting the standards.[6] Another example concerns the home construction industry. Several states are taking steps to force communities to build or improve sewage treatment facilities. Although there is a need for more housing, in some areas construction has been slowed down or even halted because of the costly sewage disposal requirements. Costs of homes have risen by as much as 30 percent.

The Alaska pipeline issue is a good illustration of a trade-off problem. Environmentalists saw the pipeline as a threat to the flora, fauna, and beauty of one of our wilderness areas. Court orders were obtained that, in effect, delayed the pipeline. As the energy crisis of 1973–74 took shape, how-

ever, many legislators began to fear that we would be trading off badly needed oil for the benefit of a relatively small part of our wilderness. The environmentalists lost out to those who feared a prolonged energy crisis. In some areas, however, environmentalists have carried the day. Some people are willing to settle for slower economic growth and even above-normal unemployment rates in order to prevent further environmental damage.

The trade-off effect often involves two industries. On Long Island, for example, there were 41 duck farms that had been accused of polluting the shellfish beds of the bay, resulting in a loss to the shellfish industry of $2.5 million a year. If the duck farms install waste treatment facilities and pass the cost on to the consumer, the consumer will be trading off ducks (the price of duck would rise) in order to enjoy more clams. These and many other trade-offs should be taken into account by consumers and citizens before they decide what public anti-pollution policies to support.

---

[6] In 1977, officials of St. Louis County in Missouri ordered the "indefinite" closing of a plant that was causing air pollution, with the result that 900 workers were idled.

LOUIE

Source: *New York Daily News*, April 14, 1972, p. 56. Reprinted by permission of Tribune Company Syndicate, Inc.

Energy Trade-Offs

As we saw in the Alaska pipeline case, there is a relationship between pollution and energy trade-offs. In Alaska, we traded off a portion of our natural environment to have more oil. Projects to promote offshore drilling in the hope of finding more petroleum always raise fears of oil spills that will pollute the oceans and the coastal areas.

To conserve energy, consumers will have to trade off some of the comforts to which they have become accustomed. Households waste millions of barrels of oil a year by keeping houses too warm, using excessively high temperatures in water heaters, failing to insulate ceilings, and having pilot lights on gas stoves. (Half the gas used in a gas stove is burned by the pilot light.)

Switching to other energy sources will involve trade-offs. Current energy consumption will have to be sacrificed for the necessary capital investment to develop such energy sources as solar or nuclear energy. The risk of a serious nuclear accident must also be taken into account, although some studies have concluded that this risk is minimal.[7] Taxes may have to be increased to finance government programs for energy research and development.[8] We may have to sacrifice some important elements of our current lifestyle—for example, switch from private automobiles to commuter trains and other forms of public transportation. Higher prices may have to be paid for existing energy supplies to encourage the development of new domestic sources.

---

[7]However, the highly publicized accident at the nuclear power plant at Three Mile Island in Pennsylvania in 1979 raised serious doubts about the validity of these studies. More disastrous by far was the accident at Chernobyl in the USSR in 1986. This disaster increased antinuclear feelings.

[8]Taxes may also be used to encourage conservation, such as the recent "gas-guzzler" tax levied on cars getting less than 22.5 miles per gallon.

 # Nuclear Power: To Be or Not To Be?

Long Island, New York, has a growing population and strong industrial development, both of which are creating the need for more electric power. The Long Island Lighting Company insists that its Shoreham nuclear power plant (built at a cost of $4.5 billion) should be allowed to operate at full capacity to meet this need. Some experts say that the plant is safe and that all we need to do is "turn on the switch." Many Island residents, however, fear that an accident at Shoreham would endanger their lives and that it would not be possible to evacuate people from the area. Some business executives, noting that Long Island electricity rates are already among the highest in the nation, are threatening to move their firms elsewhere if adequate power is not made available at reasonable rates. Of course, this would mean the loss of many jobs. What should be done in this situation? If Shoreham is not allowed to operate, who will pay the cost of the $4.5 billion plant? What are the trade-offs involved?

In summary, the costs of dealing with both the environmental problem and the energy problem will have to be borne by everyone. Economists cannot tell you what our country's policies ought to be. Economists can help to identify costs and benefits, and an economically literate citizenry should be able to avoid simplistic solutions. At the very least, careful and objective analysis needs to be made of the effects of any proposed solution. For example, the public cannot expect to continue to increase its use of electricity without creating a need for more power plants. Power plants will add to pollution unless the managers are forced to use more expensive fuels and procedures, and the cost of these will be added to the consumer's electric bill. If industry is given a tax deduction for pollution-control expenses, the cost is being passed indirectly to the general tax-paying public. To estimate the burden in this case, we would have to examine the tax system. For example, suppose that the federal government allows business firms to deduct the cost of all pollution-control devices and activities from their federal taxes. The government needs a certain amount of income, and a principal source of this income is the personal income tax, which is progressive. To the extent that those paying the personal income tax must make up for the revenue lost because of the pollution-control deductions, the burden will be somewhat progressive—that is, those with higher incomes will generally pay a greater percentage of their incomes than those at the lower levels. Suppose, on the other hand, that a state whose taxes are *regressive* grants tax deductions for pollution control. Now the lost revenue must be made up by the general taxpayer, and the people in the lower tax brackets pay a greater percentage of their income. Thus, in considering who will pay for pollution control, we must also try to find out how fairly the burden will be distributed. Economic analysis alone will not solve the problem, but applying such concepts as opportunity cost, trade-offs, and cost-benefit analysis will shed light on the situation and perhaps result in more intelligent proposals for a solution.

International Aspects

As we have already seen, both problems dealt with in this chapter—pollution and energy—are international in scope. All nations must contend with some form of environmental pollution, and pollution emanating from one country may contaminate the air or water of other countries. Some efforts have been made to bring about international cooperation, but more are clearly needed. A case in point is the Bhopal disaster in India, where a toxic gas leak killed over 2,000 people. The leak came from a U.S. company's plant in Bhopal. The problem of determining who was responsible, who should pay for the damage, and so on is a very difficult one. Some countries have claimed that the testing of nuclear weapons in other nations has produced radioactive fallout in their own territories. The nation with nuclear power might not want to admit that testing took place, let alone assume responsibility for the alleged damage.

The market for energy is worldwide. Changes in supply or demand in one part of the world will often profoundly affect supply and prices in other parts. The energy crises of recent years were particularly damaging to the developing nations, who needed increasing amounts of energy for their economic growth. World oil prices are quoted in U.S. dollars, and the oil-producing nations demand that they be paid in dollars. As the dollar rose in value (in relation to foreign currencies), other nations found oil becoming increasingly expensive. It is not surprising, then, that many countries have been willing to risk more environmental pollution for additional supplies of energy. Note that some other industrial nations have moved ahead vigorously to develop nuclear power plants, while in the United States there is strong opposition to "nukes." Between 1984 and the year 2000, world energy demand will probably increase by about 33 percent, with the developing nations accounting for about half of this increase. The developed nations, on the other hand, are expected to allow some of their energy-intensive industries (such as petrochemical manufacturing) to migrate to the poorer countries where labor and natural resource costs are lower. Energy demand (as related to gross national product) may actually decline in some developed nations. Thus, we see that complex changes are taking place. A thorough analysis of the energy situation requires an international perspective.

Chapter Highlights

1. Air and water pollution are becoming a worldwide problem, causing damage to wildlife, plants, physical property, and human health.
2. Pollution costs are the sum of public and private expenditures to avoid pollution damage plus the "welfare damage" of pollution.
3. The full effects and costs of pollution are difficult to measure.
4. Pollution is generally considered a social cost—a cost that the people as a whole bear.
5. Economic growth, industrialization, population increases, and urbanization explain the increasing pollution.
6. Private industry, government, farmers, and individuals all contribute to pollution.
7. The cost of pollution control must be weighed against the benefits to be derived therefrom.
8. Poor conservation of trees, grass, and soil have helped cause pollution.
9. The "cures" for some forms of pollution cause other kinds of pollution.
10. Pollution-control measures can bring about a reallocation of resources.
11. Negative incentives such as effluent or emission fees represent one possible means of controlling pollution; recycling, or reclaiming, waste products is another.
12. Taxes on leaded gasoline might help control air pollution, and disposal fees could encourage industries to reuse items that are now simply discarded.
13. Local and state action is often ineffective in dealing with pollution because the problems cross political lines.
14. Although the federal government passed a pollution control law over 80 years ago, only recently has it moved vigorously to deal with this problem.
15. Energy use has increased as economic activity has increased.
16. The demand for energy tends to be inelastic.
17. Heavy capital investment will be needed to increase our energy supply.
18. Pollution controls may contribute to inflation, but they may also yield benefits in the form of lower expenditures for health care and property damage.
19. Many trade-offs will be involved in controlling pollution and in increasing our energy supplies.
20. Economic analysis can help to identify the costs and benefits of various plans to control pollution and increase energy supplies and can show how actions in one part of the world are apt to affect other countries.

Study Aids

Key Terms and Names

acid rain	social indicators	effluent fees
quality of life	indirect cost	negative incentives
welfare damage	interference effects	recycling
social cost	watershed	disposal tax
external cost	thermal pollution	energy
internal cost	trade-offs	cost-benefit analysis
direct cost		

Environmental Protection	Clean Air Act	Refuse Act
Agency	Water Quality Act	

Questions

1. What are some of the main evidences of pollution damage?
2. Explain the difference between internal costs and external costs.
3. Why is the cost of pollution so difficult to measure?
4. Explain the difference between direct and indirect costs of pollution.
5. How do economic development, industrial growth, urbanization, and population increases help cause pollution?
6. List some of the specific causes of pollution and explain the effects of each.
7. Is it possible to internalize the costs of pollution? If so, how? If not, why not?
8. In what ways could attempts to control pollution bring about reallocation of resources? How would various groups be affected? How would elasticity of demand affect the allocation of resources?
9. Explain the use of negative incentives to control pollution.
10. What is recycling?
11. How can government use its tax powers to control pollution?
12. Discuss the strengths and weaknesses of local and state efforts to control pollution.
13. What are the problems involved in trying to spread the costs of pollution control so that everyone bears a fair share?
14. What factors influence the supply of and demand for energy?
15. How is cost-benefit analysis used in dealing with proposals to solve the pollution and energy problems?
16. What are some of the trade-offs relating to pollution control? To the energy supply problem? How are some of the trade-offs international in scope?

Problems

1. What are the main pollution problems of your own city, state, or area? Examine the causes, the costs of pollution damage, and the proposals for dealing with the problems. Evaluate each proposal in terms of the economic principles set forth in this chapter.
2. Examine government's role in conservation and pollution control in your area. Evaluate government actions for effectiveness and for possible allocation effects.
3. Trace the history of the U.S. government's efforts to deal with pollution and evaluate those efforts. Do the same for U.S. energy policy.
4. The Council on Wage and Price Stability once estimated that antipollution devices added $441 to the price of a car. A study made by two economists at Carnegie-Mellon University concluded that the costs of controlling air

pollution caused by motor vehicles would be more than double the measurable benefits. Yet the New York State Legislature was considering a bill to require automobile emission inspections. These inspections would cost car owners about $12 a year. Would you favor or oppose the New York State bill? What factors would you take into account in reaching your decision?

5. To reduce the use of oil and gas, auto makers are producing lighter cars by using more aluminum in place of heavier metals. This practice will increase the total demand for aluminum. Hydroelectric power in great quantities is needed to produce aluminum, but our hydroelectrical potential is virtually exhausted. The rising cost of energy is affecting the growth of our capacity to produce aluminum. What are some other aspects of this situation? What sort of economic analysis is needed to determine what the result of the increasing use of aluminum will be? What economic lessons can we learn from this problem?

6. Some economists believe that there should be no controls on oil and gas prices. If prices rise, exploration and development will be encouraged, they argue. This will reduce our dependence on foreign supplies. The higher prices will induce consumers to be less wasteful. Supporters of controls say that oil and gas companies will make high profits, and there will be an increase in the rate of infla-

tion unless controls are imposed. Which side would you support? What might be the consequences of your choice? Who would be affected, and how?

7. It is projected that by the year 2000 the United States will be using coal for 58 percent of its electricity generation, as opposed to about 54 percent now. Nuclear power's share will rise to 16 percent, from 13 percent now. Oil's share will remain at about 5 percent, and the shares accounted for by natural gas, hydroelectric power, and other sources will decline. What are the implications of these changes for our environment? For our energy supply?

8. Late in 1985 the Senate voted to approve a "Superfund" bill to provide $7.5 billion to clean up hazardous-waste dumps in the United States. President Reagan was unhappy with the bill because it would impose new taxes. (The tax would be on manufacturers and processors of raw materials—.08 percent of the value added by manufacturing or processing.) Consumers feared that the burden of the tax would fall on them. Noting that the Office of Technology Assessment had estimated that the clean-up cost would be $100 billion, environmentalists charged that the bill was not extensive enough. Discuss this problem, from the various points of view. Use economic analysis to determine who would pay for the clean-up and who would benefit.

The Unfair World

When the world thinks of the United States, it thinks of a land of affluence. Given that the United States has a GNP almost twice as large as that of the USSR, which ranks second in aggregate wealth, and that riches are visible in every section of the nation, it may seem strange that we should end our discussion of domestic economics with a chapter on "the unfair world," particularly since the "world" we refer to is the United States. Nevertheless, Michael Harrington, in his book *The Other America,* exposed a world of poverty that many Americans are blind to. Who are the poor, what causes poverty, and are there effective means for eliminating it?

Aerial photographs of our cities show the creativity, the power, the engineering skills that human beings have developed. Drop down to the street level for a closer look, and the myriad of problems will engulf you. Can cities survive the congestion, the inefficiency, the confusion in governing?

In the last section we will focus our attention on the farmers, an economic group whose economic problems stem in large part from their ever-increasing productivity. Should we alter a market that, if left undisturbed, would be perfectly competitive? Are farmers asking for more than has been given to other groups? Does helping farmers hurt consumers?

Remember, these problems do not have one "right" answer. You should regard your solutions as tentative, because as conditions change, as your understanding grows, and as your values and ideas become modified, you may want to change your opinions. Through this continuing search, you, the student and citizen, are acquiring the skills and knowledge necessary to determine what is best for you and society at large.

Chapter Objectives

When you have completed this chapter, you should be able to:

- Provide a working definition of poverty; explain why poverty is relative; and list, discuss, and evaluate the proposed solutions to the poverty problem.
- Explain what problems the city dweller faces, how those problems developed, and what solutions have been tried or proposed, and evaluate those solutions.
- Understand what the farm problem is, its historical background, suggested solutions to the problem, and the trade-off between groups with different interests.

A Poverty and Its Causes

What Is Poverty?

After a meeting of community leaders, called to organize a collective effort to fight poverty, a county supervisor approached a representative of the U.S. Department of Agriculture and asked the reason for all the concern. He had been living in his county for 20 years and knew every mile of it, and there just was no poverty to be found. There could be no doubt that he knew his constituents better than outsiders—that is, how they lived and their levels of discontent. Why stir up discontent when folks are happy with the way things are? The very low attendance at a well-publicized meeting set up for the poor people in his district proved the accuracy of the supervisor's evaluation of the image his people had of themselves.

A statistical check showed the per capita income in that county to be 59th out of 62 counties in the state, 38 percent below the average per capita income. In spite of this apparently low standard of living, only 1.6 percent of this population received public assistance, in contrast to 6.7 percent for the state. Was the county supervisor right when he denied there was poverty in his county?

The federal government defines the poverty level using an index that reflects the cost of food and the different consumption requirements of families. Factors include family size and composition, sex and age of the family head, and farm and nonfarm residence. Each year the poverty index is updated according to changes in the Consumer Price Index. In 1985 the poverty threshold for a nonfarm family of four was about $11,000.

 Most economists agree that poverty is relative, but there is a need to define it more precisely.

Given that in most countries in the world the average family income is below this figure, are we realistic when we define poverty?

Poverty is relative, determined largely by the mode of living of the community in which one lives and the level of expectations that people set for themselves. The typical welfare recipient might have a car, a television set, and a refrigerator (all purchased secondhand)—which might seem strange to some foreigners. Welfare recipients frequently appear better dressed than many college students from the middle and upper classes. They may even be suffering from malnutrition and yet be overweight from consuming too many calories. How do we explain these apparent contradictions?

Although most of the poor in the United States are well off in comparison to the poor of 50 years ago or the poor in Latin America, their income is less than half of the current median family income. The fact that the poorest 20 percent of families in this country receive 4.7 percent of our total income while the richest fifth receive 42.7 percent is reason for concern. Although some diversity may reflect differences in ability and ambition, many people believe the diversity is extreme and reflects inequalities in opportunity. Undoubtedly, very few

Americans seek absolute equality of income as their goal. Consequently we can expect to have some parts of the population poorer than others. Nevertheless, most people would probably agree that the current degree of inequality in income severely restricts equality of opportunity in education, employment, and basic services such as health care and judicial counsel. By providing greater equality of opportunity, we could lessen the gap in income between the upper and lower income groups.

Defining the Poor

It is difficult to find a definition of poverty that everybody will agree with. For the sake of convenience and because it is widely used, we accept the *poverty index figure* for nonfarm families used by the Social Security Administration. This index is a sliding scale based on family size. For farm families the figure for the poverty index is about 30 percent less than it is for nonfarm families.

This index has been criticized for many reasons, including its failure to take into account accumulated family assets, which might be considerable, and big differences in regional costs of living and individual family needs. Nevertheless, it provides a starting point.

Who Are the Poor?

In drawing a profile of the poor, one can easily distort reality, even when using facts. It is true that there are more than twice as many whites in the poverty category as blacks; it is equally true that only 11.5 percent of the white population is poor while over one third of the black population is in this category. (See Table 17–1.) Even more surprising is that half of the poor are in families in which the head of the household has worked during the year, and in more than half of these families the employed person worked for 50 or more weeks of the year. A close examination of the facts reveals that many of these families are headed by an unskilled mother who is forced to provide for her family. Others in this category are in poor health, have marginal ability, or are old.

Table 17–1 The arithmetic of poverty incidence in 1984

All persons	14.5%
Whites	11.5
Blacks	33.8
Hispanics	28.4
Preschool children	23.0
School-age children	21.0
Senior citizens (65 and older)	12.4
Female heads of household	34.5

Source: U.S. Department of Commerce.

Note: Percentages denote the proportion of persons or families within each group who are "poor."

We do know that in 1984 about one out of every seven Americans was living in poverty and that the rate fluctuates with the general level of business conditions. Strong economic growth will reduce unemployment and move people out of the poverty level (see Figure 17–1). Nevertheless, the number of "unemployables" and those whose handicaps do not permit their earnings to rise above the poverty level will be sufficient to make poverty a continuing, important problem. Nearly 50 percent of the poor live in households without a wage earner. Most are elderly, single mothers with dependent children, or handicapped.

Standards for poverty in farm areas are 30 percent below the standards for people living in cities, yet one out of every five farmers lives below even this poverty level. Migration to the city has reduced the number of rural poor, but migration may be a factor in increasing the poverty problem of the city. Government programs have done little more than make life somewhat more tolerable for these people.

The New Poor

In April 1985, while delivering a Godkin Lecture at Harvard University, Senator Daniel Patrick Moynihan pointed out that the United States may be the first post-industrial nation in history "in which the chances of being poor are far greater for a child than an adult who has left the labor

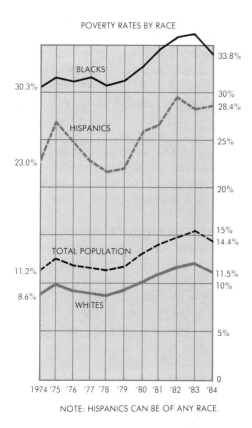

POVERTY RATES BY RACE

BLACKS

30.3%

HISPANICS

23.0%

TOTAL POPULATION

11.2%

8.6%

WHITES

33.8%

30%
28.4%

25%

20%

15%
14.4%

11.5%
10%

5%

0

1974 '75 '76 '77 '78 '79 '80 '81 '82 '83 '84

NOTE: HISPANICS CAN BE OF ANY RACE.

Figure 17–1   Rates of poverty by race
The percentage of poor rose sharply during the recessions of 1975, 1980, and 1982. The sharpest increases were for minorities.

force."[1] Most of these children are covered by Aid for Families with Dependent Children (AFDC). Unlike social security and Medicare payments, which have been protected from inflation, AFDC payments have lost about one-third of their value in real dollars since 1970. Moynihan points out that nearly one-fourth of all American children are living in poverty, that most of these children come from homes headed by women, and that over 70 percent of the poor are adult women and children. In-kind payments, when taken into consideration, reduce the number and percentage of

[1] Interview/Daniel Patrick Moynihan: We Can't Avoid Family Policy Much Longer," conducted by Richard D. Bartel, *Challenge*, September-October 1985, p. 10.

elderly poor, but increase to 32 percent the chance that a child born in 1980 will be on welfare before he or she reaches age eighteen.

 In 1970 an elderly person was more likely to be poor than was a child. Today a child is nearly six times more likely to be poor than is an elderly person.

The most tragic aspect of childhood poverty is the handicap that poor children later have as they move into the labor force. Frequently these children have low motivation, poor education, and other characteristics of a poverty culture, which may lead to a vicious cycle of poverty. The chance of escaping from the ghetto is slim when no adult is present for most of the day, when older children are saddled with unwanted responsibilities (such as taking care of younger sisters and brothers), when income arrives in the form of a welfare check, when government employees such as social workers or police officers are seen as a threat, and when school is a source of frustration and embarrassment. If the adolescent observes firsthand the ease of obtaining income quickly through illegal methods, and knows that most employment means long hours, low pay, little chance of advancement, and little job security, he or she is not likely to decide to work. Society may furnish facilities intended to improve the upward mobility of the poor, but the environment may be so confining and deadening to the individual that no real motivation ever develops.

What Are the Causes of Poverty?

Business fluctuations increase or decrease the number of persons living at the poverty level, but most of the persons affected must be considered the marginally poor. Permanent causes for poverty are (1) inadequate education, (2) physical and mental handicaps, (3) inertia, and (4) inequality of opportunity. Usually several of these causes interact in such a way that it is difficult to identify which is the primary one. Nevertheless, an examination of each cause is needed if we are to develop a plan for dealing with this problem.

Inadequate Education

In a recent study, the U.S. Bureau of the Census showed the direct relation between education and income. In 1984 the median family income for wage earners with less than eight years of education was $13,319; with eight years, $17,169; with less than four years of high school, $19,162; with high school completion, $26,528; with less than four years of college, $30,665; four years of college, $40,724; and with five or more years, $46,656. Elementary school graduates earned only 65 percent of what high school graduates earned, and high school graduates earned 65 percent of what college graduates earned. Clearly, education pays for most people.

Less education also means fewer kinds of job opportunities and higher unemployment rates. Thirty-two percent of all those who failed to complete elementary school are classified as poor. Studies have revealed, moreover, that these same people have poor buying habits. They spend their small incomes less efficiently because they know less about comparative shopping, about interest rates, and about alternatives for satisfying their needs.

Physical and Mental Handicaps

There can be little doubt that the percentage of physically and mentally handicapped is higher among those in the poverty category than in the population at large. Because physical stamina, alertness, emotional stability, and intelligence are all important for success in the job market, those who are deficient in these characteristics have difficulty competing.

The U.S. National Health Survey found the number of restricted activity days per person to be twice as high for their lowest income group as for their highest income group. The same pattern was found with respect to days spent in a hospital. The U.S. Department of Health, Education and Welfare found that the poor start out with poor health and have less opportunity to "purchase" better health.

There is a statistically significant link between poverty and people admitted to hospitals for mental disorders, although there is no acceptable theory why. Perhaps more significant is that 14 percent of the population have intelligence quotients below 85. Not many in this intelligence bracket can be expected to earn the median income, and many are handicapped in learning skills that could earn them enough to rise above the poverty level.

Inertia

Two serious causes for poverty that can be grouped under the heading of inertia are poverty culture and labor immobility. In both cases, an extra push is required to bring about positive change.

Inequality of Opportunity

Although all of the above factors can be classified as inequality of opportunity, our main concern here is with inequality related to minority groups. The median income of black families is considerably below the median income for whites. Unemployment rates for nonwhites are frequently double those for whites.

Studies reveal considerable progress in upgrading the income levels of black families in the 1960s, but almost no narrowing of the gap between whites and nonwhites. However, there are a sufficient number of instances, particularly among professionals and those in management, where comparably trained blacks receive more than whites. Colleges and corporate management responded to the charges of racism by rushing into the market and bidding up the salaries for qualified blacks. Many trade unions reacted only under severe pressure. In all instances, attempts were made to get the most "visibility" out of the blacks hired, and many blacks still level the charge of "tokenism" at employers.

Discrimination in the job market is found not only against blacks and Hispanics but also against women. The median salary of women in 1970 was $5,440, or 59 percent of the $9,184 for men. Twelve years later the median income for women had risen to $13,663, which represented 63 percent of the income earned by men. The differential in income exists not only for all age groups but, more seriously, for all comparable levels of education and training.

Some of this inequality is caused by the fact

that women have fewer years of experience working; this factor will be overcome in several years. Another factor is the relatively low pay associated with "women's jobs," such as nursing and teaching. As greater numbers of women are graduated in law, accounting, medicine, and engineering and move into managerial positions in business, the gap between male and female incomes should close.

The Market and the Economy

In each of the causes just identified, there is a mixture of economic, social, and political factors. It should be clear at this point that poverty cannot be considered an exclusively economic problem. Nevertheless, we should view it within the framework of a market economy.

The market mechanism is a primary force in allocating our resources. The fairness with which income is allocated is the subject of heated controversy not only among economists, but among all of us. Incentive and efficiency are the usual reasons advanced for allowing demand and supply to interact without interference. We have learned, however, that interference with the market mechanism is commonplace by business, labor, and government. Is the market the unbiased distributor?

Government has undertaken continuous and increasing activity to alter the market, with subsidies for business in the form of tax allowances and shelters, price supports for the farmer, minimum wages for the worker, and welfare payments for the poor. In each instance, a reallocation has taken place that would have been different if the government had not stepped in.

Businesses and working people often form their own groups to influence the market mechanism. Usually the consequences include both inefficient use of resources and extension of the inequalities of income distribution.

More recently some blacks, Hispanics, women, and the aged have tried to influence market conditions. The successful use of group pressure, which resulted in the setting of goals for minorities through affirmative action programs and the establishment of discounts for senior citizens, all distort a free market mechanism. Are these distortions less fair than those applied by other groups?

Questioning the Statistics

The Bureau of the Census has studied the effects of in-kind noncash benefits given to the poor. When the market value for all services except institutional care is considered, the poverty rate drops by 4.5 percent. When only the elderly are considered, the rate drops even more. Some scholars go so far as to say that the physical hardships associated with poverty in the past have practically disappeared. Others have shown that government programs have made the poor more financially dependent on the government. Although our programs may keep people from starving, the effects of poverty, including the vicious cycle that one generation of poor hands down to the next, cannot be ignored.

 In-kind noncash benefits, when counted as part of income, reduce the incidence of poverty, particularly for the elderly.

Proposed Solutions

Because there are many reasons for poverty, it is doubtful that any single approach will provide a satisfactory solution. Solutions must be related to causes. Consequently we must consider (1) eliminating recessions and encouraging economic growth, (2) establishing public programs to improve education and upgrade job skills, (3) rehabilitating the physically and mentally handicapped, (4) eliminating job discrimination, (5) supplementing the income of the working poor, and (6) providing income for the unemployable. Finally we will consider the issue of equality versus efficiency.

Eliminating Recessions

Our study of business cycles showed that recessions are accompanied by rising unemployment, smaller profits, increasing business failures, and a shorter workweek with little overtime pay. As the decline sets in, those immediately above the poverty line become part of the category classified as poor. As the economy begins its revival and moves upward toward prosperity, persons move up and out of the poverty category. Thus understanding and applying appropriate countercyclical policy, along with long-term economic growth, has been very important in reducing the number of poor. Since Franklin Roosevelt's cry in 1937 for a program to aid the one-third of the nation that lived in poverty, we have reduced the fraction to one-seventh. Economists have made significant strides in understanding how the economy functions, but our experiences in 1974–75 and again in the early 1980s tell us that we still have much more to learn.

If we can master the use of automatic and discretionary stabilizers so that our economy operates at its full potential, we shall have taken a big step in confining poverty. Proper use will assure that any reallocation draws on the maximum-sized GNP and will make producers out of those who are submarginal workers in a below-full-employment economy.

Education and Job Training

The U.S. Office of Education has reported in a number of ways the increasing educational attainment of the American people.

In 1940 the median number of school years completed by all persons 25 to 29 was 10.4 years. By 1985 the median number had risen to 12.9 years. For minorities, among whom the density of poor is far greater, the corresponding figures were 5.4 years for 1940 and 12.6 years for 1985. By 1984, the percentage of high school graduates who entered some form of postsecondary education was almost the same for blacks as for whites.

More recently, there has been a recognition of the differences that exist in quality of education between ghetto schools and schools in middle-class urban and suburban neighborhoods. Compensatory programs have been developed so that reading specialists, additional guidance counselors, and extra equipment could help to close this gap. Public higher education has expanded at an unprecedented rate, with several states moving toward open enrollment. New York State has provided special programs to improve basic skills of underachievers so that an open admissions program does not become a revolving door program.

Government has committed itself to providing both young and old with skills so that those outside the labor force can become part of it, and those with outdated or little-sought-after skills can upgrade them. Off-the-job training frequently fails because newly trained workers find no use for their skills. On-the-job training is somewhat better in furnishing permanent employment, particularly in the development of paraprofessionals, such as paramedics.

In 1983 Congress funded a program for providing public service jobs to help the hard-core unemployed. However, a greater emphasis is now being placed on cooperative approaches involving the government and local business and labor communities. One such program, the Community Services Administration, is designed to establish labor-intensive business enterprises in poor areas. Under this program businesses have been established in such fields as blue jeans and auto parts manufacturing and real estate.

Rehabilitation

Government involvement in both physical and mental health programs has increased each year with respect to both cost and types of programs. Free clinics and complete or partial subsidizing of hospital care by local and state governments have been accepted for many years. Medicare became part of the social security program when medical costs soared and it was recognized that the savings of the elderly could easily be wiped out through illness or accident, putting even more people into the poverty class. Medicaid, using the matching-funds technique for payment, was developed to help the poor. Social security also provides funds for blind and disabled persons. The principle of providing equal opportunities for all, which led to developing public education up to a level at which the individual could profit, is now being applied to health.

While a broad variety of statistics show that people in the United States are healthier today, the cost of medical care has soared to such heights as to threaten the continuation of Medicare as we now know it. When Medicare was first introduced, it was expected that by 1983 it would cost the federal government $8.2 billion. The real cost in constant 1983 dollars was $57.4 billion. Medicaid cost an additional $34 billion. In the Economic Report of the President the Council of Economic Advisors said that today's health problems are related more to eating, drinking, smoking, and accidents than to lack of health care. They recommended using the price mechanism to bring down costs. This approach would require patients to pay a portion of their bill—not a satisfactory solution for the poor.

 Run-away health care costs are threatening all welfare programs.

Eliminating Job Discrimination

Fair employment practices commissions have existed in a number of states for many years. They attempt to prevent any kind of discrimination based on race, religion, age, or sex. The federal government became involved through the Civil Rights Act of 1964, which prohibited discrimination by employers and unions and set up the Equal Opportunity Commission. Legislating against discrimination is the first step; enforcement is a more difficult next step.

There are some encouraging signs. The inclusion of the statement "An Affirmative Action–Equal Opportunity Employer" in classified ads has become common in many parts of the country. The number of minorities employed in the public sector has visibly improved. Blacks and Hispanics have been elected to high and prominent political positions and have attained important administrative positions, primarily in large city governments and public schools. Colleges, universities, and the smoke-stack industries such as steel and automobiles have far larger percentages of minorities than in the past. However, both public and private sectors are employing less workers than in the past.

Overall, the record on bringing minorities into the mainstream of the economy is discouraging. Note in Figure 17–1 that the percentage of blacks below the poverty line rose from 1978 to 1983. Median income in 1983 dollars has declined since 1973, and the percentage of households with

incomes of $20,000 and more has declined during this period. Moreover, the gap has widened. The median income for blacks was 58.86 percent of that for whites in 1973, 56.75 percent in 1983.

Negative Income Tax

Approximately half the poor are employed at least part of the time. If one of our main goals is to reduce the number of people living in poverty, we can best achieve this by upgrading the skills of the working poor, by supplementing the income they receive from their jobs, or by using both methods. To many economists, supplementing the income of the working poor, in such a way as to provide incentives to work, is the best and cheapest way to eliminate poverty.

The basic idea of a negative income tax is to provide financial assistance to people with incomes below a certain minimal level using the same procedures now used to collect tax revenue from people with incomes above that level.

Table 17–2 shows a possible payment schedule under the negative income tax for a family of four. This illustration provides for a minimum income of $7,500, but the amount of the subsidy (and total income) can be altered by adjusting the negative income tax rate or the negative income figure.

A family of four is entitled to tax exemptions and deductions of $10,000. A family of four that has an income of less than $10,000 would be considered to have a negative income and would be entitled to an income subsidy. The subsidy would be some proportion of the negative income; in this example, 75 percent is used. The break-even point is where the family neither receives a negative income nor pays a positive income tax. The figures used in this example can be adjusted for changes in the price level.

Professor Milton Friedman, a conservative economist who prefers to reduce government's involvement in the economy, and Professor James Tobin, a liberal economist and member of President Kennedy's Council for Economic Advisers, have endorsed this plan. Can you explain why?

The advantages of the negative income tax over our traditional programs are that it (1) makes payments to the poor a right rather than a charity,

Table 17–2   Negative Income Tax Payment Schedule for a Family of Four (hypothetical example)

1	2	3	4	5
	($10,000 − Col. 1)	(25% of Col. 2)	(Col. 2 − Col. 3)	(Col. 1 + Col. 4)
	Negative	Negative		Total
Earnings	Income	Income Tax	Subsidy	Income
$ -0-	$10,000	$2,500	$7,500	$7,500
1,000	9,000	2,250	6,750	7,750
2,000	8,000	2,000	6,000	8,000
4,000	6,000	1,500	4,500	8,500
6,000	4,000	1,000	3,000	9,000
8,000	2,000	500	1,500	9,500
10,000	-0-	-0-	-0-	10,000
		Positive		
	Positive	Income		
	Income	Tax		
12,000	12,000	308°	-0-	11,692

Note: More recent proposals have escalator clauses to adjust for inflation.
*Based on $1,000 of taxable income at 15.4 percent.

(2) is less expensive to administer than our expensive welfare programs, (3) eliminates the incentive for the poor to move to states with the highest paying welfare programs, and (4) increases the incentive for recipients to work.

Several experiments with the negative income tax were tried in different geographic locations. Using experimental and control groups, these experiments showed that when people were in the more generous programs they reduced their hours of work by over 10 percent, but when they received the lower cash payments they reduced their hours of work by only 6.2 percent. Those in favor of the program were pleased that the reduction in work hours was so minimal, and they pointed out that some people who were receiving benefits took training or searched for better jobs. Those who oppose the program pointed out that redistribution, moving in the direction of equality, reduced efficiency (i.e., work hours decreased). They also estimated that the program could cost from $10 billion to $40 billion more than present welfare.

Equality Versus Efficiency

Most economists would agree that equally distributing all income generated in our economy would produce the greatest utility for consumers.

This conclusion follows directly from the law of diminishing marginal utility. But what if that redistribution *results in less income?* Most studies show that if taxes on upper-middle and high income groups are increased significantly in order to pay for redistribution, there is a disincentive for these earners to work more and an incentive for recipients of the redistribution to work less. The result is a smaller GNP.

Equality can be bought, but it may not be worth the price—less efficiency. We should recognize that a trade-off between equality and efficiency exists and try to find policies that will do the least harm to our nation's productivity without sacrificing the welfare of the poor.

Providing for the Unemployable

Several of the plans just listed provide for income in money or in kind for persons unable to work. The concept of a guaranteed annual income, a floor below which no individual or family should drop, has been considered seriously for the last 15 years. With this country's total affluence, why should anyone be below a subsistence standard of living? The majority of Americans would probably accept this concept for those who are sufficiently handicapped that useful employment is out of the question. They would be less anxious to accept the responsibility of "subsidizing" the marginally handicapped, who are difficult to identify, and the culturally handicapped. The habit of classifying work and income together is such an integral part of our tradition that it is all too easy to accept the assumption that those on welfare are lazy. Some people in our society are questioning our basic values and wondering where responsibility should be placed for an individual's failure to become a member of the labor force. If the answer is that both the individual and the society share the responsibility, perhaps both have to make sacrifices.

B Urban Economic Problems

Today, economists and other social scientists are paying considerable attention to the problems of urban areas. In 1800 only 5.6 percent of the U.S. population lived in urban areas. By 1920 over half of the population was urbanized, and today the figure is about 74 percent. By 2000 probably 85 percent of the population will be found in urban areas.

What Is an Urban Place?

An *urban place* is one in which there are 2,500 inhabitants or more living in close proximity. All other areas are classified as *rural*. Not all of the rural inhabitants are engaged in agriculture; persons residing in rural areas but not engaged in agriculture are classed as the *rural nonfarm population*. Since World War II, the growth of population has been relatively slow in the central cities, but rapid in the suburbs. For example, in 1970 about 31.5 percent of the U.S. population resided in central cities, but by 1980 that figure had dropped to 28 percent. The suburbs and nonmetropolitan areas had gained at the expense of the large cities. During the 1970s only 12 of the nation's largest cities showed population gains.

A central city and its suburbs within commuting distance make up a *metropolitan area*. (The term *urbanized area* is also used to describe a central city and its surrounding suburbs.) The government has established several categories of metropolitan areas so that these urbanized regions can be studied as integrated social and economic units.[2] The emphasis is on economic relationship, not on political boundaries. Thus, the New York City metropolitan area goes far beyond the limits of "The Big Apple" to include other counties in New York State and even portions of Connecticut and New Jersey. These categories enable the government to gather statistical data and to study problems that pertain to an entire region.

Multiple Problems

Cities are plagued by many problems; we have space here only to identify the most difficult ones and present the solutions a few cities have tried. Of course, each problem touched on here deserves further study. The questions raised by this discussion may help steer the interested student on the right track in using the analytical approach.

Haphazard Growth

Some of our cities and towns were carefully and wisely planned, but many have grown in a haphazard fashion. Towns usually grew up along natural or constructed highways and waterways, such as harbors, branches of rivers, or intersections of roads. Some of today's business streets were once cowpaths; these winding, narrow, unplanned arteries play havoc with modern traffic. Even when

[2]For details on the various categories and how they are defined, see U.S. Bureau of the Census, *Statistical Abstract of the United States 1986,* 106th edition (Washington, D.C.: U.S. Department of Commerce, 1986), pp. 867–868.

street patterns were carefully planned, the planners could not always anticipate the needs of the future—the coming of the automobile and the need for off-street parking, the great increase in population, and the growth of urban commerce. Because there were no effective zoning laws in earlier times, industrial plants can be found in residential areas or near schools. Such conditions can have negative effects on a city's economy, but the immediate cost of correcting them is prohibitive. Of course, from the long-run point of view, the real cost of *not* correcting them will be very serious. Is the classical market mechanism for the allocation of resources responsible for this problem? Should the classical mechanism be modified, and if so, how?

Congestion

Crowding human beings and motor vehicles into small geographic areas can have serious economic consequences. New York City has a population density of 77,000 per square mile in one of its boroughs. High population density often results in high crime rates, overcrowded housing, serious traffic problems, and high disease rates.[3]

All cities, and even many small towns, are plagued by traffic congestion. Over 90 percent of all travelers in the United States use motor vehicles instead of trains or other means of transportation. Because many people insist on using private automobiles on city streets, even though public transportation is faster and cheaper, the density of registered automobiles is as high as 3,000 per square mile in some cities. Over 3 million people enter the business district of New York City daily, and of these nearly a million come by private automobiles. Yet studies have shown that railroads can carry 22 times as many people over the same distance during the same period of time as private autos can. Clearly commuter trains would be more efficient, but public policy has often

favored highways over railroads. It is not unusual to find a city devoting nearly a third of its land area to streets—land that might be used for industrial establishments or residential construction. New York City's streets, for example, take up more of its land than its residential, commercial, and industrial areas combined. Traffic congestion adds to the cost of doing business. A garment manufacturer in New York found that it took 10 people a total of 12 hours to unload a truck in the congested business district, whereas it took 2 people only 3 hours to perform the same task in a suburban area. Congestion is one of the main reasons manufacturers have been leaving central cities.

Loss of Industries

Many central cities are losing industries to the suburbs or to other areas of the nation. Whenever businesses leave central cities, the causes (sometimes called *centrifugal forces*) are similar.

1. The *spatial force,* stemming from the intense competition for space within cities, is often said to be the primary reason for the outflow of businesses from these cities. Modern industrial processes frequently demand plants that are spread out, and the available buildings in cities extend upward. Compared with the suburbs, cities have few vacant spaces. Lack of suitable space, then, is pushing many firms out of northern cities.

2. The *situational force* refers to unsatisfactory use of the available space and facilities in cities. Available buildings might be located too far from transportation facilities, sources of supply, or markets. Heavy congestion in the area where a firm is located can greatly increase the firm's production costs. Inadequate commuter services in the city can make it difficult for workers to get to their places of employment. Often, more convenient arrangements can be found in the suburbs.

3. *Antiquated facilities* no longer suitable for modern manufacturing methods can send businesses to the suburbs. It may be cheaper to build a new plant outside the city than to modernize existing structures within the city.

[3]A dwelling is said to be overcrowded if it houses more than one person per room, on the average. A *PPR Ratio* (persons per room) is obtained by dividing the number of persons living in the dwelling by the number of rooms. If the PPR ratio is greater than one, the dwelling is overcrowded.

4. *Higher labor costs* in cities are often cited by business firms as a reason for their departure. According to the National Bureau of Economic Research, a direct relation exists between the size of a city and the average hourly wage of industrial workers. For example, when the wage index in New York City had reached 197 (with 1953 as the base year), it was only 164 in Providence, Rhode Island.

It must be realized, however, that differences in wages can partly be attributed to differences in the productivity of the workers. Capital is sometimes more abundant relative to labor in large cities than in small towns. Businesses have also expressed dissatisfaction with the quality of unskilled labor in cities. In any event, the prospect of lower wages may motivate some businesses to leave large cities.

5. The *high taxes and high land values* typical in central cities can send businesses to other areas. A few years ago, the mayor of a southern town wrote to northern industrialists, offering them very low carrying charges, tax exemptions for up to 99 years, sites and buildings, and wage rates considerably below those in northern states. Lack of strong unions also attracted businesses to the South. Some of the "runaways" who accepted such offers were disappointed, however, for now the land values and taxes in small towns are getting closer to those of the cities.

6. The *general deterioration* affecting many cities is sometimes given as a reason for business departures. Such deterioration may encompass rising crime rates, the growth of slums, the exodus of middle-income people, obsolete public facilities (such as ports, roads, and commuter trains), and even "antibusiness" attitudes of some city officials.

7. New *"minicities"* have appeared near some of the older central cities, providing many of the goods and services available in the nearby central cities. At least seven such areas have developed in the suburbs of Philadelphia since 1970. One such minicity, only 20 miles from Philadelphia, contains offices, multi-unit residential facilities, large retail stores, manufacturing plants, warehouses, motels, restaurants, entertainment facilities, and a space research center. There is even a famous national park nearby (Valley Forge). This minicity offers modern buildings and attractive surroundings that Philadelphia is not able to match.

8. *Modern communications technology* has made it possible for firms to move some of their office operations out of central cities and still maintain close contact with city-based companies or facilities with which they do business. Many have moved their "back-office" functions (those that do not require face-to-face communications) to suburbs where rent, taxes, electricity, and labor costs are lower.

In some cities the loss of manufacturing is balanced by gains in other fields. Buildings no longer suitable for manufacturing can sometimes be turned into offices. There will be temporary dislocations, however, because workers who were employed in industry are not always equipped to get other jobs. And there are often more jobs being created in the suburbs than in the cities.

To assess the real significance of employment trends in a city, one must always place the data in a broad context. The United States Department of Commerce has developed the *regional share concept* for this purpose. An estimate of the number of jobs a region has gained or lost relative to other areas shows its relative attractiveness. For example, Phoenix, Arizona, would have gained 20,570 jobs in the 1950s if its industries had grown at the same rate as the nation as a whole. Actually, it gained 127,244 jobs. The difference between the two figures—106,674—is the *regional share* for Phoenix. In this case, the region did much better than the national average. Scranton, Pennsylvania, on the other hand, lost 8,594 jobs. It would have *gained* 9,754 jobs if its industries had grown at the rate of the nation as a whole. Thus, Scranton's regional share was *negative* 18,348. Most of the large losses were in the Northeast; most of the large gains were in the South, Southwest, and West.

What steps can a city take to prevent the loss of industry? Would these measures aggravate other problems? What action should the state and national governments take, if any? What noneconomic factors contribute to the loss of industry?

The Changing Population

In many of the central cities, the composition of the population is changing. For example, during one five-year period, Cleveland lost 90,000 people to the suburbs, most of whom were in the middle-income group, and gained 25,000 poor. In a one-year period, the percentage of middle-income New Yorkers dropped, while the percentage of those living below the poverty line rose. As a result, New York dropped from rank 22 to rank 45 in effective buying power per household. Between 1970 and 1980, Philadelphia's population dropped by 13.8 percent, while the percentage accounted for by members of a poor minority group rose from 34 to 40 percent.

 The shifting of population to the Sun Belt has caused major urban problems for cities whose regional shares have risen or fallen sharply.

Changes in the composition of a city's population have profound effects on its economy. People moving *out* of the city are often those who are capable of paying taxes. They are people who have relatively high levels of education and technical skills, and thus great earning power to contribute to a region's economy. They require fewer public services and assistance than do the poor who are moving in. The poor persons flocking *to* the central cities are often without the training, skills, or formal education needed to obtain the jobs available in the cities. In the poor neighborhoods of central cities, unemployment rates are often staggeringly high. An unemployment rate of 40 percent for black teenagers is not unusual.

Most poor people inhabiting central cities need more and greater services in education, health care, housing, and aid to dependent children but are unable to pay the costs. This places the burden on the middle-income or high-income residents, the very group leaving the cities. The influx of the poor and the rising taxes in the cities are reasons

often cited for the outflow of the most affluent groups. The cities, then, face a financial problem, as the cost of public services continues to rise while the tax base continues to fall. Because the productivity of industrial workers has increased greatly, they command higher wages than do the police officer, the teacher, the firefighter, the social worker, the public administrator, and other producers of services, who are producing little more than they did 30 or 40 years ago. There is a need for these service providers, however, and they too must receive higher wages if their services are to be retained. If cities attempt to solve the problem by raising taxes on existing industries, these industries often threaten to move out also. Many of the mayors of central cities are pleading for more federal aid on the ground that the problems with which they are forced to deal are essentially national. For example, they maintain that it is not the fault of the cities that impoverished and unskilled rural people are moving in.

Too Many Governments

Water that has been polluted by one city or town often flows through another city, town, county, or state. Air currents carry poisonous fumes across political boundaries. Traffic, workers, goods, services, and money capital flow from one political jurisdiction into another. There are usually dozens of separate governments in each of the metropolitan areas. The U.S. Department of Commerce defines a government as "an organized entity having governmental attributes and sufficient discretion in the management of its own affairs to distinguish it as separate from the administrative structure of any other government units."[4] If we omit school districts (which are often counted as governments), California has nearly 2,000 governments, New York State has over 2,000, and Illinois has over 4,000. One county in the New York metropolitan area has 64 villages, 3 towns, 2 cities, and nearly 300 special districts. Altogether, there are nearly 1,500 governments in the New York region. Such regional problems as air

[4]Bureau of the Census, *Governments in the United States* (Washington, D.C.: Government Printing Office, 1953), p. 6.

pollution, water supply, traffic congestion, crime, and industrial development cannot be handled efficiently when governmental responsibility is so fragmented.

Areawide problems are aggravated by the lack of one central regional authority. For example, the Bay Area Rapid Transit District, a 75-mile complex linking three counties and several cities in California, was begun in 1962, when it was realized that the area's urban transportation problems could not be solved by more freeways. (New freeways or expressways sometimes aggravate congestion by inducing more people to use cars instead of commuter trains or buses.) Delays resulted when participating communities demanded modifications in the original plans. Meanwhile, inflation increased the cost, so that the system needed millions more than originally anticipated. Even within one governmental jurisdiction, there are similar problems. Many urban governments have changed little, if at all, since colonial days. Governmental structures that were adequate in the "horse and buggy days," or that developed haphazardly, cannot cope with the overwhelming problems of today's cities. For instance, in one big city, a person attempting to establish a parking lot must deal with 21 different government agencies.

 Both economists and political scientists recommend a regional approach to solving problems.

Many city officials feel that they are being forced to carry burdens that are actually regional or national. State legislatures are often under strong rural influence, if not downright domination, and many rural representatives are unaware of city problems. It is not unusual to find that city residents pay over half of a state's taxes but receive less than half of the money spent by the state. People living in the suburbs usually use the central city's services, or rely on the city for their jobs or their businesses, but are rarely willing to help the city cope with its economic problems. Although the population of central cities is either declining or becoming less affluent, the general expenditures of the cities are rising. For example, per capita expenditures in Washington, D.C., rose about 185 percent in a recent 10-year period. New York City's welfare costs alone increased tenfold in a decade, whereas its total population remained about the same.

Possible Solutions

Some cities have made commendable progress in solving certain problems. Los Angeles has built hundreds of miles of aqueducts to provide an adequate water supply. Cooperation between Pittsburgh business leaders and city officials on air pollution control has helped revive that city's economy. With the help of federal urban renewal funds, about a third of New Haven, Connecticut, was rebuilt. San Francisco converted some of its decaying waterfront facilities into shops and restaurants. The Port of New York Authority, established in 1931 by New York and New Jersey, has built bridges, tunnels, airports, and terminals. It operates a commuter railroad and a huge world trade center. Except for the railroad, each of these facilities pays its own way. (The Port Authority has no power to tax; it can raise money only charging fees for the use of its facilities and by selling bonds.) But the Port Authority can deal with only a small fraction of the area's problems. In 1982 the Authority reported that it would take $40 billion during this decade to repair or rebuild 1,000 bridges, 4,500 buses, 6,200 miles of streets, and 6,000 miles of water lines. Its resources were too limited to deal with more than a fraction of these needs.

Perhaps the first priority for metropolitan areas is to end the fragmentation of political authority and establish some sort of areawide governmental structure. This will not be easy, however, since metropolitan areas spread out over state borders, as well as city and county lines. When critical problems threaten an area, cooperation often seems more feasible. For example, Delaware, New Jersey, New York, and Pennsylvania established the Delaware River Compact in 1961 for cooperative development and use of the Delaware River's resources. The agreement included plans for a commission to control water supply, pollution, flood protection, watershed management, recreation, and hydroelectric power. Although all the participating states have been threatened by serious water shortages and pollution, the compact was only achieved after 30 years of maneuvering. Because most governments jealously guard their sovereignty, it is likely that areawide administrative structures will be established only for specific functions and problems.

The federal government must initiate action on many urban problems and on regional cooperation. (Because the federal government was a party to the Delaware River Compact, Congress must approve all projects involving federal expenditures.) Some feel that the federal government should handle all welfare problems. This would help to eliminate the vast differences in welfare programs throughout the country and prevent one area from "exporting" its welfare problems to another. Such schemes as the Model Cities program, administered by the U.S. Department of Housing and Urban Development, can help eliminate urban slums. Although some private bankers and construction firms are attempting to promote more building in urban slums, they are being deterred by high risk and the probability of low returns. Thus government funds will be needed if we are to provide adequate housing for millions of slum dwellers. Some agree with the philosophy of the Reagan Administration, however, that the federal government should reduce its role in matters like these and let state and local governments or even private institutions and firms deal with the problems.

To stem the outflow of industry from central cities, some states and cities are providing loans and mortgage insurance, giving advice to small businesses, developing sites and constructing plants to be leased to private firms, and even training jobless workers for the kinds of positions available. Obviously, more such activity is needed.

Regional planning is essential if the haphazard growth of the past is to be avoided in the future. For example, it is useless for one town to enforce rigid zoning codes that keep out "nuisance factories" while an adjacent community permits industries to move in. A regional plan does not try to specify the use of every square foot of space, but it does take into account such factors as changing population, industrial development, transportation needs, recreation and open space, and residential construction. For example, such a plan can help a region by ensuring adequate industrial growth while protecting residents from the encroachment of noisy, smoke-producing factories. The success of regional planning depends on the cooperation of the many industries and communities involved.

Finally, all citizens must realize that urban problems will affect the entire nation. In the future it will not be possible to escape these problems by moving to other areas—there may be no "other areas." The federal government has often devoted more of its total expenditures to agriculture than to community development and housing, although over 70 percent of the population is urban and less than 3 percent is farm.

 Urban problems are national problems because everyone is affected.

If New York City's financial crisis of a few years ago had resulted in bankruptcy, the effects would have been nationwide. When Cleveland defaulted (failed to pay its debts) in late 1978, it was the first major city to do so since the Great Depression of the 1930s. Because other cities had many of the same problems as Cleveland, such as a 33-percent drop in population over a 25-year period, and because Cleveland was the eighteenth-largest city in the nation, many mayors began to tremble.

It is true that some cities have been enjoying a revival in recent years. One reason for this revival is that manufacturing is being replaced by such service industries as finance, health care, and education. Another reason is that young professionals who grew up in the suburbs after World War II have been moving to the central cities. Meanwhile, many blue-collar workers are moving to the suburbs. Nevertheless, the central cities continue to be areas with heavy concentrations of the poor and minority groups. For example, in the United States over 50 percent of blacks live in large cities, whereas only about 25 percent of whites reside in the large cities. Nearly half of the nation's poor live in central cities.

The implications of population shifts (such as the movement of more poor, black, and Hispanic people to the suburbs) will not be clear until further studies are made. Although there are signs that some cities are being revitalized, urban economic problems will be with us for a long time to come.

The Farmer

Defining the Problem

When we speak of a problem in the social sciences, we mean an unresolved controversy that can be defined and analyzed. We know that within the wide scope of any investigation, lesser related issues may exist. One long-standing problem in our economy has been "agriculture," or "the farmer." Traditionally when people spoke of "the farm problem," they were referring to the relatively low income of farmers compared with the income of other groups in the economy.

However, in 1973, when farm prices rose to unprecedented heights, consumers not only lost sympathy for the economic plight of farmers but frequently blamed them for the rise in food prices. Figure 17–2 shows how the fortunes of the farmer turned around dramatically within one year.

With few exceptions, primarily during the two world wars, farmers have lagged significantly below nonfarm individuals in income. In 1967, this income difference was over $700 after taxes. Because of a cluster of circumstances, some short run, others not, prosperity in 1973 reduced this differential to $300. In 1985 the gap widened to $1,800. Although it is difficult to project even one year in advance what the farmer's income will be compared to incomes of other people in the economy, it is reasonable to expect that the nature of the agricultural industry will continue to make it more susceptible to market forces than other industries are.

 Farm income is much more volatile than the income of other economic groups.

We face the necessity of determining what our farm policy should be. We must recognize that a large segment of our economy, the farmers, are subject to unique economic conditions and that frequent changes in policy may be called for.

A Century of Change

In the last hundred years, U.S. agriculture has, like industry, gone through great changes. Two important differences are in the number of people employed and the amount of food produced. Just before the Civil War, about one-half of our labor force was engaged in agriculture, with each farmer producing enough to feed approximately 5 people. Today about 2.3 percent of our labor force works in agriculture, and each farmer feeds 65 people. These changes have come about as a result of a technological revolution—the agricultural counterpart of the Industrial Revolution—that has increased worker output at an amazing rate. The use of machinery, improved methods, hybrid seeds, special fertilizers, and better insecticides has

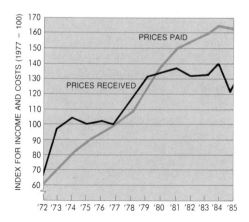

Figure 17–2   Prices received and paid by farmers

High food prices do not necessarily mean prosperity for the farmer. (Source: Department of Agriculture.)

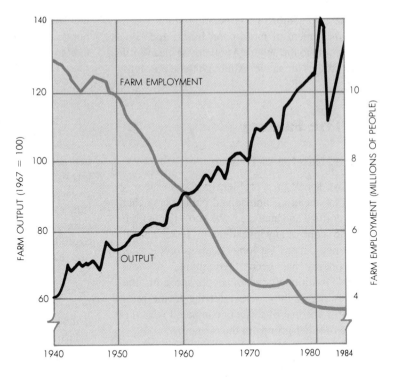

Figure 17–3   Relation of farm output to farm employment

The remarkable rise in farm output has been accompanied by an equally dramatic decline in the number of farm workers. (Source: U.S. Department of Agriculture.)

enabled fewer and fewer farmers to supply more and more food. See Figure 17–3.

These innovations have significantly changed the character of farming. One indication of this change is that farming as a "way of life" is disappearing and is being replaced by farming as a business. To be successful, modern farmers must deal with problems similar to those of the business firm. They need large amounts of capital to invest in improvement. Like single proprietors, they must have knowledge of all aspects of the total operation and be prepared to compete successfully.

Another important measure of change is the size of the farm unit. A steady reduction in the total number of small farms is in marked contrast to a corresponding increase in the importance of large operating units. Today 10 percent of the nation's farms account for 67 percent of the total

sales of farm products. A few large conglomerate corporations have gone into farming, but they account for only a small fraction of output and they have not been very successful. Although agriculture in the economy has declined in importance relative to industry, it remains the largest single producer and is this country's most productive industry.

 The number of farmers as a percentage of our working force has continued to fall.

There is one aspect of farming that has not changed in the twentieth century. Farm income still tends to fluctuate far more widely than does industrial income. For example, during the two world wars, prices rose faster for farm products than for industrial goods, and the farmer's income increased accordingly. These short periods of prosperity were more than offset by tumbling prices and income after the wars, particularly during the Great Depression in the thirties. Overall, farmers have lagged behind other groups in income.

Causes of the Farm Problem

What factors operate to make the farmers' problems different from problems of other producers? Is there anything unique in their situation that should single them out?

Of all the sectors of our economy, farming comes closest to meeting the conditions necessary for pure competition. If we disregard government action, we find in agriculture all the criteria (identified in Chapter 2) necessary for the market mechanism to work. If this is so, why has government intervention become necessary?

Inelastic Demand for Farm Products

Perhaps the single most important factor behind the farm problem is the inelastic demand for agricultural products in general, and for the main farm products in particular. Although our increasing population and larger incomes create a need for more food, until 1973 the demand for food rose more slowly that the demand for industrial products. Then, because of drought and crop failures throughout the world, the demand for U.S. crops rose, leading to an increase in exports of 60 percent from 1972 to 1973. It was this dramatic increase in world demand that changed the fortune of the U.S. farmer, not the change in demand in our own country.

The farmers' prosperity was short-lived, however, because a few years later record-breaking harvests both here and abroad caused prices to fall while the prices farmers paid continued to climb. One of the keys to explaining the farmers' problem is the inelastic demand for their product. For a graphic analysis of this problem, let us turn back to the classical model of supply and demand on page 50. Note that the demand schedules are inelastic, more vertical than horizontal. This situation exists because people in the United States can afford to buy most food products with very little reduction in other purchases even if the price

of those products rises. On the other hand, if the price of food declines, they will not increase their other purchases by large amounts.

According to the supply and demand graph on page 51, supply S intersects demand D at A, so the quantity exchanged is OQ bushels and the price is OP per bushel. The farmers' revenue is PAQO. Turning to the new supply curve, S', we see that it intersects the demand curve where OQ' is the quantity exchanged and OP' is the new price per bushel. The farmers, producing more than before, receive only $P'BQ'O$ revenue, which is less than they received before. We might conclude that farmers collectively make the greatest gain from growing less rather than more.

At first glance it appears that the solution to the farmers' problem is simple—let them all produce less! Unfortunately, this solution is an example of the fallacy of composition. The same paradox found in thrift and savings exists also for the farmer—what is good for the individual is not necessarily good for the entire group. If you were a wheat farmer, even the largest wheat producer in the nation, you would know that the amount of wheat you grew was not large enough to influence the price of wheat. Under these circumstances the more wheat you grow individually, the greater your income will be. Let the other farmers cut down!

Added Costs—The "Middleman"

No doubt you have frequently heard complaints about the cost of food. If food prices are so high, why do farmers complain about the low prices they get for their products?

As producers, farmers receive only a small part of the final retail price of food products. Much of the retail price is made up of charges for services such as processing and distributing. Those who work in this intermediate area, between producer and consumer, are known collectively as the *middleman*. Their costs have risen steadily, and new costs, such as for special packaging or processing, may have been added, resulting in even higher retail prices. The price for a package of cereal is many times greater than the value of the grain that has gone into it. In terms of the final retail price, the farmer's share may be relatively small. For bakery products and cereal, only 15 percent of the retail price goes to the farmer. For meat products, the farmer receives about 50 percent of the retail price. For all foods the farmer's share is about 36 percent. More recently the increased prices for fuel and fertilizers have driven agricultural costs up. Figure 17–4 shows the effects of these increased expenses.

Too Many Farmers

Productivity has increased at a faster rate in agriculture than in any other industry. Output per hour of farm work increased 66 percent from 1974 to 1982 alone. Because of this increased productivity and also because of the relatively slow increase in the demand for food products, fewer and fewer farmers are needed to produce an adequate domestic supply. Usually readjustments occur according to the classical model. The surplus of producers causes income to drop and directs the marginal farmer into other areas of the economy that yield a better return (remember the law of diminishing returns?). However, although it is true that the total number of farms and of farmers has declined, it has not done so at a fast enough rate.

There are several reasons for this slow rate of change. For many, farming is a way of life. Farmers are their own bosses. They can bring up their children away from what they may consider the "evils of the city." The air they breathe, the food they eat, the space they have, and the kind of work they do all bring rewards beyond mere income. In spite of the hard work and financial limitations, farmers are, by their own standards, leading the best kind of life.

The fact that there are more farmers than are needed creates a problem, which is further complicated by the higher birthrate in rural areas than in cities. Although the mobility of young people in rural communities is high and many farmers are being absorbed into urban centers, there are still too many farmers for our needs.

Prices and Competition

The prices of agricultural products reflect the highly competitive nature of farming. Were it not for government intervention, these prices would be determined in the free market. In contrast, the

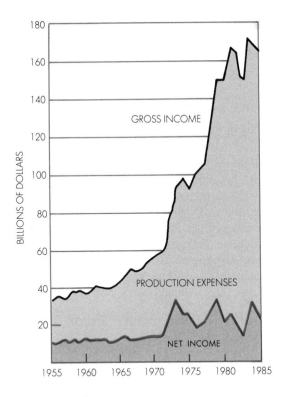

Figure 17–4   Farm income

Although gross farm income has risen sharply since 1971, increased expenses have left the farmer only slightly better off than in the past. (Sources: U.S. Departments of Agriculture and Commerce.)

prices of products farmers buy are, for the most part, not subject to the same kind of competition. (See Figure 17–4.) Many of the things farmers purchase come from industries with administered prices, where price decreases rarely occur. This difference in the extent of competition puts farmers at a disadvantage compared to other producers in the economy.

When some people complain that agricultural products get special treatment, farmers are quick to point out that many of our industries are able to keep their prices high because of tariff protection. They also accuse labor of causing higher prices because of the control unions have over the supply of labor. Why should farmers be subject to a high degree of competition when others are not?

Special Risks of Farming

Few sections of our economy are as much at the mercy of the weather as farming is. A severe storm or drought can seriously damage, or even wipe out, a farmer's crop. Insurance protection against certain disasters is available, but the cost of adequate protection is prohibitive. In any event, efforts to offset risks add to the cost of production and reduce possible profit.

The Beginning of Federal Aid

The history of federal aid to the farmer goes back over one hundred years and embraces a wide variety of projects. The Morrill Act of 1862 provided for the establishment of landgrant colleges designed primarily for educating the rural population and for promoting education in agriculture and the mechanical arts. In the 1920s, more specialized assistance was made available. Government credit agencies were established to grant the farmer low-interest loans. A Federal Farm Board was created by President Hoover to encourage crop limitation and the formation of cooperatives on a voluntary basis. A half-billion dollars was supplied to help stabilize prices. The Rural Electrification Administration was created in the 1930s to help bring the benefits of electric power to sparsely populated areas, as supply by privately owned utilities would have been uneconomical. The Agricultural Extension Service was created to do research and provide information on improving farming techniques. Crop insurance at a price below the cost to the government was started in 1938 to protect the farmer against total losses caused by weather and insects.

The government has helped the farmer through the school lunch program, food stamps, and donations of food to foreign disaster areas. It has also put pressure on the European Economic Community and Japan to drop high tariffs that insulate their inefficient farmers from less expensive U.S. farm products.

In spite of their number, such aid programs have had only limited value. They have not provided basic, long-term solutions to the farm problem. Other approaches, however, have provided more effective help. These solutions have had two

primary purposes: (1) raising the price received by farmers relative to what they must pay for goods and (2) raising farmers' income. It is usually assumed that incomes will rise if prices are increased. Placed in a setting of increasing consumer prices, any solution that would aggravate this condition would be hard to legislate.

Later Programs for Farm Aid

The depression crisis of the 1930s led to new and broader measures to help farmers. Most of these were designed to raise prices and to improve the farmers' income, although a few included other values also. Each program was initiated by federal legislation and was modified by successive administrations.

Parity and Price Supports

The key idea behind most of the chief solutions offered to solve the farm problem, from the New Deal to the present, is *parity*. Parity is an attempt to provide a basis for economic equality for the farmer relative to other groups in the economy. Specifically, it is designed to keep the purchasing power of a unit of farm production (a bushel of wheat, for example) equal to the purchasing power of the units of production that the farmer buys.

Under the New Deal, parity was based on prices for the period from 1909 to 1914, considered to be "normal" years for the economic position of farmers relative to other economic groups. If the price index of the goods farmers bought during those years averaged 100 and the average price of a bushel of wheat during this same period was $2, the attempt would be made to keep approximately the same relation between prices in future years. If in 1987 the price index of the products farmers bought was 200, what price would farmers have to receive for their bushel of wheat to maintain the same purchasing power for their unit of production?

Let us set up an equation to express the price relations involved here. The price per bushel of wheat during the base period a divided by the price index for products farmers bought during the base period b equals the parity price per bushel of wheat in the current period c divided by the price index for products farmers buy in the current period *d:*

$$\frac{a}{b} = \frac{c}{d}$$

In our example, $2/100 = x/200, or $4 per bushel of wheat. The $4 per bushel would give wheat farmers the same purchasing power for the product they sell as the real cost of the things they buy.

Now that we have seen how parity prices are arrived at, let us see how, in actual practice, payment of the parity price was made to the farmer. Farm prices above the free market price were maintained largely through the operation of the Commodity Credit Corporation, a federal agency. If the support price was $4 a bushel and the market price was $3.80, farmers put their crop into government storage and received a government loan amounting to $4 per bushel. If supply dropped sufficiently to raise the market price above $4, they took their crop out of storage, sold it, and repaid the loan. If the price failed to go to $4, they merely kept the $4 per bushel that the government lent them and the government took the loss.

Most farmers probably consider the payment of full parity fair. Rarely, however, do they receive 100 percent parity. Many other people, however, think that this system tends to favor farmers at the expense of other groups in the economy. Critics of the parity price system point out that the period from 1909 to 1914 was an unusually good time for farmers in comparison with other producers. They also emphasize that output per worker and output per acre have increased very rapidly in agriculture; as a result, abiding by parity gives higher prices to farmers than to other producers in the economy. In addition, this program has meant that not only have consumers had to pay more money in higher prices, but taxpayers have had to pay the high cost of storage.

Acreage Control and Soil Conservation

Recognizing that low farm prices for farm products are the result of inelastic demand and too great a supply, the government has based some programs on efforts to restrict the supply. Under the New Deal a program was begun that tried to restrict supply through *acreage control,* limiting the number of acres planted. Farmers were paid according to the number of acres withdrawn from cultivation as well as for the use of certain soil conservation measures.

If yield per acre had remained constant, this plan might have been effective in reducing surplus. However, a reduction of supply did not occur. Farmers withdrew their poorest acres from cultivation, used more fertilizer and the best hybrid seeds, and produced even more than before.

 Parity through price supports has been the main approach used by the government in an attempt to stabilize prices.

In recent years, other similar programs have been used and have proved only slightly more effective in reducing surpluses. The *soil bank* program of 1956 paid farmers to withdraw land from the cultivation of cash crops and to substitute the planting of timber or cover crops. The program was based on the ideas of restricting output, giving farmers an income subsidy, and conserving soil.

In general, the programs for limiting production through restricting the use of land were not very successful. No significant reduction in the supply of farm products was accomplished until the mid-1960s, when exports of commodities began to increase sharply.

Early in the 1960s, a policy was adopted that combined (1) price supports that reflected the world market levels, (2) continued acreage control to restrict production, and (3) direct payments to farmers to supplement their income. Although these policies sharply reduced surpluses, they also created a problem. Prior to 1960, direct payments by government to the farmers were generally below $1 billion per year. In 1983 the figure was $9.3 billion. It it any wonder that few consumers have shown sympathy for the farmer?

Target Prices

When the Senate Agriculture Committee looked for a new formula, they turned back to a program that had originally been introduced by Charles F.

Brannan, who was President Truman's secretary of agriculture. The legislation that emerged, the Agriculture and Consumer-Protection Act of 1973, passed easily because it was the right legislation offered at the right time.

The basic features of this act are not very different from those of the previous law except for the provision establishing target prices. This provision established a guaranteed price for wheat, corn, grain sorghum, barley, and cotton and allowed for adjustments to reflect increases in production costs. If the market price falls below target level, direct payments are made to farmers. The secretary of agriculture continues to have the right to control acreage in order to reduce production if supplies get out of balance.

 Concentrating on the farmer's income directly and letting the market set the prices for consumers is another approach.

The effect of the 1973 legislation was to remove government restraint and return to the free market system. Farmers were given the freedom to make production decisions based on their expectation of prices. Expanded agricultural exports were expected; the real test was whether relaxing restrictions could increase efficiency.

The first real test of lifting all incentives to set aside lands came in 1974. In 1972, 61.5 million acres were left idle to balance supply and demand. In 1973, the Agriculture Department, responding to almost zero reserves and growing demand, paid farmers not to grow wheat and feed grains on 16.79 million acres. In 1974, the federal government stopped paying farmers for idle land, but only 8.23 million idle acres were planted. Why did any land remain idle?

The land farmers left idle was the least productive land. After remaining idle, this marginal land required much fertilizer to make it productive. If the marginal cost for growing a bushel of wheat is less than or no more than the marginal revenue, farmers will plant their less fertile land. However, the marginal cost for producing went up with the sharp rise in the cost for fertilizer, while crop prices, the marginal revenue, started falling in the spring. The market mechanism was working.

In 1977 Congress replaced the 1973 Act with the Food and Agricultural Act. This new law raised target prices on corn and wheat, increased the amount the government could pay any one producer from $20,000 to $50,000 in any one year, and created a crop base that used as a reference the previous year's planting of the farmer. More important, it established a grain reserve with the hope that this might stabilize prices.

Farm Depression 1980-Style

For the farmer, the 1980s have been as bad as the first five years of the 1970s were good. With farm debt over $200 billion, price levels where they were nearly 10 years ago, surpluses of food worldwide, and foreign governments subsidizing their own farmers' exports, the future looks nearly as bleak to farmers as it did during the Great Depression. What brought on this disastrous picture?

The Wonderful Seventies

Take a look at Figure 17–2 on page 413. You can see that the gap between what the farmer received and what the farmer paid was very large from 1972 to 1976. These were prosperous years for the U.S. farmer because the world food shortage, brought on by extensive droughts, caused farm prices to skyrocket. Land that was submarginal at lower prices was then fertilized and put back into production. Higher prices made it economical to plant. Prices of farm land increased, reflecting the belief that the food shortage would be with the world for a long time, and the U.S. farmer was called upon to fill most of the shortage.

Interest rates were high, but with prices rising on food and land, bankers were anxious to grant farmers easy credit. What could go wrong?

Bad Times

Return to Figure 17–2 and locate the gap between prices received and prices paid from 1980. This time prices paid by the farmer are higher than prices received. In 1985 farmers' net income fell about 30 percent, and 1984 was not a very good year. Farm debt climbed to well over $200 billion. Not only were farms auctioned at a fraction of their previous value, but the banks that lent the farmers money became shaky or failed. The final blow was the impact of a strong dollar. This meant that foreigners buying U.S. farm products had to pay more in their currency to buy the U.S. dollars to pay for the grain. This gave other exporters a price advantage, and U.S. exports of grain declined. Furthermore, the value of the agricultural products the United States imported increased in the mid-1980s because of this foreign exchange problem, the rapid spread of American technology, and lower labor costs abroad.

The world was made aware of drought and hunger ravaging Africa in the mid–1980s and rose to the occasion. However, not many people were aware of the success of the "Green Revolution," an agricultural breakthrough that brought to third world countries the knowledge and ability to become or come close to becoming self-sufficient in food production. Gloomy Parson Malthus, the classical economist in Adam Smith's day, said that food production would expand in an arithmetic ratio while population grew in a geometric ratio. Not so! Using new seeds and growing technology such countries as India, China, and even Saudi Arabia have expanded their food supplies so much that they have found themselves exporting cereals. The United States, Western Europe, and Argentina are accumulating huge surpluses and sometimes engaging in a price war to sell their surpluses. In 1985 world stockpiles of grain reached nearly 200 million tons, a record. Our share of this stockpile went from 23 percent to 45 percent. Figure 17–5 shows the impact of this surplus on prices.

Disasters Bring Relief

The consequences of the 1986 nuclear disaster at Chernobyl in the USSR could have a very significant impact on the economic condition of the farmers in the U.S. Surplus milk cows, which were being prepared for slaughter under a special government program to help dairy farmers, have been saved so their milk might replace the radiated milk in the Soviet Union and Eastern Europe. How the radiation will affect cereal grains is still not known. A more important question is how long the radiation might make food grown in the Soviet's "bread basket" unusable.

It is unfortunate that tragedies such as wars, droughts, and even a nuclear disaster become the means of helping the farmer. Surely a better and more permanent solution to our agricultural problem must be found.

Contrasting Approaches

Many people throughout the world are wondering why, with a world surplus of food, consumers and citizens should subsidize the farmer. Isn't this approach encouraging even greater surpluses?

President Reagan, looking for ways to reduce expenditures and being a strong advocate of the free-market system, has sought to end subsidies. Let the market take its course. Fewer farmers, only productive land in operation, and no government interference will soon bring supply and demand into a balance that will offer the remaining farmers a good income.

This approach was attacked by politicians of farm states and later by those who recognized that the farm depression was having an impact not only on farmers, bankers, and farm equipment manufacturers, but also on all those living in the urban-rural communities that are dependent on agriculture in an indirect way. State governments began to help, and the tide swelled to provide additional government credit, direct and indirect, to keep the great majority of farmers on the farm.

A Graphic Display of the Farmers' Plight in the 1980s

In analyzing the financial condition of the farmers in the 1980s, Professor Harold Breimyer pointed out, "Of the 700,000 full-time farmers, possibly a third or more are insolvent or will become so within two or three years. They are taking hundreds of farm-supply firms and rural banks down with them."[5]

In Figures 17–5 to 17–11 the seriousness of the farmers' problems can be seen visually. Some economists say that these graphs display the true picture, which is that the relatively few farmers who hold most of the assets and produce most of the crops are being subsidized by the taxpayers to preserve the many small proprietary units.

But the question remains as to whether government should interfere with the market to help special groups. If the farmer receives help, what about the steel worker and other industries subject to international competition? This subject will take on a clearer focus when you read Chapter 18.

[5]Harold F. Breimyer, "Agriculture and the Political Economy," *Challenge*, November/December 1985, Vol. 28, No. 5, p. 19.

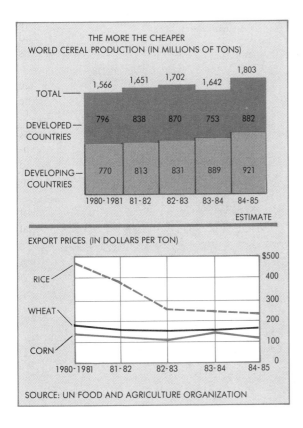

Figure 17–5
The problem starts with expanded world production.

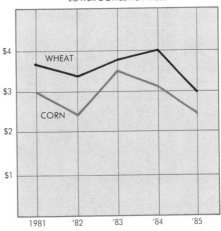

Figure 17–6
U.S. prices are influenced by world production and prices.

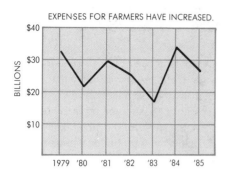

Figure 17–7

Net farm income has fluctuated because of changing crop prices and prices paid by farmers.

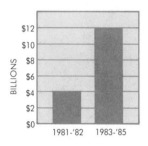

Figure 17–8

Average yearly payments to farmers have tripled.

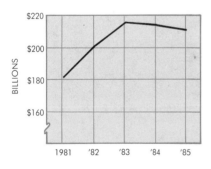

Figure 17–9

While debt continues to rise, the plateau from 1983 to 1985 was caused by some debts that were written off and lower interest rates. Over $25 billion in debts was considered uncollectable.

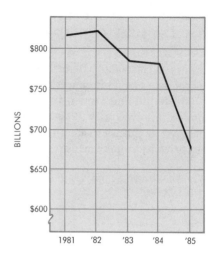

Figure 17–10

The declining value of land has threatened both banks and farm machinery dealers.

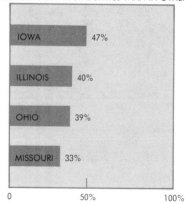

Figure 17–11

The four states above account for nearly one-fifth of the total farm income in the United States.

Chapter Highlights

1. Poverty has many meanings because it is cultural, relative, and subjective. In the United States, poverty is differently defined for rural and urban areas, and it changes with time. For practical purposes the Social Security Administration defines poverty on the basis of the number of people in the family and farm or nonfarm residence.

2. A profile of the poor shows that a disproportionately high percentage are blacks, Hispanics, and children from families headed by a single mother.

3. Business fluctuations, by affecting the marginally poor, increase or decrease the number of people living at the level of poverty.

4. Primary causes for poverty are inadequate education, physical and mental handicaps, inertia, and the inequality of opportunity.

5. Proposed solutions for poverty include eliminating recessions, increasing economic growth, improving education, upgrading job skills, rehabilitating the physically and mentally handicapped, sending government aid to depressed areas, eliminating job discrimination, and providing income or income supplements for the unemployables.

6. Little progress has been made in reducing the number of people officially listed as poor. Nearly one out of every seven Americans still lives in poverty.

7. An important plan for supplementing income is the negative income tax.

8. There is a trade-off between greater equality and more efficiency.

9. The increasing urbanization of the United States is aggravating such problems as traffic congestion, air and water pollution, and overcrowded housing.

10. Haphazard growth of urban areas, inadequate transportation systems, loss of certain industries, changing composition of the population, fragmentation of governmental authority, and lack of regional planning are creating economic problems for many metropolitan areas.

11. The farm problem is generally identified as what to do about an industry with sharply fluctuating prices and a per capita income that is frequently lower than that of nonfarm groups.

12. The technological revolution on the farm has changed farming from a way of life to a business. Small farms are disappearing. Output per worker has increased so less than 3 percent of our working force provides our food. Ten percent of our nation's farms supply 65 percent of the farm products sold.

13. The inelastic demand for farm products is largely responsible for the relative instability of farmers' incomes compared with incomes of other workers and of prices of agricultural products compared with prices of other commodities. A small change in supply brings about a major change in price.

14. Other causes of the farmer's economic problems stem from the increasing costs of the middleman, the excessive number of farmers, the competitiveness of the market, and the weather.

15. The farmer has been offered many kinds of aid, but the main solutions have been aimed at raising farm prices to raise farm income. Most solutions have been based on the concept of parity, equating the purchasing power of the farmer with the purchasing power of the units of production the farmer buys.

16. Efforts to reduce supply in order to raise prices have involved controlling acreage and soil conservation.

17. The 1970s have seen a world food crisis that resulted in an elimination of surpluses and a rise in agricultural exports. This has led to a new policy of establishing target prices with direct payments to be made to the farmer.

18. The 1980s brought a depression to the farming industry. World surpluses, declining prices, huge debt, and a strong dollar forced many farmers into bankruptcy. Rural bankers and farm machinery owners also felt the effects.

Study Aids

Key Terms and Names

new poor
working poor
poverty index
poverty culture
supplementary income
inelastic demand
middleman costs
flexible price support

target prices
subsidy
parity
acreage control
negative income tax
unemployable
soil bank program
urban place

metropolitan area
minicities
spatial force
situational force
regional share concept
model cities program
regional planning

Federal Farm Board
Rural Electrification
   Administration

Affirmative Action—Equal
   Opportunity Employer

Medicare

Questions

1. Poverty means different things to different people. Comment on the following:
   (a) Poverty is relative in time, place, and expectation.
   (b) Poverty is a culture.
   (c) Poverty is a statistic.

2. The poverty index figure has been criticized in several ways.
   (a) Do you think the Social Security Administration, which set the index, has provided a realistic scale?
   (b) Is it fair to set the farm index 30 percent below the nonfarm index?
   (c) What factors does the scale overlook?

3. Throughout your study of economics, policies have been presented for achieving the national goals of full employment without inflation. Why will the achievement of that goal not solve the poverty problem?

4. Poverty is caused by many factors. Show its relation to:
   (a) Education.
   (b) Culture.
   (c) Mobility.
   (d) Health.
5. How is the negative income tax supposed to work? What are the advantages and disadvantages of this approach?
6. Explain the ways in which urban areas are categorized and defined. What economic factors relate to these definitions? What are some of the economic problems faced by metropolitan areas? How might these problems be solved?
7. What place does mass transit have in the modern U.S. city, and what are some of the existing problems in urban transportation?
8. Why is space often mentioned as one of the basic problems of cities?
9. Explain the following statements:
   (a) "Modern technology and chemistry have changed agriculture from a way of life to a business."
   (b) "For the U.S. farmer, the last hundred years have brought many periods of unstable prices and incomes."
10. One justification for giving special aid to farmers is that many of their problems are unique.
    (a) What are some of the causes of farmers' problems that are different from the causes of other producers' problems?
    (b) Describe some of the ways that have been tried to solve the farmers' problems.
11. Explain what is meant by the idea "the paradox for the farmer is that plenty may cause poverty."
12. Programs to help the farmer have focused on raising either income or prices of farm products. Describe the methods the government and the farmer use to reduce production and to raise the price level.

Problems

1. Examine a local welfare program to determine:
   (a) Who is eligible?
   (b) Is work required of those who are capable?
   (c) What is the amount of benefits?
   (d) What is the source of welfare revenues?
   (e) Are there any restrictions on recipients? What, if anything, do you dislike about this program?
2. In the 1970s several of our largest cities were on the verge of bankruptcy. A national controversy raged over whether the federal government should bail these cities out of their financial crises. What is your position? What are your reasons?
3. Examine two industries to determine how they might benefit from government subsidies. Contrast the subsidies to industry with the subsidies farmers receive.

PART

V

International
Economics

International
Trade and Finance

In Parts One through Four, we studied the U.S. economic system and its basic theories, practices, and problems. At various points we noted the relations between our economy and the world scene. In this chapter we consider in much greater detail the importance of international trade, the mechanics of international finance, and the role of the United States in the world economy.

The subject of free trade is debated, as is the question of a freely operating market. There is apparent logic in specialization and the law of comparative advantage; at the same time international trade has often been hampered by special interest groups that have used tariffs and other restraints for selfish motives.

An added factor in determining the extent of international trade is the method that nations use in paying one another. International finance is itself complex; in addition, its patterns often reflect political motives. International financial policy can be a help to the movement of trade; however, it can also be a hindrance to trade.

In recognition of the importance of trade and finance to world economic development, institutions such as the International Monetary Fund and GATT (General Agreement on Tariffs and Trade) have been designed and developed to encourage world trade. The degree of their success in solving age-old problems will have significance for the standard of living of most of the people of the world. Regional institutions have also been developed. We shall trace the growth of one of these, the European Economic Community (the Common Market), and consider whether it poses a threat to our economy and to our participation in world trade.

Chapter Objectives

When you have completed this chapter, you should be able to:

- Explain the laws of absolute and comparative advantage and their importance to a theoretical case supporting free trade.
- Present the mercantilist, national defense, infant industries, and protection of labor arguments on behalf of trade restrictions.
- Discuss and evaluate recent U.S. tariff and trade policy.
- Explain the arguments in favor of international trade associations such as the Common Market.
- Define balance of payments.
- Describe the functions of the World Bank and the International Monetary Fund (IMF).
- Distinguish between fixed and floating exchange rates and describe what the impact of each is on the domestic economy.

A   Why Should a Nation Trade?

The Basis for Trade

The classical point of view toward trade is set forth by the English economist David Ricardo in his book *On the Principles of Political Economy and Taxation* (1817):

> Under a system of perfectly free commerce, each country naturally devotes its capital and labour to such employments as are most beneficial to each. This pursuit of individual advantage is admirably connected with the universal good of the whole. By stimulating industry, by rewarding ingenuity, and by using most efficaciously the peculiar powers bestowed by nature, it distributes labour most effectively and most economically; while, by increasing the general mass of productions, it diffuses general benefit, and binds together by one common tie of interest and intercourse, the universal society of nations throughout the civilized world. It is this principle which determines that wine shall be made in France and Portugal, that corn shall be grown in America and Poland, and that hardware and other goods shall be manufactured in England.

Ricardo's ideas formed the basis for a new concept of trade for Britain and later were adopted by many other nations. Many of Ricardo's arguments in favor of *free trade* continue to be valid, although political and economic conditions have changed greatly since his time. Let us consider some of the ideas and influences that contributed to other theories of trade.

Advantages and Problems of Specialization

As society has grown more complex, people as producers have become more specialized, exchanging the goods and services produced to satisfy more wants. Specialization increases production. Geographic regions of our country vary in terms of their climatic conditions, their skilled labor supply, or their natural resources. In the same way, nations of the world have an unequal distribution of economic factors, with varying conditions and advantages. Taking advantage of these inequalities is the basis for specialization.

Along with its obvious benefits specialization brings problems. Too great a dependence on foreign trade can be a weakness. Many nations believe that to be strong, they must try to be self-sufficient and meet their own needs as fully as possible. However, self-sufficiency for a nation is usually relative. In analyzing the economic potential of nations, we find that some nations are far closer to self-sufficiency than others. Even the United States and the USSR, with their vast territory and abundant resources, are not self-sufficient. They

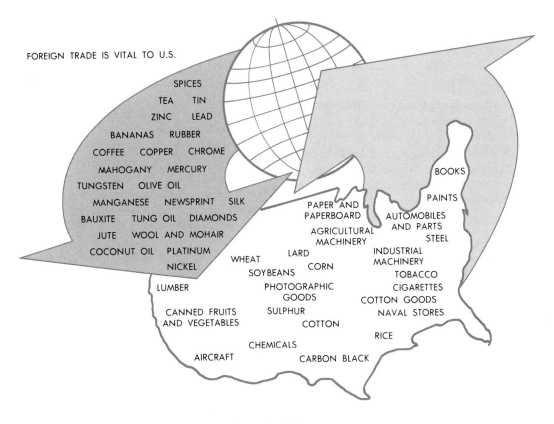

FOREIGN TRADE IS VITAL TO U.S.

SPICES
TEA   TIN
ZINC   LEAD
BANANAS   RUBBER
COFFEE   COPPER   CHROME
MAHOGANY   MERCURY
TUNGSTEN   OLIVE OIL
MANGANESE   NEWSPRINT   SILK
BAUXITE   TUNG OIL   DIAMONDS
JUTE   WOOL AND MOHAIR
COCONUT OIL   PLATINUM
NICKEL

BOOKS
PAINTS
PAPER AND PAPERBOARD
AUTOMOBILES AND PARTS
AGRICULTURAL MACHINERY
STEEL
INDUSTRIAL MACHINERY
WHEAT   LARD
SOYBEANS   CORN
TOBACCO
LUMBER
PHOTOGRAPHIC GOODS
CIGARETTES
COTTON GOODS
CANNED FRUITS AND VEGETABLES
SULPHUR
NAVAL STORES
COTTON
RICE
CHEMICALS
AIRCRAFT
CARBON BLACK

Figure 18–1   Foreign trade is vital to the United States
Many of the items we import are necessary to maintain our high standard of living. (Source: "ABC's of Foreign Trade," *U.S. Trade Policy in Brief,* Department of State Publication 7713.)

must supplement their own products and resources; moreover, they can obtain many things more cheaply by importing them than by producing them domestically. By 1986, the value of U.S. merchandise imports and exports exceeded $540 billion. If we include services, the value exceeded $800 billion. These figures do not reveal the importance of our foreign trade, however. They do not show how important many imports are to our economy, nor do they reflect the importance of our exports to the economies of other nations. (See Figure 18–1). They also fail to show how trade has grown in importance over the years. Between 1960 and 1965, trade as a proportion of our GNP was only 6.7 percent. Between 1978 and 1984, it was nearly 16 percent of our GNP.

Importance of Foreign Trade to the United States

To supplement its own natural resources, our country imports most of its uranium, rubber, manganese, nickel, tungsten, and cobalt; all of these imports are vital to our industrial machine and national defense. Most of our supply of these resources comes from foreign countries. More iron ore and copper are being obtained abroad as our own supplies grow smaller and more costly to mine. As a reflection of our rising standard of living, we also import many manufactured items of good quality in which foreign nations specialize, such as perfume, lace, china, cameras, and pieces of art. Foods that our country cannot produce are also imported. Almost all our coffee, tea, and tropical fruits are brought from abroad.

Although our nation might try to become self-sufficient in some of these areas, to do so would create new problems:

1. It would become necessary to find substitutes for some products we now enjoy.
2. More money would have to be spent to produce things that can be imported at less cost.
3. The economies of other countries that depend on our trade would be hurt. In time our exports to those nations would be correspondingly reduced.

The Law of Comparative Advantage

When one nation is able to produce a product or service more cheaply than another, that nation has an *absolute advantage*. Most people readily accept the idea that we should buy tea from Sri Lanka instead of trying to produce it ourselves; our climate and resources are not suitable for tea production. Sri Lanka can produce tea more efficiently and cheaply, and thus has an absolute advantage. If we attempted to produce our own tea, we should have to draw productive resources away from other industries in which we are relatively efficient. Because the cost of producing tea would be high, its price would soar. Other goods would become more expensive also, because by taking productive resources away from industries where they were being used efficiently, we would probably reduce the supply of goods by those industries. On the other hand, our abundant capital, technology, skilled labor, and minerals give us an absolute advantage over Sri Lanka in computer production. Obviously, it is better to buy tea from Sri Lanka and let Sri Lanka buy computers from us. Both nations benefit from the exchange.

The principle of absolute advantage is so simple and self-evident that few would dispute it. It is a different matter, however, with the *law of comparative advantage*. According to this principle, we can benefit from trade even if we produce everything more cheaply than any other country.

Let us illustrate the concept of comparative advantage with a simple example. Assume that an editor for a publishing firm is also an excellent typist. She has an absolute advantage over her secretary in both editing and typing. Why, then, does she not do both jobs herself? Say that her output as an editor is worth $30 an hour to her firm, and her output as a typist would be worth $6 per hour. Clearly it is better for her to concentrate all her efforts on editorial work and let her secretary do the typing. The secretary is not capable of doing editorial work at all, but does have considerable typing skill even though it is not as great as that of the editor.

Now apply this concept to foreign trade. Assume that the United States produces both computers and clocks more cheaply than Switzerland. We produce the computers four times as cheaply, and we produce the clocks twice as cheaply. We have an *absolute advantage* in both, but the Swiss have a *comparative advantage* in clocks. If we shift productive resources from clocks to computers, our output of computers will rise. Meanwhile, the Swiss should shift resources from computers to clocks. Because each country will be concentrating on what it does best, total output will rise. Terms of trade will develop between us so that we produce enough computers for both nations and the Swiss produce enough clocks for both nations. Total production of both items will rise because each nation is specializing in what it does most efficiently, unit costs of production will probably drop, and consumers in both countries will get more and better goods at lower cost. Of course the real-life situation is more complex, but this is the principle on which all trade is based.

 Terms of trade: the rate at which goods can be exchanged for one another in international trade.

Reasons for Interfering with Free Trade

If we consider free trade only in terms of the theoretical economic arguments involved, there can be little objection to it. However, in reality absolute free trade seldom exists, and those who oppose it are not without their reasons. Let us examine the arguments for and against free trade, recognizing that neither position is generally followed completely.

Mercantilism

From the sixteenth to the eighteenth century, a popular view was that a nation should direct its trade policy in such a way that it would accumulate gold and silver. Those who held this idea considered these precious metals to be the principal form of wealth. They sought to accomplish their goal of accumulating wealth by strict regulation of trade so that the total value of the exports of their nation would be greater than the total value of its imports. The difference in value between the shipments made and received by each of the nations would be compensated for by payment in gold by the nation that showed the deficit in imports. *Mercantilism,* as this system was called, was based on trying to gain a "favorable balance of trade" by following policies that would encourage exports and discourage imports. Much of the reasoning behind mercantilism stemmed from the falsely held belief that a nation, like a business, must sell more than it buys in order to prosper. This view was a guide for the British in governing their American colonies.

 Favorable balance of trade: a situation in which the value of a nation's exports exceeds the value of its imports.

The classical economists pointed out several obvious fallacies in mercantilist theory. There is the fact that specialization has advantages, as well as the simple fact that nations must import in order to export. Precious metals cannot always flow in one direction. Also, when a nation keeps exporting its products and importing gold, the prices of its goods and services are going to rise and it may price itself out of the international market. In the sixteenth century, mercantilist Spain found that many of the benefits of importing huge quantities of gold were dissipated by the inflation that followed. We know that real wealth is the goods and services that people want, not money per se.

Although some of the old mercantilist theories can still be heard, most of the current objections to free trade are based on political, military, and economic considerations rather than the earlier rationale. Those who want to restrict international trade are known as *protectionists.* They generally favor high tariffs and other restrictions.

National Defense

Protectionists often argue in favor of national self-sufficiency for reasons of defense. Wars can cut off goods that are essential to a nation's survival. Therefore, even though it might be more costly to produce synthetics, such as rubber substitutes, at home, the importance of protecting the industries involved in the nation's defense by restricting the importation of such goods must take priority over economic efficiency.

Critics of this position argue that such a policy encourages extreme nationalism, which is one of the causes of wars. If nations were more interdependent, not only would they understand each other better, but they would be less capable of making war.

Infant Industries

Another argument that protectionists advance is that the growth of a nation's industry must be encouraged. An industry in its early growth is at an economic disadvantage when competing with a well-established industry. For example, manufacturing was much more highly developed in England than in our country when we became independent. Our new industries could not compete with the industries of England. By giving our new industries protection, we helped them to get started.

Protection actually benefits not only the industry itself but also the consumer. The sacrifices that the consumer makes in paying higher prices are more than offset by the additional productivity of the country, the new jobs created, and the gradual lowering of prices as competition attracts more businesses into the field and efficiency increases.

The objection to this theory is that it is not only the infant industry that asks for protection.

On the contrary, Congress is besieged by the lobbies of well-established industries seeking protection. Because such industries have failed to become efficient, they look for extra protection from foreign competition.

Protecting the Wages of Labor

Labor frequently points out, and management agrees, that the high standard of living of the U.S. worker requires management to pay high wages. By contrast, foreign firms pay far lower wages. Thus the cost of production of foreign firms is kept down and these firms can sell at prices below those of U.S. firms. Protectionists argue that a large number of U.S. workers may be thrown out of work because they cannot compete with poorly paid foreign labor.

Such an argument might be valid if the output per work-hour in our country matched that of other countries. However, under these circumstances it is doubtful that we would be engaged in such production at all. The reason we were able to have a favorable balance of trade for so many years is that our costs were not higher than the costs of comparable foreign goods. During a recent year, U.S. coal miners received eight times as much per hour as foreign miners, but they produced fourteen times as much. Thus, the labor cost per unit of output was actually lower in the United States. Furthermore, between 1970 and 1977 unit labor costs in the United States rose by only 44 percent as compared with a rise of over 100 percent in most other major industrial nations. By the mid-1980s average hourly wages in several countries were higher than those of similarly employed workers in the United States.

Other costs must be considered also. In some cases where the foreign labor cost per unit is indeed lower, other costs (such as for capital and raw materials) are higher than they are in the United States. When all costs are taken into account, if the foreign country can still produce a comparable product more cheaply, most economists would argue that the United States should either take steps to increase efficiency in that industry or abandon it altogether.

Protecting the Jobs of Labor

Any threat to employment is a serious matter to both labor and business. In spite of the high average productivity of U.S. business and labor, the threat of foreign competition is ever present. It may become necessary in a competitive market to close inefficient plants, which creates a difficult situation not only for the owners and workers of the firm affected but also for the community. Representatives from areas that are particularly hard hit by foreign competition band together to lobby for the protection of the U.S. worker. It is difficult to explain to those so affected that other industries are thriving and that other workers have jobs because foreign nations have been able to increase their imports of our products by earning dollars through their sales to us. Many economists point out that it is wiser and better for all concerned to help communities hurt by foreign imports by establishing retraining programs and locating more efficient industry in their areas rather than by fighting the foreign competition.

Barriers to Trade

In establishing policies to guide economic development, nations have often turned to practices that interfere with the free flow of international trade. Protectionists have used the methods described here to accomplish their purposes, whereas people advocating free trade have tried to remove or modify the practices of protectionism.

Tariffs

The best known device for restricting imports is the *tariff*. A tariff is a tax placed on goods that move into or out of a country. Such a tax is sometimes called a *duty*. Most countries, including the United States, place duties only on imports. Duties are *specific* when the sum to be paid for each commodity is a specified amount; they are *ad valorem* when the amount to be paid varies with the value of the product. An ad valorem tariff of 25 percent on cameras would mean that a $25 duty was paid on a $100 camera and a $50 duty on a $200 camera. *Revenue tariffs*, usually placed on items not produced extensively in a country, are levied to create income; *protective tariffs* are levied to protect home industries. The higher rates of the protective tariff usually have the effect of reducing revenue because they may restrict the importation of goods.

Quota Restrictions

An *import quota* establishes the maximum amount of a particular item that can be brought into a country during a given period. It is usually even more restrictive than a tariff. One nation might willingly accept a high tariff in order to sell goods to another nation, but a quota set by the latter nation would place an absolute limit on the import of restricted items.

Other Hindrances

In addition to tariffs and quotas, other less direct devices have been developed to discourage trade. Controls may be placed on foreign exchange (foreign money or negotiable claims expressed in foreign money) so that an importer can be denied permission to purchase a product if the government wishes to prevent the entry of that particular product. Uncertainty about how an imported item is to be classified, and consequently what duty will be placed on it, can also inhibit trade. Some items may be labeled as unhealthful when the real reason for the exclusion might be that a domestic firm is seeking protection. If a government wants to discourage trade, it is possible to find a variety of ways of doing so.

Development of U.S. Trade Policies

Recognizing the need for income, the first Congress to meet under the new Constitution passed a modest revenue tariff on July 4, 1789. Essentially an agricultural nation, the United States hoped to exchange its products and raw materials for Europe's manufactured goods.

Although the nation depended heavily on the revenue it received from the tariff, protectionist rates tended to increase. An exception to this trend was the interlude of lower rates from 1833 to the Civil War, during which time the agrarian South

and West dominated Congress. The rate increases resumed again once the Civil War started, and continued until 1934, when the Trade Agreements Act was passed. Some attempts were made to lower the tariff during Cleveland's administration, and a degree of success was achieved during Wilson's first term with the lower rates of the Underwood Tariff Act. However, these attempts were in turn canceled out by even larger increases in the rates of the tariffs that followed. The climax was reached with the passage of the Hawley-Smoot Tariff Act in 1930, establishing the highest tariff rate in our history—52.8 percent on the value of all goods imported.

Difficulties in Lowering the Tariff

You might wonder at this point why Congress passed such high tariffs, when it realized that such an economic policy might do more harm than good to the country as a whole. The answer is to be found in the ways tariffs are ultimately decided on. Some Congresses have started out with the intention of lowering rates and yet have passed tariffs with duties even higher than those in effect when they started. How can such a drastic about-face occur?

An individual congressman may be interested in a general lowering of the tariff—except, perhaps, for the industries in his own district. To get the protection he seeks for those industries, he must agree to support the protection of industries in which other congressmen are interested. The result may be congressional "logrolling" and a higher tariff, which may actually be contrary to the interest of the general public.

A New Approach: Tariff Negotiation

Faced with a serious depression and declining foreign trade, President Franklin D. Roosevelt decided to try a new technique for lowering the tariff. Instead of asking Congress for a new tariff law, he asked it for authority to alter duty rates, up to 50 percent of existing rates. This power would allow the administration to negotiate trade agreements within a broadly defined area, and to enter into trade agreements with other nations without submitting these agreements for Senate approval. Each agreement made would be applicable not only to the country it was made with but also to other countries ("most-favored nation" clause).

Congress responded by passing the Trade Agreements Act of 1934, which gave the administration authority to negotiate reciprocal trade agreements. But Congress did not surrender to the president all its power to regulate tariffs. It sharply limited the duration of the law so that the president had to come to Congress regularly to ask for its renewal.

The Trade Expansion Act

With realization growing that our nation had more to gain than to lose by the expansion of world trade, President Kennedy secured bipartisan legislation that took an approach somewhat different from that of President Roosevelt. The Trade Expansion Act of 1962 gave the president the power to raise and lower duties by at least 50 percent; in addition, the act allowed rates to be reduced by as much as 100 percent on duties of less than 6 percent, on articles whose export from our nation and the European Economic Community make up 80 percent or more of free-world exports, and on tropical farm and forest products.

The president was also authorized to negotiate for entire categories of products, such as textiles, and to bargain with the Common Market nations as a single unit. To soften the effect on industries hard hit by tariff reductions, the act provided for retraining programs and resettlement allowances for workers displaced as a result of foreign competition.

Evaluation of Recent Tariff Policy

The results of our nation's policy to increase its foreign trade have been mixed. Overall, rates have been reduced considerably from what they were under the Hawley-Smoot tariff of 1930. In 1930 our rates were over 50 percent, whereas in 1980 total duties collected amounted to less than 8 percent of the value of dutiable imports. But can those who favor free (or freer) trade continue to rejoice?

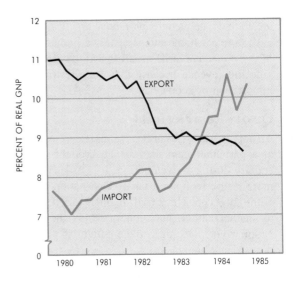

Figure 18–2   Recent trends in U.S. trade

As a percent of gross national product, U.S. exports of goods and services have been falling, and imports have been rising. This trend has caused many people to demand that the government depart from its free-trade policies. (Sources: U.S. Department of Commerce and the Federal Reserve Bank of Cleveland.)

In the years since World War II, the trends in international commerce have seemed to favor an expansion of trade. The United States can take a major portion of the credit for setting this trend. The reciprocal trade agreements and President Kennedy's Trade Expansion Act both contributed to a new atmosphere in foreign trade. Recognition was growing, in our own country and abroad, of the ideas that almost all nations have a vested interest in trade and that trade agreements bring mutual benefits. Threats to the concept of free trade emerged in the late 1970s, however, as the gap between the value of U.S. imports and exports widened (imports greatly exceeding exports) and as the value of the U.S. dollar in relation to foreign currencies declined. (See Figure 18–2.)

In late 1978, for example, Congress infuriated Europeans by failing to prevent higher U.S. duties on $400 million worth of European agricultural imports. And Taiwan feared that quotas placed on its textile exports would seriously damage its economy, which relies heavily on foreign trade. Although some protectionists argued that these moves were justified by the need to save the jobs of U.S. workers, an economist with the Brookings Institution asserted that each job preserved through trade restrictions costs the U.S. consumer $50,000 per year. Some felt that the U.S. moves were justified by protectionist actions taken by foreign governments. European governments have been protecting their farmers with export subsidies and import barriers. In 1982 the United States Commerce Department accused nine foreign governments of illegally subsidizing exports of steel to the the United States. Six nations were accused of "dumping" steel in the United States. That is, they were said to be selling steel at prices below its "fair value." Steel imports as a proportion of U.S. steel consumption rose.

In many other industries (such as radio and TV sets, shoes, and semiconductors) foreign sellers have been winning increasingly larger shares of the U.S. market. Over a million manufacturing jobs have been lost in the United States since 1979, and many blame imports for this. While many people have demanded government action to protect U.S. industries and workers from foreign competition, others have pointed out that consumers would bear the costs of such protection. A study completed in 1985 showed that trade restrictions in several commodities (including sugar, automobiles, and clothing) had added billions to the cost of these items for consumers, and the effect was regressive—the poor were hit harder than were the rich by the higher prices of the protected items.[1] Furthermore, it was feared that efforts to reduce imports would invite retaliation by other countries, thus hurting those workers and industries that export their products.

[1] Federal Reserve Bank of New York, "The Consumer Cost of U.S. Trade Restraints," *FRBNY Quarterly Review,* Summer, 1985, pp. 1–12.

B International Cooperation to Expand Trade

Many social scientists have long maintained that one of the basic causes of war—if not *the* basic cause—is the selfish, unlimited pursuit of economic gain. The struggle between "haves" and "have-nots" is not confined within the borders of a country; it frequently expresses itself between competing countries. If nations would recognize that the best way to assure their own economic well-being is to help increase the size of the world's pie, some of the tensions between nations might be significantly reduced.

World War II marked a turning point for many nations in the development of trade policies. From the horror and ravages of World War II emerged a determination never to allow such destruction to happen again. Motivated by this spirit, the United States and some European countries took giant steps to make the entire world (and failing this, the free world) more of a united economic community.

The United States Takes the Initiative

One of the innovations of the Trade Agreements Act of 1934 was the use of tariff negotiations as an instrument of government political policy in international affairs. Shortly thereafter, the close relation of economic interests and political concerns was to be further emphasized. Even before the United States entered World War II, many Americans recognized the stake we had in a world that was subject to aggression. Congress, therefore, modified our strict neutrality laws to allow an arrangement known as *lend-lease*. This trade agreement provided to Great Britain and her allies supplies desperately needed to carry on the war, and it left details of payment for a later date.

When we entered the war, we increased our aid; so by the end of the war we had handed over $50 billion in aid to our allies. These countries, in turn, supplied us with $7.8 billion worth of goods during the same period.

Aid and Loan Programs after the War

When the war ended, the only big nation in the world whose production facilities were intact was the United States. For most of the world, shortages of consumer goods presented a problem of immediate survival. Almost as pressing was the lack of capital equipment, which threatened to make it difficult for the war-torn nations to solve their problems of scarcity and reconstruction.

The American people rose to the occasion by showing a degree of altruism toward the rest of the world that no other nation has matched in peacetime. From 1945 to 1950, when our own domestic economy was in a period of scarcity (our aggregate demand was greater than our productive capacity), we gave the world over $28 billion in grants and long-term loans.

Early in 1948, we appropriated money under the European Recovery Program (ERP) to help Europe help itself. The idea was initiated by our secretary of state, George Marshall, and thus was popularly referred to as the Marshall Plan. ERP became known as the Organization for European Economic Cooperation (OEEC), and later as the Organization for Economic Cooperation and Development (OECD). Much of the thinking behind the plan was to prevent the spread of communism, which was recognized as having considerable appeal for people living in great economic uncertainty. However, there was also the belief that a strong, economically healthy Europe could eventually become important for our own progress through increased trade.

Many billions of dollars of aid and loans have been granted under other programs. Military expenditures under our alliance system have strengthened the defenses of many nations, enabling them to use more of their own resources for growth and development. Our aid to war-torn and impoverished nations not only was charitable but often had beneficial results for the United States. As the poorer nations improve their own levels of living, they are better able to buy U.S. goods and services, to carry more of the burden of their own defense, to produce goods needed by the rest of the world, and to establish internal peace and stability.

Although the U.S. government aid to foreign countries since 1945 has totaled over $251 billion, there have been other sources of assistance as well. Other developed nations have given substantial amounts of aid during the past decade. As United States development loans declined during the 1960s, commitments of the World Bank rose. United States businesses have invested billions of dollars abroad.

The percentage of our GNP devoted to foreign aid has declined sharply, however. Whereas after World War II the United States spent about 3 percent of its GNP to help other nations, the figure had dropped to well below 1 percent in 1985—below the percentages being contributed by at least 11 other industrial nations. The gap between rich and poor nations continues to widen. In 1970 the richest nations were, on the average, 23 times wealthier than the poor nations. Now they are about 40 times wealthier.

In addition to having humanitarian aspects, assisting others can often be a good investment. It has been estimated that international financial institutions spend $2 on U.S. goods and services for every dollar we contribute to them. By helping the poorer countries develop their economies, we are creating markets for our own goods. (See Figure 18–3.)

General Agreement on Tariffs and Trade

Following the close of hostilities after World War II, the United States took the initiative in expanding international trade. In 1947, along with 22 other nations, the United States signed the General Agreement on Tariffs and Trade. Under the agreement, representatives of member nations meet at regular intervals to review mutual tariff policies and to set duties on certain goods. The agreement has provided a useful framework for discussing multilateral trade agreements.

GATT, as the agreement has come to be called, is based on the ideas of (1) reducing tariffs through negotiations, (2) eliminating import quotas, and (3) applying the most-favored nation treatment so

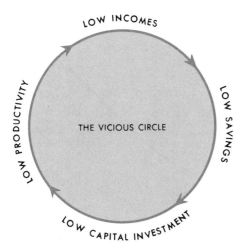

Figure 18–3 The vicious circle
Low incomes, typical in new nations, result in low savings, which in turn result in low capital investment. Low capital investment means that worker-hour productivity is low because of the lack of modern tools and equipment. Low productivity means low incomes. How can the new nations break out of this circle? What are the implications of this circle for their national economic policies? For the richer nations? What kind of aid will do the most good in the long run?

that there will be no discrimination against any nation. By 1985 90 countries had endorsed the agreement, and most of the world's trade was being carried on under GATT rules. The advantage of GATT is that trade agreements are negotiated collectively by the countries affected and not simply on a bilateral basis. Thus there is less chance that two nations will make agreements very favorable to one another but harmful to other contracting parties.

Starting in 1963, the world's biggest trading nations met in Geneva for what has come to be called the Kennedy Round of tariff talks. Each country submitted a list of its "sensitive" products that it wished excluded from negotiations. The remaining products constituted a substantial portion of what is included in world trade. When the Kennedy Round talks ended in 1967, substantial tariff cuts had been agreed to on many goods. Nontariff barriers, such as import quotas, were not affected, however. Recently, GATT officials expressed fear that protectionists were becoming

more influential than at any time since the 1930s and asked for a new effort to reduce tariffs even further.

There have been other "rounds" of trade talks, but protectionist sentiment continues to be strong among many groups in this country as well as among groups in other big trading nations. Lower tariffs on agricultural products have been particularly difficult to negotiate. In the decades since World War II, progress has been made in furthering international trade and in reducing barriers to trade. But some think that what has been accomplished is minor in comparison with what remains to be done.[2]

Developments in Europe

In the aftermath of World War II, the nations of Western Europe also decided to reappraise their economic circumstances and trade policies. They realized that if they were ever to improve their economic position, they would have to forget their past jealousies and move toward some form of economic integration. The threat of Soviet expansion on one side and the encouragement by the United States on the other brought about a spirit of cooperation among previously feuding powers. The progress of these nations under the European Recovery Program strengthened their resolve to find new directions of development, based on mutual benefit.

First Agreements

The first significant agreement on economic integration to emerge in Europe was the economic union in 1947 of Belgium, the Netherlands, and Luxembourg, called *Benelux*. Common tariff schedules were set for imports from other countries, tariffs among the three nations were reduced significantly, and plans were made for full economic integration in the future. The advantages of such an arrangement were soon evident to other countries.

[2] For instance, GATT listed over 25 nontariff barriers to trade, such as regulations for labeling and packaging goods, complex customs classifications, and export subsidies. See Sidney Golt, *The GATT Negotiations, 1973–75* (London: British-North American Committee, 1974), p. 31.

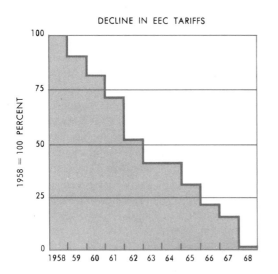

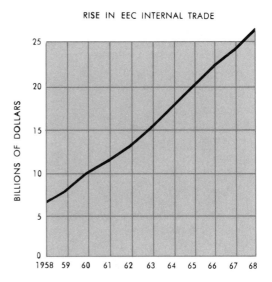

Figure 18–4   History of tariffs and trade within the Common Market

From the beginning of the Common Market to 1968, when all tariffs on industrial goods were removed for member nations, trade rose by over 400 percent. (Source: Common Market.)

In 1950, France, West Germany, and Italy joined the Benelux nations and agreed to unify their coal and steel business by forming the European Coal and Steel Community. The success of this venture and the resolution of anticipated difficulties encouraged the six nations to move toward even greater integration.

The European Common Market

The next important step toward economic integration came in 1957 when the members of the European Coal and Steel Community signed the Treaty of Rome, which launched the European Economic Community (EEC, or Common Market). These nations agreed to eliminate all tariff and other trade barriers among them and to erect a common tariff for outside nations over a period of 12 to 15 years. Furthermore, they agreed to coordinate other economic policies, such as the free flow of capital and labor within the market and a common antitrust policy, in order to encourage competition. These agreements were strongly supported by the United States.

Integration moved ahead so rapidly that the complete elimination of all internal industrial tariffs and the adoption of a common external tariff were achieved in July of 1968, eighteen months ahead of the original schedule. As Figure 18–4 shows, trade among the member nations rose as tariffs declined. The great prosperity and the economic growth rate of the EEC nations have been impressive, and six other countries have joined. (See Figure 18–5 on p. 442.)

The Common Market has not always had a smooth path, however. There have been differences over such key issues as admitting new members, forming a common defense against nuclear attack, organizing a firmer political union, and fostering relations with underdeveloped nations. Some members have changed the value of their currencies independently of the EEC's framework. Differences in tax systems and nontariff barriers have created problems. A common system of price supports for agriculture was adopted, but this led to rapidly growing farm surpluses. In 1974, higher oil and fertilizer prices helped cause unrest among the Common Market's ten million farmers, as their incomes failed to keep pace with the rising cost of living. The European Community's Common Agricultural Policy (CAP) had often been cited as its greatest achievement, for it was based on the concept that the member nations constituted a single market for agriculture and that all farmers would receive common prices and equal advantages. As farmers burned crops, blocked roads, and threatened violence, however, member nations began to take individual action to shore up farm incomes through direct subsidies.

Lack of a coordinated monetary policy was another problem of the EEC in the mid-1970s. Inflation rates differed, with Britain suffering from a 25 percent inflation rate while Germany maintained a relatively low 6.1 percent rate. Britain's balance-of-payments deficit in 1974 was about $10 billion, whereas Germany enjoyed a surplus of $4.5 billion. The energy crisis caused some nations to think first of their own immediate needs and forget that they were supposed to be part of a common economic market.

Nevertheless, the EEC has been instrumental in developing a system of support for members' currencies, moving to give the European Parliament stronger budgetary power, planning for joint management of international monetary reserves, establishing common transport policy (with such features as common licensing standards for drivers), and promoting cooperation on education.

In 1979 a European Monetary System was established to link the currencies of the EEC members and to create a European Currency Unit (ECU) that would become an international currency. But problems caused by the serious recession of 1981–82, and the fact that the economic performances of the members differed greatly, delayed the creation of the new ECU and the establishment of a European central bank.

In short, although the EEC has had many successes, it has not eliminated the economic differences among member nations, brought about uniform economic policies, or ended the divisive nationalism and political wrangling of the members.

The United States strongly supported and encouraged the Common Market from its inception. Trade with the EEC has been of vital importance. In a typical year, the 12 nations belonging to the EEC account for over 24 percent of U.S. exports. Clearly, they are important buyers of U.S. goods and services. Many U.S. banks and business firms have established branches in EEC countries. In view of the size and economic strength of the EEC, as shown in Table 18–1, the United States would be well advised to maintain positive economic and political relations with it.

Other Economic Groups

One aspect of the Common Market is that its existence can pose problems and a possible economic threat to other nations that are not members. Great Britain did not originally want to become part of the Common Market. In 1960 Britain joined Austria, Denmark, Norway, Portugal, Sweden, and Switzerland to form another economic unit in

Table 18–1 The Common Market and the United States

	EEC	United States
Area in square miles	872,211	3,615,122
Population in millions	325	240
Gross domestic product in billions of dollars*	2,408.9	3,627.9
Exports in millions of dollars	281,175	217,888
Imports in millions of dollars	338,769	314,176

*Gross domestic product (GDP) is a measure of the market value of final goods and services produced *within* a country; it excludes international flows of income and thus differs somewhat from GNP.

Source: Authors' estimates based on data for the mid-1980s obtained from the Common Market, the International Monetary Fund, and the U.S. Department of Commerce. (Portugal and Spain, the newest members of the EEC, are included.)

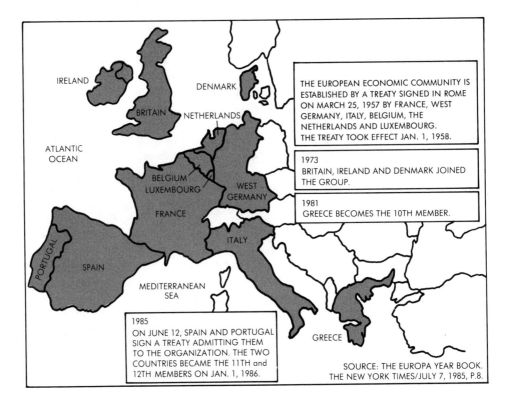

THE EUROPEAN ECONOMIC COMMUNITY IS ESTABLISHED BY A TREATY SIGNED IN ROME ON MARCH 25, 1957 BY FRANCE, WEST GERMANY, ITALY, BELGIUM, THE NETHERLANDS AND LUXEMBOURG. THE TREATY TOOK EFFECT JAN. 1, 1958.

1973
BRITAIN, IRELAND AND DENMARK JOINED THE GROUP.

1981
GREECE BECOMES THE 10TH MEMBER.

1985
ON JUNE 12, SPAIN AND PORTUGAL SIGN A TREATY ADMITTING THEM TO THE ORGANIZATION. THE TWO COUNTRIES BECAME THE 11TH and 12TH MEMBERS ON JAN. 1, 1986.

SOURCE: THE EUROPA YEAR BOOK. THE NEW YORK TIMES/JULY 7, 1985, P.8.

Figure 18–5   The growth of the European Economic Community

The fact that six other nations have joined the original founders of the Common Market is evidence of the EEC's strength and success. However, the larger membership also means increased difficulties in forming common economic and political policies. Source: The Europa Year Book; *The New York Times,* July 7, 1985.

Europe—the European Free Trade Association (EFTA). These European nations became a unit apart from the Common Market. They agreed to lower their own tariff barriers to Association members, but they made no agreements to set up a common external tariff or to integrate their economies in other ways. Although the EFTA nations made progress in lowering their tariffs and increasing their trade, they have not had as high a rate of economic growth as the Common Market nations have had. In addition, the growth of internal trade within the Common Market has been so great that there is concern that nations lying outside the market may have their exports to Market nations displaced. As Figure 18–5 shows, Britain and Denmark later decided to join the EEC.

The Council for Mutual Economic Assistance (COMECON) is the communist version of the Common Market. Its members include the USSR, East Germany, Bulgaria, Poland, Czechoslovakia, Hungary, Mongolia, and Cuba. It provides for trade agreements between the USSR and the other members, economic development, and economic cooperation.

Although the great interest shown in forming trade associations attests to the desire to break down trade barriers and promote international economic cooperation, numerous problems remain. There are bound to be differences among the members of any such group, and also grave questions over their relations with other groups and with such economic giants as the United States.

Many economists applaud the formation of common markets and free-trade areas because they see them as steps toward worldwide free trade and exchange. Others fear that they perpetuate barriers to trade with nonmembers, thus favoring inefficient producers within the group instead of increasing total welfare by dealing with more efficient nonmember producers. This so-called trade diversion away from low-cost outside producers toward high-cost inside producers reduces overall economic efficiency and welfare.

In evaluating possible U.S. policies toward regional economic groups, we must consider, among many possible factors, whether encouragement of such associations will expand markets for U.S. goods, promote worldwide economic growth, help create jobs, raise levels of living, and lead to political stability.

C International Finance: The Mechanics of Trade

Companies that do business abroad usually receive payment in their own currency. French exporters expect to be paid in French francs, English exporters in British pounds, and Japanese exporters in yen. This means that French importers buying our merchandise must find some means of obtaining dollars in order to pay us. If they cannot obtain dollars, they cannot buy our goods, and our sales overseas will be reduced. In turn, trade between the United States and France will be reduced. International payment barriers between nations thus can thwart trade. Let us see what methods and institutions have been developed to aid in selling goods in the world market.

How Foreign Transactions Are Financed

Importers and exporters in most countries need to obtain foreign currency. Suppose that you wanted to import French perfume next year. You would have to obtain some form of payment that would satisfy the French firm. Let us say that the cost of the perfume is 100,000 francs. Naturally you do not have any francs, so you go to a large bank in your city that handles foreign exchange. The bank informs you that a French franc is worth about $0.12 in U.S. money. You pay the bank $12,000 (100,000 times 0.12) plus a small commission and obtain a special check called a *bill of exchange,* which you then send to the French firm. This check is a claim on foreign currency (*foreign exchange*) and can be exchanged for other currency. The French firm takes the bill of exchange

to a bank in Paris and receives its payment of 100,000 francs. The French bank can then present the bill of exchange to a branch of the U.S. bank in France to receive its payment. If you had sold goods to a French importer, the procedure would have been reversed.

Exchange Rate under the Gold Standard

For many years gold served, at least indirectly, as the principal means of international payment. The countries of Western Europe, the United States, and many other trading nations were on the *gold standard*. Their monetary unit—for example, the dollar, the franc, the pound—was convertible to gold. If the dollar was convertible to five times as much gold as the franc and both governments were willing to convert their currency to gold on request, the *exchange rate* was 5 to 1 (five francs to one dollar). Such a system is called the *gold-par rate of exchange*.

 Exchange rate: the value of one nation's currency expressed in terms of another nation's currency.

Fluctuations of the Exchange Rate

Currency, like all scarce goods, is subject to the pressures of supply and demand. When a nation offers attractive goods for sale at reasonable prices, other nations want to buy these goods. As a result the demand for that nation's currency will be great; if the currency were to circulate in a free-exchange market for currency, its value would go up in relation to currencies that were not in such great demand. Under the gold-par rate of exchange, the value of currencies did not fluctuate much. If the demand for dollars went up in relation to that for francs, the French would merely convert their francs to gold and pay the United States in gold. There was, of course, a shipping charge for sending the gold to this country; it was this shipping charge that determined how much the exchange rates could fluctuate. Because exchange rates were quite stable under the gold standard, international traders knew what foreign currencies would be worth. Stable conditions of exchange helped facilitate trade between nations.

Devaluation of Currency

In the 1930s, as worldwide depression set off a chain reaction of declining demand, many nations tried to stimulate their international trade by devaluating their currency. To *devaluate currency* is to change the rate of exchange by reducing the value of a particular currency in relation to other currencies. When nations are on the gold standard, they accomplish a devaluation by lowering the gold content (the value in gold) of their currency.

To see the effects of a devaluation, let us assume that the value of the franc drops from $0.12 to $0.10. Now you can get 100,000 francs worth of French perfume for only $10,000 instead of $12,000. You and other importers will probably buy more French goods. Meanwhile, foreign goods will become more expensive in France. Before, a French importer could get $0.12 for one franc; now he or she can get only $0.10 for a franc. Thus a common result of a devaluation is that foreigners buy more of the goods of the country whose currency has been devalued, whereas the residents of the country with the devalued currency buy fewer foreign goods.

The effect of devaluation on trade depends upon several factors. If France devalues its currency while other nations do not, then France can expect to sell more goods to foreigners while French people will buy fewer goods from abroad. But if the other nations devalue their currencies at the same time and by the same percentage, France will gain nothing. All nations will be in the same

relative position as before. The effect of a devaluation can also be offset by changes in the prices of goods. If the price of French perfume had increased by about 20 percent at the time of the devaluation, the devaluation would not have enabled you to get the perfume cheaper, and the trade advantage that France had hoped to gain by the devaluation would have been wiped out. It is not likely that prices will rise immediately following a devaluation, but eventually they generally will climb. If the devaluation results in the sale of more goods abroad, the price of goods at home may rise because of shortages created by the rise in exports. The law of supply will then work to raise the domestic price and thus cancel some of the effects of the devaluation.

Reserve Currencies

In recent times, devaluation of the dollar or the British pound has had special meaning. When the United States agreed to buy or sell gold from other countries at $35 an ounce, our dollar was literally as good as gold. Britain, although not guaranteeing the conversion of the pounds to gold, agreed to convert pounds to dollars. This, in effect, backed the pound with gold. Because these currencies could be converted to gold directly or indirectly (until President Nixon "temporarily" suspended the convertibility of the dollar into gold in 1971) and because these currencies were so widely used in trade, many nations used the dollar and the pound as reserve currencies to back their own. As a result, a devaluation of either the pound or the dollar would affect not only these currencies but others that had dollar or pound backing.[3]

Great Britain went off the gold standard in 1931 because prices in her economy were declining as a result of the depression. To keep up with other countries in her exports, she would have had to continue to lower her prices in order to compete. Adhering to the gold standard would have

---

[3] The dollar has served as a kind of international currency. When the value of the dollar declined in world markets, nations that had accepted payments in dollars and continued to hold those dollars suffered substantial losses. This was one reason why the OPEC nations decided to raise the price of oil again in 1979. In the early 1980s, however, the value of the dollar soared again.

required depressing prices at home as well as abroad, and this would have aggravated the depression. By devaluing her currency, Britain was trying to keep her domestic prices up but at the same time lower the prices of things she exported. The lower prices on exports were designed to encourage other countries to buy more British pounds with their gold or currency.

This change in policy, however, helped Britain very little because other countries soon followed her example. Preoccupied with their own national economic problems and following a policy of economic nationalism, most nations abandoned the gold standard. They were no longer willing to adhere to the fixed exchange rates that the system required, nor were they willing to buy or sell the gold at a fixed price and in unlimited quantities.

Exchange Rates

After World War II, the "adjustable peg" system of exchange rates developed. Members of the International Monetary Fund (discussed further at the end of this chapter) agreed to define their monetary units in dollars or gold. Each member established a par rate of exchange between its own currency and the currencies of others. To keep their currencies at par (or near), nations set up stabilization funds that would hold supplies of foreign and domestic currencies. Thus, if an increase in the demand for a particular currency threatened to raise the price on the world market above the par rate, the fund could add to the supply and keep the rate stable. If the supply became too large, causing the rate to fall, the fund could buy up some of the surplus to stabilize the rate. It was hoped that these actions, along with the efforts of the IMF, would prevent competitive currency devaluations.

Governments took action to support their currencies. For example, in late 1964, after a long period during which the value of British imports exceeded the value of exports, the pound was sinking because of the decline in demand for it. The British government started using her dollar reserves to buy pounds in the world money markets in order to reduce the supply of pounds and

hold the price close to the official rate of $2.80. Fearing that a devaluation of the pound would create havoc, the United States and other big nations rallied to the support of the British with massive loans. In the fall of 1967, however, the British devalued the pound to $2.40.

The opposite type of situation occurred in Germany in late 1969. Because that nation enjoyed large trade surpluses, others demanded an upward revaluation of the mark. In October 1969, Germany complied by increasing the mark's parity by 9.3 percent. An American buying Germany goods had to pay $0.273 for each mark instead of only $0.25. This meant that German goods became more expensive to foreigners.

There were fears of a world monetary crisis in May 1971, when many people holding U.S. dollars began to think that the dollar was overvalued in relation to the German mark. Dollars poured into Germany, as speculators hoped that the mark would be revalued upward.[4] Eventually the finance ministers of the Common Market countries agreed to let West Germany "float" the mark. That is, instead of requiring Germany to maintain a fixed exchange rate with the dollar, they allowed the mark to rise in value if the demand for it increased, or drop in value if the demand declined. Suddenly U.S. tourists abroad found that they received less when they cashed in their travelers' checks for foreign currencies. Then, in August 1971, as the U.S. balance of trade headed for its first deficit since 1893 and as potential foreign claims on U.S. gold passed $55 billion (while our gold stock dropped to about $10 billion), President Nixon dramatically suspended gold payments and, in effect, ended the system of fixed exchange rates—at least for the time being. The dollar was allowed to float, and many currencies rose in value compared with the dollar.

---

[4] Another factor causing the flow of money into Germany was that the U.S. government and the Federal Reserve were trying to encourage economic expansion at home through an easy-money policy, while Germany was in the opposite position of trying to keep money tight to control inflation. Thus interest rates were high in Germany and low in the United States, and dollars poured into Germany ($1 billion in a single 40-minute period!), forcing the German central bank to reduce its discount rate.

> Floating exchange rates: currency values that are free to change in accordance with the supply of and the demand for the currency, with no interference by governments.

Floating Exchange Rates

Economists differ on the question of floating exchange rates. Some favor a perfectly "clean" (unmanaged) float. Let the laws of supply and demand determine exchange rates, with no interference from governments. Others prefer a "dirty" (managed) float.[5] A nation's currency will rise and fall in relation to others, but government may step in and take action to prevent it from dropping too low or rising too high. Some argue for a return to the old system of fixed exchange rates.

With floating exchange rates, the value of a particular currency can change continually. For example, during a relatively short period the value of the U.S. dollar in terms of the German mark went from 2.30 marks to 2.85, and then fell back to 2.50 marks. If you had been visiting Germany when the rate was $1 = 2.85 marks, you could have obtained 285 marks' worth of German goods and services for $100. If you had been there when the rate was $1 = 2.50, obviously you could have gotten only 250 marks' worth of goods and services for your $100[6]. (Assuming no change in the price of the German goods and services, you could have gotten about 12 percent fewer goods and services.) Thus, importers, exporters, banks dealing in foreign exchange, tourists, and others can be harmed by the uncertainty existing when exchange rates are free to float. In the summer of 1974, for example, a large German bank lost $190 million

through its foreign exchange trading, and the bank failed. A big U.S. bank also failed, at least partly because of losses in foreign exchange dealings. Serious international situations, such as the oil crisis of 1973–74, can cause currency values to change by as much as 4 percent a day. Over longer periods the value changes can be very great. For example, between January and October of 1978, the dollar fell by 26 percent in relation to the Japanese yen and the Swiss franc. Some reasons given for this rapid decline were that the United States (1) did not take firm action to control inflation (thus the dollar dropped in value compared with the currencies of nations with lower rates of inflation), (2) continued to have large deficits in its balance of trade (importing more than it was exporting), (3) was slow in developing a program to conserve energy and reduce oil imports, and (4) had allowed the accumulation of billions of U.S. dollars in Europe ("Eurodollars"), making the dollar plentiful abroad. Of course, these factors are interrelated.

The effects of the dollar's decline were many. Tourists abroad found that prices of foreign goods and services were staggering—at least in places like Germany, Switzerland, and Japan. United States businesses needing or wanting to import foreign products found the prices rising. Some businesses were hurt, such as a U.S. company that had borrowed 100 million Swiss francs in 1972 when the value in dollars was 26 million. Even though the company had repaid 13 million francs by 1979, it still owed the equivalent of $56 million!

The dollar's decline was halted in late 1978 when President Carter took firmer action to fight inflation and announced policies to defend the dollar. The Treasury began selling gold to help "sop up" dollars and make them scarcer. The U.S. government issued bonds denominated in foreign currencies and borrowed from the International Monetary Fund. The dollar rose sharply between 1980 and 1985, largely because the unusually high interest rates in the United States attracted heavy inflows of money from other nations where interest rates were lower. The United States had also stepped up its conservation of fuel and thus narrowed its petroleum deficit. The rate of inflation

---

[5]The noted economist Henry Wallich makes a distinction between "dirty" floats and "managed" floats, although both involve government's influencing exchange rates. To him, restrictions on trade and on capital flows are "dirty floats," whereas intervention in exchange markets, domestic action on interest rates, and policies that influence aggregate demand and therefore affect demand for imports are "managed" floats.

[6]We have used a simple example and a small sum to make the point here. Normally (except when bank failures or international crises might cause a drop in foreign exchange trading), $100 billion a day or more is handled by the foreign exchange market.

was coming down as well. Thus, foreigners were buying U.S. dollars and raising the value of the dollar in relation to their own currencies. Now it was feared that the stronger dollar would harm the nations with weaker currencies, such as France and Italy. In mid-1982, then, the U.S. government sold dollars in the foreign exchange markets to increase the supply and prop up the value of the French franc and the Italian lira. After a slight improvement, the value of these currencies continued to drop in relation to the dollar. In 1985 the United States also bought millions of dollars worth of marks, yen, and British pounds to raise the values of these currencies; and England, France, West Germany, and Japan agreed to cooperate with the United States to lower the dollar's value.

The Balance of Payments

When nations have financial dealings, it is unlikely that the total value of goods purchased by one will equal precisely the total value purchased by the other. The nation that has made the greater amount of purchases must make up the difference. To determine whether a nation must pay or be paid by other nations, a statement called a *balance of payments,* listing all transactions that a nation and its people have with all other nations, is prepared each year. Stated slightly differently, a nation's balance of payments measures the flow of payments between that nation and all other countries. *Debit items* are those for which the United States has to pay foreigners, such as the cost of French wine imported by Americans. *Credit items* are those for which foreigners pay Americans, such as the cost of U.S. wheat sold to some other nation.

People are sometimes confused by the fact that we can have a favorable balance of trade (exporting more than we import) but yet have a deficit in our balance of payments. This is because many factors enter into our dealings with other nations. First, in addition to goods, there are services. Americans flying on French planes, sleeping in French hotels, and attending the Paris Opera are paying for services provided by the French, and their payment becomes a "minus" figure in our balance of payments. If an American sends a gift of money to a relative abroad, this amount

becomes a "minus" in our balance of payments. If you purchase stocks or bonds issued by a foreign firm, your payment becomes a debit in the U.S. balance of payments. On the other hand, if you receive dividends or interest on these securities, these payments become a "plus" in our balance of payments. Direct investments, such as the purchase of a foreign factory, are also included in the balance of payments, as are loans and grants extended by our government to a foreign nation. Of course, we can have a favorable balance with one nation and an unfavorable balance with another. It is the total of all our international dealings that determines whether or not our balance of payments is in equilibrium.

Recently much has been said about balance-of-payments deficits. Indeed, the United States has often had deficits since 1950. If deficits in one year had been matched by surpluses in a later year, there would have been no need for concern about the problem, but this was not the case. Several factors account for the deficits. As Western Europe and Japan recovered from World War II, they became our strong competitors, even underselling U.S. firms in the U.S. market in many cases. The productivity of Western Europe and Japan rose more rapidly than did U.S. productivity, and therefore their production costs were kept low in relation to ours. Next, our foreign aid programs and military spending abroad contributed to the deficit. Third, U.S. companies invested large amounts in other nations, acquiring plants, oil refineries, and other costly facilities. Inflation was also a factor (especially in the late 1960s and 1970s), for it made our goods more expensive to foreigners. Some other countries used tariffs, quotas, and other impediments to reduce the influx of U.S. goods. (This was understandable when there was a shortage of dollars. However, it was more difficult to condone retaining discriminatory tariffs and the like on U.S. goods when there was a dollar glut.)

A balance of payments can involve both *autonomous transactions* and *accommodating transactions.* Let us first look at the former. Autonomous transactions include all the credits resulting from exports of U.S. goods, money spent in this country by foreign tourists, foreign purchases of U.S. securities, and so on, as well as all the debits resulting from imports of foreign goods, gifts to foreigners, U.S. loans to foreigners, and so on. If the sums of the credits and debits are equal, there is little cause for concern, as these autonomous transactions are in balance. Accommodating transactions, on the other hand, must be made when the autonomous transactions do *not* result in a balance. A simple example of an accommodating transaction would be the payment of $1 billion in gold to compensate for a $1 billion deficit in our balance of trade with another nation. Obviously, however, if gold were the only means of assuring a balance, a nation would eventually exhaust its gold supply if it continued to run deficits. Indeed, many feared this was happening to the United States. (The U.S. gold stock, valued at $24.56 billion in 1949, had dropped to only $10.89 billion by 1968.) When our autonomous transactions resulted in deficits in the 1960s and 1970s, we reduced our gold stock and other reserve assets. Foreigners acquired many billions of U.S. dollars.

Coping with Deficits

When accommodating transactions show disequilibrium in a nation's balance of payments, what steps can be taken to correct the situation? Several actions have been tried or proposed in the United States:

Controlling inflation is an important step in equalizing a nation's balance of payments, because it helps keep our prices low in relation to the prices of foreign goods and thus stimulates our exports.

Increasing productivity helps, for it enables us to produce more and better goods at lower cost. Thus, greater productivity helps to control inflation and to make the United States more competitive with foreign producers.

Both of these are positive steps that benefit our economy domestically and help promote economic growth without causing sharp rises in prices. Some of the other proposed steps are seen as negative by many economists. *Establishing tariffs, quotas, or other trade restrictions* might temporarily give us an advantage in trade, but in the long run these steps could lead to domestic price increases, inefficient use of our resources, and retaliation by other nations. (When President Johnson suggested that Americans refrain from flying on foreign airlines, the director of a large foreign airline stated that he would then have to stop buying planes from U.S. aircraft manufacturers.) The quotas that existed between 1980 and 1984 on Japanese cars added hundreds of dollars to the price of cars sold in the United States (including those made by U.S. companies).

Devaluating the dollar would make our goods cheaper to foreigners, but foreign countries might then devalue their own currencies by an equal or greater amount and nullify our action. Furthermore, any foreigner who had accepted U.S. dollars in payment for goods would be hurt, and confidence in the dollar would decline.

Controlling foreign exchange has been proposed. When U.S. exporters sell goods to others, they earn foreign exchange. The foreign exchange (say German marks or French francs) can then be used by U.S. importers to buy foreign products. Some people have thought that the government should control foreign exchange by requiring exporters to sell their foreign exchange earnings to the government. The government could then ration this foreign exchange, not only restoring equilibrium in the balance of payments but even deciding what kind of imports to favor. The critics of such a scheme point out that it destroys freedom of choice and that there would be bitter disputes over who could have the scarce foreign exchange.

Finally, *discouraging investment abroad* is a possibility. In 1963, the U.S. government did try to discourage Americans from buying foreign stocks and bonds by imposing an interest equalization tax of 15 percent (later cut to 11.5 percent) on such purchases from foreigners. Although such an action might help to curb the outflow of dollars in the short run, the United States is depriving itself of future earnings that would be derived from those investments. In addition to the tax, there was also a voluntary foreign credit restraint program (specifying ceilings on the amounts that our financial institutions could lend to foreigners) and a foreign direct investment program designed to limit direct investment outflows by U.S. firms.

CONTROVERSY IN OUR TIMES

The Dollar in World Markets

According to a leading German banker, the U.S. dollar is "the most frequently discussed economic phenomenon of our times." He adds, "... the dollar's exchange rate is at present the most important price in the world economy ...."[8] Because the dollar acts as a world currency, its value affects many nations. The central banks of many countries hold huge reserves of dollars, and over half of all world trade is priced in terms of dollars. Any shift in the dollar's exchange rate (its value in relation to the currencies of other nations) will benefit some and hurt others. Some people suggest, therefore, that the dollar's value should be more tightly controlled.

Pro

The dollar's exchange rate has been too volatile and unpredictable. Several years ago the dollar was rapidly declining in value. This made it difficult for Americans to purchase foreign goods and services. The rise in the price of foreign goods made it possible for U.S. businesses to raise the price of competing goods produced here, thus worsening inflation. Foreigners who dealt in dollars or who held dollars as reserves were hurt. People in the United States who had borrowed foreign currencies found that they had to pay back more than they borrowed because the declining dollar would buy fewer units of the foreign money. The United States lost face in the eyes of the rest of the world.

Then the dollar went soaring upward, and the situation was reversed. United States exporters found it hard to sell abroad because foreigners would have to pay more for U.S. dollars. Peo-

ple in the United States now bought the relatively cheaper foreign goods, and U.S. manufacturers complained that they could not compete. Job losses were often blamed on the "overvalued" dollar. Poor nations that had borrowed dollars found it difficult to repay both the loans and the interest because they had to use more and more of their own currencies to obtain dollars. The answer to this problem is to end the system of floating exchange rates and return to fixed rates. We might even return to the gold standard (or something much like it). At the very least, governments should intervene to keep the dollar's value stable—selling dollars in the world market when the value of the dollar goes above the desired level, and buying dollars to make them scarcer when the dollar drops below the fixed rate. This would restore stability and help to eliminate risk and uncertainty.

Con

Fixed exchange rates did not work in the past. Currency values should be determined by market conditions. A drop in the exchange value of a nation's currency means that it is importing too much, that it is too inefficient to compete in world markets, that it is permitting a high rate of inflation which makes its goods too expensive, that it is going too deeply in debt, or that others have lost confidence in the nation's stability. A nation should bring its exchange rate back up by addressing these problems, not by interfering with the money market. The fact that the U.S. dollar has soared in value shows that our federal deficit is too high—the relatively high interest rates caused by this deficit are attracting foreign investors, and their demand for dollars helps to keep the exchange rate above normal. We need to bring the deficit down. Interest rates would then

[8]Otmar Emminger, "The International Role of the Dollar," *Economic Review,* Federal Reserve Bank of Kansas City, September/October, 1985, p. 17.

CONTROVERSY IN OUR TIMES

fall, and there would be less foreign demand for U.S. dollars. No government knows what the exchange value of the dollar should be, so any fixed rate would be artificial and would soon break down under market pressures.

Consensus

Perhaps we need a middle ground, rather than the extremes of fixed exchange rates on the one hand or freely floating rates on the other. We could establish "reference zones"—ranges within which a currency would be permitted to fluctuate against other currencies. For example, the dollar might be allowed to vary by no more than

10 percent from a particular exchange rate. If it went above or below the limits set by the zones, action would be taken to reverse the trend. If the rate went too high, the government would put dollars into the world money markets, thereby increasing the supply of dollars and driving down their price (exchange rate). If the dollar dropped too low, the government would buy dollars and take them off the market to make them scarce and raise their price. Other governments would be expected to cooperate by buying or selling dollars, or by changing any fiscal or monetary policies that might be contributing to an undesirable rise or fall of the dollar's value.

These programs did help curtail financial flows, but they also shifted international financial activity away from the United States. Hoping to reverse "the decline of the United States as an important international financial center," the government terminated these programs in 1974.[7]

Seeking the cooperation of other nations has been tried. The United States has attempted to get Germany to stimulate its economy in the hope that Germans would be more prosperous and buy more U.S. goods. Because of the fear of inflation, the Germans have not been too receptive. We have also tried to convince the Japanese to buy more U.S. products and cut down on their exports to us. Although some agreements have been made, it is unrealistic to think that the burden can always be shifted to others. They have their political and economic problems too. Just as U.S. firms and workers protected by tariffs will apply pressure on the government to retain them, for example, so will foreign business and labor.

What all of this leads to is the conclusion that there is probably no nation that can "go it alone" today. Several of the steps just outlined can be taken unilaterally by a nation with a balance-of-

payments problem (increasing the rate of productivity growth, controlling domestic inflation, and so on), but international cooperation and coordination of policies are essential in the modern world. Let us now examine the international organizations that have been established to help deal with world monetary and trade problems.

International Financial Institutions

Before World War II, two important financial institutions were organized to facilitate international trade and payments. The Bank for International Settlements makes it possible for central banks to work together in arranging temporary loans to stabilize currencies. The Export-Import Bank, an agency of the U.S. government, was set up in 1934. It makes loans to help finance trade between our country and other nations. It has also stimulated private loans by guaranteeing their repayment.

Other international financial agencies were organized in the postwar years. Even before the war ended, representatives of 44 nations met at Bretton Woods, New Hampshire, and signed an agreement that created the International Bank for Reconstruction and Development, known as the

---

[7]*International Economic Report of the President,* February 1974, pp. 67–68.

World Bank, and the International Monetary Fund. The purposes of these institutions were to (1) help restore the war-ravaged nations, (2) aid under-developed nations, (3) assist in stabilizing exchange rates, and (4) facilitate trade by allowing nations to borrow currencies needed to pay for imports.

World Bank

The World Bank normally finances the foreign exchange portion of the costs of projects that, in its judgment, will contribute substantially to the productivity of the borrowing country. Loans go only to member governments, their agencies, or private firms carrying their member government's guarantee. The borrower must prove ability to ser-vice the loan and show that other sources of financing could not be obtained. The most com-mon projects financed by the bank have been highways, railroads, dams for irrigation or elec-tric power, and such industrial projects as steel mills. Fearing that poor people derived too little direct benefit from expenditures on these kinds of projects, in the late 1970s the bank began to sup-port projects that would provide immediate help to the host nation's poorest citizens. For example, money was spent to buy seeds and fertilizers for Nigerian farmers. Furthermore, the bank began to urge nations receiving bank loans to bring about a fairer distribution of income.

The World Bank has been a financial success and has earned huge profits. In fact, the bank has been criticized for conservative policies that have resulted in failure to aid poorer nations most in need but unable to meet the bank's high standards. To supplement the bank's activities, the Interna-tional Finance Corporation (IFC) was set up in 1955. The IFC makes nonguaranteed loans to pri-vate enterprise in developing countries when pri-vate capital is not available on reasonable terms. The IFC may also provide risk capital by buying stock in corporations and may invest in develop-ment banks that reloan to other institutions. When it was found that many poor nations needing hous-ing, schools, hospitals, and the like were unable to service conventional loans without seriously straining their balance-of-payments situations, the International Development Association (IDA) was created in 1960. The IDA grants "soft loans," loans made for a broader range of purposes and on more generous terms than World Bank loans. Loans are usually granted by the IDA on an interest-free basis (but with three-fourths of 1 percent annual service charge) for a maturity period of 50 years. The IDA's resources are not great, however, and the gap in wealth between rich and poor nations continues to be a cause of much concern.

International Monetary Fund

The International Monetary Fund (IMF) provides a source of international credit for short-term bor-rowing to facilitate trade. The borrowing nation must show how it expects to pay back its obliga-tions. By 1986, 148 nations had contributed gold, pounds, dollars, and other currencies to the fund in accordance with a quota assigned on the basis of ability to pay. Many countries have borrowed from the IMF, including the United States.

The short-term credit available from the fund is an aid in balancing payments. If Italy were short of dollars, for instance, she could buy dollars from the fund with her own currency. When her bal-ance-of-payments position improved, she would buy back the Italian lira with dollars or gold.

The International Monetary Fund served an additional function by obliging its members not to change the exchange rates of their currency by more than 10 percent of the original par value (value of a currency expressed in ounces of gold or dollars). It was expected that a 10-percent depreciation in the par value of a nation's currency would help overcome a deficit in balance of pay-ments. The lower prices of the nation's export goods would stimulate international sales. If this adjustment did not help, the fund could permit additional depreciation of the nation's currency.

In spite of this early effort made by the IMF to stabilize exchange rates, serious problems remained.

During 1958–68, for example, world trade more than doubled, but monetary reserves grew by only about 25 percent. Between 1965 and 1970, the gold reserves of central banks and govern-ments declined. Consequently, the IMF members decided to create a new reserve asset called *Spe-cial Drawing Rights* or SDRs.

The ability to create SDRs is like the ability

to create more money when needed. The SDRs were to be used in international monetary affairs much as gold was used; indeed SDRs are sometimes called *paper gold*. With the acceptance of SDRs by the chief trading nations, it was hoped that the world monetary system had been provided with a means of bringing about an orderly growth of reserves. The SDRs are allocated among IMF members in proportion to their existing quotas in the fund, the largest share going to the United States. SDRs could be increasingly important in the future. They were intended also to take some of the pressure off the U.S. dollar, which the world has been using as a reserve currency and as a trading and financing currency. Gold was expected to lose some of its importance, as the SDRs were to become the main growth element in world reserves.

Most economists were pleased with this development, but crises in the foreign exchange markets continued to occur. After the United States decided to stop buying and selling gold freely in its transactions with foreign monetary authorities, the system based on par values collapsed.

A situation of floating exchange rates emerged, but with governments consulting one another, intervening in the exchange markets to influence exchange rates, and coming to the aid of countries in serious trouble. For example, in 1974 ten lead-ing industrial nations decided to come to the aid of banks facing huge losses in foreign currency dealings. Also in that year the IMF established an "oil facility" to help members whose balance of payments had been seriously disrupted by the rapid rise in world oil prices. Later in the 1970s the IMF sold some of its gold in order to provide a special fund to aid the poorest countries. In 1982 Mexico faced a crisis after the downturn in the prices of oil and its other major exports forced the Mexican government to devalue the peso and made it difficult for Mexico to pay its external debts. Aid was forthcoming from the IMF, the Bank for International Settlements, many international banks, and the United States. Thus, although the 1980s brought a threat of trade "wars," the shock of the oil crises, worldwide inflation, and international recession may have convinced many world leaders that these problems could be resolved only through international cooperation.

International Economic Summit Meetings

In May of 1986, the leaders of seven major industrial nations met in Tokyo for the twelfth annual economic summit conference. During the conference the United States, Japan, West Germany, Great Britain, France, Italy, and Canada agreed to work together to meet such challenges as high

Economic Growth

A nation is growing when it is increasing its real per capita output of goods and services. The international financial institutions such as the World Bank and the IMF are instrumental in promoting growth, especially in the developing nations. The conditions that favor economic growth include political stability, a unified economy, a spirit of enterprise, a supply of natural resources, modern technology, workers who are highly motivated and trained to produce, and an adequate rate of capital formation—that is, the production of enough factories, machinery, tools, and so on, not only to replace capital goods that are wearing out or becoming obsolete, but also to provide a net increase in the stock of capital. Social capital is also needed. Such capital consists of roads, bridges, port facilities, schools, hospitals, and similar enterprises that the private sector cannot profitably provide, but that are necessary for other enterprises (such as factories and stores) to function. When any of these conditions are lacking, or are not sufficiently developed, aid from the more prosperous nations or from international agencies may be imperative if the poorer country is to grow economically.

unemployment, trade imbalances, the uncertain behavior of exchange rates, pressures to establish trade barriers, aid to the developing countries, pollution, and the effects of changes in energy prices. A new "Group of Seven" was formed, to be made up of the finance ministers of the seven nations. These officials will work more closely together and will meet more frequently between summit meetings.

The finance ministers will be expected to review the members' individual goals and economic forecasts to see if they are compatible with one another. They will attempt to coordinate policies to promote economic growth without infla-tion, encourage investment, create jobs, and bring about greater stability in exchange rates. For example, they will establish a range (or "target zone") for exchange rates for their currencies. Under this "managed float," currencies will be allowed to fluctuate only within the specified range. If a nation's currency goes above or below the range, that nation will be expected to take steps to bring the value of its currency back into the agreed-upon zone.

Although it will not be easy for these countries to coordinate their policies and their actions, they have clearly recognized their economic interdependence.

Chapter Highlights

1. Foreign trade is important because no nation is completely self-sufficient. Specialization in output by different countries offers the same advantages as it does within a country. Most nations must rely on foreign trade for materials and products that they lack entirely or cannot produce profitably.

2. The law of comparative advantage shows how total production is maximized when each nation specializes in producing things in which it has the greatest relative advantage over other nations.

3. Among the reasons protectionists give for interfering with the free flow of trade are a need for a "favorable balance of trade," requirements of national defense, protection of infant industries, and protection of wages and jobs.

4. The main barriers to trade are tariffs and quotas, although other devices are also used.

5. With few exceptions U.S. tariffs were protectionist until the passage of the Reciprocal Trade Agreements Act of 1934. Shifting power to negotiate agreements to the president has allowed tariffs to be lowered more easily, although Congress retains power to allow exceptions. The Trade Expansion Act of 1962 gave the president additional power to negotiate trade agreements.

6. After World War II, the United States took the initiative in helping to rebuild war-torn economies. It provided immediate relief with supplies of consumer goods as well as aid for long-range economic development.

7. European nations have responded well to the initiative of the United States in respect to economic integration. This integration has led to the development of the Common Market (EEC) and the European Free Trade Association (EFTA). Other regional associations have been set up in Latin America, Africa, and Asia, but none has devel-

oped as fast and completely and with such dramatic results as the Common Market.

8. International trade requires the exchange of currencies in the settlement of accounts. An importer must make payment to an exporter in the latter's national currency. If the importer's country lacks such currency, or does not have the means to buy it, trade can be hampered.

9. The rate of exchange is the value that one currency has as compared with another currency. For many years, when nations were on the gold standard, the rate of exchange was stable. Devaluation and the abandonment of the gold standard led to great fluctuations in the exchange rate.

10. After World War II, exchange rates were stabilized in several ways, including the exchanging of gold, the buying and selling of currencies by nations to keep their exchange rate in the money market close to their official exchange rate, and making valuation changes of less than 10 percent, under provisions of the International Monetary Fund.

11. A series of international monetary crises in the late 1960s and early 1970s led to a collapse of the system of fixed exchange rates, and the larger nations decided to let their currencies float, though with some government intervention to prevent rates from changing too drastically.

12. A balance of payments is a statement listing all transactions that a nation and its people have with all nations during a year. When payments are greater than receipts, a nation has a deficit. In 1950 the United States moved from a surplus to a deficit in its balance of payments. This continuing deficit became serious enough to necessitate changes in our economic policy.

13. Several international financial institutions exist to aid nations in economic development and foreign trade. Two of the most important agencies are the World Bank and the International Monetary Fund.

Study Aids

Key Terms and Names

mercantilism
infant industries
ad valorem duty
protectionists
lend-lease
exchange rate
currency devaluation

balance of payments
law of comparative advantage
favorable balance of trade
free trade
tariff
quota restriction
most-favored nation

accommodating transactions
autonomous transactions
foreign exchange
gold standard
SDRs

Benelux
EEC
Common Market
EFTA

International Monetary Fund
GATT
Export-Import Bank
World Bank

Trade Agreements Act
IFC
IDA

Questions

1. The quotation "No man is an island" may well be applied to nations and their trade. Explain how this idea might be applied specifically to the imports and exports of the United States.

2. Foreign trade is a significant factor in the U.S. economy.
   (a) Why can it be said that the standard of living in the United States partly depends on foreign trade?
   (b) Evaluate the statement "Although foreign merchandise trade represents only about 16 percent of our total economic activity, its effect is felt in every section of the United States."

3. Explain the following apparently contradictory ideas:
   (a) Nations should concentrate on producing those goods and services that they can produce most cheaply.
   (b) It is often advisable to import some goods that can be produced at home, in order to help the total economy.

4. What are the arguments for and against tariffs and other trade barriers? Evaluate each argument.

5. Differences of opinion exist on the effect of tariffs on trade.
   (a) List possible barriers to the smooth flow of international trade and explain how each works to hinder trade.
   (b) How might freer trade affect the U.S. economy?

6. Defend or refute each statement:
   (a) The huge sums spent after World War II by the United States in foreign aid were necessary for Europe's salvation and our nation's own economic health.
   (b) The cost of foreign aid might well be a small investment for a large return in friendship and world peace.
   (c) Efforts by the United States to build European economic cooperation may, in the long run, result in a serious curtailment of U.S. trade.
   (d) Multilateral trade agreements, such as those made through GATT, are preferable to bilateral trade agreements.

7. Discuss the following statements, presenting the facts involved and evaluating the general truth of each assertion.
   (a) Exports and imports are the only visible items in the balance of payments.
   (b) The invisible items may be just as important as the visible to a favorable balance of trade.
   (c) The United States was forced to reexamine its economic policies because of a continuing deficit and gold outflow.

8. Explain:
   (a) How the World Bank and the International Monetary Fund operate.
   (b) What the main differences are between the two agencies.
   (c) How these agencies contribute to world economic stability.

Problems

1. What big industries in the United States rely heavily on foreign trade? Find out approximately how many jobs in the United States depend on foreign trade. How is the average American affected by foreign trade?

2. Prepare a list of arguments to support each of these positions:
   (a) a position favoring the policies of classical mercantilism
   (b) a position favoring completely free trade

3. Study the monetary crises that led to the downfall of the fixed-exchange rate system that had been established at Bretton Woods in 1944. Consider the events of May 1971, for example, in which the German mark was allowed to float. How did the U.S. balance-of-payments problem help bring on the crises? What effect did devaluations of the U.S. dollar have on the international monetary situation? How and why did some governments bypass the IMF during these crises? What did the United States and other leading nations do about the problem?

4. As the mid-1970s approached, worldwide

inflation was a problem receiving much attention. Some economists stated that the United States had "exported" its inflation to other countries. Drawing on what you have learned about inflation, supply and demand, money and banking, and international economics, try to explain how it might be possible for the United States to export inflation. What U.S. actions and policies might cause inflation here to spread to other nations?

5. In the early 1980s several foreign nations complained that high interest rates in the United States were hurting their economies. How and why would high interest rates here hurt other countries? The U.S. government entered the foreign exchange markets and sold dollars for foreign currencies. Why might our government have done this? Would it help or hurt other nations? Explain how and why.

6. In late 1985 the growing deficit in the U.S. balance of payments and the fact that the United States had become a debtor nation for the first time since 1914 caused many people to demand that the government adopt a more protectionist stance. President Reagan attempted to adhere to a basically free-trade policy, but even some economists felt that this policy was out of touch with world realities. Examine the arguments on all sides of the issue and analyze each argument, considering the welfare of consumers, economic efficiency, the decline of some U.S. industries (and the loss of jobs therein), and U.S. relations with other nations.

Appendix: Economics in Careers

In Chapter 1 we explored the role of the professional economist as well as the contribution economics makes in preparing us to be more effective consumers and citizens. In this short appendix we will consider the role of economics in other careers and what other economics courses might be useful in preparing for those careers.

A Method of Reasoning

Probably the greatest value of studying economics lies in the method it provides for viewing almost all problems. The discipline has developed tools that permit a logical analysis of problems. As a consumer, how can we maximize our satisfaction within the constraints of our budget? As a worker, how can we determine which of several opportunities will provide us with the greatest rewards? As a business person, how can we maximize our output for a given number of dollars of input or determine which of several outputs will give the greatest revenue? As a citizen, how can we evaluate the impact on the private sector of raising taxes? Using graphs and equations, economics provides a framework for analysis of these questions and even very specific problems, such as how to maximize learning when dividing study time between history and economics. To be able to identify what has to be given up in order to get something else is to approach problem solving with clearer insight.

Business Administration

The fastest growing program in colleges during the last 10 years has been business administration or management. Women particularly have shown increased interest in this program, as affirmative action policies have opened higher level positions to them. Those majoring in business administration or management will usually take courses in accounting, finance, marketing, production, and organizational behavior. Almost all such programs require a core of economics courses: intermediate microeconomics (also called price theory and managerial economics), intermediate macroeconomics (aggregate economics), government and business (antitrust and regulation), money and banking, and statistics.

In many colleges management may be combined with other majors such as nursing, art or psychology.

Accounting

Increasing complexities in tax law have stimulated interest and job opportunities in accounting. In addition to the usual array of courses in taxes, auditing, and public- and private-sector accounting, the same core of economics courses mentioned under business administration is recommended for accounting majors.

Retail Management/Marketing

Buying, personnel, merchandising, advertising display, market research, and fashion are frequently required for a retail management major. Again a core of economics courses is required, including the intermediate theory courses.

Law

The study of economics provides an excellent background for entrance into law school. Besides intermediate theory courses, courses dealing with government regulation, antitrust law, and industrial organization are usually recommended, as well as related courses in taxes and finance.

Public Administration

Although the number of government employees has declined since 1980, when it reached a peak of 16.2 million, the decline has been small and the number of employees retiring is considerable. In addition, many nonprofit organizations require individuals with public administration training. Intermediate theory courses frequently are recommended, and some programs require courses in public finance, urban economics, and the economics of human resources.

Engineering

Engineers, like economists, are concerned with cost effectiveness. Many engineering programs require at least a basic course in economics. In addition, many colleges suggest an intermediate microeconomic theory course as well as a course in urban economics.

Interdisciplinary and Multidisciplinary Studies

Many students take dual majors to increase their job options and to reinforce their understanding. Interdepartmental majors often combine management with chemistry, mathematics, or computer science. Interdisciplinary studies in such areas as the environment and international economics are growing in popularity. The amount of economics required varies with the program and the college, but a strong economics background is considered a strong plus not only for job placement but also for career advancement.

Opportunities for Women and Minorities

Historically, few women, blacks, or Hispanics have been interested in careers in economics or related fields. On the other hand, many individuals with roots in East Asia and the Indian subcontinent have shown great interest in economics. The strength or weakness in interest has usually been correlated with quantitative skills. However, recent data indicate large increases in the numbers of women and minorities entering careers in accounting, business management, and economics.

Alice M. Rivlin, long-time head of the Congressional Budget Committee, and Juanita Kreps, former Secretary of Commerce, are noted economists who may serve as role models for aspiring women. Andrew F. Brimmer was the first black to serve on the Board of Governors of the Federal Reserve System. He is now a Professor of Economics at Harvard. Sir Arthur Lewis, Professor of Economics at Princeton, received a Nobel prize in Economics for his work in economic development. Although neither of these men is as well known as are many blacks in high-level public office, each has made substantial contributions to the world of scholarship.

Glossary of Economic Terms

Most of the terms in this glossary are found in the text. For a more extensive treatment of any term concisely defined here, use the index to find the location of the term in the text.

ability-to-pay principle: justification for taxing people with larger incomes a greater percentage of their income, based on the principle of diminishing marginal utility.

absolute advantage: an advantage that one nation has over another in trade by being able to produce a good more efficiently (at less cost).

acceleration principle: a change in sales at the consumer level will bring about a greater change in sales of producer goods.

acceptability: a characteristic of money that allows it to be accepted by individuals and businesses as a medium of exchange in a wide market.

administered price: price set under conditions of imperfect competition, where the individual firm has some degree of control.

ad valorem tax: tax applied according to the value of what is being taxed, particularly imports.

agency shop: work place in which all employees in a particular bargaining unit are required to pay union dues even though they may not want to join the union.

aggregate demand: total spending in the economy; the sum of personal consumption expenditures, business investment, and government spending.

aggregate supply: the total retail value of goods and services produced and available in a given period.

alternative cost: *See* opportunity cost.

antitrust: describes an act or a policy designed to curb monopolistic tendencies or power.

arbitration: method of settling a labor dispute in which both parties agree to accept the decision of a third party.

assessment: for taxation purposes, the official valuation of property or income.

asset: anything of value that is owned.

automatic stabilizer: tool that compensates for changes in the business cycle without requiring action by a public official or agency.

avoidance: a legal way to reduce tax payments.

balance of payments: statement listing all financial transactions that a nation and its people have with all other nations.

balance of trade: the difference between the total value of goods and services exported to other countries and the total value of goods and services imported.

balance sheet: itemized statement showing a business's assets, liabilities, and net worth on a given date.

bank reserves: amount of money a bank holds in order to meet the requirements of the Federal Reserve Bank or of a law, or the demands of its depositors. In addition to these reserves, a bank holds secondary reserves in the form of securities that can be easily converted into money.

base period: a time in the past against which changes are measured. It is used to measure price index.

benefit principle of taxation: justification for taxing people according to the benefits they received from government.

bill of exchange: written claim for foreign currency. It is the same as a foreign exchange check.

blacklist: list of workers, usually union organizers, circulated by employers in order to prevent those on the list from getting jobs.

bond: security representing indebtedness, frequently issued in $1000 denominations, and bearing a fixed rate of interest. Both governments and business firms issue bonds.

boycott: generally, a collective decision by one group to force action by another group. A boycott usually involves a union's urging its members and others not to buy from an employer in an attempt to force the latter to yield to union demands.

break-even point: point at which total revenue and total expenditure are equal.

budget: plan of expected revenue and expenditure for a specific period of time.

business cycle: expansion and contraction of the level of business activity at more or less regular intervals.

capital: a man-made instrument of production; a factor of production used in furthering the production process.

capital consumption: value of capital that is consumed in production; the depreciation of capital that is subtracted from GNP to give NNP.

capital good: a good used in the production of other goods rather than to satisfy a human want directly. It is the same as a producer good.

capitalism: economic system in which the means of production are owned and controlled by private individuals with a minimum of government interference. Allocation of resources is determined by the market mechanism.

cartel: an alliance of firms and/or countries established to control output in order to increase profits.

certificate of deposit: certificate issued by a commercial or savings bank, indicating that the depositor (who may be a corporation as well as an individual) has agreed to leave the money on deposit for a specified period of time at a particular rate of interest.

checkable deposit: a deposit in a bank or other depository institution from which the depositor may withdraw funds by writing a check or checklike instrument.

checkoff: agreement between an employer and a union by which the former deducts union dues from the employees' paychecks and turns them over to the union.

clean float: system under which a nation's currency is allowed to rise or fall in value relative to other currencies, strictly in accordance with the supply of and demand for that currency and with no interference by governments. (*See also* floating exchange rates and dirty float.)

closed shop: firm in which only workers who are already union members will be hired.

co-determination: an arrangement whereby a union has the power to veto management decisions at all levels.

collateral: something of value pledged by a borrower to secure a loan.

collective bargaining: method of reaching an agreement on the terms of a labor contract by having representatives of employers and employees discuss proposed changes.

combination: any alliance of individuals or firms established to influence market conditions. The most common types of industrial combinations in the United States have been pools, trusts, holding companies, mergers, consolidations, and conglomerates.

COMECON: Council for Mutual Economic Assistance, an organization of the USSR and several other communist nations to promote trade, economic development, and economic cooperation among the members.

command economy: an economic system in which the basic questions of *What, How,* and *For whom* are decided by a central authority.

commercial bank: financial institution whose primary function is to receive demand deposits and extend short-term loans to business firms.

common market: economic union of nations, regions, or states in which members have no trade barriers on one another's goods, but have a common tariff (or other restrictive policy) on the goods of nonmembers. The European Economic Community is an example of a common market.

common stock: the capital of a corporation, divided into shares that usually entitle the owners to voting rights and, if approved by the board of directors, dividends. (*See also* preferred stock.)

communism: economic system in which in theory all goods are owned collectively and in which payment of income is according to need. The term is used to describe the economy of the Soviet Union and of those nations that have similar ideologies. In practice the individual is given little freedom in determining *What, How,* and *For whom.*

company union: organization of employees largely under the control of management and unaffiliated with any national or international union.

comparable worth: a policy of paying workers in different jobs similar wage rates if the jobs are similar in terms of the training, experience, and responsibility required. The concept is applied particularly to low-paying jobs traditionally held by women.

comparative advantage: principle that all nations will benefit if each concentrates on producing and exporting goods in those sectors in which it has the greatest relative efficiency and on importing goods in those sectors in which it has the least relative efficiency.

compensatory countercyclical policy: program or plan designed to reverse the direction of the business cycle when it appears to be becoming inflationary or deflationary.

competition: situation in which two or more parties seek to gain an advantage over the other(s). In classical capitalism, competition protects the consumer by assuring efficiency of production.

compulsory arbitration: enforced settlement of a dispute, as between management and a union, by some government agency. This type of arbitration is practiced in New Zealand and Australia but is generally frowned on in this country.

conciliation: third-party intervention to encourage settlement of a labor-management dispute. The third party stimulates discussion that may lead to a peaceful settlement.

conglomerate: a combination of firms in unrelated industries.

conspicuous consumption: purchase and use of goods and services primarily to enhance one's social prestige rather than to satisfy material needs.

consumer good: economic good used directly to satisfy human wants rather than for resale or to further production.

consumer price index: a measure of the change in average prices of items commonly purchased by consumers.

consumer sovereignty: the central idea of Adam Smith's classical model—that production should be determined by the market's response to consumer demand.

consumption: use of goods and services to satisfy human wants.

contingent workers: part-time, temporary, or freelance workers hired to supplement a full-time regular work force.

contract: agreement between two or more parties that is recognized and enforceable by law.

contraction: decline of economic activity in the business cycle.

copyright: exclusive right to reproduce, publish, or sell what one has created, given by government to artists, authors, musicians, or their designated agents for a specified period of time.

corporate campaign: a union tactic of using public relations methods and legal maneuvers in a dispute with an employer.

corporate income tax: slightly progressive tax levied on the taxable income of corporations.

corporation: an artificial person before the law. A corporation is chartered by the state government, which gives it such powers as the right to issue stocks and bonds and to have perpetual life. The owners have only limited liability.

cost-benefit analysis: a method for comparing the dollar costs of fulfilling a want to the dollar benefits that such fulfillment provides.

cost-push inflation: rise in the price level that originates on the cost (or supply) side rather than from excess demand. It usually occurs when economic groups try to increase their relative share of the national income.

countercyclical: reversing the direction of the business cycle.

countervailing power: principle that one economic group having monopolistic power tends to balance another group having monopolistic power, as in the case of a monopolistic producer and a monopolistic buyer.

craft union: union of workers having the same or similar skills, such as electricians or plumbers. It is sometimes called a trade or horizontal union. (*See also* industrial union.)

credit: the ability to purchase or borrow with the promise to pay at some later date.

credit union: cooperative savings and loan association.

creditor nation: nation whose citizens, businesses, and government owe less to foreign creditors than foreign debtors owe to them.

crowding-out effect: a shortage of savings for private investment, resulting from heavy government borrowing.

cumulative preferred stock: stock with a stated dividend that must be paid before common stockholders receive their dividends. If the dividend is not paid, the amount owed accumulates.

currency: that part of the money supply, in the form of coins and paper bills, that is issued by the government or its agent (central bank).

customs union: agreement between nations to eliminate duties on goods traded between them and to have a common external tariff applicable to all nonmembers.

cyclical unemployment: unemployment attributable to a general decline in business activity.

debenture bonds: long-term promissory notes issued by a corporation and backed only by the good faith of the corporation.

debtor nation: nation whose citizens, businesses, and government owe more to foreign creditors than foreign debtors owe to them.

decreasing costs: costs that decline per unit as production increases.

deficit financing: condition in which government expenditure exceeds government revenue, the difference being made up by borrowing. In the United States, federal deficit financing to increase aggregate demand is sometimes used as economic policy.

deflation: decline in the general price level. It results in an increase in the purchasing power of money.

demand: the quantity of goods or services that buyers are willing to purchase at various prices at a given time.

demand deposit: deposit on account in a commercial bank on which checks can be written and from which money can be withdrawn without any advance notice. Demand deposits make up the largest part of our money supply.

demand-pull inflation: rise in the price level caused by too much money pursuing too few goods. The demand for goods is greater than the ability to supply them.

dependency ratio: ratio of nonworkers to workers; an indication of the number of nonworkers who must be supported by a given number of workers.

dependent variable: a variable that changes in value as a result of a change in the independent variable.

depreciation: reduction in the value of capital goods because of the wear and tear they undergo in producing other goods; also called capital consumption.

depression: period in the business cycle when most measurements of economic activity are at their lowest. A depression is characterized by low production, low prices, and high unemployment.

deregulation: decrease in or cessation of government regulation of an industry.

derivative deposits: those deposits that come into being as a result of people's borrowing from a bank.

devaluation: decrease in the value of the unit of money (dollars, pounds, francs, etc.) in relation to gold or other currencies.

dictatorship of proletariat: according to Karl Marx and his followers, that stage in the evolution of society that follows the overthrow of capitalism, when representatives of the working class assume complete power.

diminishing marginal utility: the gradual decline in consumer satisfaction that each additional unit of consumption of a particular good or service gives.

diminishing returns, law of: when additional units of one factor of production are added to a constant quantity of other factors, eventually each additional unit will yield less than the preceding unit.

direct foreign investment: ownership by a company based in one country of 10 percent or more of a foreign company or of an entire plant in another country (100 percent ownership).

dirty float: system under which a nation's currency is allowed to rise or fall in value relative to other currencies, but the government reserves the right to influence the rates if they are deemed to be rising or falling too sharply.

discount: interest that is paid in advance.

discretionary policy: monetary and fiscal policy designed to compensate for the business cycle by means of action by an individual or a government agency.

disinflation: a decline in the rate of inflation.

disposable income: amount of income individuals have left to spend and save; personal income minus personal taxes.

distribution: marketing or merchandising of commodities. (*See also* functional distribution.)

divestiture: the act by a firm of letting go of one of its subsidiaries.

dividend: a return to shareholders from their ownership of corporate stock, paid from profits.

divisibility: characteristic of money that allows it to be *stated* and used in fractions or multiples of the unit of money.

domestic system: system in which production takes place in the home rather than at the factory. This type of system was characteristic of production before the Industrial Revolution.

double counting: in determination of GNP by the income method, taking into account more than once the value added to products.

dumping: selling goods to other countries below cost to get rid of surpluses or to destroy foreign competition.

durability: characteristic of money that permits it to be used over a long period or to be replaced inexpensively.

econometrics: the application of statistics to the analysis of economic problems and forecasting.

economic freedom: principle that individuals have mobility in the economy in that they are guaranteed the right to choose their own jobs, to buy and sell property, and to enter into or dissolve a business.

economic good: a good that is relatively scarce and requires effort to obtain. Broadly defined, it includes services as well as physical goods.

economic growth: increase in real per capita income.

economic indicator: measurement of one or several parts of the economy that is useful for evaluating the entire economy and predicting its course. An economic indicator may be leading, coincident, or lagging depending on its relation to the economy as a whole.

economic profit: profit remaining after explicit and implicit costs are paid; sometimes called pure profit.

economic rent: after each of the other factors has been paid, the surplus paid to a resource whose supply is inelastic.

economic system: the way a society organizes itself through its institutions, guiding principles, and values to answer the central and related economic questions.

economic value: value placed on a good because of its utility and scarcity.

economics: that branch of the social sciences that is concerned with the production, distribution, and consumption of goods and services.

effective: describes a policy that accomplishes what it sets out to do.

efficient: maximizing output for a given input; productive.

elastic demand: the demand for a product when a small change in price will result in a relatively greater change in the quantity people will buy.

emerging nation: a poor country that is only beginning to develop its economic potential. The term usually refers to nations that have only recently been given their independence.

employee buyout: the purchase by workers of the company in which they are employed.

entrepreneur: one who assumes the responsibility of entrepreneurship. Management has taken over many of the functions of the entrepreneur.

entrepreneurship: that factor of production responsible for initiating production and organizing the other factors of production. It assumes the risk and receives profit as its payment.

equation of exchange: statement of the relation between the supply of money, prices, and business activity. It is $MV = PT$, where M represents the supply of money, V its velocity, P the price level, and T the number of transactions.

equilibrium: in economic theory, a condition that, once achieved, will continue unless one of the variables is changed and the change is not offset by an equal change in another variable. Equilibrium occurs at the intersection of supply and demand, the point at which aggregate demand $(C + I + G)$ crosses the 45° line, the point at which investment equals savings, and the point at which marginal cost equals marginal revenue.

escalator clause: provision in a contract permitting changes in payment to fluctuate with changes in the general price level. It is most frequently applied to wage payments.

escape clause: provision in a trade agreement allowing the United States Tariff Commission to appeal to the president to nullify the agreement if the commission finds that the trade agreement may hurt a domestic industry.

estate tax: tax placed on the value of an inherited estate.

Eurodollars: U.S. dollars on deposit in foreign banks.

European monetary system: a system established in 1979 by members of the European Economic Community (Common Market) to link their currencies and create a European Currency Unit (ECU).

evasion: illegal method of reducing tax payments.

excess profits tax: tax on business firms in addition to the normal business tax. In the United States, this tax is levied on profits above what the law designates as normal and is usually used during wartime.

excess reserves: bank reserves beyond those required by the Federal Reserve.

exchange rate: price that one nation must pay to exchange its currency for that of another nation.

exchange value: value placed on a good or service based on the amount of other goods and services it may be exchanged for.

excise tax: tax placed on a good or a service at the time of sale.

expansion: that phase of the business cycle during which activity is increasing. It is characterized by increasing employment and production.

explicit costs: costs that originate outside the firm, such as wages, rent, and interest; costs determined by the prices paid for the factors of production. (*See also* implicit costs.)

external cost: cost or burden that is placed outside the individual firm. Streams polluted by waste dumped into them are an external cost to the people.

factor market: the place or situation in which businesses obtain the factors of production—natural resources, capital, and labor.

factors of production: those ingredients necessary for producing any good or service. Most economists list four: land, labor, capital, and entrepreneurship. The term *natural resources* is frequently used for land, and *management* is sometimes used for entrepreneurship.

favorable balance of trade: condition in which the total value of a nation's exports exceeds the total value of its imports.

featherbedding: employing more workers than are needed for efficient operation, or placing limitations on the output of workers, according to provisions in a labor-management contract.

Federal Savings and Loan Insurance Corporation (FSLIC):   an agency of the federal government that insures deposits in federal savings and loan associations up to a specified amount.

fiat money: money that has no precious metal backing and circulates by order of the government.

fiscal policy: the government's planned course on budgetary matters, designed to influence economic activity.

fixed cost: cost that does not fluctuate with volume of production.

flat tax: tax in which a single rate is applied to the tax base, usually income.

floating exchange rates: exchange rates that are not rigidly controlled or fixed—the currencies of various nations are allowed to rise or fall in value on the basis of supply of and demand for each currency.

foreign exchange: process of settling claims that a country has against another country through exchange of foreign currency; the foreign money (or claims on foreign money) that a country possesses.

franchise: grant by government, giving a firm the right to carry on a particular kind of business in a certain place, often involving a monopoly or a partial monopoly; grant by a manufacturer, giving the distributor the exclusive right to handle the manufacturer's product or service in a particular place.

free trade: international trade in which all policy restrictions that may impede its flow are eliminated.

freedom of contract: in the production of goods and services, the principle that individuals have the right to enter into agreements resulting in production. Such agreements must be within the framework of the law and may not be conspiracies against society.

frictional unemployment: temporary unemployment caused by general changes in the economy. Included are new workers looking for jobs as well as workers leaving one job for another.

fringe benefits: items that increase real income but are not included in the basic wage, such as sick benefits. Fringe benefits are often included in labor contracts.

full employment: condition of the economy in which there is sufficient aggregate demand to employ all those who wish to work and are qualified to do so. In the United States, economists differ on what figure to use as full employment. Most frequently, 94 to 96 percent of the labor force are the figures mentioned. The Full Employment and Balanced Growth Act of 1978 made a 4 percent unemployment rate a national goal.

functional distribution: payment—wages, rent, interest, and profit—to the factors of production according to their contribution.

general price index: a measure of the change in average prices for all items produced in the United States; also known as the GNP deflator. (*See also* consumer price index and price index.)

general property tax: a tax on the assessed value of property, computed as a percentage of value. Specific types of property may be exempt.

general sales tax: a tax on most goods, collected at the time of their sale. Food and medicine are frequently exempt.

gift tax: a tax on the value of property that is transferred primarily to avoid payment of inheritance and estate taxes.

give-backs: agreements by unions to relinquish some benefits that had been previously granted by management.

gold certificate: in the United States, formerly a certificate issued by the government that was redeemable in gold. Gold certificates are now issued by the Treasury and held by the Federal Reserve banks as evidence of their gold holdings; these certificates are used as part of the banks' reserves against their deposits and Federal Reserve notes.

gold-par rates of exchange: fixed values of particular currencies in terms of a gold standard, used as a means of facilitating currency exchange. It was the system used primarily by the United States and Western European nations before the Great Depression.

gold standard: system in which the monetary unit is expressed in terms of gold. The government buys and sells gold freely at a fixed price.

good: defined broadly, anything that people desire.

Narrowly defined, it excludes nontangible items, which are called services.

Gresham's law: when two kinds of money are used in a country, the cheaper money will drive the relatively higher valued money out of circulation.

gross: total amount before any deductions.

gross domestic product: a measure of the market value of final goods and services produced within a country. It excludes international flows of income and thus differs somewhat from GNP.

gross national debt: total indebtedness of the national government, including the debts owed by one governmental agency to another governmental agency. *Net debt* refers only to government obligations to the public.

gross national income: GNP stated as income rather than as production.

gross national product: the total retail market value of all goods and services produced in a nation during a given period, usually a year.

gross savings: the sum of the values of capital consumption (depreciation), corporation savings, and personal savings.

guaranteed annual wage: minimum yearly payment that employers agree to make to workers. The employers agree to employ the workers for a minimum number of weeks each year and to supplement their unemployment insurance benefits if they are laid off because of insufficient demand.

holding company: a corporation organized primarily to hold stock in one or more other corporations for the purpose of control.

horizontal combination: combination formed when two or more organizations producing the same goods or performing the same services merge.

imperfect competition: any market condition that differs from pure competition.

implicit costs: costs originating within the firm that are incurred by the owner, such as those for his or her time or property employed in production. Examples are the value of the labor provided by the owner who draws no salary and that of the land he or she owns and uses in the business without receiving rental payment. (*See also* explicit costs and opportunity costs.)

import quota: limit on how much of a particular product can be imported during a specified period.

income policy: a method, voluntary or compulsory, for restraining inflation by limiting increases on wages and prices. Such a policy is usually tried when monetary and fiscal policies have not been successful.

income tax: tax on the net income of individuals or corporations, usually with progressive rates. It is the most important source of federal revenue.

independent variable: a variable that is given and can change freely in value.

index number: a measure used to express the volume of output or the price level for a given period in terms of that of the base period, the value of which is expressed as 100.

indexation: linking increases in various payments (such as old age benefits under social security, wages, and interest on bank deposits) to rises in a price index. The escalator clause in certain labor-management contracts is an example of indexation.

industrial union: labor union of which all workers in a particular industry are members, regardless of their jobs. Such a union is sometimes referred to as a vertical union.

industrywide bargaining: collective dealing in which one or several unions negotiate for a contract with virtually all the employers of an industry. In many instances, a contract worked out with a particular employer sets the pattern for the entire industry.

inelastic demand: situation in which the percentage change in the price of a product results in a smaller percentage change in the quantity demanded.

inelastic supply: situation in which the percentage change in the price of a product results in a smaller percentage change in the quantity supplied.

inflation: decrease in the purchasing power of the monetary unit caused by an increase in the price level.

inheritance tax: tax on those receiving shares of an estate.

injunction: court order restraining an individual or a group from carrying on some kind of activity. It is frequently used to prevent or stop a strike.

installment buying: acquiring goods or services by promising to make payments at regular intervals. Sometimes a small down payment is required.

installment credit: type of consumer credit in which the seller is allowed to repossess the article purchased if the buyer defaults on periodic payments.

insurance: financial operation whereby many people contribute to a fund from which those who sustain a loss are compensated.

interest: payment for the use of capital (loanable funds).

interlocking directorate: condition in which one or more members of a board of directors of one company are also members of the boards of directors of other companies.

internal cost: cost or burden that is placed within the individual firm. The expense of installing pollution (or waste) disposal units becomes part of the cost of production and therefore is an internal cost.

intrinsic value: market value of the material of which something is made, such as the value of the metal in a coin.

inventory: goods in stock and usually available for sale.

investment: when applied to an individual or a firm, the purchase of assets that will produce income; when used in macroeconomics, investment refers to capital formation and capital accumulation (capital goods produced plus inventory accumulation).

investment bank: a business that specializes in underwriting and selling new issues of stocks and bonds.

invisible exports and imports: financial transactions among nations involving services or such intangibles as shipping charges, insurance, tourist spending, and the transfer of loanable funds.

joint venture: an arrangement by which two companies agree to work together for some limited purpose, such as producing a particular model of automobile.

jurisdictional dispute: conflict between rival unions about which should have control over a given job or activity and be recognized by management.

"kinked" demand curve: a demand curve that tends to be elastic in a high price range and inelastic in a lower price range. It is usually associated with oligopolies.

L: symbol for liquidity, or the overall ability to spend; the broadest definition of our money supply, including everything in M_1, M_2, and M_3 plus most securities within 18 months of maturity. (*See also* M_1, M_2, and M_3.)

labor: the factor of production that involves human effort. Managerial activities are frequently considered a separate factor.

labor force: people 16 years of age and older who are working, looking for work, or temporarily absent from work because of such problems as labor disputes or illness.

labor union: an organization of employees that acts in their behalf, particularly in negotiating with management.

Laffer curve: Arthur Laffer's theoretical representation of the relationship between total tax revenues and tax rates.

laissez-faire: policy associated with the classical model of capitalism suggesting that the government should not interfere with the economy.

land: the factor of production from which goods originate; natural resources before people have worked on them.

law of increasing costs: in a production situation, average total unit cost increases as the volume of a business increases. This principle is not universally applicable, since in some industries unit costs are constant and in others unit costs decrease as volume of business increases.

legal reserve: percentage of deposits that depository institutions are required to post with the Federal Reserve Bank.

legal tender: form of money that the government recognizes and that creditors must legally accept as payment for debts.

liability: debt of an individual or a firm that is owed to others. It does not include capital investment by owners (stock).

limited liability: legal exemption of stockholders in a corporation from financial liability for the debts of the company beyond the amount they have invested.

limited life: characteristic of a single proprietorship or partnership that the business ceases to exist upon the death of the owner or one of the owners.

liquid assets: those assets that can easily be converted into cash, such as government bonds and other easily marketable securities.

liquidity preference: the preference that people and businesses have for holding their assets in cash rather than a less liquid form.

lockout: closing of a business by an employer in order to put pressure on a union in a labor-management dispute; the employer's counterpart of a strike.

long run: in the case of a business, a sufficiently long period to permit the business to develop its capacity to produce by adding plant and equipment.

Lorenz curve: measuring tool for plotting the degree of inequality in the distribution of income.

M_1: the narrowest definition of money. It includes money held by the public to use for current spending (transaction balances)—coins, paper currency, demand deposits in commercial banks, other checkable deposits (such as NOW accounts and share drafts in credit unions), and traveler's checks. (*See also* M_2, M_3, and L.)

M_2: M_1 plus small-denomination time deposits, savings deposits, general-purpose and broker/dealer money market fund balances, overnight repurchases, and Eurodollars. (*See also* M_1, M_3, and L.)

M_3: M_2 plus large time deposits, institutional money market fund balances, and term repurchases. (*See also* M_1, M_2, and L.)

macroeconomics: study of the economy as a whole instead of individual economic units. It is sometimes referred to as aggregate economics.

maintenance-of-membership shop: work place in which workers who are members of a union must continue their membership for the duration of the contract.

margin: in the purchase of securities, the amount of money that the buyer must deposit immediately with the broker. It is stated as a percentage of the total value of the securities.

marginal: yielding only enough value to cover the cost of production. The term may be used in reference to land, labor, or a business.

marginal analysis: analysis of economic data by studying how an additional unit of one variable affects the value of another variable.

marginal cost: additional cost for expanding output by one more unit.

marginal product: additional product derived by adding one more unit of a factor of production (like an additional worker).

marginal productivity wage theory: principle that under competitive conditions the wages of all workers will be set by the productivity, measured in money, of the last worker hired.

marginal propensity to consume: proportion of additional income that people spend.

marginal propensity to save: proportion of additional income that people save.

marginal revenue: additional revenue a firm receives from the sale of one more unit. Under pure competition in the short run, this is the same as the market price.

marginal revenue product: additional revenue a firm receives by adding one more unit of a factor of production (such as an additional worker).

market: place or situation in which buyers and sellers can meet for the purpose of exchange.

market socialism: decentralized collective ownership of the means of production with much of the decision making taking place in workers' councils. Interest and prices fluctuate with market conditions. Such a system is associated with the Yugoslav economy.

measure of value: that function of money that allows it to serve as the standard for measuring the value of production. We are using the monetary unit as the common denominator when we show the value of apples and the value of candy bars in dollars.

mediation: method of settling labor disputes in which a third party participates in a formal way in helping to bring about an agreement among the disputants. Plans offered by the mediator are not binding.

medium of exchange: the main function of money, which allows it to be used to facilitate the exchange of goods and services. A medium of exchange is needed by an economy that has specialization of production.

mercantilism: economic system most popular in the sixteenth, seventeenth, and eighteenth centuries, characterized by a highly controlled market with numerous regulations designed to increase the flow of precious metals into the treasury of the "mother country."

merger: combining of two companies into one through the dissolution of one and the sale of its assets to the other.

microeconomics: study of the economic behavior of individual units in the economy, such as business firms.

minimum wage: lowest wage that an employer can legally pay an employee. It is usually expressed as an hourly rate.

mixed capitalism: economic system in which the majority of the instruments of production are owned and operated by private enterprise and the market mechanism is the principal factor in determining the allocation of resources. Under mixed capitalism a government may provide for some ownership of, and control over, enterprise and may assume considerable responsibility for the economic well-being of the nation.

model: a theory used by social scientists to analyze economic behavior. The closer the model is to the real world, the more useful it is for analysis.

monetary base: the sum of reserves held at Federal Reserve banks plus currency and coin outside the Federal Reserve and the U.S. Treasury.

monetary policy: use of the tools of the Federal Reserve system to achieve stable prices and full employment; any policy whose direct impact is on money equilibrium.

money: medium of exchange and unit of account accepted by society. (*See also* M_1, M_2 and M_3.)

money wages: the number of dollars workers receive, as contrasted with what those dollars will buy (purchasing power).

monopolistic competition: market situation similar to pure competition but characterized by product differentiation and the fact that each firm's actions have an effect on all other firms.

monopoly: market situation in which there is only one seller of a product and there are no acceptable substitutes.

monopsony: market situation in which there is only one buyer for a product.

multinational corporation: firm with subsidiaries in many nations, usually involving important international investments.

multiplier: reciprocal of the marginal propensity to save. The extent to which injections of money into the economy create increases in income larger than the original injections.

national debt: debt owed by the federal government. It does not include the debts of state and local governments or private debt.

national income: total income payments made to the owners of the factors of production. The term is sometimes used to refer to gross or net national product.

nationalize: to take for government ownership, with or without compensation, a business or other property owned and operated privately.

natural monopoly: industry in which competition would be costly and uneconomical.

natural rate of unemployment: the unemployment rate at which wages will tend to remain stable.

natural resources: *See* land.

near-money: highly liquid assets other than M_1, such as time deposits and government securities.

negative incentives: charges, usually in the form of a tax, to discourage production or reduce the level of production. They are applied to discourage pollution.

negative income tax: a procedure for providing financial assistance to people with incomes below a certain minimum by using the income tax principle to distribute rather than collect revenue.

net: the amount left after certain designated deductions are made from the gross amount.

net national product: gross national product minus capital consumption (depreciation).

net worth: total assets minus total liabilities. It is recorded on the balance sheet of a firm.

nominal interest rate: the rate at which funds are currently being loaned; the interest rate unadjusted for inflation or deflation.

NOW account: a negotiable order of withdrawal account in a savings or commercial bank, from which people can withdraw money in much the same way as one withdraws money from a checking account. In effect, NOW accounts are interest-bearing checking accounts.

oligopoly: market situation characterized by only a few sellers of a product or the domination of the market by a few large firms.

oligopsony: market situation characterized by only a few buyers of a product.

open-market operations: the buying and selling of federal securities by the Federal Open Market Committee, usually to carry out a monetary policy.

open shop: a work place that employs workers without regard to their membership in a union.

opportunity cost: the value of what is given up or lost when a resource is used in the next best alternative way. For example, it would be the salary of the next highest paying job offered you. It is also called alternative cost.

paradox of thrift: a situation that results when people trying to save more end up saving less. The subsequent drop in aggregate demand is followed by a reduction in aggregate income, lessening their ability to save.

parity: as part of the U.S. farm policy, a plan designed to keep the purchasing power of units of farm production (for example, bushels of wheat) on a par with that of the units of production that a farmer buys, according to a ratio that existed during some selected base period.

partnership: form of business organization in which two or more individuals share ownership and operation of the business according to a contractual arrangement. Liability is unlimited.

patent: an exclusive right, granted by the government, to make and sell inventions.

payroll tax: tax on wages or salaries earned within the boundaries of a government, most frequently a city.

per capita output: GNP of a country divided by the country's population. It is sometimes used to indicate the relative standard of living of a nation.

perfect competition: *See* pure competition.

peril point: lowest figure at which a duty on imports can be set without threatening a domestic industry.

perpetual life: characteristic of a corporation, in which the death of one or more owners does not automatically bring about an end to the business.

personal consumption expenditures: money that households spend for consumer goods; disposable personal income minus savings.

personal income: total money income received by individuals before personal taxes are paid.

personal income tax: tax on the income of individuals or families. It is usually progressive.

personal savings: difference between disposable personal income and personal consumption expenditures.

Phillips curve: a curve that shows the trade-off between the rate of inflation and the rate of unemployment.

picketing: weapon used by unions during a strike— workers advertise their grievances by carrying signs and walking in lines in the neighborhood of a business, urging other workers not to work and customers not to buy.

piece rate: wage payments based on the number of units produced or work done, as contrasted with an hourly wage rate, which is a fixed amount per hour.

portability: a characteristic of money that allows it to be carried easily.

poverty index: a sliding scale based on family size and location giving the minimum income needed to meet basic family needs. The index is determined annually by the Social Security Administration.

preferential shop: work place in which management has agreed to hire union members so long as they are available.

preferred stock: that stock of a corporation that gives the owner preferential treatment in the payment of dividends and in the distribution of assets in the event the corporation is liquidated. Dividend rates are usually fixed. (*See also* common stock.)

price: exchange value of goods and services stated in a monetary unit.

price elasticity: a measurement of the responsiveness of buyers (demand) or sellers (supply) to changes in prices.

price index: device for measuring the changing value of money over a given period or the average price of a number of selected commodities and services at a given time.

price level: the average of prices paid for goods and services in a given period.

primary deposits: those deposits made by people depositing cash in the bank.

private enterprise: organization of production in which business units are owned and operated by individuals who take risks and are motivated by the desire to make a profit, as contrasted with government or collective enterprise.

private property: property that an individual owns and over which he or she has the right to exercise reasonable control. It provides incentive to produce.

private sector: all economic activity except that which is government.

producer price index: a measurement of the general price level of wholesale goods.

product differentiation: consciously trying to represent one's product as different from similar products. It is characteristic of monopolistic competition and some oligopolies.

product market: the place or situation in which goods and services are sold or traded. (*See also* factor market.)

production: any kind of activity that adds value to goods and services, including creation, transportation, and storage until used.

production function: use of the technical information that shows the amount of output capable of being created by specific inputs (factors of production).

production possibilities curve: a model that shows the full use of resources in an economy where only two goods can be produced. It demonstrates the trade-off involved in substituting one type of good for another.

productivity: output for a unit of a factor of production. It is usually expressed as output per worker-hour.

profit: payment to a business enterprise for the risks incurred; the amount left from total revenue after all costs are paid.

progressive tax: tax in which the rate of payment increases as the tax base increases.

promissory note: written statement of agreement to pay a certain sum of money to a specific person or firm at an indicated time.

propensity to consume: proportion of income that people tend to spend at different levels of income.

propensity to save: proportion of income that people tend to save at different levels of income.

proportional tax: tax in which the rate of tax does not change with a change in the tax base.

prosperity: uppermost phase of a business cycle.

protectionists: those who favor high tariffs and other restrictions on imports to the end that domestic goods will not have to compete with foreign goods.

protective tariff: tax on imported goods designed to give domestic producers protection from foreign competition.

public sector: that segment of the economy that is part of the government.

public utility: a business that provides essential services to the public and tends to be a natural monopoly. It must obtain a franchise from the government and is regulated by a government agency.

pure competition: market situation in which there are a large number of buyers and sellers acting independently and the products are homogeneous, so the entry or exit of any one buyer or seller does not affect price.

pure profit: *See* economic profit.

quality circles: groups of workers in a company who meet periodically to discuss production problems and to propose solutions.

quantity theory of money: theory that the general price level will change in response to the money supply. Stated as the equation of exchange, $MV = PT$.

ratio of concentration: the percentage of total production or sales accounted for by the four largest firms in an industry.

rational expectations: the theory asserting that efforts to affect economic activity through fiscal and monetary policies may not work as expected because people have learned to anticipate the policies of the administration and the Federal Reserve and to take actions that offset or nullify those policies.

real interest: the nominal interest rate minus the rate of inflation.

real wages: amount of goods and services that can be bought with one's money wages. It is useful for comparing changes in the standard of living, since the influence of changes in the general price level is eliminated. (*See also* money wages.)

recession: that phase of the business cycle in which there is a downswing or contraction of the economy.

recovery: that period of the business cycle that follows a depression. It is also known as an upswing or expansion.

recycling: converting waste products to usable material, usually to reduce pollution.

regressive tax: tax in which the rate of payment decreases as the tax base increases.

rent: payment for the use of land. (*See also* economic rent.)

reserve ratio: ratio of the amount of money that must be retained in a reserve account (reserve account with the Federal Reserve Bank plus vault cash) to the total demand deposits or checkable deposits of a depository institution.

revenue: income of a government or business enterprise. When deductions are made, the term is prefaced with the word *net*.

revenue sharing: the returning of a portion of revenue received by a larger unit of government with greater taxing powers to a smaller unit of government.

revenue tariffs: duties placed on imports with the objective of raising revenue rather than protecting domestic industries. Such tariffs rarely discourage international trade.

sales tax: tax placed on goods at the time of their purchase.

savings: that part of income that is not spent for consumer items.

savings and loan association: financial institution owned by share purchasers (depositors) and specializing in long-term loans to finance real estate purchases.

savings bank: financial institution specializing in small time deposits that are usually held for a considerable time.

Say's law: an assumption made by J. B. Say and supported by the classical and supply-side economists that equilibrium would be achieved at full employment without inflation because supply creates its own demand.

seasonal fluctuations: regular and predictable changes in business activity caused by changes in the season, such as the increase in construction in the spring.

secondary boycott: action by a group of workers designed to bring pressure on a firm they have a disagreement with and involving the use of third parties not involved in the dispute. An example would be the refusal on the part of workers to handle goods coming from a plant that is being struck.

secondary reserves: bank assets other than primary reserves that can be quickly converted into cash, such as government securities or commercial paper.

single proprietorship: oldest and most common type of business organization, in which the business is owned by an individual.

single tax: a plan proposed by Henry George under which all income derived from land ownership would be taxed the full amount, thereby eliminating the need to collect other taxes.

slowdown: weapon of labor in which workers purposely reduce the speed at which they work, increasing costs to the employer.

social cost: price paid by the people as a whole as a result of individual economic activities conducted by industrial producers. An example is pollution.

socialism: economic system in which much or most of the means of production are owned and controlled collectively, usually by government, and in which central planning is substituted for the market in the allocation of resources.

soil bank: in the United States, a government farm program that pays farmers for withdrawing land from cultivation.

stability of value: characteristic of money that suggests there should be little change in what a unit will buy.

stabilizer: economic tool used to reduce business fluctuations. It may be automatic, such as unemployment insurance, or discretionary, such as increasing or decreasing government spending.

stagflation: combination of declining business activity, rising unemployment, and rising price levels. The stagflation associated with the economic behavior of most industrial nations starting in 1974 was partly precipitated by the energy crisis.

standard allowable deduction: a percentage (up to a maximum amount) of gross income that may be deducted in determining taxable income. If it is used, no itemization of deductions is necessary.

standard of deferred payment: that function of money that allows it to be used to express the amount to be repaid.

standard of living: a measure of the way a family or group lives with reference to the consumer goods it has.

stock: ownership of a corporation, divided into shares and represented by certificates.

stockbroker: intermediary in the buying and selling of securities.

store of value: that function of money that allows it to be used by individuals to accumulate wealth or purchasing power.

strike: weapon of labor in which workers voluntarily stop working, thereby bringing pressure on the employer to meet their demands.

strikebreaker: worker hired to replace a striking worker.

structural unemployment: unemployment caused primarily by change in consumer preferences, technology, lack of skills, and loss of markets.

submarginal: yielding less than the cost of production. The term may be used with land, labor, or a business.

subsidy: government assistance to a program, an enterprise, or an industry frequently in the form of a money payment, generally made for the good of some special interest group. Farmers, the airlines, and the merchant marines have been subsidized at various times.

subsistence: describes the level of income necessary to maintain a minimum standard of living.

supply: the quantity of goods and services that sellers are willing to offer at various prices at a given time.

supply-side economics: a set of policies designed to stimulate productive capacity as opposed to increasing aggregate demand. The term is associated with President Reagan's economic policies.

supramarginal: yielding more than the cost of production. The term is applicable to land, labor, or a business.

surplus value: in Marxian theory, the amount charged above the cost of labor. Other economic theories consider payments made to any of the factors of production, above what the market price would call for under competitive conditions, to be surplus.

tariff: schedule of taxes on commodities imported or exported. In the United States, only imported goods are affected.

tax: compulsory charge on individuals and businesses to pay for the cost of running a government and carrying out its policies. A tax is designed to reallocate resources from the private to the public sector.

tax base: the commodity, income, or service on which a tax is levied; only that part of the value of an item that is taxed.

tax incidence: the business or individuals on whom a tax finally comes to rest.

tax rate: the specified percentage of the value of a commodity, income, or service that must be paid in tax.

taxable income: amount of income remaining after subtraction of all allowable deductions and exemptions and therefore subject to taxation.

technological unemployment: displacement of workers caused by the introduction of labor-saving machinery.

time deposit: an account in a bank or other depository institution on which interest is usually paid and the bank may legally withhold payment for a specified number of days. Technically, a time deposit differs from a savings account in that it is a loan from the depositor to the financial institution and is not redeemable on demand. The differences between time and demand deposits are disapppearing, however.

token money: circulating coins whose value is higher than the market value of the commodity (metal) they are made of.

trade association: organization of firms engaged in a common industry or business activity, established to promote their mutual interests.

trade-offs: acquiring one benefit or value at the sacrifice or partial sacrifice of another. For example, to halt air pollution we pay a higher price for unleaded gasoline, which helps us enjoy cleaner air.

trade union: *See* craft union.

transaction balances: money held by the public to use for current spending.

transfer payment: money paid by one individual or institution (particularly government) to another without the rendering of services, such as social security payments.

trust: form of business combination that became common in the 1890s, in which stockholders exchange their voting shares for trust certificates for purposes of centralizing control of an entire industry in the hands of a few.

turnover tax: form of sales tax commonly used in the Soviet Union.

two-tier wage agreements: accords permitting newly hired workers to receive a lower pay rate than older workers doing the same jobs.

underdeveloped country: technically, a nation that has realized little of its economic potential because of a lack of capital, technology, and skilled labor. More commonly, it refers to countries with a relatively low per capita income.

underground economy: economic activity that is unreported and therefore escapes taxation.

underwrite: to guarantee to furnish a definite sum of money by a definite date to a business or government in return for securities, such as stocks and bonds.

unemployment: in reference to the economy as a whole, the difference between the number of persons in the labor force and the number of persons employed. The term also refers to the number of people who are able to work and are seeking work but cannot find jobs.

unemployment insurance: that part of our social security program that provides covered employees with insurance against the complete loss of income due to unemployment. Payment comes primarily from taxes paid by employers.

unfavorable balance of trade: condition in which a nation's total value of imports exceeds its total value of exports.

union label: emblem placed on a good signifying that it was made by union workers.

union shop: a business in which the employer is free to hire any worker provided that the worker is a union member or will become a union member after a specified period of time.

unitary elasticity: the responsiveness of demand to price when the percentage change in price equals the percentage change in quantity purchased.

unit of account: the use of money as a measure or standard of value in an economy.

unlimited liability: the legal responsibility of a firm's owner or owners (with no exclusion of their personal assets) for the firm's debts—a disadvantage of a single proprietorship and of a partnership.

urban place: an area with 2500 or more inhabitants.

utility: satisfaction that one obtains, or expects to obtain, from consuming, owning, or using a good or service.

value-added tax: a tax similar to a sales tax but paid by each producer on what value he or she contributes to the final product.

variable cost: a cost that increases with an increase in production.

velocity of circulation: number of times the supply of money is turned over (spent) in a given period of time, usually a year.

vertical combination: a business organization that combines the various stages in the production of a single finished good.

wages: the prices management pays for human effort.

wealth: the total value of accumulated assets.

welfare capitalism: modified form of capitalism characterized by many social welfare programs, considerable government involvement in the economy, and legislation to provide a minimum standard of living for all citizens.

wildcat strike: work stoppage that is not sanctioned by a union.

withholding tax: tax deducted from wages and salaries by the employer. In the United States, this method is applied to personal income and social security taxes to make payments more convenient.

working poor: marginal workers whose skills and total work time do not allow them to earn an income above the poverty index.

yellow-dog contract: a wage contract in which the worker agrees before he or she is hired not to join a union during the time of employment. Such contracts are no longer legal.

Index